# ACTEX ACADEMIC SERIES

# Mathematics of Investment and Credit

## 5th Edition

SAMUEL A. BROVERMAN, PhD, ASA
UNIVERSITY OF TORONTO

ACTEX Publications, Inc.
Winsted, CT

Requests for permission should be addressed to
      ACTEX Publications
      PO Box 974
      Winsted, CT 06098


Manufactured in the United States of America

10 9 8 7 6 5 4 3 2 1

Cover design by Christine Phelps


Library of Congress Cataloging-in-Publication Data

Broverman, Samuel A., 1951-
  Mathematics of investment and credit / Samuel A. Broverman. -- 5th
ed.
     p. cm. -- (ACTEX academic series)
  ISBN 978-1-56698-767-7 (pbk. : alk. paper) 1. Interest--Mathematical
models. 2. Interest--Problems, exercises, etc. I. Title.
  HG4515.3.B76 2010
  332.8--dc22
                      2010029526


ISBN: 978-1-56698-767-7

To Sue, Alison, Amelia and Andrea

❧

"Neither a borrower nor lender be …,"

Polonius advises his son Laertes,
Act I, Scene III, Hamlet, by W. Shakespeare

# PREFACE

While teaching an intermediate level university course in mathematics of investment over a number of years, I found an increasing need for a textbook that provided a thorough and modern treatment of the subject, while incorporating theory and applications. This book is an attempt (as a 4th edition, it must be a fourth attempt) to satisfy that need. It is based, to a large extent, on notes that I developed while teaching and my use of a number of textbooks for the course. The university course for which this book was written has also been intended to help students prepare for the mathematics of investment topic that is covered on one of the professional examinations of the Society of Actuaries and the Casualty Actuarial Society. A number of the examples and exercises in this book are taken from questions on past SOA/CAS examinations.

As in many areas of mathematics, the subject of mathematics of investment has aspects that do not become outdated over time, but rather become the foundation upon which new developments are based. The traditional topics of compound interest and dated cashflow valuations, and their applications, are developed in the first five chapters of the book. In addition, in Chapters 6 to 9, a number of topics are introduced which have become of increasing importance in modern financial mathematics over the past number of years. The past decade or so has seen a great increase in the use of derivative securities, particularly financial options. The subjects covered in Chapters 6 and 8 such as the term structure of interest rates and forward contracts form the foundation for the mathematical models used to describe and value derivative securities, which are introduced in Chapter 9. This 5th edition expands on the 4th edition's coverage of the financial topics found in Chapters 8 and 9.

The purpose of the methods developed in this book is to do financial valuations. This book emphasizes a direct calculation approach, assuming that the reader has access to a financial calculator with standard financial function.

The mathematical background required for the book is a course in calculus at the Freshman level. Chapter 9 introduces a couple of topics that involve the notion of probability, but mostly at an elementary level. A very basic understanding of probability concepts should be sufficient background for those topics.

The topics in the first five Chapters of this book are arranged in an order that is similar to traditional approaches to the subject, with Chapter 1 introducing the various measures of interest rates, Chapter 2 developing methods for valuing a series of payments, Chapter 3 considering amortization of loans, Chapter 4 covering bond valuation, and Chapter 5 introducing the various methods of measuring the rate of return earned by an investment.

The content of this book is probably more than can reasonably be covered in a one-semester course at an introductory or even intermediate level. At the University of Toronto, the course on this subject is taught in two consecutive one-semester courses at the Sophomore level.

I would like to acknowledge the support of the Actuarial Education and Research Foundation, which provided support for the early stages of development of this book. I would also like to thank those who provided so much help and insight in the earlier editions of this book: John Mereu, Michael Gabon, Steve Linney, Walter Lowrie, Srinivasa Ramanujam, Peter Ryall, David Promislow, Robert Marcus, Sandi Lynn Scherer, Marlene Lundbeck, Richard London, David Scollnick and Robert Alps

I have had the benefit of many insightful comments and suggestions for this edition of the book from Keith Sharp, Louis Florence, Rob Brown, and Matt Hassett. I want to give a special mention of my sincere appreciation to Warren Luckner of the University of Nebraska, whose extremely careful reading of both the text and exercises caught a number of errors in the early drafts of this edition.

Marilyn Baleshiski is the format and layout editor, and Gail Hall is the mathematics editor at ACTEX. It has been a great pleasure for me to have worked with them on the book.

Finally, I am grateful to have had the continuous support of my wife, Sue Foster, throughout the development of each edition of this book.

Samuel A. Broverman, ASA, Ph.D.
University of Toronto
August 2010

# CONTENTS

## CHAPTER 1

### INTEREST RATE MEASUREMENT   1

## CHAPTER 2

# CHAPTER 3

## LOAN REPAYMENT  171

# CHAPTER 4

## BOND VALUATION    223

# CHAPTER 5

## MEASURING THE RATE OF RETURN OF AN INVESTMENT   263

# CHAPTER 6

## THE TERM STRUCTURE OF INTEREST RATES  **301**

# CHAPTER 7

## CASHFLOW DURATION AND IMMUNIZATION    355

# CHAPTER 8

## ADDITIONAL TOPICS IN FINANCE AND INVESTMENT    403

# CHAPTER 9

## FORWARDS, FUTURES, SWAPS, AND OPTIONS  427

# CHAPTER 1

## INTEREST RATE MEASUREMENT

*"The safest way to double your money is to fold it over and put it in your pocket."*
*– Kin Hubbard, American cartoonist and humorist (1868 - 1930)*

## 1.0 INTRODUCTION

Almost everyone, at one time or another, will be a saver, borrower, or investor, and will have access to insurance, pension plans, or other financial benefits. There is a wide variety of financial transactions in which individuals, corporations, or governments can become involved. The range of available investments is continually expanding, accompanied by an increase in the complexity of many of these investments.

Financial transactions involve numerical calculations, and, depending on their complexity, may require detailed mathematical formulations. It is therefore important to establish fundamental principles upon which these calculations and formulations are based. The objective of this book is to systematically develop insights and mathematical techniques which lead to these fundamental principles upon which financial transactions can be modeled and analyzed.

The initial step in the analysis of a financial transaction is to translate a verbal description of the transaction into a mathematical model. Unfortunately, in practice a transaction may be described in language that is vague and which may result in disagreements regarding its interpretation. The need for precision in the mathematical model of a financial transaction requires that there be a correspondingly precise and unambiguous understanding of the verbal description before the translation to the model is made. To this end, terminology and notation, much of which is in standard use in financial and actuarial practice, will be introduced.

A component that is common to virtually all financial transactions is **interest**, the "time value of money." Most people are aware that interest rates play a central role in their own personal financial situations as well as in the economy as a whole. Many governments and private enterprises

1

employ economists and analysts who make forecasts regarding the level of interest rates.

The Federal Reserve Board sets the "federal funds discount rate," a target rate at which banks can borrow and invest funds with one another. This rate affects the more general cost of borrowing and also has an effect on the stock and bond markets. Bonds and stocks will be considered in more detail later in the book. For now, it is not unreasonable to accept the hypothesis that higher interest rates tend to reduce the value of other investments, if for no other reason than that the increased attraction of investing at a higher rate of interest makes another investment earning a lower rate relatively less attractive.

---

### Irrational Exuberance

After the close of trading on North American financial markets on Thursday, December 5, 1996, Federal Reserve Board chairman Alan Greenspan delivered a lecture at The American Enterprise Institute for Public Policy Research.

In that speech, Mr. Greenspan commented on the possible negative consequences of "irrational exuberance" in the financial markets.

The speech was widely interpreted by investment traders as indicating that stocks in the US market were overvalued, and that the Federal Reserve Board might increase US interest rates, which might affect interest rates worldwide.

Although US markets had already closed, those in the Far East were just opening for trading on December 6, 1996. Japan's main stock market index dropped 3.2%, the Hong Kong stock market dropped almost 3%. As the opening of trading in the various world markets moved westward throughout the day, market drops continued to occur. The German market fell 4% and the London market fell 2%. When the New York Stock Exchange opened at 9:30 AM EST on Friday, December 6, 1996, it dropped about 2% in the first 30 minutes of trading, although the market did recover later in the day.

Sources: www.federalreserve.gov, www.pbs.org/newshour/bb/economy/december96/greenspan_12-6.html

The variety of interest rates and the investments and transactions to which they relate is extensive. Figure 1.1 was taken from the website of Bloomberg L.P. on June 6, 2007 and is an illustration of just a few of the types of interest rates that arise in practice. **Libor** refers to the London Interbank Overnight Rate, which is an international rate charged by one bank to another for very short term loans denominated in US dollars.

| KEY RATES | | | | | |
|---|---|---|---|---|---|
| | Current | 1 Month Prior | 3 Month Prior | 6 Month Prior | 1 Year Prior |
| Fed Reserve Target Rate | 5.25 | 5.25 | 5.25 | 5.25 | 5.00 |
| 3-Month Libor | 5.36 | 5.36 | 5.34 | 5.35 | 5.27 |
| Prime Rate | 8.25 | 8.25 | 8.25 | 8.25 | 8.00 |
| 5-Year AAA Banking and Finance | 5.49 | 5.07 | 4.96 | 4.93 | 5.60 |
| 10-Year AAA Banking and Finance | 5.73 | 5.39 | 5.21 | 5.23 | 5.89 |
| MORTGAGE RATES provided by Bankrate.com | | | | | |
| | Current | 1 Month Prior | 3 Month Prior | 6 Month Prior | 1 Year Prior |
| 15-Year Mortgage | 5.78 | 5.50 | 5.43 | 5.34 | 5.85 |
| 30-Year Mortgage | 6.09 | 5.77 | 5.69 | 5.58 | 6.17 |
| 1-Year ARM | 5.72 | 5.61 | 5.34 | 5.28 | 5.27 |
| USTREASURIES | | | | | |
| Bills | | | | | |
| | Coupon | Maturity Date | Current Discount/Yield | Price/Yield Change | Time |
| 3-Month | N.A. | 09/06/2007 | 4.66/4.77 | 0.02/ − .032 | 11:08 |
| 6-Month | N.A. | 12/06/2004 | 4.74/4.93 | 0.02/ − .048 | 10:41 |

www.bloomberg.com/markets/rates/index.html    Used with Permission from Bloomberg L.P.

**FIGURE 1.1**

To analyze financial transactions, a clear understanding of the concept of interest is required. Interest can be defined in a variety of contexts, and most people have at least a vague notion of what it is. In the most common context, interest refers to the consideration or rent paid by a borrower of money to a lender for the use of the money over a period of time.

This chapter provides a detailed development of the mechanics of interest rates: how they are measured and applied to amounts of principal over time to calculate amounts of interest. A standard measure of interest rates is defined and two commonly used growth patterns for investment – simple and compound interest – are described. Various alternative standard measures of interest, such as nominal annual rate of interest, rate of discount, and force of interest, are discussed. The general way in which a financial transaction is modeled in mathematical form is presented using the notions of accumulated value, present value, and equation of value.

## 1.1 INTEREST ACCUMULATION AND EFFECTIVE RATES OF INTEREST

An interest rate is most typically quoted as an annual percentage. If interest is credited or charged annually, the quoted annual rate, in    decimal fraction form, is multiplied by the amount invested or loaned to calculate the amount of interest that accrues over a one-year period. It is generally understood that as interest is credited or paid, it is reinvested. This reinvesting of interest leads to the process of compounding interest. The following example illustrates this process.

| EXAMPLE 1.1 | *(Compound interest calculation)*

The current rate of interest quoted by a bank on its savings account is 9% per annum (per year), with interest credited annually. Smith opens an account with a deposit of 1000. Assuming that there are no transactions on the account other than the annual crediting of interest, determine the account balance just after interest is credited at the end of 3 years.

| SOLUTION |

After one year the interest credited will be $1000 \times .09 = 90$, resulting in a balance (with interest) of $1000 + 1000 \times .09 = 1000(1.09) = 1090$. In common practice this balance is reinvested and earns interest in the second year, producing a balance of

$$1090 + 1090 \times .09 = 1090(1.09) = 1000(1.09)^2 = 1188.10$$

at the end of the second year. The balance at the end of the third year will be

$$1188.10 + 1188.10 \times .09 = (1188.10)(1.09) = 1000(1.09)^3 = 1295.03.$$

The following time diagram illustrates this process.

| 0 | 1 | 2 | 3 |
|---|---|---|---|
| ↑ | ↑ | ↑ | ↑ |
| 1000 | $1000 \times .09 = 90$ | $1090 \times .09 = 98.10$ | $1188.10 \times .09 = 106.93$ |
| Deposit | Interest | Interest | Interest |
| Total | $1000+90$ | $1090+98.10$ | $1188.10+106.93$ |
| | $=1090$ | $=1188.10$ | $=1295.03$ |
| | $=1000 \times 1.09$ | $=1090 \times 1.09$ | $=1188.10 \times 1.09$ |
| | | $=1000(1.09)^2$ | $=1000(1.09)^3$ |

**FIGURE 1.2** ❑

It can be seen from Example 1.1 that with an interest rate of $i$ per annum and interest credited annually, an initial deposit of $C$ will earn interest of $Ci$ for the following year. The accumulated value or future value at the end of the year will be $C + Ci = C(1+i)$. If this amount is reinvested and left on deposit for another year, the interest earned in the second year will be $C(1+i)i$, so that the accumulated balance is $C(1+i) + C(1+i)i = C(1+i)^2$ at the end of the second year. The account will continue to grow by a factor of $1+i$ per year, resulting in a balance of $C(1+i)^n$ at the end of $n$ years. This is the pattern of accumulation that results from compounding, or reinvesting, the interest as it is credited.

| 0 | 1 | 2 | $n-1$ | $n$ |
|---|---|---|---|---|
| ↑ | ↑ | ↑ | ↑ | ↑ |
| $C$ ⟶ | $Ci$ | $C(1+i)i$ | $C(1+i)^{n-2}i$ | $C(1+i)^{n-1}i$ |
| Deposit | Interest | Interest | Interest | Interest |
| | ↑ | ↑ | ↑ | ↑ |
| | $C+Ci$ | $C(1+i)$ | $= C(1+i)^{n-1}$ | $C(1+i)^{n-1}$ |
| Total | $= C(1+i)$ | $+C(1+i)i$ | | $+C(1+i)^{n-1}i$ |
| | | $= C(1+i)^2$ | | $= C(1+i)^n$ |

**FIGURE 1.3**

In Example 1.1, if Smith were to observe the accumulating balance in the account by looking at regular bank statements, he would see only one entry of interest credited each year. If Smith made the initial deposit on January 1, 2008 then he would have interest added to his account on December 31 of 2008 and every December 31 after that for as long as the account remained open.

The rate of interest may change from one year to the next. If the interest rate is $i_1$ in the first year, $i_2$ in the second year, and so on, then after $n$ years an initial amount $C$ will accumulate to $C(1+i_1)(1+i_2)\cdots(1+i_n)$, where the growth factor for year $t$ is $1+i_t$ and the interest rate for year $t$ is $i_t$. Note that "year $t$" starts at time $t-1$ and ends at time $t$.

| EXAMPLE 1.2 | *(Average annual rate of return)*

The excerpts below are taken from the 2006 year-end report of Altamira Corp., a Canadian mutual fund investment company. The excerpts below focus on the performance of the Altamira Income Fund and the Altamira Precision Dow 30 Index Fund during the five year period ending December 31, 2006.

| | **Annual Rate of Return** | | | | |
|---|---|---|---|---|---|
| | 2006 | 2005 | 2004 | 2003 | 2002 |
| Income Fund | 2.73% | 5.02% | 5.17% | 5.39% | 6.91% |
| Dow 30 Index Fund | 17.96% | − 2.33% | − 2.76% | 4.10% | − 16.49% |
| | **Average Annual Return** | | | | |
| | Inception | 1 yr% | 2 yr% | 3 yr% | 5 yr% |
| Income Fund | 02/19/70 | 2.73% | 3.87% | 4.30% | 5.04% |
| Dow 30 Index Fund | 07/14/99 | 17.96% | 7.34% | 3.86% | − .53% |

http://www.altamira.com

**FIGURE 1.4**

For the five year period ending December 31, 2006, the total compound growth in the Income Fund can be found by compounding the annual rates of return for the 5 years.

$$(1+.0273)(1+.0502)(1+.0517)(1+.0539)(1+.0691) = 1.2784$$

This would be the value on December 31, 2006 of an investment of 1 made into the fund on January 1, 2002.

This five year growth can be described by means of an average annual return per year for the five-year period. In practice the phrase "average annual return" refers to an annual compound rate of interest for the period of years being considered. The average annual return would be $i$, where $(1+i)^5 = 1.2784$. Solving for $i$ results in a value of $i = .0504$. This is the average annual return for the five year period ending December 31, 2006.

For the Dow 30 fund, an investment of 1 made January 1, 2002 would have a value on December 31, 2006 of

$$(1+.1796)(1-.0233)(1-.0276)(1+.0410)(1-.1649) = .9739$$

Solving for $i$ in the equation $(1+i)^5 = .9739$, results in $i = -.0053$, or a 5-year annual average return of $-.53\%$.

The Income Fund is described on the Altamira website as follows.

> "The Fund aims to achieve a reasonably high return (higher than that for five-year GICs) and constant income for the investor by investing mainly in fixed income securities primarily invested in Canadian (federal and provincial) government bonds and investment grade corporate bonds."

The Dow 30 fund is described as follows.

> "The Fund seeks long-term growth of capital by tracking the performance of the Dow Jones Industrial Average (Dow 30). The Dow 30 is a price-weighted index of 30 blue-chip stocks that are generally among the leaders in their industry. It has been a widely followed indicator of the US stock market." ❐

## 1.1.1 EFFECTIVE RATES OF INTEREST

In practice interest may be credited or charged more frequently than once per year. Many bank accounts pay interest monthly and credit cards generally charge interest monthly on previous unpaid balances. If a deposit is allowed to accumulate in an account over time, the algebraic form of the accumulation will be similar to the one given earlier for annual interest. At interest rate $j$ per compounding period, an initial deposit of amount $C$ will accumulate to $C(1+j)^n$ after $n$ compounding periods. (It is typical to use $i$ to denote an annual rate of interest, and in this text $j$ will often be used to denote an interest rate for a period of other than a year.)

At an interest rate of .75% per month on a bank account, with interest credited monthly, the growth factor for a one-year period at this rate would be $(1.0075)^{12} = 1.0938$. The account earns 9.38% over the full year and 9.38% is called the **effective annual rate of interest** earned on the account.

---

**Definition 1.1 – Effective Annual Rate of Interest**

The effective annual rate of interest earned by an investment during a one-year period is the percentage change in the value of the investment from the beginning to the end of the year, without regard to the investment behavior at intermediate points in the year.

---

In Example 1.2, the effective annual rates of return for two Altamira funds are given for years 2002 through 2006. Comparisons of the performance of two or more investments are often done by comparing the respective effective annual interest rates earned by the investments over a particular year. The Altamira Income Fund earned an annual effective rate of interest of 2.735% for 2006, but the Dow 30 Fund earned 17.96%. For the 5-year period from January 1, 2002 to December 31, 2006, the Income Fund earned an average annual effective rate of interest of 5.04%, but the Dow 30 average annual effective rate was −.53% (a negative rate).

### Equivalent Rates of Interest

If the monthly compounding at .75% described earlier continued for another year, the accumulated or future value after two years would be $C(1.0075)^{24} = C(1.0938)^2$. We see that over an integral number of years a month-by-month accumulation at a monthly rate of .75% is *equivalent* to annual compounding at an annual rate of 9.38%; the word "equivalent" is used in the sense that they result in the same accumulated value.

---

**Definition 1.2 - Equivalent Rates of Interest**

Two rates of interest are said to be **equivalent** if they result in the same accumulated values at each point in time.

---

### 1.1.2 COMPOUND INTEREST

When compound interest is in effect, and deposits and withdrawals are occurring in an account, the resulting balance at some future point in time can be determined by accumulating all individual transactions to that future time point.

EXAMPLE 1.3 *(Compound interest calculation)*

Smith deposits 1000 into an account on January 1, 2005. The account credits interest at an effective annual rate of 5% every December 31. Smith withdraws 200 on January 1, 2007, deposits 100 on January 1, 2008, and withdraws 250 on January 1, 2010. What is the balance in the account just after interest is credited on December 31, 2011?

SOLUTION

One approach is to recalculate the balance after every transaction. On December 31, 2006 the balance is $1000(1.05)^2 = 1102.50$;

on January 1, 2007 the balance is $1102.50 - 200 = 902.50$;

on December 31, 2007 the balance is $902.50(1.05) = 947.63$;

on January 1, 2008 the balance is $947.63 + 100 = 1047.63$;

on December 31, 2009 the balance is $1047.63(1.05)^2 = 1155.01$;

on January 1, 2010 the balance is $1155.01 - 250 = 905.01$; and

on December 31, 2011 the balance is $905.01(1.05)^2 = 997.77$.

An alternative approach is to accumulate each transaction to the December 31, 2011 date of valuation and combine all accumulated values, adding deposits and subtracting withdrawals. Then we have

$$1000(1.05)^7 - 200(1.05)^5 + 100(1.05)^4 - 250(1.05)^2 = 997.77$$

for the balance on December 31, 2011. This is illustrated in the following time line:

| 1/1/05 $\cdots$ | 1/1/07 | 1/1/08 $\cdots$ | 1/1/10 $\cdots$ | 12/31/11 |
|---|---|---|---|---|
| +1000 (initial Deposit) | | | $\longrightarrow$ | $1000(1.05)^7$ |
| | −200 | | $\longrightarrow$ | $-200(1.05)^5$ |
| | | +100 | $\longrightarrow$ | $100(1.05)^4$ |
| | | | −250 $\longrightarrow$ | $-250(1.05)^2$ |

Total $= 1000(1.05)^7 - 200(1.05)^5 + 100(1.05)^4 - 250(1.05)^2 = 997.77$.

**FIGURE 1.5**                                                                    ❏

The pattern for compound interest accumulation at rate $i$ per period results in an accumulation factor of $(1+i)^n$ over $n$ periods. The pattern of investment growth may take various forms, and we will use the general expression $a(n)$ to represent the accumulation (or growth) factor for an investment from time 0 to time $n$.

---

**Definition 1.3 – Accumulation Factor and**
**Accumulated Amount Function**

$a(t)$ is the accumulated value at time $t$ of an investment of 1 made at time 0 and defined as the accumulation factor from time 0 to time $t$. The notation $A(t)$ will be used to denote the accumulated amount of an investment at time $t$, so that if the initial investment amount is $A(0)$, then the accumulated value at time $t$ is $A(t) = A(0) \cdot a(t)$. $A(t)$ is the accumulated amount function.

---

**Compound interest accumulation at rate $i$ per period** is defined with $t$ as any positive real number.

---

**Definition 1.4 – Compound Interest Accumulation**

At effective annual rate of interest $i$ per period, the accumulation factor from time 0 to time $t$ is

$$a(t) = (1+i)^t \qquad (1.1)$$

---

The graph of compound interest accumulation is given in Figure 1.6.

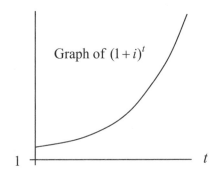

**FIGURE 1.6**

If, in Example 1.1, Smith closed his account in the middle of the fourth year (3.5 years after the account was opened), the accumulated or future value at time $t = 3.5$ would be $1000(1.09)^{3.50} = 1000(1.09)^3(1.09)^{.50} = 1352.05$, which is the balance at the end of the third year followed by accumulation for one-half more year to the middle of the fourth year.

In practice, financial transactions can take place at any point in time, and it may be necessary to represent a period which is a fractional part of a year. A fraction of a year is generally described in terms of either an integral number of $m$ months, or an exact number of $d$ days. In the case that time is measured in months, it is common in practice to formulate the fraction of the year $t$ in the form $t = \frac{m}{12}$, even though not all months are exactly $\frac{1}{12}$ of a year. In the case that time is measured in days, $t$ is often formulated as $t = \frac{d}{365}$ (some investments use a denominator of 360 days instead of 365 days, in which case $t = \frac{d}{360}$).

---

### The Magic of Compounding

Investment advice newsletters and websites often refer to the "magic" of compounding when describing the potential for investment accumulation. A phenomenon is magical only until it is understood. Then it's just an expected occurrence, and it loses its mystery.

A value of 10% is often quoted as the long-term historical average return on equity investments in the US stock market. Based on the historical data, the 30-year average return was 10% on the Dow Jones index from the start of 1970 to the end of 2000. During that period, the average annual return in the 1990s was 16.5%, in the 1980s it was 13.9%, and in the 1970's it was .5%. The 1970s were not as magical a time for investors as the 1990s.

In the 1980s heyday of multi-level marketing schemes, one such scheme promoted the potential riches that could be realized by marketing "gourmet" coffee in the following way. A participant had merely to recruit 6 sub-agents who could sell 2 pounds of coffee per week. Those sub-agents would then recruit 6 sub-agents of their own. This would continue to an ever increasing number of levels. The promotional literature stated the expected net profit earned by the "top" agent based on each number of levels of 6-fold sub-agents that could be recruited. The expected profit based on 9 levels of sub-agents was of the order of several hundred thousand dollars per week. There was no indication in the brochure that to reach this level would require over 10,000,000 ($6^9$) sub-agents. Reaching that level would definitely require some compounding magic.

Source: www.finfacts.com

When considering the equation $X(1+i)^t = Y$, given any three of the four variables $X, Y, i, t$, it is possible to find the fourth. If the unknown variable is $t$, then solving for the time factor results in $t = \dfrac{\ln(Y/X)}{\ln(1+i)}$ (ln is the natural log function). If the unknown variable is the interest rate $i$, then solving for $i$ results in $i = \left(\dfrac{Y}{X}\right)^{1/t} - 1$. Financial calculators have functions that allow you to enter three of the variables and calculate the fourth.

### 1.1.3 SIMPLE INTEREST

When calculating interest accumulation over a fraction of a year or when executing short term financial transactions, a variation on compound interest commonly known as **simple interest** is often used. At an interest rate of $i$ per year, an amount of 1 invested at the start of the year grows to $1+i$ at the end of the year. If $t$ represents a fraction of a year, then under the application of simple interest, the accumulated value at time $t$ of the initial invested amount of 1 is as follows.

---

**Definition 1.5– Simple Interest Accumulation**

The accumulation function from time 0 to time $t$ at annual simple interest rate $i$, where $t$ is measured in years is

$$a(t) \;=\; 1+it. \qquad\qquad (1.2)$$

---

As in the case of compound interest, for a fraction of a year, $t$ is usually either $m/12$ or $d/365$. The following example refers to a **promissory note**, which is a short-term contract (generally less than one year) requiring the issuer of the note (the borrower) to pay the holder of the note (the lender) a principal amount plus interest on that principal at a specified annual interest rate for a specified length of time. At the end of the time period the payment (principal and interest) is due. Promissory note interest is calculated on the basis of simple interest. The interest rate earned by the lender is sometimes referred to as the "*yield rate*" earned on the investment. As concepts are introduced throughout this text, we will see the expression "yield rate" used in a number of different investment contexts with differing meanings. In each case it will be important to relate the meaning of the yield rate to the context in which it is being used.

---

**EXAMPLE 1.4** (*Promissory note and simple interest*)

On January 31 Smith borrows 5000 from Brown and gives Brown a promissory note. The note states that the loan will be repaid on April 30 of the same year, with interest at 12% per annum. On March 1 Brown sells the promissory note to Jones, who pays Brown a sum of money in return for the right to collect the payment from Smith on April 30. Jones pays Brown an amount such that Jones' yield (interest rate earned) from March 1 to the maturity date can be stated as an annual rate of interest of 15%.

(a) Determine the amount Smith was to have paid Brown on April 30,

(b) Determine the amount that Jones paid to Brown and the yield rate (interest rate) Brown earned, quoted on an annual basis. Assume all calculations are based on simple interest and a 365 day year.

(c) Suppose instead that Jones pays Brown an amount such that Jones' yield is 12%. Determine the amount that Jones paid.

**SOLUTION**

(a) The payment required on the maturity date April 30 is
$$5000\left[1+(.12)\left(\tfrac{89}{365}\right)\right] = 5146.30$$ (there are 89 days from January 31 to April 30 in a non-leap year; financial calculators often have a function that calculates the number of days between two dates).

(b) Let $X$ denote the amount Jones pays Brown on March 1. We will denote by $j_1$ the annual yield rate earned by Brown based on simple interest for the period of $t_1 = \tfrac{29}{365}$ years from January 31 to March 1, and we will denote by $j_2$ the annual yield rate earned by Jones for the period of $t_2 = \tfrac{60}{365}$ years from March 1 to April 30. Then $X = 5000(1+t_1 j_1)$ and the amount paid on April 30 by Smith is $X(1+t_2 j_2) = 5146.30$. The following time-line diagram indicates the sequence of events.

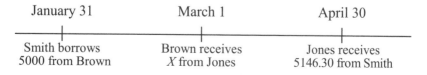

| January 31 | March 1 | April 30 |
|---|---|---|
| Smith borrows 5000 from Brown | Brown receives $X$ from Jones | Jones receives 5146.30 from Smith |

**FIGURE 1.7**

We are given $j_2 = .15$ (the annualized yield rate earned by Jones) and we can solve for $X$ from $X = \frac{5146.30}{1+t_2 j_2} = \frac{5146.30}{1+\left(\frac{60}{365}\right)(.15)} = 5022.46$. Now that $X$ is known, we can solve for $j_1$ from

$$X = 5022.46 = 5000(1+t_1 j_1) = 5000\left(1+\frac{29}{365} \cdot j_1\right)$$

to find that Brown's annualized yield is $j_1 = .0565$.

(c) If Jones' yield is 12%, then Jones paid

$$X = \frac{5146.30}{1+t_2 j_2} = \frac{5146.30}{1+\left(\frac{60}{365}\right)(.12)} = 5046.75. \qquad \square$$

In the previous example, we see that to achieve a yield rate of 15% Jones pays 5022.46 and to achieve a yield rate of 12% Jones pays 5046.75. This inverse relationship between yield and price is typical of a "**fixed-income**" investment. A fixed-income investment is one for which the future payments are predetermined (unlike an investment in, say, a stock, which involves some risk, and for which the return cannot be predetermined). Jones is investing in a loan which will pay him 5146.30 at the end of 60 days. If the desired interest rate for an investment with fixed future payments increases, the price that Jones is willing to pay for the investment decreases (the less paid, the better the return on the investment). An alternative way of describing the inverse relationship between yield and price on fixed-income investments is to say that the holder of a fixed income investment (Brown) will see the market value of the investment decrease if the yield rate to maturity demanded by a buyer (Jones) increases. This can be explained by noting that a higher yield rate requires a smaller investment amount to achieve the same dollar level of interest payments. This will be seen again when the notion of *present value* is discussed later in this chapter.

## 1.1.4 COMPARISON OF COMPOUND INTEREST AND SIMPLE INTEREST

From Equations 1.1 and 1.2 it is clear that accumulation under simple interest forms a linear function whereas compound interest accumulation forms an exponential function. This is illustrated in Figure 1.8 with a graph of the accumulation of an initial investment of 1 at both simple and compound interest.

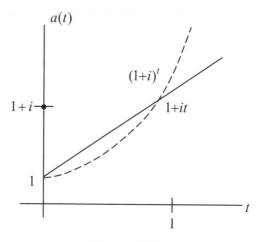

**FIGURE 1.8**

From Figure 1.8 it appears that simple interest accumulation is larger than compound interest accumulation for values of $t$ between 0 and 1, but compound interest accumulation is greater than simple interest accumulation for values of $t$ greater than 1. Using an annual interest rate of $i = .08$, we have, for example, at time $t = .25$, $1 + it = 1 + (.08)(.25) = 1.02 > 1.0194 = (1.08)^{.25}$ $= (1+i)^t$, and at $t = 2$ we have $1 + it = 1 + (.08)(2) = 1.16 < 1.1664 = (1.08)^2$ $= (1+i)^t$. The relationship between simple and compound interest is verified algebraically in an exercise at the end of this chapter.

Interest accumulation is often based on a combination of simple and compound interest. Compound interest would be applied over the completed (integer) number of interest compounding periods, and simple interest would be applied from then to the fractional point in the current interest period. For instance, under this approach, at annual rate 9%, over a period of 4 years and 5 months, an investment would grow by a factor of $(1.09)^4 \left[ 1 + \frac{5}{12}(.09) \right]$.

### 1.1.5 ACCUMULATED AMOUNT FUNCTION

When analyzing the accumulation of a single invested amount, the value of the investment is generally regarded as a function of time. For example,

$A(t)$ is the value of the investment at time $t$, with $t$ usually measured in years. Time $t = 0$ usually corresponds to the time at which the original investment was made. The amount by which the investment grows from time $t_1$ to time $t_2$ is often regarded as the amount of interest earned over that period, and this can be written as $A(t_2) - A(t_1)$. Also, with this notation, the effective annual interest rate for the one-year period from time $u$ to time $u+1$ would be $i_{u+1}$, where $A(u+1) = A(u)(1+i_{u+1})$, or equivalently,

$$i_{u+1} = \frac{A(u+1) - A(u)}{A(u)}. \tag{1.3}$$

The subscript "$u+1$" indicates that we are measuring the interest rate in year $u+1$. Accumulation can have any sort of pattern, and, as illustrated in Figure 1.9, the accumulated value might not always be increasing. The Altamira Dow 30 Index Fund in Example 1.2 has some years with negative annual effective returns.

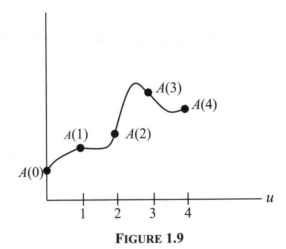

**FIGURE 1.9**

This relationship for $i_{u+1}$ shows that the effective annual rate of interest for a particular one-year period is the amount of interest for the year as a proportion of the value of the investment at the start of the year, or equivalently, the rate of investment growth per dollar invested. In other words:

*effective annual rate of interest for a specified one-year period*

$$= \frac{amount\ of\ interest\ earned\ for\ the\ one\text{-}year\ period}{value\ (or\ amount\ invested)\ at\ the\ start\ of\ the\ year}.$$

The accumulated amount function can be used to find an effective interest rate for any time interval. For example, the effective three-month interest rate for the three months from time $3\frac{1}{4}$ to time $3\frac{1}{2}$ would be

$$\frac{A\left(3\frac{1}{2}\right)-A\left(3\frac{1}{4}\right)}{A\left(3\frac{1}{4}\right)}.$$

From a practical point of view, the accumulated amount function $A(t)$ would be a step function, changing by discrete increments at each interest credit time point, since interest is credited at discrete points of time. For more theoretical analysis of investment behavior, it may be useful to assume that $A(t)$ is a continuous, or differentiable, function, such as in the case of compound interest growth on an initial investment of amount $A(0)$ at time $t = 0$, where $A(t) = A(0)(1+i)^t$ for any non-negative real number $t$.

## 1.2   PRESENT VALUE

If we let $X$ be the amount that must be invested at the start of a year to accumulate to 1 at the end of the year at effective annual interest rate $i$, then $X(1+i) = 1$, or equivalently, $X = \frac{1}{1+i}$. The amount $\frac{1}{1+i}$ is the **present value of an amount of 1 due in one year**.

---

**Definition 1.6 – One Period Present Value Factor**

If the rate of interest for a period is $i$, the present value of an amount of 1 due one period from now is $\frac{1}{1+i}$. The factor $\frac{1}{1+i}$ is often denoted $v$ in actuarial notation and is called a **present value factor** or discount factor.

---

When a situation involves more than one interest rate, the symbol $v_i$ may be used to identify the interest rate $i$ on which the present value factor is based.

The present value factor is particularly important in the context of compound interest. Accumulation under compound interest has the form $A(t) = A(0)(1+i)^t$. This expression can be rewritten as

$$A(0) \ = \ \frac{A(t)}{(1+i)^t} \ = \ A(t)(1+i)^{-t} \ = \ A(t)v^t.$$

Thus $Kv^t$ is the present value at time 0 of an amount $K$ due at time $t$ when investment growth occurs according to compound interest. This means that $Kv^t$ is the amount that must be invested at time 0 to grow to $K$ at time $t$, and the present value factor $v$ acts as a "compound present value" factor in determining the present value. Accumulation and present value are inverse processes of one another.

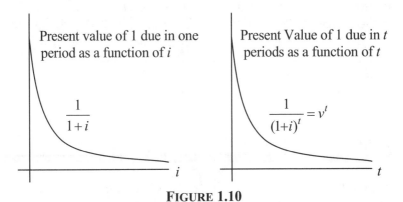

Present value of 1 due in one period as a function of $i$

$$\frac{1}{1+i}$$

Present Value of 1 due in $t$ periods as a function of $t$

$$\frac{1}{(1+i)^t} = v^t$$

**FIGURE 1.10**

The right graph in Figure 1.10 illustrates that as the time horizon $t$ increases, the present value of 1 due at time $t$ decreases (if the interest rate is positive). The left graph of Figure 1.10 illustrates the classical "inverse yield-price relationship," which states that at a higher rate of interest, a smaller amount invested is needed to reach a target accumulated value.

**EXAMPLE 1.5** (*Present value calculation*)

Ted wants to invest a sufficient amount in a fund in order that the accumulated value will be one million dollars on his retirement date in 25 years. Ted considers two options. He can invest in Equity Mutual Fund, which invests in the stock market. E.M. Fund has averaged an annual compound rate of return of 19.5% since its inception 30 years ago, although its annual growth has been as low as 2% and as high as 38%. The E.M. Fund provides no guarantees as to its future performance. Ted's other option is to invest in a *zero-coupon bond or stripped bond* (this is a bond with no coupons, only a payment on the maturity date; this concept will be covered in detail later in the book), with a guaranteed effective annual rate of interest of 11.5% until its maturity date in 25 years.

(a) What amount must Ted invest if he chooses E.M. Fund and assumes that the average annual growth rate will continue for another 25 years?

(b) What amount must he invest if he opts for the stripped bond investment?

(c) What minimum effective annual rate is needed over the 25 years in order for an investment of $25,000 to accumulate to Ted's target of one million?

(d) How many years are needed for Ted to reach $1,000,000 if he invests the amount found in part (a) in the stripped bond?

---
| SOLUTION |
---

(a) If Ted invests $X$ at $t = 0$, then $X(1.195)^{25} = 1,000,000$, so that the present value of 1,000,000 due in 25 years at an effective annual rate of 19.5% is $1,000,000v^{25} = 1,000,000(1.195)^{-25} = 11,635.96$.

(b) The present value of 1,000,000 due in 25 years at $i = .115$ is $1,000,000v^{25} = 1,000,000(1.115)^{-25} = 65,785.22$. Note that no subscript was used on $v$ in part (a) or (b) since it was clear from the context as to the interest rate being used.

(c) We wish to solve for $i$ in the equation $25,000(1+i)^{25} = 1,000,000$. The solution for $i$ is $i = \left(\frac{1,000,000}{25,000}\right)^{1/25} - 1 = .1590$.

(d) In $t$ years Ted will have $11,635.96(1.115)^t = 1,000,000$. Solving for $t$ results in $t = \dfrac{\ln\left(\frac{1,000,000}{11,635}\right)}{\ln(1.115)} = 40.9$ years.     ❑

If simple interest is being used for investment accumulation, then $A(t) = A(0)(1+it)$ and the present value at time 0 of amount $A(t)$ due at time $t$ is $A(0) = \frac{A(t)}{1+it}$. It is important to note that implicit in this expression is the fact that simple interest accrual begins at the time specified as $t = 0$. The present value based on simple interest accumulation assumes that interest begins accruing at the time the present value is being found. There is no standard symbol representing present value under simple interest that corresponds to $v$ under compound interest.

## 1.2.1 CANADIAN TREASURY BILLS

### EXAMPLE 1.6

*(Canadian Treasury bills – present value based on simple interest)*

The figure below is an excerpt from the website of the Bank of Canada describing a sale of **Treasury Bills** by the Canadian federal government on Thursday, August 28, 2003 (www.bankofcanada.ca). A **T-Bill** is a debt obligation that requires the issuer to pay the owner a specified sum (the *face amount* or *amount*) on a specified date (the *maturity date*). The issuer of the T-Bill is the borrower, the Canadian government in this case. The purchaser of the T-Bill would be an investment company or an individual. Canadian T-Bills are issued to mature in a number of days that is a multiple of 7. Canadian T-Bills are generally issued on a Thursday, and mature on a Thursday, mostly for periods of (approximately) 3 months, 6 months or 1 year.

| BANK OF CANADA | | BANQUE DE CANADA |
|---|---|---|

| | |
|---|---|
| For Release: 10:40 E.T.<br>Publication: 10 h 40 HE | OTTAWA<br>2003.08.26 |
| Treasury Bills – Regular<br>Auction Results | Bons du Trésor réguliers<br>Résultats de l'adjudication |
| On behalf of the Minister of Finance, it was announced today that tenders for Government of Canada treasury bills have been accepted as follows: | On vient d'annoncer aujourd'hui, au nom du ministre des Finances, que les soumissions suivantes ont été acceptées pour les bons du Trésor du gouvernement du Canada: |

| | | |
|---|---|---|
| Auction Date | **2003.08.26** | Date d'adjudication |
| Bidding Deadline | **10:30:00** | Heure limite de soumission |
| Total Amount | **$9,500,000,000** | Montant total |

**Multiple Price / Prix multiple**

| Amount<br>Montant | Issue<br>Émission | Maturity<br>Échéance | Outstanding<br>after Auction<br>Encours après<br>l'adjudication | (%)<br>Yield and Equivalent<br>Price Taux de<br>rendement et prix<br>correspondant | (%)<br>Allotment<br>Ratio<br>Ratio de<br>répartition | Bank of Canada<br>Purchase Achat<br>de la Banque<br>du Canada |
|---|---|---|---|---|---|---|
| 5,300,000,000<br>ISIN: CA1350Z7DL50 | 2003.08.28 | 2003.12.04 | $8,800,000,000 | Avg/Moy: 2.700  99.28029<br>Low/Bas: 2.697  99.28108<br>High/Haut: 2.704  99.27923 | 53.45667 | $500,000,000 |
| 2,100,000,0<br>00<br>ISIN: CA1350Z7D765 | 2003.08.28 | 2004.02.12 | 4,200,000,000 | Avg/Moy: 2.741  98.75411<br>Low/Bas: 2.738  98.75545<br>High/Haut: 2.744  98.75276 | 84.58961 | $250,000,000 |

**FIGURE 1.11**

Two T-Bills are described in Figure 1.11, both issued August 28, 2003. The first one is set to mature December 4, 2003, which is 98 days (14 weeks) after issue. The *yield* is quoted as 2.700% and the price (per face amount of 100) is 99.28029. The price is the present value on the issue date of 100 due on the maturity date, and present value is calculated on the basis of simple interest and a 365-day year. The quoted price based on the quoted average yield rate of 2.700% can be calculated as follows:

$$Price = 100 \times \frac{1}{1 + (.02700)\left(\frac{98}{365}\right)} = 99.28029.$$

The price of the second T-Bill can be found in a similar way. It matures February 12, 2004, which is 168 days (24 weeks) after the issue date. The quoted average yield is 2.741%. The price is

$$Price = 100 \times \frac{1}{1 + (.02741)\left(\frac{168}{365}\right)} = 98.75411.$$

Valuation of Canadian T-Bills is algebraically identical to valuation of promissory notes described in Example 1.4. ☐

Given an accumulated amount function $A(t)$, the investment grows from amount $A(t_1)$ at time $t_1$ to amount $A(t_2)$ at time $t_2 > t_1$. Therefore an amount of $\frac{A(t_1)}{A(t_2)}$ invested at time $t_1$ will grow to amount 1 at time $t_2$. In other words, $\frac{A(t_1)}{A(t_2)}$ is a generalized present value factor from time $t_2$ back to time $t_1$.

## 1.3 EQUATION OF VALUE

When a financial transaction is represented algebraically it is usually formulated by means of one or more equations that represent the values of the various components of the transaction and their interrelationships. Along with the interest rate, the other components of the transaction are the amounts disbursed and the amounts received. These amounts are called *dated cash flows*. A mathematical representation of the transaction will be an equation that balances the dated cash outflows and inflows, according to the particulars of the transaction. The equation balancing these cash flows must take into account the "time values" of these payments, the accumulated and present values of the payments made at the various time points. Such a balancing equation is called an **equation of value** for the transaction, and its formulation is a central element in the process of analyzing a financial transaction.

In order to formulate an equation of value for a transaction, it is first necessary to choose a reference time point or valuation date. At the reference time point the equation of value balances, or equates, the following two factors:

(1)   the accumulated value of all payments already disbursed plus the present value of all payments yet to be disbursed, and

(2)   the accumulated value of all payments already received plus the present value of all payments yet to be received.

### EXAMPLE 1.7    (*Choice of valuation point for an equation of value*)

Every Friday in February (the 7, 14, 21, and 28) Walt places a $1000 bet, on credit, with his off-track bookmaking service, which charges an effective weekly interest rate of 8% on all credit extended. Unfortunately for Walt, he loses each bet and agrees to repay his debt to the bookmaking service in four installments, to be made on March 7, 14, 21, and 28. Walt pays $1100 on each of March 7, 14, and 21. How much must Walt pay on March 28 to completely repay his debt?

### SOLUTION

The payments in the transaction are represented in Figure 1.12. We must choose a reference time point at which to formulate the equation of value. If we choose February 7 ($t = 0$ in Figure 1.12), then Walt receives 1000 right "now" and all other amounts received and paid are in the future, so we find their present values. The value at time 0 of what Walt will receive (on credit) is $1000(1 + v + v^2 + v^3)$, representing the four weekly credit amounts received in February, where $v = \frac{1}{1.08}$ is the weekly present value factor and $t$ is measured in weeks. The value at $t = 0$ of what Walt must pay is $1100(v^4 + v^5 + v^6) + Xv^7$, representing the three payments of 1100 and the fourth payment of $X$.

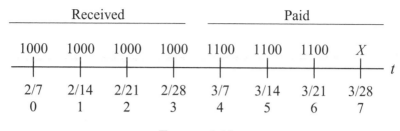

**FIGURE 1.12**

Equating the value at time 0 of what Walt will receive with the value of what he will pay results in the equation

$$1000\left(1 + v + v^2 + v^3\right) \;=\; 1100\left(v^4 + v^5 + v^6\right) + Xv^7. \tag{A}$$

Solving for $X$ results in

$$X \;=\; \frac{1000\left(1+v+v^2+v^3\right) - 1100\left(v^4+v^5+v^6\right)}{v^7} \;=\; 2273.79. \tag{B}$$

If we choose March 28 ($t = 7$) as the reference time point for valuation, then we accumulate all amounts received and paid to time 7. The value of what Walt has received is $1000\left[(1+j)^7 + (1+j)^6 + (1+j)^5 + (1+j)^4\right]$, and the value of what he has repaid is $1100\left[(1+j)^3 + (1+j)^2 + (1+j)\right] + X$, where again $j = .08$ is the effective rate of interest per week.

The equation of value formulated at $t = 7$ can be written as

$$1000\left[(1+j)^7 + (1+j)^6 + (1+j)^5 + (1+j)^4\right]$$
$$= 1100\left[(1+j)^3 + (1+j)^2 + (1+j)\right] + X. \tag{C}$$

Solving for $X$ results in

$$1000\left[(1+j)^7 + (1+j)^6 + (1+j)^5 + (1+j)^4\right]$$
$$- 1100\left[(1+j)^3 + (1+j)^2 + (1+j)\right] \;=\; 2273.79. \tag{D}$$

Note that most financial transactions will have interest rates quoted as annual rates, but in the weekly context of this example it was unnecessary to indicate an annual rate of interest. (The equivalent effective annual rate would be quite high). ❑

We see from Example 1.7 that an equation of value for a transaction involving compound interest may be formulated at more than one reference time point with the same ultimate solution. Notice that Equation C can be obtained from Equation A by multiplying Equation A by $(1+j)^7$. This corresponds to a change in the reference point upon which the equations are based, Equation A being based on $t = 0$ and Equation C being based on $t = 7$. In general, when a transaction involves only compound interest, an equation of value formulated at time $t_1$ can be translated into an equation of value formulated at time $t_2$ simply by multiplying the first equation by $(1+i)^{t_2-t_1}$. In Example 1.7, when $t = 7$ was chosen as the reference point, the solution was slightly simpler than that required for the equation of value at $t = 0$, in that no division was necessary. For most transactions there will often be one reference time point that allows a more efficient solution of the equation of value than any other reference time point.

## 1.4 NOMINAL RATES OF INTEREST

Quoted annual rates of interest frequently do not refer to the effective annual rate. Consider the following example.

### EXAMPLE 1.8 (*Monthly compounding of interest*)

Sam has just received a credit card with a credit limit of $1000. The card issuer quotes an annual charge on unpaid balances of 24%, payable monthly. Sam immediately uses his card to its limit. The first statement Sam receives indicates that his balance is 1000 but no interest has yet been charged. Each subsequent statement includes interest on the unpaid part of his previous month's statement. He ignores the statements for a year, and makes no payments toward the balance owed. What amount does Sam owe according to his thirteenth statement?

SOLUTION

Sam's first statement will have a balance of 1000 outstanding, with no interest charge. Subsequent monthly statements will apply a monthly interest charge of $\left(\frac{1}{12}\right)(24\%) = 2\%$ on the unpaid balance from the previous month. Thus Sam's unpaid balance is compounding monthly at a rate of 2% per month; the interpretation of the phrase "payable monthly" is that the quoted annual interest rate is to be divided by 12 to get the one-month interest rate. The balance on statement 13 (12 months after statement 1) will have compounded for 12 months to $1000(1.02)^{12} = 1268.23$ (this value is based on rounding to the nearest penny each month; the exact value is 1268.24). The effective annual interest rate charged on the account in the 12 months following the first statement is 26.82%. The quoted rate of 24% is a **nominal annual rate of interest, not an effective annual rate of interest**. This example shows that a *nominal annual interest rate of 24% compounded monthly* is equivalent to an effective annual rate of 26.82%. ☐

---

**Definition 1.7 – Nominal Annual Rate of Interest**

A nominal annual rate of interest compounded or convertible $m$ times per year refers to an interest compounding period of $\frac{1}{m}$ years.

$$\text{interest rate for } \frac{1}{m} \text{ period} = \frac{\text{quoted nominal annual interest rate}}{m}$$

---

Nominal rates of interest occur frequently in practice. They are used in situations which interest is credited or compounded more often than once per year. A nominal annual rate can be associated with any interest compounding period, such as six months, one month, or one week. In order to apply a quoted nominal annual rate, it is necessary to know the number of interest conversion periods in a year. In Example 1.8 the associated interest compounding period is indicated by the phrase "payable monthly," and this tells us that the interest compounding period is one month. This could also be stated in any of the following ways:

(i)    annual interest rate of 24%, compounded monthly,

(ii)   annual interest rate of 24%, convertible monthly, or

(iii)  annual interest rate of 24%, convertible 12 times per year.

All of these phrases mean that the 24% quoted annual rate is to be transformed to an effective one-month rate that is one-twelfth of the quoted annual rate, $\left(\frac{1}{12}\right)(.24) = .02$. The effective interest rate per interest compounding period is a fraction of the quoted annual rate corresponding to the fraction of a year represented by the interest compounding period.

The notion of equivalence of two rates was introduced in Section 1.1, where it was stated that rates are equivalent if they result in the same pattern of compound accumulation over any equal periods of time. This can be seen in Example 1.8. The nominal annual 24% refers to a compound monthly rate of 2%. Then in $t$ years ($12t$ months) the growth of an initial investment of amount 1 will be

$$(1.02)^{12t} = \left[(1.02)^{12}\right]^{t} = (1.2682)^{t}.$$

Since $(1.2682)^{t}$ is the growth in $t$ years at effective annual rate 26.82%, this verifies the equivalence of the two rates. The typical way to verify equivalence of rates is to convert one rate to the compounding period of the other rate, using compound interest. In the case just considered, the compound monthly rate of 2% can be converted to an equivalent effective annual growth factor of $(1.02)^{12} = 1.2682$. Alternatively, an effective annual rate of 26.82% can be converted to a compound monthly growth factor of $(1.2682)^{1/12} = 1.02$.

Once the nominal annual interest rate and compounding interest period are known, the corresponding compound interest rate for the interest conversion period can be found. Then the accumulation function follows a compound interest pattern, with time usually measured in units of effective interest conversion periods. When comparing nominal annual interest rates with differing interest compounding periods, it is necessary to convert the rates to equivalent rates with a common effective interest period. The following example illustrates this.

> **EXAMPLE 1.9**    (*Comparison of nominal annual rates of interest*)

Tom is trying to decide between two banks in which to open an account. Bank A offers an annual rate of 15.25% with interest compounded semiannually, and Bank B offers an annual rate of 15% with interest compounded monthly. Which bank will give Tom a higher effective annual growth?

SOLUTION

Bank A pays an effective 6-month interest rate of $\frac{1}{2}(15.25\%) = 7.625\%$. In one year (two effective interest periods) a deposit of amount 1 will grow to $(1.07625)^2 = 1.158314$ in Bank A.

Bank B pays an effective monthly interest rate of $\frac{1}{12}(15\%) = 1.25\%$. In one year (12 effective interest periods) a deposit of amount 1 in Bank B will grow to $(1.0125)^{12} = 1.160755$. Bank B has an equivalent annual effective rate that is almost .25% higher than that of Bank A. □

The 24% rate quoted in Example 1.8 is sometimes called an *annual percentage rate*, and the rate of 2% per month is the *periodic rate*. In practice, a credit card issuer will usually quote an "APR" (annual percentage rate), and may also quote a daily percentage rate which is $\frac{APR}{365}$. When a monthly billing cycle ends, an "average daily balance" is calculated, usually by taking the average of the account balances at the start of each day during the billing cycle. This is multiplied by the daily percentage rate, and this is multiplied by the number of days in the billing cycle. Under this approach, the monthly interest rates compounded in Example 1.8 would not be exactly 2% per month, but would be $\frac{.24}{365} \times 31 = .02038356$ for a 31 day billing cycle, $\frac{.24}{365} \times 30 = .01972603$ for a 30 day billing cycle, etc.

In order to make a fair comparison of quoted nominal annual rates with differing interest conversion periods, it is necessary to transform them to a common interest conversion period, such as an effective annual period as in Example 1.9.

---

**Payday Loans**

As long as there have been people who run short of money before their next paycheck, there have been lenders who will provide short term loans to be repaid at the next payday, usually within a few weeks of the loan. Providers of these loans seem to have become more visible in recent years with both storefront and internet based lending operations. Interest rates charged by some lenders for these loans can be surprisingly high.

The US Truth in Lending Act requires that, for consumer loans, the APR (annual percentage rate) associated with the loan must be disclosed to the borrower. The APR is generally disclosed as a nominal annual rate of interest whose conversion period is the payment period for the loan.

According to a February, 2000 report by the US-based Public Interest Research Group (USPRIG), the APR on short term loans (7 to 18 days) in states where such loans are allowed ranged from 390 to 871%.

A search of internet based lending sites turned up a lender charging a fee of $25 for a one week loan of $100. This one week interest rate of 25% is quoted as an APR of 1303.57% (this is $.25 \times \frac{365}{7}$), which is the corresponding nominal annual rate convertible every 7 days. The equivalent annual effective growth of an investment that accumulates at a rate of 25% per week with weekly compounding is $(1.25)^{365/7} = 113,022.5$, which represents an equivalent annual effective rate of interest of a little more than 11,300,000%! The lender also allows the loan to be repaid in up to 18 days for the same $25 fee for the 18 days. In this case, the APR is only 506.94%, and the equivalent annual effective rate of interest is a mere 9,128%.

Source: uspirg.org

---

### 1.4.1 ACTUARIAL NOTATION FOR NOMINAL RATES OF INTEREST

There is *standard actuarial notation* for denoting nominal annual rates of interest, although this notation is not generally seen outside of actuarial practice. In actuarial notation, the symbol $i$ is generally reserved for an effective annual rate, and the symbol $i^{(m)}$ is reserved for a nominal annual rate with interest compounded $m$ times per year. Note that the superscript is for identification purposes and is not an exponent. The notation $i^{(m)}$ is taken to mean that interest will have a compounding period of $\frac{1}{m}$ years and compound rate per period of $\frac{1}{m} \cdot i^{(m)} = \frac{i^{(m)}}{m}$.

In Example 1.8, $m = 12$, so the nominal annual rate would be denoted as $i^{(12)} = .24$. The information indicated by the superscript "(12)" in this notation is that there are 12 interest conversion periods per year, and that the effective rate of 2% per month is $\frac{1}{12}$ of the quoted rate of 24%. Similarly, in Example 1.9 the nominal annual rates would be $i_A^{(2)} = .1525$ and $i_B^{(12)} = .15$ for Banks A and B, respectively.

In Example 1.8 the equivalent effective annual growth factor is $1 + i = \left(1 + \frac{.24}{12}\right)^{12} = 1.2682$. In Example 1.9 the equivalent effective annual growth factors for Banks A and B, respectively, are

$$1 + i_A = \left(1 + \frac{.1525}{2}\right)^2 = 1.158314$$

and

$$1 + i_B = \left(1 + \frac{.15}{12}\right)^{12} = 1.160755.$$

The general relationship linking equivalent nominal annual interest rate $i^{(m)}$ and effective annual interest rate $i$ is

$$1 + i = \left[1 + \frac{i^{(m)}}{m}\right]^m. \tag{1.4}$$

The comparable relationships linking $i$ and $i^{(m)}$ can be summarized in the following two equations

$$i = \left[1 + \frac{i^{(m)}}{m}\right]^m - 1 \quad \text{and} \quad i^{(m)} = m\left[(1+i)^{1/m} - 1\right]. \tag{1.5}$$

Note that $(1+i)^{1/m}$ is the $\frac{1}{m}$-year growth factor, and $(1+i)^{1/m} - 1$ is the equivalent effective $\frac{1}{m}$-year compound interest rate.

It should be clear from general reasoning that with a given nominal annual rate of interest, the more often compounding takes place during the year, the larger the year-end accumulated value will be, so the larger the equivalent effective annual rate will be as well. This is verified algebraically in an exercise at the end of the chapter. The following example considers the relationship between equivalent $i$ and $i^{(m)}$ as $m$ changes.

EXAMPLE 1.10

(*Equivalent effective and nominal annual rates of interest*)

Suppose the effective annual rate of interest is 12%. Find the equivalent nominal annual rates for $m = 1, 2, 3, 4, 6, 8, 12, 52, 365, \infty$.

SOLUTION

$m = 1$ implies interest is convertible annually ($m = 1$ time per year), which implies the effective annual interest rate is $i^{(1)} = i = .12$. We use Equation (1.5) to solve for $i^{(m)}$ for the other values of $m$. The results are given in Table 1.1.

TABLE 1.1

| $m$ | $(1+i)^{1/m} - 1$ | $i^{(m)} = m\left[(1+i)^{1/m} - 1\right]$ |
|---|---|---|
| 1 | .1200 | .12 |
| 2 | .0583 | .1166 |
| 3 | .0385 | .1155 |
| 4 | .0287 | .1149 |
| 6 | .0191 | .1144 |
| 8 | .0143 | .1141 |
| 12 | .0095 | .1139 |
| 52 | .00218 | .1135 |
| 365 | .000311 | .113346 |
| $\infty$ | | $\displaystyle\lim_{m\to\infty} m\left[(1+i)^{1/m} - 1\right] = \ln(1+i) = .113329$ |

Note that $(1.12)^{1/2} - 1 = .0583$ is the effective 6-month rate of interest that is equivalent to an effective annual rate of interest of 12% (two successive 6-month periods of compounding at effective 6-month rate 5.83% results in one year growth of $(1.0583)^2 = 1.12$). The limit in the final line of Table 1.1 is a consequence of l'Hospital's Rule. It can also be seen from Table 1.1 that the more frequently compounding takes place (i.e., as $m$ increases), the smaller is the equivalent nominal annual rate. The change is less significant, however, in going from monthly to weekly or even daily compounding, so we see that there is a limit to the benefit of compounding. With an effective annual rate of 12%, the minimum equivalent nominal annual rate is never less than 11.333% no matter how often compounding takes place. The limiting case $(m \to \infty)$ in Example 1.10 is called *continuous compounding* and is related to the notions of *force of interest* and instantaneous growth rate of an investment. This is discussed in detail in Section 1.6.

A nominal rate, although quoted on an annual basis, might refer to only the immediately following fraction of a year. For instance, in Example 1.9 Bank B's quoted nominal annual rate of 15% with interest credited monthly might apply only to the coming month, after which the quoted rate (still credited monthly) might change to something else, say 13.5%. Thus when interest is quoted on a nominal annual basis, the actual rate may change during the course of the year, from one interest period to the next.

## 1.5 EFFECTIVE AND NOMINAL RATES OF DISCOUNT

### 1.5.1 EFFECTIVE ANNUAL RATE OF DISCOUNT

In previous sections of this chapter, interest amounts have been regarded as paid or charged at the end of an interest compounding period, and the corresponding interest rate is the ratio of the amount of interest paid at the end of the period to the amount of principal at the start of the period. Interest rates and amounts viewed in this way are sometimes referred to as *interest payable in arrears* (payable at the end of an interest period). This is the standard way in which interest rates are quoted, and it is the standard way by which interest amounts are calculated. In many situations it is the method required by law.

Occasionally a transaction calls for *interest payable in advance*. In this case the quoted interest rate is applied to obtain an amount of interest which is payable at the start of the interest period. For example, if Smith borrows 1000 for one year at a quoted rate of 10% with interest payable in advance, the 10% is applied to the loan amount of 1000, resulting in an amount of interest of 100 for the year. The interest is paid at the time the loan is made. Smith receives the loan amount of 1000 and must immediately pay the lender 100, the amount of interest on the loan. One year later he must repay the loan amount of 1000. The net effect is that Smith receives 900 and repays 1000 one year later. The effective annual rate of interest on this transaction is $\frac{100}{900} = .1111$, or 11.11%. This 10% payable in advance is called the **rate of discount** for the transaction. The rate of discount is the rate used to calculate the amount by which the year end value is reduced to determine the present value.

The effective annual rate of discount is another way of describing investment growth in a financial transaction. In the example just considered we see that an effective annual interest rate of 11.11% is equivalent to an effective annual discount rate of 10%, since both describe the same transaction.

---

**Definition 1.8 – Effective Annual Rate of Discount**

In terms of an accumulated amount function $A(t)$, the general definition of the effective annual rate of discount from time $t = 0$ to time $t = 1$ is

$$d = \frac{A(1) - A(0)}{A(1)}. \tag{1.6}$$

---

This definition is in contrast with the definition for the effective annual rate of interest, which has the same numerator but has a denominator of $A(0)$. Effective annual interest measures growth on the basis of the initially invested amount, whereas effective annual discount measures growth on the basis of the year-end accumulated amount. Either measure can be used in the analysis of a financial transaction.

### 1.5.2 EQUIVALENCE BETWEEN DISCOUNT AND INTEREST RATES

Equation (1.6) can be rewritten as $A(0) = A(1) \cdot (1-d)$, so we see that $1-d$ acts as a present value factor. The value at the start of the year is the principal amount of $A(1)$ minus the interest payable in advance, which is $d \cdot A(1)$. On the other hand, on the basis of effective annual interest we have $A(0) = A(1) \cdot v$. We see that for $d$ and $i$ to be equivalent rates, present values under both representations must be the same, so we must have $\frac{1}{1+i} = v = 1-d$, or equivalently, $d = \frac{i}{1+i}$, or $i = \frac{d}{1-d}$.

Equivalent rates of interest and discount $i$ and $d$ are:

$$d = \frac{i}{1+i} \quad \text{and} \quad i = \frac{d}{1-d} \tag{1.7}$$

With $d = .10$ in the situation outlined above, we have $i = \frac{.1}{1-.1} = .1111$, or 11.11%. The relationships between equivalent interest and discount rates for periods of other than a year are similar. Suppose that $j$ is the effective rate of interest for a period of other than one year. Then $d_j = \frac{j}{1+j}$ where $d_j$ is the equivalent effective rate of discount for that period.

The present value of 1 due in $n$ years can be represented in the form $v^n = (1-d)^n$, so that present values can be represented in the form of *compound discount*. This underlines the fact that the concepts of discount rate and compound discount form an alternative to the concepts of interest rate and compound interest in describing the behavior of an investment.

From a practical point of view, $A(0)$ in Equation (1.6) will not be less than 0. If $A(1) > A(0)$, an effective rate of discount can be no larger than 1 (100%). Note that an effective discount rate of $d = 1$ (100%), implies a present value factor of $1-d = 1-1 = 0$ at the start of the period (an investment of 0 growing to a value of 1 at the end of a year would be a very profitable arrangement). In the equivalence between $i$ and $d$ we see that $\lim_{i \to \infty} d = 1$, so that very large effective interest rates correspond to equivalent effective discount rates near 100%.

### 1.5.3 SIMPLE DISCOUNT AND VALUATION OF US T-BILLS

One of the main practical applications of discount rates occurs with United States Treasury Bills. In Section 1.2 it was seen that Canadian T-Bills are quoted with prices and annual yield rates, where an annual yield rate is applied using simple interest for the period to the maturity of the T-Bill. The pricing of US T-Bills is based on **simple discount**.

---

**Definition 1.9 – Simple Discount**

With a quoted annual discount rate of $d$, based on simple discount the present value of 1 payable $t$ years from now is $1-dt$. Simple discount is generally only applied for periods of less than one year.

---

| EXAMPLE 1.11 | (*US Treasury Bill*) |

Quotations for US T-Bills are based on a maturity amount of $100. The table below was excerpted from the website of the United States Bureau of the Public Debt in June, 2004. The website provides a brief description of how the various quoted values are related to one another.

### Examples of Treasury Bill Auction Results

| Term | Issue Date | Maturity Date | Discount Rate% | Investment Rate% | Price Per $100 | CUSIP |
|------|------------|---------------|----------------|------------------|----------------|-------|
| 12-day | 06/3/2004 | 06/15/2004 | 0.965 | 0.974 | 99.968 | 912795QP9 |
| 28-day | 06/3/2004 | 07/01/2004 | 0.940 | 0.952 | 99.927 | 912795QR5 |
| 91-day | 06/3/2004 | 09/02/2004 | 1.130 | 1.150 | 99.714 | 912795RA1 |
| 182-day | 06/3/2004 | 12/02/2004 | 1.400 | 1.430 | 99.292 | 912795RP8 |

(www.publicdebt.treas.gov/sec/secpry.htm)

The "Price Per $100" is the present value of $100 due in the specified number of days. The relationship between the quoted price and the discount rate is based on simple discount in which a fraction of a year is calculated on the basis of a 360-day year. The quoted discount and investment rates are annual rates.

For instance, the price for the 182-day bill issued June 3, 2004 and maturing December 2, 2004 is found from the relationship $P = 100(1-dt)$. With discount rate $d = .01400$, and fraction of a year $t = \frac{182}{360}$, we have

$$P = 100\left[1-(.01400)\left(\tfrac{182}{360}\right)\right] = 99.292 \text{ (rounded to the 3}^{\text{rd}} \text{ decimal place,}$$

which is the practice for quoting T-Bill prices).

The "Investment Rate" is an annual rate of simple interest that is equivalent to the return over the 182-day period. The investment growth for the 182-day period is $\frac{100}{99.292} = 1.0071305$. If this is converted to an annual return based on simple interest for a 365-day year (not the 360 day year used with the discount rate), the corresponding return for 365 days is $.00713 \times \frac{365}{182} = .01430$ which can be quoted as a rate of 1.430%. Calculations for the other T-Bills quoted above are done in the same way. □

The US government's Truth in Lending legislation requires that financial institutions making loans based on discount rates make clear to borrowers the equivalent interest rate being charged. Thus an annual effective discount rate of 8% cannot be presented as a loan rate of 8%, but must instead be presented as the equivalent interest rate, $i = \frac{d}{1-d} = \frac{.08}{1-.08} = .0870$.

---

**Investing In Treasury Bills**

According to the website of the US Bureau of Public Debt, on May 31, 2006, the total US public debt outstanding was a little over $8.35 trillion ("little" in this case is around $7 billion). About $4.8 trillion of that total is publicly held by banks, private investors, insurance companies and foreign investors. Of the $4.8 trillion, about $952 billion is in Treasury Bills.

For over 20 years, the US Treasury Department has sold T-Bills, notes and bonds directly to the public in amounts that are multiples of $1000. Recently, the Treasury Department has allowed individuals to open internet based accounts through which treasury securities can be purchased.

Source: www.publicdebt.treas.gov

---

### 1.5.4 NOMINAL ANNUAL RATE OF DISCOUNT

---

**Definition 1.10 – Nominal Annual Rate of Discount**

A nominal annual rate of discount compounded $m$ times per year refers to a discount compounding period of $\frac{1}{m}$ years,

$$\text{discount rate for } \frac{1}{m} \text{ period} = \frac{\text{quoted nominal annual discount rate}}{m}$$

---

In actuarial notation, the symbol $d$ is generally used to denote an effective annual discount rate, and the symbol $d^{(m)}$ is reserved for denoting a nominal annual discount rate with discount compounded (or convertible) $m$ times per year. The notation $d^{(m)}$ is taken to mean that discount will have a compounding period of $\frac{1}{m}$ years and compound rate per period of $\frac{1}{m} \cdot d^{(m)} = \frac{d^{(m)}}{m}$.

The relationship between equivalent nominal and effective annual discount rates parallels the relationship between nominal and effective annual interest rates. The $\frac{1}{m}$-year present value factor would be $1 - \frac{d^{(m)}}{m}$. For instance, the notation $d^{(4)} = .08$ refers to a 3-month discount rate of $\frac{.08}{4} = .02$, and a 3-month present value factor of $1 - .02 = .98$. This would be compounded 4 times during the year to an effective annual present value factor of $(.98)^4 = .9224$. This annual present value factor could then be described as being equivalent to an effective annual discount rate of 7.76%.

With $d^{(m)}$ in effect, there would generally be $m$ compounding periods during the year, so the equivalent effective annual present value factor would be $\left(1 - \frac{d^{(m)}}{m}\right)^m$. If $d$ is the equivalent effective annual rate of discount, then we have the relationship

$$1 - d = \left(1 - \frac{d^{(m)}}{m}\right)^m. \tag{1.8}$$

### EXAMPLE 1.12

(*Equivalent effective and nominal annual rates of discount*)

Suppose that the effective annual rate of discount is $d = .107143$. Find the equivalent nominal annual discount rates $d^{(m)}$ for

$$m = 1, 2, 3, 4, 6, 8, 12, 52, 365, \infty.$$

### SOLUTION

Using Equation (1.8) we solve for $d^{(m)} = m\left[1 - (1-d)^{1/m}\right]$. The numerical results are tabulated below in Table 1.2.

**TABLE 1.2**

| $m$ | $1-(1-d)^{1/m}$ | $d^{(m)} = m\left[1-(1-d)^{1/m}\right]$ |
|---|---|---|
| 1 | .107143 | .107143 |
| 2 | .0551 | .1102 |
| 3 | .0371 | .1112 |
| 4 | .0279 | .1117 |
| 6 | .0187 | .1123 |
| 8 | .0141 | .1125 |
| 12 | .0094 | .1128 |
| 52 | .0022 | .1132 |
| 365 | .0003 | .11331 |
| $\infty$ | $\lim_{m\to\infty} m\left[1-(1-d)^{1/m}\right] = -\ln(1-d) = .113329$ | |

❑

Note that in Example 1.12, $1-(1-.107143)^{1/2} = .055089$ is the effective 6-month rate of discount that is equivalent to an effective annual rate of discount of 10.7143% (two 6-month periods of compounding at effective 6-month discount rate 5.5089% results in one year present value of $(1-.055089)^2 = 1-.107143$).

Note also in Table 1.2 that as $m$ increases, $d^{(m)}$ increases with upper limit $d^{(\infty)}$. Thus if $m > n$ then $d^{(m)} > d^{(n)}$ for equivalent rates. This is the opposite of what happens for equivalent nominal interest rates (see Example 1.10). This can be explained by noting that interest compounds on amounts increasing in size whereas discount compounds on amounts decreasing in size.

The effective annual discount rate used in Example 1.12 is $d = .107143$, which is equivalent to an effective annual interest rate of $i = .12$. It was chosen to facilitate comparison with the table in Example 1.10. The exercises at the end of the chapter examine in more detail the numerical relationship between equivalent nominal annual interest and discount rates, and refer to the equivalent rates in the tables from Examples 1.10 and 1.12. We see that the nominal annual interest rate convertible continuously from Example 1.10 is $i^{(\infty)} = .1133$, which is equal to $d^{(\infty)}$ in Example 1.12. In general, for equivalent rates $i$ and $d$ it is always the case that $d^{(\infty)} = i^{(\infty)}$, equal to the force of interest.

## 1.6 THE FORCE OF INTEREST

Financial transactions occur at discrete time points. Many theoretical financial models are based on events that occur in a continuous time framework. The famous Black-Scholes option pricing model (which will be briefly reviewed in Chapter 9) was developed on the basis of stock prices changing continuously as time goes on. In this section we describe a way to measure investment growth in a continuous time framework.

Continuous processes are usually modeled mathematically as limits of discrete time processes, where the discrete time intervals get smaller and smaller. This is how we will approach measuring continuous growth of an investment.

### 1.6.1 CONTINUOUS INVESTMENT GROWTH

Suppose that the accumulated value of an investment at time $t$ is represented by the function $A(t)$, where time is measured in years. The amount of interest earned by the investment in the $\frac{1}{4}$-year period from time $t$ to time $t+\frac{1}{4}$ is $A\left(t+\frac{1}{4}\right) - A(t)$, and the $\frac{1}{4}$-year interest rate for that period is $\frac{A\left(t+\frac{1}{4}\right) - A(t)}{A(t)}$. The $\frac{1}{4}$-year interest rate can be described in terms of a nominal annual interest rate by multiplying the $\frac{1}{4}$-year interest rate by 4. The nominal annual interest rate compounded quarterly $\left(i^{(4)}\right)$ is $4 \times \frac{A\left(t+\frac{1}{4}\right) - A(t)}{A(t)}$ We are again using a (nominal) annual interest rate measure to describe what occurs in the $\frac{1}{4}$-year period from time $t$ to time $t+\frac{1}{4}$ with the understanding that the rate may change from one quarter to the next.

The $\frac{1}{4}$-year example can be generalized to any fraction of a year. The interest rate earned by the investment for the $\frac{1}{m}$-year period from time $t$

to time $t + \frac{1}{m}$ is $\frac{A\left(t+\frac{1}{m}\right)-A(t)}{A(t)}$. This rate can be described in terms of a nominal annual rate of interest compounded $m$ times per year. The nominal annual rate would be found by scaling up the $\frac{1}{m}$-year rate by a factor of $m$ so that $i^{(m)} = m \times \frac{A\left(t+\frac{1}{m}\right)-A(t)}{A(t)}$. Again, although described as an annual rate, $i^{(m)}$ is the quoted nominal annual rate of interest based on the investment performance from time $t$ to time $t + \frac{1}{m}$.

If $m$ is increased, the time interval $\left[t, t + \frac{1}{m}\right]$ decreases, and we are focusing more and more closely on the investment performance during an interval of time immediately following time $t$. Taking the limit of $i^{(m)}$ as $m \to \infty$ results in

$$i^{(\infty)} = \lim_{m \to \infty} i^{(m)} = \lim_{m \to \infty} m \times \frac{A\left(t+\frac{1}{m}\right)-A(t)}{A(t)}.$$

This limit can be reformulated by making the following variable substitution. Define the variable $h$ to be $h = \frac{1}{m}$, so that $h \to 0$ as $m \to \infty$. The limit can then be written in the form

$$i^{(\infty)} = \frac{1}{A(t)} \cdot \lim_{h \to 0} \frac{A(t+h) - A(t)}{h} = \frac{1}{A(t)} \cdot \frac{d}{dt} A(t) = \frac{A'(t)}{A(t)}. \quad (1.9)$$

$i^{(\infty)}$ is a nominal annual interest rate compounded infinitely often or **compounded continuously.** $i^{(\infty)}$ is also interpreted as the instantaneous rate of growth of the investment per dollar invested at time point $t$ and is called the **force of interest at time $t$.** Note that $A'(t)\,dt$ represents the instantaneous growth of the invested amount at time point $t$ (just as $A(t+1) - A(t)$ is the *amount* of growth in the investment from $t$ to $t+1$), whereas $\frac{A'(t)}{A(t)}$ is the relative instantaneous rate of growth per unit amount invested at time $t$ (just as $\frac{A(t+1) - A(t)}{A(t)}$ is the relative rate of growth from $t$ to $t+1$ per unit invested at time $t$).

The force of interest may change as $t$ changes. The actuarial notation that is used for the force of interest at time $t$ is usually $\delta_t$ instead of $i^{(\infty)}$. In order for the force of interest to be defined, the accumulated amount function $A(t)$ must be differentiable (and thus continuous, because any differentiable function is continuous). Continuous investment growth models have been central to the analysis and development of financial models with important practical applications, most notably for models of investment derivative security valuation such as stock options.

---

**Definition 1.11 – Force of Interest**

For an investment that grows according to accumulated amount function $A(t)$, the force of interest at time $t$, is defined to be

$$\delta_t = \frac{A'(t)}{A(t)} \tag{1.10}$$

---

### 1.6.2 INVESTMENT GROWTH BASED ON THE FORCE OF INTEREST

The following example shows the force of interest that corresponds to (a) simple interest, and (b) compound interest.

**EXAMPLE 1.13**  (*Force of interest*)

Derive an expression for $\delta_t$ if accumulation is based on

(a) simple interest at annual rate $i$, and

(b) compound interest at annual rate $i$.

**SOLUTION**

(a)  $A(t) = A(0) \cdot [1 + i \cdot t]$, so $A'(t) = A(0) \cdot i$. Then $\delta_t = \dfrac{A'(t)}{A(t)} = \dfrac{i}{1 + i \cdot t}$.

(b)  $A(t) = A(0) \cdot (1+i)^t$, so that $A'(t) = A(0) \cdot (1+i)^t \cdot \ln(1+i)$, and then

$\delta_t = \dfrac{A'(t)}{A(t)} = \ln(1+i)$. This was the form of force of interest denoted earlier as $i^{(\infty)}$. In the case of compound interest growth, the force of interest is constant as long as the effective annual interest rate is constant. In the case of simple interest, $\delta_t$ decreases as $t$ increases.  □

The force of interest can be used to describe investment growth. Using Equation (1.10) we have $\delta_t = \frac{A'(t)}{A(t)} = \frac{d}{dt}\ln[A(t)]$. Integrating this equation from time $t = 0$ to time $t = n$, we get

$$\int_0^n \delta_t \, dt = \int_0^n \frac{d}{dt}\ln[A(t)]dt = \ln[A(n)] - \ln[A(0)] = \ln\left[\frac{A(n)}{A(0)}\right].$$

This can be rewritten in the form

$$\exp\left[\int_0^n \delta_t \, dt\right] = \frac{A(n)}{A(0)} \qquad (1.10a)$$

or

$$A(n) = A(0) \cdot \exp\left[\int_0^n \delta_t \, dt\right] \qquad (1.10b)$$

or

$$A(0) = A(n) \cdot \exp\left[-\int_0^n \delta_t \, dt\right] \qquad (1.10c)$$

The general form of the accumulation factor from time $t = n_1$ to time $t = n_2$ (where $n_1 \le n_2$) is $e^{\int_{n_1}^{n_2} \delta_t \, dt}$ and the general form of the present value factor for the same period of time is $e^{-\int_{n_1}^{n_2} \delta_t \, dt}$. In the case in which $\delta_t$ is constant with value $\delta$ from time $n_1$ to time $n_2$, the accumulation factor for that period simplifies to $e^{(n_2-n_1)\delta}$ and the present value factor is $e^{-(n_2-n_1)\delta}$.

Example 1.13(a) showed that for simple interest accumulation at annual interest rate $i$, with accumulation function $A(t) = A(0) \times (1+it)$, the force of interest is $\delta_t = \frac{i}{1+it}$. For an investment of 1 made at time $n_1$, the growth factor for the investment to time $n_2$ is

$$\exp\left(\int_{n_1}^{n_2} \frac{i}{1+it}\,dt\right) = \exp\left[\ln(1+n_2 i) - \ln(1+n_1 i)\right] = \frac{1+n_2 i}{1+n_1 i}.$$

In practice however, when simple interest is being applied, it is assumed that simple interest accrual for an investment begins at the time that the investment is made, so that an investment made at time $n_1$ will grow by a factor of $1+(n_2-n_1)\times i$ to time $n_2$, which is not the same as the growth factor found using the force of interest $\delta_t = \frac{i}{1+it}$. The reason for this is that this force of interest has a starting time of 0, and later deposits must accumulate based on the force of interest at the later time points, whereas in practice, each time a deposit or investment is made, the clock is reset at time 0 for that deposit, and simple interest begins anew for that deposit.

Another identity involving the force of interest is based on the relationship $\frac{d}{dt}A(t) = A(t)\cdot\delta_t$. $A(t)\cdot\delta_t$ is the instantaneous amount of interest earned by the investment at time $t$. Integrating both from time 0 to time $n$ results in

$$\int_0^n A(t)\cdot\delta_t\,dt = \int_0^n \frac{d}{dt}A(t)\,dt = A(n) - A(0). \qquad (1.11)$$

This is the amount of interest earned from time 0 to time $n$.

EXAMPLE 1.14   (*Force of interest*)

Given $\delta_t = .08 + .005t$, calculate the accumulated value over five years of an investment of 1000 made at each of the following times:

(a) Time 0, and
(b) Time 2.

SOLUTION

(a) In this case, $A(0) = 1000$ and $A(5) = A(0)\cdot\exp\left[\int_0^5 \delta_t\,dt\right]$, so that the accumulated value is

$$1000\cdot\exp\left[\int_0^5 (.08+.005t)\,dt\right],$$

which is

$$1000 \cdot \exp\left[(.08)(5) + (.0025)(25)\right] = 1000 \cdot e^{.4625} = 1588.04.$$

(b) This time we have $A(2) = 1000$ and $A(7) = A(2) \cdot \exp\left[\int_2^7 \delta_t \, dt\right]$, so that the accumulated value at time 7 is

$$1000 \cdot \exp\left[\int_2^7 (.08 + .005t) \, dt\right],$$

leading to

$$1000 \cdot \exp[(.08)(7-2) + (.0025)(49-4)] = 1669.46.$$

Note that both (a) and (b) involve 5 year periods, but the accumulations are different as a result of the non-constant force of interest. □

### 1.6.3 CONSTANT FORCE OF INTEREST

It was shown in Example 1.13 that if the effective annual interest rate $i$ is constant then $\delta_t = \ln(1+i)$. Let us now suppose the force of interest $\delta_t$ is constant with value $\delta$ from time 0 to time $n$. Then

$$A(n) = A(0) \cdot e^{\int_0^n \delta_t \, dt} = A(0) \cdot e^{n\delta} = A(0) \cdot (e^\delta)^n.$$

This form of accumulation is algebraically identical to compound interest accumulation of the form $A(n) = A(0) \cdot (1+i)^n$, where $e^\delta = 1 + i$, or equivalently, where $\delta = \ln(1+i)$.

A constant effective annual interest rate $i$ is equivalent to constant force of interest $\delta$ according to the relationship

$$1 + i = e^\delta, \text{ or equivalently, } \delta = \ln(1+i) \qquad (1.12)$$

Example 1.13 illustrates the relationship that $\delta$ and $i$ must satisfy in order to be equivalent rates. This relationship was already seen in Examples 1.10 and 1.12, where an effective annual rate of $i = .12$ was used to find equivalent nominal annual rates $i^{(m)}$ for various values of $m$. For $m = \infty$ the rates $i^{(\infty)}$ and $d^{(\infty)}$ were found to be $i^{(\infty)} = \ln(1+i) = \ln(1.12) = .1133$, the constant force of interest that is equivalent to $i = .12$.

The explicit use of the force of interest does not often arise in a practical setting. For transactions of very short duration (a few days or only one day), a nominal annual interest rate convertible daily, $i^{(365)}$, might be used. This rate is approximately equal to the equivalent force of interest, as illustrated in Table 1.1. Major financial institutions routinely borrow and lend money among themselves overnight, in order to cover their transactions during the day. The interest rate used to settle these one day loans is called the *overnight* rate. The interest rate quoted will be a nominal annual rate of interest compounded every day ($m = 365$).

---

**EXAMPLE 1.15** | (*Overnight Rate*)

Bank A requires an overnight (one-day) loan of 10,000,000 and is quoted a nominal annual rate of interest convertible daily of 12% by Bank B.

(a) Calculate the amount of interest Bank A must pay for the one-day loan.

(b) Suppose the loan was quoted at an annual force of interest of 12%. Calculate the interest Bank A must pay in this case.

---

**SOLUTION**

(a) With $i^{(365)} = .12$, the one-day rate of interest is $\frac{.12}{365} = .000328767$, so that interest on 10,000,000 for one day will be 3,287.67 (to the nearest cent).

(b) If $\delta = .12$, then interest for one day will be

$$10,000,000(e^{.12/365} - 1) = 3,288.21.$$

The difference between these amounts of interest is 0.54 (a very small fraction of the principal amount of 10,000,000). ❑

---

## 1.7 INFLATION AND THE "REAL" RATE OF INTEREST

Along with the level of interest rates, one of the most closely watched indicators of a country's economic performance and health is the rate of inflation. A widely used measure of inflation is the change in the *Con-*

*sumer Price Index* (CPI), generally quoted on an annual basis. The change in the CPI measures the (effective) annual rate of change in the cost of a specified "basket" of consumer items. Alternative measures of inflation might be based on more specialized sectors in the economy. Inflation rates vary from country to country. They may be extremely high in some economies and almost insignificant in others. It is sometimes the case that an economy experiences deflation for a period of time (negative inflation), characterized by a decreasing CPI. Politicians and economists have been involved in numerous debates on the causes and effects of inflation, its relationship to the country's economic health, and how best to reduce or prevent inflation.

Investors are also concerned with the level of inflation. It is clear that a high rate of inflation has the effect of rapidly reducing the value (purchasing power) of currency as time goes on. It is not surprising then that periods of high inflation are usually accompanied by high interest rates, since the rate of interest must be high enough to provide a "real" return on investment. The study of the cause and effect relationship between interest and inflation is the concern of economists. We are concerned here with analyzing the relationship between interest and inflation in terms of the measurement of return on investments.

We have used the phrase *real return* a few times already without being very specific as to its meaning. The **real rate of interest** refers to the *inflation-adjusted* return on an investment.

---

**Definition 1.12 – Real Rate of Interest**

With annual interest rate $i$ and annual inflation rate $r$, the real rate of interest for the year is

$$i_{real} = \frac{value\ of\ amount\ of\ real\ return\ (yr\text{-}end\ dollars)}{value\ of\ invested\ amount\ (yr\text{-}end\ dollars)} = \frac{i-r}{1+r}, \quad (1.13)$$

---

The simple and commonly used measure of the real rate of interest is $i-r$, where $i$ is the annual rate of interest and $r$ is the annual rate of inflation. This measure is often seen in financial newspapers or journals. As a precise measure of the real growth of an investment, or real growth in purchasing power, $i-r$ is not theoretically correct. This is made clear in the following example.

---

| EXAMPLE 1.16 | *(The "real" rate of interest)*

Smith invests 1000 for one year at effective annual rate 15.5%. At the time Smith makes the investment, the cost of a certain consumer item is 1. One year later, when interest is paid and principal returned to Smith, the cost of the item has become 1.10. What is the annual growth rate in Smith's purchasing power with respect to the consumer item?

| SOLUTION |

At the start of the year, Smith can buy 1000 items. At year end he receives $1000(1.155) = 1155$, and is able to buy $\frac{1155}{1.10} = 1050$ items. Thus Smith's purchasing power has grown by 5% (i.e., $\frac{50}{1000}$). Regarding the 10% increase in the cost of the item as a measure of inflation, we have $i - r = .155 - .10 = .055$, so, in this case, $i - r$ is not a correct representation of the "real" return earned by Smith.  ❒

In Example 1.16 Smith would have to receive 1100 at the end of the year just to stay even with the 10% inflation rate. He actually receives interest plus principal for a total of 1155. Thus Smith receives

$$1000(1+i) - 1000(1+r) \;=\; 1000(i-r) \;=\; 55$$

more than necessary to stay even with inflation, and this 55 is his "real" return on his investment. To measure this as a percentage, it seems natural to divide by 1000, the amount Smith initially invested. This results in a rate of $\frac{55}{1000} = .055 = i - r$, which is the simplistic measure of real growth mentioned prior to Example 1.16. A closer look, however, shows that the 55 in real return earned by Smith is paid in end-of-year dollars, whereas the 1000 was invested in beginning-of-year dollars. The dollar value at year end is not the same as that at year beginning, so that to regard the 55 as a percentage of the amount invested, we must measure the real return of 55 and the amount invested in equivalent dollars (dollars of equal value). The 1000 invested at the beginning of the year is equal in value to 1100 after adjusting for inflation at year end. Thus, based on end-of-year dollar value, Smith's real return of 55 should be measured as a percentage of 1100, the inflation-adjusted equivalent of the 1000 invested at the start of the year. On this basis the real rate earned by Smith is $\frac{55}{1100} = .05$, the actual growth in purchasing power.

In general, with annual interest rate $i$ and annual inflation rate $r$, an investment of 1 at the start of a year will grow to $1+i$ at year end. Of this $1+i$, an amount of $1+r$ is needed to maintain dollar value against inflation, i.e., to maintain purchasing power of the original investment of 1. The remainder of $(1+i) - (1+r) = i - r$ is the "real" amount of growth in the investment, and this real return is paid at year end. The investment of 1 at the start of the year has an inflation-adjusted value of $1+r$ at year end in end-of-year dollars.

Notice that the lower the inflation rate $r$, the closer $1+r$ is to 1, and so the closer $i-r$ is to $\frac{i-r}{1+r}$. On the other hand, if inflation is high, (it has been known to reach levels of a few hundred percent in some countries) then the denominator $1+r$ becomes an important factor in $\frac{i-r}{1+r}$. For instance, if inflation is at a rate of 100% ($r=1$) and interest is at a rate of 120% ($i=1.2$), then $i-r = .20$ but $i_{real} = \frac{i-r}{1+r} = .10$. It is usually the case that the rate of interest is greater than inflation.

---

### Hyperinflation

Hyperinflation refers to the very rapid, very large increase in price levels. In Germany between January 1922 and November 1923, price levels grew by a factor of about twenty billion. This pales in comparison to the inflation rate in Hungary in July of 1946, which was in excess of four quintillion percent. That rate of inflation corresponds to prices doubling every fifteen hours for the entire month.

Between 1990 and 1994, after several revaluations of the Yugoslavian currency, the Dinar, one pre-1990 Dinar was equal in value to $1.2 \times 10^{27}$ 1994 Dinars.

Hyperinflation of the type described in the previous paragraph is usually associated with a wartime economy during which consumer items may become scarce or unavailable. The US experienced a record peacetime rate of increasing consumer prices of 13.3% in 1979. Government monetary policy resulted in a significant increase in interest rates over the next few years and the annual US inflation had decreased to less than 4% by 1983.

---

One more point to note is that inflation rates are generally quoted as the rate that has been experienced in the year just completed, whereas interest rates are usually quoted as those to be earned in the coming year. In order to make a meaningful comparison of interest and inflation, both rates should refer to the same one-year period. Thus it may be more appropriate to use a projected rate of inflation for the coming year when inflation is considered in conjunction with the interest rate for the coming year.

## 1.8 SUMMARY OF DEFINITIONS AND FORMULAS

### Definition 1.1 – Effective Annual Rate of Interest

The effective annual rate of interest earned by an investment over the one year period from time $t$ to time $t+1$ is $\frac{A(t+1)-A(t)}{A(t)}$, where $A$ denotes the accumulation function for the investment.

### Definition 1.2 – Equivalent Rates of Interest

Two rates of interest are said to be **equivalent** if they result in the same accumulated values at each point in time.

### Definition 1.3 – Accumulation Factor
### and Accumulated Amount Function

$a(t)$ is the accumulated value at time $t$ of an investment of 1 made at time 0. $a(t)$ is referred to as the accumulation **factor** from time 0 to time $t$. It is the factor by which an investment has grown from time 0 to time $t$.

The notation $A(t)$ will be used to denote the accumulated **amount** of an investment at time $t$, so that if the initial investment amount is $A(0)$, then the accumulated value at time $t$ is $A(t) = A(0) \cdot a(t)$. $A(t)$ is the accumulated amount function.

### Definition 1.4 – Compound Interest Accumulation

At effective annual rate of interest $i$ per period, the accumulation factor from time 0 to time $t$ is
$$a(t) = (1+i)^t \qquad (1.1)$$

### Definition 1.5 – Simple Interest Accumulation

The accumulation factor from time 0 to time $t$ at annual simple interest rate $i$, where $t$ is measured in years is
$$a(t) = 1+it. \qquad (1.2)$$

### Definition 1.6 – Present Value

If the rate of interest for a period is $i$, the present value of an amount of 1 due one period from now is $\frac{1}{1+i}$. The factor $\frac{1}{1+i}$ is often denoted $v$ in actuarial notation and is called a **present value factor** or discount factor. The present value at time 0 of an amount $K$ due at time $t$ is $\frac{K}{(1+i)^t} = Kv^t$.

### Definition 1.7 – Nominal Annual Rate of Interest

A nominal annual rate of interest compounded $m$ times per year refers to an interest compounding period of $\frac{1}{m}$ years. In actuarial notation the symbol $i^{(m)}$ is reserved for denoting a nominal annual rate with interest compounded (or convertible) $m$ times per year. The notation $i^{(m)}$ is taken to mean that interest will have a compounding period of $\frac{1}{m}$ years and compound rate per period of $\frac{1}{m} \cdot i^{(m)} = \frac{i^{(m)}}{m}$.

### Relationship Between Equivalent Nominal Annual and Effective Annual Rates of Interest

The general relationships linking equivalent nominal annual interest rate $i^{(m)}$ and effective annual interest rate $i$ are

$$1+i = \left[1 + \frac{i^{(m)}}{m}\right]^m , \qquad (1.4)$$

and

$$i = \left[1 + \frac{i^{(m)}}{m}\right]^m - 1 \quad \text{and} \quad i^{(m)} = m\left[(1+i)^{1/m} - 1\right]. \qquad (1.5)$$

### Definition 1.8 – Effective Annual Rate of Discount

In terms of an accumulated amount function $A(t)$, the general definition of the effective annual rate of discount from time $t = 0$ to time $t = 1$ is

$$d = \frac{A(1) - A(0)}{A(1)}. \qquad (1.6)$$

### Equivalent Rates of Interest and Discount $i$ and $d$

$$d = \frac{i}{1+i} \quad \text{and} \quad i = \frac{d}{1-d} \qquad (1.7)$$

**Definition 1.9 – Simple Discount**

With a quoted annual discount rate of $d$, based on simple discount the present value of 1 payable $t$ years from now is $1 - dt$. Simple discount is generally only applied for periods of less than one year.

**Definition 1.10 – Nominal Annual Rate of Discount**

A nominal annual rate of discount compounded $m$ times per year refers to a discount compounding period of $\frac{1}{m}$ years. In actuarial notation the symbol $d^{(m)}$ is reserved for denoting a nominal annual discount rate with discount compounded (or convertible) $m$ times per year. The notation $d^{(m)}$ is taken to mean that discount will have a compounding period of $\frac{1}{m}$ years and compound rate per period of $\frac{1}{m} \cdot d^{(m)} = \frac{d^{(m)}}{m}$. We also have the relationship

$$1 - d = \left( 1 - \frac{d^{(m)}}{m} \right)^m. \tag{1.8}$$

**Definition 1.11 – Force of Interest**

For an investment that grows according to accumulation amount function $A(t)$, the force of interest at time $t$ is defined to be

$$\delta_t = \frac{A'(t)}{A(t)} \tag{1.10}$$

$$A(n) = A(0) \cdot \exp\left[ \int_0^n \delta_t \, dt \right]$$

**Definition 1.12 – Real Rate of Interest**

With annual interest rate $i$ and annual inflation rate $r$, the real rate of interest for the year is

$$i_{real} = \frac{value\ of\ amount\ of\ real\ return\ (yr\text{-}end\ dollars)}{value\ of\ invested\ amount\ (yr\text{-}end\ dollars)} = \frac{i - r}{1 + r} \tag{1.13}$$

## 1.9 NOTES AND REFERENCES

Standard International Actuarial Notation was first adopted in 1898 at the 2nd International Actuarial Congress, and has been updated periodically since then. The current version of the notation is found in the article "International Actuarial Notation," on pages 166-176 of Volume 48 (1947) of the *Transactions of the Actuarial Society of America*.

Governments at all levels (federal, state, provincial, and even municipal) have statutes regulating interest rates. These include usury laws limiting the level of interest rates and statutes specifying interest rate disclosure and interest calculation. For example, Section 347 of Part IX of the Canadian Criminal Code contains a law limiting interest to an effective annual rate of 60%, and the US Government's Truth in Lending legislation of 1968 requires nominal interest disclosure for most consumer borrowing.

Vaguely worded statutes regulating interest rates can result in legal disputes as to their interpretation. Section 4 of Canada's century-old *Interest Act* states that "Except as to mortgages on real estate, whenever interest is…made payable at a rate or percentage per day, week, month, or…for any period less than a year, no interest exceeding…five per cent per annum shall be chargeable unless the contract contains an express statement of the yearly rate or percentage to which such other rate…is equivalent." This legislation has resulted in numerous civil suits over which of nominal and effective annual rates are to be interpreted as satisfying the requirement of being equivalent to an interest rate quoted per week or month. The Canadian courts have mostly ruled that either nominal or effective annual rates satisfy the requirements of Section 4.

The book *Standard Securities Calculation Methods* published by the Securities Industry Association in 1973 was written as a reference for "the entire fixed-income investment community" to provide a "readily available source of the formulas, standards, and procedures for performing calculations." Included in that book are detailed descriptions of the various methods applied in practice in finding $t$ for simple interest calculations.

A great deal of information on financial theory and practice can be found on the internet.

## 1.10 EXERCISES

The exercises without asterisks are intended to comprehensively cover the material presented in the chapter. Exercises with a asterisk can be regarded as supplementary exercises which cover topics in more depth, either theoretically or computationally, than those without a asterisk. Those with an S come from old Society of Actuaries or Casualty Actuarial Society exams.

### SECTION 1.1

1.1.1   Alex deposits 10,000 into a bank account that pays an effective annual interest rate of 4%, with interest credited at the end of each year. Determine the amount in Alex's account just after interest is credited at the end of the $1^{st}$, $2^{nd,}$ and $3^{rd}$ years, and also determine the amount of interest that was credited on each of those dates.

1.1.2   2500 is invested. Find the accumulated value of the investment 10 years after it is made for each of the following rates:

(a)  4% annual simple interest;
(b)  4% effective annual compound interest;
(c)  6-month interest rate of 2% compounded every 6 months;
(d)  3-month interest rate of 1% compounded every 3 months.

1.1.3   Bob puts 10,000 into a bank account that has monthly compounding with interest credited at the end of each month. The monthly interest rate is 1% for the first 3 months of the account and after that the monthly interest rate is .75%. Find the balance in Bob's account at the end of 12 months just after interest has been credited. Find the average compound monthly interest rate on Bob's account for the 12 month period.

1.1.4S  Carl puts 10,000 into a bank account that pays an effective annual interest rate of 4% for ten years, with interest credited at the end of each year. If a withdrawal is made during the first five and one-half years, a penalty of 5% of the withdrawal is made. Carl withdraws $K$ at the end of each of years 4, 5, 6 and 7. The balance in the account at the end of year 10 is 10,000. Calculate $K$.

1.1.5    (a) Unit values in a mutual fund have experienced annual growth rates of 10%, 16%, –7%, 4%, and 32% in the past five years. The fund manager suggests the fund can advertise an average annual growth of 11% over the past five years. What is the actual average annual compound growth rate over the past five years?

      (b) A mutual fund advertises that average annual compound rate of returns for various periods ending December 31, 2005 are as follows:

         10 years - 13%; 5 years - 17%; 2 years - 15%; 1 year - 22%.

      Find the 5-year average annual compound rates of return for the period January 1, 1996 to December 31, 2000, and find the annual rate of return for calendar year 2004.

  * (c) Using the fact that the geometric mean of a collection of positive numbers is less than or equal to the arithmetic mean, show that if annual compound interest rates over an $n$-year period are $i_1$ in the first year, $i_2$ in the second year,$\ldots,i_n$ in the $n^{th}$ year, then the average annual compound rate of interest for the $n$-year period is less than or equal to $\frac{1}{n} \cdot \sum_{k=1}^{n} i_k$.

1.1.6S   Joe deposits 10 today and another 30 in five years into a fund paying simple interest of 11% per year. Tina will make the same two deposits, but the 10 will be deposited n years from today and the 30 will be deposited $2n$ years from today. Tina's deposits earn an effective annual rate of 9.15%. At the end of 10 years, the accumulated amount of Tina's deposits equals the accumulated amount of Joe's deposits. Calculate $n$.

1.1.7    Smith has just filed his income tax return and is expecting to receive, in 60 days, a refund check of 1000.

      (a) The tax service that helped Smith fill out his return offers to buy Smith's refund check from him. Their policy is to pay 85% of the face value of the check. What annual simple interest rate is implied?

(b) Smith negotiates with the tax service and sells his refund check for 900. To what annual simple interest rate does this correspond?

(c) Smith decides to deposit the 900 in an account which earns simple interest at annual rate of 9%. What is the accumulated value of the account on the day he would have received his tax refund check?

(d) How many days would it take from the time of his initial deposit of 900 for the account to reach 1000?

1.1.8   Smith's business receives an invoice from a supplier for 1000 with payment due within 30 days. The terms of payment allow for a discount of 2.5% if the bill is paid within 7 days. Smith does not have the cash on hand 7 days later, but decides to borrow the 975 to take advantage of the discount. What is the largest simple interest rate, as an annual rate, that Smith would be willing to pay on the loan?

1.1.9   (a) Jones invests 100,000 in a 180-day short term guaranteed investment certificate at a bank, based on simple interest at annual rate 7.5%. After 120 days, interest rates have risen to 9% and Jones would like to redeem the certificate early and reinvest in a 60-day certificate at the higher rate. In order for there to be no advantage in redeeming early and reinvesting at the higher rate, what early redemption penalty (from the accumulated book value of the investment certificate to time 120 days) should the bank charge at the time of early redemption?

(b) Jones wishes to invest funds for a one-year period. Jones can invest in a one-year guaranteed investment certificate at a rate of 8%. Jones can also invest in a 6-month GIC at annual rate 7.5%, and then reinvest the proceeds at the end of 6 months for another 6-month period. Find the minimum annual rate needed for a 6-month deposit at the end of the first 6-month period so that Jones accumulates at least the same amount with two successive 6-month deposits as she would with the one-year deposit.

1.1.10 (a) At an effective annual interest rate of 12%, calculate the number of years (including fractions) it will take for an investment of 1000 to accumulate to 3000.

(b) Repeat part (a) using the assumption that for fractions of a year, simple interest is applied.

(c) Repeat part (a) using an effective monthly interest rate of 1%.

(d) Suppose that an investment of 1000 accumulated to 3000 in exactly 10 years at effective annual rate of interest $i$. Calculate $i$.

(e) Repeat part (d) using an effective monthly rate of interest $j$. Calculate $j$.

1.1.11 For each of the following pairs of rates, determine which one results in more rapid investment growth.

(a) 17-day rate of $\frac{3}{4}\%$ or 67-day rate of 3%

(b) 17-day rate of $\frac{3}{2}\%$ or 67-day rate of 6%

1.1.12 Smith has 1000 with which she wishes to purchase units in a mutual fund. The investment dealer takes a 9% "front-end load" from the gross payment. The remainder is used to purchase units in the fund, which are valued at 4.00 per unit at the time of purchase.

(a) Six months later the units have a value of 5.00 and the fund managers claim that "the fund's unit value has experienced 25% growth in the past 6 months." When units of the fund are sold, there is a redemption fee of 1.5% of the value of the units redeemed. If Smith sells after 6 months, what is her 6-month return for the period?

(b) Suppose instead of having grown to 5.00 after 6 months, the unit values had dropped to 3.50. What is Smith's 6-month return in this case?

*1.1.13 Suppose that $i > 0$. Show that

(i) if $0 < t < 1$ then $(1+i)^t < 1 + i \cdot t$, and

(ii) if $t > 1$ then $(1+i)^t > 1 + i \cdot t$.

*1.1.14 Investment growth is sometimes plotted over time with the vertical axis transformed to an exponential scale, so that the numerical value of $y$ is replaced by $e^y$ or $10^y$ at the same position on the vertical axis. Show that the graph of compound interest growth over time with the vertical axis transformed in this way is linear.

## SECTION 1.2 and 1.3

1.2.1 Bill will receive $5000 at the end of each year for the next 4 years. Using an effective annual interest rate of 6%, find today's present value of all the payments Bill will receive.

1.2.2S The parents of three children aged 1, 3, and 6 wish to set up a trust fund that will pay 25,000 to each child upon attainment of age 18, and 100,000 to each child upon attainment of age 21. If the trust fund will earn effective annual interest at 10%, what amount must the parents now invest in the trust fund?

1.2.3 A magazine offers a one-year subscription at a cost of 15 with renewal the following year at 16.50. Also offered is a two-year subscription at a cost of 28. What is the effective annual interest rate that makes the two-year subscription equivalent to two successive one-year subscriptions?

1.2.4 What is the present value of 1000 due in 10 years if the effective annual interest rate is 6% for each of the first 3 years, 7% for the next 4 years, and 9% for the final 3 years?

1.2.5 Payments of 200 due July 1, 2012 and 300 due July 1, 2014 have the same value on July 1, 2009 as a payment of 100 made on July 1, 2009 along with a payment made on July 1, 2013. Find the payment needed July 1, 2013 assuming effective annual interest at rate 4%?

1.2.6S  Ed buys a TV from Al for 480 by paying 50 in cash, 100 every three months for one year (four payments of 100), and a final payment in 15 months (three months after the final quarterly payment). Find the amount of the final payment if Al earns a 3-month compound interest rate of 3%. What is the final payment if Al earns a one-month rate of 1%?

1.2.7S  David can receive one of the following two payment streams:

(i)  100 at time 0, 200 at time $n$, and 300 at time $2n$.

(ii) 600 at time 10

At an effective annual interest rate of $i$, the present values of the two streams are equal. Given $v^n = 0.75941$, determine $i$.

1.2.8  A manufacturer can automate a certain process by replacing 20 employees with a machine. The employees each earn 24,000 per year, with payments on the last day of each month, with no salary increases scheduled for the next 4 years. If the machine has a lifetime of 4 years and interest is at a monthly rate of .75%, what is the most the manufacturer would pay for the machine (on the first day of a month) in each of the following cases?

(a)  The machine has no scrap value at the end of 4 years.

(b)  The machine has scrap value of 200,000 after 4 years.

(c)  The machine has scrap value of 15% of its purchase price at the end of 4 years.

1.2.9S  A contract calls for payments of 750 every 4 months for several years. Each payment is to be replaced by two payments of 367.85 each, one to be made 2 months before, and one to be made at the time of, the original payment. Find the 2-month rate of interest implied by this proposal if the new payment scheme is financially equivalent to the old one.

1.2.10 Fisheries officials are stocking a barren lake with pike, whose number will increase annually at the rate of 40%. The plan is to prohibit fishing for two years on the lake, and then allow the removal of 5000 pike in each of the third and fourth years, so that the number remaining after the fourth year is the same as the original number stocked in the lake. Find the original number, assuming that stocking takes place at the start of the year and removal takes place at midyear.

1.2.11 Smith lends Jones 1000 on January 1, 2007 on the condition that Jones repay 100 on January 1, 2008, 100 on January 1, 2009, and 1000 on January 1, 2010. On July 1, 2008, Smith sells to Brown the rights to the remaining payments for 1000, so Jones makes all future payments to Brown. Let $j$ be the 6-month rate earned on Smith's net transaction, and let $k$ be the 6-month rate earned on Brown's net transaction. Are $j$ and $k$ equal? If not, which is larger?

1.2.12 Smith has debts of 1000 due now and 1092 due two years from now. He proposes to repay them with a single payment of 2000 one year from now. What is the implied effective annual interest rate if the replacement payment is accepted as equivalent to the original debts?

1.2.13 Calculate each of the following derivatives.

(a) $\frac{d}{di}(1+i)^n$      (b) $\frac{d}{di}v^n$      (c) $\frac{d}{dn}(1+i)^n$      (d) $\frac{d}{dn}v^n$

1.2.14 A 182-day Canadian T-bill for 100 has a quoted price of 94.771 and a quoted yield rate of 11.07%. Show that any price from 94.767 to 94.771 inclusive has a corresponding yield rate of 11.07%. This shows that the yield rate quote to .01% is not as accurate a measure for the T-bill as is the price to $10^{ths}$ of a cent.

1.2.15 Smith just bought a 100,000 182-day Canadian T-bill at a quoted yield rate of 10%.

(a) Find the price, $P$, that Smith paid for the T-bill.

(b) Find $\frac{dP}{di}$ . Use the differential to approximate the change in the price of the T-bill if the yield rate changes to 10.1% immediately after Smith purchases it.

(c) Suppose the T-bill matures in 91 days instead of 182 days. Find the price and $\frac{dP}{di}$ at a quoted nominal yield of 10%. What happens to $\frac{dP}{di}$ as a T-bill approaches its due date?

*1.2.16 At time 0 a balance of amount $B_0$ is in an account earning simple interest at rate $i$ per period, paid at the end of the period. Various deposits and withdrawals are made during the period, with a transaction of amount $a_k$ made at time $t_k$ for $k = 1, 2, ..., n$ where $0 < t_k < 1$. ( $a_k > 0$ indicates a deposit to the account, and $a_k < 0$ indicates a withdrawal). Assume that $t = 1$ is the reference point (focal date) for the account and interest on deposits and withdrawals begins accruing at the time of the deposit or withdrawal.

(a) Find an expression for $B_1$, the account balance at $t = 1$.

(b) Find an expression for $B$, the average balance in the account during the period from time 0 to time 1.

(c) Show that $B_1 = B_0 + \sum\limits_{k=1}^{n} a_k + \overline{B} \cdot i$.

*1.2.17 Smith wishes to buy a TV set and is offered a time payment plan whereby he makes 24 monthly payments of 30 each starting now. Smith wants the payments to start in 2 months rather than now. If interest is at a one-month interest rate of 1%, what is the present value now of the saving to Smith if the seller agrees to Smith's terms?

*1.2.18 Smith receives a paycheck of 3500 on the last day of each month, and immediately deposits all but 1000 of it in a bank account. The first deposit is on December 31, 2004. Smith deposits an additional 1000 on the $15^{th}$ of every month. The account pays an annual interest rate of 10%. Find the balance in the account on March 31, 2005, after the deposit is made and interest is credited, in each of the following cases.

(a) Simple interest based on minimum monthly balance and credited on the last day of March (no interest in January or February)

(b) Simple interest based on minimum daily balance and credited on the last day of March (no interest in January or February)

(c) Same as (a) but with interest credited on the last day of every month

(d) Same as (b) but with interest credited on the last day of every month

It follows from Exercise 1.2.18 that use of minimum daily balances for simple interest calculations is equivalent to using average balances.

## SECTION 1.4

1.4.1   Suppose the nominal annual rate is 12%. Find the equivalent effective annual rates for $m = 1, 2, 3, 4, 6, 8, 12, 52, 365, \infty$.

1.4.2   Find the present value of 1000 due at the end of 10 years if

(a) $i^{(2)} = .09$,

(b) $i^{(6)} = .09$, and

(c) $i^{(12)} = .09$.

1.4.3   Mountain Bank pays interest at rate $i^{(2)} = .15$. River Bank pays interest compounded daily. What minimum nominal annual rate must River Bank pay in order to be as attractive as Mountain Bank?

1.4.4S   Eric deposits $X$ into a savings account at time 0, which pays interest at a nominal rate of $i$, compounded semiannually. Mike deposits $2X$ into a different savings account at time 0, which pays simple interest at an annual rate of $i$. Eric and Mike earn the same amount of interest during the last 6 months of the $8^{th}$ year. Calculate $i$.

1.4.5    Smith receives income from his investments in Japanese curren-
         cy (yen). Smith does not convert the yen to dollars, but invests
         the yen in a term deposit that pays interest in yen. He finds a
         bank that will issue such a term deposit, but it charges a 1%
         commission on each initial placement and on each rollover. The
         current interest rate on the yen deposits is a nominal annual rate
         of 3.25% convertible quarterly for a 3-month deposit. To keep
         his yen available, Smith decides to roll over the deposit every 3
         months. What is the effective annual after-commission rate that
         Smith earns?

1.4.6    The nominal interest rate $i^{(m)}$ can be defined for values of
         $m < 1$. Algebraically the definition follows the relationship in
         Equation (1.4). If we see the phrase "interest is compounded
         once every two years", this means that the annually quoted rate
         is a nominal rate with $m = .5$.

         If $i = .10$, find the equivalent $i^{(.5)}$, $i^{(.25)}$, $i^{(.1)}$, and $i^{(.01)}$. Rank
         the values in increasing size, and compare with the relationship
         $i^{(m)} < i$ for $m > 1$.

1.4.7    Smith buys a 1000 Canada savings bond, with an issue date of
         November 1, paying interest at 11.25% per year. The bond can
         be cashed in anytime after January 1 of the following year, and it
         will pay simple interest during the first year of $\frac{1}{12}$ of the annual
         interest for every completed month since November 1. The gov-
         ernment allows purchasers to pay for their bonds as late as No-
         vember 9, with full interest still paid for November. Smith pays
         1000 on November 9 and cashes in the bond on the following
         January 1. What is his equivalent effective annual rate of interest
         for his transaction?

*1.4.8   A Canadian GIC has an interest rate guaranteed for the term of
         the certificate, a significant penalty for redemption prior to the
         specified maturity date, and principal and interest usually se-
         cured by a government deposit insurance program. Smith buys a

one-year guaranteed investment certificate with principal of $X$. The annual interest rate quoted on the certificate is 9%, with interest payable monthly, on the monthly anniversary date of the certificate. Immediately upon receiving an interest payment. Smith reinvests it in an account earning a nominal annual rate of 9% convertible monthly, with interest compounded from a deposit date. Show that after one year Smith has the same total that she would have had if she had deposited the full $X$ in the account and left it on deposit for the year.

*1.4.9 (a) Show that if $j > 0$ then the function $f(m) = \left(1 + \frac{j}{m}\right)^m$ is an increasing function of $m$.

 (b) Show that if $j > 0$ then $g(m) = m\left[(1+j)^{1/m} - 1\right]$ is a decreasing function of $m$.

 (c) Use l'Hospital's Rule to show that $\lim_{m \to \infty} f(m) = e^j$ for the function $f(m)$ defined in part (a).

 (d) Show that $\lim_{m \to \infty} g(m) = \ln(1+j)$ for the function $g(m)$ defined in part (b).

*1.4.10 Bank A has an effective annual rate of 18%. Bank B has a nominal annual rate of 17%. What is the smallest whole number of times per year that Bank B must compound its interest in order that the rate at Bank B be at least as attractive as that at Bank A on an effective annual basis? Repeat the exercise with a nominal rate of 16% at Bank B.

## SECTION 1.5

1.5.1 A discounted note of face amount $X$, due in one-half year, is valued today at 4992. Find $X$ under each of the following interest calculation methods.

 (a) Compound interest at effective annual rate 8%
 (b) Simple interest at annual rate 8%
 (c) Compound discount at effective annual rate 8%
 (d) Simple discount at annual rate 8%

1.5.2    The table of US T-Bill values in Example 1.11 has 1 91-day T-Bill. Verify the relationships between the quoted discount rate, investment rate and price.

1.5.3    Let $j$ be the compound interest rate for the $T$-year period from time $r$ to time $r+T$, and let $d_j$ be the corresponding rate of discount for that time period. Show that (a) $d_j = \frac{j}{1+j}$ and (b) $j = \frac{d_j}{1-d_j}$.

1.5.4    A store has a normal markup of 30% on the purchase price of goods bought at wholesale. During a promotion the markup is only 15%. What percent reduction in the retail price will result?

1.5.5S   Bruce and Robbie each open up new bank accounts at time 0. Bruce deposits 100 into his bank account, and Robbie deposits 50 into his. Each account earns an effective annual discount rate of $d$. The amount of interest earned in Bruce's account during the $11^{th}$ year is equal to $X$. The amount of interest earned in Robbie's account during the $17^{th}$ year is also equal to $X$. Calculate $X$.

1.5.6    Given an effective annual discount rate of $d$, show that, with compounding, the accumulated value after $n$ years of an initial investment of amount 1 is $(1-d)^{-n}$. In other words, if an amount $X$ due in $n$ years has present value 1, then $X = (1-d)^{-n}$.

1.5.7S   Jeff deposits 10 into a fund today and 20 fifteen years later. Interest is credited at a nominal discount rate of $d$ compounded quarterly for the first 10 years, and at a nominal interest rate of 6% compounded semiannually thereafter. The accumulated balance in the fund at the end of 30 years is 100. Calculate $d$.

1.5.8    (a) Smith has a promissory note due in $n$ days. A bank will buy the note from Smith using a simple discount rate $d$. What is the equivalent simple interest rate $i$ earned by the bank over the period? What happens to $i$ as $n$ increases?

         (b) A lender wishes to earn interest at an annual simple rate of 11%. What annual simple discount rate should be charged on a loan for 1 year? for 6 months? for 1 month?

1.5.9 Smith buys a 182-day US T-Bill at a price which corresponds to a quoted annual discount rate for 182-day T-bills of 10%. 91 days later Smith sells the T-Bill, at which time the prevailing quoted annual discount rate of 91-day T-Bills is also 10%. Find the actual rate of return (91-day interest rate) that Smith earned during the time he held the T-Bill.

1.5.10 Show that equivalent nominal interest and discount rates $i^{(m)}$ and $d^{(m)}$ satisfy the relationships

(a) $d^{(m)} = \dfrac{i^{(m)}}{1 + \frac{i^{(m)}}{m}}$ and (b) $i^{(m)} = \dfrac{d^{(m)}}{1 - \frac{d^{(m)}}{m}}$,

and show that these relationships are consistent with the results of Exercise 1.5.2 and Examples 1.10 and 1.12.

*1.5.11 Bob borrows 1000 from Ed at effective annual interest rate $i$, agreeing to repay in full at the end of one year. When the year is up, Bob has no money, but they agree that he can repay one year later in such a way that the effective annual discount rate $d$ in the second year *is numerically equal* to the interest rate $i$ in the first year. At the end of the second year Bob pays 1200. What is $i$ in the first year?

*1.5.12 Smith has 960 to invest on January 1. He has the following two investment options.

(a) He can buy a 6-month 1000 T-bill for a purchase price of 960, and reinvest the proceeds on July 1 at a 6-month interest rate $j$.

(b) He can buy a one-year 1000 T-bill for a purchase price of 920 and invest the remaining 40 in an account earning interest at the same effective 6-month interest rate $j$ as in option (a).

If options (a) and (b) result in the same accumulated amount on December 31, including interest and T-bill maturity, find the value of $j$ (assuming $j < 10\%$). The period from January 1 to July 1 is regarded as exactly ½-year and the time from January 1 to December 31 is regarded as exactly 1 year for time measurement.

## SECTION 1.6

1.6.1    For the period from time 0 to time 2, the force of interest is defined as follows:

$$\delta_t = \begin{cases} .05 \text{ for } 0 < t \le 1 \\ .05 + .02(t-1) \text{ for } 1 < t \le 2 \end{cases}$$

10,000 is invested at time 0. Find the accumulated value at time 1 and at time 2.

1.6.2S  A customer is offered an investment where interest is calculated according to the following force of interest:

$$\delta_t = \begin{cases} .02t & 0 \le t \le 3 \\ .045 & t > 3 \end{cases}$$

The customer invests 1000 at time $t = 0$. What nominal rate of interest, compounded quarterly, is earned over the first four-year period?

1.6.3S  At time $t = 0$, 1 is deposited into each of Fund $X$ and Fund $Y$. Fund $X$ accumulates at a force of interest $\delta_t = \frac{t^2}{k}$. Fund $Y$ accumulates at a nominal rate of discount of 8% per annum convertible semiannually. At time $t = 5$, the accumulated value of Fund $X$ equals the accumulated value of Fund $Y$. Determine $k$.

1.6.4S  Tawny makes a deposit into a bank account which credits interest at a nominal interest rate of 10% per annum, convertible semiannually. At the same time, Fabio deposits 1000 into a different bank account, which is credited with simple interest. At the end of 5 years, the forces of interest on the two accounts are equal, and Fabio's account has accumulated to $Z$. Determine $Z$.

1.6.5S  Ernie makes deposits of 100 at time 0, and $X$ at time 3. The fund grows at a force of interest $\delta_t = \frac{t^2}{100}$, $t > 0$. The amount of interest earned from time 3 to time 6 is $X$. Calculate $X$.

1.6.6S  Bruce deposits 100 into a bank account. His account is credited interest at a nominal rate convertible semiannually. At the same time, Peter deposits 100 into a separate account. Peter's account is credited interest at a force of interest of $\delta$. After 7¼ years, the value of each account is 200. Calculate $i - \delta$.

1.6.7S  An investment of 1000 accumulates to 1360.86 at the end of 5 years. If the force of interest is $\delta$ during the first year and $1.5\delta$ in each subsequent year, find the equivalent effective annual interest rate in the first year.

1.6.8   Smith forecasts that interest rates will rise over a 5-year period according to a force of interest function given by $\delta_t = .08 + \frac{.025t}{t+1}$ for $0 \le t \le 5$.

(a) According to this scheme, what is the average annual compound effective rate for the 5-year period?

(b) What are the equivalent effective annual rates for each of years 1, 2, 3, 4, and 5?

(c) What is the present value at $t = 2$ of 1000 due at $t = 4$?

1.6.9S  The present value of $K$ payable after 2 years is 960. If the force of interest is cut in half, the present value becomes 1200. What is the present value if the effective annual discount rate is cut in half?

1.6.10  If the force of interest is doubled, are the corresponding equivalent effective annual interest and discount rates more or less than doubled?

*1.6.11    On January 1 Smith deposits 1000 into an account earning $i^{(4)} = .08$ with interest credited on the last day of March, June, September, and December. If Smith closes the account during the year, simple interest is paid on the balance from the most recent interest credit date.

(a) What is Smith's close-out balance on July 19?

(b) Suppose all four quarters in the year are considered equal, and time is measured in years. Derive expressions for Smith's accumulated amount function $A(t)$, the close-out balance at time $t$. Consider separately the four intervals $0 \le t \le .25$, $.25 \le t \le .50$, $.50 \le t \le .75$ and $.75 \le t \le 1$.

(c) Using part (b), show that if $0 \le t \le .25$, then it follows that $\delta_t = \delta_{t+.25} = \delta_{t+.50} = \delta_{t+.75}$.

*1.6.12 (a) Find an expression for the $\frac{1}{m}$-year discount rate from time $t$ to time $t + \frac{1}{m}$ in terms of an accumulated amount function $A$.

(b) If $d^{(m)}$ is the nominal annual discount rate corresponding to the rate in part (a), find an expression for $d^{(m)}$ in terms of $A$.

(c) Take the limit as $m \to \infty$ of the expression for $d^{(m)}$ in part (b) to show that $d^{(\infty)} = \dfrac{A'(t)}{A(t)} = \delta_t$.

*1.6.13 (a) Suppose an accumulated amount function is a polynomial of the form $A(t) = a_0 + a_1 \cdot t + \cdots + a_n \cdot t^n$, where $a_n > 0$ and $n > 0$. Show that $\lim\limits_{t \to \infty} \delta_t = 0$.

(b) Let $\delta_t = \dfrac{k}{\sqrt{t}}$, $K > 0$. Find an expression for the accumulation function $A(t)$, where $A(0) = 1$. Show $\lim\limits_{t \to \infty} \dfrac{A(t)}{1+it} = \infty$ for any $i > 0$, and $\lim\limits_{t \to \infty} \dfrac{A(t)}{(1+i)^t} = 0$.

## SECTION 1.7

1.7.1    Suppose that for the coming year inflation is forecast at an effective annual rate of $r = .15$ and interest is forecast at effective annual rate $i = .10$. What will be the corresponding real, or inflation-adjusted rate of interest for the coming year?

1.7.2    A person's savings earn an effective rate of $i = .12$ on which 45% income tax is paid. If the inflation rate is 10% per year, what is the annual after-tax real rate of return?

1.7.3    Smith earned gross income of 40,000 last year. According to the income tax structure, taxes are 25% of the first 20,000 of gross income plus 50% of the excess over 20,000. Thus Smith paid 15,000 in taxes and had after-tax income (ATI) of 25,000. Inflation is forecast at 5% this year, and Smith's gross income will rise by 5% to 42,000. The government is considering a new tax structure of 25% of the first 21,000 plus 50% of the excess over 21,000 (full indexing).

(a) Show that if the government adopts the new tax structure then the real annual rate of growth in both Smith's ATI and in his paid taxes is 0%.

(b) Find the real annual rate of growth in Smith's ATI and his taxes paid if the government continues with the old scheme (no indexing).

1.7.4    Using the values of $r$ and $i$ in Exercise 1.7.1 suppose Smith borrows 100,000 for a year at $i = .10$, and buys 100,000 units of a certain item that has a current cost of 1 per unit. Suppose the price of this item is tied to the rate of inflation ($r = .15$). One year from now Smith sells the items at the inflated price. What is his net gain on this transaction? (This illustrates that during times when inflation rates exceed interest rates, there is great incentive to borrow at the negative real rate of interest. This demand by borrowers is a factor in the inevitable correction that leads to the interest rate becoming larger than the inflation rate.)

1.7.5 If the force of interest for the coming year will be $\delta$ and the force of inflation will be $\delta_r$, show that the inflation-adjusted force of interest is $\delta - \delta_r$.

1.7.6 The newly independent nation of Falkvinas has a unit of currency called the Britarg. In the coming year inflation in Falkvinas will be 100%, whereas Canada's inflation rate will be 14%. A Canadian investor can earn interest in Canada on Canadian dollars at an annual rate of 18%. What effective annual rate must an investor earn on Britargs in Falkvinas in order that his real rate of interest match the real rate earned by an investor in Canadian dollars?

1.7.7 Smith will need 1000 US dollars one year from now. He can invest funds in a US dollar account for the next year at 9%. Alternatively Smith can now buy Canadian dollars at the exchange rate of 0.73 US = 1 CDN, and invest in a Canadian dollar account for the next year at 10%. If both of these alternatives require the same amount of currency today, what is the implied exchange rate between the two currencies one year from now?

1.7.8 Show that the present value of $(1+r)^n$ due in $n$ years at effective annual rate $i$ is equal to the present value of 1 due in $n$ years at effective annual rate $\frac{i-r}{1+r}$.

*1.7.9 (a) In an attempt to reduce interest rates during times of high inflation, a government allows banks to issue "indexed term deposits" upon which only the "real" interest earned is taxed. If inflation is at rate $r$, and the bank pays interest at real rate $i'$, then on a one-year deposit of initial amount 1 an investor receives inflation-adjusted principal of $1+r$, plus "real interest" on the inflation-adjusted principal of $i'(1+r)$, for a total amount paid at year end of $(1+r)(1+i')$. The investor pays tax only on the real interest paid [i.e., on $i'(1+r)$.] This is compared to the usual term-deposit situation in which interest at rate $i$ is paid at the end of the year. Derive expressions in terms of $i$, $i'$, $r$ and $t_x$, (where $0 < t_x < 1$ is the investor's tax rate) for the real after-tax rates of return on the indexed term deposit and on the standard term deposit.

(b) Suppose $r = 12\%$ and a bank offers inflation-adjusted term deposits at a real rate of 2%. What rate of interest would an investor have to earn on a standard term deposit in order to have the same after-inflation, after-tax return as on the indexed term deposit if the investor has a tax rate of

(i) 0%,         (ii) 25%,        (iii) 40%,        (iv) 60%?

# CHAPTER 2

## VALUATION OF ANNUITIES

*"A nickel ain't worth a dime anymore."*

*– Yogi Berra*

Many financial transactions involve a series of payments, such as periodic dividend payments to someone owning common stock, monthly payments on a loan, or annual interest payments on a coupon bond. It is often the case (as in the loan and bond examples) that the payments are made at regularly scheduled intervals of time. In the examples in Chapter 1 that dealt with transactions involving more than one payment, each payment was treated and valued separately. When a transaction involves a number of payments made in a systematic way, it is often possible to apply algebraic methods to simplify the valuation of the series. In this chapter we will develop methods for valuing a series of payments.

Prior to the availability of sophisticated calculators and computer spreadsheet programs, it was important to have algebraic representations for series of payments that required as little calculation by hand as possible. Many of the methods developed in the past are no longer important for calculation purposes, but some remain useful for the insight that they may provide in analyzing and valuing a series of payments.

The generic term used to describe a series of periodic payments is **annuity**. In a life insurance context, an annuity is a "life-contingent" series of payments that are contingent on the survival of a specific individual or group of individuals. The more precise term for a series of payments that are not contingent on the occurrence of any specified events is **annuity-certain** (an annuity whose payments will definitely be made). Since this book deals almost entirely with annuities-certain, we shall use the term annuity to refer to an annuity-certain, unless otherwise specified.

The calculations in many of the examples presented here can be done in an efficient way using a financial calculator or computer spreadsheet program. The presentation here emphasizes understanding the underlying principles and algebraic relationships involved in annuity valuation.

A key algebraic relationship used in valuing a series of payments is the geometric series summation formula

$$1 + x + x^2 + \cdots + x^k = \frac{1 - x^{k+1}}{1 - x} = \frac{x^{k+1} - 1}{x - 1}. \tag{2.1}$$

This is illustrated in the following example.

**EXAMPLE 2.1** (*Accumulation of a level payment annuity*)

The federal government sends Smith a family allowance payment of $30 every month for Smith's child. Smith deposits the payments in a bank account on the last day of each month. The account earns interest at the annual rate of 9% compounded monthly and the interest is paid into the account on the last day of each month. If the first payment is deposited on May 31, 1998, what is the account balance on December 31, 2009, including the payment just made and interest paid that day?

**SOLUTION**

The following line diagram illustrates the accumulation in the account from one deposit to the next.

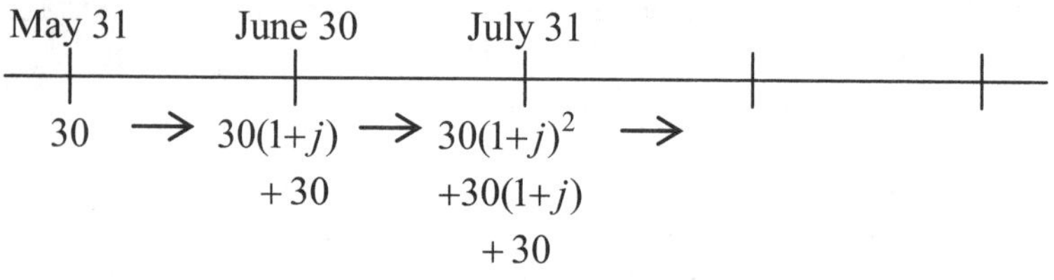

**FIGURE 2.1**

The one-month compound interest rate is $j = .0075$. The balance in the account on June 30, 1998, including the payment just deposited and the accumulated value of the May 31 deposit is

$$C_2 = 30(1+j) + 30 = 30[(1+j) + 1].$$

The balance on July 31, 1998 is

$$C_3 = C_2(1+j) + 30 = 30[(1+j)+1](1+j) + 30 = 30\left[(1+j)^2 + (1+j) + 1\right].$$

Continuing in this way we see that the balance just after the $m^{th}$ deposit is $C_m = 30\left[(1+j)^{m-1} + \cdots + (1+j)^2 + (1+j) + 1\right]$, the accumulation of those first $m$ deposits. By applying the geometric series formula, the balance on December 31, 2009, just after the $140^{th}$ deposit is

$$30\left[(1+j)^{139} + (1+j)^{138} + \cdots + (1+j) + 1\right]$$

$$= 30\left[\frac{(1+j)^{140} - 1}{(1+j) - 1}\right] = 30\left[\frac{(1.0075)^{140} - 1}{.0075}\right] = 7385.91. \quad \Box$$

## 2.1 LEVEL PAYMENT ANNUITIES

### 2.1.1 ACCUMULATED VALUE OF AN ANNUITY

In Example 2.1, the expression for the aggregate accumulated value on December 31, 2009 is

$$30(1+j)^{139} + 30(1+j)^{138} + \cdots + 30(1+j) + 30.$$

This is the sum of the accumulated values of the individual deposits. $30(1+j)^{139}$ is the accumulated value on December 31, 2009 of the deposit made on May 31, 1998, $30(1+j)^{138}$ is the accumulated value on December 31, 2009 of the deposit made on June 30, 1998, and so on.

Let us consider a series of $n$ payments (or deposits) of amount 1 each, made at equally spaced intervals of time, and for which interest is at compound rate $i$ per payment period, with interest credited on payment dates. The accumulated value of the series of payments, valued at the time of (and including) the final payment, can be represented as the sum of the accumulated values of the individual payments. This is

$$(1+i)^{n-1} + (1+i)^{n-2} + \cdots + (1+i) + 1 = \frac{(1+i)^n - 1}{(1+i) - 1} = \frac{(1+i)^n - 1}{i} \quad (2.2)$$

This is illustrated in the following diagram. We can see from the diagram that since the valuation point is the time that the $n^{th}$ deposit is made, this is actually $n-1$ periods after the first deposit. Therefore the first deposit has grown with compound interest for $n-1$ periods.

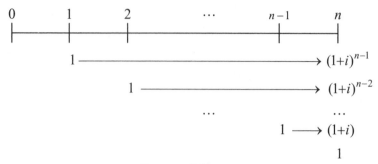

**FIGURE 2.2**

This annuity has standard actuarial notation and terminology associated with it.

---

**Definition 2.1 – Accumulated Value of an *n*-Payment Annuity-Immediate of 1 Per Period**

The symbol $s_{\overline{n}|i}$ denotes the accumulated value, at the time of (and including) the final payment of a series of $n$ payments of 1 each made at equally spaced intervals of time, where the rate of interest per payment period is $i$.

$$s_{\overline{n}|i} = (1+i)^{n-1} + (1+i)^{n-2} + \cdots + (1+i) + 1$$

$$= \sum_{t=0}^{n-1}(1+i)^t = \frac{(1+i)^n - 1}{i} \qquad (2.3)$$

---

The symbol $s_{\overline{n}|i}$ and other related annuity symbols can be used to efficiently represent transactions that involve a series of level payments. If there is no possibility of confusion with other interest rates in a particular situation, the subscript $i$ is omitted from $s_{\overline{n}|i}$ and the accumulated value is denoted $s_{\overline{n}|}$, without the subscript $i$. The number of payments in the series is called the term of the annuity, and the time between successive payments is called the payment period, or **frequency**. Note that for any interest rate $i$, $s_{\overline{1}|i} = 1$, but if $i > 0$ and $n > 1$, then $s_{\overline{n}|i} > n$ because of interest on earlier deposits.

It should be emphasized that the $s_{\overline{n}|i}$ notation can be used to express the accumulated value of an annuity provided the following conditions are met:

(1) the payments are of equal amount;

(2) the payments are made at equal intervals of time, with the same frequency as the interest rate is compounded;

(3) the accumulated value is found at the time of and including the final payment.

This series of payments is referred to in actuarial terminology as an accumulated **annuity-immediate**. We often see a series of payments described with the phrase "payments occur at the end of each year (or month)," with a valuation made at the end of $n$ years. The conventional interpretation of this phrase is to regard the valuation as an accumulated annuity-immediate.

Figure 2.3 plots the accumulated value of the annuity as a function of the number of annuity payments (using a 10% interest rate).

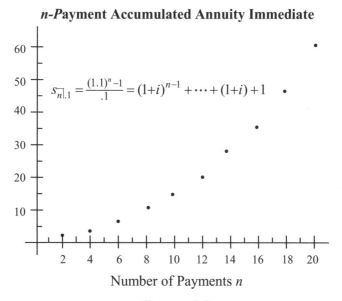

**$n$-Payment Accumulated Annuity Immediate**

$$s_{\overline{n}|.1} = \frac{(1.1)^n - 1}{.1} = (1+i)^{n-1} + \cdots + (1+i) + 1$$

Number of Payments $n$

**FIGURE 2.3**

General reasoning suggests that if the interest rate is increased, accumulated values increase. Figure 2.4 plots the accumulated value of a 20-payment annuity as a function of the interest rate. If the interest rate is 0, then there is no interest accumulation, and the accumulated value of the annuity is just the sum of the annuity payments.

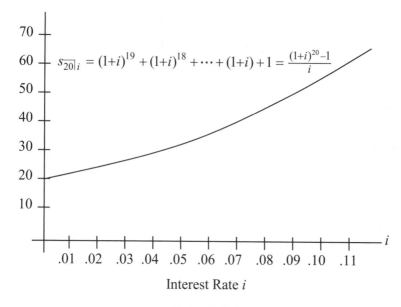

$$s_{\overline{20}|i} = (1+i)^{19} + (1+i)^{18} + \cdots + (1+i) + 1 = \frac{(1+i)^{20}-1}{i}$$

Interest Rate $i$

**FIGURE 2.4**

Equation 2.3 can be rewritten as

$$(1+i)^n = i \times s_{\overline{n}|i} + 1 = i \times \left[(1+i)^{n-1} + (1+i)^{n-2} + \cdots + (1+i) + 1\right] + 1.$$

We can interpret this expression in the following way. Suppose that a single amount of 1 is invested at time 0 at periodic interest rate $i$, so that an interest payment of $i$ is generated at the end of each period. Suppose further that each interest payment is reinvested and continues to earn interest at rate $i$. This is allowed to continue for $n$ periods. Then the accumulation of the reinvested interest, along with the return of the initial amount 1 invested (the right hand side of the equation above), must be equal to the compound accumulation of 1 at rate $i$ per period invested for $n$ periods.

EXAMPLE 2.2 *(Accumulated value of an annuity-immediate)*

What level amount must be deposited on May 1 and November 1 each year from 2008 to 2015, inclusive, to accumulate to 7000 on November 1, 2015 if the nominal annual rate of interest compounded semi-annually is 9%?

SOLUTION

A first step in translating the verbal description of this annuity into an algebraic form is to determine the number of deposits being made. There are a total of 16 deposits (2 per year for each of the 8 years from 2008 to 2015 inclusive) and they occur every $\frac{1}{2}$-year. As a second step, we note that the $\frac{1}{2}$-year interest rate is 4.5%, and the $\frac{1}{2}$-year payment period corresponds to the $\frac{1}{2}$-year interest compounding period. If the level amount deposited every $\frac{1}{2}$-year is denoted by $X$, the accumulated value of the deposits at the time of the $16^{th}$ deposit is

$$X \cdot \left[ (1.045)^{15} + (1.045)^{14} + \cdots + 1.045 + 1 \right]$$
$$= X \cdot \frac{(1.045)^{16} - 1}{.045} = X \cdot s_{\overline{16}|.045} = 22.719337X$$

(note that the factor $(1.045)^{15}$ arises as a result of there being 15 half-year periods from the time of the first deposit on May 1, 2008 to the time of the $16^{th}$ deposit on November 1, 2015). Then

$$X = \frac{7000}{s_{\overline{16}|.045}} = \frac{7000}{22.719337} = 308.11. \qquad \square$$

All financial calculators have functions that calculate the accumulated value of an annuity at the time of the final payment if the payment amount, number of payments, and interest rate are known.

### 2.1.1.1 *Accumulated Value of an Annuity Some Time after the Final Payment*

After a series of deposits is completed, the balance can continue to accumulate with interest only. The following example illustrates this.

EXAMPLE 2.3

(*Accumulated value of an annuity some time after the final payment*)

Suppose that in Example 2.1, Smith's child is born in April, 1998 and the first payment is received and deposited at the end of May. The payments continue and the deposits are made at the end of each month until (and including the month of) the child's $16^{th}$ birthday. The payments cease after the $16^{th}$ birthday, but the balance in the account continues to accumulate with interest until the end of the month of the child's $21^{st}$ birthday. What is the balance in the account at that time?

---

**SOLUTION**

At the end of the month of the child's $16^{th}$ birthday, Smith makes the $192^{nd}$ deposit into the account. This is at the end of April, 2014 (there are 12 deposits per year for 16 years for a total of 192 deposits). The accumulated value at that time is

$$30\left[(1.0075)^{191} + (1.0075)^{190} + \cdots + (1.0075) + 1\right]$$

$$= 30 \times s_{\overline{192}|.0075} = 30 \times \frac{(1.0075)^{192} - 1}{.0075} = 12,792.31.$$

Five years (60 months) later, at the end of the month of the child's $21^{st}$ birthday, the account will have grown, with interest only, to

$$12,792.31(1.0075)^{60} = 20,028.68. \qquad \square$$

We have seen that the value at the time of the $n^{th}$ deposit of a series of $n$ deposits of amount 1 each is $\frac{(1+i)^n - 1}{i} = s_{\overline{n}|}$. If there are no further deposits, but the balance continues to grow with compound interest, then the accumulated value $k$ periods after the $n^{th}$ deposit is

$$[(1+i)^{n-1} + (1+i)^{n-2} + \cdots + (1+i) + 1] \times (1+i)^k$$

$$= (1+i)^{n+k-1} + (1+i)^{n+k-2} + \cdots + (1+i)^{k+1} + (1+i)^k$$

$$= \frac{(1+i)^n - 1}{i} \times (1+i)^k$$

$$= s_{\overline{n}|} \times (1+i)^k$$

$$= \textit{Value at time } n \times \textit{growth factor from time } n \textit{ to time } n+k.$$

This can be also be represented in the following way.

$$s_{\overline{n}|} \times (1+i)^k = \frac{(1+i)^n - 1}{i} \times (1+i)^k$$

$$= \frac{(1+i)^{n+k} - (1+i)^k}{i}$$

$$= \frac{(1+i)^{n+k} - 1}{i} - \frac{(1+i)^k - 1}{i} = s_{\overline{n+k}|} - s_{\overline{k}|}. \qquad (2.4)$$

Using Equation (2.4), the accumulated value of the account on April 30, 2019 in Example 2.3 can be written as $30\left[s_{\overline{252}|} - s_{\overline{60}|}\right]$.

Figures 2.5a and 2.5b below illustrate the formulations given in Equation 2.4. If the annuity payments had continued to time $n+k$, which is the time of valuation, the accumulated value would be $s_{\overline{n+k}|}$. Since there are not any payments actually made for the final $k$ payment periods, $s_{\overline{n+k}|}$ must be reduced by $s_{\overline{k}|}$, the accumulated value of $k$ payments of 1 each ending at time $n+k$.

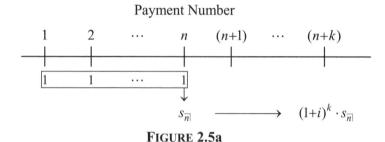

**FIGURE 2.5a**

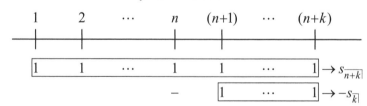

**FIGURE 2.5b**

Equation (2.4) can be reformulated as

$$s_{\overline{n+k}|} \;=\; s_{\overline{n}|}(1+i)^k + s_{\overline{k}|} \;=\; s_{\overline{k}|}(1+i)^n + s_{\overline{n}|}. \tag{2.5}$$

Equation 2.5 shows that a series of payments can be separated into components, and the accumulated value of the entire series at a valuation point can be represented as the sum of the accumulated values (at that valuation point) of the separate component series.

### 2.1.1.2 *Accumulated Value of an Annuity with Non-Level Interest Rates*

The concept of dividing a series of payments into subgroups and valuing each subgroup separately can be applied to find the accumulated value of an annuity when the periodic interest rate changes during the term of the annuity. This is illustrated in the following modification of Example 2.1.

### EXAMPLE 2.4

*(Annuity accumulation with non-level interest rates)*

Suppose that in Example 2.1 the nominal annual interest rate earned on the account changes to 7.5% (still compounded monthly) as of January 1, 2004. What is the accumulated value of the account on December 31, 2009?

### SOLUTION

In a situation in which the interest rate is at one level for a period of time and changes to another level for a subsequent period of time, it is necessary to separate the full term into separate time intervals over which the interest rate is constant. We first calculate the accumulated value in the account on December 31, 2003, since the nominal interest rate is level at 9% up until this point. This accumulated value is

$$30 \cdot \frac{(1.0075)^{68} - 1}{.0075} \ = \ 30 \times s_{\overline{68}|.0075} \ = \ 2,648.50.$$

From January 1, 2004 onward, the accumulation in the account can be separated into two components: the accumulation of the 2648.50 that was on balance as of January 1, 2004, and the accumulation of the continuing deposits from January 31, 2004 onward. The 2648.50 accumulates to

$$2,648.50 \times (1.00625)^{72} = 4,147.86$$

as of December 31, 2009, and the remaining deposits continuing from January 31, 2004 accumulate to

$$30 \times \frac{(1.00625)^{72} - 1}{.00625} \ = \ 30 \times s_{\overline{72}|.00625} \ = \ 2,717.36,$$

for a total of 6865.22. The accumulated value on December 31, 2009 can be written as

$$30 \times \left[ s_{\overline{68}|.0075} \times (1.00625)^{72} + s_{\overline{72}|.00625} \right]. \qquad \square$$

We can generalize the concept presented in the Example 2.4. Suppose that we consider an $n+k$-payment annuity with equally spaced payments of 1 per period and with an interest rate of $i_1$ per payment period up to the time of the $n^{th}$ payment, followed by an interest rate of $i_2$ per payment period from the time of the $n^{th}$ payment onward. The accumulated value of the annuity at the time of the final payment can be found in the following way.

(a) The accumulated value of the first $n$ payments valued at the time of the $n^{th}$ payment is $s_{\overline{n}|i_1}$.

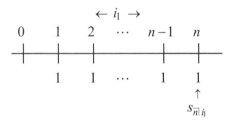

(b) The accumulated value found in part (a) grows with compound interest for an additional $k$ periods at compound periodic interest rate $i_2$, to a value of $s_{\overline{n}|i_1} \times (1+i_2)^k$ as of time $n+k$.

(c)    The accumulated value of the final $k$ payments is $s_{\overline{k}|i_2}$.

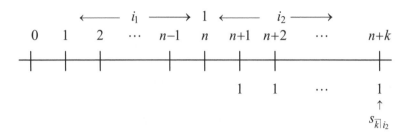

(d)    The total accumulated value at time $n+k$ is the sum of (b) and
(c), and equals $s_{\overline{n}|i_1} \times (1+i_2)^k + s_{\overline{k}|i_2}$.

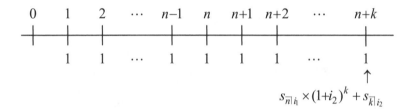

Note that if the interest rate is level over the $n+k$ periods, so that
$i_2 = i_1$, then Equation 2.5 is the same as the expression in (d). This method can be extended to situations in which the interest rate changes
more than once during the term of the annuity.

### 2.1.1.3 *Accumulated Value of an Annuity With a Changing Payment*

The relationship in Equation 2.5 can also be used to find the accumulated
value of an annuity for which the payment amount changes during the
course of the annuity. The following example illustrates this point.

| EXAMPLE 2.5 |

*(Annuity whose payment amount changes during annuity term)*

Suppose that 10 monthly payments of 50 each are followed by 14 monthly
payments of 75 each. If interest is at an effective monthly rate of 1%, what
is the accumulated value of the series at the time of the final payment?

SOLUTION

Using the same technique as in Example 2.3 for finding the accumulated value of an annuity some time after the final payment, at the time 24 (months) the accumulated value of the first 10 payments is

$$50s_{\overline{10}|.01} \times (1.01)^{14} = 601.30.$$

The value of the final 14 payments, also valued at time 24 is

$$75s_{\overline{14}|.01} = 1,121.06.$$

The total accumulated value at time 24 is 1722.36. There is an alternative way of approaching this situation. Note in Figure 2.6 that the original (non-level) sequence of payments can be decomposed into two separate level sequences of payments, both of which end at time 24.

| Time | 0 | 1 | 2 | $\cdots$ | 10 | 11 | 12 | $\cdots$ | 24 |
|------|---|----|----|----------|----|----|----|----------|----|
| Original Series | | 50 | 50 | $\cdots$ | 50 | 75 | 75 | $\cdots$ | 75 |
| New Series 1 | | 50 | 50 | $\cdots$ | 50 | 50 | 50 | $\cdots$ | 50 |
| New Series 2 | | | | | | 25 | 25 | $\cdots$ | 25 |

FIGURE 2.6

The accumulated value (at time 24) of the alternate form of the series is

$$50s_{\overline{24}|.01} + 25s_{\overline{14}|.01} = 1,348.67 + 373.69 = 1,722.36. \qquad \square$$

### 2.1.2 PRESENT VALUE OF AN ANNUITY

The discussion above has been concerned with formulating and calculating the accumulated value of a series of payments. We now consider the present value of an annuity, which is a valuation of a series of payments some time before they begin

EXAMPLE 2.6 (*Present value of a series of payments*)

Smith's grandchild will begin a four year college program in one year. Smith wishes to open a bank account with a single deposit today so that her grandchild can withdraw $1000 each year for four years from the account, with the first withdrawal taking place one year from now, and subsequent withdrawals each year after that. The account has an effective annual interest rate of 6% and the deposit is calculated so that the account balance will be reduced to 0 when the fourth withdrawal is made four years from now. Determine the amount of the deposit Smith makes today.

SOLUTION

Suppose that the amount of the initial deposit is $X$. If we track the account balance after each withdrawal, we see the following:

Balance after $1^{st}$ withdrawal:

$$X(1.06) - 1000$$

Balance after $2^{nd}$ withdrawal:

$$[X(1.06) - 1000](1.06) - 1000 \quad = \quad X(1.06)^2 - 1000(1.06) - 1000$$

Balance after $3^{rd}$ withdrawal:

$$[X(1.06)^2 - 1000(1.06)](1.06) - 1000$$
$$= X(1.06)^3 - 1000(1.06)^2 - 1000(1.06) - 1000$$

Balance after $4^{th}$ withdrawal:

$$X(1.06)^4 - 1000(1.06)^3 - 1000(1.06)^2 - 1000(1.06) - 1000.$$

In order for the balance to be 0 just after the $4^{th}$ withdrawal, we must have

$$X(1.06)^4 = 1000(1.06)^3 + 1000(1.06)^2 + 1000(1.06) + 1000,$$

or equivalently,

$$X = \frac{1000}{1.06} + \frac{1000}{(1.06)^2} + \frac{1000}{(1.06)^3} + \frac{1000}{(1.06)^4}$$
$$= 1000[v + v^2 + v^3 + v^4]$$
$$= 3,465.11. \qquad \square$$

It can be seen from Example 2.6 that the deposit amount needed is the combined present value of the four withdrawals that will be made. The present value of an annuity of payments is the value of the payments at the time, or some time before, the payments begin. Consider again a series of $n$ payments of amount 1 each, made at equally spaced intervals for which interest is at effective interest rate $i$ per payment period. The present value of the series of payments, valued **one period before** the first payment, can be represented as the sum of the present values of the individual payments:

$$\frac{1}{(1+i)} + \frac{1}{(1+i)^2} + \cdots + \frac{1}{(1+i)^{n-1}} + \frac{1}{(1+i)^n}$$

$$= v + v^2 + \cdots + v^{n-1} + v^n = v\left[1 + v + \cdots + v^{n-1}\right]$$

$$= v \times \frac{1-v^n}{1-v} = \frac{1-v^n}{(1+i)(1-\frac{1}{1+i})} = \frac{1-v^n}{1+i-1} = \frac{1-v^n}{i}. \quad (2.6)$$

Applying Equation 2.6 to Example 2.6 we see that the present value of the four payment annuity received by Smith's grandchild is:

$$1000\left[v + v^2 + v^3 + v^4\right] = 1000\left[\frac{1-v_{.06}^4}{.06}\right] = 3,465.11.$$

It is often the case that, as in Example 2.6, a valuation of a series of payments is done one period before the first payment. There is a specific actuarial symbol that represents the present value of a such an annuity.

---

**Definition 2.2 – Present Value of an $n$-Payment Annuity-Immediate of 1 Per Period**

The symbol $a_{\overline{n}|i}$ is specifically used to denote the present value of a series of equally spaced payments of amount 1 each when the valuation point is one payment period before the payments begin.

$$a_{\overline{n}|i} = v + v^2 + \cdots + v^n = \sum_{i=1}^{n} v^t = \frac{1-v^n}{i}. \quad (2.7)$$

---

This valuation is illustrated in the following line diagram.

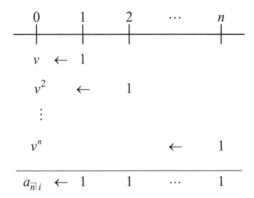

Similar to the use of the notation $s_{\overline{n}|}$, the symbol $a_{\overline{n}|}$, can be used to express the present value of an annuity provided the following conditions are met.

(1) There are $n$ payments of equal amount.

(2) The payments are made at equal intervals of time, with the same frequency as the frequency of interest compounding.

(3) The valuation point is one payment period before the first payment is made.

A typical situation in which the present value of an annuity-immediate arises is the repayment of a loan. In financial practice, a loan being repaid with a series of payments is structured so that the original loan amount advanced to the borrower is equal to the present value of the loan payments to be made by the borrower, and the first loan payment is made one period after the loan is made. The present value is calculated using the loan interest rate.

EXAMPLE 2.7 (*Loan repayment*)

Brown has bought a new car and requires a loan of 12,000 to pay for it. The car dealer offers Brown two alternatives on the loan:

(a) monthly payments for 3 years, starting one month after purchase, with an annual interest rate of 12% compounded monthly, or

(b) monthly payments for 4 years, also starting one month after purchase, with annual interest rate 15%, compounded monthly.

Find Brown's monthly payment and the total amount paid over the course of the repayment period under each of the two options.

SOLUTION

We denote the monthly payment under option (a) by $P_1$ and under option (b) by $P_2$. "12% compounded monthly" refers to a one month interest rate of 1%, and alternative (b) refers to a one-month interest rate of 1.25%. Since payments begin one month (one payment period) after the loan, the equations of value for the two options are

(a) $12,000 = P_1 \times a_{\overline{36}|.01}$ and

(b) $12,000 = P_2 \times a_{\overline{48}|.0125}$.

Then $P_1 = \dfrac{12,000}{a_{\overline{36}|.01}} = \dfrac{12,000(.01)}{1-(1.01)^{-36}} = \dfrac{12,000}{30.107505} = 398.57$, and

$$P_2 = \dfrac{12,000}{a_{\overline{48}|.0125}} = \dfrac{12,000}{35.931363} = 333.97.$$

The total paid under option (a) would be $36P_1 = 14,348.52$, and under option (b) it would be $48 \times P_2 = 16,030.56$. □

The following two graphs illustrate the present value of an annuity-immediate first as a function the rate of interest, and then as a function of the number of payments. The first graph is an illustration of the fact that as interest rates increase, present value decreases. The second graph shows that the present value of a payment made far in the future is small.

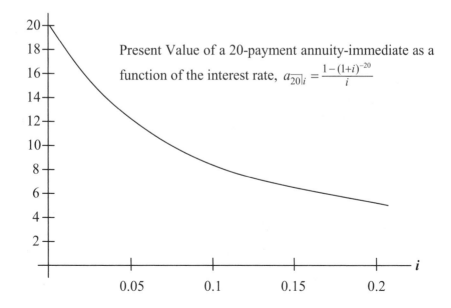

Present Value of a 20-payment annuity-immediate as a function of the interest rate, $a_{\overline{20}|i} = \dfrac{1-(1+i)^{-20}}{i}$

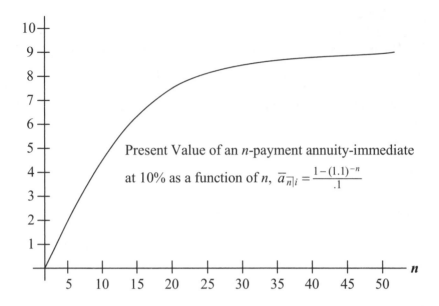

Present Value of an $n$-payment annuity-immediate at 10% as a function of $n$, $\overline{a}_{\overline{n}|i} = \dfrac{1-(1.1)^{-n}}{.1}$

### 2.1.2.1 *Present Value of an Annuity Some Time Before Payments Begin*

As in the case of an accumulated annuity in which the value was found some time after the final payment, it may be necessary to find the present value of a series of payments some time before the first payment is made. This is illustrated in the following modification of Example 2.7.

**EXAMPLE 2.8**

(*Valuation of an annuity some time before payments begin*)

Suppose that in Example 2.7 Brown can repay the loan, still with 36 payments under option (a) or 48 payments under option (b), with the first payment made 9 months after the car is purchased in either case. Assuming interest accrues from the time of the car purchase, find the payments required under options (a) and (b).

**SOLUTION**

We denote the new payments under options (a) and (b) by $P_1'$ and $P_2'$, respectively. Then the equation of value for option (a) is

$$12,000 = P_1' \times \left[ v^9 + v^{10} + \cdots + v^{44} \right] = P_1' \times v^8 \cdot a_{\overline{36}|.01},$$

which leads to

$$P_1' = \frac{12,000}{v^8 \cdot a_{\overline{36}|.01}} = (1.01)^8 \cdot \frac{12,000}{a_{\overline{36}|.01}} = (1.01)^8 \cdot P_1 = 431.60.$$

In a similar manner,

$$P_2' = (1.0125)^8 \times \frac{12,000}{a_{\overline{48}|.0125}} = (1.0125)^8 \times P_2 = 368.86.$$

Since the payments are deferred for 8 months as compared to the situation in Example 2.7, it should not be surprising that in each of cases (a) and (b) the new payment is equal to the old payment multiplied by an 8-month accumulation factor. ❏

Suppose an $n$-payment annuity of 1 per period is to be valued $k+1$ payment periods before the first payment is made. The present value can be expressed as $v^{k+1} + v^{k+2} + \cdots + v^{k+n}$, which can be reformulated as

$$v^k \times [v + v^2 + \cdots + v^n] = v^k \times a_{\overline{n}|}.$$

Since $a_{\overline{n}|}$ represents the present value of the annuity one period before the first payment, the value $k$ periods before that (for a total of $k+1$ periods before the first payment) should be $v^k \times a_{\overline{n}|}$. With a derivation similar to that for Equation (2.4), we have

$$v^k \times a_{\overline{n}|} = a_{\overline{n+k}|} - a_{\overline{k}|}. \tag{2.8}$$

Such an annuity is called a **deferred annuity**. The annuity considered in Equation (2.8) is usually called a $k$-period deferred, $n$-payment annuity of 1 per period. This present value may be denoted by $_k|a_{\overline{n}|}$. Note that for a $k$-period deferred annuity-immediate, the first payment comes $k+1$ periods after the valuation date, not $k$ periods after. Equation (2.8) can be rewritten in the form

$$a_{\overline{n+k}|} = a_{\overline{k}|} + v^k \times a_{\overline{n}|} = a_{\overline{n}|} + v^n \times a_{\overline{k}|}. \tag{2.9}$$

### 2.1.2.2 *Present Value of an Annuity with Non-Level Interest Rates*

Just as Equation (2.5) can be used for accumulated annuities, Equation (2.9) can be applied to find the present value of an annuity for which the interest rate changes during the term of the annuity. If we consider an $n+k$-payment annuity with equally spaced payments, with an interest rate of $i_1$ per period up to the time of the $n^{th}$ payment followed by a rate of $i_2$ per period from the $n^{th}$ payment onward, the present value of the annuity one period before the first payment can be found in the following manner.

(a) The present value of the first $n$ payments valued one period before the first payment is $a_{\overline{n}|i_1}$.

(b) The present value of the final $k$ payments valued at time $n$ (one period before the first of the final $k$ payments) at rate $i_2$ is $a_{\overline{k}|i_2}$.

(c) The value of (b) at time 0 (one period before the first payment of the entire series) at interest rate $i_1$ per period over the first $n$ periods is $v_{i_1}^n \times a_{\overline{k}|i_2}$.

(d) The total present value at time 0 is the sum of (a) and (c), which is $a_{\overline{n}|i_1} + v_{i_1}^n \times a_{\overline{k}|i_2}$.

This is illustrated in the following line diagram.

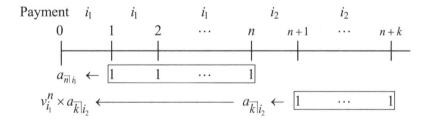

**FIGURE 2.7**

### 2.1.2.3 *Relationship Between $a_{\overline{n}|i}$ and $s_{\overline{n}|i}$*

We now return to annuities with a level interest rate. The valuation point for an $n$-payment accumulated annuity-immediate is the time of the $n^{th}$ payment and the accumulated value at that time is $s_{\overline{n}|i}$. The valuation point for the present value of an $n$-payment annuity-immediate is one period before the first payment, and the present value is $a_{\overline{n}|i}$. We see that the valuation point for the present value of the annuity is $n$ periods earlier than the valuation point for the accumulated value. Then it follows that

$$s_{\overline{n}|i} = (1+i)^n \times a_{\overline{n}|i} \tag{2.10}$$

and

$$a_{\overline{n}|i} = v^n \times s_{\overline{n}|i}. \tag{2.11}$$

This can be easily verified algebraically by observing that

$$v^n \times s_{\overline{n}|i} = v^n \times \left[ \frac{(1+i)^n - 1}{i} \right] = \frac{1-v^n}{i} = a_{\overline{n}|i}.$$

For a particular value of $i$, both $s_{\overline{n}|i}$ and $a_{\overline{n}|i}$ increase as $n$ increases. Furthermore $s_{\overline{n}|i} = 1 + (1+i) + \cdots + (1+i)^{n-1}$ increases as $i$ increases (a higher interest rate results in greater accumulated values of the payments). However, since $v = \frac{1}{1+i}$ decreases as $i$ increases, we can see that $a_{\overline{n}|i} = v + \cdots + v^n$ decreases as $i$ increases. This again illustrates the inverse relationship between the present value of an income stream and the interest rate used for valuation.

### 2.1.2.4 *Valuation of Perpetuities*

It was pointed out in Chapter 1 that if $i > 0$, then $v^n$ decreases as $n$ increases, and, in fact, $v^n \to 0$ as $n \to \infty$. Furthermore it was noted earlier in this section that $a_{\overline{n}|i}$ increases as $n$ increases. As $n \to \infty$ it is easy to see that

$$\lim_{n \to \infty} a_{\overline{n}|i} = \lim_{n \to \infty} \frac{1-v^n}{i} = \frac{1}{i}. \tag{2.12}$$

This expression can also be derived by summing the infinite series of present values of payments $v + v^2 + v^3 + \cdots$. The infinite series becomes $v + v^2 + v^3 + \cdots = v \times \frac{1}{1-v} = \frac{1}{i}$. The infinite period annuity that results as $n \to \infty$ is called a **perpetuity**, and a notation that may be used to represent the present value of this perpetuity is $a_{\overline{\infty}|i} = \frac{1}{i}$. Since the valuation of the perpetuity occurs one period before the first payment, it would be referred to as a perpetuity-immediate.

This notion of perpetuity can be considered from another point of view. Suppose that $X$ is the amount that must be invested at interest rate $i$ per period in order to generate a perpetuity of 1 per period. In order to generate a payment of 1 without taking anything away from the existing principal amount $X$, the payment of 1 must be generated by interest alone. Therefore $X \cdot i = 1$, or equivalently, $X = \frac{1}{i}$.

---

**EXAMPLE 2.9**   (*Perpetuity*)

At an annual effective interest rate of 8%, a deposit of $10,000 will generate interest of $800 at the end of a year. If that interest payment is "withdrawn" from the account, but the principal amount of $10,000 is allowed to remain in the account for another year, it will generate another interest payment of $800 at the end of the second year. This can go on indefinitely, as long as the only amount withdrawn at the end of each year is the interest generated for that year. Another way of seeing this is that 10,000 is the present value at 8% of payments of 800 at the end of each year forever,
$$10,000 = 800 a_{\overline{\infty}|.08}.$$

```
  |———————————+———————————————+———————————————+——————  - - -
10,000   →  10,000(1.08)
            – 800
            = 10,000    →    10,000(1.08)
                             – 800
                             = 10,000    →    10,000(1.08)   - - -
```

Note that it is not possible to formulate the accumulated value of a perpetuity. ⬚

---

**EXAMPLE 2.10**   (*Valuation of a perpetuity*)

A perpetuity-immediate pays $X$ per year. Brian receives the first $n$ payments, Colleen receives the next $n$ payments, and Jeff receives the remaining payments. Brian's share of the present value of the original perpetuity is 40%, and Jeff's share is $K$. Calculate $K$.

SOLUTION

The present value of the perpetuity is $Xa_{\overline{\infty}|i} = \frac{X}{i}$. The present value of Brian's portion of the perpetuity is $Xa_{\overline{n}|i} = X\left(\frac{1-v^n}{i}\right)$, which we are told is 40% of $\frac{X}{i}$. Therefore, $1-v^n = .4$, so that $v^n = .6$. The present value of Colleen's portion of the perpetuity is $Xv^n a_{\overline{n}|i} = .6Xa_{\overline{n}|i} = (.6)(.4)\frac{X}{i}$, which is 24% of the value of the original perpetuity. Therefore, Jeff's share of the perpetuity is $(100-40-24)\% = 36\%$. Alternatively, note that Jeff's share can be formulated as

$$Xv^{2n}a_{\overline{\infty}|i} = (.6)^2 Xa_{\overline{\infty}|i} = (.36)\frac{X}{i}. \qquad \square$$

It is possible to interpret a level $n$-payment annuity as the "difference" between two perpetuities. The present value of a perpetuity-immediate of 1 per year is $a_{\overline{\infty}|i} = \frac{1}{i}$. An "$n$-year deferred" perpetuity-immediate of 1 per year would have payments starting in $n+1$ years, and would have present value $v^n \times a_{\overline{\infty}|i} = \frac{v^n}{i}$. Subtracting the second present value from the first, we get $a_{\overline{\infty}|i} - v^n \times a_{\overline{\infty}|i} = \frac{1-v^n}{i} = a_{\overline{n}|i}$. Subtracting the deferred perpetuity cancels all payments after the $n^{th}$ payment, leaving an $n$-payment annuity-immediate.

### 2.1.3 ANNUITY-IMMEDIATE AND ANNUITY-DUE

To make a valuation of a level series of equally spaced payments, the information needed is

(1)    the number of the payments,
(2)    the valuation point, and
(3)    the interest rate per payment period.

There are a few particular valuation points that arise frequently in practice, and there is actuarial notation and terminology to represent those valuations. For a level series of payments of 1 each, we have already seen $s_{\overline{n}|}$ and **annuity-immediate** valuations. Annuity-immediate is often identified by the phrase "payments are made at the end of each period." When deposits are made into a bank account it is usually the case that an accumulated value is calculated at the time of a deposit, so the valuation is an accumulated annuity-immediate. In general, if we are told that an annuity has $n$ payments made at the end of each period, this is interpreted as the payments being made at times 1 (end of $1^{st}$ period), 2 (end of $2^{nd}$ period),..., $n$ (end of $n^{th}$ period). It would also be understood that the present value of the annuity is found at the beginning of the $1^{st}$ period, which is time 0 (one period before the first payment), and the accumulated value would be found at the end of the $n^{th}$ period, which is time $n$. Most financial calculators have a setting denoted "END" which will set the calculator for annuity-immediate calculations.

Another standard annuity form is that of the **annuity-due**. This form occurs most frequently in the context of life annuities, but can also be defined in the case of annuities-certain. In the case of present value, an annuity-due refers to the valuation of the annuity **at the time of (and including)** the first payment. In the case of accumulated value, annuity-due refers to the valuation of the annuity **one payment period after the final payment**. If an annuity is described as having payments occurring at the beginning of each period, the implication is that annuity-due valuation is intended. There would be payments at time 0 (beginning of the $1^{st}$ period), time 1 (beginning of $2^{nd}$ period),..., time $n-1$ (beginning of $n^{th}$ period). The present value of the annuity would be found at time 0 and the accumulated value would be found at time $n$. The calculator setting "BEGIN" or "BGN" sets annuity valuation in the form of annuity-due.

---

**Definition 2.3  Annuity-Due**

For $n$-payment annuities with payments of amount 1 each, the annuity-due present value is at the time of the first payment,

$$\ddot{a}_{\overline{n}|i} = 1 + v + v^2 + \cdots + v^{n-1} = \frac{1-v^n}{1-v} = \frac{1-v^n}{d}, \quad (2.13)$$

and the accumulated value is one period after the final payment,

$$\ddot{s}_{\overline{n}|i} = (1+i) + (1+i)^2 + \cdots + (1+i)^n$$

$$= (1+i)\left[\frac{(1+i)^n - 1}{i}\right] = \frac{(1+i)^n - 1}{d}, \quad (2.14)$$

---

where $d$ is the discount rate equivalent to interest rate $i$. Figure 2.8 summarizes the annuity-immediate and annuity-due valuation points.

Payment No.

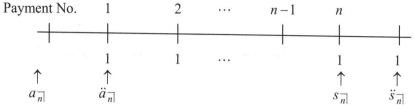

**FIGURE 2.8**

Note that for both the present value and accumulated value of the annuity-due, the valuation point is one period after the valuation point for the corresponding annuity-immediate. This leads to the relationships

$$\ddot{a}_{\overline{n}|i} = (1+i)a_{\overline{n}|i} \qquad (2.15a)$$

and

$$\ddot{s}_{\overline{n}|i} = (1+i)s_{\overline{n}|i}. \qquad (2.15b)$$

A perpetuity-due of 1 per year has present value

$$\ddot{a}_{\overline{\infty}|i} = 1 + v + v^2 + \cdots = \frac{1}{1-v} = \frac{1}{d}$$

$$= \frac{1+i}{i} = (1+i)a_{\overline{\infty}|i} = 1 + a_{\overline{\infty}|i} \qquad (2.16)$$

---

**EXAMPLE 2.11** (*Annuity due*)

Jim began saving money for his retirement by making monthly deposits of 200 into a fund earning 6% interest compounded monthly. The first deposit occurred on January 1, 1995. Jim became unemployed and missed making deposits 60 through 72. He then continued making monthly deposits of 200. How much did Jim accumulate in his fund, including interest on December 31, 2009, assuming payments continued through to December 1, 2009?

**SOLUTION**

The savings plan originally called for a total of 180 deposits (15 years of monthly deposits). We note that 13 deposits will be missed, the $60^{th}$ to the $72^{nd}$, inclusive. The $60^{th}$ deposit would have occurred on December 1, 1999, and the $72^{nd}$ deposit would have occurred on December 1, 2000. The valuation point is December 31, 2009, which is one month after the final deposit on December 1, 2009. If none of the deposits had been missed, then there would have been 180 deposits and the accumulated value one month after the $180^{th}$ monthly deposit can be expressed as an annuity-due. The interest rate is .5% per month, so the accumulated value on December 31, 2009 would be

$$200 \times \left[ (1.005)^{180} + (1.005)^{179} + \cdots + (1.005) \right]$$
$$= 200 \ddot{s}_{\overline{180}|.005}$$
$$= 200 \times \frac{(1.005)^{180} - 1}{.005} \times (1.005) = 58,454.56.$$

The actual accumulated value is 58,454.56 minus the accumulated value of the missed payments. The first missed payment was December 1, 1999, and the valuation date of December 31, 2009 is 121 months later. The value on December 31, 2009 of the missed payments is

$$200 \times \left[ (1.005)^{121} + (1.005)^{120} + \cdots + (1.005)^{109} \right]$$
$$= 200 \times (1.005)^{109} \times \left[ (1.005)^{12} + (1.005)^{11} + \cdots + 1 \right]$$
$$= 200 \times (1.005)^{109} \times \frac{(1.005)^{13} - 1}{.005}$$
$$= 200 \times (1.005)^{109} \times s_{\overline{13}|.005} = 4,614.73.$$

Note that the accumulated value of the missed payments could also be formulated as $200 \times (1.005)^{108} \cdot \ddot{s}_{\overline{13}|.005}$ (this follows from the relationship $(1.005) \times s_{\overline{13}|.005} = \ddot{s}_{\overline{13}|.005}$), which can be interpreted as the accumulated value of the 13 missed payments valued on December 31, 2000 (one month after the $13^{th}$ missed payment) and then accumulating this amount for another 9 years (108 months).

The value of the deposits made is $58,454.56 - 4,614.73 = 53,839.83.$  ☐

A series of payments can be valued at any time. Annuity-immediate and annuity due, accumulated and present value, are based on the most frequently used valuation points. We have seen that annuities can be valued some time after they end or some time before they begin. Valuations can also be done within the term of the annuity, so that we would find the accumulated value of payments already made combined with the present value of payments yet to be made. The general term to refer to the value of an annuity at any point in time is *current value*.

## 2.2 LEVEL PAYMENT ANNUITIES – SOME GENERALIZATIONS

### 2.2.1 DIFFERING INTEREST AND PAYMENT PERIOD

In the annuities considered in Section 2.1 it had been assumed that the quoted compounding interest period is the same as the annuity payment period. It may often be the case that the quoted interest rate has a compounding period that does not coincide with the annuity payment period. For the purpose of a numerical evaluation of the annuity, we focus on the annuity payment period and determine and use the interest rate per payment period that is equivalent to the quoted interest rate. What is meant by equivalence here is "compound equivalence" as defined in Chapter 1. The following example illustrates this.

**EXAMPLE 2.12**  (*Differing interest and payment period*)

On the last day of every March, June, September, and December, Smith makes a deposit of 1000 into a savings account. The first deposit is March 31, 1995 and the final one is December 31, 2010. Find the balance in Smith's account on January 1, 2011 in each of the following two cases. A calendar quarter is regarded as exactly $\frac{1}{4}$-year.

(a)   Interest is quoted at a 9% nominal annual interest rate compounded monthly.

(b)   Interest is quoted at an effective annual rate of 10%, with compound interest paid for amounts on deposit for a fraction of a year.

**SOLUTION**

Smith makes a total of 64 deposits (4 per year for 16 years). If the effective 3-month rate $j$ were known, then the accumulated value just after the final deposit would be $1000 \times \frac{(1+j)^{64}-1}{j} = 1000 s_{\overline{64}|j}$. In case (a), from the quoted nominal annual rate we see that the effective 1-month rate is .0075, so $j$ satisfies the relationship $1+j = (1.0075)^3$; this is the "compound equivalence" relationship relating the effective 3-month interest rate $j$ to the effective 1-month rate .0075. Solving for $j$ results in $j = .02266917$. The accumulated value of the annuity is then

$$1000 \times \frac{(1.02266917)^{64}-1}{.02266917} = 1000 s_{\overline{64}|.02266917} = 141,076.$$

In case (b), $j$ satisfies the relationship $1 + j = (1.10)^{1/4} = 1.02411369$; the effective 3-month rate is found by compounding the effective annual rate for a $\frac{1}{4}$-year period. The accumulated value of the annuity is

$$1000 \times \frac{(1.02411369)^{64} - 1}{.02411369} = 1000 s_{\overline{64}|.02411369} = 149,084. \qquad \square$$

The payment period for the annuity in Example 2.12 is 3 months, so for each of the two parts of the example, the quoted interest rate was converted to an equivalent 3-month interest rate. This is the way in which such a situation is dealt with in practice. Most mortgage loans are set up to have monthly payments, but the interest rate may not be quoted as a monthly rate.

Round-off error can occur if an approximate interest rate is used. Note that in Example 2.12 if we had used approximate values of $j$ rounded to the nearest .01%, for (a) $j = .0227$ and for (b) $j = .0241$, then the accumulated values would be 141,242 in case (a) and 149,006 in case (b). Calculators generally have at least 8 digits of accuracy, which is sufficient for all practical purposes.

---

**Canada's Registered Education Savings Plan (RESP)**

In the early 1980s, the Government of Canada introduced a reduced-tax savings plan to encourage parents to save for a child's postsecondary education. The plan allows deposits of up to $167 at the start of each month. A bonus amount equal to 20% of each deposit is a contribution from the federal government as an added incentive to contribute to the plan. Contributions can be made up to the child's 21$^{st}$ birthday.

The tax incentive in the plan is that when the child begins postsecondary studies and begins to withdraw funds from the RESP account, any amounts withdrawn above the original deposits made by the parents are regarded as income to the child. It is anticipated that the child will be in a low tax bracket while pursuing post-secondary studies, and will pay less tax than the parents otherwise would have paid on any earned interest.

An illustration of the accumulation of an RESP is given on the website of the Bank of Nova Scotia. The illustration assumes that the parents make the maximum deposit of $167 at the beginning of each month from the date of the child's birth until one month before the child's

18$^{th}$ birthday. The illustration indicates that at an annual effective rate of interest of 7%, the deposits (including the bonus deposit) will accumulate to $84,672 as of the child's 18$^{th}$ birthday. This can be formulated as $200\ddot{s}_{\overline{216}|j}$, where $j$ is the monthly rate of interest equivalent to an annual effective interest rate of 7%.

At the current time this book is being written, the Bank of Nova Scotia is advertising an annual effective interest rate of 2.75% on RESP deposit plans. At that rate, the deposits would accumulate to $55,759.

## 2.2.2 m-THLY PAYABLE ANNUITIES

When the quoted interest rate is an effective annual rate of interest and the payments are made more frequently than once per year, the actuarial concept of an $m^{thly}$ payable annuity can be applied. Part (b) of Example 2.12 can be used as an illustration. There are $m = 4$ payments per year of 1,000 each, and the interest rate is quoted as an effective annual rate of 10%. The total paid per year is 4,000 for 16 years. The actuarial notation $4000s_{\overline{16}|.10}^{(4)}$ can be used to represent the accumulated value at the time of the final quarterly payment of 1,000. The coefficient 4000 is the total paid per year, and the superscript "(4)" indicates that this total of 4,000 is split into 4 payments of 1,000 each to be made at the end of each quarter. In the exercises it is shown that $s_{\overline{16}|.10}^{(4)} = \frac{(1.10)^{16}-1}{i^{(4)}} = s_{\overline{16}|.10} \cdot \frac{i}{i^{(4)}}$, where $i^{(4)}$ is the nominal annual rate of interest compounded 4 times per year that is equivalent to the effective annual rate of $i = .10$.

The general form of an accumulated $m^{thly}$ payable annuity-immediate is $Ks_{\overline{n}|i}^{(m)}$, which is interpreted as follows. The effective annual interest rate is $i$ and payments of amount $\frac{K}{m}$ each occur at the end of every $\frac{1}{m}$-year period (total amount paid per year is $K$). $Ks_{\overline{n}|i}^{(m)}$ denotes the accumulated value of this series of payments at the end of $n$ years of payments; there would be a total of $m \times n$ payments, and the valuation point is the time of the final payment. There is a similar notation for the present value of an $m^{thly}$ payable annuity. For the same set of payments just described, $Ka_{\overline{n}|i}^{(m)}$ denotes the present value of the series one *payment period* (or

$\frac{1}{m}$-year ) before the first payment. In the exercises at the end of this chapter it is shown that

$$a_{\overline{n}|i}^{(m)} = \frac{1 - v_i^n}{i^{(m)}} = a_{\overline{n}|i} \cdot \frac{i}{i^{(m)}}. \qquad (2.17)$$

This $m^{thly}$ payable annuity notation arises in a life-annuity context, where it is more likely to be used.

### 2.2.3 CONTINUOUS ANNUITIES

The annuities considered up to now all have specified individual payments at specified points in time. They are *discrete annuities* and frequently occur in practical situations. For theoretical purposes and for modeling complex situations, it is sometimes useful to consider *continuous annuities,* those which have payments made continuously over a period of time.

In part (b) of Example 2.12 an annuity has quarterly payments and interest is quoted on an effective annual basis. The exercises at the end of the chapter consider a generalization of this situation in which payments are made every $\frac{1}{m}^{th}$ of a year. As $m$ becomes larger the time between successive payments becomes smaller. Although it would not be physically possible to reach the limit of this payment pattern as $m \to \infty$, the interpretation of that limit would be an annuity *payable continuously.*

Suppose an annuity has a level rate of continuous payment of 1 per period, and an effective rate of interest of $i$ per period. Then the amount paid during the interval from time $t_1$ to time $t_2$ (measured using the period as the unit of time) is equal to $t_2 - t_1$. Suppose the payment continues for $n$ periods, measured from time 0 to time $n$. In order to find the accumulated value of the $n$ periods of payment, it is not possible to add up the accumulated values of individual payments as was done for the discrete annuities considered earlier. But we can determine the accumulated value at time $n$ of the infinitesimal amount paid between time $t_1$ and time $t_2$ using differential calculus. The accumulated value as of time $n$ of this amount is $(1+i)^{n-t_1} dt$. These accumulated amounts are "added up" by means of an integral, so that the accumulated value of the continuous annuity, paid at rate 1 per period for $n$ periods, denoted by $\overline{s}_{\overline{n}|i}$, is given by

$$\overline{s}_{\overline{n}|i} = \int_0^n (1+i)^{n-t}\, dt. \tag{2.18a}$$

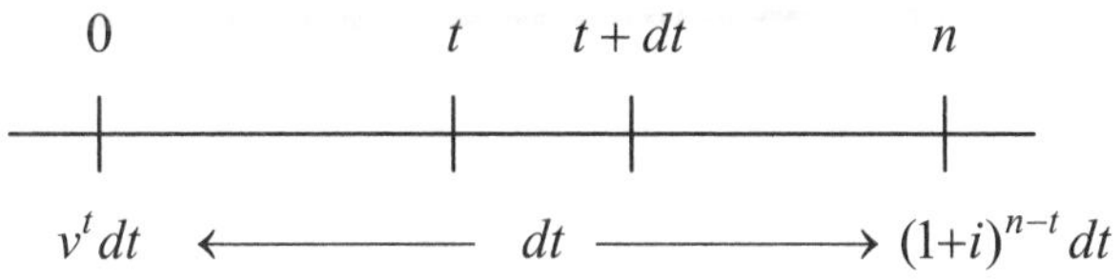

FIGURE 2.9

Integrating the right side of (2.18a) we obtain

$$\overline{s}_{\overline{n}|i} = \frac{-(1+i)^{n-t}}{\ln(1+i)}\bigg|_0^n = \frac{(1+i)^n - 1}{\delta}$$

$$= \frac{e^{n\delta} - 1}{\delta} = \frac{(1+i)^n - 1}{i} \cdot \frac{i}{\delta} = \frac{i}{\delta} \cdot s_{\overline{n}|i}. \tag{2.18b}$$

Note also that $\overline{s}_{\overline{n}|i} = \frac{(1+i)^n - 1}{\delta} = \lim_{m\to\infty} \frac{(1+i)^n - 1}{i^{(m)}} = \lim_{m\to\infty} s_{\overline{n}|i}^{(m)}$. The interpretation of this relationship is that as $m$ gets larger, the annuity payment is more frequent and is spread more evenly throughout the year, with the limit being a continuous distribution of payment throughout the year.

EXAMPLE 2.13   (*Continuous annuity*)

In 2004 and 2005 Smith deposits 12 every day into an account and in 2006 he deposits 15 every day into the account. The account earns interest from the exact time of the deposit, with interest quoted as an effective annual rate. The rates are 9% in 2004 and 2005, and 12% in 2006. Find the amount in the account, including interest, on December 31 2006 (a) exactly based on the daily deposits, and (b) using the approximation that deposits are made continuously.

SOLUTION

(a)   $j_1$ denotes the equivalent daily compound interest rate in 2004 and 2005, and $j_2$ denotes the equivalent daily compound interest rate in 2006. It then follows that $j_1 = (1.09)^{1/365} - 1 = .00023631$, and $j_2 = (1.12)^{1/365} - 1$. Using the approach illustrated in part (b) of Example 2.12, the accumulated value on December 31, 2006 is

$$12s_{\overline{730}|j_1}(1.12)+15s_{\overline{365}|j_2}$$

$$= 12(1.12)\left[\frac{(1.09)^2-1}{j_1}\right]+15\left[\frac{(1.12)-1}{j_2}\right]$$

$$= 10,706.19+5,796.40$$

$$= 16,502.59.$$

(b)  If deposits are made continuously, then the total paid per year in 2004-2005 is $12\times365=4380$, and in 2006 it is $15\times365=5475$.

The accumulated value would be

$$4380(1.12)\bar{s}_{\overline{2}|.09}+5475\cdot\bar{s}_{\overline{1}|.12}$$

$$= 4380(1.12)\left[\frac{(1.09)^2-1}{\ln(1.09)}\right]+5475\left[\frac{(1.12)-1}{\ln(1.12)}\right]$$

$$= 10,707.45+5,797.30 = 16,504.75.$$

Note that the difference between (a) and (b) is about \$2 in a total of about \$16,500.  ❏

The present value, at the time payment begins, of a continuous annuity paying a total of 1 per period at effective periodic interest rate $i$ is

$$\bar{a}_{\overline{n}|i} = \int_0^n v^t\, dt \qquad\qquad (2.19a)$$

$$= \frac{1-v^n}{\ln(1+i)} = \frac{1-v^n}{\delta} = \frac{1-e^{-n\delta}}{\delta}$$

$$= \frac{i}{\delta}\cdot a_{\overline{n}|i} = \lim_{m\to\infty} a_{\overline{n}|i}^{(m)}. \qquad\qquad (2.19b)$$

The relationships in Equations (2.4), (2.5), (2.6), (2.8), (2.9), (2.10), and (2.11) are also valid for a continuous annuity.

Suppose a general accumulation function is in effect, where $a(t_1,t_2)$ is the accumulated value at time $t_2$ of an amount 1 invested at time $t_1$. Then $\int_{t_0}^{t_e} a(t,t_e)\,dt$ and $\int_{t_0}^{t_e}\frac{1}{a(t_0,t)}\,dt$ represent the accumulated value at time $t_e$ and the present value at time $t_0$, respectively, of a continuous annuity of 1 per unit time, payable from time $t_0$ to time $t_e$. If accumulation is based on force of interest $\delta_r$, then

$$a(t_1, t_2) = \exp\left[\int_{t_1}^{t_2} \delta_r \, dr,\right] \tag{2.20}$$

and we have present and accumulated annuity values at time 0 and time $n$, respectively, given by

$$\bar{a}_{\overline{n}|\delta_r} = \int_0^n e^{-\int_0^t \delta_r dr} \, dt \tag{2.21a}$$

and

$$\bar{s}_{\overline{n}|\delta_r} = \int_0^n e^{\int_t^n \delta_r dr} \, dt, \tag{2.21b}$$

along with the relationship

$$\bar{s}_{\overline{n}|\delta_r} = \bar{a}_{\overline{n}|\delta_r} \cdot e^{\int_0^n \delta_r dr}. \tag{2.21c}$$

### 2.2.4 SOLVING FOR THE NUMBER OF PAYMENTS IN AN ANNUITY (UNKNOWN TIME)

Suppose we consider the basic relationship for the accumulated value, $M$, of an annuity-immediate with $n$ level payments of amount $J$ each with an interest rate of $i$ per payment period. The relationship is

$$M = J\left[(1+i)^{n-1} + (1+i)^{n-2} + \cdots + (1+i) + 1\right] = J\left[\frac{(1+i)^n - 1}{i}\right] = J s_{\overline{n}|i}.$$

We can regard $M$, $J$, $i$, and $n$ as "variables" in this equation, and given any three of these variables it is possible to solve for the fourth. In examples considered so far, either we have been given $J$, $i$, and $n$, and solved for $M$, or we have been given $M$, $i$, and $n$, and solved for $J$. We can solve for the unknown time factor $n$ algebraically as follows:

$$M = J \times \frac{(1+i)^n - 1}{i} \quad \rightarrow \quad (1+i)^n = 1 + \frac{Mi}{J} \quad \rightarrow \quad n = \frac{\ln\left[1 + \frac{Mi}{J}\right]}{\ln(1+i)}.$$

In general, it will not be possible to solve algebraically for the unknown interest rate factor $i$. In either case, the solution would be done using appropriate functions on a financial calculator. Most financial calculators have functions that solve for the fourth variable if any three of $M$, $J$, $i$, and $n$ are known. The same comments apply to the present value of a level payment annuity-immediate,

$$L = K[v + v^2 + \cdots + v^n] = K\left[\frac{1 - v^n}{i}\right]$$

where the four variables are the present value $L$, the payment amount $K$, the number of payments $n$, and the interest rate $i$. Solving for $n$ results in $n = \dfrac{\ln\left[1 - \frac{Li}{K}\right]}{\ln[v]}$. Calculator functions also allow the distinction between annuity-immediate and annuity-due.

Solving for the unknown time will usually result in a value for $n$ that is not an integer. The integer part will be the number of full periodic payments required, and there will be an additional fractional part of a payment required to complete the annuity. This additional fractional payment may be made at the time of the final full payment (called a "balloon payment") or may be made one period after the final full payment. The following examples illustrate these ideas.

**EXAMPLE 2.14** (*Finding the unknown number of payments*)

Smith wishes to accumulate 1000 by means of semiannual deposits earning interest at nominal annual rate $i^{(2)} = .08$ .

(a) The regular deposits will be 50 each. Find the number of regular deposits required and the additional fractional deposit in each of the following two cases:

  (i) the additional fractional deposit is made at the time of the last regular deposit, and

  (ii) the additional fractional deposit is made six months after the last regular deposit.

(b) Repeat the problem with a regular deposit amount of 25.

SOLUTION

(a) We solve the relationship $1000 = 50 \cdot s_{\overline{n}|.04}$ for $n$. Writing this equation as

$$1000 = 50 \times \frac{(1.04)^n - 1}{.04}$$

results in a value of $n = \frac{\ln(1.8)}{\ln(1.04)} = 14.9866$. Thus 14 deposits of the full amount of 50 are required. The accumulated amount on deposit at the time of, and including, the $14^{th}$ deposit is $50s_{\overline{14}|.04} = 914.60$. If the additional fractional deposit is made at the time of the $14^{th}$ regular deposit, then it must be $1000 - 914.60 = 85.40$, which is actually larger than the regular semiannual deposit. If the account is allowed to accumulate another half-year, then the accumulated amount in the account six months after the $14^{th}$ deposit, is $50\ddot{s}_{\overline{14}|.04} = 50(1.04)s_{\overline{14}|.04}$ $= 951.18$. In this case an additional fractional deposit (also called a *balloon payment*) of amount $1000 - 951.18 = 48.82$ is required to bring the amount on deposit to a total of 1000.

(b) With the problem repeated at a deposit amount of 25, solving $1000 = 25s_{\overline{n}|.04}$ results in $n = 24.3624$. The accumulated amount at the time of the $24^{th}$ deposit is $25s_{\overline{24}|.04} = 977.07$, so that the additional fractional deposit required would be 22.93, if it were made at the time of the $24^{th}$ deposit. The accumulated amount six months after the $24^{th}$ deposit is $25\ddot{s}_{\overline{24}|.04} = 1016.15$. No additional fractional (or *drop*) payment would be required since the accumulated value is already 16.15 larger than the target value of 1000.  ❑

In situations not so elementary as those in Example 2.14, an unknown time problem may not have an analytic solution for $n$. In that case some sort of approximation technique must be applied. The following example illustrates this.

EXAMPLE 2.15   (*Unknown Time*)

Smith makes a gross contribution of 100 per month to a retirement fund earning $i^{(12)} = .09$, with interest credited on the last day of each month. At the time each deposit is made, the fund administrators deduct 10 from the deposit for expenses and administration fees. The first deposit is made on the last day of January 2010. In which month does the accumulated value of the fund become greater than the total gross contribution to that point?

| SOLUTION |

We wish to solve for the smallest integer $n$ for which the inequality $90s_{\overline{n}|.0075} \geq 100n$ is true. The net deposit is 90 and the monthly rate is $j = \frac{.09}{12} = .0075$. The relationship $90\left[\frac{(1.0075)^n - 1}{.0075}\right] \geq 100n$ is equivalent to $(1.0075)^n \geq 1 + .008333n$, which we cannot solve analytically. An elementary approach to a solution is by "trial-and-error," where we try various values of $n$ until the inequality is satisfied. From an inspection of the inequality, since the exponential factor $(1.0075)^n$ ultimately increases faster than the linear factor $1 + .008333n$, we see that the inequality will eventually be satisfied (for a large enough $n$). With the arbitrary choice of $n = 10$, we have $(1.0075)^{10} = 1.077583$ and $1 + .008333(10) = 1.08333$, so the inequality is not satisfied. We try a larger $n$, say $n = 20$, in which case $(1.0075)^{20} = 1.161184$ and $1 + .008333(20) = 1.1666$, so the inequality is still not satisfied. Continuing in this way we obtain the results shown in Table 2.1.

TABLE 2.1

| $n$ | $(1.0075)^n$ | $1 + .008333n$ | Satisfied |
|-----|--------------|----------------|-----------|
| 10 | 1.0775825 | 1.08333 | No |
| 20 | 1.1611841 | 1.16666 | No |
| 30 | 1.2512720 | 1.24999 | Yes |
| 25 | 1.2053870 | 1.20833 | No |
| 28 | 1.2327120 | 1.23332 | No |
| 29 | 1.2419570 | 1.24166 | Yes |

Therefore $n = 29$ is the smallest $n$ for which the inequality is satisfied The $29^{th}$ deposit occurs at the end of May 2012. Note that Table 2.1 could be generated in a computer spreadsheet program. The "Solver" function in an EXCEL spreadsheet could also be used to solve for $n$.  ☐

The solution for $n$ in the equation $L = Ka_{\overline{n}|i}$ was seen to be $n = \frac{\ln[1-(Li/K)]}{\ln[v]}$. It is implicitly assumed that $1 - \frac{L \times i}{K} > 0$, since otherwise it would be impossible to find the natural logarithm. Upon closer inspection, if $1 - \frac{L \times i}{K} \leq 0$, then $K \leq L \cdot i$, so the loan payment will at most cover the periodic interest due on the loan and will never repay any principal. Therefore, if the loan payment isn't sufficient to cover the periodic interest due, the loan will never be repaid and $n = \infty$.

### 2.2.5 SOLVING FOR THE INTEREST RATE IN AN ANNUITY (UNKNOWN INTEREST)

It is generally necessary to use a calculator function or computer routine to solve for an unknown interest rate.

The following is based on an example of an Individual Retirement Account (IRA) found on the website of the Western & Southern Financial Group (Cincinnati, OH). An IRA is a deposit account in which funds accumulate tax-deferred until withdrawn at the time of retirement. There may also be some income tax reduction at the time of each deposit. An excerpt from the website is below.

**IRA Advantage: Tax-Favored Compounding**

This chart assumes a $3,000 annual contribution at the beginning of each year, a hypothetical 6% average rate of return, and a 30% combined federal and state income tax bracket.

This example assumes deductible contributions. Earnings grow tax-deferred until withdrawn at the end of the period.

Should the IRA be withdrawn as a lump sum at the end of the period, its value would be $359,941 after 30% taxes.

$514,201

$317,817

Fully Taxable

Tax-Deferred IRA

Tax-deferred IRA versus fully taxable growth of $3,000 annual contributions over 40 years assuming 6% growth.

www.westernsouthernlife.com

**FIGURE 2.10**

### EXAMPLE 2.16

*(Individual Retirement Account – Unknown Interest)*

Verify the numerical values shown in Figure 2.10 above.

### SOLUTION

For the tax-deferred accumulation in the IRA, with deposits of $3,000 at the start of each year for 40 years, at a 6% effective annual rate of interest, the deposits should accumulate to

$$3000\ddot{s}_{\overline{40}|.06} = 3000(1.06) \times \frac{(1.06)^{40} - 1}{.06} = 492,143$$

at the end of the $40^{th}$ year. This is not the stated amount of $514,201 in Figure 2.10 above. We can find the effective annual interest rate $i$ which results in the stated accumulated value: $3000\ddot{s}_{\overline{40}|i} = 514,201$.

Using a financial calculator, we get the value $i = 6.17\%$. This is the effective annual rate that is equivalent to a nominal annual rate of 6% compounded monthly (.5% per month). This is not explicitly stated on the webpage.

Figure 2.10 also has an example of fully taxable accumulation with an indicated tax rate of 30%. This means that any interest earned on the deposits will be taxed at that rate. The before-tax .5% monthly rate of interest becomes an after-tax rate of $.5\% \times .7 = .35\%$.

The equivalent effective annual after-tax rate of interest is

$$(1.0035)^{12} - 1 = .042818\,(4.28\%).$$

The fully taxable accumulated value at the end of 40 years is

$$3000\ddot{s}_{\overline{40}|.042818} = 3000(1.042818) \times \frac{(1.042818)^{40} - 1}{.042818} = 317,817,$$

as indicated in Figure 2.10. ❑

Part of the solution to Example 2.16 involved finding an interest rate in a transaction with level deposits. Solving for the interest rate in a more general financial transaction whose payments are not level can lead to significant complications. For many standard financial transactions, such as loans, there is often only one non-negative solution to the unknown interest rate. Occasionally a complicated situation may arise in which it is not clear whether there is any solution for $i$, and if so whether it is unique. These considerations will be addressed in Chapter 5.

There are a few points to keep in mind when considering a situation involving an unknown rate of interest. It can be assumed that interest rates are greater than or equal to $-100\%$, since at a rate of $-100\%$ the accumulated value of 1 would be 0 at any future point except in unusual circumstances. One such circumstance would be where an investor has at risk more than the amount invested (such as with "leveraged" investments or when investing on "margin"). Another situation would be where the investment consists of a series of varying cashflows, each one of which can be either positive and negative (i.e., disbursements and receipts). We will consider the determination of the unknown interest rate, also called the *internal rate of return* in a more general context in Chapter 5.

## 2.3 ANNUITIES WITH NON-CONSTANT PAYMENTS

There are a number of situations which involve a non-level series of payments. In order to value the annuity if the payment amounts do not follow any uniform pattern, it would be necessary to value the payments individually and then add the values of the individual payments. This can be done in a straightforward way. Suppose we consider a series of $n$ payments that are separated by equal intervals of time and suppose that the payment amounts are $K_1, K_2, \ldots, K_n$. If the valuation rate of interest is $i$ per payment period, then the accumulated value of the series valued at the time of the final payment is $K_1(1+i)^{n-1} + K_2(1+i)^{n-2} + \cdots + K_{n-1}(1+i) + K_n$. The present value of the series of payments valued one payment period before the first payment would be $K_1 v + K_2 v^2 + \cdots + K_{n-1} v^{n-1} + K_n v^n$. Both the TI BA II PLUS and the HP-12C calculators have cashflow worksheet functions which compute accumulated and present values of a series of up to 20 different payment amounts.

### 2.3.1 ANNUITIES WHOSE PAYMENTS FORM
####       A GEOMETRIC PROGRESSION

When there is some systematic way in which the payments of an annuity vary, it may be possible to algebraically simplify the present or accumulated value. Retirement annuities often have a "cost-of-living" increase or inflation-adjustment provision. This means that the annuity payment is adjusted periodically (usually annually) to account for inflation. Algebraically, such an annuity would have payments that tend to increase geometrically. Inflation is unlikely to be constant from year to year, but if we consider a simplified situation where there is a level rate of inflation of $r$ every year, then an inflation adjusted annuity would have payments which grow by a factor of $1+r$ each year. Many insurance companies sell indexed annuities with a fixed index rate $r$. The following example illustrates this idea.

> EXAMPLE 2.17

(*Annuity whose payments form a geometric progression*)
Smith wishes to purchase a 20-year annuity with annual payments beginning one year from now. The annuity will be valued at an effective annual rate of 11%. Smith anticipates an effective annual inflation rate over the next 20 years of 4% per year, so he would like each payment after the first to be 4% larger than the previous one. If Smith's first payment is to be 26,000, what is the present value of the annuity?

> SOLUTION

The series of payments is

$$26,000; 26,000(1.04); 26,000(1.04)^2; \ldots; 26,000(1.04)^{19},$$

and has present value

$$26,000v_{.11} + 26,000(1.04)v_{.11}^2 + 26,000(1.04)^2 v_{.11}^3$$
$$+ \cdots + 26,000(1.04)^{19} v_{.11}^{20}.$$

This can be written as $26,000v\left[1 + 1.04v + (1.04v)^2 + \cdots + (1.04v)^{19}\right]$, which then simplifies to $26,000v\left[\dfrac{1-(1.04v)^{20}}{1-1.04v}\right] = 270,484.$   ❑

The important point to note is that when payments form a geometric progression, the ratio in the progression combines with the present value factor so that the present value of the annuity reduces to another geometric progression.

There is a basic geometric payment annuity valuation formula that can be applied in most such situations. Suppose that a series of $n$ periodic payments has a first payment of amount 1 and all subsequent payments are $(1+r)$ times the previous payment. At a rate $i$ per payment period, one period before the first payment, the present value of the series can be written as

$$v + (1+r)v^2 + (1+r)^2 v^3 + \cdots + (1+r)^{n-1} v^n$$

$$= v \times \left[ 1 + \frac{1+r}{1+i} + \left( \frac{1+r}{1+i} \right)^2 + \cdots + \left( \frac{1+r}{1+i} \right)^{n-1} \right]$$

$$= \frac{1}{1+i} \times \frac{1 - \left( \frac{1+r}{1+i} \right)^n}{1 - \frac{1+r}{1+i}} = \frac{1 - \left( \frac{1+r}{1+i} \right)^n}{i - r} \tag{2.22}$$

and the accumulated value at the time of the final payment can be expressed as

$$\frac{1 - \left( \frac{1+r}{1+i} \right)^n}{i - r} \cdot (1+i)^n = \frac{(1+i)^n - (1+r)^n}{i - r}. \tag{2.23}$$

Applying this formula to Example 2.17, we see that the present value of the annuity with $i = .11$, $r = .04$, and $n = 20$, produces a present value of

$$26{,}000 \times \frac{1 - \left( \frac{1.04}{1.11} \right)^{20}}{.11 - .04}.$$

We now show that the present value of the series above at the time of the first payment can be written as $\ddot{a}_{\overline{n}|j}$ for an appropriately defined interest rate $j$. The present value of the series at the time of the first payment is

$$1 + (1+r)v_i + \left[(1+r)v_i\right]^2 + \cdots + \left[(1+r)v_i\right]^{n-1}$$

$$= \frac{1 - \left[(1+r)v_i\right]^n}{1 - (1+r)v_i} = \frac{1 - \left(\frac{1+r}{1+i}\right)^n}{1 - \frac{1+r}{1+i}}.$$

We can formulate this as $\ddot{a}_{\overline{n}|j} = \frac{1-v_j^n}{1-v_j}$ , if we let $v_j = \frac{1+r}{1+i}$. The present value will be of the proper form, and $\frac{1}{1+j} = v_j = \frac{1+r}{1+i}$, so that $1+j = \frac{1+i}{1+r}$, and $j = \frac{i-r}{1+r}$. This shows that the present value of an annuity-due whose payments form a geometric progression can be formulated as an annuity with level payments valued at a modified rate of interest (an *inflation-adjusted* rate of interest), as described in Section 1.6. In most practical situations $i$ would be larger than $r$, so that $j$ would be positive.

### 2.3.1.1 *Differing Payment Period and Geometric Frequency*

It is possible that the geometric increase period (or frequency) and the payment period do not coincide. In such a situation it is usually necessary to modify the payment period to coincide with the geometric increase period; in other words we find an equivalent payment per geometric increase period. We can then apply one of the expressions just given for present and accumulated values. The following example illustrates this.

---

| EXAMPLE 2.18 | (*Differing payment period and increase period*)

Smith's child was born January 1, 2001. Smith receives monthly family allowance payments on the last day of each month, beginning January 31, 2001. The payments are increased by 12% each calendar year to meet cost-of-living increases. Monthly payments are constant during each calendar year at 25 each month in 2001, rising to 28 each month in 2002, 31.36 each month in 2003, and so on. Immediately upon receipt of a payment, Smith deposits it in an account earning $i^{(12)} = .12$ with interest credited on the last day of each month. Find the accumulated amount in the account on the child's $18^{th}$ birthday.

---

SOLUTION

The change in payment amount occurs once each year, but the payments are made monthly. The accumulated value on January 1, 2019, the $18^{th}$

birthday, can be written as the sum of the accumulated values of each of the deposits as

$$25(1.01)^{215} + 25(1.01)^{214} + \cdots + 25(1.01)^{204}$$
$$+25(1.12)(1.01)^{203} + 25(1.12)(1.01)^{202} + \cdots + 25(1.12)(1.01)^{192}$$
$$+25(1.12)^2(1.01)^{191} + 25(1.12)^2(1.01)^{190} + \cdots + 25(1.12)^2(1.01)^{180}$$
$$+\cdots + 25(1.12)^{17}(1.01)^{11} + 25(1.12)^{17}(1.01)^{10} + \cdots + 25(1.12)^{17}.$$

A way of simplifying this sum is to first group the deposits on an annual basis, and for each year find the accumulated value of that year's deposits at the end of that year, as shown in Table 2.2.

**TABLE 2.2**

| Year | Accumulated Value of Deposits on December 31 |
|------|----------------------------------------------|
| 2001 | $25s_{\overline{12}|.01} = X$ |
| 2002 | $28s_{\overline{12}|.01} = 25(1.12)s_{\overline{12}|.01} = (1.12)X$ |
| 2003 | $31.36s_{\overline{12}|.01} = 25(1.12)^2 s_{\overline{12}|.01} = (1.12)^2 X$ |
| $\vdots$ | |
| 2018 | $25(1.12)^{17} s_{\overline{12}|.01} = (1.12)^{17} X$ |

The monthly deposits are equivalent to 18 geometrically increasing annual deposits of $X$, $(1.12)X$, $(1.12)^2 X, \ldots, (1.12)^{17} X$. The accumulated value at the time of the final deposit is

$$(1+i)^{17} X + (1+i)^{16}(1.12)X + (1+i)^{15}(1.12)^2 X + \cdots + (1+i)^0 (1.12)^{17} X.$$

This is the accumulated value of a geometric payment annuity with $n = 18$ payments, geometric growth rate $1 + r = 1.12$, effective annual interest rate $i = (1.01)^{12} - 1$, and initial payment $25s_{\overline{12}|.01} = X$. We can use Equation 2.23 to find the accumulated value at the end of 18 years (time of the final payment), with $r = .12,$, $1 + i = (1.01)^{12}$, and $n = 18$.

$$X\left[\frac{(1+i)^{18}-(1+r)^{18}}{i-r}\right] = 25 \cdot s_{\overline{12}|.01} \times \frac{(1.01)^{216}-(1.12)^{18}}{(1.01)^{12}-1-.12}.$$

Since $X = 25s_{\overline{12}|.01} = 317.06$, the accumulated value is 41,282.55. ❑

If $i = r$, then Equation 2.22 (and 2.23) involve division by 0. In this case, the present value one period before the first payment is

$$v+(1+r)v^2+(1+r)^2 v^3 + \cdots + (1+r)^{n-1}v^n = v+v+\cdots v = nv,$$

and the accumulated value at the time of the final payment is

$$nv(1+i)^n = n(1+i)^{n-1}.$$

### 2.3.1.2 Dividend Discount Model for Valuing a Stock

An elementary model for the value of a share of stock is the **dividend discount model**. Using this model, the value of a share of stock is the present value of the future dividends that will be paid on the stock. A basic form of this model assumes a constant rate of increase in the amount of the dividend paid, so that the future stream of dividends forms a geometric payment perpetuity. We make the following assumptions:

(i)    the next dividend payable one year from now is of amount $K$,
(ii)   the annual compound growth rate of the dividend is $r$, and
(iii)  the interest rate used for calculating present values is $i$.

The present value one payment period before the first dividend payment is

$$K \times \left[\frac{1}{1+i} + \frac{1+r}{(1+i)^2} + \frac{(1+r)^2}{(1+i)^3} + \cdots\right].$$

This present value can be formulated as

$$\frac{K}{1+i} \times \left[ 1 + \left( \frac{1+r}{1+i} \right) + \left( \frac{1+r}{1+i} \right)^2 + \cdots \right]$$

$$= \frac{K}{1+i} \times \frac{1}{1 - \frac{1+r}{1+i}} = \frac{K}{i-r}. \tag{2.24}$$

This value of stock is sometimes referred to as the *theoretical price* of the stock. Note that this is just the limit as $n \to \infty$ of $\frac{1 - \left( \frac{1+r}{1+i} \right)^n}{i-r}$, the finite geometric payment annuity-immediate considered earlier. In this derivation, there is an implicit assumption that $i > r$ in order for the infinite geometric series to converge (sum to a finite number). It would be prudent for an investor to assume that there is some risk as to whether or not the anticipated future dividends will actually be paid. This would be reflected by using a "risk-adjusted" interest rate for finding the present value of the future dividends. The risk-adjusted rate would be larger than interest rates on (essentially) riskless government securities.

### EXAMPLE 2.19   (*The theoretical price of a stock*)

Common stock $X$ pays a dividend of 50 at the end of the first year, with each subsequent annual dividend being 5% greater than the preceding one. John purchases the stock at a price to earn an expected effective annual yield of 10%. Immediately after receiving the $10^{th}$ dividend, John sells the stock for a price of $P$. His effective annual yield over the 10-year period was 8%. Calculate $P$.

### SOLUTION

The initial price paid by John to buy the stock is the theoretical price based on a first dividend of amount 50 to be paid in one year, with subsequent dividends growing by $r = 5\%$ per year, and with valuation based on a yield rate of $i = 10\%$ per year. The theoretical price of the stock is $\frac{50}{.10 - .05} = 1,000$. John sells the stock for amount $P$ at the end of 10 years. To say that John's yield over the 10 year period is 8% per year is to say that his investment of 1,000 is equal to the present value of what he receives, using a valuation rate of 8%. What he receives is the 10 years of dividends and the sale price $P$ at the end of 10 years. The dividends form a 10-year geometrically increasing annuity-immediate, with first payment $K = 50$ and geometric growth rate $r = 5\%$. The present value at $j = 8\%$ of the 10 years of dividends is $K \times \left[ \dfrac{1 - \left(\frac{1+r}{1+j}\right)^{10}}{j - r} \right] = 50 \times \left[ \dfrac{1 - \left(\frac{1.05}{1.08}\right)^{10}}{.08 - .05} \right] = 409.18$. The present value at time 0 of the sale price $P$ (received when the stock is sold at the end of 10 years) is $Pv_{.08}^{10} = .46319P$. Then,

$$1,000 = 409.18 + .46319P,$$

so that

$$P = 1,275.54. \qquad \square$$

### 2.3.2 ANNUITIES WHOSE PAYMENTS FORM AN ARITHMETIC PROGRESSION

Another systematic pattern of payment that can arise is one in which the payments follow an arithmetic progression. We consider two basic forms of annuities with arithmetic payments.

#### 2.3.2.1 *Increasing Annuities*

We first consider an $n$-payment annuity whose first payment is 1 and with each subsequent payment increasing by 1. With an interest rate of $i$ per period and equally spaced payments, the present value of the series of payments valued one period before the first payment can be expressed as

$$v + 2v^2 + 3v^3 + \cdots + (n-1)v^{n-1} + nv^n.$$

The typical algebraic method of simplifying a series that involves an arithmetic component is as follows. We let $X$ denote the series above. Then

$$(1+i)X = 1 + 2v + 3v^2 + \cdots + nv^{n-1}.$$

Subtracting the first series from the second results in

$$iX = 1 + v + v^2 + \cdots + v^{n-1} - nv^n.$$

The first part of the right hand side of this expression happens to be the present value of an $n$-payment annuity-due. Therefore

$$X = \frac{1+v+v^2+\cdots+v^{n-1}-nv^n}{i} = \frac{\ddot{a}_{\overline{n}|}-nv^n}{i}. \tag{2.25}$$

In a similar way, the accumulated value of the series of payments valued at the time of the final payment can be shown to be equal to $\frac{\ddot{s}_{\overline{n}|}-n}{i}$. The present and accumulated values just calculated have standard actuarial notation and terminology to denote them. The phrase **$n$-payment increasing annuity immediate** is used to refer to an annuity whose payments are the sequence of integers from 1 to $n$. The present value, $X$, of the increasing series is denoted $(Ia)_{\overline{n}|i}$. The accumulated value is denoted $(Is)_{\overline{n}|i}$.

---

| EXAMPLE 2.20 | (*Reinvested interest and increasing annuity*) |

Mary makes deposits of 1000 into an account at the **end** of each year for 5 years. John makes deposits of 1000 into an account at the **beginning** of each year for 5 years. Each year, just after interest is credited to each account, they withdraw only the interest and redeposit it into a second account (they each have their own second accounts). Mary's primary account has an effective annual rate of 9% and John's has a rate of 10%. Mary's secondary account has an effective annual interest rate of 9% and John's secondary account has an effective annual interest rate of 8%. At the end of 5 years Mary's investment has a value of $X$, and John's has a value of $Y$. Calculate $Y - X$.

---

| SOLUTION |

At the end of 5 years, the value of Mary's investment is the sum of the 5 deposits of 1000 each and the accumulated reinvested interest. Since Mary's first deposit of 1000 into her primary account is at the end of the first year, the first interest payment from the primary account is at the end of the second year for amount 90; this is deposited into the secondary account (but the original deposit of 1000 stays in the primary account). At the end of the second year she adds 1000 to the primary account to bring the balance to 2000, and the interest generated from the primary account at the end of the third year is 180.

Each year she adds 1000 to the primary account, so each year the interest generated by that account is 90 more than the previous year. The interest generated by the primary account is 90, 180, 270, and 360 at the end of the

$2^{nd}, 3^{rd}$, and $4^{th}$ and $5^{th}$ years. These interest payments are deposited into the secondary account (which also earns interest at a rate of 9%). The time diagram representation of Mary's investment is as follows:

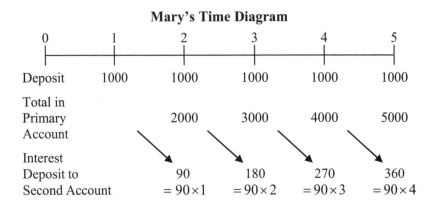

**Mary's Time Diagram**

Mary's total investment at the end of 5 years is

$$X = 5000 + 90(Is)_{\overline{4}|.09} = 5,984.71.$$

Note that since the reinvestment rate for the interest payments is 9%, which is the same as the interest rate on the initial deposits, Mary's accumulation at the end of 5 years can also be formulated as $1000s_{\overline{5}|.09} = 5,984.71$; it is the same as if she had left the interest payments in the primary account to accumulate at the 9% rate. This can be seen algebraically as follows.

$$5000 + 90(Is)_{\overline{4}|.09} = 5000 + 90 \times \frac{\ddot{s}_{\overline{4}|.09} - 4}{.09}$$

$$= 5000 + 1000(\ddot{s}_{\overline{4}|.09} - 4)$$

$$= 1000 + 1000\ddot{s}_{\overline{4}|.09} = 1000(1 + \ddot{s}_{\overline{4}|.09}) = 1000s_{\overline{5}|.09}$$

John's deposits are made at the beginning of each year, so the first interest payment from John's primary account occurs at the end of the first year, and the amount of that interest payment is 100; it is deposited into the secondary account earning 8%. John's subsequent interest payments are then 200, 300, 400 and 500 at the ends of years 2, 3, 4 and 5. The time diagram for John's investment is as follows.

**John's Time Diagram**

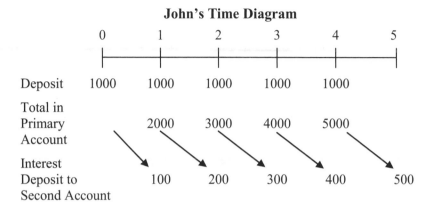

John's accumulated investment at the end of year 5 is

$$Y = 5000 + 100(Is)_{\overline{5}|.08} = 6,669.91,$$

Then, $Y - X = 685.20$. □

If the payments in an increasing annuity immediate are allowed to continue forever, the result is an *increasing perpetuity immediate*, whose present value is

$$(Ia)_{\overline{\infty}|i} = v + 2v^2 + 3v^3 + \cdots = \lim_{n \to \infty} (Ia)_{\overline{n}|i} = \lim_{n \to \infty} \frac{\ddot{a}_{\overline{n}|} - nv^n}{i}.$$

From l'Hospital's rule of limits it follows that

$$\lim_{n \to \infty} nv^n = \lim_{n \to \infty} \frac{n}{(1+i)^n} = \lim_{n \to \infty} \frac{1}{(1+i)^n \ln(1+i)} = 0.$$

Also, since $\ddot{a}_{\overline{\infty}|i} = \frac{1}{d}$, it follows that

$$(Ia)_{\overline{\infty}|i} = \frac{1}{id} = \frac{1+i}{i^2} = \frac{1}{i^2} + \frac{1}{i}. \tag{2.26}$$

---

**EXAMPLE 2.21** (*Increasing Perpetuity*)

Perpetuity $X$ has annual payments of $1, 2, 3, \ldots$ at the end of each year. Perpetuity $Y$ has annual payments of $q, q, 2q, 2q, 3q, 3q, \ldots$ at the ends of successive years. The present value of $X$ is equal to the present value of $Y$ at an effective annual interest rate of 10%. Calculate $q$.

| SOLUTION |
|---|

Perpetuity $X$ has present value

$$v + 2v^2 + 3v^3 + \cdots = (Ia)_{\overline{\infty}|.1} = \tfrac{1}{i^2} + \tfrac{1}{i} = \frac{1}{(.1)^2} + \frac{1}{.1} = 110.$$

Perpetuity $Y$ can be separated into two groups of payments, those at the ends of years $1,3,5,7,9,\ldots$ of amounts $q, 2q, 3q, \ldots$, and those at the ends of years $2,4,6,8,10,\ldots$ also of amounts $q, 2q, 3q, \ldots$ . The second set of payments forms an increasing perpetuity-immediate payable every second year. The effective 2-year rate of interest equivalent to the effective annual rate of 10% is $j = (1.1)^2 - 1 = .21\,(21\%)$. The present value of the second set of payments is

$$q(v_{.21} + 2v_{.21}^2 + 3v_{.21}^3 + \cdots) = q(Ia)_{\overline{\infty}|.21} = q\left(\frac{1}{.21} + \frac{1}{(.21)^2}\right) = 27.44q.$$

Since the first set of payments is identical to the second, except that it starts one year earlier, its present value will be 1.1 times larger (one less year of present value factor), so that the present value of the first series of payments is $27.44q(1.1) = 30.18q$. The total present value of perpetuity $Y$ is $27.44q + 30.18q = 57.62q$. We are told that this is the same present value as the value of perpetuity $X$ of 110, so that $q = 1.91$. □

### 2.3.2.2 Decreasing Annuities

Another basic annuity with payments that follow an arithmetic progression is the **$n$-payment decreasing annuity immediate**. This annuity has a first payment of amount $n$ and each subsequent payment is of amount 1 less than the previous payment. The standard actuarial notation used for this annuity is **$(Da)_{\overline{n}|i}$**, and this represents the present value of the sequence of payments of amounts $n, n-1, n-2, \ldots, 2, 1$, with payment starting one period from now. The formulation given for $(Da)_{\overline{n}|}$ given in Equation (2.27) below can be derived as we did with Equation (2.25).

$$(Da)_{\overline{n}|} = nv + (n-1)v^2 + (n-2)v^3 + \cdots + 2v^{n-1} + v^n = \frac{n - a_{\overline{n}|}}{i}. \quad (2.27)$$

If this same decreasing series is valued at the time of the final payment, then we get the accumulated value of the $n$-payment decreasing annuity immediate, $(Ds)_{\overline{n}|} = \frac{n(1+i)^n - s_{\overline{n}|}}{i} = (Da)_{\overline{n}|} \cdot (1+i)^n$. There are a number of algebraic relationships involving the increasing and decreasing annuities that are considered in the exercises at the end of the chapter. The following example illustrates how the basic increasing and decreasing annuities can be used to formulate valuations of more general annuities with payments that follow an arithmetic progression.

---

**EXAMPLE 2.22**   (*Increasing annuity*)

Jeff bought an increasing perpetuity-due with annual payments starting at amount 5 and increasing by 5 each year until the payment amount reaches 100. The payments remain at 100 thereafter. The effective annual interest rate is 7.5%. Determine the present value of this perpetuity.

---

**SOLUTION**

There are at least two ways in which this perpetuity present value can be formulated.

(i) We can separate the first 20 payments (increasing from 5 to 100) from the $21^{st}$ payment and beyond (level at 100). The present value as a perpetuity-due (valued at the time of the first payment) is

$$5(I\ddot{a})_{\overline{20}|.075} + v^{20} \cdot 100 \ddot{a}_{\overline{\infty}|.075} = 5(1.075)(Ia)_{\overline{20}|.075} + v^{20} \cdot 100 \ddot{a}_{\overline{\infty}|.075}$$

$$= 5(1.075)\left(\frac{\ddot{a}_{\overline{20}|} - 20v^{20}}{.075}\right) + v^{20} \cdot \frac{100}{d}$$

$$= 447.975 + 337.426 = 785.40.$$

Note that the 20-payment increasing annuity-due can be formulated as

$$(I\ddot{a})_{\overline{20}|} = \frac{\ddot{a}_{\overline{20}|} - 20v^{20}}{d} = \frac{\ddot{a}_{\overline{20}|} - 20v^{20}}{i/(1+i)} = (1+i) \cdot \frac{\ddot{a}_{\overline{20}|} - 20v^{20}}{i} = (1+i)(Ia)_{\overline{20}|}.$$

The overall valuation is illustrated in the following time-diagram.

| 0 | 1 | 2 | $\cdots$ | 18 | 19 | 20 | 21 | ... |
|---|---|---|---|---|---|---|---|---|
| [5 | 10 | 15 | ... | 95 | 100] | [100 | 100 | ... |

$5(I\ddot{a})_{\overline{20|}}$ $\qquad\qquad\qquad\qquad\leftarrow\qquad$ $100\ddot{a}_{\overline{\infty|}}$

(ii) We can separate the series into a combination of a level perpetuity-due minus a 19 year decreasing annuity-due.

| Original series is equivalent to | 5 | 10 | 15 | $\cdots$ | 95 | 100 | 100 | 100 | $\cdots$ |
|---|---|---|---|---|---|---|---|---|---|

| Level perp-due combined with | 100 | 100 | 100 | $\cdots$ | 100 | 100 | 100 | 100 | $\cdots$ |
|---|---|---|---|---|---|---|---|---|---|

| Decreasing annuity-due | $-95$ | $-90$ | $-85$ | $\cdots$ | $-5$ |
|---|---|---|---|---|---|

Note the negative payments on the decreasing annuity-due. The present value of the two combined series is

$$100\ddot{a}_{\overline{\infty|}} - 5(D\ddot{a})_{\overline{19|}}$$

$$= 100\left(\frac{1}{d}\right) - 5\left[\frac{19 - a_{\overline{19|}}}{d}\right] = 1,433.333 - 647.933 = 785.40. \quad \square$$

### 2.3.2.3 *Continuous Annuities with Varying Payments*

The general form of a varying annuity defined at the start of this section had a payment of amount $K_t$ payable at time $t$. The value of a continuous annuity with varying payments can also be formulated in a general context. In this case the payment pattern is described by a continuous function $h(t)$, which represents the *instantaneous rate* or *density of payment* being made at time $t$. Then, incorporating the continuous annuity concept defined in Section 2.2.3, $h(t)\, dt$ would be the instantaneous payment at time $t$, all of whose present or accumulated values would be "added," in the form of an integral, from time 0 to time $n$, producing

$$\int_0^n h(t) \cdot v^t \, dt \tag{2.28a}$$

for the present value at time 0, and

$$\int_0^n h(t) \cdot (1+i)^{n-t} \, dt \qquad (2.28b)$$

for the accumulated value at time $n$. Corresponding to the standard increasing annuity in the discrete case is the continuously increasing annuity, for which $h(t)$ replaces $t$. The notation used for the present value of this annuity is

$$(\overline{I}\,\overline{a})_{\overline{n}|i} = \int_0^n t \cdot v^t \, dt \qquad (2.29a)$$

and for the accumulated value is

$$(\overline{I}\,\overline{s})_{\overline{n}|i} = \int_0^n t \cdot (1+i)^{n-t} \, dt. \qquad (2.29b)$$

These can be simplified by applying integration by parts, producing

$$(\overline{I}a)_{\overline{n}|i} = \frac{\overline{a}_{\overline{n}|} - nv^n}{\delta} \qquad (2.30a)$$

and

$$(\overline{I}\,\overline{s})_{\overline{n}|i} = \frac{\overline{s}_{\overline{n}|} - n}{\delta}, \qquad (2.30b)$$

where $\delta = \ln(1+i)$. If the force of interest is varying as well, say $\delta_t$ at time $t$, then the more general expressions for the present and accumulated values of the annuities at times 0 and $n$, respectively, are

$$\int_0^n h(t) \cdot e^{-\int_0^t \delta_r \, dr} \, dt \qquad (2.\,31a)$$

and

$$\int_0^n h(t) \cdot e^{\int_t^n \delta_r \, dr} \, dt. \qquad (2.\,31b)$$

### 2.3.2.4 *Unknown Interest Rate for Annuities with Varying Payments*

In Section 2.2 we considered methods of determining an unknown interest rate. For the cases considered there, and for varying annuities as well, it is generally true that there is a unique solution for $i$. The following example shows this.

---

| EXAMPLE 2.23 | (*Unique solution for i.*)

Suppose that an annuity consists of payments $K_1, K_2, \ldots, K_n$ made at times $0 < t_1 < t_2 < \cdots < t_n$, where each $K_r > 0$. Suppose also that $L > 0$. Show that there is a unique $i$ ($i > -1$) for which $L$ is the present value at time 0 of the given series of payments, where $i$ is the interest rate per time unit measured by $t$.

| SOLUTION |

With $v = \frac{1}{1+i}$, the present value at time 0 of the series of payments is $f(i) = K_1 v^{t_1} + K_2 v^{t_2} + \cdots + K_n v^{t_n}$. Since the $K_r$'s and $t_r$'s are all $> 0$, it follows that $f(i)$ is a decreasing function of $i$, since $v^{t_k}$ decreases as $i$ increases. But $\lim_{i \to \infty} f(i) = 0$, since each $v^{t_k} \to 0$ as $i \to \infty$, and $\lim_{i \to -1} f(i) = +\infty$, since $v^{t_k} \to +\infty$ as $i \to -1$. Then since $0 < L < +\infty$ and $f(i)$ decreases from $+\infty$ to 0 as $i$ goes from $-1$ to $+\infty$, it follows that there is a unique $i > -1$ for which $L = f(i)$. Note that $i > 0$ if $L < \sum_{r=1}^{n} K_r$ and $i < 0$ if $L > \sum_{r=1}^{n} K_r$. ◻

In a more general setting, a financial transaction may involve a series of disbursements (payments made out) and payments received. A computer routine such as "Solver" in EXCEL would be needed to solve for the unknown interest rate in a general setting. Financial calculators are usually limited to finding the unknown interest rate when payments are level (or with a balloon payment) or have a limited number of varying payments. Solving for an unknown interest rate, yield rate, or internal rate of return in a general setting is considered in Chapter 5.

## 2.4 APPLICATIONS AND ILLUSTRATIONS

### 2.4.1 YIELD RATES AND REINVESTMENT RATES

Suppose that a single amount $L$ is invested for an $n$ year period and the value of the investment at the end of $n$ years is $M$. A reasonable definition of the annual yield rate earned by the investment over the $n$ year period is the rate $i$ that satisfies the equation $L(1+i)^n = M$.

Now suppose that a loan of amount $L$ is made at effective annual interest rate $i$ and is repaid by $n$ level annual payments of amount $K$ each. The equation of value for the loan is $L = K \cdot a_{\overline{n}|i}$. Suppose that we regard the loan as an investment from the point of view of the lender. We would like to have a measure of the annual rate of return or interest rate or yield rate earned by the lender over the $n$ year period. In order to use the yield rate definition given in the previous paragraph, we would need a value of the investment at the end of $n$ years. This implicitly suggests that the lender is reinvesting the loan payments as they are being received, and has accumulated an amount $M$ at the end of $n$ years.

In order for the lender to realize an annual yield rate of $i$ (the original loan rate) over the $n$ year period, the lender should have accumulated $L(1+i)^n$ as of time $n$. In order for this to occur, it can be seen from the equation of value for the loan that the amount the lender must have accumulated as of time $n$ is $L(1+i)^n = Ka_{\overline{n}|i}(1+i)^n = Ks_{\overline{n}|i}$. We see that in order for the lender to realize an annual yield rate of $i$ (the loan rate), the annual rate of interest earned by the reinvested payments must also be $i$. If reinvestment is at a rate other than $i$, then the lender's annual yield will be different from $i$.

Consider the case of a 10-year loan of 10,000 at $i = .05$. We look at three ways in which the loan can be repaid.

(1) Ten level annual payments of $\dfrac{10,000}{a_{\overline{10}|.05}} = 1295.05$. If these payments are reinvested at 5% as they are received, the accumulated value at the time of the tenth payment is $1295.05 s_{\overline{10}|.05} = 16,288.95$. Since $10,000(1.05)^{10} = 16,288.95$, the lender realizes an annual compound rate of return (or yield) of 5%.

(2) Ten level annual interest payments of 500, plus a return of the entire 10,000 principal at the end of ten years. If the payments of 500 are reinvested at 5%, the accumulated value after ten years is $500 s_{\overline{10}|.05} = 6,288.95$. Along with the payment of 10,000 at time 10, the accumulated value is again 16,288.95 (this also follows from the relationship $1 + i \times s_{\overline{n}|i} = (1+i)^n$), which indicates an annual compound rate of return of 5%.

(3) A single payment of $10,000(1.05)^{10} = 16,288.95$. In this case it is clear that the lender receives an annual compound rate of return of 5%.

As long as the reinvestment rate is 5%, then for any repayment schedule for which the present value of the payments is 10,000 at $i = .05$, the accumulated value of the reinvested payments will be 16,288.95.

Now let us assume instead that the interest rate earned on reinvested payments is 3%. A reinvestment rate is irrelevant in Case (3), since no reinvestment takes place. In Case (1) the accumulated value of the reinvested payments is $1295.05s_{\overline{10}|.03} = 14,846.30$. In Case (2) the accumulated value is $500s_{\overline{10}|.03} + 10,000 = 15,731.94$. In Cases (1) and (2) the accumulated value does not give an annual rate of 5% compounded for 10 years on an initial investment of 10,000. For Case (1), the average annual compound rate of return $j$ is found from $10,000(1+j)^{10} = 14,846.30$, which results in $j = .0403$, and for Case (2) the average return is found from $10,000(1+j)^{10} = 15,731.94$, which results in $j = .0464$. The reason the average rate is less than 5% is that the reinvestment rate is less than 5%. Furthermore, the less reinvestment that takes place, the less of a reduction there is below 5%. In other words Case (3) has no reinvestment and results in an annual compound rate of 5%, and Case (2) has more reinvestment than Case (3), but less reinvestment than Case (1) which has the lowest average compound return.

An important measure of rate of return on an investment is the **internal rate of return (IRR) on a transaction.** In the context of a loan regarded as an investment, the internal rate of return is the rate of interest for which the loan amount is equal to present value of the loan payments. In other words, the internal rate of return on a loan transaction is simply the interest rate at which the loan is made. The internal rate of return can be applied to more general financial transactions, and will be considered in some detail in Chapter 5. In each of Cases (1), (2) and (3) above, the internal rate of return is 5%, since in each case, the present value, at 5%, of the loan payments is 10,000. The reinvestment rate is relevant to the determination of the <u>yield rate</u> on a transaction as defined above, but the reinvestment rate is irrelevant in determining the <u>internal rate of return</u>.

| EXAMPLE 2.24 | *(Yield rates)* |

Smith owns a 10,000 savings bond that pays interest monthly at $i^{(12)} = .06$. Upon receipt of an interest payment, he immediately deposits it into an account earning interest, payable monthly, at a rate of $i^{(12)} = .12$. Find the accumulated value of this account just after the $12^{th}$, $24^{th}$, and $36^{th}$ deposit. In each case find Smith's average annual yield $i^{(12)}$ based on his initial investment of 10,000. Assume that the savings bond may be cashed in at any time for 10,000.

---

| SOLUTION |
|---|

The savings bond pays interest of 50 per month, so the accumulated values in the account are $50s_{\overline{12}|.01} = 634.13$, $50s_{\overline{24}|.01} = 1348.67$, and $50s_{\overline{36}|.01} = 2153.84$ after 12, 24 and 36 months, respectively. If $j$ is the average monthly yield rate earned on the initial 10,000 investment, then if Smith was to cash in his bond at the end of 12 months, $j$ would be the solution to the equation

$$10,000(1+j)^{12} = 10,634.13,$$

resulting in $j = .00514$ and $i^{(12)} = 12j = .0616$. For the 24-month period $10,000(1+j)^{24} = 11,348.67$, so that $j = .00529$ and $i^{(12)} = .0634$; for the 36-month period we find $j = .00543$ and $i^{(12)} = .0652$.     ❏

In general if an amount $L$ is invested and generates interest at rate $i$ per period which is then reinvested at rate $j$, the accumulated value of the reinvested interest at time $n$ will be $L \times i \times s_{\overline{n}|j}$, and the total value of the investment will be $L + L \times i \times s_{\overline{n}|j} = L\left[1 + i \times s_{\overline{n}|j}\right]$ (initial principal plus reinvested interest).

---

| EXAMPLE 2.25 | (*Yield rates*)
|---|---|

Suppose that Smith, on a payroll savings plan, buys a savings bond for 100 at the end of every month, with the bond paying monthly interest at $i^{(12)} = .06$. The interest payments generated are reinvested in an account earning $i^{(12)} = .12$. Find the accumulated value in the deposit account at the end of 12 months, 24 months and 36 months. Find the yield rate in the form $i^{(12)}$ that Smith realizes over each of these time periods on his investment.

## SOLUTION

At the end of 12 months Smith will have bought 1200 in bonds. The first 100 bond was bought at the end of the first month, so Smith received interest of 0.50 at the end of the second month, at which time he bought the second 100 bond, bringing his total in bonds to 200. At the end of the third month Smith receives 1.00 (monthly interest on the 200 in bonds), and buys a third 100 bond. At the end of the fourth month he receives 1.50 in interest and buys a fourth 100 bond. Therefore the interest Smith receives from the bonds is $0.50, 1.00, 1.50, 2.00, \ldots, 5.50$ at the ends of months $2, 3, 4, 5, \ldots, 12$. The accumulated value in the deposit account after 12 months is $.50 \times (Is)_{\overline{11}|.01} = 34.13$, after 24 months it is

$$.50 \times (Is)_{\overline{23}|.01} = 148.67,$$

and after 36 months the accumulated value is

$$.50 \times (Is)_{\overline{35}|.01} = 353.84.$$

What is meant by the monthly yield rate $j$ is the rate at which the original payments must be invested to accumulate to the actual amount that Smith has at the later point in time. Smith's monthly yield $j$ on the 1200 (100 per month) invested over 12 months is the solution of $100 s_{\overline{12}|j} = 1234.13$, for which the solution is $j = .00508$, or $i^{(12)} = .061$. Over 24 months $j$ is found from $100 s_{\overline{24}|j} = 2548.67$, which gives $j = .00518$, or $i^{(12)} = .0622$. Over 36 months we have $100 s_{\overline{36}|j} = 3953.84$, which gives $j = .00529$, or $i^{(12)} = .0634$. ◻

As a general approach to the situation in Example 2.25, suppose that a series of $n$ deposits of amount 1 each generate interest at rate $i$ per payment period, and that the interest is reinvested as it is received at rate $j$ per period. The first interest payment is $i$, which comes one period after the first of the original deposits. The second interest payment is $2i$ and is paid one period after the second of the original deposits. The following table illustrates the original deposits and the interest generated by them.

**TABLE 2.3**

| Time | 0 | 1 | 2 | 3 | 4 | ⋯ | $n-2$ | $n-1$ | $n$ | | Total |
|---|---|---|---|---|---|---|---|---|---|---|---|
| Payment | 1 | 1 | 1 | 1 | | ⋯ | 1 | 1 | 1 | → | $n$ |
| Interest | | | $i$ | $2i$ | $3i$ | ⋯ | $(n-3)i$ | $(n-2)i$ | $(n-1)i$ | → | $i \times (Is)_{\overline{n-1}|j}$ |

The interest is reinvested at rate $j$ per period, with the interest payments forming an increasing annuity since interest at rate $i$ is being earned on an increasing principal amount. The total accumulated value of the reinvested interest is $i \times (Is)_{\overline{n-1}|j}$, which, along with the original $n$ deposits of 1 each, results in a total of $n + i \times (Is)_{\overline{n-1}|j}$ at time $n$.

## 2.4.2 DEPRECIATION

Among the various assets owned by a business may be an automobile. As time goes on, the resale value of the automobile decreases, and eventually the automobile may be worth nothing. Tax and accounting rules generally allow the business to take as an expense the annual reduction in value of the asset. Each year the business would make an accounting for the reduction in value (or **depreciation**) of the asset, and the value after the depreciation has been applied. Eventually, the asset will be sold for some amount (the "salvage value") which could be zero.

To set up a schedule of depreciation for an asset, we would need to have the following information:

(i)  the initial value or purchase price of the asset, say $P_0$,

(ii) the number of years over which the asset will be depreciated, say $n$, and

(iii) the salvage value of the asset at the end of the asset's useful lifetime, say $P_n$.

A depreciation schedule would provide the year-by-year sequence of depreciated values, $P_0, P_1, P_2, \ldots, P_{n-1}, P_n$, where $P_t$ denotes the depreciated value at time $t$. The amounts of depreciation year-by-year would be $D_1, D_2, \ldots, D_{n-1}, D_n$, where $D_t$ denotes the amount of depreciation for the $t^{th}$ year. $D_t$ is the amount of reduction in asset value from the end of the

$t-1^{st}$ year to the end of the $t^{th}$ year, so that $D_t = P_{t-1} - P_t$, and $P_t = P_{t-1} - D_t$. We see that over the course of the $n$ years we have the following relationships:

$$P_0 - D_1 - D_2 - \cdots - D_{n-1} - D_n$$
$$= P_0 - (P_0 - P_1) - (P_1 - P_2) - \cdots - (P_{n-2} - P_{n-1}) - (P_{n-1} - P_n) = P_n$$

and

$$P_t - P_{t+k} = D_{t+1} + D_{t+2} + \cdots + D_{t+k} \qquad (2.32)$$

(the reduction in asset value from one point in time to another is the sum of the yearly depreciation charges during that time interval).

There are several conventional methods for constructing the schedule of annual depreciation amounts and depreciated values. We consider four depreciation methods.

### 2.4.2.1 Depreciation Method 1 – The Declining Balance Method

The declining balance method (also known as the constant percentage method, or the compound discount method) requires the assumption of an annual discount factor $d$.

The factor is applied each year to the previous year-end's depreciated value to calculate this year's amount of depreciation, so that $D_t = P_{t-1} \cdot d$. We get the following sequence of depreciation amounts and depreciated values.

Starting asset value $\qquad\qquad\qquad\qquad P_0$

Amount of depreciation in $1^{st}$ year $\qquad D_1 = P_0 \cdot d$

$1^{st}$ year-end depreciated value $\qquad P_1 = P_0 - D_1 = P_0 \cdot (1-d)$

Amount of depreciation in $2^{nd}$ year $\quad D_2 = P_1 \cdot d = P_0 \cdot (1-d) \cdot d$

$2^{nd}$ year-end depreciated value $\qquad P_2 = P_1 - D_2 = P_1 \cdot (1-d) = P_0 \cdot (1-d)^2$

The pattern continues in this way, so that the depreciated value at the end of $t$ years is

$$P_t = P_0 \times (1-d)^t, \qquad (2.33a)$$

and the amount of depreciation for the $t^{th}$ year is

$$D_t = P_0 \times (1-d)^{t-1} \cdot d. \qquad (2.33b)$$

Note that the salvage value is $P_n = P_0 \times (1-d)^n$.

### 2.4.2.2 Depreciation Method 2 – The Straight-Line Method

The straight-line method is quite simple. The total amount of depreciation that occurs over the $n$-year period is $P_0 - P_n$. In the straight-line method, the amount of depreciation each year for $n$ years is $\frac{1}{n}^{th}$ of the $n$ year total depreciation charge, so that

$$D_t = \frac{1}{n}(P_0 - P_n) \qquad (2.34a)$$

for each year, $t = 1, 2, ..., n$. The depreciated value at the end of $t$ years will be the initial value minus the $t$ years of depreciation charges, so that

$$P_t = P_0 - (D_1 + D_2 + \cdots + D_t) = P_0 - t \times \frac{1}{n} \times (P_0 - P_n). \qquad (2.34b)$$

Notice that this can be rewritten in the form $P_t = \frac{n-t}{n} \times P_0 + \frac{t}{n} \times P_n$; this shows that the depreciated value is just the linearly interpolated value $\frac{t}{n}$ of the way from the asset value at time 0 to the asset value at time $n$ (not surprising, since there is a constant annual reduction in asset value).

### 2.4.2.3 Depreciation Method 3 – The Sum of Years Digits Method

In this method, the amount of depreciation for a particular year is a fraction of the total $n$-year depreciation charge, $P_0 - P_n$. We define the following factor, $S_k = 1 + 2 + \cdots + k = \frac{k(k+1)}{2}$; this is the sum of the integers from 1 to $k$.

In the first year, the amount of depreciation taken is $\frac{n}{S_n} \times (P_0 - P_n)$, and in the second year, the amount of depreciation taken is $\frac{n-1}{S_n} \cdot (P_0 - P_n)$. In the $t^{th}$ year, the amount of depreciation taken is

$$D_t = \frac{n-t+1}{S_n} \times (P_0 - P_n). \qquad (2.35a)$$

In the exercises, you are asked to show that the depreciated value at the end of the $t^{th}$ year is

$$P_t = P_n + \frac{S_{n-t}}{S_n} \times (P_0 - P_n). \qquad (2.35b)$$

For instance, with a 20-year depreciation period, the depreciated value at the end of 8 years would be $P_8 = P_{20} + \frac{S_{12}}{S_{20}} \times (P_0 - P_{20}) = P_{20} + \frac{78}{210} \times (P_0 - P_{20})$, since

$$S_{12} = 1 + 2 + \cdots + 12 = \frac{12 \times 13}{2} = 78$$

and

$$S_{20} = 1 + 2 + \cdots + 20 = \frac{20 \times 21}{2} = 210.$$

### 2.4.2.4 Depreciation Method 4 – The Compound Interest Method

This method may also be called the sinking fund method and it requires the assumption of an interest rate $i$. The amount of depreciation in the $t^{th}$ year is

$$D_t = \frac{(1+i)^{t-1}}{s_{\overline{n}|i}} \times (P_0 - P_n) \qquad (2.36a)$$

and the depreciated value at the end of $t$ years is

$$P_t = P_0 - \frac{s_{\overline{t}|i}}{s_{\overline{n}|i}} \times (P_0 - P_n). \qquad (2.36b)$$

Note that in this method, the annual depreciation charges are getting larger as time goes on. For the compound discount method and the sum of years digits method, the depreciation charge is largest in the first year and decreases as time goes on. The Compound Interest Method is rarely used in practice.

EXAMPLE 2.26 (*Depreciation*)

An asset has a purchase price of 1,000 and a salvage value of 100 at the end of 10 years. For each of the depreciation methods presented above, create tables for the depreciated value and amount of depreciation for each of the 10 years of the life of the asset. For the declining balance method use a discount factor of 20.56% and for the compound interest method use an interest rate of 10%.

SOLUTION

Depreciated Values

| $t$ | DB(1) $1000(.7944)^t$ | SL(2) $1000 - 90t$ | SY(3) $100 + \frac{900S_{\overline{10-t}}}{55}$ | CI(4) $1000 - \frac{900s_{\overline{t}.1}}{15.937}$ |
|---|---|---|---|---|
| 1 | 794.40 | 910 | 836.36 | 943.53 |
| 2 | 631.07 | 820 | 689.09 | 881.41 |
| 3 | 501.32 | 730 | 558.18 | 813.08 |
| ⋮ | ⋮ | ⋮ | ⋮ | ⋮ |
| 9 | 125.99 | 190 | 116.36 | 233.13 |
| 10 | 100 | 100 | 100 | 100 |

Yearly Amounts of Depreciation

| $t$ | DB(1) $205.60(.7944)^{t-1}$ | SL(2) $90$ | SY(3) $\frac{900(10-t+1)}{55}$ | CI(4) $\frac{900(1.1)^{t-1}}{15.937}$ |
|---|---|---|---|---|
| 1 | 205.60 | 90 | 163.64 | 56.47 |
| 2 | 163.32 | 90 | 147.27 | 62.12 |
| 3 | 129.75 | 90 | 130.91 | 68.33 |
| ⋮ | ⋮ | ⋮ | ⋮ | ⋮ |
| 9 | 32.61 | 90 | 32.73 | 121.05 |
| 10 | 25.90 | 90 | 16.36 | 133.16 |

❑

### 2.4.3 CAPITALIZED COST

An asset needed for a production process may have a finite lifetime, after which it will need to be replaced. The asset may have some salvage value at the end of its lifetime. Even if it is not necessary to borrow in order to obtain the asset, there will be an interest cost or interest loss because funds have to be used to purchase the asset. The asset may also have periodic maintenance costs. We define the asset's capitalized cost to be the original cost of the asset, plus the present value of an infinite number of replacements, plus the present value of maintenance costs in perpetuity. In other words, it is the present value of the costs involved in having use of the asset forever.

The components of the asset purchase and maintenance can be summarized as follows:

- initial asset value is $P$
- lifetime of the asset is $n$ years
- salvage value at the end of $n$ years is $S$
- interest rate cost is $i$ (sometimes called the required annual yield rate)
- periodic (usually end of each year) maintenance cost is $M$

The cashflows required to maintain the asset indefinitely are:

(i)   a payment of amount $P$ at time 0,
(ii)   payments of amount $P-S$ at times $n, 2n,\ldots,$ forever,
(iii)   payments of amount $M$ each year forever starting one year from now.

The capitalized cost of the asset is then

$$C = P + (P-S)\left(v^n + v^{2n} + \cdots\right) + M\left(v + v^2 + \cdots\right).$$

This can be reformulated as

$$C = P + \frac{P-S}{i \times s_{\overline{n}|i}} + \frac{M}{i}, \tag{2.37}$$

since

$$v^n + v^{2n} + \cdots = \frac{v^n}{1-v^n} = \frac{1}{(1+i)^n - 1} = \frac{1}{i \times s_{\overline{n}|i}}.$$

| EXAMPLE 2.27 | (*Capitalized Cost*)

Machines $X$ and $Y$ each sell for 100,000 and each has a life of 17 years. Machine $X$ produces 1000 units per year, has an annual maintenance expense of 1000 and a salvage value of 33,750. Machine $Y$ produces $U$ units per year, has an annual maintenance expense of 1100 and no salvage value. At an effective annual rate of interest of 8%, a buyer is indifferent between the two machines. Determine $U$.

| SOLUTION |

To say that the buyer is indifferent means that the capitalized cost per unit produced (annual) is the same for both machines. The capitalized cost of Machine $X$ is

$$100,000 + \frac{100,000 - 33,750}{(1.08)^{17} - 1} + \frac{1,000}{.08} = 137,037.$$

The capitalized cost of Machine $Y$ is

$$100,000 + \frac{100,000}{(1.08)^{17} - 1} + \frac{1,100}{.08} = 150,787.$$

The capitalized cost per unit produced annually is $\frac{137,037}{1000} = 137$ for Machine $X$, and is $\frac{150,787}{U}$ for Machine $Y$. In order for the buyer to be indifferent between the two machines, the unit costs must be the same, so that $\frac{150,787}{U} = 137$, from which we get $U = 1100$. ☐

Related to the capitalized cost is the *periodic charge* to maintain the asset. The periodic charge is equal to the capitalized cost multiplied by the interest rate, so that

$$\text{Periodic Charge} = \left( P + \frac{P - S}{i \times s_{\overline{n}|i}} + \frac{M}{i} \right) \times i = Pi + \frac{P - S}{s_{\overline{n}|i}} + M. \quad (2.38)$$

We can interpret this periodic charge as being composed of the annualized interest on the initial purchase price ($P \times i$), plus the annual cost to make up the shortfall between purchase price and salvage value that will occur when the asset has to be repurchased in $n$ years $\left(\frac{P-S}{s_{\overline{n}|i}}\right)$, plus the annual maintenance cost $(M)$.

### 2.4.4 Book Value and Market Value

An investor considering the purchase of an annuity (or series of cash-flows) at time $t_0$ will typically calculate the present value of the series of cashflows at some interest rate $i_0$. This rate would be related to rates in effect for similar investments at the time of valuation. The investor's *yield-to-maturity* on the series of cashflows is $i_0$ if the series is received for its full term. At any intermediate point during the term of the series of cashflows, the present value of the remaining payments in the series based on the original rate $i_0$ is called the **book value** of the cashflow at that time. Such a valuation might be needed for accounting purposes. If the investor decides at time $t_1 > t_0$ to sell the remainder of the series of cashflows that he is entitled to receive, an appropriate interest rate, called the market rate $i_1$, would be used at $t_1$ for the valuation. The present value of the remaining series at $t_1$ based on the market rate is called the market value of the series of cashflows. These notions of book value and **market value** arise in the context of loan amortization (Chapter 3) and in the valuation of bonds (Chapter 4).

---

| EXAMPLE 2.28 | *(Book value and market value)* |

Smith borrows 10,000 at effective annual interest rate $i_0 = .10$. The loan will be repaid by 10 annual payments of amounts $2000, 1900, 1800, \ldots,$ 1100, with the first payment made one year after the loan. Determine the book value and the market value of the loan payments just after the $5^{th}$ payment if the market rate of interest is then 12%.

---

| SOLUTION |

Note that the present value at $t = 0$ of the loan payments at $i_0 = .10$ is $1000a_{\overline{10}|.10} + 100(Da)_{\overline{10}|.10} = 10,000$. The book value just after the $5^{th}$ payment is $BV_5 = 1000a_{\overline{5}|.10} + 100(Da)_{\overline{5}|.10} = 5000$, and the market value is $MV_5 = 1000a_{\overline{5}|.12} + 100(Da)_{\overline{5}|.12} = 4767.46$. $\qquad\square$

## 2.4.5 THE SINKING FUND METHOD OF VALUATION

A situation may arise in which a lender is considering the purchase of an annuity (a specified series of payments). In previous sections of this chapter we have considered the valuation of the series of payments in the form of the present value of the series at some interest rate $i$ per payment period. However, as noted earlier, in order to actually realize a return of $i$ per period to the end of the term, we must have a reinvestment rate of $i$ as well. In practice, the rate $i$ on a loan would tend to be larger than the rate $j$ earned on reinvestment, such as in a deposit account. The **sinking fund method** is a way for an investor to value the annuity when $j \neq i$. The sinking fund method of valuing a level annuity of $K$ per period for $n$ periods allows an investor to receive a periodic return of $i$ per period while recovering his initial investment amount (the principal) in a sinking fund (deposit account). The idea is that the investor pays an amount $P$ for the series of payments, and receives a periodic return at rate $i$ on the initial outlay, which would be $P \times i$ per period. The actual payment being received from the annuity is $K$ per period, so the amount of the payment in excess of the periodic return is $K - P \times i$. This excess is the amount that is deposited into the sinking fund at rate $j$. At the end of the $n$-period term, the sinking fund has accumulated to $(K - P \times i)s_{\overline{n}|j}$. This accumulated amount should be just enough to repay the investor's initial outlay, allowing him to recover the principal. This scenario is illustrated in Table 2.4.

### TABLE 2.4

| Time | 0 | 1 | 2 | $\cdots$ | $n$ |
|---|---|---|---|---|---|
| Initial Outlay | $P$ | | | $\cdots$ | |
| Interest per period | | $P \cdot i$ | $P \cdot i$ | $\cdots$ | $P \cdot i$ |
| Actual payment | | $K$ | $K$ | $\cdots$ | $K$ |
| Sinking fund deposit | | $K - P \cdot i$ | $K - P \cdot i$ | $\cdots$ | $K - P \cdot i$ |
| | | | | | $\rightarrow (K - P \cdot i)s_{\overline{n}|j}$ |
| | | | | | $= P$ |

Then we see that

$$(K - P \times i)s_{\overline{n}|j} = P \tag{2.39a}$$

or, equivalently,

$$P = \frac{K \times s_{\overline{n}|j}}{1 + i \times s_{\overline{n}|j}}. \tag{2.39b}$$

This situation is similar to Case (2) considered at the start of this section, where the 10,000 loan is repaid by interest alone and the principal is returned at the end of the term. In this case the initial investment of $P$ earns interest of $P \times i$ per period, and the principal amount is returned at the end of the term by means of the accumulated sinking fund.

---

| EXAMPLE 2.29 | (*Sinking fund*) |

A manufacturer is considering the purchase of some equipment that will generate income of 15,000 per year, payable at the end of the year. The equipment has a lifetime of 8 years and no salvage value. What price should be paid for this equipment in order to realize an annual return of 10% while recovering the principal in a sinking fund earning 7 % per annum?

| SOLUTION |

We can apply Equation (2.39b) with $K = 15,000$, $n = 8$, $i = .10$, and $j = .07$, obtaining $P = \dfrac{15,000 s_{\overline{8}|.07}}{1 + .10 \times s_{\overline{8}|.07}} = 75,961.77$ as the solution of the equation $(15,000 - .10P) s_{\overline{8}|.07} = P$. Note that the income of 15,000 per year can be split into 7596.18 plus 7403.82, and the 8 deposits of 7403.82 accumulate to 75,961.73 at 7%. The present value of the income at $i = .10$ is $15,000 a_{\overline{8}|.10} = 80,023.89$. ❑

Exercises at the end of this chapter relate to various aspects of the sinking fund approach to valuing a series of payments. The relationship between the usual present value method of valuing an annuity and the sinking fund method is considered in the following example.

---

| EXAMPLE 2.30 | (*Valuation methods*) |

Let $P_1$ be the present value of an $n$-payment level annuity-immediate valued in the usual way at a periodic interest rate of $i$ per period. Let $P_2$ be the "present" value of the annuity based on the sinking fund method with annual return of $i > 0$ (the same interest rate as in the calculation of $P_1$) to the investor along with recapture of principal in a sinking fund at rate $j > 0$. (The quotation marks around "present" indicate that present value is not being found in the usual sense with a present value factor $v$ at some specified rate of interest.) Derive each of the relationships

(a) $i = j \rightarrow P_1 = P_2$, (b) $i > j \rightarrow P_1 > P_2$, and (c) $i < j \rightarrow P_1 < P_2$.

## SOLUTION

Let the periodic payment be 1. Then $P_1 = a_{\overline{n}|i}$ and $P_2 = \dfrac{s_{\overline{n}|j}}{1 + i \cdot s_{\overline{n}|j}}$. If $i = j$,

then $P_2 = \dfrac{s_{\overline{n}|i}}{1 + i \cdot s_{\overline{n}|i}} = \dfrac{s_{\overline{n}|i}}{(1+i)^n} = a_{\overline{n}|i} = P_1$, establishing relationship (a). Note

that $P_2$ can be rewritten in the form $P_2 = \dfrac{1}{i} \times \left[ 1 - \dfrac{1}{1 + i s_{\overline{n}|j}} \right]$. Then we have

the following sequence of implications:

$$i > j \ \rightarrow \ s_{\overline{n}|i} > s_{\overline{n}|j}$$

$$\rightarrow \ 1 + i \times s_{\overline{n}|i} > 1 + i \times s_{\overline{n}|j}$$

$$\rightarrow \ \frac{1}{1 + i \times s_{\overline{n}|i}} < \frac{1}{1 + i \times s_{\overline{n}|j}}$$

$$\rightarrow \ P_1 = a_{\overline{n}|i} = \frac{1}{i} \times \left[ 1 - \frac{1}{1 + i \times s_{\overline{n}|i}} \right] > \frac{1}{i} \times \left[ 1 - \frac{1}{1 + i \times s_{\overline{n}|j}} \right] = P_2,$$

which establishes relationship (b). Relationship (c) is established in the same way as (b), except that all inequalities are reversed. ❏

The sinking fund method of valuation can be applied to a varying series of payments $K_1, K_2, \ldots, K_n$ made at times $1, 2, \ldots, n$. Suppose $L$ is the purchase price to provide a return of $i$ per payment period while allowing the recapture of principal in a sinking fund at rate $j$. Then $L$ must be the accumulated value at time $n$ of the series of sinking fund deposits, where the sinking fund deposit at time $t$ is $K_t - L \cdot i$. Then

$$L = (K_1 - L \times i)(1 + j)^{n-1} + (K_2 - L \times i)(1 + j)^{n-2}$$

$$+ \cdots + (K_{n-1} - L \times i)(1 + j)^1 + (K_n - L \times i)(1 + j)^0$$

$$= \sum_{t=1}^{n} K_t (1 + j)^{n-t} - L \times i \times s_{\overline{n}|j}.$$

Solving for $L$ results in

$$L = \frac{\displaystyle\sum_{t=1}^{n} K_t (1 + j)^{n-t}}{1 + i \times s_{\overline{n}|j}}. \tag{2.40}$$

The most general case would also allow for varying rates of return $i_1, i_2, \ldots, i_n$ and sinking fund rates $j_1, j_2, \ldots, j_n$.

## 2.5 SUMMARY OF DEFINITIONS AND FORMULAS

**Finite Geometric Series**

$$1 + x + x^2 + \cdots + x^k = \frac{1 - x^{k+1}}{1-x} = \frac{x^{k+1} - 1}{x - 1}. \tag{2.1}$$

**Definition 2.1 – Accumulated value of a level $n$-payment annuity-immediate of 1 per period**

$$s_{\overline{n}|i} = (1+i)^{n-1} + (1+i)^{n-2} + \cdots + (1+i) + 1 = \sum_{t=0}^{n-1} (1+i)^t = \frac{(1+i)^n - 1}{i}. \tag{2.3}$$

**Accumulated value $k$ periods after the $n^{th}$ deposit of an $n$-payment annuity-immediate**

$$\frac{(1+i)^n - 1}{i} \times (1+i)^k$$
$$= s_{\overline{n}|} \times (1+i)^k$$
$$= s_{\overline{n+k}|} - s_{\overline{k}|} \quad \textit{Value at time } n \times \textit{growth}$$
$$\textit{factor from time } n \textit{ to time } n+k. \tag{2.4}$$

**Separation of an accumulated annuity-immediate into two payment groups**

$$s_{\overline{n+k}|} = s_{\overline{n}|} \times (1+i)^k + s_{\overline{k}|} = s_{\overline{k}|} \times (1+i)^n + s_{\overline{n}|}. \tag{2.5}$$

**Definition 2.2 – Present value of a level $n$-payment annuity-immediate of 1 per period**

$$a_{\overline{n}|i} = v + v^2 + \cdots + v^n = \sum_{i=1}^{n} v^t = \frac{1 - v^n}{i}. \tag{2.7}$$

## Separation of the present value of an annuity-immediate into two payment groups

$$a_{\overline{n+k}|} = a_{\overline{k}|} + v^k \times a_{\overline{n}|} = a_{\overline{n}|} + v^n \times a_{\overline{k}|}. \tag{2.9}$$

Present value of an annuity with non-level interest rates for an $n+k$-payment annuity with equally spaced payments, with an interest rate of $i_1$ per period up to the time of the $n^{th}$ payment followed by a rate of $i_2$ per period from the $n^{th}$ payment onward, the present value of the annuity one period before the first payment is $a_{\overline{n}|i_1} + v_{i_1}^n \times a_{\overline{k}|i_2}$.

## Present value of a perpetuity-immediate

$$a_{\overline{\infty}|i} = \frac{1}{i}. \tag{2.12}$$

## Definition 2.3 – Annuity-due

$$\ddot{a}_{\overline{n}|i} = 1 + v + v^2 + \cdots + v^{n-1} = \frac{1-v^n}{d}, \tag{2.13}$$

$$\ddot{s}_{\overline{n}|i} = (1+i) + (1+i)^2 + \cdots + (1+i)^n = \frac{(1+i)^n - 1}{d} \tag{2.14}$$

$$\ddot{a}_{\overline{n}|i} = (1+i)a_{\overline{n}|i} \quad \text{and} \quad \ddot{s}_{\overline{n}|i} = (1+i)s_{\overline{n}|i}. \tag{2.15}$$

$$\ddot{a}_{\overline{\infty}|i} = 1 + v + v^2 + \cdots = \frac{1}{1-v}$$

$$= \frac{1}{d} = \frac{1+i}{i} = (1+i)a_{\overline{\infty}|i} = 1 + a_{\overline{\infty}|i} \tag{2.16}$$

## Continuous annuities

$$\overline{s}_{\overline{n}|i} = \int_0^n (1+i)^{n-t}\, dt = \frac{(1+i)^n - 1}{\delta} \tag{2.18}$$

$$\overline{a}_{\overline{n}|i} = \int_0^n v^t\, dt = \frac{1-v^n}{\delta} = \frac{1-e^{-n\delta}}{\delta} \tag{2.19}$$

**Annuity whose payments follow a geometric series**

A series of $n$ periodic payments has first payment of amount 1, and all subsequent payments are $(1+r)$ times the size of the previous payment. At a rate of interest $i$ per payment period, the present value of the series one period before the first payment is

$$v + (1+r)v^2 + (1+r)^2 v^3 + \cdots + (1+r)^{n-1} v^n = \frac{1 - \left(\frac{1+r}{1+i}\right)^n}{i - r}, \qquad (2.22)$$

and the accumulated value at the time of the final payment is

$$\frac{1 - \left(\frac{1+r}{1+i}\right)^n}{i - r} \times (1+i)^n = \frac{(1+i)^n - (1+r)^n}{i - r}. \qquad (2.23)$$

If $i = r$ then the present value one period before the first payment is

$$v + (1+r)v^2 + (1+r)^2 v^3 + \cdots + (1+r)^{n-1} v^n = v + v + \cdots v = nv$$

**Dividend discount model for valuing a stock**

If the next dividend payable one year from now is of amount $K$, and the annual compound growth rate of the dividend is $r$, and the interest rate used for calculating present values is $i$, the present value one payment period before the first dividend payment is $\frac{K}{i-r}$. $\qquad (2.24)$

**$n$-payment increasing annuity-immediate and increasing perpetuity-immediate**

$$\begin{aligned} (Ia)_{\overline{n}|i} &= v + 2v^2 + 3v^3 + \cdots + (n-1)v^{n-1} + nv^n \\ &= \frac{\ddot{a}_{\overline{n}|i} - nv^n}{i}, \end{aligned} \qquad (2.25)$$

$$(Is)_{\overline{n}|} = \frac{\ddot{s}_{\overline{n}|} - n}{i},$$

$$(Ia)_{\overline{\infty}|} = \frac{\ddot{a}_{\overline{\infty}|}}{i} = \frac{1}{id} = \frac{1}{i} + \frac{1}{i^2} \qquad (2.26)$$

## Decreasing annuities

$$(Da)_{\overline{n}|} = nv + (n-1)v^2 + (n-2)v^3 + \cdots + 2v^{n-1} + v^n$$

$$= \frac{n - a_{\overline{n}|}}{i} \qquad (2.27)$$

$$(Ds)_{\overline{n}|} = \frac{n(1+i)^n - s_{\overline{n}|}}{i}$$

$$= (Da)_{\overline{n}|} \times (1+i)^n.$$

## 2.6 NOTES AND REFERENCES

A finite difference approach to simplifying the present value of a varying annuity is discussed in the *Theory of Interest*, by S. Kellison. Chapter 2 of *Compound Interest* by M. Butcher and C. Nesbitt contains an extensive collection of numerical and algebraic problems on annuities.

## 2.7 EXERCISES

### SECTION 2.1

2.1.1   50,000 can be invested under two options:

Option 1

> Deposit the 50,000 into a fund earning an annual effective rate of $i$; or

Option 2

> Purchase an annuity-immediate with 24 level annual payments at an annual effective rate of 10%.

The payments under Option 2 are deposited into a fund earning an annual effective rate of 5%. Both options produce the same accumulated value at the end of 24 years. Calculate $i$.

2.1.2 Bob wants to purchase a perpetuity paying 1000 per year with the first payment due at the end of year 11. He can purchase it by either:

(i) paying 900 per year at the end of each year for 10 years; or

(ii) paying $K$ per year at the end of each year for the first 5 years and nothing for the next 5 years.

Calculate $K$.

2.1.3 Write the annuity $s_{\overline{n+k}|i}$ in series form (assume $n$ and $k$ are integers). Group separately the accumulated values (as of the time of the final payment) of the first $n$ payments and final $k$ payments. Use this formulation to derive Equation (2.4).

2.1.4 Smith makes deposits of 1000 on the last day of each month in an account earning interest at rate $i^{(12)} = .12$. The first deposit is January 31, 2005 and the final deposit is December 31, 2029. The accumulated account is used to make monthly payments of $Y$ starting January 31, 2030 with the final one on December 31, 2054. Find $Y$.

2.1.5 Since June 30, 2007 Smith has been making deposits of 100 each into a bank account on the last day of each month. For all of 2007 and 2008 Smith's account earned nominal interest compounded monthly at an annual rate of 9%. For the first 9 months of 2009 the account earned $i^{(12)} = .105$, and since then the account has been earning $i^{(12)} = .12$.

Find the balance in the account on each of the following days:

(i) January 1, 2008,

(ii) January 1, 2009, and

(iii) February 1, 2010

Find the amount of interest credited on February 28, 2010.

2.1.6S To accumulate 8000 at the end of $3n$ years, deposits of 98 are made at the end of each of the first $n$ years and 196 at the end of each of the next $2n$ years. The effective annual rate of interest is $i$. You are given $(1+i)^n = 2.0$. Determine $i$.

2.1.7 (a) In a series of 40 payments the first 10 payments are 10 each, the second 10 payments are 20 each, the third ten payments are 30 each, and the final 10 payments are 40 each. The payments are equally spaced and the interest rate is 5% per payment period. Find the accumulated value at the time of the final payment.

(b) Show that the accumulated value of the series is equal to
$$10\left[ s_{\overline{10}|.05} + s_{\overline{20}|.05} + s_{\overline{30}|.05} + s_{\overline{40}|.05} \right].$$

2.1.8S Given $s_{\overline{10}|.10} = S$, find the value of $\sum_{t=1}^{10} s_{\overline{t}|.10}$ in terms of $S$.

2.1.9 A deposit of 1 is made at each of times $t = 1, 2, \ldots, n$ to an account earning interest at rate $i$ per payment period. Let $I_t$ denote the interest payable at time $t$. Find an expression for $I_t$, and show that $\sum_{t=1}^{n} I_t = s_{\overline{n}|i} - n$. What is the interpretation of this relationship?

2.1.10 Smith buys 100 shares of stock ABC at the same time Brown buys 100 shares of stock XYZ. Both stocks are bought for 10 per share. Smith receives a dividend of .80 per share, payable at the end of each year, for 10 years, at which time (just after receiving the $10^{th}$ dividend) he sells his stock for 2 per share. Smith invests his dividends at annual rate 6%, and invests the proceeds of the sale of his stock at the same rate. Brown receives no dividends for the first 10 years, but starts receiving annual dividends of .40 per share at the end of 11 years. Brown also invests his dividends in an account earning 6%. If Brown sells his shares $n$ years after purchase, what should be the sale price per share in order that his accumulated investment matches that of Smith, for each of $n = 15, 20$ and 25?

2.1.11S  (a) If $s_{\overline{n}|} = 70$ and $s_{\overline{2n}|} = 210$, find the values of $(1+i)^n$, $i$, and $s_{\overline{3n}|}$.

(b) If $s_{\overline{3n}|} = X$ and $s_{\overline{n}|} = Y$, express $v^n$ in terms of $X$, $Y$ and constants.

(c) If $s_{\overline{n}|} = 48.99$, $s_{\overline{n-2}|} = 36.34$, and $i > 0$, find $i$.

2.1.12S  An $m+n$ year annuity of 1 per year has $i = 7\%$ during the first $m$ years and has $i = 11\%$ during the remaining $n$ years. If $s_{\overline{m}|.07} = 34$ and $s_{\overline{n}|.11} = 128$, what is the accumulated value of the annuity just after the final payment?

2.1.13S  Chuck needs to purchase an item in 10 years. The item costs 200 today, but its price inflates 4% per year. To finance the purchase, Chuck deposits 20 into an account at the beginning of each year for 6 years. He deposits an additional $X$ at the beginning of years 4, 5, and 6 to meet his goal. The effective annual interest rate is 10%. Calculate $X$.

2.1.14  Show that Equation (2.7) can be written as $1 = v^n + i \cdot a_{\overline{n}|i}$, and give an interpretation of this relationship.

2.1.15  For the situation described in Exercise 2.1.5, find the present value of the series on June 1, 2007.

2.1.16  A scholarship fund is started on January 1, 2000 with an initial deposit of 100,000 in an account earning $i^{(2)} = .08$, with interest credited every June 30 and December 31. Every January 1 from 2001 on, the fund will receive a deposit of 5000. The scholarship fund makes payments to recipients totaling 12,000 every July 1 starting in 2000. What amount is in the scholarship account just after the 5000 deposit is made on January 1, 2010?

2.1.17S  At an effective annual interest rate of $i, i > 0$, both of the following annuities have a present value of $X$:

(a)  a 20-year annuity-immediate with annual payments of 55

(b)  a 30-year annuity-immediate with annual payments that pays 30 per year for the first 10 years, 60 per year for the second 10 years, and 90 per year for the final 10 years.

Calculate $X$.

2.1.18  10,000 can be invested under two options:

Option 1.  Deposit the 10,000 into a fund earning an effective annual rate of $i$; or

Option 2.  Purchase an annuity-immediate with 24 level annual payments at an effective annual rate of 10%. The payments are deposited into a fund earning an effective annual rate of 5%.

Both options produce the same accumulated value at the end of 24 years. Calculate $i$.

2.1.19S  Dottie receives payments of $X$ at the end of each year for $n$ years. The present value of her annuity is 493. Sam receives payments of $3X$ at the end of each year for $2n$ years. The present value of his annuity is 2748. Both present values are calculated at the same effective annual interest rate. Determine $v^n$.

2.1.20  A loan of 10,000 is being repaid by 10 semiannual payments, with the first payment made one-half year after the loan. The first 5 payments are $K$ each, and the final 5 are $K + 200$ each. What is $K$ if $i^{(2)} = .06$?

2.1.21  Show that $a_{\overline{n}|}$ can be written as the difference between a perpetuity-immediate and an $n$-year deferred perpetuity-immediate.

*2.1.22  Derive Equation (2.8): (a) by means of a line diagram similar to the derivation of Equation (2.4), and (b) by considering the series forms of the annuities in Equation (2.8).

*2.1.23 For the series of part (a) of Exercise 2.1.7, find the present value one payment period before the first payment. Show that this present value can be written as

$$10\left[4 \cdot a_{\overline{40}|.05} - a_{\overline{10}|.05} - a_{\overline{20}|.05} - a_{\overline{30}|.05}\right].$$

*2.1.24 Suppose an annuity of $n+k$ equally-spaced payments (where $n$ and $k$ are integers) of amount 1 each is subject to interest at rate $i$ per payment period until the $n^{th}$ payment, and at rate $j$ per payment period starting just after the $n^{th}$ payment. If $Y$ is the accumulated value of the series at the time of the final payment and $X$ is the present value of the series one period before the first payment, show that $Y = (1+i)^n (1+j)^k \cdot X$.

*2.1.25 Derive the relationship $\dfrac{1}{a_{\overline{n}|i}} = \dfrac{1}{s_{\overline{n}|i}} + i.$

*2.1.26 For an annuity of $3n$ payments of equal amount at periodic interest rate $i$, it is found that one period before the first payment the present value of the first $n$ payments is equal to the present value of the final $2n$ payments. What is the value of $v^n$?

*2.1.27 Derive the following identities:

(a) $\ddot{a}_{\overline{n}|i} = (1+i)a_{\overline{n}|i} = a_{\overline{n}|i} + 1 - v^n = 1 + a_{\overline{n-1}|i}$

(b) $\ddot{s}_{\overline{n}|i} = (1+i)s_{\overline{n}|i} = s_{\overline{n}|i} - 1 + (1+i)^n = s_{\overline{n+1}|i} - 1$

*2.1.28 A loan of 5000 can be repaid by payments of 117.38 at the end of each month for $n$ years ($12n$ payments), starting one month after the loan is made. At the same rate of interest, $12n$ monthly payments of 113.40 each accumulate to 10,000 one month after the final payment. Find the equivalent effective annual rate of interest.

*2.1.29  (a) A perpetuity pays 1 every January 1 starting in 2015. The effective annual rate of interest will be $i$ in odd-numbered years and $j$ in even-numbered years. Find an expression for the present value of the perpetuity on January 1, 2014.

(b) A perpetuity starting January 1, 2015 pays 1 every January 1 in odd years and 2 every January 1 in even years. Find an expression for the present value at rate $i$ per year of the perpetuity on (i) January 1, 2014, and (ii) January 1, 2015.

*2.1.30  (a) Three schemes are considered for the repayment of a loan of amount $L$ which is to be repaid with 10 annual payments. Scheme (i) has 5 payments of $X$ each followed by 5 payments of $2X$ each, scheme (ii) has 10 payments of $Y$ each, and scheme (iii) has 5 payments of $2Z$ each followed by 5 payments of $Z$ each. For each scheme the first payment is made one year after the loan. Assuming that $i > 0$, show that $X > \frac{2Y}{3} > Z$.

(b) A loan of amount $L$ is to be repaid by $n > 1$ equal annual payments, starting one year after the loan. If interest is at effective annual rate $i$ the annual payment is $P_1$, and if interest is at effective annual rate $2i$ the annual payment is $P_2$. Show that $P_2 < 2P_1$.

*2.1.31  Smith borrows 5000 on January 1, 2005. She repays the loan with 20 annual payments starting January 1, 2006. The payments in even-numbered years are $Y$ each and the payments in odd-numbered years are $X$ each. If $i = .08$ and the total of all 20 loan payments is 10,233, find $X$ and $Y$.

*2.1.32  A loan of 11,000 is made with interest at a nominal annual rate of 12% compounded monthly. The loan is to be repaid by 36 monthly payments of 367.21 over 37 months, starting one month after the loan is made, there being a payment at the end of every month but one. At the end of which month is the missing payment?

*2.1.33  Derive the following identities assuming $t < n$.

(a)  $v^t \cdot s_{\overline{n}|} = a_{\overline{t}|} + s_{\overline{n-t}|} = \ddot{a}_{\overline{t+1}|} + \ddot{s}_{\overline{n-t-1}|}$

(b)  $(1+i)^t \cdot \ddot{a}_{\overline{n}|} = \ddot{s}_{\overline{t}|} + \ddot{a}_{\overline{n-t}|} = s_{\overline{t+1}|} + a_{\overline{n-t-1}|}$

Formulate corresponding expressions for the case $t > n$.

## SECTION 2.2

2.2.1  A 50,000 loan made on January 1, 2010 is to be repaid over 25 years with payments on the last day of each month, beginning January 31, 2010.

(a) If $i^{(2)} = 10\%$, find the amount of the monthly payment $X$.

(b) Starting with the first payment, the borrower decides to pay an additional 100 per month, on top of the regular payment of $X$, until the loan is repaid. An additional fractional payment might be necessary one month after the last regular payment of $X + 100$. On what date will the final payment of $X + 100$ be made, and what will be the amount of the additional fractional payment?

2.2.2  The following is an excerpt from the website of the Bank of Montreal (www4.bmo.com). The website gives some examples of accumulation over 25 years in a Registered Retirement Savings Plan (the Canadian version of an IRA).

Derek, Ira, and Anne each contribute $1,200 annually to their RRSPs earning a 6% average annual compounded return.

- Derek contributes $1,200 at the beginning of each calendar year.
- Ira contributes $100 at the start of each month throughout the year.
- Anne contributes $1,200 each year on the very last day for RRSP contributions deductible in the tax year (assume that this is the last day of the calendar year).

Determine the accumulated values in the three numerical examples given.

2.2.3 Jerry will make deposits of 450 at the end of each quarter for 10 years. At the end of 15 years, Jerry will use the fund to make annual payments of $Y$ at the beginning of each year for 4 years, after which the fund is exhausted. The effective annual rate of interest is 7%. Determine $Y$.

2.2.4S Kathryn deposits 100 into an account at the beginning of each 4-year period for 40 years. The account credits interest at an effective annual interest rate of $i$. The accumulated amount in the account at the end of 40 years is $X$, which is 5 times the accumulated amount in the account at the end of 20 years. Calculate $X$.

2.2.5S A perpetuity paying 1 at the beginning of each 6-month period has a present value of 20. A second perpetuity pays $X$ at the beginning of every 2 years. Assuming the same effective annual interest rate, the two present values are equal. Determine $X$.

2.2.6S Sally lends 10,000 to Tim. Tim agrees to pay back the loan over 5 years with monthly payments at the end of each month. Sally can reinvest the payments from Tim in a savings account paying interest at 6%, compounded monthly. The yield rate earned on Sally's investment over the five-year period turned out to be 7.45%, compounded semi-annually. What nominal rate of interest, compounded monthly, did Sally charge Tim on the loan?

2.2.7 A sum of 10,000 was invested on September 1, 1970 at an effective annual interest rate of 5% in order to provide an annual scholarship of 2000 every September 1 forever, starting as soon as possible. In what year will the first payment of 2000 be made? What smaller payment could be made one year earlier while still permitting the annual scholarships of 2000 thereafter? Assume that interest is credited every August 31.

2.2.8   On the first day of each month, starting January 1, 1995, Smith deposits 100 in an account earning $i^{(12)} = .09$, with interest credited the last day of each month. In addition, Smith deposits 1000 in the account every December 31. On what day does the account first exceed 100,000?

2.2.9   On the first day of every January, April, July and October Smith deposits 100 in an account earning $i^{(4)} = .16$. He continues the deposits until he accumulates a sufficient balance to begin withdrawals of 200 every 3 months, starting 3 months after the final deposit, such that he can make twice as many withdrawals as he made deposits. How many deposits are needed?

2.2.10  Ten annual deposits of 1000 each are made to Account A, starting on January 1, 1986. Annual deposits of 500 each are made to Account B indefinitely, also starting on January 1, 1986. Interest on both accounts is at rate $i = .05$, with interest credited every December 31. On what date will the balance for Account B first exceed the balance for Account A? Assume that the only transactions to the accounts are deposits and interest credited every December 31.

2.2.11  A loan of 1000 is repaid with 12 annual payments of 100 each starting one year after the loan is made. The effective annual interest rate is 3.5% for the first 4 years. Find the effective annual interest rate $i$ for the final 8 years.

2.2.12  An insurance company offers a "capital redemption policy" whereby the policyholder pays annual premiums (in advance) of 3368.72 for 25 years, and, in return, receives a redemption amount of 250,000 one year after the $25^{th}$ premium is paid. The insurer has determined that administrative expenses are 20% of the first premium and 10% of all remaining premiums, and these expenses are incurred at the time the premium is paid. The insurer anticipates investing the net (after expenses) premiums received at an effective annual interest rate of 12.5%. What is the insurer's accumulated profit just after the policy matures and the redemption amount of 250,000 is paid? Find the effective annual rate of return earned by the policyholder for the 25-year period.

2.2.13 Smith is negotiating to purchase a car, and he determines that he must borrow 12,000 to complete the purchase. He is offered financing at a nominal interest rate of $i^{(12)}$ with monthly payments beginning one month after the loan is made. He can repay the loan over a 2-year period (24 payments) at 592.15 per month, or over a 3-year period (36 payments) at 426.64 per month (the same interest rate in both cases). Find $i^{(12)}$ and the monthly amount payable if he were able to repay the loan over a 4-year period (still at the same interest rate).

*2.2.14S At an effective annual interest rate of $i, i > 0$, the present value of a perpetuity paying 10 at the end of each 3-year period, with the first payment at the end of year 6, is 32 . At the same effective annual rate of $i$, the present value of a perpetuity-immediate paying 1 at the end of each 4-month period is $X$. Calculate $X$.

*2.2.15 Payments of 25 each are made every 2 months from June 1, 2003 to April 1, 2009, inclusive. Find the value of the series (a) 2 months before the first payment at effective annual interest rate $i = .06$, (b) 10 months before the first payment at nominal annual rate $i^{(3)} = .06$, (c) 2 months after the final payment at nominal annual rate $d^{(2)} = .06$, and (d) 1 year after the final payment at annual force of interest $\delta = .06$.

*2.2.16 A perpetuity consists of monthly payments. The payment pattern follows a repeating 12-month cycle of eleven payments of 1 each followed by a payment of 2. The effective monthly interest rate is $j$. Show that the present value of the perpetuity valued one month before the first payment is $\frac{1}{j}\left[1 + \frac{1}{s_{\overline{12}|j}}\right]$.

*2.2.17 Find the present value at time 0 of an $n$-year continuous annuity based on force of interest $\delta_t = p + \frac{s}{1 + re^{st}}$.

*2.2.18 A loan of amount $L$ is to be repaid with $n$ periodic payments of amount $K$ each at periodic interest rate $i > 0$, where $n$ is even. The same loan can be repaid by $\frac{n}{2}$ payments if the periodic payment is increased to an amount larger than $K$. Determine whether the new payment is exactly double, more than double, or less than double the value of $K$.

*2.2.19 Deposits of 500 each are made into an account on the first day of every January and July beginning on January 1,1999.

    (a) If $i^{(6)} = .06$ and interest is credited on the last day of every February, April, June, August, October and December, on what date does the account balance first exceed 10,000?

    (b) Suppose instead that $i = .04$ and interest is credited only on December 31 each year, with simple interest credited for fractions of a year. On what date should the account be closed in order that the closing balance be nearest 10,000?

*2.2.20 Find the smallest integer $n$ for which deposits of 1 per period accumulate to at least 100 in each of the following cases.

    (a) 20 deposits at 3% followed by $n$ deposits at 4%

    (b) $n$ deposits at 3% followed by $n$ deposits at 4%

*2.2.21 Apply the following approximation method to find $n$ in Example 2.14. Take natural logarithms of both sides of the equation

$$(1.0075)^n = 1 + .008333n,$$

and use the Taylor expansion of $\ln(1+.008333n)$ to: (i) 2 terms and (ii) 3 terms.

*2.2.22 Solve for $i$ and $n$ in terms of $A$ and $B$, where $A = s_{\overline{n}|i}$ and $B = s_{\overline{n+1}|i}$.

*2.2.23 (a) For the equation $L = K \cdot a_{\overline{n}|i}, L, K, n > 0,$ note that $L = n \cdot K$ if $i = 0$. Use the following principles:

(i) $\lim_{i \to \infty} a_{\overline{n}|i} = 0,$

(ii) $\lim_{i \to -1} a_{\overline{n}|i} = \infty,$ and

(iii) $a_{\overline{n}|i}$ is a decreasing function of $i$

to show that the equation has a unique solution for $i$ between $-1$ and $\infty$ if $L, K$ and $n$ are given. Also show that $i > 0$ if $L < n \cdot K$ and $i < 0$ if $L > n \cdot K$.

(b) Derive a result similar to that in part (a) for the accumulated annuity relationship $M = J \cdot s_{\overline{n}|i}$.

*2.2.24 A fund has value $A$ at the start of a year, $B$ at the end of the year, and interest of $I$ earned for the year. Assuming that interest income accrues continuously on the fund, use the approximate relationship $\frac{i}{\delta} \approx 1 + \frac{i}{2}$ to show that the annual interest rate earned by the fund is approximately $\frac{2I}{B + A - I}$.

*2.2.25 An annuity has $n$ annual payments of amount 1 each. Interest is quoted at a nominal annual rate of $i^{(m)}$. Let $j = \frac{i^{(m)}}{m}$. Express the equivalent effective annual rate of interest $i$ in terms of $j$.

(a) Show that (i) $s_{\overline{n}|i} = \frac{(1+j)^{m \cdot n} - 1}{(1+j)^m - 1}$, (ii) $\ddot{a}_{\overline{n}|i} = \frac{1 - v_j^{m \cdot n}}{1 - v_j^m}$.

(b) Let $P = \frac{1}{s_{\overline{m}|j}}$ be the payment required every $\frac{1}{m}^{th}$ of a year for one year to accumulate to 1 at the end of the year (i.e., at the time of the $m^{th}$ payment of $P$) at interest rate $j$ per $\frac{1}{m}^{th}$ of a year. Show that $s_{\overline{n}|i}$ from part (b) is equal to $P \cdot s_{\overline{m \cdot n}|j} = s_{\overline{n}|i}$.

(c) If the quoted rate is $i^{(\infty)} = \delta$, the annual force of interest, show that $s_{\overline{n}|i} = \frac{e^{n\delta} - 1}{e^{\delta} - 1}$.

(d) Repeat part (b) for the present value of perpetuities, both immediate and due.

*2.2.26  An annuity has level payments of $\frac{1}{m}$ every $\frac{1}{m}^{th}$ of a year for $n$ years (a total of $n \cdot m$ payments). Interest is at effective annual rate $i$. Let $j$ denote the interest rate for $\frac{1}{m}^{th}$ of a year that is equivalent to $i$.

(a) Show that the accumulated value of the annuity at the time of the final payment is

$$\frac{1}{m} \cdot s_{\overline{n \cdot m}|j} = \frac{1}{m} \cdot \frac{(1+i)^n - 1}{(1+i)^{1/m} - 1}.$$

(b) Show each of the following:

(i)  $\dfrac{1}{m} \cdot a_{\overline{n \cdot m}|j} = \dfrac{1 - v_i^n}{i^{(m)}} = a_{\overline{n}|i} \cdot \dfrac{i}{i^{(m)}}$

(ii)  $\dfrac{1}{m} \cdot \ddot{s}_{\overline{n \cdot m}|j} = \dfrac{(1+i)^n - 1}{d^{(m)}} = s_{\overline{n}|i} \cdot \dfrac{i}{d^{(m)}}$

*2.2.27  (a) Show that $\lim\limits_{m \to \infty} s_{\overline{n}|i}^{(m)} = \lim\limits_{m \to \infty} \ddot{s}_{\overline{n}|i}^{(m)} = \ddot{s}_{\overline{n}|i}^{(\infty)} = s_{\overline{n}|i}^{(\infty)} = \overline{s}_{\overline{n}|i}$.

(b) If $i > 0$ and $m > 1$, rank the following values in increasing order: $a_{\overline{n}|i}$, $\ddot{a}_{\overline{n}|i}$, $a_{\overline{n}|i}^{(m)}$, $\ddot{a}_{\overline{n}|i}^{(m)}$, $\overline{a}_{\overline{n}|i}$.

(c) Assuming simple interest at rate $i$, find $\overline{s}_{\overline{n}|i}$.

## SECTION 2.3

2.3.1 Stan elects to receive his retirement benefit over 20 years at the rate of 2000 per month beginning one month from now. The monthly benefit increases by 5% each year. At a nominal interest rate of 6% convertible monthly, calculate the present value of the retirement benefit.

2.3.2 The first of a series of 30 annual payments is 1000 and each subsequent payment is 1% smaller than the previous one. What is the accumulated value of this series at the time of the final payment if (i) $i = 1\%$, (ii) $i = 5\%$, and (iii) $i = 10\%$?

2.3.3 Jeff and Jason spend $X$ dollars each to purchase annuities. Jeff buys a perpetuity-immediate, which makes annual payments of 30. Jason buys a 10-year annuity-immediate, also with annual payments. The first payment is 53, with each subsequent payment $k\%$ larger than the previous year's payment. Both annuities use an effective annual interest rate of $k\%$. Calculate $k$.

2.3.4S Mike buys a perpetuity-immediate with varying annual payments. During the first 5 years, the payment is constant and equal to 10. Beginning in year 6, the payments start to increase. For year 6 and all future years, the current year's payment is $K\%$ larger than the previous year's payment. At an effective annual interest rate of 9.2%, the perpetuity has a present value of 167.50. Calculate $K$, given $K < 9.2$.

2.3.5S A senior executive is offered a buyout package by his company that will pay him a monthly benefit for the next 20 years. Monthly benefits will remain constant within each of the 20 years. At the end of each 12-month period, the monthly benefits will be adjusted upwards to reflect the percentage increase in the CPI. You are given:

(i) The first monthly benefit is $R$ and will be paid one month from today.

(ii) The CPI increases 3.2% per year forever.

At an effective annual interest rate of 6%, the buyout package has a value of 100,000. Calculate $R$.

2.3.6   (a) Show that the accumulated value one period after the final payment of the annuity on page 111 is $(1+r)^n \cdot \ddot{s}_{\overline{n}|j}$.

   (b) Show that the present value one period before the first payment of the annuity on page 111 is $\frac{1}{1+r} \cdot a_{\overline{n}|j}$.

2.3.7   Smith has 100,000 with which she buys a perpetuity on January 1, 2005. Suppose that $i = .045$ and the perpetuity has annual payments beginning January 1, 2006. The first three payments are 2000 each, the next three payments are $2000(1+r)$ each,..., increasing forever by a factor of $1 + r$ every three years. What is $r$?

2.3.8   An employee serves 37 years before retiring on a pension. His initial salary was 18,000 per year and increased by 4% each year. Assume that the whole year's salary is paid at the middle of each year.

   (a) If his pension is 70% of his average annual salary over his entire career, what is his ultimate pension?

   (b) If the pension is 2.5% of career average salary multiplied by years of service, what is his ultimate pension?

   (c) If his pension is 2.5% of his average salary over the final 10 years he worked, multiplied by his total years of service, then what is his ultimate pension?

   (d) If he contributes 3% of his salary (at the time it is paid), matched by an equal contribution from his employer, to an account earning annual interest at rate $i = .06$, and the accumulated value (at the end of his $37^{th}$ year of employment) is used to purchase a 20-year annuity-due with annual payments, valued at $i = .06$, find the annual payment from the annuity.

2.3.9   The following is an excerpt from The Hartford Insurance Company website (http://institutional.hartfordlife.com/). It describes a "structured settlement" in which an income stream is to be paid out over time. Verify that the total payout over the 20 years is $644,889.

### Installment Payment Example

**Situation**:  A young man, 25 years old, is injured in an automobile accident.

**Needs:**   Financial Security to provide young man with funds to satisfy **current obligations** and guaranteed payments to provide for **future needs** such as:
   - **Replacement of Lost Income** ($2,000 per month with 3% annual cost of living increase)

**Claim Summary**

| Future Needs | Structured Settlement | | |
| --- | --- | --- | --- |
| | Guaranteed Payout | Life Expectancy Payout | Annuity Cost |
| **Replace Loss Income** Age 25-45 monthly payment range $2,000 to $3,507 | **$644,889** | **$644,889** | **$346,851** |

Find the effective annual rate of interest that was used to get the present value of $346,851 (this will require a numerical approximation routine such as the EXCEL Solver program).

2.3.10S   Susan invests $Z$ at the end of each year for seven years at an effective annual interest rate of 5%. The interest credited at the end of each year is reinvested at an effective annual rate of 6%. The accumulated value at the end of seven years is $X$. Lori invests $Z$ at the end of each year for 14 years at an effective annual interest rate of 2.5%. The interest credited at the end of each year is reinvested at an effective annual rate of 3%. The accumulated value at the end of 14 years is $Y$. Calculate $Y/X$.

2.3.11S  Sandy purchases a perpetuity-immediate that makes annual payments. The first payment is 100, and each payment thereafter increases by 10. Danny purchases a perpetuity-due which makes annual payments of 180. Using the same effective annual interest rate, $i > 0$, the present value of both perpetuities are equal. Calculate $i$.

2.3.12S  Olga buys a 5-year increasing annuity for $X$. Olga will receive 2 at the end of the first month, 4 at the end of the second month, and for each month thereafter the payment increases by 2. The nominal interest rate is 9% convertible quarterly. Calculate $X$.

2.3.13S  1000 is deposited into Fund $X$, which earns an effective annual rate of 6%. At the end of each year, the interest earned plus an additional 100 is withdrawn from the fund. At the end of the tenth year, the fund is depleted. The annual withdrawals of interest and principal are deposited into Fund $Y$, which earns an effective annual rate of 9%. Determine the accumulated value of Fund $Y$ at the end of year 10.

2.3.14S  A perpetuity costs 77.1 and makes annual payments at the end of the year. The perpetuity pays 1 at the end of year 2, 2 at the end of year 3,..., $n$ at the end of year $(n+1)$. After year $(n+1)$, the payments remain constant at $n$. The effective annual interest rate is 10.5%. Calculate $n$.

2.3.15  A loan of 12,000 is repaid by 36 monthly payments starting one month after the loan. The first 12 payments are $395 + X$ each, the next 12 payments are 395 each, and the final 12 payments are $395 - X$ each. If $i^{(12)} = .12$, find $X$.

2.3.16  What series of payments is represented by the present value $A \cdot a_{\overline{n}|} + B \cdot (Da)_{\overline{n}|}$? Formulate the present value of a 25-year decreasing annuity-immediate with first payment of 100 and subsequent payments decreasing by 3 per period.

2.3.17S    Victor invests 300 into a bank account at the beginning of each year for 20 years. The account pays out interest at the end of every year at an effective annual interest rate of $i\%$. The interest is reinvested at an effective annual rate of $\frac{i}{2}\%$. The yield rate on the entire investment over the 20 year period is 8% effective annual. Determine $i$.


2.3.18S    Joe can purchase one of two annuities:

Annuity 1:    A 10-year decreasing annuity-immediate, with annual payments of $10, 9, 8, \ldots, 1$.

Annuity 2:    A perpetuity-immediate with annual payments. The perpetuity pays 1 in year 1, 2 in year 2, 3 in year 3,..., and 11 in year 11. After year 11, the payments remain constant at 11.

At an effective annual interest rate of $i$, the present value of Annuity 2 is twice the present value of Annuity 1. Calculate the value of Annuity 1.


*2.3.19   A government provides each citizen over the age of 65 with a monthly pension payable for life. The current monthly payment is 400. The payment is indexed to inflation so that every year there is an adjustment to reflect the rate of inflation for the year (but payments within a year are level). The government proposes a cost-cutting measure whereby the payments will be "partially de-indexed," so that the payment increase will be the excess of the inflation rate over 3%. The increase is 0 if the inflation is less than 3%. As a simplified model the government regards the lifetime payments as a perpetuity. What are the pension present values both before and after de-indexing under each of the following annual interest/inflation scenarios?

(i)   $i = .12, r = .09$    (ii)  $i = .12, r = .03$
(iii) $i = .09, r = .06$    (iv)  $i = .06, r = .03$

*2.3.20  On January 1, 2005 Smith deposits 500,000 in an account earning a effective monthly rate of 1%, with interest credited on the last day of each month. Withdrawals are made on the first day of each month starting February 1, 2005, with an initial withdrawal of 1000. Each subsequent withdrawal is 1% larger than the previous one, continuing in this pattern for as long as possible.

(a) When does the account finally become exhausted, and what is the amount of the last regular withdrawal?

(b) What is the maximum amount the account balance reaches during this process?

*2.3.21  For 100,000, Smith purchases a 20-payment annuity-immediate with annual payments. For each of the following cases find the unknown interest rate $i$.

(a) The first payment is 7000 and each subsequent payment is 750 more than the previous one.

(b) The first payment is 7000 and each subsequent payment is 10% larger than the previous one.

This problem requires a numerical approximation routine such as the EXCEL Solver program.

*2.3.22  (a)  Write out the terms of the series for $(Is)_{\overline{n}|i}$.

Show $(Is)_{\overline{n}|i} = \frac{\ddot{s}_{\overline{n}|i} - n}{i}$.

(b) Draw a line diagram and explain verbally why $s_{\overline{n+1}|i}$ must equal $(n+1) + i \cdot (Is)_{\overline{n}|i}$.

*2.3.23 Show that the following relationships are valid, and illustrate them using line diagrams:

(a) $(Ia)_{\overline{n}|} + (Da)_{\overline{n}|} = (n+1) \cdot a_{\overline{n}|}$

(b) $(Ia)_{\overline{n}|} = \sum_{k=0}^{n-1} {}_k|a_{\overline{n-k}|}$ and $(Is)_{\overline{n}|} = \sum_{k=1}^{n} s_{\overline{k}|}$

(c) $(I\ddot{s})_{\overline{n}|} = (Is)_{\overline{n}|} + \ddot{s}_{\overline{n}|} - n$

(d) $(D\ddot{a})_{\overline{n}|} = (Da)_{\overline{n}|} + n - a_{\overline{n}|}$

(e) $(Da)_{\overline{n}|} = \sum_{k=1}^{n} a_{\overline{k}|}$

*2.3.24 Show that if $i > 0$ then $(Ia)_{\overline{\infty}|} = \dfrac{1}{i} + \dfrac{1}{i^2} = \dfrac{1}{i \cdot d} = a_{\overline{\infty}|} \cdot \ddot{a}_{\overline{\infty}|}$. Give a verbal interpretation for the final expression.

*2.3.25 (a) Show that

(i) $\dfrac{d}{di} a_{\overline{n}|i} = -v \cdot (Ia)_{\overline{n}|}$,

(ii) $\dfrac{d}{di} s_{\overline{n}|i} = (Ds)_{\overline{n-1}|}$, and

(iii) $\dfrac{d}{d\delta} \overline{a}_{\overline{n}|i} = -(\overline{I}\,\overline{a})_{\overline{n}|}$.

(b) Find expressions for $\dfrac{d}{dn} \overline{a}_{\overline{n}|}$ and $\dfrac{d}{dn} \overline{s}_{\overline{n}|}$.

*2.3.26 Smith is arranging a mortgage loan of 100,000 to be repaid with monthly payments over 25 years, with the first payment due one month after the loan is made. Interest is quoted at a nominal annual rate compounded semiannually of $i^{(2)}$. The loan will not be issued for several months, and the interest rate will be set at the time of the loan. Smith, in determining the sensitivity of his monthly payment to the interest rate, calculates $\dfrac{d}{di^{(2)}} K$, where $K$ is the monthly payment. Find the value of this derivative for the following values of $i^{(2)}$: 21%, 13%, 10%, 5%.

*2.3.27 Smith retires on January 1, 2004. She deposits 500,000 in an account earning effective annual interest at $i = .10$, with interest credited every December 31. Smith withdrawals $\frac{1}{19}$ of the balance in the account on January 1, 2005, $\frac{1}{18}$ of the balance on January 1, 2006,..., $\frac{1}{2}$ of the balance on January 1, 2022, and the entire balance on January 1, 2023. Find an expression for the amount of the withdrawal on January 1, $2004 + t$, for $t = 1, 2, ..., 19$.

*2.3.28 On January 1 Smith deposits 100,000 in an account earning interest at rate $i^{(12)} = .09$, credited on the final day of each month.

(a) Suppose Smith withdraws 1000 on the first day of each month starting on February 1. Smith continues the withdrawals as long as possible with a smaller withdrawal one month after the final regular withdrawal of 1000. Find the number of regular withdrawals and the date and amount of the final smaller withdrawal.

(b) Instead of level withdrawals of 1000 each, let Smith's monthly withdrawals start at 1000 on February 1, and increase by 10 each month (March 1 is 1010, April 1 is 1020, and so on). Withdrawals continue in this pattern for as long as possible with a final smaller withdrawal one month after the last regular increasing withdrawal. Find the number of regular withdrawals and the date and amount of the final smaller withdrawal.

(c) Repeat part (b) assuming that the withdrawals grow by 1% per month, so that March 1 is 1010, April 1 is 1020.10, and so on.

(d) For each of parts (a), (b), and (c) find the total amount withdrawn, and explain the relationship among the three totals.

*2.3.29    Each year on Smith's child's birthday, Smith makes a deposit of 100 multiplied by the child's age (100 on the $1^{st}$ birthday, 200 on the $2^{nd}$, and so on) to an account earning effective annual interest rate $i$. The final deposit is on the child's $12^{th}$ birthday. The account continues to accumulate, and on the child's $18^{th}$ birthday the balance is 17,177.70. Find $i$. The solution requires the use of a program such as EXCEL Solver or the cashflow worksheet of the BA II PLUS calculator.

*2.3.30    For $i > 0$ and $n > 1$, show that $(Ia)_{\overline{n}|} < \left(\frac{n+1}{2}\right) a_{\overline{n}|} < (Da)_{\overline{n}|}$.

*2.3.31    (a) An increasing perpetuity at effective annual interest rate $i$ has a payment once every $k$ years, with payment amounts $1, 2, 3, \ldots$ . Show that the present value of the perpetuity at the time of the first payment is $\dfrac{1}{\left(i \cdot a_{\overline{k}|}\right)^2}$.

(b) Find an expression for the present value of an increasing perpetuity-due with annual payments whose first $k$ payments are 1 each, next $k$ payments are 2 each, and so on, increasing in this way forever. Assume effective annual interest rate $i$.

*2.3.32    Show in Example 2.23 that $i > 0$ if $L < \sum\limits_{s=1}^{n} K_s$, and $i < 0$ if $L > \sum\limits_{s=1}^{n} K_s$.

*2.3.33    Suppose that $K_1, K_2, \ldots, K_n$ are payments made to an account at times $0 < t_1 < t_2 < \cdots < t_n$. Show that if $L > 0$, then there is a unique interest rate $i > -1$ for which $L$ is the accumulated value of the series of payments at time $t_n$.

*2.3.34   A perpetuity-due with annual payments pays 1 now, $1+2=3$ in one year, $1+2+3 = 6$ in two years,..., $1+2+\cdots+n$ in $n-1$ years, and so on. Show that the present value of this perpetuity-due is $\ddot{a}_{\overline{\infty}|} \cdot (I\ddot{a})_{\overline{\infty}|}$.

*2.3.35   A $(2n-1)$-payment annuity has payments in the pattern $1, 2, \ldots,$ $n-1, n, n-1, n-2, \ldots, 2, 1$. Show that the present value of this annuity one payment period before the first payment is $\ddot{a}_{\overline{n}|} \cdot a_{\overline{n}|}$.

*2.3.36   Show that $\frac{\ddot{a}_{\overline{n}|}}{i}$ is the present value of a perpetuity-immediate whose payments increase by 1 per period for n periods, from 1 to $n$, and then remain level at $n$ forever.

*2.3.37   (a) Show that $\lim_{m \to \infty} (I^{(m)}a)_{\overline{n}|}^{(m)} = (\overline{I}\,\overline{a})_{\overline{n}|}$.

(b) $\lim_{m \to \infty} (Ia)_{\overline{n}|}^{(m)}$ is denoted $(I\overline{a})_{\overline{n}|}$. Give a verbal description of this expression.

*2.3.38   A general continuous annuity has rate of payment $h(t)$ at time $t$, $t > 0$, and had an initial discrete payment of $F_0$ at time 0. If the force of interest is $\delta$ and $F_t$ denotes the accumulated value in the fund at time $t$, show that $\frac{d}{dt} F_t = \delta \cdot F_t + h(t)$.

*2.3.39   (a) If $h(t) = n - t, 0 \le t \le n$, in the general continuously varying annuity, the present value is denoted $(\overline{D}\overline{a})_{\overline{n}|}$. Using integration by parts, derive an expression for $(\overline{D}\overline{a})_{\overline{n}|}$. Show that $(\overline{I}\overline{a})_{\overline{n}|} + (\overline{D}\overline{a})_{\overline{n}|} = n \cdot \overline{a}_{\overline{n}|}$.

(b) Show that $(\overline{I}\overline{a})_{\overline{n}|} = \int_0^n {}_t|\overline{a}_{\overline{n-t}|}\, dt$ and $(\overline{D}\overline{a})_{\overline{n}|} = \int_0^n \overline{a}_{\overline{t}|}\, dt$.

*2.3.40    An $n$-payment annuity has the following series of payments:

$$A, A+B, A+2B, \ldots, A+(n-1)B$$

Formulate expressions in terms of level and increasing annuity notation for the present value of the series of payments one period before the first payment, and the accumulated value of the series at the time of the final payment.

## SECTION 2.4

2.4.1    Jones buys from Smith the right to receive 20 annual payments of 1000 each beginning 1 year hence.

(a) In their discussion regarding this transaction, Smith and Jones consider three ways of determining the amount Jones must pay to Smith. Find this amount according to each of the following approaches:

(i)  The present value at $i = .12$.

(ii) A price to yield Jones an annual return of 12% while recovering his principal in a sinking fund earning an annual rate of 6%.

(iii) Accumulate the payments at 6% and then find the present value at 12% of that accumulated value.

(b) Jones calculates his annual rate of return a number of different ways. In case (iii) of part (a) Jones earns an annual rate of return of 12% for the 20 years  Find his annual "yield" according to each of the following approaches.

(i)  In part (a)(i) above, assume that Jones can reinvest the payments at 6% per year; find Jones' average annual compound rate of return based on the accumulated amount after 20 years compared to his initial investment.

(ii) Using the amount invested based on the approach in (a)(ii) as the present value of the annuity, find the unknown interest rate (internal rate of return).

(iii) Assuming that the full 1000 is deposited in the sinking fund at 6%, find the average annual compound rate of return over the 20 years based on the accumulated value of the sinking fund and the initial amount invested in (a)(ii).

2.4.2　A loan is set up at periodic interest rate $i$, to be repaid by $n$ periodic payments of amount $K$ each. As the lender receives the payments, he reinvests them at interest rate $j$. Show that the average compound periodic rate of interest earned by the lender based on his initial outlay and his accumulated amount at time $n$ is $i'$, where $i'$ is the solution of the equation $(1+i')^n = \frac{s_{\overline{n}|j}}{a_{\overline{n}|i}}$.

Show also that $i'$ is between $i$ and $j$ (i.e., if $j < i$ then $j < i' < i$; if $i < j$ then $i < i' < j$; if $i = j$ then $i = i' = j$).

2.4.3　An investor is considering the purchase of an annuity of $K$ per year for $n$ years, starting one year from the purchase date. He calculates a purchase price on each of two bases: (i) the present value of the annuity at rate $i$ per year, resulting in price $P_1$, and (ii) the sinking fund method with annual return of $i$ per year (same $i$ as in (i)), recovering the principal in a sinking fund with an accumulation rate of $j$ per year, resulting in price $P_2$.

Derive the following relationships by comparing $\frac{1}{P_1}$ and $\frac{1}{P_2}$ and using the identity $\frac{1}{s_{\overline{n}|k}} + k = \frac{1}{a_{\overline{n}|k}}$.

(i)　$P_1 = P_2$ if $i = j$

(ii)　$P_1 > P_2$ if $i > j$

(iii)　$P_1 < P_2$ if $i < j$

2.4.4　Repeat Example 2.29 in each of the following cases

(a) If the equipment has a salvage value after 10 years of 10,000, find the purchase price based on the sinking fund method using the same $i$ and $j$ as before.

(b) Find the salvage value for which the purchase price would be 85,000 based on the sinking fund method using the same $i$ and $j$ as before.

2.4.5　Repeat Example 2.30 by showing that $\frac{d}{dj} P_2 > 0$.

2.4.6   The average periodic compound yield rate earned over an $n$-period term on an annuity of 1 per period whose payments earn initial interest of $i$ per period which is then reinvested at rate $j$ is $i'$, where $s_{\overline{n}|i'} = n + i \cdot (Is)_{\overline{n-1}|j}$. Show that $i'$ lies between $i$ and $j$, and that if $i = j$ then $i' = i = j$.

2.4.7   A purchaser pays 245,000 for a mine which will be exhausted at the end of 18 years. What level annual revenue (received at the end of each year) is required in order for the purchaser to receive a 5% annual return on his investment if he can recover his principal in a sinking fund earning 3.5% per year?

2.4.8   Smith wishes to purchase an increasing annuity with 20 annual payments of 1000, 2000, 3000,..., 20,000. Smith considers the following three methods of valuing the annuity one period before the first payment. Find the purchase price in each case.

(a) Present value method at $i = .10$.

(b) Sinking fund method, earning annual interest of 10% on the initial investment and recovering the initial investment in a sinking fund earning 6% per year. (Note that this involves negative sinking fund deposits for several years, which is algebraically feasible but unrealistic from a practical point of view.)

(c) Capitalizing unpaid interest each year at rate 10%: with initial investment $P_0$ the outstanding balance at time 1 is $P_1 = P_0(1.10) - 1000$; at time 2 it is $P_2 = P_1(1.10) - 2000$, and so on. This continues until $P_t$ is such that the payments are large enough to support the sinking fund method with a purchase price of $P_t$, and Smith earns 10% per year on $P_t$ for the remaining years while accumulating $P_t$ in a sinking fund earning interest at 6%.

2.4.9   Machine I costs $X$, has a salvage value of $\frac{X}{8}$, and is to be depreciated over 10 years using the declining balance method.

Machine II costs $Y$, has a salvage value of $\frac{X}{8}$, and is to be depreciated over 10 years using the sum-of-the-years digits method.

The total amount of depreciation in the first seven years for Machine I equals the total amount of depreciation in the first seven
years for Machine II. Calculate $\frac{Y}{X}$.

2.4.10   A copier costs $X$ and will have a salvage value of $Y$ after $n$ years.

(i)   Using the straight line method, the annual depreciation expense is 1000.

(ii)  Using the sum of the years digits method, the depreciation
expense in year 3 is 800.

(iii) Using the declining balance method, the depreciation expense is
33.125% of the book value in the beginning of the year.

Calculate $X$.

2.4.11   A manufacturer buys a machine for 20,000. The manufacturer estimates that the machine will last 15 years. It will be depreciated using
the constant percentage method with an annual depreciation rate of
20%. At the end of each year, the manufacturer deposits an amount
into a fund that pays 6% annually. Each deposit is equal to the depreciation expense for that year. How much money will the manufacturer have accumulated in the fund at the end of 15 years?

2.4.12   A machine is purchased for 5000 and has a salvage value of $S$ at
the end of 10 years. The machine is depreciated using the sum-
of-the-years-digits method.

At the end of year 4, the machine has a book value of 2218. At
that time, the depreciation method is changed to the straight-line
method for the remaining years. Determine the new depreciation
charge for year 8.

# CHAPTER 3

## LOAN REPAYMENT

*"Before borrowing money from a friend, decide which you need most."*
*– American Proverb*

When a loan is being repaid by a series of payments, the total of all payments must retire the original amount of the loan (the principal) as well as provide interest on the loan. It is usually the case that each loan payment can be separated into two components, the amount of interest and the amount of principal. There are several ways in which a loan repayment scheme can be set up, each of which specifies the division of payments into interest and principal. In this chapter we will consider various loan repayment methods. The most common one is the **amortization method**.

## 3.1 THE AMORTIZATION METHOD OF LOAN REPAYMENT

The definition and basic properties of an amortized loan can best be described by means of a simple illustration. We consider a loan of amount 1000 with an interest rate of 10% per year. Suppose that there is a payment of 200 at the end of 1 year, a payment of 500 at the end of 2 years, and a final payment at the end of 3 years to completely repay the loan. At the end of the first year, before the first payment is made, the amount owed, including interest, is $1000(1.10) = 1100$. The payment of 200 reduces the amount owed to 900 just after the first payment; this is the outstanding balance on the loan just after the first payment is made. At the end of the second year, before the second payment is made, the amount owed is $900(1.10) = 990$. The payment of 500 reduces the outstanding balance to 490 just after the second payment. At the end of the third year, before the third payment is made, the amount owed is $490(1.10) = 539$. This is the amount needed to completely repay the loan at the end of the third year.

This illustration captures a defining feature of an amortized loan. Each time a payment is made, the outstanding balance from the previous payment point is accumulated with interest to the current payment point, and the new pay-

171

ment is subtracted from that accumulated amount, resulting in the new outstanding balance at the current point.

Another important aspect of an amortized loan is the separation of each payment into interest and principal. Continuing the illustration, we see that at the end of the first year there will be interest of 100 owed on the loan, along with the previous original loan balance of 1000. The amortization method requires that whenever a payment is made, interest is paid first, and any amount remaining is applied toward reducing the loan balance. Therefore, for the payment of 200 made at the end of the first year, 100 is interest paid, and the remaining 100 is principal repaid. The outstanding loan balance is reduced by 100 from 1000 to 900. At the end of the second year there will be interest of 90 (10% of 900). Using the amortization method, the payment of 500 at the end of the second year is composed of an interest payment of 90, and the principal repaid is 410. The outstanding balance after the second payment is 490 (the previous balance of 900 minus the 410 in principal just paid). At the end of the third year there will be interest due of 49 (10% of 490). The total payment required to completely repay the loan at the end of the third year is the interest payment of 49 plus the principal amount of 490 still owed; the total payment required is 539.

Considering this illustration a little further we see that the outstanding loan balance can be updated from one point to the next as follows.

$$1000(1.10) - 200 = 900, \ 900(1.10) - 500 = 490, \ 490(1.10) - 539 = 0.$$

Combining these expressions, we get

$$1000(1.10)^3 - 200(1.10)^2 - 500(1.10) - 539 = 0.$$

This can also be written in the form $1000 = 200v + 500v^2 + 539v^3$. We have illustrated another important aspect of the loan amortization method, the original loan amount is equal to the present value of the loan payments using the loan interest rate above.

Another point to note about the example is that the total amount paid is 1239, which is 239 above the original loan amount of 1000. Therefore, the total amount of interest paid over the loan period is 239. We also saw that interest paid in the three payments was 100, 90, and 49 for a total amount of 239 during the course of the loan.

### 3.1.1 THE GENERAL AMORTIZATION METHOD

---

**Definition 3.1 – Amortized Loan**

An amortized loan of amount $L$ made at time 0 at periodic interest rate $i$ and to be repaid by $n$ payments of amounts $K_1, K_2, \ldots, K_n$ at times $1, 2, \ldots, n$ (where the payment period corresponds to the interest period) is based on the equation

$$L = K_1 v + K_2 v^2 + \cdots + K_n v^n. \tag{3.1}$$

---

The simplest example of a loan repayment is one in which a loan made at a specified point in time is to be repaid by a single payment at some later point in time. If a loan is to be repaid one interest period later, the amount of that single payment is $L(1+i) = L + L \cdot i$. It is clear that in this payment $L$ represents the repayment of the original principal on the loan, and $L \cdot i$ is a payment of interest due. Just before the payment is made the accumulated amount owed is $L(1+i)$, and the payment of that amount reduces the amount owed to zero.

Suppose that the payment made after one period, say $K_1$, is somewhat less than $L(1+i)$. In this case the loan is not fully repaid by the payment of $K_1$, and there remains a balance owed, called the **outstanding balance** or *outstanding principal*. The amount of the outstanding balance just after that first payment is the unpaid part of the loan, so that

$$OB_1 = L(1+i) - K_1. \tag{3.2}$$

The process involved in the amortization method of loan repayment can be described by reformulating Equation (3.2) as

$$OB_1 = L(1+i) - K_1 = L - (K_1 - Li). \tag{3.3}$$

$Li$ represents the accrued interest on the original principal amount for the period. The payment of $K_1$ is regarded as first paying the accrued interest, $Li$, and the remainder of the payment, $K_1 - Li$, is applied to reduce the principal, or balance owed. Therefore the outstanding balance that remains is equal to the initial balance owed minus the amount of principal repaid. Thus $L - (K_1 - Li) = OB_1$. In the example presented in the previous section with $L=1000$, $i=.10$ and $K_1 = 200$, we see that $OB_1 = 1000(1.10)-200 = 900$, $Li = 1000(.1) = 100$ is the interest paid in the first payment, and $K_1 - Li = 200-100 = 100$ is the principal paid in the first payment.

We will now denote the initial loan amount $L$ by $OB_0$, the outstanding balance at time 0. At the end of the first period the loan has accumulated, with interest, to $OB_0(1+i)$. The payment of amount $K_1$ is then applied, so that the resulting outstanding balance at time 1 (just after the first payment) is $OB_1 = OB_0(1+i) - K_1$. This relationship can also be written as $OB_1 = OB_0 - (K_1 - OB_0 \times i)$, where $OB_0 \times i = I_1$ represents the amount of **interest paid** at the end of the first period, and $K_1 - OB_0 \times i = K_1 - I_1 = PR_1$ represents the amount applied to reduce the outstanding balance. Thus $PR_1$ is the amount of **principal repaid** by the first payment. Then we have

$$OB_1 \;=\; OB_0 - (K_1 - OB_0 \times i) \;=\; OB_0 - (K_1 - I_1) \;=\; OB_0 - PR_1.$$

This process can now be extended to the end of the second payment period, where we have an accumulated balance of $OB_1(1+i)$ which is then reduced by the second payment $K_2$, resulting in an outstanding balance just after the second payment of $OB_2 = OB_1(1+i) - K_2$. This can be rewritten as

$$\begin{aligned} OB_2 \;=\; OB_1(1+i) - K_2 \;&=\; OB_1 - (K_2 - OB_1 \times i) \\ &=\; OB_1 - (K_2 - I_2) \;=\; OB_1 - PR_2. \end{aligned}$$

In this expression, $I_2 = OB_1 \times i$ is the interest due at the end of the second period, and $PR_2 = K_2 - I_2$ is applied to repay principal. This process continues from one payment period to the next. Just after the $t^{th}$ payment there will be an outstanding balance of $OB_t$. During the following period this outstanding balance will accumulate with interest to $OB_t(1+i)$, at which time the $t+1^{st}$ payment $K_{t+1}$ is made so that the outstanding balance is

$$OB_{t+1} \;=\; OB_t(1+i) - K_{t+1}. \tag{3.4}$$

This can be rewritten as

$$OB_{t+1} = OB_t - (K_{t+1} - OB_t \times i) = OB_t - (K_{t+1} - I_{t+1}) = OB_t - PR_{t+1}. \tag{3.5}$$

The interest due at the end of the $t+1^{st}$ period is

$$I_{t+1} = OB_t \times i \qquad (3.6)$$

The part of the $t+1^{st}$ payment which is applied to repay principal is

$$PR_{t+1} = K_{t+1} - I_{t+1} \qquad (3.7)$$

This pattern of interest paid and principal reduction continues until the time of the $n^{th}$, and final, payment, which reduces the outstanding balance to zero. That is, $OB_n = OB_{n-1}(1+i) - K_n = 0$. Therefore, we see that each payment can be decomposed into a part that pays the interest that has accrued since the last payment and a part that repays some of the principal outstanding. The following time diagram illustrates the successive outstanding balances as the amortization progresses.

| 0 | 1 | 2 | $\cdots$ | $t-1$ | | $t$ $\cdots$ |
|---|---|---|---|---|---|---|
| $OB_0 \longrightarrow$ | $OB_0(1+i)$ | $OB_1(1+i)$ | | | | $OB_{t-1}(1+i)$ |
| | $-K_1$ ↗ | $-K_2$ ↗ $\cdots$ | | ↗ | | $-K_t$ |
| | $= OB_1$ | $= OB_2$ | | $OB_{t-1}$ | | $= OB_t$ |

FIGURE 3.1

---

**Definition 3.2 – Components of a General Amortized Loan**

**Loan Amount L:**

Loan amount $L$ at interest rate $i$ per period, to be repaid by $n$ payments of amounts $K_1, K_2, \ldots, K_n$ at the end of $n$ successive periods.

**Outstanding balance just after payment at time $t$:**
$OB_t$ is the amount still owed on the loan just after the payment is made.

**Interest due in the payment at time $t$:**
$I_t$ is the interest on the outstanding balance since the previous payment was made.

**Principal repaid in the payment at time $t$:**
$PR_t$ is the part of the payment $K_t$ that is applied toward repaying loan principal.

### 3.1.2 THE AMORTIZATION SCHEDULE

The amortization of a loan as described above can be summarized in an *amortization schedule*, which sets out at each point in time the outstanding balance just after the payment made at that time, the interest paid, and the principal repaid. For the example from the previous section with $L = 1000$, $i = .10$, $K_1 = 200$, $K_2 = 500$ and $K_3 = 539$, we can summarize the various components of the amortization as follows.

**TABLE 3.1**

| $t$ | Payment | Interest Due | Principal Repaid | Outstanding Balance |
|---|---|---|---|---|
| 0 | – | – | – | $L = OB_0 = 1000$ |
| 1 | **200** | $I_1 = OB_0 \times i$ $= 1000(.1)$ $= 100$ | $PR_1 = K_1 - I_1$ $= 200 - 100$ $= 100$ | $OB_1 = OB_0 - PR_1$ $= 1000 - 100$ $= 900$ |
| 2 | **500** | $I_2 = OB_1 \times i$ $= 900(.1)$ $= 90$ | $PR_2 = K_2 - I_2$ $= 500 - 90$ $= 410$ | $OB_2 = OB_1 - PR_2$ $= 900 - 410$ $= 490$ |
| 3 | **539** | $I_3 = OB_2 \times i$ $= 490(.1)$ $= 49$ | $PR_3 = K_3 - I_3$ $= 539 - 49$ $= 490$ | $OB_3 = OB_2 - PR_3$ $= 490 - 490$ $= 0$ |

Table 3.2 illustrates the entries in an amortization table in a general way.

**TABLE 3.2**

| $t$ | Payment | Interest Due | Principal Repaid | Outstanding Balance |
|---|---|---|---|---|
| 0 | – | – | – | $L = OB_0$ |
| 1 | $K_1$ | $I_1 = OB_0 \times i$ | $PR_1 = K_1 - I_1$ | $OB_1 = OB_0 - PR_1$ |
| 2 | $K_2$ | $I_2 = OB_1 \times i$ | $PR_2 = K_2 - I_2$ | $OB_2 = OB_1 - PR_2$ |
| ⋮ | ⋮ | ⋮ | ⋮ | ⋮ |
| $t$ | | | | $OB_t$ |
| $t+1$ | $K_{t+1}$ | $I_{t+1} = OB_t \times i$ | $PR_{t+1} = K_{t+1} - I_{t+1}$ | $OB_{t+1} = OB_t - PR_{t+1}$ |
| ⋮ | ⋮ | ⋮ | ⋮ | ⋮ |
| $n$ | $K_n$ | $I_n = OB_{n-1} \times i$ | $PR_n = K_n - I_n$ | $OB_n = OB_{n-1} - PR_n$ |

From Table 3.2 we see that the total amount paid during the course of repaying the loan is $K_T = \sum_{t=1}^{n} K_t$, of which $I_T = \sum_{t=1}^{n} I_t$, is the total interest paid over the course of the loan, and the total principal repaid is $K_T - I_T = \sum_{t=1}^{n} (K_t - I_t) = L = OB_0$. Note that total interest paid $I_T$ can be written as

$$I_T = \sum I_t = \sum (OB_{t-1} \times i)$$
$$= i \times \sum OB_{t-1} = i[OB_0 + OB_1 + \cdots + OB_{n-1}]. \quad (3.8)$$

If the final loan payment occurs at time $n$ to completely repay the loan, then $OB_n = 0$.

| EXAMPLE 3.1 | (*Amortization table*)

A loan of amount 1000 at a nominal annual interest rate of 12% compounded monthly is repaid by 6 monthly payments, starting one month after the loan is made. The first three payments are amount $X$ each and the final three payments are amount $2X$ each. Construct the amortization schedule for this loan.

| SOLUTION |

To solve for $X$ we have $1000 = Xa_{\overline{3}|.01} + 2Xv^3 a_{\overline{3}|.01}$ as the equation of value, so that $X = 115.61$ to the nearest cent and $2X = 231.21$ to the nearest cent. The amortization schedule, with $t$ measured in months, is given in Table 3.3. The exact value of $OB_6$ is 0, and the value of $-.01$ in the schedule is due to roundoff error which accumulates in the calculation of all quantities to the nearest cent. In practice the final payment would have been increased by 1 cent to 231.22 in order to reduce $OB_6$ to zero. If $X$ and the various quantities in the schedule had been calculated with a few additional digits of accuracy, the value of $OB_6$ would be closer to its exact value of zero. The total amount paid on the loan is 1040.46, of which 40.47 is interest and 1000 (999.99 because of roundoff) is principal repayment.

TABLE 3.3

| $t$ | Payment | Interest Due | Principal Repaid | Outstanding Balance |
|---|---|---|---|---|
| 0 | – | – | – | $L = OB_0 = 1000$ |
| 1 | $K_1 = 115.61$ | $I_1 = OB_0 \times i$ $= 10$ | $PR_1 = K_1 - I_1$ $= 105.61$ | $OB_1 = OB_0 - PR_1$ $= 894.39$ |
| 2 | $K_2 = 115.61$ | $I_2 = OB_1 \times i$ $= 8.94$ | $PR_2 = K_2 - I_2$ $= 106.67$ | $OB_2 = OB_1 - PR_2$ $= 787.72$ |
| 3 | $K_3 = 115.61$ | $I_3 = OB_2 \times i$ $= 7.88$ | $PR_3 = K_3 - I_3$ $= 107.73$ | $OB_3 = OB_2 - PR_3$ $= 679.99$ |
| 4 | $K_4 = 231.21$ | $I_4 = OB_3 \times i$ $= 6.80$ | $PR_4 = K_4 - I_4$ $= 224.41$ | $OB_4 = OB_3 - PR_4$ $= 455.58$ |
| 5 | $K_5 = 231.21$ | $I_5 = OB_4 \times i$ $= 4.56$ | $PR_5 = K_5 - I_5$ $= 226.65$ | $OB_5 = OB_4 - PR_5$ $= 228.93$ |
| 6 | $K_6 = 231.21$ | $I_6 = OB_5 \times i$ $= 2.29$ | $PR_6 = K_6 - I_6$ $= 228.92$ | $OB_6 = OB_5 - PR_6$ $= .01$ |
| Totals | 1040.46 | 40.47 | 999.99 | |

❐

### 3.1.3 RETROSPECTIVE FORM OF THE OUTSTANDING BALANCE

If we follow the amortization process from one period to the next for the general $n$-payment loan we see that the successive outstanding balance amounts can be formulated as

$$OB_1 = OB_0(1+i) - K_1$$
$$OB_2 = OB_1(1+i) - K_2 = OB_0(1+i)^2 - K_1(1+i) - K_2$$
$$OB_3 = OB_2(1+i) - K_3 = OB_0(1+i)^3 - K_1(1+i)^2 - K_2(1+i) - K_3$$
$$\vdots$$
$$OB_t = OB_0(1+i)^t - K_1(1+i)^{t-1} - K_2(1+i)^{t-2} - \cdots - K_{t-1}(1+i) - K_t$$
$$\vdots$$
$$OB_n = OB_0(1+i)^n - K_1(1+i)^{n-1} - K_2(1+i)^{n-2} - \cdots - K_{n-1}(1+i) - K_n = 0.$$

The general relationship given by

$$OB_t = OB_0(1+i)^t - K_1(1+i)^{t-1} - K_2(1+i)^{t-2} - \cdots - K_{t-1}(1+i) - K_t \quad (3.9)$$

is the **retrospective method** of formulating the outstanding balance of the loan just after the $t^{th}$ payment. The retrospective method formulates $OB_t$ as the amount of the original loan accumulated to time $t$ $\left(L(1+i)^t = OB_0(1+i)^t\right)$, minus the accumulated value of all payments to time $t$, up to and including $K_t$.

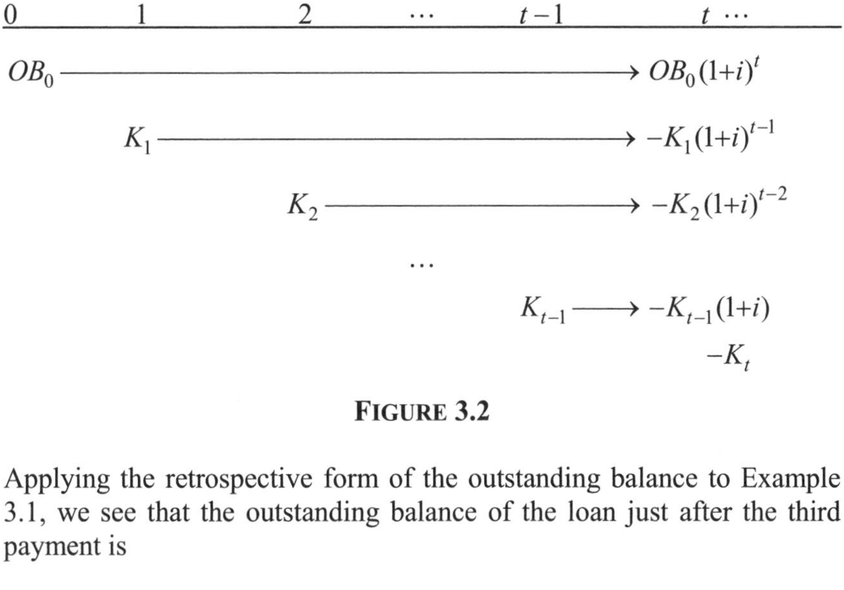

| 0 | 1 | 2 | $\cdots$ | $t-1$ | $t$ $\cdots$ |

$OB_0 \longrightarrow OB_0(1+i)^t$

$K_1 \longrightarrow -K_1(1+i)^{t-1}$

$K_2 \longrightarrow -K_2(1+i)^{t-2}$

$\cdots$

$K_{t-1} \longrightarrow -K_{t-1}(1+i)$

$-K_t$

**FIGURE 3.2**

Applying the retrospective form of the outstanding balance to Example 3.1, we see that the outstanding balance of the loan just after the third payment is

$$OB_3 = 1000(1.01)^3 - 115.61(1.01)^2 - 115.61(1.01) - 115.61$$
$$= 1000(1.01)^3 - 115.61 s_{\overline{3}|.01} = 679.99.$$

In a general amortization, the loan is completely repaid by the $n^{th}$ payment, so

$$OB_n = OB_0(1+i)^n - K_1(1+i)^{n-1} - K_2(1+i)^{n-2} - \cdots - K_{n-1}(1+i) - K_n = 0.$$

Multiplying both sides of this equation by $v^n$ and rearranging the terms we have

$$L = OB_0 = K_1v + K_2v^2 + \cdots + K_nv^n. \tag{3.1}$$

This is a restatement of the relationship showing that the loan amount is equal to the present value of the loan payments.

### 3.1.4 PROSPECTIVE FORM OF THE OUTSTANDING BALANCE

The general retrospective form of the outstanding balance at time $t$ is given by Equation (3.9). If we replace $OB_0$ in that equation by

$$OB_0 = K_1v + K_2v^2 + \cdots + K_nv^n,$$

from Equation (3.1), then Equation (3.9) is transformed into

$$OB_t = \left[ K_1v + K_2v^2 + \cdots + K_tv^t + K_{t+1}v^{t+1} + \cdots + K_nv^n \right](1+i)^t$$
$$- K_1(1+i)^{t-1} - K_2(1+i)^{t-2} - \cdots - K_{t-1}(1+i) - K_t$$
$$= K_{t+1}v + K_{t+2}v^2 + \cdots + K_nv^{n-t}. \tag{3.10}$$

Thus we see that $OB_t$ is equal to the present value, *at time t*, of all remaining payments from time $t+1$ onward, but not including the payment just made at time $t$. This is the **prospective form** of the outstanding balance, and it is algebraically equivalent to the retrospective form. Just as the original loan amount is the present value of the loan payments, the amount owed at any point in time is the present value of the remaining payments.

| 0 | 1 | 2 | $\cdots$ | $t$ | $t+1$ | $t+2$ | $\cdots$ | $n$ |
|---|---|---|---|---|---|---|---|---|
| | | | | $\uparrow$ | | | | |
| | | | | $OB_t$ | $K_{t+1}$ | $K_{t+2}$ | $\cdots$ | $K_n$ |

**FIGURE 3.3**

In Example 3.1 we can apply the prospective form to find $OB_3$ as

$$OB_3 = 231.21v + 231.21v^2 + 231.21v^3 = 231.21a_{\overline{3}|.01} = 679.98,$$

where the difference from the retrospective $OB_3$ value of 679.99 is due to roundoff error.

### 3.1.5 ADDITIONAL PROPERTIES OF AMORTIZATION

#### 3.1.5.1 *Non-Level Interest Rate*

In the discussion of the amortization method given above, it was assumed that the interest rate on the loan remained unchanged from one period to the next. The amortization method can also be applied when the interest rate changes over time. Let $i_1$ denote the interest rate for the first period, which runs from time 0 to time 1, $i_2$ denotes the interest rate for the second period, and so on, with the interest rate for the $t+1^{st}$ period denoted by $i_{t+1}$. Then the amortization relationships become

$$
\begin{aligned}
OB_1 &= OB_0(1+i_1) - K_1 \\
&= OB_0 - (K_1 - OB_0 \times i_1) = OB_0 - (K_1 - I_1) \\
&= OB_0 - PR_1,
\end{aligned} \tag{3.11}
$$

and, in general,

$$
\begin{aligned}
OB_{t+1} &= OB_t - (K_{t+1} - OB_t \times i_{t+1}) \\
&= OB_t - (K_{t+1} - I_{t+1}) \\
&= OB_t - PR_{t+1}.
\end{aligned} \tag{3.12}
$$

---

| EXAMPLE 3.2 | *(Non-level interest rates)* |

A loan of amount 1000 is repaid by 6 monthly payments, starting one month after the loan is made. The interest rate for the first three months is a nominal annual rate of 12% compounded monthly, and the interest rate for the next three months is a nominal annual rate of 6% compounded monthly. The first three payments are amount $X$ each and the final three payments are amount $2X$ each. Construct the amortization schedule for this loan.

---

**SOLUTION**

To solve for $X$ we have $1000 = Xa_{\overline{3}|.01} + 2X v_{.01}^3 \, a_{\overline{3}|.005}$ as the equation of value, so that $X = 114.85$ to the nearest cent and $2X = 229.71$ to the nearest cent. The amortization table for this loan is in Table 3.4.

**TABLE 3.4**

| $t$ | Payment | Interest Due | Principal Repaid | Outstanding Balance |
|---|---|---|---|---|
| 0 | – | – | – | $L = OB_0 = 1000$ |
| 1 | $K_1 = 114.85$ | $I_1 = OB_0 \times i$ $= 10$ | $PR_1 = K_1 - I_1$ $= 104.85$ | $OB_1 = OB_0 - PR_1$ $= 895.15$ |
| 2 | $K_2 = 114.85$ | $I_2 = OB_1 \times i$ $= 8.95$ | $PR_2 = K_2 - I_2$ $= 105.90$ | $OB_2 = OB_1 - PR_2$ $= 789.25$ |
| 3 | $K_3 = 114.85$ | $I_3 = OB_2 \times i$ $= 7.89$ | $PR_3 = K_3 - I_3$ $= 106.96$ | $OB_3 = OB_2 - PR_3$ $= 682.29$ |
| 4 | $K_4 = 229.71$ | $I_4 = OB_3 \times i$ $= 3.41$ | $PR_4 = K_4 - I_4$ $= 226.30$ | $OB_4 = OB_3 - PR_4$ $= 455.99$ |
| 5 | $K_5 = 229.71$ | $I_5 = OB_4 \times i$ $= 2.28$ | $PR_5 = K_5 - I_5$ $= 227.43$ | $OB_5 = OB_4 - PR_5$ $= 228.56$ |
| 6 | $K_6 = 229.71$ | $I_6 = OB_5 \times i$ $= 1.14$ | $PR_6 = K_6 - I_6$ $= 228.57$ | $OB_6 = OB_5 - PR_6$ $= -.01$ |
| Totals | 1033.68 | 33.67 | 1000.01 | |

❑

### 3.1.5.2 *Capitalization of Interest*

In Example 3.1 the interest amounts are relatively small compared to the actual loan payments, and the excess of the total payment amount over the interest due, $K_t - I_t$, is equal to the principal repaid in that payment, $PR_t$. It is possible that during the repayment of a loan by the amortization method, a particular payment is not large enough to cover the interest due $(K_t < I_t)$, so there is a shortfall of $I_t - K_t$ in the payment of interest. For instance, this will happen if an originally scheduled payment is missed. In this case $PR_t$, the amount of principal repaid, is negative $(PR_t < 0)$. Algebraically the new outstanding balance just after the $t^{th}$ payment is $OB_t = OB_{t-1} - PR_t$, and since $PR_t < 0$ we find that $OB_t = OB_{t-1} - (K_t - I_t) = OB_{t-1} + (I_t - K_t) > OB_{t-1}$. In other words the *outstanding balance increases by the amount of unpaid interest*. The unpaid interest is **capitalized** and added to the balance still owed. For the purpose of dividing payments into interest and principal, the unpaid interest, which will accumulate as time goes on, should still be regarded as interest when payments are made at a later time.

| EXAMPLE 3.3 | *(Capitalization of interest)*

A loan of 100,000 has payments at the end of each month for 12 years. For the first 6 years the payments are $Z$ each month, and for the final 6 years the payments are $2Z$ each month. Interest is at a nominal annual rate of 12% compounded monthly. Find the outstanding balance at the end of the first year.

| SOLUTION |

The initial amortization relationship is

$$100,000 = Z\, a_{\overline{72}|.01} + 2Z\, v_{.01}^{72}\, a_{\overline{72}|.005}$$

Solving for $Z$ results in $Z = 988.89$.

The interest due at the end of the first month is 1000, but the payment is only 988.89. The shortfall of 11.11 is added to the loan amount so that $OB_1 = 100,011.11$. This can also be seen algebraically from

$$OB_1 = OB_0(1+i) - Z_1 = 100,000(1.01) - 988.89 = 100,011.11.$$

The outstanding balance at the end of the first year (just after the $12^{th}$ monthly payment) can be expressed retrospectively as

$$OB_{12} = 100,000(1.01)^{12} - 988.89\, s_{\overline{12}|.01} = 100,140.90. \qquad \square$$

### 3.1.5.3 *Amortization with Level Payments of Principal*

Repayment via level payments is the most common form of repaying a loan. In such a case, the amounts of principal repaid increase from one payment to the next in a systematic way and the amounts of interest due decrease. Occasionally a loan repayment is structured to have specified amounts of principal repaid with each payment, along with payment of interest due on the previous period's outstanding balance. This is illustrated in the following example.

---

**EXAMPLE 3.4** (*Loan with level payments of principal*)

A loan of 3000 at an effective quarterly interest rate of $j = .02$ is amortized by means of 12 quarterly payments, beginning one quarter after the loan is made. Each payment consists of a principal repayment of 250 plus interest due on the previous quarter's outstanding balance. Construct the amortization schedule.

---

**SOLUTION**

With an initial outstanding balance of $L = OB_0 = 3000$, we have interest due at the end of the first quarter of amount $I_1 = 3000(.02) = 60$. Since the principal paid in the first payment is $PR_1 = 250$, the total amount of the first payment is $K_1 = I_1 + PR_1 = 310$. Then

$$OB_1 = OB_0 - PR_1 = 3000 - 250 = 2750.$$

Table 3.5 gives the full amortization schedule, where $t$ counts quarters.

**TABLE 3.5**

| $t$ | Payment | Interest Due | Principal Repaid | Outstanding Balance |
|---|---|---|---|---|
| 0 | – | – | – | $L = OB_0 = 3000$ |
| 1 | $K_1 = 310$ | $I_1 = OB_0 \times i = 60$ | $PR_1 = 250$ | $OB_1 = OB_0 - PR_1 = 2750$ |
| 2 | 305 | 55 | 250 | 2500 |
| 3 | 300 | 50 | 250 | 2250 |
| 4 | 295 | 45 | 250 | 2000 |
| 5 | 290 | 40 | 250 | 1750 |
| 6 | 285 | 35 | 250 | 1500 |
| 7 | 280 | 30 | 250 | 1250 |
| 8 | 275 | 25 | 250 | 1000 |
| 9 | 270 | 20 | 250 | 750 |
| 10 | 265 | 15 | 250 | 500 |
| 11 | 260 | 10 | 250 | 250 |
| 12 | 255 | 5 | 250 | 0 |

The total interest paid during the course of the loan is $60+55+\cdots+5 = 390$. Note that the present value, at quarterly rate 2%, of all payments is equal to 3000, satisfying the requirement of an amortized loan. ☐

### 3.1.5.4 *Interest Only With Lump Sum Principal Payment at the End*

Occasionally a loan will call for periodic payments of interest only, and a single payment of the full principal amount at the end of a specified term. Such a loan has interest payments of $I_1 = I_2 = \cdots = I_n = L \times i$, and principal payments of

$$PR_1 = PR_2 = \cdots = PR_{n-1} = 0 \quad \text{and} \quad PR_n = L. \qquad (3.13)$$

The outstanding balances are

$$OB_0 = L,$$
$$OB_1 = OB_0 - PR_1 = L,$$
$$OB_1 = L,\ldots,OB_{n-1} = L,$$
$$OB_n = OB_{n-1} - PR_n = L - L = 0. \qquad (3.14)$$

In this situation the borrower might accumulate the principal amount $L$ by means of deposits into an account during the lifetime or term of the loan. The deposit account is called a **sinking fund**, and this method of loan repayment is called the **sinking fund method**, and it is similar to the theory described in Chapter 2. The sinking fund method of loan repayment is considered in detail in Section 3.3.

## 3.2 AMORTIZATION OF A LOAN WITH LEVEL PAYMENTS

A loan is typically repaid with level payments, and if this is the case the amortization schedule has a systematic form. The original loan amount, based on the amortization method, is the present value of the payments. Suppose that each payment is of amount 1, so that $L = OB_0 = a_{\overline{n}|i}$, and $K_1 = K_2 = \cdots = K_n = 1$. The prospective form of the outstanding balance just after the $t^{th}$ payment is $OB_t = a_{\overline{n-t}|i}$, the present value of the remaining $n-t$ payments of amount 1 each. The retrospective form of the outstanding balance just after the $t^{th}$ payment is

$$OB_t = L(1+i)^t - Ks_{\overline{t}|i}.$$

This is algebraically equivalent to the prospective form:

$$OB_t = L(1+i)^t - Ks_{\overline{t}|i} = a_{\overline{n}|i}(1+i)^t - s_{\overline{t}|i}$$

$$= s_{\overline{t}|} + a_{\overline{n-t}|} - s_{\overline{t}|} = a_{\overline{n-t}|}. \qquad (3.15)$$

The full amortization schedule is shown in Table 3.6.

**TABLE 3.6**

| $t$ | Payment | Interest Due | Principal Repaid | Outstanding Balance |
|---|---|---|---|---|
| 0 | – | – | – | $L = OB_0 = a_{\overline{n}|}$ |
| 1 | $K_1 = 1$ | $\begin{aligned} I_1 &= OB_0 \times i \\ &= i\,a_{\overline{n}|} \\ &= 1 - v^n \end{aligned}$ | $\begin{aligned} PR_1 &= K_1 - I_1 \\ &= v^n \end{aligned}$ | $\begin{aligned} OB_1 &= OB_0 - PR_1 \\ &= a_{\overline{n}|} - v^n \\ &= a_{\overline{n-1}|} \end{aligned}$ |
| 2 | $K_2 = 1$ | $\begin{aligned} I_2 &= OB_1 \times i \\ &= i\,a_{\overline{n-1}|} \\ &= 1 - v^{n-1} \end{aligned}$ | $\begin{aligned} PR_2 &= K_2 - I_2 \\ &= v^{n-1} \end{aligned}$ | $\begin{aligned} OB_2 &= OB_1 - PR_2 \\ &= a_{\overline{n-1}|} - v^{n-1} \\ &= a_{\overline{n-2}|} \end{aligned}$ |
| ⋮ | | ⋮ | ⋮ | ⋮ |
| $t-1$ | | | | $OB_{t-1} = a_{\overline{n-t+1}|}$ |
| $t$ | $K_t = 1$ | $\begin{aligned} I_t &= OB_{t-1} \times i \\ &= i\,a_{\overline{n-t+1}|} \\ &= 1 - v^{n-t+1} \end{aligned}$ | $\begin{aligned} PR_t &= K_t - I_t \\ &= v^{n-t+1} \end{aligned}$ | $\begin{aligned} OB_t &= OB_{t-1} - PR_t \\ &= a_{\overline{n-t+1}|} - v^{n-t+1} \\ &= a_{\overline{n-t}|} \end{aligned}$ |
| ⋮ | | ⋮ | ⋮ | ⋮ |
| $n$ | $K_n = 1$ | $\begin{aligned} I_n &= OB_{n-1} \times i \\ &= i\,a_{\overline{1}|} \\ &= 1 - v \end{aligned}$ | $\begin{aligned} PR_n &= K_n - I_n \\ &= v \end{aligned}$ | $\begin{aligned} OB_n &= OB_{n-1} - PR_n \\ &= a_{\overline{1}|} - v \\ &= 0 \end{aligned}$ |

The total amount paid during the term of the loan is $K_T = n$ ($n$ payments of 1). The total amount of interest paid is

$$I_T = (1-v^n)+(1-v^{n-1})+\cdots+(1-v) = n-a_{\overline{n}|}, \qquad (3.16)$$

and the total principal repaid is

$$K_T - I_T = n-(n-a_{\overline{n}|}) = a_{\overline{n}|} = L, \qquad (3.17)$$

the original amount of the loan.

Another point to note about this amortization schedule concerns the principal repaid column. Moving down this column from time 1 to time 2 and onward, we see that

$$PR_2 = v^{n-1} = v^n(1+i) = PR_1(1+i),$$

and, in general,

$$PR_t = v^{n-t+1} = v^n(1+i)^{t-1} = PR_1(1+i)^{t-1}. \qquad (3.18)$$

This relationship involving the principal repaid amounts is valid provided the payments and the interest rate remain level. In Exercise 3.1.7 it is shown that if two successive payments on an amortized loan are equal ($K_t = K_{t+1}$) and if the corresponding periodic interest rates are also equal ($i_t = i_{t+1} = i$), then $PR_{t+1} = PR_t(1+i)$. In Example 3.1 where $K_1 = K_2 = K_3$, we expect that $PR_2 = PR_1(1+j)$ and $PR_3 = PR_2(1+j)$. This is easily verified since

$$PR_2 = 105.61(1.01) = 106.67$$

and

$$PR_3 = 106.67(1.01) = 107.74.$$

Furthermore, since $K_4 = K_5 = K_6$, we have $PR_4(1+j) = PR_5$ and $PR_5(1+j) = PR_6$. Note that $\frac{PR_4}{PR_3} = \frac{224.41}{107.74} = 2.083 \neq 1+j$, since $K_3 \neq K_4$.

---

**EXAMPLE 3.5**   (*A 30-year mortgage*)

A homebuyer borrows $250,000 to be repaid over a 30-year period with level monthly payments beginning one month after the loan is made. The interest rate on the loan is a nominal annual rate of 9% compounded monthly. Find each of the following:

(a) the amount of interest and the amount of principal paid in the first year,

(b) the amount of interest and the amount of principal paid in the $30^{th}$ year.

---

SOLUTION

The monthly interest rate is .75%, and the monthly payment is $K$, where $Ka_{\overline{360}|.0075} = 250,000$. Then $K = 2,011.556542$. In practice, the actual payment by the borrower would be rounded to the nearest .01 (cent). For the purpose of consistency in the algebraic relationships being illustrated, calculations will be based on full calculator accuracy without rounding.

(a) The outstanding balance at the end of the first year (12 months) is (prospectively) $2,011.556542\, a_{\overline{348}|.0075} = 248,292.0073$. The amount of principal paid in the first year is the amount by which the outstanding balance was reduced

$$250,000 - 248,292.0073 = 1,707.9927.$$

The total amount paid in the first year is the 12 payments of 2,011.556542 for a total of 24,138.6785. Of that total, 1,707.9927 was principal repaid, so the remaining

$$24,138.6785 - 1,707.9927 = 22,430.6858$$

was interest paid in the first year.

(b) The outstanding balance at the end of the $29^{th}$ year is (prospectively) $2,011.556542 a_{\overline{12}|.0075} = 23,001.9734$. Since the loan is completely repaid at the end of the $30^{th}$ year, the amount of principal repaid during the $30^{th}$ year must be the total amount of 23,001.9734 still outstanding when the $30^{th}$ year begins. The total amount paid in the $30^{th}$ year is still 12 payments of 2011.556542 for a total of 24,138.6785. Therefore, the total amount of interest paid in the $30^{th}$ year is

$$24,138.6785 - 23,001.9734 = 1,136.7051.$$

Notice that since this is a level payment amortization, the amount of principal repaid grows by a factor of 1.0075 from one month to the next. Therefore, for each payment in the $30^{th}$ year, the amount of principal repaid is $(1.0075)^{348}$ times as large as the principal paid in the corresponding payment in the first year (29 years or 348 months earlier). Therefore, the total principal paid in the $30^{th}$ year should be $1,707.9927 \times (1.0075)^{348} = 23,001.9728$. The amount of principal paid in the $30^{th}$ year calculated in (b) above is 23,001.9734. The difference from the value of 23,001.9728 is due to roundoff error within the calculator.

In practice, any discrepancies that arise due to roundoff error would be corrected when the loan is finally settled. For instance, if the payment is 2,011.56, the retrospective outstanding balance calculation at the end of the first year would be

$$250,000(1.0075)^{12} - 2,011.56s_{\overline{12}|.0075} = 248,291.96.$$

There is a difference of .05 between this value and the value found in part (a) based on more accuracy in the payment amount.

Some entries in the amortization table for this loan are in the following table.

TABLE 3.7

| $t$ | Payment | Interest Due | Principal Repaid | Outstanding Balance |
|---|---|---|---|---|
| 0 | 2011.56 | – | – | 250,000.00 |
| 1 | 2011.56 | 1875.00 | 136.56 | 249,863.44 |
| 2 | 2011.56 | 1873.98 | 137.58 | 249,725.86 |
| 3 | 2011.56 | 1872.94 | 138.62 | 249,587.25 |
| 4 | 2011.56 | 1871.90 | 139.65 | 249,447.60 |
| 5 | 2011.56 | 1870.86 | 140.70 | 249,306.90 |
| 6 | 2011.56 | 1869.80 | 141.75 | 249,165.14 |
| ⋮ | | ⋮ | ⋮ | ⋮ |
| 240 | 2011.56 | 1197.08 | 814.48 | 158,795.68 |
| ⋮ | | ⋮ | ⋮ | ⋮ |
| 300 | 2011.56 | 736.34 | 1275.22 | 96,903.46 |
| ⋮ | | ⋮ | ⋮ | ⋮ |
| 348 | 2011.56 | 186.20 | 1825.35 | 23,001.97 |
| ⋮ | | ⋮ | ⋮ | ⋮ |
| 358 | 2011.56 | 44.59 | 1966.97 | 3978.30 |
| 359 | 2011.56 | 29.84 | 1981.72 | 1996.58 |
| 360 | 2011.56 | 14.97 | 1996.58 | 0 |

❐

Figure 3.4 below shows two graphs of the outstanding balance over the lifetime of the loan in Example 3.5. The first graph was generated by a computer routine, and the second graph was taken from the financial calculation website www.dinkytown.net/java/SimpleLoan.html.

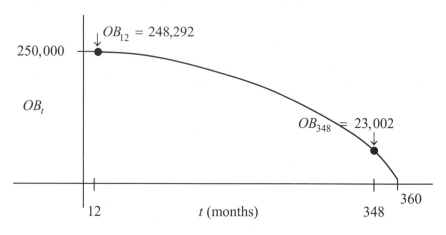

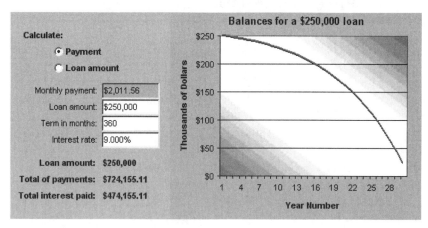

www.dinkytown.net/java/SimpleLoan.html

**FIGURE 3.4**

### 3.2.1 *Mortgage Loans in Canada*

**The Canada Interest Act of 1900**

The following is paragraph 6 of this statute first enacted by the federal parliament of Canada in 1900.

"**6.** Whenever any principal money or interest secured by mortgage on real property or hypothec on immovables is, by the mortgage or hypothec, made payable on a sinking fund plan, on any plan under which the payments of principal money and interest are blended or on any plan that involves an allowance of interest on stipulated repayments, no interest whatever shall be chargeable, payable or recoverable on any part of the principal money advanced, unless the mortgage or hypothec contains a statement showing the amount of the principal money and the rate of interest chargeable on that money, calculated yearly or half-yearly, not in advance."

As a result of this law, the interest rate on a mortgage on property in Canada must be quoted as either an annual effective rate of interest or a nominal annual rate of interest compounded semiannually, although almost all Canadian mortgages call for monthly payments. Canadian mortgage lenders almost universally quote mortgage interest rates as nominal annual rates compounded semiannually.

Source: Consolidated Statutes of Canada

If the loan in Example 3.5 was a Canadian mortgage, and if the interest rate of 9% was a nominal annual rate compounded semi-annually, then the equivalent monthly rate of interest would be $j = (1.045)^{1/6} - 1 = .00736312$. The monthly payment would be 1,982.08.

### 3.2.2 *Mortgage Loans in the US*

The loan interest rate quoted for a mortgage in the United States is, by law, a nominal annual rate of interest compounded monthly. This is the rate that is used to calculate the monthly payment on the loan. When a mortgage loan is arranged, there may be some fees and other costs associated with the loan. The *Annual Percentage Rate* (APR) is a measure of the cost of the loan in terms of an interest rate that takes into account the fees that must be paid.

Suppose that a loan is to be repaid with monthly payments for 30 years, and suppose that the quoted annual **loan rate** of $i$ is compounded monthly. Suppose that the loan has associated fees of amount $F$, that are payable at the time the loan is made. The result of the payment of these fees up front is that the borrower receives a net amount of $L - F$. The APR for the loan is a nominal annual rate of interest compounded monthly, say $i'$, with a corresponding monthly rate of $j' = \frac{i'}{12}$, and which satisfies the relationship $L - F = K a_{\overline{360}|j'}$. Note that the payment amount originally calculated based on the loan rate is used in the APR calculation. The APR will be larger than the loan rate when there are fees on the loan, because a larger interest rate is needed to make the present value smaller than the loan amount $L$.

**EXAMPLE 3.5 continued**    (*APR for a 30- year mortgage*)

Suppose that the loan has fees of $5,000 that are paid at the time of the loan. Find the APR on the loan.

**SOLUTION**

The APR will be $i'$, with corresponding monthly rate $j' = \frac{i'}{12}$, satisfying the relationship $250,000 - 5,000 = 2,011.56 a_{\overline{360}|j'}$. Using a calculator unknown interest function, we get $j' = .007689577$, so that the APR is $i' = 12 j' = .0922749$ (nominal annual rate of interest compounded monthly).

❑

A **fixed rate mortgage** (FRM) is a loan for which the interest rate is set for a specified period of time. For instance, a fixed rate, 30-year mortgage with monthly payments would have an interest rate specified in advance, and payments calculated so that the loan will be repaid in 30 years. An **adjustable rate mortgage** (ARM) is a loan for which the interest rate will be reset periodically (as often as every month, or perhaps only every 3 years). When the interest rate is reset, the payment is recalculated based on the current outstanding balance so that the loan will still be paid off in the originally scheduled time. An ARM generally has a lower initial interest rate than an FRM, but the ARM carries the risk that interest rates, and therefore payment amounts, will rise at some time during the lifetime of the loan.

The original loan may have a provision which allows the borrower to fully repay the loan prior to the original ending date. In such a case, there might be a pre-specified penalty that the borrower must pay to "prepay" the loan. In spite of a possible penalty for prepayment of the loan, this might be an attractive option for the borrower if the borrower can find a loan at an interest rate that is significantly lower than the original loan rate (or if the borrower wins the lottery and wants to repay all debts she has).

---

**The Subprime Loan Crisis of 2007**

The subprime mortgage crisis began in 2006 and is continuing through 2008 at the time this book is being written. A subprime borrower is one who is a relatively high credit risk. Low interest rate adjustable rate mortgage loans made to subprime borrowers in the early 2000s along with increasing interest rates and a bursting of the bubble in housing prices that occurred later in the decade had resulted in an increasing number of loan defaults and foreclosures on properties. This resulted in an unwillingness on the part of investors to make mortgage loans. As a result, even the more creditworthy borrowers found it difficult to obtain financing for mortgages, and this in turn had the effect of depressing the housing market further.

---

## 3.3 THE SINKING-FUND METHOD OF LOAN REPAYMENT

The final comments in Section 3.1 considered the case of a loan which called for periodic payments of interest only during the term of the loan, along with repayment of the full principal amount at the end of the term. For such a loan, the borrower would have to make a series of $n$ interest payments to the lender, each of amount $L \cdot i$, along with a payment of $L$ at time $n$. The borrower has an obligation to pay the single lump sum of amount $L$ at time $n$, and may wish to meet this obligation by accumulating that amount during the term of the loan by means of $n$ periodic deposits into an interest-bearing savings account called a *sinking fund*. This method of loan repayment is called the **sinking-fund method**.

There is no guarantee that the rate earned in the sinking fund, say $j$, is the same as the periodic interest rate on the loan, $i$. In a practical situation it would usually be the case that the interest rate charged by the lender is larger than the rate that can be earned in a deposit account, so that $i > j$.

A standard way of accumulating the principal amount in the sinking fund is by using level deposits. If this is the case, then for the loan situation just described the borrower's payment would be $L \times i$, which is the interest payment to the lender, plus $\frac{L}{s_{\overline{n}|j}}$, which is the level sinking fund deposit, producing a total periodic outlay of $L\left[i + \frac{1}{s_{\overline{n}|j}}\right]$.

EXAMPLE 3.6    (*Sinking fund*)

A loan of 100,000 is to be repaid by ten annual payments beginning one year after the loan is made. The lender wants annual payments of interest at a rate of 10% and repayment of the principal in a single lump sum at the end of 10 years. The borrower can accumulate the principal in a sinking fund earning an annual interest rate of 8%, and decides to do this by means of 10 level deposits starting one year after the loan is made.

(a) Find the borrowers' total annual outlay and compare this to the level annual payment required by the amortization method at 10%. Find the annual rate of interest $i'$ for which the amortization method at rate $i$ results in the same total annual outlay as the borrower pays in the sinking fund method in this example.

(b) Suppose that the lender's rate is 8% and the sinking fund rate is 10%. Repeat part (a), comparing this to the amortization method at 8%.

SOLUTION

(a) The total annual outlay under the sinking fund method is $100,000\left[.1 + \frac{1}{s_{\overline{10}|.08}}\right] = 16,902.95$, and the annual payment under amortization at 10% is $\frac{100,000}{a_{\overline{10}|.10}} = 16,274.54$. To find $i'$ we have $100,000 = 16,902.95\, a_{\overline{10}|i'}$, which results in $i' = .1089$.

(b) The total annual outlay under the sinking fund method is $100,000\left[.08 + \frac{1}{s_{\overline{10}|.10}}\right] = 14,274.54$, and the annual payment under amortization at 8% is $\frac{100,000}{a_{\overline{10}|.08}} = 14,902.95$. To find $i'$ we have $100,000 = 14,274.54\, a_{\overline{10}|i'}$, which results in $i' = .0706$. ☐

As deposits are made to the sinking fund, the fund balance grows toward the target value of $L$. For instance, in part (a) of Example 3.6, just after the fifth deposit into the sinking fund, the fund balance is $6902.95 \cdot s_{\overline{5}|.08} = 40,496.85$. This is the accumulated value after five years in the fund that will eventually pay back the principal amount. The value of the net debt outstanding after 5 years can be regarded as the initial loan amount minus the amount for repayment of principal that has already been accumulated to that point. This is

$$100,000 - 40,496.85 = 59,503.15.$$

This can be regarded as $OB_5$. Similarly $OB_6$ would be 100,000 minus the accumulated value of the sinking fund just after the sixth deposit, so $OB_6 = 100,000 - 6902.95 \cdot s_{\overline{6}|.08} = 49,360.45$. The principal repaid in the sixth year is the amount by which the value of the debt decreases, which is $PR_6 = OB_5 - OB_6 = 10,142.70$.

Also in Example 3.6 we see that the amount of interest paid to the lender is $100,000(.1) = 10,000$ each year. This amount is offset by the interest earned in the sinking fund for the year. For the sixth year the amount of interest earned by the sinking fund is equal to .08 multiplied by the balance in the account at the end of the fifth year, producing $(.08)(40,496.85) = 3239.75$. Then the net interest paid for the sixth year is the amount paid to the lender minus the amount earned in the sinking fund, which is $I_6 = 10,000 - 3239.75 = 6760.25$. It then follows that $I_6 + PR_6 = 6760.25 + 10,142.70 = 16,902.95$, which is the total annual payment made by the borrower. It is possible to construct a schedule showing the principal repaid for each period (growth in the sinking fund for that period) and the net interest paid for each period (interest paid to the lender for the period minus interest earned in the sinking fund that period). This is the equivalent of an amortization schedule in the context of loan repayment by the sinking fund method. This idea is outlined in the next paragraph.

### 3.3.1 SINKING-FUND METHOD SCHEDULE

To construct the schedule, we know that the net amount of the debt at the end of the $t^{th}$ period, just after the $t^{th}$ deposit, is

$$OB_t = L - \frac{L}{s_{\overline{n}|j}} \times s_{\overline{t}|j} = L\left[1 - \frac{s_{\overline{t}|j}}{s_{\overline{n}|j}}\right], \qquad (3.19)$$

and, similarly, $OB_{t-1} = L\left[1 - \frac{s_{\overline{t-1}|j}}{s_{\overline{n}|j}}\right]$.

The principal repaid in the $t^{th}$ period is

$$PR_t = OB_{t-1} - OB_t = L\left[\frac{s_{\overline{t}|j} - s_{\overline{t-1}|j}}{s_{\overline{n}|j}}\right] = \frac{L(1+j)^{t-1}}{s_{\overline{n}|j}}. \qquad (3.20)$$

Note that if the sinking fund deposits are level, then the amount of principal repaid grows by a factor of $1+j$ per period, which is similar to the growth of $PR_t$ in the amortization method when payments are level.

The net interest paid in the $t^{th}$ payment is

$$I_t = L \cdot i - \frac{L \cdot s_{\overline{t-1}|j}}{s_{\overline{n}|j}} \times j = L\left[i - \frac{(1+j)^{t-1}-1}{s_{\overline{n}|j}}\right]. \qquad (3.21)$$

Note that $I_t + PR_t = L\left[i + \frac{1}{s_{\overline{n}|j}}\right]$, the borrower's total periodic outlay.

## 3.4 APPLICATIONS AND ILLUSTRATIONS

### 3.4.1 MAKEHAM'S FORMULA

We have seen examples of loans in which the lender receives payments of only interest each period, and then receives the full amount of principal after several periods. For a loan of this type, with principal repaid after $n$ periods, the sequence of payments received by the lender is $Li, Li, \ldots, Li, Li+L$, where there are $n$ terms in this sequence. Suppose the lender sells the loan to an investor, and the investor values the sequence of payments at the time the loan is purchased by finding the present value at periodic interest rate $j$. The investor will pay the original lender an amount equal to the present value of the payments, with the valuation based on interest rate $j$; the investor has purchased the right to receive the payments. This present value is $A = Lv_j^n + Lia_{\overline{n}|j}$, where the first term is the present value of the principal amount repaid at time $n$, and the second term is the present value of the interest payments. This present value can be written as

$$
\begin{aligned}
A &= Lv_j^n + Lia_{\overline{n}|j} \\
&= Lv_j^n + Li\left(\frac{1-v_j^n}{j}\right) \\
&= Lv_j^n + \frac{i}{j}\left(L - Lv_j^n\right) = K + \frac{i}{j}\left(L - K\right).
\end{aligned}
\tag{3.22}
$$

where $K = L \cdot v_j^n$ is the present value of the repayment of principal. Equation (3.22) is called **Makeham's formula** for valuing the original series of cashflows at rate $j$. Note that if $j = i$, then the total present value of principal and interest payments reduces to $L$, the original loan.

Makeham's formula provides a useful method for valuing a loan for which there is a schedule of repayments of principal at various points in time, along with payments of interest every period on the outstanding balance. The example considered above involves a single repayment of principal, with interest payable up to and including the time of that payment of principal. Suppose that a loan of amount $L$ is to be repaid by $m$ payments of principal of amounts $L_1, L_2, \ldots, L_m$ to be made at times $t_1, t_2, \ldots, t_m$ so that $L_1 + L_2 + \cdots + L_m = L$, with payments of interest at rate $i$ on the outstanding balance at the end of every period. This situation can be regarded as $m$ separate loans, all issued at the same time and each of the type described in the previous paragraph, and is illustrated in the following figure.

| 0 | 1 | 2 | $\cdots$ | $t_1$ | $\cdots$ | $t_2$ | $\cdots$ | $t_m$ |
|---|---|---|---|---|---|---|---|---|
| $L_1 \rightarrow L_1 i$ | $L_1 i$ | $\cdots$ | $L_1 i + L_1$ | | | | | |
| $L_2 \rightarrow L_2 i$ | $L_2 i$ | $\cdots$ | $L_2 i$ | $\cdots$ | $L_2 i + L_2$ | | | |
| $\vdots \quad \vdots$ | $\vdots$ | | $\vdots$ | | $\vdots$ | | | |
| $L_m \rightarrow L_m i$ | $L_m i$ | $\cdots$ | $L_m i$ | $\cdots$ | $L_m i$ | $\cdots$ | $L_m i + L_m$ | |

**FIGURE 3.5**

Note again that the interest payments on the original loan are at rate $i$ but the valuation rate is $j$ for the series of principal and interest payments. The present value of the $s^{th}$ loan at rate of interest $j$ per period is found from Makeham's formula to be

$$A_s = L_s v_j^{t_s} + L_s i\, a_{\overline{t_s}|j} = K_s + \frac{i}{j}\left(L_s - K_s.\right)$$

The present value of the entire loan is then the sum of the present values of the $m$ parts of the loan. This total present value is

$$A = \sum_{s=1}^{m} A_s = \sum_{s=1}^{m}\left[L_s v_j^{t_s} + L_s i\, a_{\overline{t_s}|j}\right]$$

$$= \sum_{s=1}^{m}\left[K_s + \frac{i}{j}\left(L_s - K_s\right)\right] = K + \frac{i}{j}(L - K), \quad (3.23)$$

where $K = \sum_{s=1}^{m} K_s$ and $L = \sum_{s=1}^{m} L_s$. We see that the form of the present value (at rate $j$) in Equation (3.23) is also valid if the principal is repaid in a series of payments. However $K$ now represents the total present value of all principal payments, $\frac{i}{j}(L-K)$ represents the present value of all interest payments, and $L$ represents the total amount of principal. Note that Makeham's formula applies if the interest rate $i$ on the original loan remains constant throughout the course of the loan (if not, the loan would have to be broken into separate loans each at the associated interest rate), and the investor's valuation rate $j$ also remains constant for the term of the payments. The investor's valuation rate must be based on the same compounding period as are the payments of interest.

### EXAMPLE 3.7 (Makeham's formula)

A loan of 100,000 is to be repaid with 10 annual payments of principal of 10,000 each, starting one year after the loan is made, plus monthly interest payments on the outstanding balance. The interest rate is $i^{(12)} = .12$. Two years after the loan is made (just after the second principal payment and monthly interest payment) the lender sells the loan to an investor. Find the price paid by the investor if he values the remaining payments at a nominal annual rate of interest convertible monthly of (a) 6%, (b) 12%, and (c) 18%.

SOLUTION

(a) At the time the loan is sold, the outstanding balance is $L = 80,000$ with $m = 8$ annual principal payments of $L_1 = L_2 = \cdots = L_8 = 10,000$ and monthly interest payments at 1% per month on the outstanding balance. The present value of the principal payments is

$$K = K_1 + K_2 + \cdots + K_8 = 10,000\left(v^{12} + v^{24} + \cdots + v^{96}\right)$$

$$= 10,000\left(\frac{v^{12} - v^{108}}{1 - v^{12}}\right) = 61,687.68,$$

where $v$ is at $\frac{1}{2}\%$. The price paid by the investor is then

$61,687.68 + \frac{.01}{.005}(80,000 - 61,687.68) = 98,312.33$.

(b) In this case the monthly interest rate is $j = .01$, so $K = 48,513.85$ and the investor pays $48,513.85 + \frac{.01}{.01}(80,000 - 48,513.85) = 80,000$.

(c) In this case $j = .015$, so $K = 38,878.04$ and the investor pays 66,292.68. ∎

## 3.4.2 THE MERCHANT'S RULE

According to the **Merchant's Rule** of loan repayment, all amounts advanced and all loan repayments made are accumulated with simple interest until the settlement date, at which time the aggregate accumulated values of the amounts advanced must be equal to the aggregate accumulated values of the repayments made. Example 3.8 illustrates the Merchant's Rule.

EXAMPLE 3.8 | (*Merchant's Rule*)

Smith borrows 2000 on January 17 and makes payments of 800 each on the last day of each month, starting January 31. On March 15, he borrows an additional 2000. He continues the payments of 800 through May 31, and then pays the remainder of the obligation on June 30. What payment must be made on June 30 if the annual interest rate is 13% and the loan is based on the Merchant's Rule? (Assume a non-leap year.)

---

| SOLUTION |

All loan amounts and payments are accumulated with simple interest to the settlement date of June 30. Let $X$ denote the payment required at that time. Then the equation of value is

$$2000\left[2+(.13)\times\frac{164+107}{365}\right] = 800\left[5+(.13)\times\frac{150+122+91+61+30}{365}\right]+X,$$

which has the solution $X = 63.68$. ☐

### 3.4.3 THE US RULE

As with most transactions involving simple interest, the Merchant's Rule would not normally be used in transactions whose duration is more than one year. Another method for calculating the loan repayment is the **United States Rule**, also known as the **actuarial method**. According to this method, interest is computed each time a payment is made or an additional loan amount is disbursed. The interest calculation is based on simple interest from the time the previous payment or additional loan disbursement is made. The balance on the loan after the current payment is the previous balance, plus interest accrued, minus the current payment (or plus the current addition to the loan).

| EXAMPLE 3.9 | (*US Rule*)

Solve for $X$ in Example 3.8 assuming the loan calculations are based on the US rule.

| SOLUTION |

The interest and outstanding balance calculations are summarized in the Table 3.8 below.

The payment required on June 30 is 65.76. A typical calculation made in Table 3.8 is the one for January 31. The amount of accrued interest is $2000(.13)\left(\frac{14}{365}\right)=9.97$, so the outstanding balance is

$$2000+9.97-800 = 1209.97.$$

**TABLE 3.8**

| Date | Accrued Interest | Payment | Outstanding Balance |
|--------|------|--------|---------|
| Jan 17 | – | (2000) | 2000.00 |
| Jan 31 | 9.97 | 800 | 1209.97 |
| Feb 28 | 12.07 | 800 | 422.04 |
| Mar 15 | 2.25 | (2000) | 2424.29 |
| Mar 31 | 13.82 | 800 | 1638.11 |
| Apr 30 | 17.50 | 800 | 855.61 |
| May 31 | 9.45 | 800 | 65.06 |
| Jun 30 | .70 | 65.76 | 0 |

The US Rule is essentially amortization in which the interest rate for the fraction of a year from one transaction point to the next is the corresponding fraction of the annually quoted interest rate. $\square$

## 3.5 SUMMARY OF DEFINITIONS AND FORMULAS

**Definition 3.1 – Amortized Loan**

An amortized loan of amount $L$ made at time 0 at periodic interest rate $i$ and to be repaid by $n$ payments of amounts $K_1, K_2, ..., K_n$ at times $1, 2, ..., n$ (where the payment period corresponds to the interest period) satisfies the equation

$$L = K_1 v + K_2 v^2 + \cdots + K_n v^n. \tag{3.1}$$

**Definition 3.2 – Components of an Amortized Loan**

**Loan Amount L:**
Loan amount $L$ at interest rate $i$ per period, to be repaid by $n$ payments of amounts $K_1, K_2, ..., K_n$ at the end of $n$ successive periods.

**Outstanding balance just after payment at time $t$:**
$OB_t$ is the amount still owed just after the payment is made.

**Interest due in the payment at time $t$:**
$I_t$ is the interest on the outstanding balance since the previous payment was made.

**Principal repaid in the payment at time $t$:**

$PR_t$ is the part of the payment $K_t$ that is applied toward repaying loan principal.

$$OB_{t+1} = OB_t(1+i) - K_{t+1}. \qquad (3.4)$$

$$I_{t+1} = OB_t \times i \qquad (3.6)$$

$$PR_{t+1} = K_{t+1} - I_{t+1} \qquad (3.7)$$

**Retrospective form of outstanding balance**

$$
\begin{aligned}
OB_t = \; & OB_0(1+i)^t - K_1(1+i)^{t-1} \\
& - K_2(1+i)^{t-2} \\
& - \cdots - K_{t-1}(1+i) \\
& - K_t
\end{aligned}
\qquad (3.9)
$$

**Prospective form of outstanding balance**

$$OB_t = K_{t+1} \times v + K_{t+2} \times v^2 + \cdots + K_n \times v^{n-t}. \qquad (3.10)$$

**Amortization with $n$ level payments of amount $K$ each**

$$
\begin{aligned}
OB_t = L(1+i)^t - Ks_{\overline{t}|i} &= K(a_{\overline{n}|i}(1+i)^t - s_{\overline{t}|i}) \\
&= K(s_{\overline{t}|} + a_{\overline{n-t}|} - s_{\overline{t}|}) = K(a_{\overline{n-t}|}).
\end{aligned}
$$

$$I_t = K(1 - v^{n-t+1})$$

$$PR_t = Kv^{n-t+1}$$

$$PR_t = PR_{t-1}(1+i) = PR_1(1+i)^{t-1}.$$

## 3.6 NOTES AND REFERENCES

There are a number of websites with information on loan amortization. An online mortgage and APR calculator with accelerated payment options can be found at www.dinkytown.net. A search of the internet for loan amortization examples can return some interesting results and examples, some of which may have incorrect calculations.

The subprime loan crisis that is unfolding as this book is being written may have some serious economic effects. Credit difficulties in the United States have significant impact in other countries whose financial institutions are involved in investments and loans in the United States.

The "double-up option" for loan repayment of Exercise 3.2.19 and the weekly repayment scheme in Exercise 3.2.23 are based on actual loan repayment options of financial institutions. These have been promoted in times of high interest rates because of the significant reduction in repayment time and interest paid. The situation in Exercise 3.2.35 in which a loan is amortized at a rate of interest higher than the lender's rate, with the difference used for an insurance premium or sales commission, is considered in detail in *Mathematics of Compound Interest*, by Butcher and Nesbitt.

## 3.7 EXERCISES

### SECTION 3.1

3.1.1 An amortized loan has 10 annual payments at the end of each year starting one year from now. The first 5 payments are $1000 each and the final 5 payments are $500 each. Interest is at an effective annual rate of 10%. Find each of the following:

   (i)   the initial loan amount

   (ii)  the outstanding balance just after the $3^{rd}$ payment

   (iii) the interest and principal in the $4^{th}$ payment

   (iv)  the outstanding balance just after the $8^{th}$ payment.

3.1.2S  A loan is amortized over five years with monthly payments at a nominal interest rate of 9% compounded monthly. The first payment is 1000 and is to be paid one month from the date of the loan. Each succeeding monthly payment will be 2% lower than the prior payment. Calculate the outstanding loan balance immediately after the $40^{th}$ payment is made.

3.1.3   Verify that at quarterly interest rate $j = .02$, the total payments in Example 3.4 (i.e., $310, 305, \ldots, 255$) have present value 3000.

3.1.4   Smith borrows 20,000 to purchase a car. The car dealer finances the purchase and offers Smith two alternative financing plans, both of which require monthly payments at the end of each month for 4 years starting one month after the car is purchased.

   (i)  0% interest rate for the first year followed by 6% nominal annual interest rate compounded monthly for the following three years.

   (ii) 3% nominal annual interest rate compounded monthly for the first year followed by 5% nominal annual interest compounded monthly for the following three years.

   For each of (i) and (ii) find the monthly payment and the outstanding balance on the loan at the end of the first year.

3.1.5S  Betty borrows 19,800 from Bank $X$. She repays the loan by making 36 equal payments of principal at the end of each month. She also pays interest on the unpaid balance each month at a nominal rate of 12%, compounded monthly. Immediately after the $16^{th}$ payment is made, Bank $X$ sells the rights to future payments to Bank $Y$. Bank $Y$ wishes to yield a nominal rate of 14%, compounded semi-annually, on its investment. What price does Bank $X$ receive?

3.1.6   For the general loan of amount $L$ that is amortized over $n$ periods by payments $K_1, K_2, \ldots, K_n$ at interest rate $i$ per payment period (see Table 3.2), show that $K_T - I_T = L$.

3.1.7   Suppose that during the course of a loan, two successive periods have the same interest rate $(i_t = i_{t+1} = i)$. Show that $PR_{t+1} = PR_t(1+i) + K_{t+1} - K_t$. It then follows that if $K_{t+1} = K_t$ and $i_t = i_{t+1} = i$, then $PR_{t+1} = PR_t(1+i)$.

3.1.8   A loan at rate $i^{(12)} = .12$ is repaid with 120 monthly payments starting one month after the loan. The amount of the first payment is 600 and each subsequent payment is 5 larger than the previous payment. Find the original amount of the loan. Find $PR_1$ and use the result of Exercise 3.1.7 to show that $PR_t = PR_1(1.01)^{t-1} + 5 \cdot s_{\overline{t-1}|i}$. Find $OB_{60}$ prospectively, retrospectively, and by verifying that $OB_{60} = L - \sum_{k=1}^{60} PR_k$, using the form of $PR_k$ found earlier in this exercise. Find $I_{61}$. Find $PR_{61}$ using the formula above and also from $PR_{61} = K_{61} - I_{61}$, and verify that they are equal.

3.1.9S   A 30-year loan of 1000 is repaid with payments at the end of each year. Each of the first ten payments equals the amount of interest due. Each of the next ten payments equals 150% of the amount of interest due. Each of the last ten payments is $X$. The lender charges interest at an effective annual rate of 10%. Calculate $X$.

3.1.10   A loan of amount $L$ at rate $i$ per period calls for payments of interest only (at the end of each period) for $n$ periods, plus a single repayment of principal of amount $L$ at the end of $n$ periods. Show that the present value at periodic rate $i$ of the interest and principal payments is equal to $L$.

*3.1.11 Example 3.1 is modified so that monthly payments are made for 12 years starting one month after the loan. The monthly payment is $K$ for the first 6 years (72 payments) and $2K$ for the last 6 years (72 payments).

    (a) Find $K$ and construct the amortization table for the first year.

    (b) Verify that the result in Exercise 3.1.7 applies here, although the $PR$ amounts are negative during this period.

    (c) Using monthly payment amounts rounded to the nearest penny, find the amount of the final payment required at $t = 144$ to retire the debt.

*3.1.12 Plot the $OB_t$ functions for Example 3.1 and Example 3.2.

*3.1.13 A loan of amount $L$ is repaid by 15 annual payments starting one year after the loan. The first 6 payments are 500 each and the final 9 payments are 1000 each. Interest is at effective annual rate $i$. Show that each of the following is a correct expression for $PR_6$.

    (a) $500\left(2v^{10} - v\right)$

    (b) $500\left(\left[1 - i\left(2a_{\overline{10}|} - v\right)\right]\right)$

    (c) $(500 - L \cdot i)(1+i)^5$

## SECTION 3.2

3.2.1    A loan of $L$ is amortized by $n$ level payments of amount $K$ at rate $i$ per period. Show that

$$OB_t \;=\; L(1+i)^t - K \cdot s_{\overline{t}|i} \;=\; Ka_{\overline{n-t}|i} \;=\; L - PR_1 \cdot s_{\overline{t}|i}$$

3.2.2    Suppose the loan in Example 3.4 is repaid by 12 level quarterly payments at rate $j = .02$. Find the total amount of interest paid over the course of the loan. This total is larger than the total in Example 3.4. Provide a non-algebraic justification for this by general reasoning.

3.2.3   Fill in the blanks of the following amortization schedule for a loan with level 5 level payments.

| $t$ | $OB_t$ | $I_t$ | $PR_t$ |
|---|---|---|---|
| 0 | — | | |
| 1 | 706.00 | 43.10 | 156.00 |
| 2 | — | — | — |
| 3 | — | — | — |
| 4 | — | — | — |
| 5 | 0 | — | — |

3.2.4   A 5-year loan made on July 1, 2004 is amortized with 60 level monthly payments starting August 1, 2004. If interest is at $i^{(12)} = .12$, find the date on which the outstanding balance first falls below one-half of the original loan amount.

3.2.5   (a) A 5-year loan is amortized with semiannual payments of 200 each, starting 6 months after the loan is made. If $PR_1 = 156.24$, find $i^{(12)}$.

(b) A loan is repaid by 48 monthly payments of 200 each. The interest paid in the first 12 payments is 983.16 and the principal repaid in the final 12 payments is 2215.86. Find $i^{(12)}$.

3.2.6   A loan is amortized by level payments every February 1, plus a smaller final payment. The borrower notices that the interest paid in the February 1, 2004 payment was 103.00, and the interest in the February 1, 2005 payment will be 98.00. The rate of interest on the loan is $i = .08$.

(a) Find the principal repaid in the 2005 payment.

(b) Find the date and amount of the smaller final payment made one year after the last regular payment.

3.2.7S   Iggy borrows $X$ for 10 years at an effective annual rate of 6%. If he pays the principal and accumulated interest in one lump sum at the end of 10 years, he would pay 356.54 more in interest than if he repaid the loan with 10 level payments at the end of each year. Calculate $X$.

3.2.8S  A 10-year loan of 2000 is to be repaid with payments at the end of each year. It can be repaid under the following two options:

(i)  Equal annual payments at an effective annual rate of 8.07%.

(ii)  Installments of 200 each year plus interest on the unpaid balance at an effective annual rate of $i$.

The sum of the payments under option (i) equals the sum of the payments under option (ii). Determine $i$.

3.2.9  A person borrows money at $i^{(12)} = .12$ from Bank A, requiring level payments starting one month later and continuing for a total of 15 years (180 payments). She is allowed to repay the entire balance outstanding at any time provided she also pays a penalty of $k$% of the outstanding balance at the time of repayment. At the end of 5 years (just after the $60^{th}$ payment) the borrower decides to repay the remaining balance, and finances the repayment plus penalty with a loan at $i^{(12)} = .09$ from Bank B. The loan from Bank B requires 10 years of level monthly payments beginning one month later. Find the largest value of $k$ that makes her decision to refinance correct.

3.2.10  (a)  For each of Examples 3.1 and 3.4 find the total present value (at the time of the loan) of the interest payments and principal payments separately.

(b)  For a loan of amount $L$ repaid by $n$ level payments, find the total present value of the interest payments and principal payments separately.

3.2.11  A loan is being repaid with level payments of $K$ every 6 months. The outstanding balances on three consecutive payment dates are 5190.72, 5084.68, and 4973.66. Find $K$.

3.2.12 Smith wishes to sell his house for 200,000. Jones has 100,000 available for a down payment, and can take a bank loan with monthly payments at $i^{(12)} = .15$. Smith offers to "take back" the mortgage for 100,000 with monthly payments at $i^{(12)} = .12$, based on a 25-year amortization period, with a provision that Jones will refinance the outstanding balance of the loan elsewhere after 3 years. Jones accepts Smith's offer. Immediately after the transaction Smith sells the loan to a broker for a price that yields the broker $i^{(12)} = .15$ over the 3-year period. (The broker becomes entitled to the 3 years of monthly payments as well as the outstanding balance.) What is the net amount that Smith receives for the house?

3.2.13 A loan of amount $L$ is to be repaid by $n$ payments, starting one period after the loan is made, with interest at rate $i$ per period. Two repayment schemes are considered:

(i) level payments for the lifetime of the loan;

(ii) each payment consists of principal repaid of $\frac{L}{n}$ plus interest on the previous outstanding balance.

Find the total interest repaid under each scheme and show algebraically that the interest paid under scheme (i) is larger than that paid under scheme (ii). Show that for each $t = 1, 2, \ldots, n-1$, $OB_t$ is larger under scheme (i) than under scheme (ii). Verify algebraically that $L$ is the present value at the time of the loan, at rate of interest $i$ per payment period, of all payments made under scheme (ii).

3.2.14 An estate of 1,000,000, invested at an annual interest rate of 5%, is being shared by A, B, and C. Starting 1 year after the estate is established, A receives 125,000 of principal each year for 5 years, B receives 75,000 of principal each year for 5 years, and C receives the interest each year. Find the present values of the shares of A, B, and C at 5%, and verify that their sum is 1,000,000.

*3.2.15 A loan of 1000 at interest of $i = .01$ per period is amortized by payments of 100 per period, starting one period after the loan, for as long as necessary, plus a final smaller payment one period after the last regular payment. Solve for the number of regular payments and the final smaller payment by constructing the amortization table.

*3.2.16 Smith has two options to repay a loan at effective annual interest rate $i > 0$ over an $n$-year period: (i) $n$ level annual payments starting one year after the loan, or (ii) $12n$ level monthly payments starting one month after the loan.

(a) Show that on each annual anniversary of the loan, the outstanding balance just after payment is made is the same under both options.

(b) Show that the total interest paid under scheme (i) is greater than under scheme (ii).

*3.2.17 A loan is being repaid by $2n$ level payments, starting one year after the loan. Just after the $n^{th}$ payment the borrower finds that she still owes $\frac{3}{4}$ of the original amount. What proportion of the next payment is interest?

*3.2.18 An amortized loan of 1000 is to be repaid with 24 monthly payments starting one month after the loan. The nominal interest rate convertible monthly is 9% for the first 18 months and 12% for the final 6 months. Construct the amortization table for this loan, and find the amount of principal repaid in the first year (first 12 payments).

*3.2.19  On July 1, 2005 Smith will borrow 75,000 at rate $i^{(12)} = .12$. He has three amortization options for repayment with monthly payments starting August 1, 2005.

(i) A standard 25-year loan with monthly payment $K$.

(ii) A "double up" option, with the same monthly payment $K$ as in (i), except that every $6^{th}$ payment is $2K$. Payments continue in this pattern for as long as necessary plus a final smaller payment one month after the last regular payment.

(iii) Constant principal of 250 per month for 25 years plus a monthly payment of interest on the previous month's outstanding balance.

For each option find the total amount of interest paid during the lifetime of the loan, and for part (ii) find when the loan is repaid and the final smaller payment required.


*3.2.20  A loan at $i = .05$ is to be repaid by $n$ level annual payments of $p$ each starting one year after the loan. The borrower misses the $5^{th}$ and $6^{th}$ payments. He is told that if he pays $1.16p$ for each of the remaining payments, the loan will be repaid at the originally scheduled time. Find the number of payments on the original loan. Give a verbal explanation of the equation $s_{\overline{2}|} = .16 \cdot a_{\overline{n-6}|}$ which arises in this situation.


*3.2.21  A loan of amount $L$ is being repaid by $n$ level payments of amount $K$ each at interest rate $i$ per period. If $t + u \leq n$, show that $OB_{t+u} = OB_t \cdot (1+i)^u - K \cdot s_{\overline{u}|}$. Formulate a general version of this relationship for a loan repayment scheme with payment amounts $K_1, K_2, \ldots, K_n$.

*3.2.22  A loan of 10,000 at effective annual rate $i = .08$ is to be repaid with 20 level annual payments of amount $K$ each. The borrower is unable to make the $6^{th}$, $7^{th}$, and $8^{th}$ payments. The lender allows the payments to be missed on the condition that the loan will still be repaid on time by increasing the $9^{th}$ through $20^{th}$ payments to $K + X$. Show that $X = \dfrac{K \cdot s_{\overline{3}|}}{a_{\overline{12}|}}$. Find the difference in the total interest paid between this repayment scheme and the repayment scheme in which no payments are missed.

*3.2.23  In times of high interest rates, lending institutions may offer some variations in repayment schemes. Suppose a loan of amount $L$ is to be amortized with level monthly payments of $K$ each for 25 years. The lender offers an alternate repayment plan with weekly payments, starting one week after the loan is made. The borrower is offered two choices for the payment: (i) $B_1 = \dfrac{K}{4}$ and (ii) $B_2 = \dfrac{12K}{52}$. The weekly payments continue for as long as necessary with an additional final smaller payment. Suppose that $L = 100,000$. The one-week rate $j_w$ is $j_w = (1+i)^{7/365} - 1$, where $i$ is the equivalent effective annual rate. For each of cases (i) and (ii) find the term of repayment and the reduction in interest paid over the course of the loan as compared to the monthly repayment scheme for each of the interest rates $i^{(12)} = 6\%$, and 24%.

*3.2.24  A loan of amount L is amortized according to scheme (ii) in Exercise 3.2.13.

(a) Show that $K_t = \dfrac{L}{n} + L \cdot i \cdot \left(\dfrac{n-t+1}{n}\right)$.

Use the result of Exercise 3.1.7 to show that $PR_k = \dfrac{L}{n}$.

(b) Use part (a) to show that $\sum\limits_{t=1}^{n}\left[1 + (n-t+1) \cdot i\right] \cdot v^t = n$.

Give a verbal interpretation of this identity.

(c) Show that $\sum\limits_{t=1}^{n}\left[1 + (n-t) \cdot d\right] \cdot v^{t-1} = n$, and give a verbal interpretation.

*3.2.25  A loan of amount $L$ is being amortized by level continuous payments over $n$ interest periods, with interest rate of $i$ per period. The amount of payment per period is $\frac{L}{a_{\overline{n}|i}}$. Find the rate at which principal is being repaid at time t, the rate at which interest is being paid at time $t$, and $OB_t$. Find the amount of principal and interest paid in the interval from time $t$ to time $t+1$. Show that $\frac{d^2}{dt^2} OB_t < 0$, so that the $OB_t$ curve is concave downward.

*3.2.26S  A bank customer borrows $X$ at an effective annual rate of 12.5% and makes level payments at the end of each year for $n$ years.

(i)  The interest portion of the final payment is 153.86.

(ii) The total principal repaid as of time $(n-1)$ is 6009.12.

(iii) The principal repaid in the first payment is $Y$.

Calculate $Y$.

*3.2.27  (a)  A loan of amount $L$ at interest rate $i$ per period is repaid by $n-1$ level periodic payments of $K$ each, starting one period after the loan is made, followed by a single payment of amount $B$ at time $n$ to completely repay the loan. Show that the principal repaid in the $t^{th}$ payment $(t < n)$ is

$$K \cdot v^{n-t+1} + (K-B) \cdot v^{n-t} \cdot d.$$

(b)  Apply the result in part (a) to Exercise 3.2.15, after finding the final payment $B$, to show that $PR_1 = 90$.

*3.2.28  Find the form of $OB_t$, $I_t$, and $PR_t$ for each of the following loans.

(a)  $L = (Ia)_{\overline{n}|i}$, with $n$ payments $K_1 = 1, K_2 = 2, ..., K_n = n$.

(b)  $L = (Da)_{\overline{n}|i}$, with $n$ payments $K_1 = n, K_2 = n-1, ..., K_n = 1$.

*3.2.29   (a) Show that a loan of amount $n$ at interest rate $i$ per period can be repaid by the series of $n$ geometrically increasing payments $K_1 = (1+i)$, $K_2 = (1+i)^2, \ldots, K_n = (1+i)^n$, with the first payment made one period after the loan.

(b) Show that $OB_t = (n-t)(1+i)^t$.

*3.2.30   (a) A loan of amount $L$ at interest rate $i$ per period, with equivalent force of interest $\delta$ is repaid by means of continuous payment for $n$ periods, at rate of payment $K_t$ at time $t$, so that $L = \int_0^n K_s \cdot v^s \, ds$. Formulate the prospective and retrospective outstanding balance at time $t$ and show that $\frac{d}{dt} OB_t = \delta \cdot OB_t - K_t$.

(b) Find an expression for the amount of principal repaid and the amount of interest paid between times $t_0$ and $t_1$ on the loan in part (a).

*3.2.31   (a) A loan of 10,000 at effective annual rate $i = .08$ is to be repaid with 20 level annual payments of amount $K$ each. At the time of the $5^{th}$ payment, the borrower makes an additional payment of amount $PR_6 + PR_7 + PR_8$. The regular payments of amount $K$ continue as usual from time 6 onward, for as long as necessary. Show that the loan will be repaid with the $17^{th}$ payment, as measured from the date of the loan, and show that the amount of interest paid is $I_6 + I_7 + I_8$ less than would have been paid under the original scheme.

(b) Generalize part (a) for a loan of amount $L$ at interest rate $i$ to be repaid by $n$ level payments, where, at the time of the $t_0^{th}$ payment, the borrower makes an additional payment of $PR_{t_0+1} + PR_{t_0+2} + \cdots + PR_{t_0+m}$. Show that the loan is repaid with the $(n-m)^{th}$ payment, and the interest is $I_{t_0+1} + I_{t_0+2} + \cdots + I_{t_0+m}$ less than would have been paid under the original scheme.

*3.2.32 A loan of 10,000 is to be repaid by 10 annual payments of 1000 of principal, starting one year after the loan, plus periodic payments of interest on the outstanding balance. Find the total amount of interest paid in each of the following cases.

(a) Annual interest payments at effective annual rate of interest .12550881%.

(b) Semiannual interest payments at effective 6-month rate of 6.09%

(c) Quarterly interest payments at effective 3-month rate of 3%.

Show that at rate $i^{(4)} = .12$ the present values on the loan issue date of the interest payments in each of cases (a), (b) and (c) are equal. Explain why this is so.

*3.2.33 A loan of amount $L$ is made at interest rate $i$ per period to be repaid by $n$ periodic payments of amounts $K_1, K_2, \ldots, K_n$. When a payment is made, there is income tax payable at rate $r < 1$ on the interest portion of the payment; thus at the time of the $t^{th}$ payment the lender receives a net payment of $K_t - r \cdot I_t$. Show that the present value of the net after-tax payments received by the lender are equal to $L$ at interest rate $i(1-r)$.

*3.2.34 An amortized loan for 10,000 has interest at 8% per year on the first 5000 of outstanding balance, and 10% per year on the $OB$ in excess of 5000. Suppose that annual payments are 1500 for as long as necessary. Construct the amortization table for the loan.

*3.2.35 A loan of 100,000 at effective annual rate 12% is to be repaid by level annual payments for 10 years. Part of each payment is an insurance premium to insure the loan against default due to the death of the borrower. In each payment the amount of the insurance premium is 2% of the previous year's outstanding balance, so the net amount of interest paid to the lender is 10% of the previous year's outstanding balance. The principal repaid in each payment is the same as in an ordinary amortization at 12%. Construct a table showing the net amount of interest and principal received in each payment, and show that the present value at $i = .10$ of the principal plus net interest payments is 100,000.

## SECTION 3.3

3.3.1   The lender of a loan of 100,000 receives annual interest payments at 12% per year for 10 years, and, in addition, will receive a lump-sum repayment of the principal along with the $10^{th}$ interest payment. The borrower will pay the annual interest to the lender and accumulate the 100,000 by annual deposits to an 8% sinking fund. The borrower wishes to schedule the deposits so that his total annual outlay is $X$ for each of the first 5 years, and $2X$ for each of the final 5 years. Find $X$. Construct a table listing "outstanding balance," "principal repaid" and "net interest paid" for each $t$ from 1 to 10.

3.3.2   (a) With reference to part (a) of Example 3.6, suppose the loan amount of 100,000 was not given, but rather that the borrower's total annual outlay of 16,902.95 was given. Show that the loan amount is 100,000.

   (b) A borrower's total annual outlay is $K$ per period for $n$ periods, including interest at rate $i$ to the lender on a loan of $L$, and accumulating the principal in a sinking fund at rate $j$ with $n$ level periodic deposits. Solve for $L$ in terms of $K, n, i$ and $j$.

3.3.3   The borrower of a loan of 10,000 makes monthly interest payments to the lender at rate $i^{(12)} = .15$, and monthly deposits of 100 to a sinking fund earning $i^{(12)} = .09$. When the sinking fund reaches 10,000 the borrower will repay the principal and discharge the loan. Find the total amount paid by the borrower over the course of the loan.

3.3.4   Smith can repay a loan of 250,000 in one of two ways:

   (i)  30 annual payments based on amortization at $i = .12$;

   (ii) 30 annual interest payments to the lender at rate $i = .10$, along with 30 level annual deposits to a sinking fund earning rate $j$.

   Find the value of $j$ to make the schemes equivalent.

3.3.5　(a) The borrower's annual outlay in part (a) of Example 3.6 is 16,902.95. Suppose that an investor wishes to purchase a 10-payment annuity of 16,902.95, starting one year after the purchase date, and is willing to pay a price that will yield 10% per year on his investment while allowing him to recover his principal (purchase price) in a sinking fund earning 8% per year. Find the purchase price the investor will pay.

(b) On a loan of amount $L$ the lender receives interest only at rate $i$ per period and a lump-sum principal repayment of amount $L$ at the end of $n$ periods. The borrower plans to accumulate the lump-sum payment by means of $n$ level deposits into a sinking fund earning interest at rate $j$. An investor considers purchasing the right to receive the annuity formed by the series of total annual outlays (interest plus sinking fund deposit) by the borrower for the $n$ periods. The investor will pay a price $P$ so that he can receive a return of $i$ per period (same as lender's rate) on his investment, while recovering his initial investment in a sinking fund earning interest at rate $j$ (same rate as the borrower's sinking fund). Show that $P = L$. (In this situation the investor is the lender in the sense that he loans out an amount $P$, but the investor also plays the role of "borrower" accumulating the initial loan amount in a sinking fund.)

3.3.6S　John borrows 1000 for 10 years at an annual effective interest rate of 10%. He can repay this loan using the amortization method with payments of $P$ at the end of each year. Instead, John repays the 1000 using a sinking fund that pays an annual effective rate of 14%. The deposits to the sinking fund are equal to $P$ minus the interest on the loan and are made at the end of each year for 10 years. Determine the balance in the sinking fund immediately after the repayment of the loan.

3.3.7    A business currently produces 9000 units of its product each month, which sells for 85 per unit at the end of the month. The company considers an alternative process which has a startup cost of 1,500,000 and continuing monthly costs (on top of previous monthly costs) of 15,816 incurred at the end of each month. The alternative process will result in monthly production of 12,000 units. The company can borrow the 1,500,000 on an interest-only loan at monthly rate 1.5%, with the principal repayable after 40 months. The company can accumulate the principal in a sinking fund earning interest at 1% per month over the 40-month period. The company can reduce the selling price of the product to $X$ per unit and still make a profit that is 30,000 more per month than it was before the new process was implemented. Find $X$.

*3.3.8   A loan is made so that the lender receives periodic payments of interest only at rate $i$ per period for $n$ periods plus the return of principal in a single lump-sum payment at the end of the $n$ periods. The borrower will accumulate the principal by means of $n$ level periodic deposits to a sinking fund earning periodic interest rate $j$, such that the accumulated value in the sinking fund is equal to the principal just after the $n^{th}$ level deposit is made. The borrower's total annual outlay is the same as if the loan were being amortized at periodic rate $i'$. Show that if $j < i$ then $i' > i$, and if $j = i$ then $i' = i$. An approximation to $i'$ in terms of $i$ and $j$ is $i' \approx i + \frac{1}{2}(i-j)$. Compare the exact values for $i'$ found in Example 3.6 to the approximate values found by this formula. Try various combinations of $i, j$ and $n$, and compare the exact value of $i'$ to that found by the formula.

*3.3.9   In repaying a loan of amount $L$, the total periodic outlay made by a borrower at time $t$ is $K_t$ for $t = 1, 2, \ldots, n$. The borrower pays interest on $L$ at rate $i$, with the rest of the outlay going into a sinking fund earning rate $j$ to accumulate to $L$ at time $n$. Solve for $L$ in terms of $i, j, n,$ and the $K_t$'s. Let $X$ be the present value of the $K_t$'s at rate $j$ per period. Show that $L$ can be written in the form $\frac{X}{Y}$, and solve for $Y$. Show that $Y = 1$ if $i = j$.

*3.3.10   Show that the borrower's total outlay for a standard sinking-fund method repayment as described at the start of Section 3.3 can be written as $L\left[\dfrac{1}{a_{\overline{n}|i}}+\left(\dfrac{1}{s_{\overline{n}|j}}-\dfrac{1}{s_{\overline{n}|i}}\right)\right]$, and use this to compare to amortization at rate $i$.

*3.3.11   A loan of 100,000 is to be repaid by 20 level annual payments. The lender wishes to earn 12% per year on the full loan amount and will deposit the remainder of the annual payment to a sinking fund earning 8% annually.

(a) Find the amount of the level annual payment.

(b) Just after receiving the $10^{th}$ payment, the lender sells the remaining 10 payments. The purchaser considers two ways of valuing the remaining payments:

   (i)   amortization at 10% per year, or

   (ii)  earning an annual return of 12% on his investment while recovering his principal in a sinking fund earning 8%.

Find the amount in the original lender's sinking fund at the time the remainder of the loan is sold, and in each of cases (i) and (ii) find the amount paid by the investor to the original lender.

(c) In each of cases (i) and (ii) of part (b), the original lender wants to calculate the average annual return (internal rate of return) on his investment for the 10 years. He uses two different approaches:

   ($\alpha$) Equating 100,000 to the present value (at rate $i_\alpha$) of the 10 annual payments of 12,000 plus the present value of the accumulated amount in the sinking fund and the proceeds of the sale at time 10;

   ($\beta$) Equating 100,000 to the present value (at rate $i_\beta$) of the 10 actual payments received plus the present value of the proceeds of the sale at time 10.

For each of cases (i) and (ii), find $i_\alpha$ and $i_\beta$.

## SECTION 3.4

3.4.1 Solve part (a) of Example 3.7 by setting up the full cashflow sequence and finding the present value. There would be 12 monthly payments of 800 each plus a payment of 10,000 with the $12^{th}$ payment, followed by 12 monthly payments of 700 each plus a payment of 10,000 with the $12^{th}$ payment, and so on.

3.4.2 A loan of 15,000 is repaid by annual payments of principal starting one year after the loan is made, plus quarterly payments of interest on the outstanding balance at a quarterly rate of 4%. Find the present value of the payments to yield an investor a quarterly rate of 3% if the principal payments are

(a) 1000 per year for 15 years; or
(b) 1000 in the $1^{st}$ year, 2000 in the $2^{nd}$ year,..., 5000 in the $5^{th}$ year; or
(c) 5000 in the $1^{st}$ year, 4000 in the $2^{nd}$ year,..., 1000 in the $5^{th}$ year.

3.4.3 An amortized loan of amount $a_{\overline{n}|i}$ at rate $i$ per period has $n$ periodic payments of 1 each. Show that if the payments on the loan are valued at rate $j$ per period, then the present value of the interest payments on the original loan is

$$a_{\overline{n}|j} - \frac{v_i^n - v_j^n}{j-i} = \frac{i}{j}\left(a_{\overline{n}|i} - \frac{v_i^n - v_j^n}{j-i}\right).$$

3.4.4 A home builder offers homebuyers a financing scheme whereby the buyer makes a down payment of 10% of the price at the time of purchase. At the end of each year for 5 years the buyer makes principal payments of 2% of the original purchase price, as well as monthly payments of interest on the outstanding balance at a monthly rate of $\frac{1}{2}$%. Just after the fifth annual principal payment, the full outstanding balance is due (the homebuyer will negotiate with a bank for a loan of this amount). The cost of the home to the builder is 200,000, and the builder will be selling the buyer's 5-year loan to an investor who values the loan at $i^{(12)} = .15$. What should the builder set as the purchase price of the house so as to realize a net profit of 40,000 after the sale of the loan to the investor?

3.4.5 (Alternative derivation of Makeham's Formula) A loan of amount $L$ is repaid by a series of principal payments along with interest on the outstanding balance at the end of each period. If the rate of interest is $i$ per period and the loan is valued on the issue date at a rate of $j$ per period, denote the present value on the issue date by $A_j(i)$.

Let $K_j$ denote the present value at rate $j$ of the principal payments. Then $A_j(i) - K_j$ is the present value (at rate $j$) of the interest payments. Show that (i) $\frac{A_j(i) - K_j}{A_j(i') - K_j} = \frac{i}{i'}$, and (ii) $A_j(j) = L$. Use (i) and (ii) to show that $A_j(i) = K_j + \frac{i}{j}(L - K_j)$.

3.4.6 A loan of 500,000 is to be repaid by 25 annual principal payments of 20,000 each, starting one year after the loan, along with quarterly interest payments on the outstanding balance at a nominal annual rate of $i^{(4)} = .10$. An investor purchases the loan just after issue. Find the nominal annual yield convertible quarterly realized by the investor if the purchase price is (a) 450,000, (b) 500,000, or (c) 550,000. This will require the use of a computer routine such as Excel Solver.

3.4.7 Using Equation (3.22), show that $A < L$ is equivalent to $j > i$, $A = L$ is equivalent to $j = i$, and $A > L$ is equivalent to $j < i$.

3.4.8 Suppose the investor in Exercise 3.4.2 is subject to a tax on all interest payments at the time they are made. Find the net present value to the investor who is subject to a tax rate of (i) 25%, (ii) 40%, or (iii) 60%.

3.4.9 Smith borrows 1000 on January 1 (of a non-leap year) at $i = .10$, and repays the loan with 5 equal payments of amount $X$ each. The payments are made every 73 days, so that the final payment is made exactly one year after the loan was made. Calculate $X$ based on the Merchant's Rule, and then based on the US Rule.

3.4.10    Suppose that a loan of amount $L$ is made at time 0, and payments of $A_1, A_2, \ldots, A_{n-1}$ are made at times $0 < t_1 < t_2 < \cdots t_{n-1}$. Show that if $i > 0$, $A_k > 0$ for each $k$, and $\sum_{k=1}^{n-1} A_k < L$, then the amount $A_n$, required to repay the loan at time $t_n, t_n > t_{n-1}$, is larger under the US Rule than it is under the Merchant's Rule.

3.4.11    A corporation wishes to issue a zero-coupon bond due in 20 years with maturity value of 1,000,000 and compound annual yield rate of 9%. The corporation wants to charge the interest expense on an annualized basis and plans to use a straight-line approach (i.e., the difference between the proceeds of the bond and the maturity value is divided into 20 equal parts, one part to be charged as an expense in each of the 20 years). The tax authorities insist that the "actuarial method" is the appropriate way of determining the annual interest charge (i.e., the interest charge for year $k$ is the amount of compound interest accrued on the debt in year $k$). For each of the first year and the $20^{th}$ year, what is the interest charge under each of the two methods? In what year would the interest charges under the two methods be most nearly equal?

3.4.12    Smith has a *line of credit* with a bank, allowing loans up to a certain limit without requiring approval. Interest on the outstanding balance on the loan is based on an annual simple interest rate of 15%. Interest is charged to the account on the last day of each month, as well as the day on which the line of credit is completely repaid (the month-end balance is the accrued outstanding balance from the start of the month minus accrued payments). On January 15 Smith borrows 1000 from his line of credit, and borrows an additional 500 on March 1. Smith pays 250 on the $15^{th}$ of March, April, May, June, and July. What payment is required to repay the line of credit on August 15? Suppose that instead of charging interest on the last day of each month, the line of credit bases calculations on (a) the US Rule, or (b) the Merchant's Rule. In each of cases (a) and (b) find the payment required on August 15.

# CHAPTER 4

## BOND VALUATION

*"Gentlemen prefer bonds."*
*– Andrew Mellon, 1855-1937*

It is often necessary for corporations and governments to raise funds to cover planned expenditures. Corporations have two main ways of doing so; one is to issue **equity** by means of common (or preferred) shares of ownership (stocks) which usually give the shareholder a vote in deciding the way in which the corporation is managed. The other is to issue **debt**, which is to take out a loan requiring interest payments and repayment of principal. For borrowing in the short term, the corporation might obtain a *demand loan* (a loan that must be repaid at the lender's request with no notice) or a *line of credit* (an account which allows the borrower to maintain outstanding balances up to a specified maximum amount, with periodic interest payable). For longer term borrowing it is possible to take out a loan that is amortized in the standard way, but this would usually be done only for loans of a relatively small amount. To borrow large amounts over a longer term a corporation can issue a **bond**, also called a *debenture*. A bond is a debt that usually requires periodic interest payments called **coupons** (at a specified rate) for a stated term and also requires the return of the principal at the end of the term. It will often be the case that the amount borrowed is too large for a single lender or investor, and the bond is divided into smaller units to allow a variety of investors to participate in the issue.

---

**Definition 4.1 – Bond**

A bond is an interest-bearing certificate of public (government) or private (corporate) indebtedness.

---

Governments generally have the option of raising funds via taxes. Governments also raise funds by borrowing, in the short term by issuing Treasury bills, and in the longer term by issuing coupon bonds (called Treasury notes for maturities of 10 years or less). Government *savings bonds* pay periodic interest and might not have a fixed maturity date, and can usually be redeemed by the owner of the bond at any time for the return of principal and any accrued interest. Savings bonds would be purchased and held by individual investors, while government T-Bills and coupon bonds are held by individuals, financial institutions such as insurance companies and banks, and other investors. Bonds are crucial components in government and corporate financing.

The initial purchaser of a bond might not retain ownership for the full term to maturity, but might sell the bond to another party. Ownership of the bond refers to the right to receive the payments specified by the bond. There is a very active and liquid secondary market in which bonds are bought and sold. Through this market bonds also provide an important investment vehicle, and can make up large parts of pension funds and mutual funds. Bonds issued by corporations are usually backed by various corporate assets as collateral, although a type of bond called a *junk bond* has been used with little or no collateral, often to raise funds to finance the takeover of another company. Bonds issued by financially and politically stable governments are virtually risk-free and are a safe investment option. There are agencies that rate the risk of default on interest and principal payments associated with a bond issuer. The purchaser of a bond will take into account the level of risk associated with the bond when determining its value.

The risk of loss of principal or loss of a financial reward stemming from a borrower's failure to repay a loan or otherwise meet a contractual obligation is referred to as **credit risk**. Credit risk arises whenever a borrower is expecting to use future cash flows to pay a current debt, such as in the case of a bond. Investors are compensated for assuming credit risk by way of interest payments from the borrower or issuer of a debt obligation. Credit risk is closely tied to the potential return of an investment, the most notable being that the yields on bonds correlate strongly to their perceived credit risk.

## 4.1 DETERMINATION OF BOND PRICES

A bond is a contract that specifies a schedule of payments that will be made by the issuer to the bondholder (purchaser). The most common type of bond issue is the *straight-term bond*, for which the schedule of payments is similar to that of a loan with regular payments of interest plus a single payment of principal at the end of the term of the loan. A bond specifies a **face amount** and a *bond interest rate*, also called the **coupon rate**, which are analogous to the principal amount of a loan and rate at which interest is paid. The bond also specifies the *maturity date* or **term to maturity** during which the *coupons* (bond interest payments) are to be paid, and the **redemption amount** that is to be repaid on the maturity date. It is generally the case that the face amount and the redemption amount on a bond are the same, and this will be assumed to be the case throughout this chapter unless specified otherwise.

For bonds issued in Canada and the United States, the coupons are nearly always paid semiannually, with the coupon rate quoted on a nominal annual basis. (Some bonds issued in some European countries have coupons payable annually). Unless specified otherwise, when coupon rates are quoted in this chapter they will refer to annual rates payable semiannually, with the first coupon payable one period after the bond is issued, and with coupons payable up to and including the time at which the redemption amount is paid. Note that bonds may be issued on a non-coupon date, in which case the first coupon is paid less than one coupon period after issue.

The website of the US Bureau of the Public Debt has a great deal of information about bonds issued by the US Government. At that website, a historical record of all bonds (and T-Bills) issued by the US Government is available. An excerpt is included in Table 4.1.

**TABLE 4.1**

| Historical Securities Search Results Treasury Notes | | | | | | | |
|---|---|---|---|---|---|---|---|
| Security Term | Auction Date | Issue Date | Maturity Date | Interest Rate % | Yield % | Price Per $100 | CUSIP |
| 2-YR | 01-24-2007 | 01-31-2007 | 01-31-2009 | 4.875 | 4.930 | 99.896458 | 912828GE4 |
| 5-YR | 01-25-2007 | 01-31-2007 | 01-31-2012 | 4.750 | 4.855 | 99.538790 | 912828GF1 |

The first bond in the website excerpt has the following characteristics:

| | |
|---|---|
| Issue Date: | January 31, 2007 |
| Maturity Date: | January 31, 2009 |
| Interest Rate: | 4.875% |
| Yield Rate: | 4.930% |
| Price per $100: | 99.896 |

This describes a 2-year Treasury Note with *face amount* of $100. The purchaser of this bond will receive payments of $\frac{1}{2} \times 4.875 = 2.4375$ every July 31 and January 31, starting July 31, 2007 and ending January 31, 2009 (the maturity date of the bond). The purchaser will also receive $100 on January 31, 2009. This payment of $100 is the *redemption value* or *maturity value* of the bond.

The "interest rate" in the table is the coupon rate on the bond, quoted on an annual basis. It is understood in practice that coupons are paid semi-annually, so that the coupon rate is divided by 2 to calculate the actual coupon amount of 2.4375. The purchaser will pay a price that is equal to the present value of the series of payments based on a rate of return, or **yield rate,** that is indicated by current financial market conditions. For this example, at the time of purchase, it is indicated that the yield rate is 4.930%. This is the rate used by the purchaser to calculate the present value of the series of bond payments. It is the convention that bond yield rates, like coupon rates, are quoted as nominal annual interest rates compounded twice per year. Therefore, the yield rate per half-year is 2.465%. It should be emphasized again that the phrase "interest rate" in Table 4.1 is the rate used to determine the coupons that the bond will pay, and the phrase "yield rate" is the rate which is used to calculate the present value of the stream of coupons and redemption amount. During the lifetime of the bond, the coupon rate will not change; it is a part of the contract describing the stream of payments that the bond will make. The yield rate is set by market conditions, and will fluctuate as time goes on and market conditions change.

The following time diagram describes the payments made by the first bond in Table 4.1.

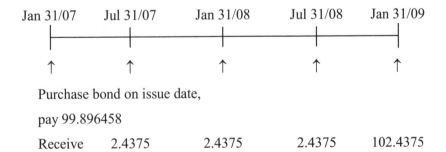

If we regard the period from the issue date to the first coupon (January 31, 2007 to July 31, 2007) and the time from one coupon period to the next each as exactly one-half year, then the present value of the bond payments is

$$100 \times \frac{1}{(1.02465)^4} + 2.4375$$

$$\times \left[ \frac{1}{1.02465} + \frac{1}{(1.02465)^2} + \frac{1}{(1.02465)^3} + \frac{1}{(1.02465)^4} \right] = 99.896.$$

This is the listed purchase price of the bond. It is an anomaly of financial practice that if the details of this bond were to be quoted in the financial press, all quantities would be described as listed above, except for the price, which would be quoted as 99.29. This does not mean a price of 99 dollars and 29 cents. For US government bond issues, the fractions of a dollar in price are quoted in multiples of $\frac{1}{32}^{nds}$ of a dollar, so that 99.29 refers to a price of $99\frac{29}{32}$ dollars, which is \$99.906 (the difference between this price and the actual price of 99.896 is due to rounding to the nearest $\frac{1}{32}$).

### 4.1.1 THE PRICE OF A BOND ON A COUPON DATE

The following notation will be used to represent the various parameters associated with a bond:

$F$ – The face amount (also called the par value) of the bond

$r$ – The coupon rate per coupon period (six months unless otherwise specified)

$C$ – The redemption amount on the bond (equal to $F$ unless otherwise noted)

$n$ – The number of coupon periods until maturity or *term* of the bond

The coupons are each of amount $Fr$, and the sequence of payments associated with the bond is shown in the following time diagram

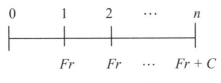

**FIGURE 4.1**

The purchase price of the bond is determined as the present value, on the purchase date, of that series of payments. There will be a number of factors that influence the yield rate used by the purchaser to find the price of the bond. We will not explore here the relationship between economic factors and interest rates on investments. We will simply accept that "market forces" determine the interest rate used to value the bond and thus to determine the purchase price. We will use $j$ to denote the six-month yield rate.

It is now a straightforward matter to formulate the price of the bond on a coupon date using the notation defined above:

$$P = C \times \frac{1}{(1+j)^n} + Fr\left[\frac{1}{1+j} + \frac{1}{(1+j)^2} + \cdots + \frac{1}{(1+j)^n}\right] = Cv_j^n + Fra_{\overline{n}|j}. \quad (4.1)$$

The first term on the right hand side of the equation is the present value of the redemption amount to be received by the bondholder in $n$ coupon periods. The second term is the present value of the annuity of coupons to be received until the bond matures. Note that it is being assumed that the next coupon is payable one full coupon period from the valuation point (hence the annuity-immediate symbol), and there are $n$ coupon periods until the bond matures.

It is usually the case that the redemption amount and the face amount are the same $(C = F)$. If this is so, the bond price can be expressed as

$$P = Fv_j^n + Fr\, a_{\overline{n}|j}. \quad (4.2)$$

Using the identity $v_j^n = 1 - ja_{\overline{n}|j}$, Equation 4.1 becomes

$$P = C + (Fr - Cj)a_{\overline{n}|j}. \quad (4.3)$$

Alternatively, writing $a_{\overline{n}|j}$ in Equation (4.1) as $a_{\overline{n}|j} = \frac{1 - v_j^n}{j}$, and letting the present value of the redemption amount be denoted by $K = Fv_j^n$, Equation (4.1) becomes

$$P = Fv_j^n + \frac{r}{j}\left(F - Fv_j^n\right) = K + \frac{r}{j}(F - K). \quad (4.4)$$

Equation (4.4) is known as *Makeham's Formula*, which is the same as Equation (3.22) with $F$ replacing the loan amount $L$, and $r$ replacing the interest rate $i$ in Equation (3.22). Note that, as in Equation (3.22), Equation (4.4) requires $r$ and $j$ to be based on the same period.

Equation (4.2) was used in finding the price of the US Treasury note in the previous section. For that note, the price was found on the issue date January 31, 2007 for a bond with a face and redemption amount of $F = C = 100$. The coupons were payable semiannually at rate $r = .024375$ (this is the six-month coupon rate found from the annual quoted coupon rate of 4.875%. The bond matures on January 31, 2009, which is $n = 4$ coupon periods after the issue date. The yield rate is quoted as 4.930% (compounded semi-annually), which corresponds to a yield rate of $j = .02465$ every six months. The prices of the other bond in Table 4.1 can be found in the same way.

| EXAMPLE 4.1 | *(Price of a bond on a coupon date)*

A 10% bond with semiannual coupons has a face amount of 100,000,000 and was issued on June 18, 1990. The first coupon was paid on December 18, 1990, and the bond has a maturity date of June 18, 2010.

(a) Find the price of the bond on its issue date using $i^{(2)}$ equal to

    (i) 5%,   (ii) 10%,  and  (iii) 15%.

(b) Find the price of the bond on June 18, 2000, just after the coupon is paid, using the yield rates of part (a).

| SOLUTION |

(a) We have $F = C = 100,000,000$, $r = .05$, and $n = 40$. Using Equation (4.2), we see that the price of the bond is

$$P = 100,000,000 v_j^{40} + (100,000,000)(.05) a_{\overline{40}|j}.$$

With (i) $j = .025$, (ii) $j = .05$, and (iii) $j = .075$, the bond prices are (i) $P = 162,756,938$, (ii) $P = 100,000,000$, and (iii) $P = 68,513,978$.

(b) We still have $F = C = 100,000,000$ and $r = .05$, but now $n = 20$ (since there are 10 years, or 20 coupons, remaining on the bond). Using Equation (4.2), we have

$$P = 100,000,000 + 100,000,000(.05 - j)a_{\overline{20}|j}.$$

This results in prices of (i) 138,972,906, (ii) 100,000,000, and (iii) 74,513,772. ❑

Note that as the yield rate is increased in Example 4.1 the bond price decreases. This is due to the inverse relationship between interest rate and present value; the bond price is the present value of a stream of payments valued at the yield rate.

In the Canadian financial press bond prices are generally quoted as a value per 100 of face amount, to the nearest .001 and yield rates are quoted to the nearest .001% (one-thousandth of a percent). Thus the quoted prices in Example 4.1 would be (i) 162.757, (ii) 100.000, and (iii) 68.514 in part (a), and (i) 138.972, (ii) 100.000, and (iii) 74.514 in part (b).

In the US there is a variety of quotation procedures. US government bond prices are quoted to the nearest $\frac{1}{32}$ per 100 of face amount, and yields are quoted to the nearest .01%. For corporate bonds, price quotations are to the nearest $\frac{1}{8}$ per 100 of face amount and **current yields** are also quoted. The current yield is the coupon rate divided by the bond's price.

### 4.1.2 BONDS BOUGHT OR REDEEMED AT A PREMIUM OR DISCOUNT

In looking at the bond price formulation of Equation (4.3) it is clear that the relative sizes of the bond price and face amount are directly related to the relative sizes of the coupon rate and yield rate. We have the relationships

$$P > F \quad \leftrightarrow \quad r > j, \tag{4.5a}$$

$$P = F \quad \leftrightarrow \quad r = j, \tag{4.5b}$$

and

$$P < F \quad \leftrightarrow \quad r < j, \tag{4.5c}$$

These relationships are similar to the ones between the loan amount $L$ and the price paid for the loan based on Makeham's Formula in Section 3.4. The terminology associated with these relationships between $P$ and $F$ is as follows.

---

**Definition 4.2 – Bond Purchase Value**

(a) If $P > F$, the bond is said to be bought **at a premium**.
(b) If $P = F$, the bond is said to be bought **at par**.
(c) If $P < F$, the bond is said to be bought **at a discount**.

---

Equation (4.3) can be rewritten as $P - F = F(r - j)a_{\overline{n}|j}$. Suppose that the bond is bought at a premium so that $P > F$. The rewritten version of Equation (4.3) indicates that the amount of premium in the purchase price $(P-F)$ is regarded as a loan (from the buyer to the seller) repaid at rate $j$ by $n$ payments of $F(r-j)$, the excess of coupon over yield.

We can also see from Equation (4.3) that if $r > j$ and the time $n$ until maturity is increased, then the bond price $P$ increases, but if $r < j$ then $P$ decreases as $n$ increases. This can be seen another way. If $r > j$ then $P > F$, so that the bondholder will realize a *capital loss* of $P - F$ at the time of redemption. Having the capital loss deferred would be of some value to the bondholder, so he would be willing to pay a larger $P$ for such a bond with a later maturity date. The reverse of this argument applies if $r < j$. In any event, the level of bond yield rates would influence a bond issuer in setting the coupon rate and maturity date on a new issue, since both coupon rate and maturity date have an effect on the actual price received for the bond by the issuer.

In the case where $F$ and $C$ are not equal, an additional parameter can be defined, called the *modified coupon rate* and denoted by $g = \frac{F \cdot r}{C}$, so that $Cg = Fr$. Exercise 4.1.18 develops alternative formulations for bond prices when $C \neq F$ that are equivalent to Equations (4.2), (4.3) and (4.4). When $C = F$ the bond is said to be *redeemed at par*, when $C > F$ the bond is said to be *redeemed at a premium*, and when $C < F$ the bond is said to be *redeemed at a discount*.

---

**The US Treasury Department "Halloween Surprise" of October 31, 2001**

On October 31, 2001, the US Department of the Treasury announced that it would no longer be issuing 30-year treasury bonds. The yield on a 30-year treasury bond had become a bellweather for long term interest rates. The announcement resulted in a surge in demand for the long-term bonds, prices rose and yield rates fell oń 30-year bonds by about 33 basis points (.33%) that day (yields on 2-year Treasury bonds fell only 4 basis points that day). Among the reasons given by the Treasury Department to discontinue the 30-year bonds were

(i)  they were expensive for the government (30 year yields at that time were about 5.25% and 10-year yields were below 4.25%; yield represents a measure of the cost to the bond issuer) and

(ii) the government was running a large budget surplus and government borrowing needs had diminished.

The US deficit is expected to be over $200 billion in 2007 and this has resulted in increased borrowing needs. On February 15, 2006, the Treasury Department reintroduced 30-year bonds with a $14 billion issue. Yields on the 30-year bonds are at about the same level as yields on 10-year T-bonds, so by that measure of cost, in February of 2006 the 30-year bonds were no more costly to issue than 10-year bonds.

---

### 4.1.3  BOND PRICES BETWEEN COUPON DATES

We have thus far considered only the determination of a bond's price on its issue date or at some later coupon date. In practice bonds are traded daily, and we now consider the valuation of a bond at a time between coupon dates. Let us regard the coupon period as the unit of time, and suppose that we wish to find the purchase price $P_t$ of a bond at time $t$, where $0 \leq t \leq 1$, with $t$ measured from the last coupon payment. The value of the bond is still found as the present value at the yield rate of all future payments (coupons plus redemption). Suppose that there are $n$ coupons remaining on the bond, including the next coupon due. At yield rate $j$ per coupon period, the value $P_1$ of the bond *just after* the next coupon could be found using one of Equations (4.2), (4.3) or (4.4). Then the value of the bond at time $t$ is the present value of the amount $P_1 + Fr$ due at time 1 (the present value of both the coupon due then and the future coupons and redemption), so that

$$P_t = v_j^{1-t}[P_1 + Fr]. \qquad (4.6a)$$

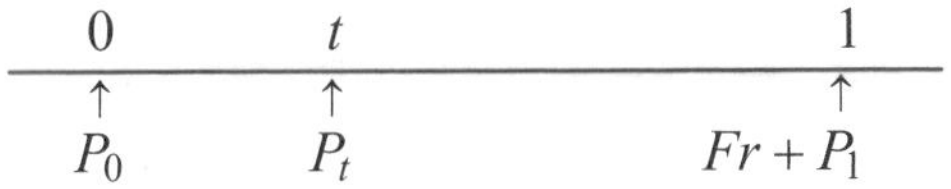

**FIGURE 4.2**

Alternatively, if we define $P_0$ to be the value of the bond just after the last coupon, then (see Exercise 4.1.27) we also have

$$P_t = P_0(1+j)^t. \qquad (4.6b)$$

The value $P_t$ given by Equations (4.6a) and (4.6b) is the purchase price paid for the bond at time $t$, and it is also called the **price-plus-accrued** of the bond. Price-plus-accrued may also be referred to as the "full price," the "flat price" or the "dirty price" of the bond.

In the calculation involved in Equations (4.6a) and (4.6b), the value of $t$ is between 0 and 1 and measures the time since the last coupon was paid as a fraction of a coupon period. Given the coupon dates and the date of time $t$, the numerical value of $t$ is

$$t = \frac{number\ of\ days\ since\ last\ coupon\ paid}{number\ of\ days\ in\ the\ coupon\ period}. \qquad (4.7)$$

The price given by Equations (4.6a) and (4.6b), with $t$ defined by Equation (4.7), is not the price that would be quoted for the bond in a financial newspaper. This quote price is called the market **price** (or simply "price" or "clean price"), and is equal to the price-plus-accrued minus the fraction of the coupon accrued to time $t$ (throughout this section, the terms *market price* and *purchase price* will have the specific meanings given here). This fractional coupon is proportional to the fractional part of the coupon period that has elapsed since the last coupon was paid, so the fractional coupon is $t \times F \times r$. The market price of the bond is then

$$Price_t = Price\text{-}plus\text{-}accrued_t - tFr = P_0(1+j)^t - tFr. \qquad (4.8)$$

This is the market price of the bond as calculated in practice. It is sometimes called the "actual/actual" method of calculating the market price. There is a variation to this calculation in which $P_0(1+j)^t$ is replaced by $P_0(1+jt)$ (a simple interest approximation).

| EXAMPLE 4.2 | (*Bond price between coupon dates*)

For each of the yield rates (i), (ii), and (iii) in Example 4.1, find both the purchase price and market price on August 1, 2000. Quote the prices (to the nearest .001) per 100 of face amount.

| SOLUTION |

Using the results in part (b) of Example 4.1, we see that on the last coupon date, June 18, 2000, the value of the bond was (i) 138,972,906, (ii) 100,000,000, and (iii) 74,513,772. The number of days from June 18 to August 1 is 44, and the number of days in the coupon period from June 18 to December 18 is 183. Using Equation (4.6b), with $t = \frac{44}{183}$, we have purchase prices of

(i) $138,972,906(1.025)^{44/183} = 139,800,445,$

(ii) $100,000,000(1.05)^{44/183} = 101,180,005,$ and

(iii) $74,513,772(1.075)^{44/183} = 75,820,791.$

Per 100 of face amount, the purchase prices, to the nearest .001, are

(i) 139.800,     (ii) 101.180,     and     (iii) 75.821.

The market prices are:

(i)     $139,800,445 - (44/183)(.05)(100,000,000) = 138,598,259,$

(ii)     $101,180,004 - (44/183)(.05)(100,000,000) = 99,977,818,$ and

(iii)     $75,820,791 - 44/13)(.05)(100,000,000) = 74,618,605.$

Per 100 of face we have quoted prices of

(i)     138.598,

(ii)     99.978, and

(iii)     74.619.     ❑

## 4.1.4  BOOK VALUE OF A BOND

In reporting the value of assets at a particular time, a bondholder would have to assign a value to the bond at that time. This value is called the *book value* of the bond, and is usually taken as the current price of the bond valued at the original yield rate at which the bond was purchased. For accounting purposes the accrued interest since the last coupon would be considered as a separate item from the book value of the bond. The next section of this chapter looks at book value in more detail.

Figure 4.3 below displays the graph of the purchase price and the market price of a bond over several consecutive coupon periods (all prices are calculated at the original yield rate of the bond). Nodes in the graph indicate the price just after a coupon is paid. The upper line in the graph is the purchase price or book value, and the lower line is the price without the accrued coupon. This graph is for a bond bought at a premium. The graph for a bond bought at a discount would be rising, but otherwise would be similar. Note that the market price (without the accrued coupon) is approximately the linear interpolation between two successive coupon dates (see Exercise 4.1.26), and the purchase price readjusts back to the market price on the coupon dates.

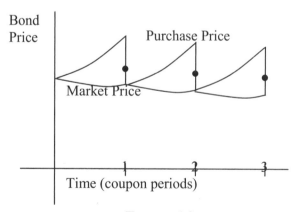

**FIGURE 4.3**

A bond trader would often be comparing the relative values of different bonds, and would want an equitable basis on which to compare, at a specific point in time, bonds with different calendar coupon dates. The price without accrued coupon (see Figure 4.3) provides a smooth progression of bond values from one coupon date to the next, and it is this price that is used by bond traders to compare relative bond values. This can easily be seen if we consider a bond for which $r = j$. We see from Equation (4.3) that if $r = j$ (the coupon and yield rates are equal), then on a coupon date the price of the bond would be $F$ (the bond is bought at par). However the purchase price of the bond grows from $P_0 = F$ at $t = 0$ to $P_0(1+j)$ just before the coupon is paid at $t = 1$, and just after that coupon is paid the price drops to $P_1 = F$ (see Exercise 4.1.28). For a bond trader comparing two bonds with different coupon dates, but both with $r = j$, it would be appropriate to compare using market price, since this price has eliminated a "distortion" caused by the accrued coupon included in the purchase price.

The notion, introduced earlier, of a bond bought at a premium, at par, or at a discount just after a coupon is paid was based on comparing the bond price with the face amount. To describe a bond as being bought at a premium, par or discount when bought at a time between coupon dates, the comparison is made between the market price and the face amount. It was pointed out that just after a coupon payment, a bond is priced at a premium, par or discount according to whether $r > j$, $r = j$, or $r < j$, respectively. This relationship remains valid when comparing the market price with the face amount at a time between coupon dates.

### 4.1.5 FINDING THE YIELD RATE FOR A BOND

When bonds are actually bought and sold on the bond market, the trading takes place with buyers and sellers offering "bid" and "ask" prices, respectively, with an intermediate settlement price eventually found. The amount by which the ask price exceeds the bid is the "spread." This is the difference in price between the highest price that a buyer is willing to pay for an asset and the lowest price for which a seller is willing to sell it. This terminology applies to investments of all types, bonds, equities (Chapter 8), derivative investments (Chapter 9). Some assets are more liquid than others and this may affect the size of the spread.

We have considered bond valuation mainly from the point of view of calculating the price of a bond when the coupon rate, time to maturity and yield rate are known. In practice, bond prices are settled first, and the corresponding yield rate is then determined and made part of the overall quotation describing the transaction. The determination of the yield rate from the price becomes an unknown interest rate problem which would be solved using an unknown interest function, a bond yield function on a financial calculator, or a spreadsheet program.

For a bond with face amount $F$, coupon rate $r$, with $n$ coupons remaining until maturity, and bought at a purchase price $P$ one period before the next coupon is due, the yield rate $j$ is the solution of the equation $P = Fv_j^n + Fr\,a_{\overline{n}|j}$. $j$ is the yield rate, or *internal rate of return* for this transaction, and there is a unique positive solution, $j > 0$. If the bond is bought at time $t$, $0 < t < 1$, measured from the last coupon, and there are $n$ coupons remaining, then $j$ is the solution of the equation $P = [Fv_j^n + Fr\,a_{\overline{n}|j}](1+j)^t$, where $P$ is the purchase price of the bond. Again, there will be a unique positive solution, $j > 0$.

| EXAMPLE 4.3 | (*Finding the yield rate from the price of a bond*) |

A 20-year 8% bond has semi-annual coupons and a face amount of 100. It is quoted at a purchase price of 70.400 (in decimal form, not $\frac{1}{32}$ form).

(a) Find the yield rate.

(b) Suppose that the bond was issued January 15, 2000, and is bought by a new purchaser for a price of 112.225 on January 15, 2005 just after a coupon has been paid.

   (i) Find the yield rate for the new purchaser.

   (ii) Find the yield rate (internal rate of return) earned by the original bondholder.

   (iii) Suppose that the original bondholder was able to deposit coupons into an account earning an annual interest rate of 6% convertible semi-annually. Find the average effective annual rate of return earned by the original bond purchaser on his 5-year investment. Assume that interest on the deposit account is credited every January 15 and July 15.

(c) Suppose that the bond was issued January 15, 2000, and is bought by a new purchaser on April 1, 2005 for a market price of 112.225.

   (i) Find the yield rate for the new purchaser.

   (ii) Find the yield rate (internal rate of return) earned by the original bondholder.

SOLUTION

(a) We solve for $j$, the 6-month yield rate, in the equation

$$70.400 = 100v_j^{40} + 4a_{\overline{40}|j}$$

(40 coupon periods to maturity, each coupon amount is 4). Using a financial calculator returns a value of $j = .059565$. This would be a quoted yield rate of 11.913% (compounded semi-annually).

(b) (i) There are 30 coupons remaining when the new purchaser buys the bond. We solve for $j$, the 6-month yield rate, in the equation $112.225 = 100v_j^{30} + 4a_{\overline{30}|j}$ (30 coupon periods to maturity). Using a financial calculator returns a value of $j = .033479$. This would be a quoted yield rate of 6.696% (compounded semi-annually).

(ii) The original bondholder received 10 coupons plus the purchase price of 112.225 on January 15, 2005. The original bondholder's equation of value for that 5-year (10 half-years) period is $70.400 = 112.225v_j^{10} + 4a_{\overline{10}|j}$. A financial calculator returns a value of $j = .09500$ (6-month yield of 9.5%) or a quoted nominal annual yield compounded semiannually of 19.0%.

(iii) On January 15, 2005, just after the coupon is deposited, the balance in the deposit account is $4s_{\overline{10}|.03} = 45.86$. Along with the sale of the bond, the original bondholder has a total of $45.86 + 112.225 = 158.08$. For the five year period, the annualized return is $i$, the solution of the equation $158.08 = 70.40(1+i)^5$. Solving for $i$ results in a value of $i = 17.6\%$.

(c) (i) There are 76 days from January 15, 2005 (the time of the most recent coupon) to April 1, 2005. The entire coupon period from January 15, 2005 to July 15, 2005 is 181 days. The purchase price of the bond on April 1, 2005 at yield rate $j$ per coupon period is $\left[100v_j^{30} + 4a_{\overline{30}|j}\right](1+j)^{76/181}$. The market price is 112.225, so the purchase price is $112.225 + \frac{76}{181} \times 4 = 113.905$. The new purchaser's 6-month yield is $j$, the solution of the equation $113.905 = \left[100v_j^{30} + 4a_{\overline{30}|j}\right](1+j)^{76/181}$. This is an awkward equation. Using a financial calculator with a function for calculating the yield rate on a bond, we get $j = .033421$ (annual yield rate of 6.684%, compounded semi-annually).

(ii) The original purchaser will receive 10 coupons of amount 4 each, plus a payment of 113.905 on April 1, 2005. The payment of 113.905 is made $10\frac{76}{181} = 10.420$ coupon periods after the bond was originally purchased. The original purchaser's 6-month yield $j$, is the solution of the equation $70.400 = 113.905 v_j^{10.420} + 4a_{\overline{10}|j}$. Standard financial calculator functions will not be capable of solving for $j$, and some approximate computer routine such as EXCEL Solver would be needed. The resulting solution is $j = .093054$ (9.31% is the 6-month yield rate). ☐

Several exercises at the end of the chapter look at various methods for approximating the yield rate. These methods may provide some insight into the price-yield relationship, but they are no longer used in practice.

## 4.2 AMORTIZATION OF A BOND

For taxation and other accounting purposes, it may be necessary to determine the amount of interest received and principal returned in a bond coupon or redemption payment. This can be done by viewing the bond as a standard amortized loan.

The purchaser of the bond can be thought of as the lender and the issuer of the bond is the borrower. The purchase price of the bond, $P$, can be thought of as the loan amount, and the coupon and redemption payments are the loan payments made by the borrower (the bond issuer) to the lender (the bondholder). For an amortized loan, the loan amount is the present value of the loan payments using the loan interest rate for present value calculation. Since the bond purchase price is the present value of the coupon and redemption payments using the yield rate, the **yield rate is the loan rate** when thinking of the bond purchase as a loan. An amortization schedule for the bond would be constructed algebraically like the general amortization schedule in Table 3.2.

The payment amounts in the bond amortization schedule will be the coupon amounts $Fr$ up to the $n-1^{st}$ coupon and the $n^{th}$ payment is a coupon plus the redemption amount, $Fr + C$. The prospective form of the outstanding balance just after a coupon payment is the present value of all future coupons plus redemption amount, valued at the "loan interest rate" which is the yield rate on the bond from when it was originally purchased, and is equal to the bond's book value.

The algebraic relationships for loan amortization also apply to bond amortization. One of the basic loan amortization relationships from Chapter 3 was Equation 3.4, $OB_{t+1} = OB_t(1+i) - K_{t+1}$. The corresponding bond amortization relationship up to the $n-1^{st}$ coupon is

$$BV_{t+1} = BV_t(1+j) - Fr \qquad (4.9)$$

$BV$ denotes the book value (or amortized value) and $j$ is the yield rate. We can also formulate the interest paid and principal repaid:

$$I_{t+1} = BV_t \times j \qquad (4.10)$$

$$PR_{t+1} = Fr - I_{t+1} \qquad (4.11)$$

The bond amortization schedule for a bond purchased on a coupon date (just after the coupon is paid) is given in the following table.

**TABLE 4.2**

| $K$ | Outstanding Balance (Book Value after Payment) | Pay-ment | Interest Due | Principal Repaid |
|---|---|---|---|---|
| 0 | $P = F[1+(r-j)\cdot a_{\overline{n}|}]$ | – | – | – |
| 1 | $F[1+(r-j)\cdot a_{\overline{n-1}|}]$ | $Fr$ | $F[j+(r-j)(1-v_j^n)]$ | $F(r-j)\cdot v_j^n$ |
| 2 | $F[1+(r-j)\cdot a_{\overline{n-2}|}]$ | $Fr$ | $F[j+(r-j)(1-v_j^{n-1})]$ | $F(r-j)\cdot v_j^{n-1}$ |
| $\vdots$ | $\vdots$ | $\vdots$ | $\vdots$ | $\vdots$ |
| $k$ | $F[1+(r-j)\cdot a_{\overline{n-k}|}]$ | $Fr$ | $F[j+(r-j)(1-v_j^{n-k+1})]$ | $F(r-j)\cdot v_j^{n-k+1}$ |
| $\vdots$ | $\vdots$ | $\vdots$ | $\vdots$ | $\vdots$ |
| $n-1$ | $F[1+(r-j)\cdot a_{\overline{1}|}]$ | $Fr$ | $F[j+(r-j)(1-v_j^2)]$ | $F(r-j)\cdot v_j^2$ |
| $n$ | 0 | $Fr+F$ | $F[j+(r-j)(1-v_j)]$ | $F[1+(r-j)\cdot v_j]$ |

Notice that since the payments are level throughout the term of the bond, except for the final payment, the principal repaid column forms a geometric progression with ratio $1+j$. The following example illustrates a bond amortization.

| EXAMPLE 4.4 | *(Bond amortization)*

A 10% bond with face amount 10,000 matures 4 years after issue. Construct the amortization schedule for the bond over its term for nominal annual yield rates of (a) 8%, (b) 10%, and (c) 12%.

| SOLUTION |

(a) The entries in the amortization schedule are calculated as they were in Table 4.2, where $k$ counts coupon periods. With a nominal yield rate of 8% the purchase price of the bond is 10,673.27. Then $I_1 = (10,673.27)(.04) = 426.93$, and so on. The complete schedule is shown in Table 4.3a.

## TABLE 4.3a

| $k$ | Outstanding Balance | Payment | Interest Due | Principal Repaid |
|---|---|---|---|---|
| 0 | 10,673.27 | – | – | – |
| 1 | 10,600.21 | 500 | 426.93 | 73.07 |
| 2 | 10,524.22 | 500 | 424.01 | 75.99 |
| 3 | 10,445.19 | 500 | 420.97 | 79.03 |
| 4 | 10,363.00 | 500 | 417.81 | 82.19 |
| 5 | 10,277.52 | 500 | 414.52 | 85.48 |
| 6 | 10,188.62 | 500 | 411.10 | 88.90 |
| 7 | 10,096.16 | 500 | 407.54 | 92.46 |
| 8 | 0 | 10,500 | 403.85 | 10,096.15 |

Note that since $OB_7 = 10,096.16$ and $PR_8 = 10.096.15$ we should have $OB_8 = .01$. Of course $OB_8 = 0$ and the one cent discrepancy is due to rounding. The values of $OB_k$ decrease to the redemption value as $k$ approaches the end of the term. The entry under Principal Repaid is called **the amount for amortization of premium** for that particular period. The amortization of a bond bought at a premium is also referred to as **writing down a bond**. If we sum the entries in the principal repaid column for $k$ from 1 to 7 along with 96.15 at time 8 (the principal repaid before the redemption payment of 10,000), we get a total of 673.27

which is the total premium above redemption value at which the bond was originally purchased. The coupon payments are amortizing the premium, reducing the book value to 10,000 as of time 8 and then the redemption payment of 10,000 retires the bond debt.

(b) With a nominal yield rate of 10% the purchase price is 10,000. The schedule is shown in Table 4.3b.

**TABLE 4.3b**

| k | Outstanding Balance | Payment | Interest Due | Principal Repaid |
|---|---|---|---|---|
| 0 | 10,000.00 | – | – | – |
| 1 | 10,000.00 | 500 | 500.00 | 0 |
| 2 | 10,000.00 | 500 | 500.00 | 0 |
| 3 | 10,000.00 | 500 | 500.00 | 0 |
| 4 | 10,000.00 | 500 | 500.00 | 0 |
| 5 | 10,000.00 | 500 | 500.00 | 0 |
| 6 | 10,000.00 | 500 | 500.00 | 0 |
| 7 | 10,000.00 | 500 | 500.00 | 0 |
| 8 | 0 | 10,500 | 500.00 | 10,000 |

(c) With a nominal yield rate of 12% the purchase price is 9379.02; the schedule is shown in Table 4.3c.

**TABLE 4.3c**

| k | Outstanding Balance | Payment | Interest Due | Principal Repaid |
|---|---|---|---|---|
| 0 | 9379.02 | — | — | — |
| 1 | 9441.76 | 500 | 562.74 | – 62.74 |
| 2 | 9508.27 | 500 | 566.51 | – 66.51 |
| 3 | 9578.77 | 500 | 570.50 | – 70.50 |
| 4 | 9653.50 | 500 | 574.73 | – 74.73 |
| 5 | 9732.71 | 500 | 579.21 | – 79.21 |
| 6 | 9816.67 | 500 | 583.96 | – 83.96 |
| 7 | 9905.67 | 500 | 589.00 | – 89.00 |
| 8 | 0 | 10,500 | 594.34 | 9905.66 |

Round-off error again gives a value of $OB_8 = .01$, when it should be zero. Note that $OB_k$ *increases* to the redemption amount as $k$ approaches the end of the term. The principal repaid column entries are negative. This occurs because the coupon payment of 500 is not large enough to pay for the interest due, so the shortfall is added to the outstanding balance (amortized value). The negative of the principal repaid entry is called the **amount for accumulation of discount** when a bond is bought at a discount. This amortization is also referred to as **writing up a bond.** □

Since a bond amortization is algebraically the same as a loan amortization, calculator functions for amortization can be used to calculated bond amortization quantities.

## 4.3 APPLICATIONS AND ILLUSTRATIONS

### 4.3.1 CALLABLE BONDS: OPTIONAL REDEMPTION DATES

A bond issuer may wish to add flexibility to a bond issue by specifying a range of dates during which redemption can occur, at the issuer's option. Such a bond is referred to as a **callable bond**. For a specific yield rate, the price of the bond will depend on the time until maturity, and for a specific bond price, the yield rate on the bond will depend on the time until maturity. The following example illustrates the way in which a callable bond is priced.

---

**Definition 4.3 – Callable Bond**

A callable bond is one for which there is a range of possible redemption dates. The redemption is chosen by the bond issuer. ·

---

EXAMPLE 4.5 *Finding the price of a callable bond*)

(a) A 10% bond with semi-annual coupons and with face and redemption amount 1,000,000 is issued with the condition that redemption can take place on any coupon date between 12 and 15 years from the issue date. Find the price paid by an investor wishing a minimum yield of (i) $i^{(2)} = .12$, and (ii) $i^{(2)} = .08$.

(b) Suppose the investor pays the maximum of all prices for the range of redemption dates. Find the yield rate if the issuer chooses a redemption date corresponding to the minimum price in each of cases (i) and (ii) of part (a).

(c) Suppose the investor pays the minimum of all prices for the range of redemption dates. Find the yield rate if the issuer chooses a redemption date corresponding to the maximum price in each of cases (i) and (ii) of part (a).

(d) Suppose the investor pays 850,000 for the bond and holds the bond until it is called. Find the minimum yield that the investor will obtain.

## SOLUTION

(a) (i) From Equation (4.3) $P = 1,000,000\left[1 + (.05 - .06) \cdot a_{\overline{n}|.06}\right]$, where $n$ is the number of coupons until redemption, $n = 24, 25, \ldots, 30$. The price range for these redemption dates is from 874,496 for redemption at $n = 24$ to 862,352 for redemption at $n = 30$. It is most prudent for the investor to offer a price of 862,352.

(ii) The range of prices is from 1,152,470 if redemption occurs at 12 years, to 1,172,920 if redemption is at 15 years The prudent investor would pay 1,152,470.

(b) If the investor in (i) pays the maximum price of 874,496 (based on redemption at $n = 24$), and the bond is redeemed at the end of 15 years, the actual nominal yield is 11.80%. If the investor in (ii) pays 1,172,920 (based on redemption at $n = 30$), and the bond is redeemed at the end of 12 years, the actual nominal yield is 7.76%.

(c) If the investor in (i) pays 862,352 (based on 15 year redemption) and the bond is redeemed after 12 years, the actual nominal yield is 12.22%, and if the investor in (ii) pays 1,152,470 (based on 12 year redemption) and the bond is redeemed after 15 years, the actual nominal yield is 8.21%.

(d) We use the equation $850,000 = 1,000,000 v_j^n + 50,000 a_{\overline{n}|j}$.

For each $n$ from 24 to 30, we can find the corresponding 6-month yield rate $j$. For $n = 24$, the 6-month yield rate is $j = .0622$, which corresponds to a nominal annual yield of 12.44%. For $n = 30$, the 6-month yield rate is .0610 (nominal annual 12.20%). If we check the yield rate for $n = 25, 26, 27, 28, 29$, we will see that the minimum yield occurs if redemption is at $n = 30$, and this yield is 12.20%.

❏

For a callable bond, if a minimum yield $j$ is desired, there are some general rules that can be established for finding the purchase price that will result in a yield rate of at least $j$. Using the bond price formula $P = C\left[1 + (r - j) \cdot a_{\overline{n}|j}\right]$, we have seen that for a given yield rate $j$, if $r < j$, then $P < C$ (the bond is bought at a discount). Also, in this case, since $r - j < 0$, the minimum price will occur at the maximum value of $n$ (latest redemption date), because $(r - j) \cdot a_{\overline{n}|j}$ is most negative when $n$ is largest. This can also be seen from general reasoning, because if a bond is bought at a discount, then it is most advantageous to the bond purchaser to receive the large redemption amount $C$ as soon as possible, so the bond has greatest value if redemption occurs at the earliest redemption date and the bond has least value if redemption occurs at the latest date. Using similar reasoning, if $r > j$ (bond bought at a premium), the minimum price will occur at the minimum value of $n$. This is illustrated in part (a) of Example 4.5.

Similar reasoning to that in the previous paragraph provides a general rule for determining the minimum yield that will be obtained on a callable bond if the price is given. If a bond is bought at a discount for price $P$, then there will be a "capital gain" of amount $C - P$ when the bond is redeemed. The sooner the bondholder receives this capital gain, the greater will be the yield (return) on the bond, and therefore, the minimum possible yield would occur if the bond is redeemed on the latest possible call date. This is illustrated in part (d) of Example 4.5. In a similar way, we see that for a bond bought at a premium, there will be a "capital loss" of amount $P - C$ when the bond is redeemed. The earlier this loss occurs, the lower the return received by the bondholder, so the minimum yield occurs at the earliest redemption date.

If an investor pricing the bond desires a minimum yield rate of $j$, the investor will calculate the price of the bond at rate $j$ for each of the redemption dates in the specified range. The minimum of those prices will be the purchase price. If the investor pays more than that minimum price, and if the issuer redeems at a point such that the price is the minimum price, then the investor has "overpaid" and will earn a yield less then the minimum yield originally desired. This is illustrated in parts (b) and (c) of Example 4.5.

When the first optional call date arrives, the bond issuer, based on market conditions and its own financial situation, will make a decision on whether or not to call (redeem) the bond prior to the latest possible redemption date. If the issuer is not in a position to redeem at an early date, under appropriate market conditions, it still might be to the issuer's advantage to redeem the bond and issue a new bond for the remaining term. As a simple illustration of this point, suppose in Example 4.5(a) that 12 years after the issue date, the yield rate on a new 3-year bond is 9%. If the issuer redeems the bond and immediately issues a new 3-year bond with the same coupon and face amount, the issuer must pay 1,000,000 to the bondholder, but then receives 1,025,789 for the new 3-year bond, which is bought at a yield rate of 9%.

A callable bond might have different redemption amounts at the various optional redemption dates. It might still be possible to use some of the reasoning described above to find the minimum price for all possible redemption dates. In general, however, it may be necessary to calculate the price at several (or all) of the optional dates to find the minimum price.

### Example 4.6 (*Varying redemption amounts for a callable bond*)

A 15-year 8% bond with face amount 100 is callable (at the option of the issuer) on a coupon date in the $10^{th}$ to $15^{th}$ years. In the $10^{th}$ year the bond is callable at par, in the $11^{th}$ or $12^{th}$ years at redemption amount 115, or in the $13^{th}$, $14^{th}$ or $15^{th}$ years at redemption amount 135.

(a) What price should an investor pay in order to ensure a minimum nominal annual yield to maturity of (i) 12%, and (ii) 6%?

(b) Find the investor's minimum yield if the purchase price is (i) 80, and (ii) 120.

### Solution

(a) (i) Since the yield rate is larger than the coupon rate (or modified coupon rate for any of the redemption dates), the bond will be bought at a discount. Using Equation (4.3E) from Exercise 4.1.18, we see that during any interval for which the redemption amount is level, the lowest price will occur at the latest redemption date. Thus we must compute the price at the end of 10 years, 12 years and 15 years. The corresponding prices are 77.06, 78.60 and 78.56. The lowest price corresponds to a redemption date of 10 years, which is near the earliest possible redemption date. This example indicates that the principal of pricing a bond bought at a discount by using the latest redemption date may fail when the redemption amounts are not level.

(ii) For redemption in the $10^{th}$ year and the $11^{th}$ or $12^{th}$ years, the yield rate of 3% every six months is smaller than the modified coupon rate of 4% (for redemption in year 10) or $\frac{100(.04)}{115} = .0348$ (for redemption in years 11 or 12). The modified coupon rate is $.0296 < 3\%$ for redemption in the $13^{th}$ to $15^{th}$ years. Thus the minimum price for redemption in the $10^{th}$ year occurs at the earliest redemption date, which is at $9\frac{1}{2}$ years, and the minimum price for redemption in the $11^{th}$ or $12^{th}$ years also occurs at the earliest date, which is at $10\frac{1}{2}$ years. Since $g < j$ in the $13^{th}$ to $15^{th}$ years, the minimum price occurs at the latest date, which is at 15 years. Thus we must calculate the price of the bond for redemption at $9\frac{1}{2}$ years, $10\frac{1}{2}$ years and 15 years. The prices are 114.32, 123.48, and 134.02. The price paid will be 114.32, which corresponds to the earliest possible redemption date.

(b) (i) Since the bond is bought at a discount (to the redemption value), it is to the investor's disadvantage to have the redemption at the latest date. Thus we find the yield based on redemption dates of 10 years, 12 years and 15 years. These nominal yield rates are 11.40%, 11.75% and 11.77% The minimum yield is 11.40%.

(ii) Since the bond is bought at a premium to the redemption value in the $10^{th}$ year and in the $11^{th}$ and $12^{th}$ years, the minimum yield to maturity occurs at the earliest redemption date for those periods. This is $9\frac{1}{2}$ years for the $10^{th}$ year and $10\frac{1}{2}$ years for the $11^{th}$ and $12^{th}$ years. The bond is bought at a discount to the redemption amount in the $13^{th}$ to $15^{th}$ years, so the minimum yield occurs at the latest redemption date, which is 15 years. We find the yield based on redemption at $9\frac{1}{2}$ years, $10\frac{1}{2}$ years and 15 years. These nominal yield rates are 5.29%, 6.38% and 7.15% The minimum is 5.29%.  ❏

Through the latter part of the 1980s, bonds callable at the option of the issuer became less common in the marketplace. The increased competition for funds by governments and corporations during that period produced various incentives that are occasionally added to a bond issue. One such incentive is a retractable-extendible feature, which gives the *bondholder* the option of having the bond redeemed (retracted) on a specified date, or having the redemption date extended to a specified later date. This is similar to a callable bond with the option in the hands of the bondholder rather than the bond issuer. Another incentive is to provide warrants with the bond. A warrant gives the bondholder the option to purchase additional amounts of the bond at a later date at a guaranteed price.

### 4.3.2 SERIAL BONDS AND MAKEHAM'S FORMULA

A bond issue may consist of a collection of bonds with a variety of redemption dates, or redemption in installments. This might be done so that the bond issuer can stagger the redemption payments instead of having a single redemption date with one large redemption amount. Such an issue can be treated as a series of separate bonds, each with its own redemption date, and it is possible that the coupon rate differs for the various redemption dates. It may also be the case that purchasers will want different yield rates for the different maturity dates. This bond is called a *serial bond* since redemption occurs with a series of redemption payments.

Suppose that a serial bond has redemption amounts $F_1, F_2, \ldots, F_m$, to be redeemed in $n_1, n_2, \ldots, n_m$ coupon periods, respectively, and pays coupons at rates $r_1, r_2, \ldots, r_m$, respectively, Suppose also that this serial bond is purchased to yield $j_1, j_2, \ldots, j_m$, respectively, on the $m$ pieces. Then the price of the $t^{th}$ piece can be formulated using any one of Equation (4.2), (4.3) or (4.4). Using Makeham's bond price formula given by Equation (4.4), the price of the $t^{th}$ piece is

$$P_t = K_t + \frac{r_t}{j_t}(F_t - K_t), \qquad (4.12)$$

where $K_t = F_t \cdot v_{j_t}^{n_t}$. The price of the total serial issue would be $P = \sum_{t=1}^{m} P_t$. In the special case where the coupon rates and yield rates on all pieces of the serial issue are the same, the total price of the issue can be written in a compact form using Makeham's Formula:

$$P = \sum_{t=1}^{m} P_t = \sum_{t=1}^{m} \left[ K_t + \frac{r}{j}(F_t - K_t) \right] = K + \frac{r}{j}(F - K), \quad (4.13)$$

where $K = \sum_{t=1}^{m} K_t$ is the present value of all redemption amounts for the

entire issue, and $F = \sum_{t=1}^{m} F_t$ is the total redemption amount for the issue.

If the series of redemptions has a systematic form, such as a level amount every period for a number of periods, then $K$ can be conveniently formulated as the present value of the annuity formed by the series of redemption amounts. Note that Equation (4.13) requires a uniform coupon rate and yield rate for all redemption dates in the issue.

---

**EXAMPLE 4.7** (*Serial bond*)

On August 15, 2000 a corporation issues a 10% serial bond with face amount 50,000,000. The redemption is scheduled to take place at 5,000,000 every August 15 from 2010 to 2014 and 25,000,000 on August 15, 2015. Find the price of the entire issue on the issue date at a yield of $i^{(2)} = .125$.

**SOLUTION**

The present value of all of the redemption payments is

$$K = 5,000,000 \left[ v^{20}_{.0625} + v^{22}_{.0625} + v^{24}_{.0625} + v^{26}_{.0625} + v^{28}_{.0625} \right]$$
$$+ 25,000,000 \cdot v^{30}_{.0625} = 9,976,960.$$

Then the price of the serial bond is

$$P = K + \frac{r}{j}(F-K)$$
$$= 9,976,960 + \frac{.05}{.0625}(50,000,000-9,976,960) = 41,995,392. \quad \square$$

## 4.4 DEFINITIONS AND FORMULAS

---

**Definition 4.1 – Bond**

A bond is an interest-bearing certificate of public (government) or private (corporate) indebtedness.

---

## Bond notation

$F$ – The face amount (also called the par value) of the bond
$r$ – the coupon rate per coupon period (six months unless otherwise specified)
$C$ – the redemption amount on the bond (equal to $F$ unless otherwise noted)
$n$ – the number of coupon periods until maturity
$j$ – the yield rate per coupon period

## Bond price on a coupon date

$$P = C\frac{1}{(1+j)^n} + Fr\left[\frac{1}{1+j} + \frac{1}{(1+j)^2} + \cdots + \frac{1}{(1+j)^n}\right]$$

$$= Cv_j^n + Fr\, a_{\overline{n}|j} \tag{4.1}$$

$$= C + (Fr - Cj)a_{\overline{n}|j} \tag{4.3}$$

---

**Definition 4.2 – Bond Purchase Value**

(a) If $P > F$, the bond is said to be bought **at a premium**.
(b) If $P = F$, the bond is said to be bought **at par**.
(c) If $P < F$, the bond is said to be bought **at a discount**.

---

## Bond price between coupon dates

$P_t = P_0(1+j)^t$ is the price including accrued coupon at fraction $t$ into the coupon period, where $P_0$ is the price just after the last coupon. The market price is $P_0(1+j)^t - Frt$ (the purchase price minus accrued coupon).　(4.8)

$$t = \frac{number\ of\ days\ since\ last\ coupon\ paid}{number\ of\ days\ in\ the\ coupon\ period}. \tag{4.7}$$

## Amortization of a Bond

$BV$ denotes the book value (or amortized value) and $j$ is the yield rate.

$$BV_{t+1} = BV_t(1+j) - Fr \tag{4.9}$$

$$I_{t+1} = BV_t \times j \tag{4.10}$$

$$PR_{t+1} = Fr - I_{t+1} \tag{4.11}$$

---

**Definition 4. 3 – Callable Bond**

A callable bond is one for which there is a range of possible redemption dates. The redemption is chosen by the bond issuer.

---

## 4.5 NOTES AND REFERENCES

The reference book *Standard Securities Calculation Methods*, provides a comprehensive collection of calculation and quotation methods used in financial practice. *The Handbook of Fixed Income Securities*, by F. Fabozzi covers a wide range of topics on bonds and other fixed income investments. The text by Butcher and Nesbitt details several numerical procedures for approximating yield rates, and provides additional references on the subject.

## 4. 6 EXERCISES

Unless specified otherwise, it is assumed that all coupon rates are quoted as annual rates but payable semiannually, all yield rates are nominal annual rates convertible semiannually, and bonds are valued just after a coupon has been paid.

### SECTION 4.1

4.1.1 Find the prices of the following bonds, all redeemable at par. Show how to compare their prices without actually calculating the numerical values.

(a) A 10-year 100, 5% bond yielding 7.2%
(b) A 10-year 100, 5½ % bond yielding 7.7%
(c) A 12-year 100, 5% bond yielding 7.2%
(d) A 12-year 100, 5½ % bond yielding 7.7%

4.1.2 A twelve-year 100 par value bond pays 7% coupons semiannually. The bond is priced at 115.84 to yield an annual nominal rate of 6% compounded semiannually. Calculate the redemption value of the bond.

4.1.3   A zero-coupon bond pays no coupons and only pays a redemption amount at the time the bond matures. Greta can buy a zero-coupon bond that will pay 10,000 at the end of 10 years and is currently selling for 5,083.49. Instead she purchases a 10% bond with coupons payable semi-annually that will pay 10,000 at the end of 10 years. If she pays $X$ she will earn the same annual effective interest rate as the zero coupon bond. Calculate $X$.

4.1.4   A 6% bond maturing in 8 years with semiannual coupons to yield 5% convertible semiannually is to be replaced by a 5.5% bond yielding the same return. In how many years should the new bond mature? (Both bonds have the same price, yield rate and face amount).

4.1.5   Don purchases a 1000 par value 10-year bond with 8% semiannual coupons for 900. He is able to reinvest his coupon payments at a nominal rate of 6% convertible semiannually. Calculate his nominal annual yield rate convertible semiannually over the ten-year period.

4.1.6   A 25-year bond with a par value of 1000 and 10% coupons payable quarterly is selling at 800. Calculate the annual nominal yield rate convertible quarterly.

4.1.7   An investor borrows an amount at an annual effective interest rate of 7% and will repay all interest and principal in a lump sum at the end of 10 years. She uses the amount borrowed to purchase a 1000 par value 10-year bond with 10% semiannual coupons bought to yield 8% convertible semiannually. All coupon payments are reinvested at a nominal rate of 6% convertible semiannually. Calculate the net gain to the investor at the end of 10 years after the loan is repaid.

4.1.8   In the table in Section 4.1 excerpted from the U.S. Bureau of Public Debt, a 5-year treasury bond is listed as having been issued on January 31, 2007 and maturing on January 31, 2012. The coupon rate is 4.75%, the yield rate at issue is listed as 4.855%, and the price at issue is listed as 99.539. Verify that this is the correct price for this bond.

4.1.9    The *National Post* ©, a Canadian daily newspaper, has listings after each trading day of the closing prices and yields of a number of bonds that traded the previous day. In the March 2, 2004 edition, there was the following listing for a Government of Canada bond:

| Coupon | Maturity Date | Bid $ | Yield % |
|--------|---------------|-------|---------|
| 4.25   | Sep 01/09     | 102.76 | 3.69   |

(a) Verify that this is the correct price for the bond.

(b) In this listing, the price per $100 is rounded to the nearest $.01, and the yield rate is rounded to the nearest .01%. The quoted yield rate could be any number from 3.685% to 3.695% (and would be rounded to 3.69%, we can think of 3.695% as 3.6949999%). Find the resulting prices at the two ends of that range of yield rates.

(c) The bid price of 102.76 could have been rounded from an actual price between 102.755 and 102.765. Find the yield rates that correspond to those prices.

4.1.10   An $n$-year 4.75% bond is selling for 95.59. An $n$-year 6.25% bond at the same yield would sell for 108.82. The face and redemption amount of the bond is 100. Find the yield rate.

4.1.11   Bond A has $n$ coupons remaining at rate $r_1$ each, and sells to yield rate $i_1$ effective per coupon period. Bond B has the same face value and number of coupons remaining as Bond A, but the coupons are at rate $r_2$ each and the yield rate is $i_2$ effective per period. If $i_2 \cdot r_1 = i_1 \cdot r_2$ and $i_2 > i_1 > r_1$, which of the following statements are true?

    I.   The price of Bond B exceeds the price of Bond A.

    II.  The present value of Bond B's coupons on the purchase date exceeds the present value of Bond A's coupons.

    III. The present value of the redemption amount for Bond B exceeds the corresponding present value for Bond A.

4.1.12  Two bonds, each of face amount 100, are offered for sale at a combined price of 240. Both bonds have the same term to maturity but the coupon rate for one is twice that of the other. The difference in price of the two bonds is 24. Prices are based on a nominal annual yield rate of 3%. Find the coupon rates of the two bonds.

4.1.13  A 7% bond has a price of 79.30 and a 9% bond has a price of 93.10, both per 100 of face amount. Both are redeemable in $n$ years and have the same yield rate. Find $n$.

4.1.14  When a certain type of bond matures, the bondholder is subject to a tax of 25% on the amount of discount at which he bought the bond. A 1000 bond of this type has 4% *annually* paid coupons and is redeemable at par in 10 years. No tax is paid on coupons. What price should a purchaser pay to realize an effective annual yield of 5% after taxes?

4.1.15  Smith purchases a 20-year, 8%, 1000 bond with semiannual coupons. The purchase price will give a nominal annual yield to maturity, of 10%. After the $20^{th}$ coupon, Smith sells the bond. At what price did he sell the bond if his actual nominal annual yield is 10%?

4.1.16  Show that Equations (4.6a) and (4.6b) are algebraically equivalent.

4.1.17  In the bond quotations of a financial newspaper, a quote was given for the price on February 20, 2004 of an 11% bond with face amount 100 maturing on April 1, 2023. The yield was quoted as 11.267%. Find the quoted price to the nearest .001.

4.1.18  Suppose the redemption amount $C$ is not necessarily equal to the face amount $F$ on a bond. Using $g = \frac{Fr}{C}$ as the *modified coupon rate*, show that Equations (4.2), (4.3) and (4.4) become

$$P \;=\; C \cdot v_j^n + Cg \cdot a_{\overline{n}|j}, \qquad (4.2E)$$

$$P \;=\; C + C(g-j) \cdot a_{\overline{n}|j}, \qquad (4.3E)$$

and

$$P = K + \frac{g}{j}(C-K). \qquad (4.4E)$$

Describe the relationship linking the relative sizes of $P$ and $C$ to the relative sizes of $g$ and $j$.

4.1.19 A 1000 bond bearing coupons at annual rate 6.5%, payable semiannually, and redeemable at 1050 is bought to yield a nominal rate of 8%. If the present value of the redemption amount is 210, what is the price to the nearest 10?

4.1.20 A company issues 1,000,000 in bonds. The prevailing yield rate on the bonds is 12%. The company considers having coupons at 8% and a maturity of 15 years. On second thought, the company decides on a maturity date of 20 years. What coupon rate must the bond issue have in order for the company to raise the same amount of revenue as it would have on the 15-year issue? Suppose the company issued the bonds with a maturity date of 10 years. What coupon rate is required to raise the same amount as under the other two issues?

4.1.21S You have decided to invest in two bonds. Bond $X$ is an $n$-year bond with semi-annual coupons, while bond $Y$ is zero-coupon bond, which is redeemable in $n/2$ years. The desired yield rate is the same for both bonds. You also have the following information:

**Bond $X$**

- Par value is 1000.
- The ratio of the semi-annual bond rate to the desired semi-annual yield rate, $\frac{r}{i}$ is 1.03125.
- The present value of the redemption value is 381.50.

**Bond $Y$**

- Redemption value is the same as that of bond $X$.
- Price to yield is 647.80.

What is the price of bond $X$?

*4.1.22 Consider two bonds, each with face amount 1. One bond matures 6 months from now and carries one coupon of amount $r_1$. The other bond matures 1 year from now and carries two semiannual coupons of amount $r_2$ each. Both bonds have the same selling price to yield nominal annual $i^{(2)}$. Find a formulation for $i^{(2)}$ in terms of $r_1, r_2$ and constants.

*4.1.23 A bond issue carries quarterly coupons of 2% of the face amount outstanding. An investor uses Makeham's Formula to evaluate the whole outstanding issue to yield an effective annual rate of 13%. Find the value of $H$ used in the formula $P = K + H(C-K)$.

*4.1.24 A bond with face and redemption amount of 3000 with *annual* coupons is selling at an effective annual yield rate equal to twice the annual coupon rate. The present value of the coupons is equal to the present value of the redemption amount. What is the selling price?

*4.1.25 On November 1, 1999 Smith paid 1000 for a government savings bond of face amount 1000 with annual coupons of 8%, with maturity to occur on November 1, 2011. On November 1, 2005 the government issues new savings bonds with the same maturity date of November 1, 2011, but with annual coupons of 9.5% (Smith's bond will still pay 8%). The government offers Smith a cash bonus of $X$ to be paid on the maturity date if he holds his old bond until maturity. Smith can cash in his old bond on November 1, 2005 and buy a new bond for 1000. If both options yield 9.5% from November 1, 2005 to November 1, 2011, find $X$.

*4.1.26 Show that if $(1+j)^t$ is approximated by $1+jt$, then the quoted price of a bond at time $t$, $0 \le t \le 1$, since the last coupon is the linearly-interpolated value at $t$ between $P_0$ and $P_1$. (This is the linearly interpolated price exclusive of the accrued coupon.)

*4.1.27 Show that $P_0(1+j) - Fr = P_1$. Then assuming that $r = j$ and $P_0 = F$, show that $P_1 = F$.

*4.1.28 Suppose that a bond has semiannual coupons of amount $Fr$ each. At six-month effective yield rate $j$, a continuous payment for six months equivalent to a semiannual coupon is $\bar{r} \cdot F = (Fr / \bar{s}_{\overline{1}|j})$.

Suppose that the quoted price at time $t$ (where $0 \le t \le 1$ is measured since the last coupon) is redefined to be the price-plus-accrued minus $\bar{r} \cdot F \cdot \bar{s}_{\overline{t}|j}$. Show that the quoted price in part (ii) of Example 4.2 would then become exactly 100 per 100 of face amount. Show that $\bar{r} \cdot \bar{s}_{\overline{t}|j}$ is approximately equal to $t \cdot Fr$.

*4.1.29 During the time when compound interest calculations were done by hand and with reference to interest tables, bond tables were constructed listing prices at issue (per 100 of face amount) of bonds with varying maturity dates, coupon rates and yield rates. Thus the bond price $P(n,r,j)$ is written as a function of $n$, $r$ and $j$. Show that $P(n,r,j)$ is a linear function of $r$ but not of $n$ or $j$. Thus linear interpolation with respect to the coupon rate gives exact results, but linear interpolation with respect to the yield rate gives approximate results.

*4.1.30 Let $n \ge 1$, $0 \le t \le 1$, and $g(j) = [F \cdot v_j^n + Fr \cdot a_{\overline{n}|j}](1+j)^t$.

(a) Show that $g(j)$ is strictly decreasing and convex (i.e.,

$$g'(j) < 0 \text{ and } g''(j) > 0).$$

(b) Show that $\lim_{j \to -0} g(j) = +\infty$ and $\lim_{j \to \infty} g(j) = 0$.

(c) Use parts (a) and (b) to show that if $P > 0$ the equation

$$P = [F \cdot v_j^n + Fr \cdot a_{\overline{n}|j}](1+j)^t$$

has a unique solution for $j$.

## SECTION 4.2

4.2.1   Find the total amount paid, the total interest and the total principal repaid in the amortization of Table 4.2.

4.2.2   Graph $OB_k$ for each of the three cases in Example 4.4.

(a) Show that for a bond bought at a premium, the graph of $OB_k$ is concave downward.

(b) Show that for a bond bought at a discount, the graph of $OB_k$ is convex upward.

4.2.3   A 10% bond has face amount 10,000. For each combination of the following number of coupon periods and six-month yield rates, use a computer spreadsheet program to construct the amortization table and draw the graph of $OB_k$:   $n = 1, 5, 10, 30$;   $j = .025, .05, .075$.

4.2.4   The amortization schedule for a 100, 5% bond with yielding a nominal annual rate of $i^{(2)} = 6.6\%$ gives a value of 90.00 for the bond at the beginning of a certain 6-month period just after a coupon has been paid. What is the book value at the start of the next 6-month period?

4.2.5   A bond of face amount 100 is purchased at a premium of 36 to yield 7%. The amount for amortization of premium in the $5^{th}$ coupon is 1.00. What is the term of the bond?

4.2.6   A bondholder is subject to a tax of 50% on interest payments at the time interest is received, and a tax (or credit) of 25% on capital gains (or losses) when they are realized. Assume that the capital gain (or loss) on the bond is the difference between the purchase price and the sale price (or redemption amount if held to maturity), and the full amount of each coupon is regarded as interest. For each of the cases in Example 4.4, find the bond's purchase price so that the stated yield is the *after-tax* yield (based on the bond being held to maturity).

4.2.7 Among a company's assets and accounting records, an actuary finds a 15-year bond that was purchased at a premium. From the records, the actuary has determined the following:

(i)   The bond pays semi-annual interest.

(ii)  The amount for amortization of the premium in the $2^{nd}$ coupon payment was 977.19.

(iii) The amount for amortization of the premium in the $4^{th}$ coupon payment was 1046.79.

What is the value of the premium?

*4.2.8 Using Table 4.2, show that the bond payments can be regarded as payments on two separate loans. The first loan is of amount $F$ with interest only at rate $j$ (per coupon period) for $n$ periods, plus return of $F$ at the end of $n$ periods. The second loan is an amortization of $P - F$ over $n$ periods at effective rate $j$ (per coupon period), with payments of $F(r-j)$ per coupon period. This second loan is the amortization of premium if $P > F$.

*4.2.9 A 30-year bond with face amount 10,000 is bought to yield $i^{(2)} = .08$. In each of the following cases find the purchase price of the bond and the bond's coupon rate.

(a) The final entry in the amortization schedule for accumulation of discount is 80.

(b) The first entry in the amortization schedule for amortization of premium is 80.

(c) The final entry in the schedule for interest due is 500.

## SECTION 4.3

4.3.1 A 10% bond with face amount 100 is callable on any coupon date from 15½ years after issue up to the maturity date which is 20 years from issue.

(a) Find the price of the bond to yield a minimum nominal annual rate of (i) 12%, (ii) 10%, and (iii) 8%.

(b) Find the minimum annual yield to maturity if the bond is purchased for (i) 80, (ii) 100, and (iii) 120.

4.3.2 Repeat Exercise 4.3.1 assuming that the bond is callable at a redemption amount of 110, including the redemption at maturity.

4.3.3S A 1000 par value bond pays annual coupons of 80. The bond is redeemable at par in 30 years, but is callable any time from the end of the 10th year at 1050. Based on her desired yield rate, an investor calculates the following potential purchase prices $P$:

(i) Assuming the bond is called at the end of the $10^{th}$ year, $P = 957$.
(ii) Assuming the bond is held until maturity, $P = 897$.

The investor buys the bond at the highest price that guarantees she will receive at least her desired yield rate regardless of when the bond is called. The investor holds the bond for 20 years, after which time the bond is called. Calculate the annual yield rate the investor earns.

4.3.4 On June 15, 2005 a corporation issues an 8% bond with a face value of 1,000,000. The bond can be redeemed, at the option of the corporation, on any coupon date in 2016 or 2017 at par, on any coupon date in 2018 through 2020 for amount 1,200,000, or on any coupon date in 2021 through June 15, 2023 at redemption amount 1,300,000.

(a) Find the price to yield a minimum nominal annual rate of (i) 10% and (ii) 6½%.

(b) Find the minimum nominal annual yield if the bond is bought for (i) 800,000, (ii) 1,000,000, or (iii) 1,200,000.

4.3.5 An 8% serial bond of face amount 2,000,000 issued June 15, 2000 is to be redeemed by 10 semiannual installments of 100,000 each starting June 15, 2005, followed by 5 semiannual installments of 200,000 each starting June 15, 2010. Find the price of the entire issue to yield $i^{(2)} = .10$.

4.3.6 An *annuity bond* has level payments (coupon plus redemption) every coupon period. Thus it is a serial bond, but the redemption amounts decrease every period. A 10-year 10% annuity bond with face amount 100,000 has semiannual payments of $\dfrac{100,000}{a_{\overline{20}|.05}}$, of which some would be coupon payment and some would be redemption payment. A purchaser wishes a yield of $i^{(2)} = .12$. Find the price of the bond and construct the amortization schedule for the first 2 years.

4.3.7 Suppose that a serial bond has redemption amounts of $C_1, C_2, \ldots, C_m$ (not necessarily equal to $F_1, F_2, \ldots, F_m$). Show that if $\dfrac{r \cdot F_t}{C_t} = g$ for all $t = 1, 2, \ldots, m$, then the price can be written as $P = K + \dfrac{g}{j}(C - K)$, where $K$ is the present value of the redemption amounts at yield rate $j$.

# CHAPTER 5

## MEASURING THE RATE OF RETURN
## OF AN INVESTMENT

*"Save a little money at the end of each month,*
*and at the end of the year you'll be surprised at how little you have."*
*– Ernest Haskins,*

In the previous chapters we have looked at valuing various series of cash-flows. The inverse relationship between interest rates and present value should be clear from the examples of previous chapters. From general reasoning, it seems that when calculating the present value of a series of cash-flows, the interest rate used for valuation can be thought of as a "rate of return" by either party in the transaction (the purchaser and the seller of the series of cashflows).

In many circumstances, the valuation rate can be used to determine a preference for one transaction over another. For example, suppose that an investor has $100,000 available with which to purchase a 20-year annual payment annuity-immediate. Financial Institution X offers annual payments of $8,024.26, and Financial Institution Y offers payments of $8,718.46. The investor would choose Financial Institution Y, which offers a larger annual payment. We can find the effective annual interest rate for each of the two annuities by solving for $i$ in the equation $100,000 = Ka_{\overline{20}|i}$, where

$K$ is the payment amount. The interest rates are 5% for Institution X and 6% for Institution Y, and we see that the investor has chosen the annuity that has the higher interest rate. This interest rate may be called the "yield rate" or the **internal rate of return** on the transaction.

# 5.1 INTERNAL RATE OF RETURN AND NET PRESENT VALUE

## 5.1.1 INTERNAL RATE OF RETURN DEFINED

A general financial transaction involves a number of cashflows out (payments made) at various points in time as well as a number of cash-flows in (payments received). The **internal rate of return (IRR)** for the transaction is the interest rate at which the value of all cashflows out is equal to the value of cashflows in. Any valuation point can be used in setting up an equation of value to solve for an internal rate of return on a transaction, although there will usually be some natural valuation point, such as the starting date or the ending date of the transaction. The yield-to-maturity for coupon bonds presented in Chapter 4 is an example of an the internal rate of return, because it is the rate at which the price paid for the bond is equal to the present value of the coupon and redemption payments to be received.

Suppose that a transaction consists of a single amount $L$ invested at time 0, and several future payments $K_1, K_2, \ldots, K_n$ to be received at times $1, 2, \ldots, n$, with each $K_j > 0$. Then for the equation of value $L = K_1 \cdot \frac{1}{1+i} + K_2 \cdot \frac{1}{(1+i)^2} + \cdots + K_n \cdot \frac{1}{(1+i)^n}$, there is only one solution for $i$ that satisfies $i > -100\%$. If $L < \sum_{j=1}^{n} K_j$, then this unique solution is posi-tive, $i > 0$. For instance, with the annuity-immediate from Institution Y described at the start of this chapter, the amount invested is $L = 100,000$, there are $n = 20$ payments received, and the total amount received is $\sum_{j=1}^{n} K_j = 20 \times 8,718.46 = 174,369.20 > 100,000 = L$. It follows that there is a unique positive solution for $i$ to the equation $100,000 = 8,718.46 a_{\overline{20}|i}$ (that solution is $i = 6\%$).

It is possible to extend this notion of IRR to more complex transactions. Let us consider the situation in which there are payments received of amounts $A_0, A_1, A_2, \ldots, A_n$ at times $0 = t_0 < t_1 < t_2 < \cdots < t_n$, and disbursements (payments made out) of amounts $B_0, B_1, B_2, \ldots, B_n$ at the same points in time, where all $A_j \geq 0$ and all $B_j \geq 0$. The net amount received at time $k$ is

$C_k = A_k - B_k$, which can be positive or negative. If a payment of $B_j$ is disbursed at time $t_j$ but there is no payment received at that time, then $A_j = 0$. Conversely, if there is a payment received of $A_k$ at time $t_k$ but no payment disbursed at that time, then $B_k = 0$. In the context of the annuity example presented at the start of this chapter, from the point of view of Institution Y selling the annuity, $A_0 = 100,000$ (the company receives the 100,000 from the purchaser of the annuity) and

$$A_1 = A_2 = \cdots = A_n = 0; \quad B_0 = 0$$

and

$$B_1 = B_2 = \cdots = B_{20} = 8,718.46,$$

the net amounts received by the company are

$$C_0 = 100,000$$

and

$$C_1 = C_2 = \cdots = C_{20} = -8,718.46.$$

---

**Definition 5.1 – Internal Rate of Return**

Suppose that a transaction has net cashflows of amounts $C_0, C_1, ..., C_n$ at times $0, 1, ..., n$. The internal rate of return for the transaction is any rate of interest satisfying the equation $\sum_{k=0}^{n} C_k \cdot v^{t_k} = 0.$ (5.1)

---

In general we wish to find the compound interest rate $i$ for which the value of the series of cashflows out is equal to the value of the series of cashflows in at any point in time. The equation of value at time 0 for this general situation is

$$A_0 + A_1 \cdot v^{t_1} + A_2 \cdot v^{t_2} + \cdots + A_n \cdot v^{t_n}$$
$$= B_0 + B_1 \cdot v^{t_1} + B_2 \cdot v^{t_2} + \cdots + B_n \cdot v^{t_n}, \quad (5.1a)$$

or, equivalently,

$$\sum_{k=0}^{n} C_k \cdot v^{t_k} = 0. \quad (5.1)$$

Recall that as long as compound interest is in effect, the equation of value can be set up at any time point $t$, and the value(s) of $i$ for which the equation holds would be the same. For instance, the equation of value set up at time $t_n$ is

$$C_0(1+i)^{t_n} + C_1(1+i)^{t_n-t_1} + \cdots + C_{n-1}(1+i)^{t_n-t_{n-1}} + C_n$$

$$= \sum_{k=0}^{n} C_k(1+i)^{t_n-t_k} = 0. \qquad (5.2)$$

An alternative definition of **internal rate of return** is a solution for $i$ in Equation (5.1) or (5.2). The strict definition of the internal rate of return does not depend on any reinvestment options that might be available during the transaction. It can be seen, however, from Equation (5.2) that the interpretation of $i$ as the periodic yield rate for the entire transaction is equivalent to an implicit assumption that all amounts are reinvested at rate $i$ at all times during the transaction.

For instance, one interpretation that the rate of return earned by the annuitant is 6% for the 20-year annuity described at the start of this chapter is that the invested amount of $100,000 should grow to $100,000(1.06)^{20} = 320,713.55$ at the end of 20 years. In order for this to occur, as each annuity payment is received it must be reinvested into an account earning 6% per year, so that at the end of 20 years the accumulated value of the reinvested deposits is $8,718.46 s_{\overline{20}|.06} = 320,714$.

| EXAMPLE 5.1 | (*Internal rate of return*)

Smith buys 1000 shares of stock at 5.00 per share and pays a commission of 2%. Six months later he receives a cash dividend of .20 per share, which he immediately reinvests commission-free in shares at a price of 4.00 per share. Six months after that he buys another 500 shares at a price of 4.50 per share, and pays a commission of 2%. Six months after that he receives another cash dividend of .25 per share and sells his existing shares at 5.00 per share, again paying a 2% commission. Find Smith's internal rate of return for the entire transaction in the form $i^{(2)}$.

| SOLUTION |

At the time of the original share purchase, $A_0 = 0$ and $B_0 = 5100$, the initial outlay including commission. Measuring time in 6-month intervals, we have

$t=1$ at 6 months with $A_1 = 200$ and $B_1 = 200$, since he receives and immediately reinvests the dividend of 200, buying an additional 50 shares. Then $t=2$ is at 12 months with $A_2 = 0$ and $B_2 = 2295$ (buying an additional 500 shares and now owning a total of 1550 shares), and $t=3$ is at 18 months with $A_3 = 387.50 + 7595 = 7982.50$ (the dividend on 1550 shares plus the proceeds from the sale of the shares after commission) and $B_3 = 0$. The net amounts received are $C_0 = -5100$, $C_1 = 0$, $C_2 = -2295$, and $C_3 = 7982.5$. We wish to solve the equation, $-5100 - 2295 \cdot v^2 + 7982.5 \cdot v^3 = 0$, or, equivalently,

$$f(j) = 5100(1+j)^3 + 2295(1+j) - 7982.5 = 0,$$

where the $v$ and $j$ factors are based on 6-month interest rates so that $i^{(2)} = 2j$. Using a financial calculator with multiple cashflow capability, the unknown interest rate is found to be $j = 3.246\%$, or equivalently, $i^{(2)} = 6.49\%$.  □

Note that the transaction in Example 5.1 has a unique positive solution for $j$, the effective 6-month internal rate of return. This is true because the function $f(j)$ is a strictly increasing function of $j$, $f(0) < 0$, and $\lim\limits_{j \to \infty} f(j) = \infty$, and therefore there is a unique $j > 0$ that solves the equation $f(j) = 0$. The internal rate of return on a transaction can be a meaningful measure when comparing the relative advantages of two or more financial transactions.

### 5.1.2 UNIQUENESS OF THE INTERNAL RATE OF RETURN

We saw in Example 2.23 that for certain financial transactions there is a unique solution for internal rate of return that is greater than $-100\%$. It is possible in a more general situation that there are no real solutions for the internal rate of return, or that there are several real solutions all of which are greater than $-100\%$. The following example illustrates this.

---

EXAMPLE 5.2 *(Internal rate of return)*

Smith has a line of credit account that allows him to make withdrawals from or payments to the account at any time. The balance may be negative (indicating the amount that he owes to the account) or positive (indicating the amount the account owes him). Balances in the account, whether positive or negative, earn interest at rate $i$ per period. Solve for $i$ for each of the following sets of transactions on Smith's line of credit. Assume the line of credit was opened at time 0 and was closed with a balance of zero at time 2, and that the $A$s are withdrawals from the line of credit, and the $B$s are payments to the line of credit. Thus the payment of $B_2$ made to the line of credit clears the outstanding balance on the account.

(a)    $t_1 = 1, t_2 = 2, A_0 = 0, A_1 = 2.3, A_2 = 0, B_0 = 1, B_1 = 0, B_2 = 1.33$

(b)    $t_1 = 1, t_2 = 2, A_0 = 0, A_1 = 2.3, A_2 = 0, B_0 = 1, B_1 = 0, B_2 = 1.32$

(c)    $t_1 = 1, t_2 = 2, A_0 = 0, A_1 = 2.3, A_2 = 0, B_0 = 1, B_1 = 0, B_2 = 1.3125$

(d)    $t_1 = 1, t_2 = 2, A_0 = 0, A_1 = 2.3, A_2 = 0, B_0 = 1, B_1 = 0, B_2 = 1.2825$

SOLUTION

(a) $C_0 = -1, C_1 = 2.3,$ and $C_2 = -1.33,$ so that the equation of value at time 0 is $-1 + 2.3 \cdot v - 1.33 \cdot v^2 = 0$. Solving this quadratic equation produces only imaginary roots for $v$, and thus no real roots for $i$.

(b) $C_0 = -1, C_1 = 2.3,$ and $C_2 = -1.32,$ The equation of value at time 2 (remember that it can be set up at any point of time) is $-(1+i)^2 + 2.3(1+i) - 1.32 = 0$, which is a quadratic equation in $1+i$. Solving the quadratic results in $i = .1$ or $.2$, so both interest rates of 10% and 20% are solutions.

(c) $C_0 = -1, C_1 = 2.3, C_2 = -1.3125$. The equation of value at time 2 is $-(1+i)^2 + 2.3(1+i) - 1.3125 = 0$, producing $i = 5\%$ or $25\%$.

(d) $C_0 = -1, C_1 = 2.3, C_2 = -1.2825$. The equation of value at time 2 is $-(1+i)^2 + 2.3(1+i) - 1.2825 = 0$, so that $i = -5\%$ or $35\%$.    □

For the simple annuity transaction discussed at the start of this section, it was possible to do a meaningful comparison of the two annuities by comparing their internal rates of return. The situations described in Example 5.2 illustrate the difficulties that can arise when solving for an internal rate of return on a transaction, and the limitations that occur when using only the IRR as a measure of the relative performance of investments. Since $C_0$ and $C_1$ are the same for all four transactions, it is easy to compare the transactions by comparing the $C_2$ values. We see that transaction (a) has the largest amount to pay off the line of credit at time 2, with the final payment getting progressively smaller as we consider (b), (c), and (d). Therefore to minimize his cost in repaying the line of credit, Smith would prefer (d), although this is not readily apparent by comparing the internal rates of return. Later in this section we will consider alternative methods for measuring the return on a financial transaction and for comparing financial transactions.

It is useful to be able to identify conditions on a financial transaction that imply a unique internal rate of return greater than $-100\%$. We continue to describe a financial transaction using the cashflow series $C_0, C_1, ..., C_n$, where $C_t$ denotes the net amount received at time $t$. It is possible to formulate conditions on the $C_k$ that guarantee a unique $i > -1$..

Example 2.23 illustrates one basic, but common situation in which there is a unique IRR. If $C_0 > 0$ and $C_k < 0$ for $k = 1, 2, ..., n$, then there is a unique internal rate of return that is greater than $-100\%$. Furthermore, if $\sum_{k=0}^{n} C_k < 0$ then the unique internal rate of return is strictly positive. The typical transactions that correspond to this situation are loans of a single amount repaid by one or more payments in the future, or annuity purchases made with a single payment followed by annuity payments in the future. Additional conditions that result in a unique internal rate of return are considered in Exercise 5.1.6.

It is not possible to compare the relative merits of two transactions on the basis of IRR alone if one of the transactions does not have a real-valued rate. Even if each of two transactions has a unique internal rate, it may not be the case that a comparison of those rates is sufficient to decide which transaction is preferable (see Exercise 5.1.4).

**Criminal Interest Rate in Canada**

Section 347 of the Criminal Code of Canada passed by the federal government of Canada in 1985 defines a "criminal rate" of interest on a financial transaction to be "an effective annual rate of interest calculated in accordance with generally accepted actuarial practices and principles that exceeds sixty percent."

The Canadian Institute of Actuaries is the professional organization responsible for setting standards of actuarial practice in Canada. Section 4400 of the CIA's (Canadian Institute of Actuaries) Consolidated Standards of Practice outlines the procedure for computation of a criminal rate of interest. The internal rate of return, as defined earlier in this chapter, is the rate that is used under this procedure. Section 4400 also states "If the calculation produces only one result, then the actuary would report that result. If the calculation produces more than one result, then the actuary would report only those which are positive and real."

### 5.1.3 PROJECT EVALUATION USING NET PRESENT VALUE

An alternative way of comparing transactions is by means of **net present value** (NPV). Suppose that an individual is trying to choose between two possible sets of cashflows. Assume the two sets of cashflows being considered have no risk associated with them. It can be postulated that at a particular point in time (labeled time 0), each individual has an interest rate $i$ (sometimes called the individual's **interest preference rate**) that is the appropriate rate for valuing (discounting) the two sets of cashflows. To compare two transactions whose net cashflow vectors are $\mathbf{C} = (C_0, C_1, \ldots, C_n)$ and $\mathbf{C}' = (C_0', C_1', \ldots, C_n')$, we compare $P_i(\mathbf{C}) = \sum_{k=0}^{n} C_k \cdot v_i^{t_k}$ with $P_i(\mathbf{C}') = \sum_{k=0}^{n} C_k' \cdot v_i^{t_k}$. The cashflow vector whose present value is larger is preferable.

Note that in the transactions of Example 5.2, for any interest preference rate that exceeds $-1$, we have $P_i(C_a) < P_i(C_b) < P_i(C_c) < P_i(C_d)$ (see Exercise 5.1.2). The same is true for the two annuities considered at the start of this section. Exercise 5.1.4 provides an example of two transactions for which one is preferable at certain interest preference rates, and the other is preferable at other interest preference rates.

The approach described above is a commonly used method in capital budgeting; it is also called the **net present value method.**

---

**Definition 5.2 – Net Present Value Method**

The net present value method ranks possible investment alternatives by the present value of all net amounts received. An interest rate, sometimes called the *cost of capital* or *interest preference rate* must first be chosen, and then used in the present value calculations.

---

A simple criterion that is used to determine whether or not an investment project is acceptable is based on the sign of the NPV. A positive NPV indicates that the investment will be profitable, while a negative NPV indicates that it will not be profitable. Note that the IRR is the interest rate for which the NPV is 0. Figure 5.1 shows the graphs of the NPVs of the four cases considered in Example 5.2 at different interest preference rates.

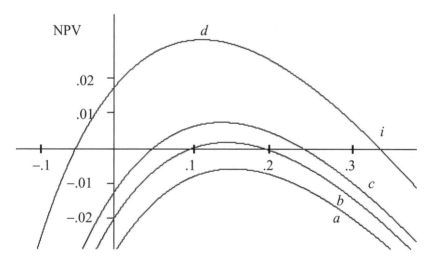

**FIGURE 5.1**

Example 5.2 was constructed to highlight some anomalous behavior that can occur when considering IRR and NPV. For instance, it may be difficult to interpret why 5.2(b) should be rejected due to negative NPV when the valuation rate $i$ is either less than 10% or greater than 20%. IRR and NPV are the most commonly used methods for evaluating financial projects, but there are other methods than can be applied.

### 5.1.4 ALTERNATIVE METHODS OF VALUING INVESTMENT RETURNS

**Capital budgeting** refers to the financial management process whereby criteria are set for evaluating alternative investment opportunities. Comparing investments via their internal rates of return or via their net present values are two of several standard capital budgeting methods.

The internal rate of return and the net present value are two examples of *discounted cash-flow procedures.* There are a number of project appraisal methods that make use of the "cost of capital," which can be regarded as the cost of borrowing to fund a project. We now consider a few more project appraisal methods.

#### 5.1.4.1 *Profitability Index*

At a specified rate of interest $i$ (cost of capital), calculate the ratio

$$I = \frac{present\ value\ of\ cash\ inflows}{present\ value\ of\ outflows},$$

where each present value is calculated at the beginning of the project. This ratio is an index measuring the return per dollar of investment. This method is often used when the "outflow" is a single amount invested at time 0 and the "inflow" is a series of payments to be received in the future. As a simple illustration, suppose that an investment of 1,000 can be made into one of two projects. The first project will generate income of 250 per year for 5 years starting in one year, and the second project will generate income of 140 per year for 10 years. If the cost of capital is $i = 5\%$ then the profitability indexes for the two projects are:

Project 1: $I = \frac{250a_{\overline{5}|.05}}{1000} = 1.0824$ and Project 2: $I = \frac{140a_{\overline{10}|.05}}{1000} = 1.0810.$

Project 1 would be preferable to Project 2 since it has a higher profitability index. Note that the preference may reverse if the cost of capital is changed. For example, with a cost of capital of 4%, Project 2 will have a higher profitability index than Project 1.

Note that if the internal rate of return is used to find the present value, then $I = 1$, because then the present value of cash inflows is equal to the present value of cash outflows.

### 5.1.4.2 Payback Period

If the investment consists of a series of cash outflows followed by a series of cash inflows $(C_0, C_1, C_2, \ldots, C_t < 0$ and $C_{t+1}, C_{t+2}, \ldots, C_n > 0)$ the payback period is the number of years required to recover the original amounts invested. Thus the first $k$ for which $-\sum_{s=0}^{t} C_s \leq \sum_{r=t+1}^{k} C_r$ is the payback period. In the two project example considered under the Profitability Index method, we see that for Project 1 we have $C_0 = -1000$ and $C_1 = \cdots = C_5 = 250$, and the payback period is 4 years (the 1000 is paid back after 4 payments of 250). For Project 2 the payback period is just over 7 years.

A variation on this method is the *discounted payback period* method, which incorporates a cost of capital $i$. In that case, the payback period is the first $k$ for which

$$-\sum_{s=0}^{t} C_s \, v_i^s \leq \sum_{r=t+1}^{k} C_r \cdot v_i^r.$$

If the cost of capital is $i = .05$ and $k = 4$ we have

$$-\sum_{s=0}^{t} C_s v^s = -C_0 = 1000$$

and

$$\sum_{r=t+1}^{k} C_r \cdot v^{k-r} = \sum_{r=1}^{4} C_r \cdot v^r = 250 a_{\overline{4}|.05} = 886.49,$$

but for $k = 5$ we have

$$\sum_{r=t+1}^{k} C_r \cdot v^r = \sum_{r=1}^{5} C_r \cdot v^r = 250 a_{\overline{5}|.05} = 1082.37,$$

Therefore, discounted payback for Project 1 occurs sometime during the $5^{th}$ year.

### 5.1.4.3 Modified Internal Rate of Return (MIRR)

Calculation of the MIRR uses a cost of capital rate $i$. To find the MIRR, say $j$, we formulate two accumulated values at the time the project ends. The first is the value of all payments made, accumulated at the (unknown) MIRR $j$. The second is the accumulated value of all payments received, accumulated at the cost of capital $i$. We set the two accumulated values equal and solve for $j$. The rationale behind this method is that payments received will be reinvested and the return on these reinvested amounts should be at least the cost of capital (note that if we assume that the reinvestment is at rate $j$ instead of rate $i$, the solution would give us the original IRR). With a single payment made of 1000 and 5 annual payments received of 250 starting one year from now, and with a cost of capital of $i = 5\%$, the MIRR equation is

$$1000(1+j)^5 = 250s_{\overline{5}|.05} = 1381.41,$$

from which we get $j = 6.68\%$

### 5.1.4.4 *Project Return Rate and Project Financing Rate*

During the course of a project with cash inflows and outflows, at some points in time the investor may be a "net borrower" with money being owed by the investor, and at other times the investor may be a "net lender" with a positive balance invested. Suppose that the cost of borrowing, the *project financing rate*, is $i$ during the period of time that the investor is a net borrower. Suppose that the return on the investment, the *project return rate*, is $j$ during the period of time the investor is a net lender. If the net value of the project is set to 0 at the time of completion of the project, it is possible to establish an algebraic relationship between $i$ and $j$. Solving for $j$ from $i$ would give a minimum project return needed for the project to break even at the time of completion. This approach is only meaningful if there are different times at which the investor is in a net lending position and in a net borrowing position.

Part (a) of Example 5.2 can be used as an illustration. Suppose that we assume a project financing rate of $i$. Let us suppose that at time 0 the investor is in a net lender position with an amount of 1 invested. At time 1 the value of the investment is $1+j$, since the project return rate has been earned during the time the investor is in a lender position. At time 1, the investor receives 2.3 from his line of credit and is in a net borrower position with amount owed $1+j-2.3$. At time 2, this amount owed is $(j-1.3)(1+i)$. The investor returns to a breakeven position by investing 1.33 at time 2. The investor's net position at time 2 can be expressed as $(j-1.3)(1+i)+1.33 = 0$. Solving for $j$ results in $j = 1.3 - \frac{1.33}{1+i}$. We can see that as the project financing rate $i$ increases, the project return rate needed for a breakeven position increases as well.

## 5.2 DOLLAR-WEIGHTED AND TIME-WEIGHTED RATE OF RETURN

Managers of investment funds often report the return or yield of a fund on an annual basis. There are two standard methods for measuring the annual return on a fund that are adaptations of concepts that have already been developed.

### 5.2.1 DOLLAR-WEIGHTED RATE OF RETURN

The **dollar-weighted rate of return** is the internal rate of return for the fund, but it is based on an equation of value using simple interest applied from each transaction to the year-end for which the rate is being measured. In this section, when dollar-weighted return is referenced, it will be assumed that we are referring to this simple interest form.

To find the dollar-weighted rate of return on a fund over the course of a year, the following information is needed:

(i)   the amount in the fund at the start of the year,

(ii)  the amounts and times of all deposits to, and withdrawals from the fund during the year, and

(iii) the amount in the fund at the end of the year.

An equation of value is created in the following form:

  Amount of initial fund balance plus all deposit amounts accumulated to the end of the year with simple interest

  −   amount of all withdrawals from the fund accumulated to the end of the year with simple interest

  =   fund balance at the end of the year (after all deposits/withdrawals have taken place).

If all times and amounts of deposits and withdrawals are known, along with the initial fund balance and the final fund balance, then it is straightforward to solve for the interest rate that makes the equation valid. Note that this equation of value is the same one we would use to solve for the internal rate of return, but for IRR we would use compound interest instead of simple interest. For periods of less than a year, the difference between compound and simple interest in the dollar-weighted equation will not usually be large.

| EXAMPLE 5.3 | (*Dollar-weighted return*)

A pension fund receives contributions and pays benefits from time to time. The fund began the year 2009 with a balance of $1,000,000. There were contributions to the fund of $200,000 at the end of February and again at the end of August. There was a benefit of $500,000 paid out of the fund at the end of October. The balance remaining in the fund at the start of the year 2010 was $1,100,000. Find the dollar-weighted return on the fund, assuming each month is $\frac{1}{12}$ of a year.

| SOLUTION |

The equation of value for the dollar-weighted return is

$$1,000,000(1+i) + 200,000\left(1+\frac{10}{12}i\right)$$
$$+200,000\left(1+\frac{4}{12}i\right) - 500,000\left(1+\frac{2}{12}i\right) = 1,100,000.$$

The initial balance of 1,000,000 earns interest for a full year. For the deposit of 200,000 at the end of February, we have applied simple interest for the 10 months remaining until the end of the year. Similar comments apply to the other deposit and the withdrawal. Solving for $i$ results in

$$i = \frac{1,100,000 + 500,000 - 1,000,000 - 200,000 - 200,000}{1,000,000 + 200,000\left(\frac{10}{12}\right) + 200,000\left(\frac{4}{12}\right) - 500,000\left(\frac{2}{12}\right)}$$

$$= \frac{200,000}{1,150,000} = .1739.$$

Note that the amount 200,000 in the numerator is the net amount of interest earned during the year. It is the net amount by which the account increased after combining all deposits and withdrawals. The account started at 1,000,000, there was a net withdrawal during the year of

100,000, but the balance at the end of the year had risen by 100,000 from the balance at the start of the year. Therefore, 200,000 must have been investment (or interest) income added to the account. The denominator is the "average amount on deposit during the year." In the expression for $i$ above, the initial balance of 1,000,000 is "on deposit for the full year," the deposit of 200,000 at the end of February is on deposit for the remaining $\frac{10}{12}$ of the year (10 months), and the deposit of 200,000 at the end of August is on deposit for the remaining $\frac{4}{12}$ of the year (4 months). Withdrawals reduce the average balance on deposit during the year; so the 500,000 withdrawal made at the end of October reduces the average balance on deposit for the remaining $\frac{2}{12}$ of the year. ◻

---

**Definition 5.3 – Dollar-Weighted Return For a One-Year Period**

Suppose the following information is known:

(i)  the balance in a fund at the start of the year is $A$,

(ii) for $0 < t_1 < t_2 < \cdots < t_n < 1$, the net deposit at time $t_k$ is amount $C_k$ (positive for a net deposit, negative for a net withdrawal), and

(iii) the balance in the fund at the end of the year is $B$.

Then the net amount of interest earned by the fund during the year is

$I = B - \left[ A + \sum_{k=1}^{n} C_k \right]$, and the dollar-weighted rate of return earned by the fund for the year is

$$\frac{I}{A + \sum_{k=1}^{n} C_k (1 - t_k)}. \tag{5.3}$$

---

An approximation to this dollar-weighted rate can be found by assuming that the total net deposits/withdrawals are uniformly spread throughout the year, and are approximated as occurring at mid-year. The total net deposit/withdrawal for the year is still $C = \sum_{k=1}^{n} C_k$, and the approximate dollar-weighted return is $\frac{I}{A+\frac{1}{2}C}$. Using this approximation, the dollar-weighted rate of return in Example 5.3 becomes

$$\frac{200,000}{1,000,000 + \frac{1}{2}(-100,000)} = .2105.$$

In this case this is a poor approximation because the deposits and withdrawals are not equally spread over the year (deposits are early, withdrawal is late).

If compound interest had been used in setting up the equation of value in Example 5.3, the resulting equation would be

$$1,000,000(1+i) + 200,000(1+i)^{10/12} + 200,000(1+i)^{4/12}$$
$$-500,000(1+i)^{2/12} = 1,100,000.$$

The solution to this equation is the internal rate of return $i = .1740$ (very close to the dollar-weighted return of .1739 found in Example 5.3).

## 5.2.2 TIME-WEIGHTED RATE OF RETURN

The **time-weighted rate of return** for a one year period is found by compounding the returns over successive parts of the year. Suppose that during the course of a year, the following interest rates occur: 6-month rate of 4%, followed by 3-month rate of 3%, followed by 3-month rate of 2%. If we assume reinvestment in successive periods, then an investment of 1 made at the start of the year will grow to $(1.04)(1.03)(1.02) = 1.0926$. The time-weighted rate of return for the year would be 9.26%, which is found by compounding the rates in successive fractions of the year. Notice that the fact that the first fraction of the year was 6 months, and the second and third were 3 months each, was not relevant. The important point in this example is that the year was broken into 3 successive pieces, with rates of 4%, 3% and 2% in the three successive pieces, which compounded to 1.0926.

**Definition 5.4 – Time-Weighted Return For a One-Year Period**

Suppose the following information is known:

(i)     the balance in a fund at the start of the year is $A$,

(ii)    for $0 < t_1 < t_2 < \cdots < t_n < 1$, the net deposit at time $t_k$ is amount $C_k$ (positive for a net deposit, negative for a net withdrawal),

(iii)   the value of the fund **just before the net deposit at time** $t_k$ is $F_k$, and

(iv)    the balance in the fund at the end of the year is $B$.

The time-weighted return rate earned by the fund for the year is

$$\left[ \frac{F_1}{A} \times \frac{F_2}{F_1 + C_1} \times \frac{F_3}{F_2 + C_2} \times \cdots \times \frac{F_k}{F_{k-1} + C_{k-1}} \times \frac{B}{F_k + C_k} \right] - 1 \quad (5.4)$$

In general, in order to find the time-weighted rate of return, we need the return for each piece of the year. The time length of each piece of the year is irrelevant. It is typical to break the year into the pieces defined by the points at which deposits or withdrawals occur, as indicated in the definition above. The factor $\frac{F_j}{F_{j-1} + C_{j-1}}$ is the growth factor for the period from $t_{j-1}$ to $t_j$. The time-weighted return is found by compounding the successive growth factors over the course of the year.

We adapt the situation presented in Example 5.3 to provide an example for the time-weighted return.

EXAMPLE 5.4    (*Time-weighted rate of return*)

A pension fund receives contributions and pays benefits from time to time. The fund value is reported after every transaction and at year end. The details during the year 2009 are as follows:

|  | Date | Amount |
|---|---|---|
| Fund values: | 01/1/09 | 1,000,000 |
|  | 03/1/09 | 1,240,000 |
|  | 09/1/09 | 1,600,000 |
|  | 11/1/09 | 1,080,000 |
|  | 01/1/10 | 900,000 |
|  |  |  |
| Contributions received: | 02/28/09 | 200,000 |
|  | 08/31/09 | 200,000 |
| Benefits paid: | 10/31/09 | 500,000 |
|  | 12/31/09 | 200,000 |

Find the time-weighted rate of return.

| SOLUTION |

The fund's earned rates for various parts of the year are as follows:

01/1/09 to 02/28/09: $\dfrac{1,240,000-200,000-1,000,000}{1,000,000} = .04$

03/1/09 to 08/31/09: $\dfrac{1,600,000-200,000-1,240,000}{1,240,000} = .1290$

09/1/09 to 10/31/09: $\dfrac{1,080,000+500,000-1,600,000}{1,600,000} = -.0125$

11/1/09 to 12/31/09: $\dfrac{900,000+200,000-1,080,000}{1,080,000} = .0185$

Then the time-weighted rate of return for 2009 is

$$i_T = (1.04)(1.1290)(.9875)(1.0185) - 1 = .1809.$$

This can also be formulated as

$$i_T = \left(\frac{1,040,000}{1,000,000}\right)\left(\frac{1,400,000}{1,240,000}\right)\left(\frac{1,580,000}{1,600,000}\right)\left(\frac{1,100,000}{1,080,000}\right) - 1 = .1809$$

❏

The information in Example 5.4 adds some detail to the information provided in Example 5.3. In Example 5.4 we are given the updated fund value after each transaction. This allows us to find the fund value just before each deposit and withdrawal, and therefore we can find the return earned by the fund for each transaction period. For instance, the fund balance on January 1 was 1,000,000. Just before the deposit on February 28, the fund balance was 1,040,000 (the March first balance of 1,240,000 minus the deposit of 200,000 made on February 28). Therefore, the growth factor in the fund from January 1 to February 28 is $\frac{1,040,000}{1,000,000} = 1.04\,(4\%)$. We make similar calculations for each successive transaction period, and compound them over the full year.

An investment fund manager generally does not have control over the timing or amounts of cash inflows and outflows for the fund. The time-weighted return is often used to compare the relative performance of various investment fund managers since the method eliminates the impact of money flows in and out of the fund.

Dollar-weighted and time-weighted returns are generally applied for periods of a year or less. It is possible to apply the methods to estimate a rate of return for a period of longer than one year, but since simple interest is usually not applied beyond a one year period, the dollar-weighted return would be replaced by the usual internal rate of return calculation for longer periods.

## 5.3 APPLICATIONS AND ILLUSTRATIONS

### 5.3.1 THE PORTFOLIO METHOD AND THE INVESTMENT YEAR METHOD

It is possible that when new funds are added to an existing investment account, the "new money" is kept segregated from the rest of the fund for some period of time. The existing fund may be earning interest at one rate in the coming year, and the new money might earn interest at a different rate. "New money" may be segregated every year for several years in terms of the interest rate earned before being integrated into a larger pooled fund. For instance, an existing investment fund may be scheduled to earn a 4% return in 2003, a 4.2% return in 2004 and a 4.5% return in 2005, but new contributions might be segregated from the main fund for 2 years and scheduled to earn 5% in 2003 and 4.8% in 2004. In 2005 and thereafter, the "new money" contributed in 2003 earns the same as the "main" fund. Under this situation, there may be a 2-year segregation period for all new contributions, so that new money that is contributed in 2004 might earn a different rate of return than the 4.8% return in 2004 earned by money that was new in 2003.

The "portfolio year rate" refers to the interest rate earned by the main or pooled fund, and would be classified by the year the interest is earned only. In the example above, the 4% return in 2003 would be the portfolio rate for 2003 and the 4.2% return in 2004 would be the portfolio rate for 2004. The "investment year rate" refers to the interest rate earned by "new money" before it has been incorporated into the pooled fund. The investment year rate on new money would be classified by (i) the year in which new money was received, and (ii) the current year interest is earned. The 5% rate is the investment year rate in 2003 for new money received in 2003, and 4.8% would be the investment year rate in 2004 for new money that had been received in 2003. The following example illustrates this idea.

## EXAMPLE 5.5

(*Investment Year Method and Portfolio Year Method*)

You are given the following table of interest rates:

| Calendar Year of Original Investment | Investment Year Rates (in %) | | | | | Portfolio Rates (in %) |
|---|---|---|---|---|---|---|
| $y$ | $i_1^y$ | $i_2^y$ | $i_3^y$ | $i_4^y$ | $i_5^y$ | $i^{y+5}$ |
| 1992 | 8.25 | 8.25 | 8.40 | 8.50 | 8.50 | 8.35 |
| 1993 | 8.50 | 8.70 | 8.75 | 8.90 | 9.00 | 8.60 |
| 1994 | 9.00 | 9.00 | 9.10 | 9.10 | 9.20 | 8.85 |
| 1995 | 9.00 | 9.10 | 9.20 | 9.30 | 9.40 | 9.10 |
| 1996 | 9.25 | 9.35 | 9.50 | 9.55 | 9.60 | 9.35 |
| 1997 | 9.50 | 9.50 | 9.60 | 9.70 | 9.70 | |
| 1998 | 10.00 | 10.00 | 9.90 | 9.80 | | |
| 1999 | 10.00 | 9.80 | 9.70 | | | |
| 2000 | 9.50 | 9.50 | | | | |
| 2001 | 9.00 | | | | | |

Suppose that the amount in a fund is 1000 on January 1, 1997. Let the following be the accumulated value of the fund on January 1, 2000:

$P$: under the investment year method

$Q$: under the portfolio yield method

$R$: if the balance is withdrawn at the end of every year and is reinvested at the new money rate.

Determine the ranking of $P$, $Q$, and $R$.

SOLUTION

For a new investment in 1997, under the investment year method, the rates earned in successive years are found in the row for 1997 in the table. The rate earned in 1997 is 9.50%, the rate earned in 1998 is 9.50%, and the rate earned in 1999 is 9.60%.

The portfolio rates are found in the final column of the table. For 1997 we use $i^{1992+5} = 8.35\%$, for 1998 we use $i^{1993+S} = 8.60\%$, etc.

The new money rates are from the first column of the investment year table for years 1997, 1998 and 1999 ($i_1^y$). A new investment made in 1997 earns 9.50% in 1997, a new investment made in 1998 earns 10.00% in 1998, and a new investment made in 1999 earns 10.00% in 1999.

Under the three methods, the deposit grows according to the following rates.

|   | 1997 | 1998 | 1999 |
|---|------|------|------|
| $P$ | 9.50% | 9.50% | 9.60% |
| $Q$ | 8.35% | 8.60% | 8.85% |
| $R$ | 9.50% | 10.00% | 10.00% |

$P = 1000(1.095)(1.095)(1.096) = 1314,$

$Q = 1000(1.0835)(1.086)(1.0885) = 1281,$

$R = 1000(1.095)(1.10)(1.10) = 1325.$

We see that $R > P > Q$. This relationship could be determined by comparing the interest rates in the table above without doing the actual calculations. ❐

## 5.3.2 INTEREST PREFERENCE RATES FOR BORROWING AND LENDING

In Section 5.1 the concept of an individual's interest preference rate was introduced as the rate at which that individual would value future payments. It might also be the cost of capital at which the individual could borrow. In using such a rate ($i_P$) for valuation, when a transaction is regarded as taking place in an account with amounts credited and debited from that account (such as a line of credit), it is implicitly assumed that over the term of the transaction the individual would receive interest credited at rate $i_P$ when the account is in a net surplus position and pay interest at rate $i_P$ when the account is in a net deficit position. It is reasonable to extend the notion of interest preference rates somewhat further by attributing a pair of rates to the individual, one rate at which the account would pay interest when in a surplus position ($i_S$), and another rate at which the account would charge interest when in a deficit position ($i_D$). In this framework it would be possible to compare two transactions by comparing the amount (net profit) in the account at the end of each transaction.

**EXAMPLE 5.6** (*Interest preference rates*)

A line of credit loan of 10,000 is to be used for investment purposes. There are two investment alternatives. The first will provide payments of 3000 each year for 10 years starting one year from now. The second will provide payments of 8000 two years and five years from now, and 7000 seven years and ten years from now. The investor plans to deposit all proceeds from the investment into the line of credit account. When there is a balance owed in the account, interest is charged at 15% per year, and when there is surplus in the account interest is credited at 9% per year. Find the account balance after 10 years for each investment alternative.

**SOLUTION**

Investment 1 results in the following sequence of account balances:

$t = 0: -10,000$

$t = 1: -10,000(1.15) + 3000 = -8500$

$t = 2: -8,000(1.15) + 3000 = -6775$

$t = 3: -4791.25$

$t = 4: -2509.94$

$t = 5: 113.57$

$t = 6: 113.57(1.09) + 3000 = 3123.79$

$$\vdots$$

$t = 10: 3123.79(1.09)^4 + 3000 \cdot s_{\overline{4}|.09} = 18,129$

Investment 2 results in the following sequence:

$$t = 2 : -10,000(1.15)^2 + 8000 = -5225$$
$$t = 5 : -5225(1.15)^3 + 8000 = 53.43$$
$$t = 7 : 53.43(1.09)^2 + 7000 = 7063.48$$
$$t = 10 : 7063.48(1.09)^3 + 7000 = 16,147$$

The first investment would result in a larger gain at the end of the tenth year.

□

### 5.3.3 ANOTHER MEASURE FOR THE YIELD ON A FUND

We now consider the case of a fund which has deposits and withdrawals made continuously, and investment income earned continuously.

Suppose that a fund is observed over time, and the amount in the fund at time $t$ is $F(t)$. The fund earns interest and also receives and/or makes payments from time to time. If we wish to find the average annualized yield earned by the fund from time $t_1$ to time $t_2$ measured in years, we can formulate the yield as the internal rate of return), where

$$F(t_2) = F(t_1)(1+i)^{t_2-t_1} + \sum_t c_t (1+i)^{t_2-t} + \int_{t_1}^{t_2} \overline{c}(t)(1+i)^{t_2-t} \, dt,$$

$c_t$ represents the net amount received $(+)$ or paid out $(-)$ at time $t$, and $\overline{c}(t)$ is the net continuous rate of payment (received or paid out) at time $t$.

The relationship between $F(t_1)$ and $F(t_2)$ can be more simply stated as

$$F(t_2) = F(t_1) + I_{t_1 t_2} + N_{t_1 t_2}, \tag{5.5}$$

where $I$ represents interest earned for the period on the initial $F(t_1)$ as well as on contributions (less interest lost on withdrawals), and $N$ represents the net amount of new money received by the fund during the period where

$$N_{t_1 t_2} = \sum_t c_t + \int_{t_1}^{t_2} \overline{c}(t) \, dt. \tag{5.6}$$

Suppose that the time interval from $t_1$ to $t_2$ is one year, and let us make the simplifying assumption that $N$ is uniformly received during the course of the year. Then $F(t_2)$ is a combination of the accumulated value of $F(t_1)$ after one year and the accumulated value of a continuous one-year level annuity paying $N$ during the year, so that $F(t_2) = F(t_1)(1+i) + N \cdot \overline{s}_{\overline{1}|i}$ Using Equation (5.5) it follows that

$$F(t_2) = F(t_1)(1+i) + [F(t_2) - F(t_1) - I] \cdot \overline{s}_{\overline{1}|i}.$$

Since $\overline{s}_{\overline{1}|i} = \int_0^1 (1+i)^s \, ds = \frac{i}{\delta}$, it is not possible to solve exactly for $i$. A simple approximation often used in practice is based on the trapezoidal rule for approximate integration, which gives $\int_0^1 (1+i)^s \, ds \approx 1 + \frac{i}{2}$. With this approximation we see that

$$F(t_2) \approx F(t_1)(1+i) + [F(t_2) - F(t_1) - I]\left(1 + \frac{i}{2}\right), \qquad (5.7)$$

from which it follows that

$$i \approx \frac{2I}{F(t_1) + F(t_2) - I}. \qquad (5.8)$$

It is possible to generalize Equation (5.8) as follows:

$$i \approx \frac{2I}{2 \cdot \int_{t_1}^{t_2} F(t) \, dt - I}. \qquad (5.9)$$

It may be the case that $F(t)$ is changing continuously for part of the period from $t_1$ to $t_2$ (say from $t_1$ to $t'$), and there is then a significant payment (or withdrawal) at time $t'$, with $F(t)$ again changing continuously from $t'$ to $t_2$. Then $F(t)$ is piecewise continuous from $t_1$ to $t_2$. In such a case the integral in Equation (5.9) can be approximated by approximating $\int_{t_1}^{t'}$ and $\int_{t'}^{t_2}$ separately.

| EXAMPLE 5.7 | (*Yield on a fund*)

A large pension fund was valued at 350,000,000 on January 1, 2010. During 2010 the contributions to the fund totaled 80,000,000, benefit payments totaled 20,000,000, and the fund recorded interest income of 40,000,000. Estimate the yield on the fund for 2010 in each of the following cases.

(a) Contributions, benefit payments, and interest income occur uniformly and continuously throughout the year.

(b) Benefit payments, interest income, and 20,000,000 of the contributions are uniformly spread throughout the year, but there is a lump sum contribution of 60,000,000 on September 1, 2010.

(c) Same as (b) except that the lump sum contributions are 50,000,000 on May 1 and 10,000,000 on September 1, 2010.

| SOLUTION |

(a) Let January 1, 2010 be $t = 0$ and January 1, 2011 be $t = 1$. Note that $F(1) = 350 + 80 - 20 + 40 = 450$ (million). Equation (5.6) can be directly applied, producing $i \approx \frac{2(40)}{350 + 450 - 40} = .1053$.

(b) The lump-sum contribution is made at $t = \frac{2}{3}$. Since the part of the contributions other than the lump sum, along with the benefits and interest income, are uniformly spread over the year, then just before this lump-sum contribution the approximate value of the fund is $F_-\left(\frac{2}{3}\right) = 350 + \frac{2}{3}(80-60) - \frac{2}{3}(20) + \frac{2}{3}(40) = 376.67$. Just after the lump-sum contribution the value of the fund is

$$F_+\left(\frac{2}{3}\right) = 376.67 + 60 = 436.67,$$

and the value of the fund at the end of the year is the same as in (a), $F(1) = 450$. We can assume that $F(t)$ is linear from $t = 0$ to $t = \frac{2}{3}$ (just before the lump sum payment) and from $t = \frac{2}{3}$ (just after the lump sum payment) to $t = 1$. Based on the method described in the comments following Equation (5.7), we approximate $\int_0^1 F(t)\,dt$ by approximating each of the integrals $\int_0^{2/3} F(t)\,dt$ and $\int_{2/3}^1 F(t)\,dt$. Using the trapezoidal rule the approximate values of the integrals are

$$\int_0^{2/3} F(t)\,dt = \frac{2/3}{2}[350+376.67] = 242.22$$

and

$$\int_{2/3}^1 F(t)\,dt = \frac{1/3}{2}[436.67+450] = 147.78,$$

so that the approximation to $\int_0^1 F(t)\,dt$ is 390. Then using Equation (5.9) we have $i \approx \dfrac{2(40)}{2(390)-40} = .1081.$

(c) Just before the lump sum contribution at $t=\frac{1}{3}$ the fund value is

$$F_-\left(\frac{1}{3}\right) = 350 + \frac{1}{3}(80-60) - \frac{1}{3}(20)\frac{1}{3}(40) = 363.33, \text{ and it is}$$

$$F_+\left(\frac{1}{3}\right) = 363.66 + 50 = 413.33$$

just after that contribution. Just before the lump sum contribution at $t=\frac{2}{3}$ the fund value is

$$F_-\left(\frac{2}{3}\right) = 413.33 + \frac{1}{3}(80-60) - \frac{1}{3}(20) + \frac{1}{3}(40) = 426.66,$$

and we have $F_+\left(\frac{2}{3}\right) = 426.66 + 10 = 436.66$ just after that contribution. As in parts (a) and (b) we have $F(1) = 450$. Then

$$\int_0^1 F(t)\,dt = \int_0^{1/3} F(t)\,dt + \int_{1/3}^{2/3} F(t)\,dt + \int_{2/3}^1 F(t)\,dt.$$

The trapezoidal rule for approximate integration is applied as follows:

$$\int_a^b g(x)\,dx \approx \frac{b-a}{2}[g(a)+g(b)].$$

Applying the trapezoidal rule to each integral as in part (b), we find

$$\int_0^1 F(t)\,dt = 118.89 + 140 + 147.78 = 406.67,$$

so that

$$i \approx \frac{2(40)}{2(406.66)-40} = .1034. \qquad \square$$

## 5.4   DEFINITIONS AND FORMULAS

**Definition 5.1 – Internal Rate of Return**

Suppose that a transaction has net cashflows of amounts $C_0, C_1, ..., C_n$ at times $0, 1, ..., n$. The internal rate of return for the transaction is any rate of interest satisfying the equation

$$\sum_{k=0}^{n} C_k \cdot v^{t_k} = 0. \tag{5.1}$$

**Definition 5.2 – Net Present Value Method**

The net present value method ranks possible investment alternatives by the present value of all net amounts received. An interest rate, sometimes called the *cost of capital* must first be chosen, and then used in the present value calculations.

**Definition 5.3 – Dollar-Weighted Return For a One-Year Period**

Suppose the following information is known:

(i)    the balance in a fund at the start of the year is $A$,

(ii)   for $0 < t_1 < t_2 < \cdots < t_n < 1$, the net deposit at time $t_k$ is amount $C_k$ (positive for a net deposit, negative for a net withdrawal), and

(iii)  the balance in the fund at the end of the year is $B$.

Then the net amount of interest earned by the fund during the year is $I = B - \left[ A + \sum_{k=1}^{n} C_k \right]$, and the dollar-weighted rate of interest earned by the fund for the year is

$$\frac{I}{A + \sum_{k=1}^{n} C_k (1-t_k)}. \tag{5.3}$$

**Definition 5.4 – Time-Weighted Return For a One-Year Period**

Suppose the following information is known:

(i)  the balance in a fund at the start of the year is $A$;

(ii) for $0 < t_1 < t_2 < \cdots < t_n < 1$, the net deposit at time $t_k$ is amount $C_k$ (positive for a net deposit, negative for a net withdrawal),

(iii)   the balance in the fund **just before the net deposit at time** $t_k$ is $F_k$, and

(iv)   the balance in the fund at the end of the year is $B$.

The time-weighted rate of interest earned by the fund for the year is

$$\left[\frac{F_1}{A} \times \frac{F_2}{F_1 + C_1} \times \frac{F_3}{F_2 + C_2} \times \cdots \times \frac{F_k}{F_{k-1} + C_{k-1}} \times \frac{B}{F_k + C_k}\right] - 1. \quad (5.4)$$

## 5.5  Notes and References

Several books contain a discussion of conditions relating to the existence and uniqueness of yield rates for financial transactions. Discussions can be found in Butcher and Nesbitt, in *The Theory of Interest*, by Kellison, and also in *An Introduction to the Mathematics of Finance*, by McCutcheon and Scott. The notion of interest preference rates introduced in the paper "A New Approach to the Theory of Interest" in *TSA*, Volume 32 (1980), by D. Promislow provides a fresh and useful alternative to yield rates as a way of comparing investments. An idea similar to that of interest preference rates is discussed in McCutcheon and Scott.

The internal rate of return and discounted cashflow methods of capital budgeting are analyzed in considerable detail in the papers "Mathematical Analysis of Rates of Return under Certainty" and "An Analysis of Criteria for Investment and Financing Decisions under Certainty," by Teicherow, Robichek, and Montalbano, which appeared in *Management Science*, Volumes 11 and 12 (1965). The notation $F_t(k,r)$ is introduced there to denote the future value at time $t$ of a cashflow with $k$ as the project financing rate of interest (the rate charged when the investment is in a deficit or loan outstanding position) and $r$ as the project investment rate (the rate earned when the investment is in a surplus position). This is similar to the pair of interest preference rates discussed in Section 5.3.2.

The paper "Axiomatic Characterization of the Time-weighted Rate of Return," by K.B. Gray and R.B. Dewar in *Management Science*, Volume 18, No. 2 (1971) argues that the time-weighted rate of return is "the only measure appropriate for measuring the performance of fund managers."

# 5.6 EXERCISES

## SECTION 5.1

5.1.1 Repeat part (a) of Example 5.2 by setting up the equation of value at time $t_2 = 2$, and repeat part (b) by setting up the equation of value at time 0.

5.1.2 Show that for any $i > -1$, for the transactions in Example 5.2 we have $P_i(C_a) < P_i(C_b) < P_i(C_c) < P_i(C_d)$.

5.1.3 Repeat Example 5.1 removing all commission expenses on the purchase and sale of shares.

5.1.4 Transactions A and B are to be compared. Transaction A has net cashflows of

$$C_0^A = -5, \quad C_1^A = 3.72, \quad C_2^A = 0, \quad C_3^A = 4$$

and Transaction B has net cashflows

$$C_0^B = -5, \quad C_1^B = 3, \quad C_2^B = 1.7, \quad C_3^B = 3.$$

Find the yield rate for each transaction to at least 6 decimal places. Show that Transaction A is preferable to B at interest preference rates less than 11.11% and at interest preference rates greater than 25%, and Transaction B is preferable at interest preference rates between 11.11% and 25%.

5.1.5   A project requires an initial capital outlay of 30,000 and will return the following amounts (paid at the ends of the next 5 years):

14,000,    12,000,    6,000,    4,000,    2,000.

Solve for each of the following.

(a) Internal rate of return.

(b) Modified internal rate of return assuming a cost of capital of 10% per year.

(c) Net present value based on a cost of capital of 10% per year.

(d) The payback period.

(e) The discounted payback period assuming a cost of capital of 10% per year.

(f) The profitability index.


*5.1.6  (a) Suppose there is a $k$ between 0 and $n$ such that either

(i) $C_0, C_1, \ldots, C_k \leq 0$ and $C_{k+1}, C_{k+2}, \ldots, C_n \geq 0$ (i.e., all the negative net cashflows precede the positive net cashflows), or

(ii) $C_0, C_1, \ldots, C_k \geq 0$ and $C_{k+1}, C_{k+2}, \ldots, C_n \leq 0$ (i.e., all the positive net cashflows precede the negative net cashflows).

Assuming that $C_0 \neq 0$, show that there is a unique $i > -1$ for which $\sum_{s=1}^{n} C_s \cdot v^{t_s} = 0$. (Hint: show that the function

$$\sum_{s=0}^{k} C_s \cdot (1+i)^{t_k - t_s} + \sum_{s=k+1}^{n} C_s \cdot (1+i)^{t_k - t_s}$$

is monotonic, either increasing for all $i$ or decreasing for all $i$, and check the limits as $i \to \infty$ and $i \to -1$.)

(b) Let $C_0, C_1, \ldots, C_n$ be an arbitrary sequence of net cash-flows, and let $F_0 = C_0$, $F_1 = C_0 + C_1$, $F_2 = C_0 + C_1 + C_2$, $F_t = C_0 + C_1 + \cdots + C_t$, $F_n = C_0 + C_1 + \cdots + C_n$, so that $F_t$ is the cumulative total net cashflow at the $t^{th}$ cash-flow point. Suppose that both $F_0$ and $F_n$ are non-zero, and that the sequence $\{F_0, F_1, \ldots, F_n\}$ has exactly one change of sign. Show that there is a unique $i > 0$ for which $\sum\limits_{s=0}^{n} C_s \cdot v^{t_s} = 0$, although there may be one or more negative roots.

(c) Show that the transaction in Example 5.1 satisfies both (a) and (b) above, but none of the transactions in Example 5.2 satisfy these conditions.

(d) *Descartes' rule of signs* (discovered by $16^{th}$ Century mathematician Rene Descartes) states that for a polynomial of the form $P(x) = C_n x^n + C_{n-1} x^{n-1} + \cdots + C_1 x + C_0$, the number of positive roots of $P(x)$ is less than or equal to the number of sign changes in the sequence $C_n, C_{n-1}, \ldots, C_1, C_0$, and the number of negative roots of $P(x)$ is less than or equal to the number of sign changes in the sequence

$$(-1)^n C_n, \quad (-1)^{n-1} C_{n-1}, \ldots, (-1)C_1, C_0.$$

Show that Descartes Rule of signs concludes that the transaction in Example 5.1 has at most one positive root and no negative roots.

*5.1.7 Smith buys an investment property for 900,000 by making a down payment of 150,000 and taking a loan for 750,000. Starting one month after the loan is made Smith must make monthly loan payments, but he also receives monthly rental payments, set for 2 years such that his net outlay per month is 1200. In addition there are taxes of 10,000 payable 6 months after the loan is made and annually thereafter as long as Smith owns the property. Two years after the original purchase date Smith sells the property for $Y \geq 741,200$, out of which he must pay the balance of 741,200 on the loan.

(a) Show that part (a) of Exercise 5.1.6 guarantees a unique yield rate on the 2-year transaction.

(b) Use part (b) of Exercise 5.1.6 to find the minimum value of $Y$ that guarantees a unique positive rate of return over the two year period.

5.1.8  Suppose $Y = 1,000,000$ in Exercise 5.1.7. Apply various approximation methods to find the yield rate in the form $i^{(12)}$.

*5.1.9  An investment company offers a 15-year "double your money" savings plan, which requires a deposit of 10,000 at the start of each year for 15 years. At the end of 15 years each participant receives 300,000. If a participant opts out of the plan, he gets back his deposits accumulated at 4% up to the time he opts out. Opting out occurs at the start of a year when a new payment is due, from the start of the $2^{nd}$ to the start of the $15^{th}$ year.

The company's experience shows that out of 100 new participants, the numbers that opt out each year are 5 at the start of the $2^{nd}$ year, 4 at the start of each of the $3^{rd}$ and $4^{th}$ years, 3 at the start of each of the $5^{th}$ and $6^{th}$ years, 2 at the start of each of the $7^{th}$ through $9^{th}$ years, and 1 at the start of each of the $10^{th}$ through $15^{th}$ years. The deposits received by the company can be reinvested at effective annual rate $i$.

(a) Assuming 100 initial participants, find the company's net profit at the end of 15 years, after all plans have been settled, as a function of $i$, and show that it is an increasing function of $i$.

(b) What value of $i$ gives no net profit to the company?

*5.1.10 (a) The cashflows from Exercise 5.1.6 are "indexed to infla-
tion" at periodic rate $r$, so that the transaction is modified to
$C_0' = C_0$, $C_1' = C_1(1+r)$, $C_2' = C_2(1+r)^2, \ldots$, $C_n' = C_n(1+r)^n$.
Show that $i_0' = (1+r) \cdot i_0 + r$ is a yield rate for the new transaction.

(b) Smith can borrow 10,000 at $i = 12\%$ and repay the loan
with 15 annual payments beginning one year after the loan
is made. He will invest the 10,000 in equipment that will
generate revenue at the end of each year for 15 years. He
expects revenue of 1200 after one year, and he expects
subsequent revenue to increase by an inflationary factor of
$1 + r$ per year thereafter. He will apply the full amount of
his annual revenue as an annual loan payment, until the
loan is repaid. Find the smallest value of $r$ that will allow
repayment of the loan in 15 years.

*5.1.11 When net cashflow occurs continuously, say at rate $\overline{C}(t)$ at
time $t$, then the equation of value for a yield rate (force of interest) for the transaction over the period from 0 to $n$ is

$$\int_0^n \overline{C}(t) \cdot e^{-\delta t} \, dt = 0.$$

The overall equation of value for yield rate is

$$\sum_{s=0}^{n} C_s \cdot e^{-\delta \cdot t_s} + \int_0^n \overline{C}(t) \cdot e^{\delta t} \, dt = 0.$$

Suppose a company is marketing a new product. The production
and marketing process involves a startup cost of 1,000,000 and
continuing cost of 200,000 per year for 5 years, paid continuously. It is forecast that revenue from the product will begin one
year after startup, and will continue until the end of the original
5-year production process. Revenue (which will be received continuously) is estimated to start at a rate of 500,000 per year and
increase linearly (and continuously) over a two-year period to a
rate of 1,000,000 per year at the end of the $3^{rd}$ year, and then decrease to a rate of 200,000 per year at the end of the $5^{th}$ year.
Solve for the yield rate $\delta$ earned by the company over the 5-year
period.

*5.1.12 A loan of 100,000 is to be repaid by the sinking fund method over a 25-year period. The lender receives annual interest payments at rate 10% per year, and the borrower accumulates the principal by means of annual deposits in a sinking fund earning annual interest at rate 6%. After the 10th deposit to the sinking fund, the rate is increased to 8%.

(a) At the time the loan is issued, the borrower is not aware of the future interest rate change in the fund, and decides to make level annual deposits (starting one year after the loan) under the assumption that the interest rate will stay at 6% for the full 25 years. When the rate change is announced after 10 years, the borrower changes the level of future deposits so that the accumulated value will be 100,000 at the time of the $25^{th}$ deposit. Find the borrower's yield rate on this transaction.

(b) Suppose that the rate change after 10 years is known by the borrower on the issue date of the loan, and he calculates a level deposit which will accumulate to 100,000 based on the 25-year schedule of interest rates. Find the borrower's yield rate in this case.

## SECTION 5.2

5.2.1 The details regarding fund value, contributions and withdrawals from a fund are as follows:

|  | Date | Amount |
|---|---|---|
| Fund Values: | 1/1/05 | 1,000,000 |
|  | 7/1/05 | 1,310,000 |
|  | 1/1/06 | 1,265,000 |
|  | 7/1/06 | 1,540,000 |
|  | 1/1/07 | 1,420,000 |
| Contributions Received: | 6/30/05 | 250,000 |
|  | 6/30/06 | 250,000 |
| Benefits Paid: | 12/31/05 | 150,000 |
|  | 12/31/06 | 150,000 |

Find the effective annual time-weighted rate of return for the two-year period of 2005 and 2006.

5.2.2S  You are given the following information about an investment account:

| Date | Value Immediately Before Deposit | Deposit |
|------|----------------------------------|---------|
| January 1 | 10 | |
| July 1 | 12 | $X$ |
| December 31 | $X$ | |

Over the year, the time-weighted return is 0%, and the dollar-weighted return is $Y$. Calculate $Y$.

5.2.3  On January 1, 2005, an investment account is worth 100,000. On April 1, 2005, the value has increased to 103,000 and 8,000 is withdrawn. On January 1, 2007, the account is worth 103,992. Assuming a dollar-weighted method for 2005 and a time-weighted method for 2006, the effective annual interest rate was equal to $x$ for both 2005 and 2006. Calculate $x$.

5.2.4S  An investor deposits 50 in an investment account on January 1. The following summarizes the activity in the account during the year:

| Date | Value Immediately Before Deposit | Deposit |
|------|----------------------------------|---------|
| March 15 | 40 | 20 |
| June 1 | 80 | 80 |
| October 1 | 175 | 75 |

On June 30, the value of the account is 157.50. On December 31, the value of the account is $X$. Using the time-weighted method, the equivalent effective annual yield during the first 6 months is equal to the (time-weighted) effective annual yield during the entire 1-year period. Calculate $X$.

5.2.5    Fund X has unit values which are 1.0 on January 1, 2005, .8 on July 1, 2005 and 1.0 on January 1, 2006. A fund manager receives contributions of 100,000 on January 1, 2005 and 100,000 on July 1, 2005 and immediately uses the entire contributions to purchase units in Fund X. Find the time-weighted and dollar-weighted rates of return for 2005.

5.2.6    You are given the following information about the activity in two different investment accounts:

| Date | Account K Fund Value Before Activity | Deposit | Withdrawal |
|------|------|------|------|
| 1/1/1999 | 100.0 | | |
| 7/1/1999 | 125.0 | | X |
| 10/1/1999 | 110.0 | 2X | |
| 12/31/ 1999 | 125.0 | | |

| Date | Account L Fund Value Before Activity | Deposit | Withdrawal |
|------|------|------|------|
| 1/1/1999 | 100.0 | | |
| 7/1/1999 | 125.0 | | X |
| 12/31/1999 | 105.8 | | |

During 1999, the dollar weighted return for investment Account $K$ equals the time weighted return for investment Account $L$, which equals $i$. Calculate $i$.

## SECTION 5.3

5.3.1    A large pension fund has a value of 500,000,000 at the start of the year. During the year the fund receives contributions of 100,000,000, pays out benefits of 40,000,000 and has interest income of 60,000,000. Estimate the yield rate on the fund for each of the following circumstances:

(a) Contributions, benefits and interest are uniformly spread throughout the year.

(b) Benefits and interest are uniformly spread throughout the year, and the contributions are made in one lump-sum at time (i) $t = 0$, (ii) $t = \frac{1}{4}$, (iii) $t = \frac{1}{2}$, (iv) $t = \frac{3}{4}$, or (v) $t = 1$.

5.3.2    Suppose a fund receives new money of amount $N$ in two equal installments, one at the beginning of the year and one at the end of the year. Show that Equation (5.8) is an exact measure of $i$ for the year.


*5.3.3 Suppose the first investment in Example 5.6 pays $X$ per year. Find the value of $X$ for which the balance at the end of 10 years is the same as it is for the second investment.

# CHAPTER 6

## THE TERM STRUCTURE OF INTEREST RATES

*"A billion here, a billion there, and pretty soon you're talking about real money."*
— *Everett Dirksen, U.S. Senator from Illinois, 1896-1969*

When a borrower arranges to take a loan, there are a number of factors that the lender will consider in setting the interest rate on the loan. For instance, the lender would be concerned with the *credit rating* of the borrower, which is a measure of how likely the borrower is to be able to make the scheduled loan payments. The lender would also likely be concerned with the length of time over which the loan is to be repaid. An investor in a fixed-term deposit with some financial institution would have similar concerns. If the investment is in a government security such as a Treasury bill or Treasury bond, then there would not likely be any concern with the credit rating of the government, and the main consideration in determining the desired return would be the length of time until maturity of the investment. The relationship between the time to maturity and the yield rate on fixed income securities such as Treasury bills and coupon bonds is referred to as the **term structure of interest rates**, and a graph representing that relationship is called a **yield curve**.

The term structure changes from day to day as a result of changing economic conditions, but it is usually the case that longer term investments have higher associated rates of return than shorter term investments. This is called a *normal term structure*. For example, the following excerpt from the Bloomberg © website on March 12, 2004 illustrates a graph of yield-to-maturity versus time to maturity for US Treasury bills (less than one year maturity), Treasury notes (up to 10 year maturity) and Treasury bonds (over 10 year maturity). There is a clear increasing trend in the yield rate as the time to maturity increases.

| U.S. TREASURIES | | | | | |
|---|---|---|---|---|---|
| **Bills** | | | | | |
| | COUPON | MATURITY DATE | CURRENT PRICE/YIELD | PRICE/YIELD CHANGE | TIME |
| **3-Month** | N.A. | 06/10/2004 | 0.93/0.94 | 0.01/0.006 | 03/12 |
| **6-Month** | N.A. | 09/09/2004 | 0.97/0.99 | 0.01/0.01 | 03/12 |
| **Notes/Bonds** | | | | | |
| | COUPON | MATURITY DATE | CURRENT PRICE/YIELD | PRICE/YIELD CHANGE | TIME |
| **2-Year** | 1.625 | 02/28/2006 | 100-06/1.5 | -0-03/0.048 | 03/12 |
| **3-Year** | 2.250 | 02/15/2007 | 100-29/1.9 | -0-05/0.054 | 03/12 |
| **5-Year** | 2.625 | 03/15/2009 | 99-16/2.72 | -0-11/0.074 | 03/12 |
| **10-Year** | 4.000 | 02/15/2014 | 101-26/3.76 | -0-17/0.065 | 03/12 |
| **30-Year** | 5.375 | 02/15/2031 | 109-31/4.71 | -0-25/0.048 | 03/12 |

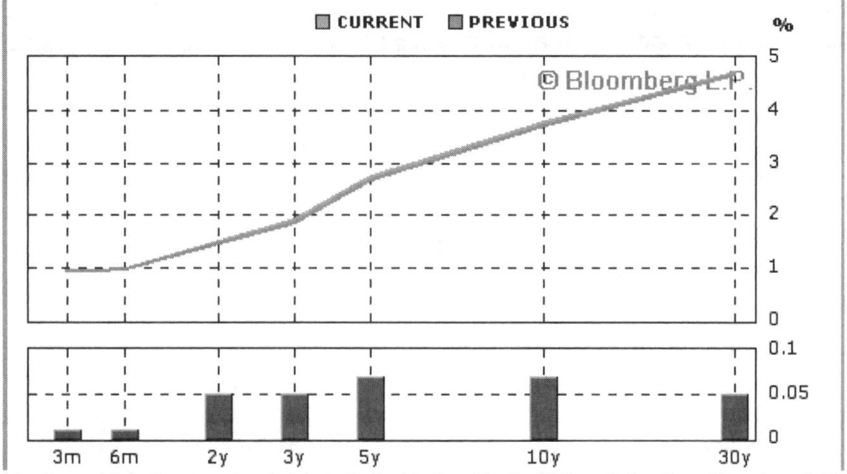

http://www.bloomberg.com/markets/rates/index.html     Used with Permission from Bloomberg L.P.

**FIGURE 6.1**

The following yield curves were taken from the website of Stockcharts.com © and represent the term structure of US Treasury securities at several points in time. We see that during the year from May, 2000 to April, 2001, the term structure changed from being *inverted* (in May and August, 2000), meaning that yield rates are lower for long term than for short term investments, to a *flat* term structure in September, to a more normal increasing term structure by April

2001. The one year period that was chosen for this illustration is somewhat of an anomaly. Prior to early 2000, the term structure had a normal shape for several years, and from early 2001 to the time of publication of this book it has had a normal shape.

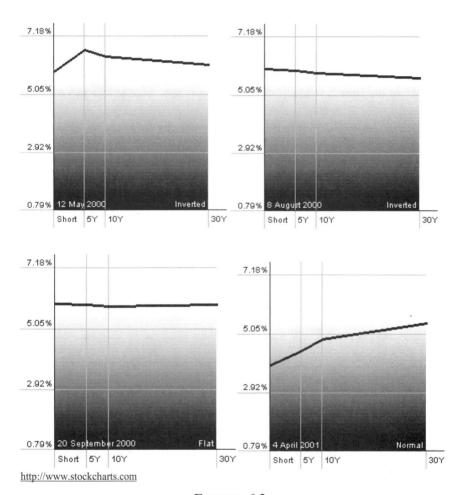

**FIGURE 6.2**

There are various theories that attempt to relate the shape of the yield curve to economic conditions and investor behavior. We will not look into such theories in this book, but we will be concerned with the relationship between the yield curve and pricing of fixed income securities.

In the Bloomberg website excerpt above, prices and yields of a few representative Treasury securities are given in the table. The actual yield curve would be based on a more complete collection of Treasury securities that traded on March 12, 2004.

Governments issue bonds of various terms to maturity on a regular basis, and over time there may be bonds issued at different times that mature on the same date. One of the bonds listed in the Bloomberg website excerpt is a 2.25% coupon Treasury note maturing on February 15, 2007. In a more complete listing of Treasury notes, one would find another one also maturing on February 15, 2007 that has a 6.25% coupon. Figure 6.3 was taken from the Yahoo © website based on the close of trading on March 12, 2004. We see the 2.25% bond listed along with the 6.25% bond. The 6.25% bond has a larger coupon and therefore will have a higher price than the 2.25% bond. The two bonds mature at the same time, and so we might anticipate that they should have the same yield rate. The yield rates on the two bonds differ very slightly, and we might attribute the difference to some roundoff error, or perhaps to slightly changed market conditions between the last trade of the 2.25% bond and the last trade of the 6.25% bond on March 12, 2004. Keep in mind the conventions describing coupon bonds that were discussed in Chapter 4. In particular, recall that coupon rate and yield rates are quoted as nominal annual rates compounded semi-annually

|  | Coupon | Maturity | Yield | Price |
|---|---|---|---|---|
| T-Note (3-yr) | 2.25 | 02-15-2007 | 1.913 | 100.950 |
| T-Note | 6.25 | 02-15-2007 | 1.909 | 112.259 |

http://bond.finance.yahoo.com

**FIGURE 6.3**

There are many other examples of bonds that mature on the same date but have different coupon and yield rates. From the financial pages of the *Globe and Mail* © newspaper from Canada reporting on closing bond prices and yields for March 12, 2004, there are quotations for two Government of Canada bonds that both mature on June 1, 2010. There is a 5.50% bond priced at 109.50 with a yield of 3.77%, and there is a 9.50% bond priced at 131.80 with a yield of 3.72%. Again, the difference between the yield rates on the two bonds is small. A more careful look at each of the pairs of bonds that mature simultaneously reveals a consistency in the difference between the yield rates. For both pairs we see that the bond with the higher coupon rate has the lower yield to maturity. We might expect that bonds from the same issuer with the same maturity date should have the same yield rates, but we shall shortly see why this is not (theoretically) the case.

The payments on a coupon bond consist of the coupon payments and the redemption payment on the maturity date. Due to amortization of a bond, in a sense, a coupon bond "matures a little bit" every time a coupon is paid, so we are mixing maturity dates over the course of the series of bond payments.

---

**Definition 6.1 – Zero Coupon Bond**

A zero coupon bond is a bond which has no coupons and has a single payment made at the time of maturity. It is also referred to as a **discount bond** or a pure discount bond. A Treasury Bill is an example of a zero coupon bond since it consists of a single payment made at the time the T-Bill matures.

---

For a zero coupon bond, the yield to maturity would be a clear measure of yield rate for single payments made at that particular date. If we know the pricing of zero coupon bonds for many maturity terms from very short term to very long term, we can always represent a given set of cashflows as an appropriate series of zero coupon bonds, and the total present value of the set of cashflows is the sum of the present values of the component zero coupon bonds. Example 6.1 on page 311 illustrates this idea.

---

**Definition 6.2 – Term Structure of Interest Rates**

The term structure of interest rates at the current point in time is the set of yield rates on zero coupon bonds of all maturities. This is the set $\{s_0(t)\}_{t>0}$, where $s_0(t)$ is the annual effective yield rate as of time 0 for a zero coupon bond maturing at time $t$. The term structure is also called the **zero coupon bond yield curve**. In the notation, the subscript indicates the current point in time from which interest rates are being measured.

---

When we speak of the term structure of interest rates, we can loosely mean the more vague relationship between the term of an investment and the rate of return, where we could have a different relationship for different risk-classes of investments. We can have a term structure for US Treasury issues, or we can have a term structure for AA risk rated corporate bonds, etc. The generally accepted definition of the term structure is the relationship between the time to maturity and the yield to maturity of zero coupon bonds of a particular risk class.

---

**Definition 6.3 – Spot Rate of Interest**

The yield to maturity on a zero coupon bond is called the spot rate of interest for that time to maturity. $s_0(t)$ is the spot rate for a $t$-year maturity zero coupon bond. The price at time 0 of a $t$-year zero coupon bond is $\dfrac{1}{(1+s_0(t))^t}$ for a maturity value of 1.

---

The algebraic description of the term structure and spot rates is as follows. At the present moment, we consider a zero coupon bond maturing $t$ years from now, with a spot rate of $s_t$ measured as an effective annual rate of interest. The present value of a payment of 1 due in $t$ years is $(1+s_0(t))^{-t}$. Any set of future cashflows can be valued now using the term structure. Suppose that payments of amounts $C_1, C_2, \ldots, C_n$ are due in $t_1, t_2, \ldots, t_n$ years from now. The total present value of the series of cashflows is

$$C_1(1+s_0(t_1))^{-t_1} + C_2(1+s_0(t_2))^{-t_2} + \cdots + C_n(1+s_0(t_n))^{-t_n}. \quad (6.1)$$

## 6.1 Spot Rates of Interest

Bond issuers do not usually issue zero coupon bonds directly, but in the secondary market, investors are allowed to separate and resell individually each of the coupon and redemption payments that will be made by the issuer of the bond. The US Treasury describes this procedure program in the following excerpt from the US Treasury website.

## Treasury STRIPS

The Treasury STRIPS program was introduced in January 1985. STRIPS is the acronym for Separate Trading of Registered Interest and Principal of Securities. The STRIPS program lets investors hold and trade the individual interest and principal components of eligible Treasury notes and bonds as separate securities.

## What is a stripped security?

When a Treasury fixed-principal or inflation-indexed note or bond is stripped, each interest payment and the principal payment becomes a separate zero coupon security. Each component has its own identifying number and can be held or traded separately. For example, a Treasury note with 10 years remaining to maturity consists of a single principal payment at maturity and 20 interest payments, one every six months for 10 years. When this note is converted to STRIPS form, each of the 20 interest payments and the principal payment becomes a separate security. STRIPS are also called zero coupon securities because the only time an investor receives a payment during the life of a STRIP is when it matures.

## How do I buy STRIPS?

The Treasury does not issue or sell STRIPS directly to investors. STRIPS can be purchased and held only through financial institutions and government securities brokers and dealers.

## Why do investors hold STRIPS?

STRIPS are popular with investors who want to receive a known payment at a specific future date. For example, some State lotteries invest the present value of large lottery prizes in STRIPS to be sure that funds are available when needed to meet annual payment obligations that result from the prizes. Pension funds invest in STRIPS to match the payment flows of their assets with those of their liabilities.

STRIPS are also referred to as "coupons and residuals" (the residuals being payments that come at maturity). Each day there are quotations of prices and yields of STRIPS for Treasury issues, with payments due in a few months to many years. These yields make up the term structure (for that day) for "risk-free" investments (risk-free in the sense that the US government guarantees that the payments will be made) and are called

**spot rates of interest** for the various terms to maturity. The price of a STRIP is quoted in the financial press as the present value of $100 payable at that STRIPS' payment point. The price per dollar can be used as a present value factor for payments due at that time point.

TABLE 6.1

| Globe and Mail © | | | | |
|---|---|---|---|---|
| Issuer | Coupon | Maturity | Price | Yield |
| CMHC | 0.000 | 12/01/2004 | 98.67 | 1.90 |
| Canada | 0.000 | 03/01/2005 | 97.98 | 2.15 |
| Canada | 0.000 | 06/01/2005 | 97.45 | 2.15 |
| Canada | 0.000 | 10/01/2005 | 96.54 | 2.30 |
| Canada | 0.000 | 03/01/2006 | 95.38 | 2.43 |
| Canada | 0.000 | 04/01/2006 | 95.05 | 2.50 |
| Canada | 0.000 | 09/15/2006 | 93.62 | 2.66 |
| Canada | 0.000 | 10/01/2006 | 93.50 | 2.66 |
| Canada | 0.000 | 12/01/2006 | 92.64 | 2.84 |
| Canada | 0.000 | 06/01/2007 | 91.43 | 2.81 |
| Canada | 0.000 | 10/01/2007 | 89.90 | 3.03 |
| Canada | 0.000 | 03/15/2008 | 88.12 | 3.19 |
| Canada | 0.000 | 06/01/2008 | 86.86 | 3.38 |
| Canada | 0.000 | 10/01/2008 | 85.84 | 3.39 |
| Canada | 0.000 | 12/01/2008 | 85.05 | 3.47 |
| Canada | 0.000 | 03/01/2009 | 83.86 | 3.58 |
| Canada | 0.000 | 12/01/2009 | 80.48 | 3.84 |
| Canada | 0.000 | 12/01/2010 | 76.18 | 4.10 |
| Canada | 0.000 | 06/01/2011 | 73.91 | 4.24 |
| Canada | 0.000 | 12/01/2011 | 72.11 | 4.29 |
| Canada | 0.000 | 06/01/2012 | 69.76 | 4.44 |
| Canada | 0.000 | 12/01/2012 | 68.13 | 4.46 |
| Canada | 0.000 | 12/01/2013 | 64.58 | 4.56 |
| Canada | 0.000 | 12/01/2014 | 61.09 | 4.66 |
| Canada | 0.000 | 06/01/2015 | 59.37 | 4.71 |
| Canada | 0.000 | 12/01/2016 | 54.22 | 4.88 |
| Canada | 0.000 | 06/01/2017 | 52.28 | 4.97 |
| Canada | 0.000 | 12/01/2017 | 50.74 | 5.01 |
| Canada | 0.000 | 12/01/2018 | 47.88 | 5.07 |
| Canada | 0.000 | 06/01/2019 | 46.48 | 5.10 |
| Canada | 0.000 | 06/01/2020 | 43.99 | 5.13 |
| Canada | 0.000 | 06/01/2021 | 41.33 | 5.20 |
| Canada | 0.000 | 06/01/2022 | 38.84 | 5.26 |
| Canada | 0.000 | 06/01/2025 | 33.45 | 5.23 |

The convention of a nominal annual rate compounded semi-annually applies to the quotation of yields on STRIPS. Tables 6.1 and 6.2 are excerpts from the *Globe and Mail* © and *Wall Street Journal* © for closing prices March 12, 2004 for Canadian Treasury STRIPS and US Treasury STRIPS, respectively.

TABLE 6.2

## Wall St. Journal ©

### US Treasury Strips

| Maturity | Type | Bid | Asked | Chg | Ask Yld | Maturity | Type | Bid | Asked | Chg | Ask Yld |
|---|---|---|---|---|---|---|---|---|---|---|---|
| May | 04 | Ci | 99.27 | 99.27 | ··· | 0.93 | Aug | 06 | ci | 96.00 | 96.02 | −4 | 1.67 |
| May | 04 | np | 99.27 | 99.27 | ··· | 0.93 | Oct | 06 | np | 95.18 | 95.19 | −1 | 1.75 |
| Jul | 04 | Ci | 99.21 | 99.21 | ··· | 1.03 | Nov | 06 | ci | 95.10 | 95.12 | ··· | 1.79 |
| Aug | 04 | Ci | 99.19 | 99.19 | ··· | 0.95 | Nov | 06 | np | 95.11 | 95.12 | ··· | 1.78 |
| Aug | 04 | np | 99.19 | 99.19 | ··· | 0.97 | Feb | 07 | ci | 94.14 | 94.16 | −1 | 1.95 |
| Nov | 04 | Ci | 99.09 | 99.10 | ··· | 1.05 | Feb | 07 | np | 94.19 | 94.20 | −1 | 1.90 |
| Nov | 04 | bp | 99.10 | 99.10 | ··· | 1.04 | May | 07 | ci | 93.22 | 93.24 | −1 | 2.05 |
| Nov | 04 | np | 99.10 | 99.10 | ··· | 1.04 | May | 07 | np | 93.23 | 93.25 | −1 | 2.04 |
| Jan | 05 | Ci | 99.14 | 99.14 | −1 | 0.67 | Aug | 07 | np | 93.00 | 93.02 | −1 | 2.12 |
| Feb | 05 | Ci | 99.02 | 99.03 | −1 | 1.01 | Aug | 07 | ci | 92.24 | 92.26 | −1 | 2.19 |
| Feb | 05 | np | 99.00 | 99.00 | −3 | 1.09 | Aug | 07 | np | 92.30 | 93.00 | −1 | 2.13 |
| May | 05 | Ci | 98.26 | 98.27 | ··· | 1.01 | Nov | 07 | ci | 92.02 | 92.05 | −1 | 2.24 |
| May | 05 | bp | 98.23 | 98.24 | ··· | 1.09 | Nov | 07 | np | 92.09 | 92.11 | −1 | 2.19 |
| May | 05 | np | 99.22 | 98.22 | ··· | 1.13 | Feb | 08 | ci | 91.03 | 91.01 | −1 | 2.38 |
| May | 05 | np | 98.22 | 98.22 | ··· | 1.13 | Feb | 08 | np | 91.10 | 91.12 | −1 | 2.32 |
| Jul | 05 | Ci | 98.30 | 98.31 | ··· | 0.78 | May | 08 | ci | 90.01 | 90.04 | −1 | 2.52 |
| Aug | 05 | Ci | 98.13 | 98.14 | ··· | 1.12 | May | 08 | np | 90.09 | 90.12 | −1 | 2.45 |
| Aug | 05 | bp | 98.07 | 98.08 | −1 | 1.25 | Aug | 08 | ci | 89.09 | 89.11 | −1 | 2.57 |
| Aug | 05 | np | 98.09 | 98.10 | ··· | 1.12 | Nov | 08 | ci | 88.07 | 88.10 | −1 | 2.68 |
| Nov | 05 | Ci | 97.25 | 97.26 | ··· | 1.34 | Nov | 08 | np | 88.14 | 88.16 | −1 | 2.63 |
| Nov | 05 | Ci | 97.25 | 97.26 | ··· | 1.34 | Feb | 09 | ci | 87.05 | 87.08 | −2 | 2.80 |
| Nov | 05 | np | 97.25 | 97.26 | ··· | 1.34 | May | 09 | ci | 86.07 | 86.10 | −2 | 2.87 |
| Jan | 06 | Ci | 98.01 | 98.02 | ··· | 1.07 | May | 09 | np | 86.23 | 86.26 | −1 | 2.76 |
| Feb | 06 | Ci | 97.10 | 97.11 | ··· | 1.40 | Aug | 09 | ci | 85.23 | 85.16 | −1 | 2.91 |
| Feb | 06 | bp | 97.08 | 97.09 | ··· | 1.44 | Aug | 09 | np | 85.18 | 85.21 | −1 | 2.88 |
| Feb | 06 | np | 97.08 | 97.10 | ··· | 1.43 | Nov | 09 | ci | 84.29 | 84.28 | −1 | 2.92 |
| May | 06 | np | 98.20 | 96.21 | ··· | 1.57 | Nov | 09 | bp | 83.26 | 83.29 | −2 | 3.12 |
| Jul | 06 | Ci | 96.29 | 96.30 | −4 | 1.33 | Feb | 10 | ci | 83.02 | 83.05 | −2 | 3.14 |
| Jul | 06 | np | 96.03 | 96.09 | ··· | 1.63 | May | 10 | np | 82.04 | 82.07 | ··· | 3.20 |

Table 6.2 is a partial listing of the Treasury Strips quotations for March 12, 2004. A more complete listing would have maturities ranging up to about 30 years. The term structure graph in Figure 6.1 on page 302 is a plot of time versus yield to maturity for the complete set of Treasury

securities for all maturity dates. In the listing of US Treasury STRIPS, we see, for example, that the present value (the ask price) on March 12, 2004 of a payment of $100 to be made on May 15, 2010 is quoted as $82.07, which is $82$\frac{7}{32}$ = $82.22 (treasury note payments and maturities usually take place on the $15^{th}$ of a month, and price quotations give fractions of a dollar in increments of $\frac{1}{32}$). This can be regarded as a zero coupon bond maturing on May 15, 2010.

The quoted yield rate for that ask price is 3.20%. As of March 12, 2004, there were 6 years, 2 months and 3 days until the payment is made. This corresponds to 12 full half-year periods plus (approximately) 2.1 months for a total of $12 + \frac{2.1}{6} = 12.35$ interest (half-year) periods. The present value of $100 due in 12.35 interest periods at a rate of 1.60% per interest period is $100(1.016)^{-12.35} = $82.20$. The quoted price of $82.22 is within the roundoff error range for interest rates quoted to the nearest .01%.

There seem to be some anomalies in the quoted values in Tables 6.1 and 6.2. For instance, in what appears to be a fairly steady increasing trend in the yield rates with increasing time to maturity, we see that the yield rate for the January, 2006 US Treasury STRIP is 1.07%, which is noticeably lower than the yield rate of 1.34% for the November, 2005 STRIP. There are also different STRIPS that mature at the same time but have different yields. These differences may be due to a number of factors. If a STRIP payment has a callable feature, it may end earlier than the maturity date stated, and the price and yield would be quoted on the basis of its earliest call date. It would be listed in the table, however, by its latest call date. The size of the payment available may have some implications in the market as to the liquidity (demand and/or availability) for that amount of a STRIP.

The yield rates in the excerpts are market versions of the term structure of interest rates (for government securities) in the US and in Canada on March 12, 2004. Although the quotations listed are not a complete description of the term structure, we have enough information to calculate the present value of most risk-free sets of cashflows. For example, the Bloomberg website excerpt in Figure 6.1 lists a 2.25% bond maturing February 15, 2007 as having a price of $100.91 and a yield to maturity of 1.9%. This bond would make payments of $1.125 on August 15, 2004, February 15 and August 15 in both 2005 and 2006 and February 15, 2007, along with a payment of $100 on February 15, 2007.

We can find the present value of each of these payments separately using the term structure represented in the STRIPS quotations.

Theoretically, the sum of the separate present values of these payments should be the same as the price of the full bond. This is sometimes referred to as the **Law of One Price**. The Law of One Price is an economic rule which states that in an *efficient market*, a security must have a single price, no matter how that security is created. The Law of One Price is closely related to the concept of arbitrage which will be introduced later in this chapter.

**EXAMPLE 6.1** *(Using the term structure to price a bond)*

Suppose that the current term structure has the following yields on zero coupon bonds.

| Term | ½ Year | 1 Year | 1 ½ Year | 2-Year |
|------|--------|--------|----------|--------|
| Zero Coupon Bond Rate | 8% | 9% | 10% | 11% |

Find the price per $100 face amount and yield to maturity of each of the following 2-year bonds (with semi-annual coupons):

   (i)   zero coupon bond,
   (ii)  5% annual coupon rate,
   (iii) 10% annual coupon rate.

**SOLUTION**

(i)   Price is $100\left(1+\frac{.11}{2}\right)^{-4} = 80.72$ and yield to maturity is (nominal) 11%.

(ii)  Price is $2.5\left[(1.04)^{-1}+(1.045)^{-2}+(1.05)^{-3}\right]+102.5(1.055)^{-4} = 89.59.$
     Yield to maturity is (nominal) 10.9354%.

(iii) Price is $5\left[(1.04)^{-1}+(1.045)^{-2}+(1.05)^{-3}\right]+105(1.055)^{-4} = 98.46.$
     Yield to maturity is (nominal) 10.8775%.       ❏

For the 2.25% Treasury Note from Figure 6.1, pricing the note using Treasury STRIPS does not quite replicate the quoted price because of distortions in the pricing of STRIPS that was mentioned earlier. Using the average price for simultaneous maturities in Table 6.2, we have the following present value factors on March 12, 2004 for various payment dates.

## TABLE 6.3

| Payment Date | Present Value Factor |
|---|---|
| August 15, 2004 | .9959 |
| February 15, 2005 | .9903 |
| August 15, 2005 | .9831 |
| February 15, 2006 | .9728 |
| August 15, 2006 | .9600 |
| February 15, 2007 | .9451 |

The entry in Table 6.3 for August 15, 2004 is based on the STRIP quote from Table 6.2 of a price of 99.19 for an August 2004 STRIP maturity. The value 99.19 refers to a price of $99\frac{19}{32} = 99.59$ for a STRIP of face amount 100. This corresponds to a present value factor of .9959. The average of the two bid entries for the Aug 04 maturity were used. The other entries in Table 6.3 are found in a similar way using bid values averaged over STRIPS with the same maturity date.

Using these zero-coupon bond values, the present value of the bond payments would be

$$1.125(.9959+.9903+.9831+.9728+.9600) + 101.25(.9451) = 101.21.$$

To get the quoted price, we subtract the accrued coupon, which is $\frac{26}{182} \times 1.125 = .16$ (26 days from February 15, 2004 to March 12, 2004, out of a coupon period of 182 days from Feb. 15 to Aug. 15, 2004). According to this method of pricing the bond, the quoted price should be 101.05. This is somewhat different from the quoted price on the Bloomberg website of 100.91. The bond price for March 12, 2004 was quoted in the *Wall Street Journal* at a price of 100.97, still a little different from 101.05. The difference between the Bloomberg quote and the *Wall Street Journal* quote might be due to different times at which the quotes were taken.

In Chapter 4 bond valuation was presented with prices calculated using the yield to maturity. The yield to maturity of a coupon bond is a single interest rate that is applied to find the present value of all payments to be made by the bond. The yield to maturity is actually an average of the spot rates for the payment periods represented by the bond.

## 6.2 THE RELATIONSHIP BETWEEN SPOT RATES OF INTEREST AND YIELD TO MATURITY ON COUPON BONDS

We have seen that we can find the present value of a series of payments if the term structure is known. We can also find the price of a bond if the yield to maturity is known. These two alternative valuation methods for a coupon bond lead to a relationship between spot rates and yield to maturity. The following is an exaggerated example to illustrate the relationship.

**EXAMPLE 6.2** (*Spot rates vs. yield to maturity*)

Suppose that the term structure of interest rates has the following schedule of spot rates for maturities of 1, 2, 3 and 4 years:

| Maturity | 1 Year | 2 Year | 3 Year | 4 Year |
|----------|--------|--------|--------|--------|
| Spot Rate | .05 | .10 | .15 | .20 |

Use this term structure to find the price and yield to maturity for a 5% annual coupon bond maturing in (i) 1 year, (ii) 2 years, (iii) 3 years, and (iv) 4 years. Also use this term structure to find the price and yield to maturity for a 4 year 10% annual coupon bond.

**SOLUTION**

1-year bond: The bond pays 105 in 1 year, so the price is $(105)(1.05)^{-1} = 100$.

The bond is bought at par because the coupon rate and the spot rate are the same, 5%.

2-year bond: The bond pays 5 in 1 year, and 105 in 2 years. The price is $5(1.05)^{-1} + 105(1.10)^{-2} = 91.54$. The yield to maturity for this 2-year bond is .0987. Note that this yield to maturity for the 2-year bond is smaller than the spot rate of .10 for a zero coupon bond with a 2-year maturity. The yield rate is also larger than the 1-year spot rate of 5%.

3-year bond: The bond pays 5 in 1 year, 5 in 2 years, and 105 in 3 years. The price is $5[(1.05)^{-1} + (1.10)^{-2}] + 105(1.15)^{-3} = 77.93$. The yield to maturity for this 3-year bond is .1460. Again, note that this yield to maturity for the 3 year bond is smaller that the spot rate of .15 for a zero coupon bond with a 3-year maturity.

4-year bond: The bond pays 5 in 1, 2 and 3 years, and 105 in 4 years. The price is $5\left[(1.05)^{-1} + (1.10)^{-2} + (1.15)^{-3}\right] + 105(1.20)^{-4} = 62.82$. The yield to maturity for this 4-year bond is .1912. Again, this yield to maturity for the 4-year bond is smaller that the spot rate of .20 for a zero coupon bond with a 4-year maturity.

4 year, 10% bond: The bond pays 10 in 1, 2 and 3 years, and 110 in 4 years. The price is $10[(1.05)^{-1} + (1.10)^{-2} + (1.15)^{-3}] + 110(1.20)^{-4} = 77.41$. The yield to maturity for this 4-year bond is .1848. Again, this yield to maturity for the 4 year bond is smaller that the spot rate of .20 for a zero coupon bond with a 4-year maturity. ☐

We can identify some patterns that occur in Example 6.2. Example 6.2 has an increasing term structure. We note that the yield to maturity for the 4-year 5% bond was 19.12% and for the 4-year 10% bond it was 18.48%. This is consistent with the behavior we have seen in some bonds quoted in the previous section. We saw quotes as of March 12, 2004 for U.S. Treasury notes maturing February 15, 2007. The 2.25% note had a yield to maturity of 1.913% and the 6.25% note had a yield to maturity of 1.909%. This phenomenon of the higher coupon bond with the same maturity date having a lower yield to maturity will always occur **when the term structure of spot interest rates is increasing** (in other words, for a normal yield curve). In the case of a zero coupon bond maturing in $n$ periods, the yield to maturity is the same as the spot rate, say $s_n$. If a bond has non-zero coupons, there will be payments occurring both before and at time $n$, and payments before time $n$ will be valued at a lower spot rate than $s_n$ (since the spot rates will be increasing up to $s_n$). The yield to maturity is the single interest rate such that the present value of all payments at that rate is equal to the bond price. The yield to maturity is a weighted average of the spot rates up to time $n$, where the weight is related to the size of the payments occurring before time $n$. A higher coupon bond makes larger payments earlier and puts more weight on early payments, and therefore puts more weight on earlier spot rates. Since we are assuming an increasing term structure, the smaller spot rates occur at the earlier payment times, and putting more weight on those smaller spot rates brings the average yield to maturity down. We can describe this algebraically in the following way. Suppose that the coupon is $r$ per year in Example 6.2(iv). Then the price of the bond is

$$r\left[(1.05)^{-1} + (1.10)^{-2} + (1.15)^{-3}\right] + (100+r)(1.20)^{-4} \qquad (6.1)$$

Suppose that we denote the yield to maturity as $y_r$ for this bond. The price can also be formulated as

$$r\left[(1+y_r)^{-1} + (1+y_r)^{-2} + (1+y_r)^{-3}\right] + (100+r)(1+y_r)^{-4}.$$

We can see that $.05 < y_r < .20$, since any yield larger than $.20$ must result in a present value smaller than (1), and any yield smaller than $.05$ must result in a present value greater than (1). $y_r$ is an average rate of return for the 2-year period, but the average is weighted by how much emphasis is made on each payment. As $r$ increases from 0, the yield decreases from .20. That is why in Example 6.2, we see the yield to maturity for the 4-year bond dropping as the coupon rate rises. The reverse behavior would occur in the case of a decreasing term structure (an inverted yield curve).

Economic conditions and the investment climate are constantly changing. Each day there will be changes in investor perceptions, and one of the ways that these changes can be observed is in yield rates in the bond market. The term structure will evolve from day to day. Earlier in this chapter, graphs of the term structure were presented for various points in time. These graphs were excerpted from the internet site Stockcharts.com. On that website (www.stockcharts.com/charts/YieldCurve.html) there is a "Dynamic Yield Curve" graphic, which shows the term structure evolving through time, day by day, for a period of several years.

## 6.3 FORWARD RATES OF INTEREST

### 6.3.1 FORWARD RATES OF INTEREST AS DEFERRED BORROWING OR LENDING RATES

Suppose that the current term structure has spot rates of $s_0(1) = .08$ for a one year maturity and $s_0(2) = .09$ for a two year maturity. An investment of amount 1 right now in a one-year zero coupon bond will grow to 1.08 in one year, while an investment of 1 right now in a two-year zero coupon bond will grow to $(1.09)^2 = 1.1881$ in two years. Let us suppose that we are able to borrow money at the same rate at which we can invest in zero coupon bonds (not a realistic assumption for me personally, but more realistic for a large financial institution).

Suppose that we borrow an amount of 1 today for <u>one year</u> so that we are committed to pay 1.08 back in <u>one year</u>. We invest that amount of 1 in a <u>two-year</u> zero coupon bond which will pay 1.1881 <u>two years</u> from now. Our net outlay right now is 0 (borrow 1 and immediately invest it) and one year from now when the one year loan is due, we pay 1.08, so we have a net outlay of 1.08 one year from now. This transaction is summarized in Figure 6.4. The net effect of this transaction is that we invest 1.08 one year from now and receive 1.1881 two years from now. We have postponed, for one year, a one year investment, and our one year return on that postponed investment is $\frac{1.1881}{1.08} - 1 = .1001$. This rate of 10.01% is a **one year forward rate of interest**.

This one year forward rate of interest may also be described as the one year forward rate of interest for year 2, or the one year forward rate of interest for the one-year period from time 1 to time 2. Generalizations of this notion will be presented a little later.

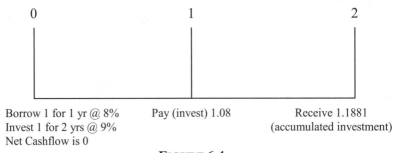

**FIGURE 6.4**

We can "reverse" the transaction just described by borrowing 1 today for two years so that we are committed to pay 1.1881 at the end of two years. We invest the borrowed amount of 1 for one year at 8% so that we received 1.08 at the end of one year. Our net outlay now is still 0, one year from now we receive 1.08, and two years from now we pay 1.1881. We have arranged a one year loan that begins one year from now at effective annual interest rate 10.01%.

### 6.3.2 Arbitrage with Forward Rates of Interest

The two transactions just described both show that borrowing or investing for one year starting one year from now can be arranged at the annual rate of 10.01% by using an appropriate combination of zero coupon bonds. If it were possible to arrange now to take a one year loan starting one year from now at an interest rate of less than 10.01% then it would be possible to make an arbitrage gain (guaranteed positive return for net investment of 0). For instance, suppose that a lender offers to lend you money for one year, starting one year from now at a rate of 9.5%. You arrange to borrow 1.08 in one year and pay back $1.08 \times 1.095 = 1.1826$ two years from now. You also borrow 1 for one year at 8% and invest it for two years at 9%. At the end of one year you pay back the one year loan with the 1.08 you arranged to borrow. At the end of two years, your investment pays 1.1881 and you pay 1.1826 on the loan. With a net outlay of 0, you have made a gain of .0055. This is an example of arbitrage gain.

In a similar way, if it is possible to arrange now to make a one year investment starting one year from now with an interest rate of more than 10.01%, then it is possible to make an arbitrage gain. Arbitrage will be discussed in more detail in the next section of this chapter.

One interpretation of a forward rate of interest is that it is the interest rate that we expect to be in effect in the future based on the current interest rate environment. We would make decisions about arranging now to borrow or invest at future points in time based on the forward rates that we currently see. Interest rates change from time to time, so the related forward rates would change over time as well. For instance, even though the current spot rates of 8% for one year and 9% for two years implies a one year forward rate of 10.01%, it is possible that one year from now interest rates may have changed and when this year elapses the one year rate at that time might not be 10.01%. On the other hand, an important point regarding a forward rate of interest is that we can arrange a transaction right now through an appropriate combination of borrowing and investing in zero coupon bonds that guarantees a return of 10.01% for an investment to be made one year from now.

### 6.3.3 GENERAL DEFINITION OF FORWARD RATES OF INTEREST

In the example above, we see that if $s_0(1)$ and $s_0(2)$ are known, we can borrow 1 for one year and pay back $1 + s_0(1)$ in one year, and we can invest the 1 now for two years and receive $(1 + s_0(2))^2$ two years from now. The net effect is that we invest $1 + s_0(1)$ one year from now and receive $(1 + s_0(2))^2$ two years from now. The rate of return for the one year period starting one year from now is

$$\frac{(1+s_0(2))^2}{1+s_0(1)} - 1 = i_0(1,2). \tag{6.2}$$

$i_0(1,2)$ is the one-year forward rate of interest for the one year period starting one year from now. The subscript indicates the current point in time, and the starting and ending point for the forward rate are in the parenthesis.

This can be generalized to any forward length of time. If we know the value of $s_0(t)$ for all times $t > 0$, then we can calculate forward rates of interest for any period of time in the future. An investment of 1 made now in an $(n-1)$-year zero coupon bond will grow to $(1 + s_0(n-1))^{n-1}$ at the end of $n-1$ years. An investment of 1 now in an $n$-year zero coupon bond will grow to $(1 + s_0(n))^n$ at the end of $n$ years. This implies that an investment of amount $(1 + s_0(n-1))^{n-1}$ made $n-1$ years from now should grow to $(1 + s_0(n))^n$ one year later ($n$ years from now), and this in turn implies that the interest rate that should be used to arrange transactions that will take place between $n-1$ and $n$ years from now is $\dfrac{(1+s_0(n))^n}{(1+s_0(n-1))^{n-1}} - 1$.

---

**Definition 6.4 – Forward Rate of Interest**

Given the term structure of zero coupon bond yield rates, $\{s_0(t)\}_{t>0}$, the time 0, $n-1$-year forward, one year interest rate for the year from time $n-1$ to time $n$ is denoted by the symbol $i_0(n-1,n)$, and satisfies the relationship

$$1 + i_0(n-1,n) = \frac{(1+s_0(n))^n}{(1+s_0(n-1))^{n-1}}. \qquad (6.3)$$

The forward rate for the period from time 0 to time 1 is $i_0(0,1) = s_0(1)$ (not really a forward rate, since "forward rate" refers to a rate on a transaction that starts in the future, not now).

---

There is no standard notation in financial practice for describing forward rates of interest. Other references may use the notation $f_1$ or $f_{[1,2]}$ or $_1f_1$ as alternative notation to this textbook's notation of $i_0(1,2)$.

Rewriting the equation for $i_{n-1,n}$ above we have

$$\left(1 + s_0(n-1)\right)^{n-1} \cdot \left(1 + i_0(n-1,n)\right) = \left(1 + s_0(n)\right)^n. \qquad (6.4)$$

Then starting with $i_{0,1} = s_1$, we can express accumulated values into the future with forward rates of interest as an alternative to the term structure rates:

AV in 1 year $\quad 1 + s_0(1) = 1 + i_0(0,1)$

AV in 2 year $\quad (1 + s_0(2))^2 = ((1 + s_0(1))(1 + i_0(1,2)))$

$$= (1 + i_0(0,1))(1 + i_0(1,2))$$

AV in 3 years $\quad (1 + s_0(3))^3 = (1 + s_0(2))^2(1 + i_0(2,3))$

$$= (1 + i_0(0,1))(1 + i_0(1,2))(1 + i_0(2,3))$$

The general expression that we get is

$$(1 + s_0(n))^n = (1 + i_0(0,1))(1 + i_0(1,2))\cdots(1 + i_0(n-1,n)) \qquad (6.5)$$

for the accumulated value at time $n$ of an investment of 1 made now.

This equation can be interpreted as saying that the accumulated value at the end of $n$ years of 1 invested now is found by compounding with successive 1 year interest rates. The successive 1 year interest rates are the forward rates of interest that the current interest rate structure implies.

"Time 0" usually refers to right now, the current time point. A forward rate of interest is tied to the current time point. The effective annual one year forward rate of interest for the period from time 1 to time 2 is an interest rate that takes effect one year from now. After the current year passes, "time 0" will be redefined to describe the time point that is actually one year from now, and we can define forward rates from our new reference time point. The general notation $i_k(t, t+1)$ refers to a $t$-year forward, one year effective annual rate of interest for the one year period starting $t$ years after time $k$; it is a forward rate from reference time point $k$.

**EXAMPLE 6.3** (*Spot rates vs. forward rates*)

For the term structure of interest in Example 6.2, find the one year forward rates of interest for years 1, 2, 3 and 4.

**SOLUTION**

$s_0(1) = .05$, $s_0(2) = .10$, $s_0(3) = .15$, $s_0(4) = .20$ are the term structure rates.

$i_0(0,1)$ is always the current one year rate of interest for this coming year, so it is always equal to $s_0(1)$. Therefore

$$i_0(0,1) = s_0(1) = .05, \ i_0(1,2) = \frac{\left(1+s_0(2)\right)^2}{1+s_0(1)} - 1 = \frac{(1.1)^2}{1.05} - 1 = .1524,$$

$$i_0(2,3) = \frac{\left(1+s_0(3)\right)^3}{\left(1+s_0(2)\right)^2} - 1 = \frac{(1.15)^3}{(1.1)^2} - 1 = .2596, \text{ and}$$

$$i_0(3,4) = \frac{\left(1+s_0(4)\right)^4}{\left(1+s_0(3)\right)^3} - 1 = \frac{(1.20)^4}{(1.15)^3} - 1 = .3634.$$

are the forward rates for each of the four years. ◻

Example 6.3 is rather extreme, but we can identify some patterns from it. The term structure is increasing and the forward rate for each future year (after the first year) is greater than the zero coupon yield for maturities at the end of that year; i.e.,

$$i_0(1,2) = .1524 > .10 = s_0(2),$$
$$i_0(2,3) = .2596 > .15 = s_0(3),$$

and $i_0(3,4) = .3634 > .20 = s_0(4)$. It is not difficult to see why this is always the case when the term structure rates $s_t$ are increasing as $t$ increases. In fact, if $s_0(n) > s_0(n-1)$ then

$$i_0(n-1,n) = \frac{\left(1+s_0(n)\right)^n}{\left(1+s_0(n-1)\right)^{n-1}} - 1$$

$$= \frac{\left(1+s_0(n)\right)^{n-1}}{\left(1+s_0(n-1)\right)^{n-1}} \times \left(1+s_0(n)\right) - 1 > s_0(n),$$

since $\dfrac{1+s_0(n)}{1+s_0(n-1)} > 1$.

An increasing term structure will result in increasing forward rates for the first few years, but there is no guarantee that the forward rates themselves will continue to increase. Exercises 6.3.1 and 6.3.2 at the end of the chapter will show the variations that can occur in forward interest rate behavior, and how forward rates are related to spot rates.

## 6.4 APPLICATIONS AND ILLUSTRATIONS

### 6.4.1 ARBITRAGE

Artbitrage can be described in a number of ways. A standard dictionary definition is the following.

---

**Definition 6.5 – Arbitrage**

An arbitrage is a simultaneous purchase and sale of securities in different markets in order to profit from price discrepancies.

---

Another description of an arbitrage is that it is a financial transaction which returns a positive amount on an investment of amount 0 with no risk. It is also an investment with no risk which has a return greater than the risk-free rate (the risk-free rate is the rate of return on federal government investments).

An arbitrage is a "free lunch," or something for nothing. For example, if the stock of XYZ corporation has a quoted market price of US $100 on the New York Stock Exchange, and at the same time has a quoted price that is equivalent to US $101 on the Toronto Stock Exchange, it would be possible to "buy low and sell high" at the same instant making a profit of $1 per share. Such an imbalance in markets is unlikely to occur, and if it does occur, it is unlikely to last long. In most models of financial market behavior, it is assumed that no arbitrage opportunities exist, since investors are rational and would immediately exploit any market imbalance. It is not unusual to see small price differences in financial instruments trading on different markets, but it would take a large amount invested to make any significant profit on the difference, and there is a risk that during the time it takes to make such investments the price differential may disappear.

---

**Sport Betting Arbitrage**

There are many (legal) ways to gamble. It is estimated that Americans bet $12 billion in online gambling in 2005. A significant component of online gambling is betting on the outcome of sporting events.

Denmark was one of the countries participating in the 2006 Winter Olympics in Turin, Italy, On February 6, 2006, "SportingUSA.com," an online betting casino, offered (British) odds of 2.5 to 1 that Denmark would not win any medals. This means a bet of $1 would pay back $2.5+$1 = $3.5 if Denmark won no medals and $0 if Denmark won at least one medal. On the same date, the online casino "Bet365.com" offered odds of 1.875 to 1 that Denmark would win at least one medal.

Suppose that on Feb. 6, 2006 a gambler bet $451 with SportingUSA that Denmark would win no medals, and at the same time bet $549 with Bet365 that Denmark would win at least one medal. If Denmark wins no medals, the gambler ends up with $3.5 \times \$451 = \$1,578.50$ (the gambler would lose the $549 bet with Bet365). If Denmark wins at least one medal, the gambler ends up with $2.875 \times \$549 = \$1,578.38$. For an "investment" (the bet) of $1,000, there is a guaranteed gain of $578.

This example of a sports betting arbitrage was given on an online service (arbhunters.co.uk), that seeks out sports betting arbitrage opportunities.

---

When the assumption is made that no arbitrage opportunities exist, it is usually also assumed that financial transactions can be arranged by any investor to buy or to sell, at the same price, any financial instrument. In considering the term structure of interest rates earlier in this chapter, we saw that the term structure of spot rates for zero coupon bonds implied the existence of forward rates. For example, a one-year effective annual spot rate of $s_0(1) = .08$ and a two-year spot rate of $s_0(2) = .09$ implies a one year forward, one-year effective annual rate of $i_0(1,2) = \frac{(1.09)^2}{1.08} - 1 = .1001$.

If we assume that there are no arbitrage opportunities, then right now, the only rate at which someone can arrange a one-year forward loan for a one year period is at 10.01%. If any other interest rate is offered for a one-year forward one year loan or investment, then an arbitrage opportunity will exist.

EXAMPLE 6.4 (*Arbitrage on forward interest rates*)

Suppose that the one-year zero coupon bond yield rate is 8% and the two-year zero coupon bond yield rate is 9% (both effective annual rates). For each of the situations in (a) and (b), construct transactions that provide an arbitrage gain, i.e., a positive profit for a net investment of 0. Assume that it is possible to borrow or lend at the zero coupon rates for their maturity periods.

(a) A borrower offers to pay you an interest rate $i$ above 10.01% for a one year investment starting one year from now.

(b) A lender offers to lend you money for one year at rate $j$ starting one year from now at an interest rate less than 10.01%.

SOLUTION

(a) Borrow 1000 at the two-year zero coupon yield rate of 9%, so that you must repay $1000(1.09)^2 = 1,188.10$ two years from now. Invest the 1000 in a one-year zero coupon bond for one year at the one-year rate of 8%, so that you receive 1080 one year from now. Arrange to lend that amount to the borrower at rate $i$ starting one year from now. You have made a net investment of 0, and at the end of two years the borrower pays you $1080(1+i)$. Since $i > .1001$ it follows that the amount you receive from the borrower at the end of two years is

$$1080(1+i) > 1080(1.1001) = 1188.10.$$

You have more than you need to repay your two year loan. You have made a guaranteed positive gain on an investment of 0.

(b) Borrow 1000 at the one-year zero coupon yield rate of 8%. You must repay 1080 in one year. Invest the 1000 at the two-year zero coupon yield of 9%, so that you will receive 1881.10 in two years. Arrange to borrow 1080 from the lender one year from now at the one-year rate of $j$. At the end of one year, when you receive 1080 from the lender, you pay the 1080 as repayment of your own one-year loan. At the end of two years you receive 1881.10 from your two-year investment, and you have to repay $1080(1+j)$ to the lender from whom you borrowed 1080. Since $j < .1001$, the amount you must repay at the end of two years is $1080(1+j) < 1080(1.1001) = 1881.10$. Therefore, the proceeds of your two year investment is more than enough to repay your loan and the difference is a guaranteed profit to you, having invested a net amount of 0.

In both cases (a) and (b) you have made an arbitrage profit.　　□

## 6.4.2 FORWARD RATE AGREEMENTS

In Section 6.3 we saw that a one-year spot rate of 8% and a two-year spot rate of 9% implies a one-year forward, effective annual interest rate of 10.01%. It was shown that the combination of selling a two-year zero coupon bond and using the proceeds to buy a one-year zero coupon bond has the net effect of arranging a loan that begins in one year and matures in two years and earns the one-year forward rate from time 1 to time 2.

It is possible in the over-the-counter market (a market that is not associated with an exchange such as the NYSE) to make forward loan arrangements. Often a financial interemediary can bring together a borrower and a lender (investor) to arrange a forward loan. There are a variety of forward arrangements that can be made that are referred to as **forward rate agreements**.

---

**Definition 6.6 – Forward Rate Agreement (FRA)**

A forward rate agreement is a contract that guarantees a borrowing or lending rate for a specific amount of principal (sometimes called the **notional amount**) for a specified time period that begins at a future date.

---

A FRA can be used to arrange a new forward loan or to modify the terms of an existing loan. Suppose that at time 0, the borrower wishes to arrange with a lender a forward loan to begin at time $t$ for a one year period. A simple version of an FRA would have the borrower and lender agreeing to some rate, say $j_0(t,t+1)$, on the loan for that future period.

Alternatively, a borrower may have an existing **floating rate**, interest only loan from Bank A for which the interest rate is reset at the start of each year based on the market conditions at that time. In another version of an FRA, a financial intermediary (not necessarily Bank A) would specify the guaranteed rate on the loan for the future period from time $t$

to time $t+1$, say $j_0(t,t+1)$. When time $t$ arrives, the actual one-year loan rate (the floating rate) might be $u_{t,t+1}$, and this is the rate which the borrower must pay Bank A for the following year. Under the FRA (arranged at time 0), the financial intermediary agrees to pay the borrower at time $t+1$ the difference between the actual (floating) loan rate $u_{t,t+1}$ and the FRA loan rate $j_0(t,t+1)$. This makes $j_0(t,t+1)$ the borrower's net interest rate for the year, and it makes the intermediary's net interest rate $u_{t,t+1} - j_0(t,t+1)$ (which may be positive or negative). Figure 6.5 illustrates the forward rate agreement.

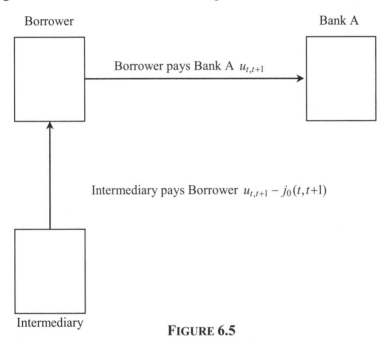

Borrower

Bank A

Borrower pays Bank A $u_{t,t+1}$

Intermediary pays Borrower $u_{t,t+1} - j_0(t,t+1)$

Intermediary

**FIGURE 6.5**

As we have seen earlier, at time 0 when a forward loan is arranged (the simple FRA mentioned above), in order for there to be no arbitrage possibility, the rate at which the loan will be made is the forward rate $i_0(t,t+1)$ that is implied by the current term structure at time 0.

In the case of the other version of FRA mentioned above in which a borrower wishes to arrange with an intermediary to substitute existing floating rate payments on a loan for fixed forward rates, the amount that the financial intermediary pays the borrower depends upon whether the FRA is settled at the time the loan is made (time $t$) or at the time the loan is repaid (time $t+1$). In the example above, it was assumed that the intermediary settled the FRA at time $t+1$. It is also possible to settle the FRA at time $t$.The following example illustrates this.

**EXAMPLE 6.5** (*Forward rate agreement*)

Suppose that the one-year zero coupon bond yield rate is 8% and the two-year zero coupon bond yield rate is 9% (both effective annual rates). The implied one-year forward, one-year effective annual rate of interest is 10.01%. A borrower has a one-year forward floating rate loan with notional amount $100,000 with a bank, with interest to be paid two years from now. Based on a one-year forward loan rate of 10.01% guaranteed by a financial intermediary using an FRA, describe in each of the following cases the payments that will be made (or received) by a financial intermediary to (or from) the borrower.

(a) The FRA is settled at the time the loan is repaid (time 2).

(b) The FRA is settled at the time the loan is made (time 1).

**SOLUTION**

When the first year is over, the actual one year lending rate for the next year (time 1 to time 2) is known, say $u_{1,2}$. That is the one-year rate on the loan of 100,000 taken at time 1.

(a) The borrower will have to pay $100,000(1+u_{1,2})$ at time 2. The financial intermediary pays the difference between the actual loan interest due and the loan interest that was guaranteed by the FRA. The intermediary pays $100,000(u_{1,2}-.1001)$. For instance, if $u_{1,2}=.105$, the intermediary would pay $100,000(.105-.1001)=490$ to the borrower at time 2 to cover the additional .49% in borrowing cost for the year. On the other hand, if $u_{1,2}=.0975$, the financial intermediary would pay the borrower $100,000(.0975-.1001)=-260$. The negative sign means that the borrower would pay the intermediary 260 to bring the borrowing cost up to 10.01% from 9.75%.

(b) If the FRA is settled at time 1, the intermediary would pay the present value at time 1 of the amount in part (a). This is $\dfrac{100,000(u_{1,2}-.1001)}{1+u_{1,2}}$.

The one-year interest rate $u_{1,2}$ is known at time 1, so any amount due at time 2 is discounted using that rate. Using the numerical values from part (a), we see that if $u_{1,2} = .105$, the intermediary would pay the borrower $\frac{100,000(.105-.1001)}{1.105} = 443.43$ at time 1. ❑

It is possible for the intermediary to create the cash flows needed in an FRA with an appropriate combination of buying and selling zero coupon bonds. In the previous example, the financial intermediary can sell for $92,593 a two-year zero coupon bond with 9% annual yield maturing at $110,010 and invest the $92,593 in a one-year zero coupon bond with 8% annual yield. At the end of one year, the one-year bond matures at $100,000 and can be loaned out at $u_{1,2}$. At the end of two years, the intermediary receives $100,000(1+u_{1,2})$ when that loan is repaid. Also, at the end of two years, the intermediary must pay $110,010 to pay the maturity on the two-year zero coupon bond that was sold at time 0. The intermediary receives a net amount of $100,000(u_{1,2}-.1001)$. This combination replicates the payments that the intermediary must make under the FRA. It is referred to as a **synthetic FRA.** It is summarized in the following time diagram.

| Time 0 | Time 1 | Time 2 |
|---|---|---|
| Intermediary arranges FRA with borrower, no money is paid | | |
| Intermediary sells 110,010 2-year zero, receives 92,593 | | Intermediary pays 110,010 when 2-year zero matures |
| Intermediary uses 92,593 to buy 100,000 1-year zero | 1-year zero matures, Intermediary receives 100,000 and lends out that amount for one year at rate $u_{1,2}$ | Intermediary receives $100,000(1+u_{1,2})$ when one-year loan is repaid |
| Net Cashflow Received by Intermediary | | |
| 0 | 0 | $100,000(u_{1,2}-.1001)$ |

This shows how an intermediary can use zero coupon bonds and lending at the floating rate to create the cashflow needed that exactly matches what the intermediary needs to pay under the FRA. The intermediary can always arrange to lend (invest) at the floating rate $u_{1,2}$ when time 1 arrives, so what the intermediary is really doing is arranging the combination of one-year and two-year zeros that corresponds to a one-year investment at a rate of 10.01% starting at time 1.

Note that the primary borrower is responsible for the principal and the fixed forward interest on the loan. The financial intermediary is responsible only for the interest difference between the floating rate and the fixed forward rate. Rather than creating the synthetic FRA, in practice the intermediary might engage in two separate FRAs that offset each other. In one FRA, the intermediary is paying $100,000(u_{1,2}-.1001)$ to a party that has a one-year forward loan at the floating rate $u_{1,2}$ and wants to exchange it for a one-year forward loan at the fixed rate 10.01%, and in the other FRA, the intermediary is paying $100,000(.1001-u_{1,2})$ to a party who wants to exchange a one-year forward loan at the fixed rate 10.01% for a one year forward loan at the floating rate rate $u_{1,2}$. The intermediary would charge a fee to each party, and would have the payments from the two FRAs exactly offset one another.

### 6.4.3 Interest Rate Swaps

---

**Definition 6.7 – Interest Rate Swaps**

An **interest rate swap** is a contractual agreement between two parties to exchange a series of payments for a stated period of time.

---

Interest rate swaps may be implemented for a number of reasons. An interest rate swap can be used to convert *floating-rate liability* into *fixed-rate liability* or vice-versa. The **floating rate of interest** is a short-term interest rate that changes periodically, depending on the transaction to which it is being applied. The 1-month yield on a US T-Bill is an example of a floating rate of interest. A loan that requires monthly interest at a floating rate will have each month's new interest rate based on market conditions for the new month. A floating rate mortgage usually has monthly interest charges using an updated rate each month, with updated rates related to a market interest rate such as the prime rate or LIBOR rate. A swap can also change the risk characteristics of assets or liabilities that are associated with the swap.

### 6.4.3.1 *A Comparative Advantage Interest Rate Swap*

Consider two borrowers, $A$ and $B$. In the following discussion, the prime rate of interest refers to the short-term interest rate that banks charge their most creditworthy borrowers. Borrower $A$ has a high credit rating, and can borrow in the medium to long-term bond market at a rate of 8%, or in the floating-rate market (short-term or spot market) at prime plus 1%. Borrower $B$ has a medium credit rating and can borrow in the fixed-rate market at 9% or in the floating-rate market at prime plus 1.5%. Borrower $A$ wishes to borrow an amount in the floating-rate market and $B$ wishes to borrow the same amount in the fixed-rate market. It is possible to construct an arrangement between $A$ and $B$ that will allow both of them to borrow at lower rates than those described above. The two borrowers construct the following swap.

$A$ borrows in the fixed-rate market at 8% and loans the funds to $B$ at a rate of 8.5%. $B$ borrows in the floating-rate market at prime plus 1.5% and loans the funds to $A$ at prime plus 1.25%. The net effect for borrower $A$ is that borrower $A$ pays 8% on the fixed-rate loan, receives 8.5% from $B$ and pays prime plus 1.25% to $B$, for a net payment rate of prime plus .75%. The net effect for borrower $B$ is that $B$ pays prime plus 1.5% on the floating-rate loan, $B$ receives prime plus 1.25% from $A$ and $B$ pays 8.5% to $A$, for a net payment rate of 8.75%. $A$'s net payment rate of prime plus .75% is .25% below the floating rate that $A$ would pay directly, and $B$'s net payment rate of 8.75% is .25% below the fixed-rate that $B$ would pay directly.

What allows this arrangement to be made is that the differential between fixed and floating rates for $A$ is not the same as that for $B$, and the two borrowers are able to take advantage of that by taking parallel loans (or back-to-back loans) and swapping them. Borrower $A$ has a comparative advantage in the floating rate market, and borrower $B$ has a comparative advantage in the fixed rate market.

This situation is an arrangement between borrowers $A$ and $B$ without making use of a financial intermediary to make the swap arrangements. In practice, a financial intermediary would make the swap arrangements for them, and would receive as income a percentage of the principal involved. In the example above, the swap administered by the financial intermediary could be structured as follows:

(i) borrower $A$ borrows at fixed rate 8% (not necessarily from the intermediary);

(ii) borrower $B$ borrows at floating rate prime plus 1.5% (also not necessarily from the intermediary);

(iii) the intermediary agrees with $A$ to accept from $A$ floating rate interest payments at prime at the same time as paying $A$ fixed interest at 7.2%;

(iv) the intermediary agrees with $B$ to accept from $B$ fixed interest payments at 7.3% at the same time as paying $B$ floating rate interest payments at prime.

The net effect for borrower $A$ is that $A$ pays prime plus .8%;

The net effect for borrower $B$ is that $B$ pays a fixed rate of 8.8%;

The net effect for the intermediary is the receipt of "spread income" that is equal to .1% of the principal amount. This is income earned by the intermediary as a result of the spread rates between borrowers $A$ and $B$; it is not interest on an amount invested in the usual sense.

More generally, suppose that borrower $A$ can borrow at fixed rate $i_A$ and floating rate $j_A$ = prime rate + $f_A$, and borrower $B$ can borrow at fixed rate $i_B$ and floating rate $j_B$ = prime rate + $f_B$. If $i_B - i_A > f_B - f_A$ then an interest rate swap can be constructed between $A$ and $B$ that allows $A$ to borrow at floating rate prime rate + $r_A$ and allows $B$ to borrow at fixed rate $r_B$, where $r_A < f_A$ and $r_B < i_B$. This is done as follows:

(i) Let $c = (i_B - i_A) - (f_B - f_A)$;

(ii) $A$ borrows at fixed rate $i_A$ and lends the funds to $B$ at fixed rate $i_B - c$;

(iii) $B$ borrows at floating rate prime rate + $f_B$ and lends the funds to $A$ at a floating rate of prime rate + $f_B - \frac{c}{2}$.

The net effect for $A$ is that $A$ pays

$$i_A - (i_B - c) + \text{prime} + f_B - \frac{c}{2} = \text{prime} + i_A - i_B + f_B + \frac{c}{2}$$
$$= \text{prime} + f_A - \frac{c}{2}$$
$$= \text{prime} + r_A < \text{prime} + f_A. \qquad (6.6a)$$

The net effect for $B$ is that $B$ pays

$$\text{prime} + f_B - \left(\text{prime} + f_B - \frac{c}{2}\right) + i_B - c = i_B - \frac{c}{2} = r_B < i_B. \quad (6.6b)$$

If $d < c$, then it is possible for an intermediary to receive a fee at rate $d$ under the following arrangement:

(i) $A$ borrows at fixed rate $i_A$;

(ii) $B$ borrows at floating rate $\text{prime} + f_B$;

(iii) the intermediary agrees with $A$ to accept from $A$ floating rate interest payments at prime at the same time as paying $A$ fixed interest at rate $i_A - \left(f_A - \frac{c}{2} + \frac{d}{2}\right)$;

(iv) the intermediary agrees with $B$ to accept from $B$ fixed interest payments at $i_B - f_B - \frac{c}{2} + \frac{d}{2}$ at the same time as paying $B$ floating rate interest payments at prime.

The net effect for borrower $A$ is that $A$ pays

$$i_A + \text{prime} - \left[i_A - \left(f_A - \frac{c}{2} + \frac{d}{2}\right)\right] = \text{prime} + f_A - \frac{c}{2} + \frac{d}{2};$$

the net effect for borrower $B$ is that $B$ pays

$$\text{prime} + f_B + i_B - f_B - \frac{c}{2} + \frac{d}{2} - \text{prime} = i_B - \frac{c}{2} + \frac{d}{2};$$

the net effect for the intermediary is that the intermediary receives a fee of

$$\text{prime} - \left[i_A - \left(f_A - \frac{c}{2} + \frac{d}{2}\right)\right] + i_B - f_B - \frac{c}{2} + \frac{d}{2} - \text{prime}$$

$$= (i_B - i_A) - (f_B - f_A) - c + d = d.$$

### 6.4.3.2 Swapping a Floating Rate Loan for a Fixed Rate Loan

Another scenario in which an interest rate swap may be arranged is one in which a borrower has a floating rate loan that will take place for a certain period of time, and would like to convert it to a fixed rate loan for that period of time (this will be the **swap term**). One way to deal with this is to arrange a FRA for each particular interest payment.

We have seen in Section 6.4.2 that a FRA can be used to change a borrower's future floating interest rate payment to a fixed interest rate payment. In order that there are no arbitrage opportunities, the FRA will have a fixed rate equal to the forward rate of interest implied by the current term structure. An FRA can also be regarded as an interest rate swap, because the borrower's future interest payment based on a floating rate is being swapped for a future interest payment based on a fixed rate. No money exchanges hands at the time the swap (or FRA) is arranged, but there may be a payment from the borrower to the financial intermediary arranging the swap (or vice-versa) when the future interest period ends (or begins).

---

| EXAMPLE 6.6 | *(Forward rate agreement as an interest rate swap)*

A borrower has a floating rate loan that has payments of interest only at the end of each year for the next three years. Suppose that the current term structure has effective annual zero coupon bond yields for one, two and three years of 8%, 9% and 9.5%, respectively. The borrower arranges an FRA for each year's interest to exchange floating interest payments for fixed interest payments. Find the fixed interest rates that will be arranged under each FRA, assuming that no arbitrage opportunities are created by any of the FRAs.

---

| SOLUTION |

The fixed interest rate for a particular year's FRA will be the forward rate for that year implied by the current term structure. Note that the one-year yield of 8% will be the floating rate for the first year. There is no FRA for the first year, because the first year's interest rate is known. The FRA for the second year's interest payment will have a fixed rate of

$i_0(1,2) = \frac{(1.09)^2}{1.08} - 1 = .1001$ (the one-year forward effective annual interest rate). The FRA for the third year's interest payment will have a fixed rate of $i_0(2,3) = \frac{(1.095)^3}{(1.09)^2} - 1 = .1051$ (the two-year forward effective annual interest rate). The financial intermediary will pay the difference between $u_{1,2}$ (the floating rate for the second year) and 10.01% at the end of the second year. For the third year, the payment will be the difference between $u_{2,3}$ and 10.51%. ☐

Suppose that the notional amount of the loan in Example 6.6 is $10,000,000. The interest payment at the end of the first year will be

$800,000. As a result of the FRAs for the second and third year interest, the borrower will have a net fixed interest payment at the end of the second year of $1,001,000, and $1,051,000 at the end of the third year.

### 6.4.3.3 *The Swap Rate*

A variation on the interest rate swap in Example 6.6 is for the borrower to arrange with the financial intermediary that the borrower's net interest rate is level for each of the three years. Assuming no arbitrage opportunities are created by the arrangement, we can find a fixed level effective annual interest rate $j$ for the three year period that is an appropriate (or equivalent) substitute for the rates found in the separate FRAs. With a notional amount of $10,000,000, we saw the previous paragraph the resulting fixed interest payments for the three years in the previous paragraph. We use the term structure to find the present value at time 0 of those fixed interest payments:

$$PV_0 = \frac{800,000}{1.08} + \frac{1,001,000}{(1.09)^2} + \frac{1,051,000}{(1.095)^2} = 2,383,761.$$

If these interest payments are swapped for level interest payments of $10,000,000j$ at the end of each year for three years, the present value at time 0 of the level payments is

$$PV_0 = 10,000,000j \times \left[ \frac{1}{1.08} + \frac{1}{(1.09)^2} + \frac{1}{(1.095)^2} \right].$$

The appropriate rate $j$ should result in the same present value. Therefore,

$$10,000,000j \times \left[ \frac{1}{1.08} + \frac{1}{(1.09)^2} + \frac{1}{(1.095)^2} \right] = 2,383,761,$$

and solving for $j$ results in $j = 9.42\%$. This 9.42% rate of interest is referred to as the **swap rate**.

The following three sets of cash flows can be swapped for one another:

(i)  floating rate interest payments,

(ii)  varying fixed rate interest payments based on the forward rates of interest implied by the current term structure, and

(iii)  level fixed interest payments based on the swap rate.

We have seen that the swap rate is a level interest rate on an interest only loan that results in level interest payments that have the same present value as interest payments based on the forward rates of interest. Suppose that the current term structure implies the following set of effective annual forward rates of interest for the next $n$ years: $i_0(0,1), i_0(1,2), \ldots, i_0(n-1,n)$. A loan with floating rate interest can be swapped for a loan with fixed interest based on the forward rates, which, in turn, can be swapped for a loan with level interest at the swap rate $j$. The swap rate is found by setting equal the present values at time 0 of the floating rate interest payments and the swap rate interest payments. This can be expressed in the equation

$$
j \times \left[ \frac{1}{1+s_0(1)} + \frac{1}{\left(1+s_0(2)\right)^2} + \cdots + \frac{1}{\left(1+s_0(n)\right)^n} \right]
$$
$$
= \frac{i_0(0,1)}{1+s_0(1)} + \frac{i_0(1,2)}{\left(1+s_0(2)\right)^2} + \cdots + \frac{i_0(n-1,n)}{\left(1+s_0(n)\right)^n}. \quad (6.7)
$$

The swap rate $j$ can be interpreted as a weighted average of the forward rates. This can be seen by reformulating Equation 6.7:

$$
j = w_1 i_0(0,1) + w_2 i_0(1,2) + \cdots + w_n i_0(n-1,n),
$$

where

$$
w_t = \frac{\dfrac{1}{\left(1+s_0(t)\right)^t}}{\dfrac{1}{1+s_0(1)} + \dfrac{1}{\left(1+s_0(2)\right)^2} + \cdots + \dfrac{1}{\left(1+s_0(n)\right)^n}} \quad (6.8)
$$

We can follow the progress of the level payment swap from the point of view of the financial intermediary using this example. The first year interest rate is 8%, so the financial intermediary receives a net amount of $\$942,473.77 - \$800,000 = \$142,473.77$ at the end of the first year (the level interest payment received from the borrower minus the floating interest payment paid to the borrower). This amount is not necessarily a gain made by the intermediary. In fact, if interest rates evolve over time in a way that is consistent with the original term structure at time 0, this amount will disappear over the three year term of the swap.

When the swap was initiated at time 0, the forward rates were $i_0(0,1) = .1001$ and $i_0(2,3) = .1051$. When the first year is done, there will be a term structure as of that time. Suppose that the term structure at the end of the first year has one-year zero yield of $s_1(2) = 10.01\%$ and two-year zero yield at $s_1(3) = 10.26\%$. This implies a one-year forward rate of $i_1(2,3) = \frac{(1.1026)^2}{1.1001} - 1 = .1051$. If a new two year swap was initiated at time 1, it would call for fixed payments of $1,001,000 at time 2 and $1,051,000 at time 3. The original level payment swap has payments of $942,473.77 at time 2 and time 3. The present value at time 1 of the difference between what the intermediary will receive and what a new swap would have the intermediary receive at times 2 and 3 is

$$\frac{942,473.77 - 1,001,000}{1.1001} + \frac{942,473.77 - 1,051,000}{(1.1026)^2} = -142,469.$$

This cancels out the $142,473 balance after the first year swap payment.

This suggests a way in which the value to the intermediary of the swap can be found some time after the swap is made. Using the example above, suppose that the term structure at the end of the first year is $s_1(2) = 9\%$ and $s_1(3) = 10\%$. The forward rates as of time 1 implied by this term structure are $i_1(1,2) = .09$ and $i_1(2,3) = \frac{(1.10)^2}{1.09} - 1 = .1101$.

A two year swap initiated at time 1 would have fixed payments of $900,000 at the end of the second year, and $1,101,000 at the end of the third year. The value of the original swap at time 1 is equal to the $142,473 plus the present value of the difference between the actual swap payments that will be received and the swap payments that are implied by the new term structure:

$$142,473 + \frac{942,473 - 900,000}{1.09} + \frac{942,473 - 1,101,000}{(1.10)^2} = 50,425.$$

If interest rates had risen significantly as of time 1, the swap would have a smaller value, possibly becoming negative.

---

**The Growing Swap Market**

The practice of interest rate swapping began in the late 1970s. It has grown incredibly quickly since that time. An estimate of 1992 activity in interest rate and currency swaps is 5 trillion dollars (US), and an estimate of the same activity in 2005 is over 60 trillion dollars.

---

### 6.4.4 THE FORCE OF INTEREST AS A FORWARD RATE

Now imagine a situation in which we know the zero coupon yield rate for any time to maturity $t$ (including fractional times). If for instance we have zero coupon yields for maturities monthly into the future, then it is possible to find forward rates in effect for one month starting any number of months from now.

Suppose that for any maturity time $t$ in the future, we know the zero coupon bond yield rate as a continuously compounded rate. For a zero coupon bond that matures at time $t$, let us denote by $\alpha_t$ the continuously compounded yield rate, so that the present value of 1 due at time $t$ is $(e^{-\alpha_t})^t = e^{-t \cdot \alpha_t}$. Alternatively, an investment of 1 can be made now to accumulate to $a(t) = e^{t \cdot \alpha_t}$ at time $t$.

In Chapter 1, the force of interest was defined as a nominal annual rate that is compounded continuously. For an investment whose value at time $t$ is $a(t)$ (and is continuously changing), the force of interest at time $t$ was defined to be $\delta_t = \dfrac{a'(t)}{a(t)}$. It was seen in Chapter 1 that the value of the investment at time $t$ can be expressed as $a(t) = e^{\int_0^t \delta_u \, du}$. The force of interest is describing how the investment will be growing (instantaneously) at time $t$ in the future, so it is a continuously compounded version of a $t$-period forward rate of interest.

We can now relate $\alpha_t$, the continuously compounded term structure yield on zero coupon bonds, to $\delta_t$ the force of interest (continuously compounded forward rate) at time $t$. It is possible to formulate the term structure if the force of interest is known, and the reverse is true as well. From the two representations of $a(t)$ we have

$$a(t) = e^{t \cdot \alpha_t} = e^{\int_0^t \delta_u \, du},$$

so that

$$t \cdot \alpha_t = \int_0^t \delta_u \, du$$

and

$$\alpha_t = \frac{1}{t} \cdot \int_0^t \delta_u \, du.$$

We see that the continuously compounded term structure rate for maturity at time $t$ is an average of the force of interest over the period from time 0 to time $t$. This is similar to what occurs with effective annual rates for the relationship between the term structure and forward rates. We saw in Section 6.3 that

$$(1+s_0(n))^n = (1+i_0(0,1))(1+i_0(2,3)) \cdots (1+i_0(n-1,n)),$$

so that

$$1 + s_0(n) = \left[ (1+i_0(0,1))(1+i_0(1,2)) \cdots (1+i_0(n-1,n)) \right]^{1/n};$$

this is the geometric mean of the year-by-year forward growth factors $1+i_0(0,1), 1+i_0(1,2), \ldots, 1+i_0(n-1,n)$ ($s_n$ is the zero coupon yield for an $n$-year maturity, and $i_0(k-1,k)$ is the $k-1$ year forward rate for the one year period from time $k-1$ to time $k$).

If we differentiate both sides of the equation $t \cdot \alpha_t = \int_0^t \delta_u \, du$ with respect to $t$, we get $\alpha_t + t \cdot \frac{d\alpha_t}{dt} = \delta_t$. Note that if the term structure is "flat," i.e. $\alpha_t = \alpha$ (constant) for all $t$, then the force of interest is also constant, $\delta_t = \alpha_t + t \cdot \frac{d\alpha_t}{dt} = \alpha + 0 = \alpha$ for all $t$. Also, if the force of interest is constant at $\delta_t = \delta$ for all $t$, then $\alpha_t = \frac{1}{t} \cdot \int_0^t \delta_u \, du = \delta$ for all $t$.

Suppose that the continuous term structure rate $\alpha_t$ is increasing as $t$ increases (meaning that $\frac{d\alpha_t}{dt} > 0$); then $\delta_t > \alpha_t$, and the reverse inequality is true if the term structure is falling for maturities at time $t$. This is similar to the behaviour that we saw for the effective annual versions of term structure and forward rates in Section 6.3, where forward rates of interest are larger than zero coupon yields if the term structure of zero coupon yields is increasing with time to maturity.

| EXAMPLE 6.7 | *(Continuous Term Structure and Forward Rates)*

Suppose that the yield to maturity for a zero coupon bond maturing at time $t$ is $\alpha_t = .09 - (.08)(.94)^t$, a continuously compounded rate.

(a) Find the related forward rate $\delta_t$.

(b) A borrower plans to borrow 1000 in one year and repay the loan with a single payment at the end of the second year. Determine the amount that will have to be paid back based on the stated term structure.

| SOLUTION |

(a) The forward rate at time $t$ is

$$\delta_t = \alpha_t + t \cdot \frac{d\alpha_t}{dt} = .09 - (.08)(.94)^t - (.08)(.94)^t (\ln .94) \cdot t.$$

(b) The forward loan can be arranged by selling a one-year zero coupon bond with face amount 1000. When the bond is sold, an amount of $1000e^{-\alpha_1} = 1000e^{-[.09 - (.08)(.94)]} = 985.31$ is received. This amount is invested in a two-year zero coupon bond, which will mature at a value of

$$985.31e^{2\alpha_2} = 985.31e^{2[.09 - (.08)(.94)^2]} = 1024.11.$$

We can also solve for the amount outstanding by using the continuously compounded forward rate (which is the force of interest). The amount outstanding at the end of the second year will be

$$1000e^{\int_1^2 \delta_t \, dt} = 1000e^{\int_1^2 [.09 - (.08)(.94)^t - (.08)(.94)^t (\ln .94) \cdot t] dt} = 1024.11. \quad \square$$

### 6.4.5 AT-PAR YIELD

We have seen that if the term structure of zero coupon yield rates is either rising or falling, then two bonds with the same maturity date but different coupon rates will have different yield to maturity values. There is another measure of bond yield that relates to the term structure, and that is the **at-par yield**.

---

**Definition 6.7 – At-Par Yield**

Given a term structure of zero coupon yield rates, the at-par yield rate for a coupon bond maturing at time $t$ is defined to be the rate $r_t$ such that a bond with coupon rate $r_t$ that matures at time $t$ has a yield to maturity that is also $r_t$, so that the bond will be priced at par.

---

For a given term structure it is not difficult to find the at-par yield for any maturity time $t$. Suppose that the term structure spot rates are $\{s_0(t): t = 1, 2, ...\}$ for zero coupon bonds maturing in $1, 2, ...$ years, and suppose that the at-par yield is $r_n$ for an $n$-year coupon bond with annual coupons. Since this is the at-par yield, the coupon rate is also $r_n$ and the bond price is 1 (for a bond with face amount 1) so that

$$(1+s_0(n))^{-n} + r_n \cdot \sum_{k=1}^{n} (1+s_0(k))^{-k} = 1,$$

and then $r_n = \dfrac{1-(1+s_0(n))^{-n}}{\sum_{k=1}^{n}(1+s_0(k))^{-k}}.$

EXAMPLE 6.8   (*Finding the at-par yield*)

Using the term structure from Example 6.2, find the at-par yield for bonds with annual coupons that mature in 1, 2, 3 and 4 years.

SOLUTION

The key point in finding the at-par yield is that the price of the bond should be 100 for a face amount of 100.

1-Year Bond: $100 = 100(1+r_1)\left(\frac{1}{1.05}\right)$. Solving for $r_1$ results in $r_1 = .05$.

2-Year Bond:

$$100 = 100r_2\left(\frac{1}{1.05}\right) + 100(1+r_2)\left(\frac{1}{1.10}\right)^2$$

Solving for $r_2$ results in $r_2 = .0976$.

3-Year Bond:

$$100 = 100r_3\left(\frac{1}{1.05}\right) + 100r_3\left(\frac{1}{1.10}\right)^2 + 100(1+r_3)\left(\frac{1}{1.15}\right)^3$$

Solving for $r_3$ results in $r_3 = .1406$.

4-Year Bond:

$$100 = 100r_4\left(\tfrac{1}{1.05}\right) + 100r_4\left(\tfrac{1}{1.10}\right)^2 + 100r_4\left(\tfrac{1}{1.15}\right)^3 + 100(1+r_4)\left(\tfrac{1}{1.20}\right)^4$$

Solving for $r_4$ results in $r_4 = .1774$. ◻

When a government issues a coupon bond, the coupon rate is usually chosen so that the bond is priced at, or close to par. This will depend on prevailing rates in the financial markets at the time the bond is issued. The at-par yield that prevails at the time a coupon bond is issued is the coupon rate that should be chosen in order for the bond to be priced at par when it is issued.

It is also interesting to note the relationship between the at-par yield and the swap rate on a interest rate swap. From equation (6.7), the swap rate is $j$, from the equation

$$j \times \left[ \frac{1}{1+s_0(1)} + \frac{1}{\left(1+s_0(2)\right)^2} + \cdots + \frac{1}{\left(1+s_0(n)\right)^n} \right]$$

$$= \frac{i_0(0,1)}{1+s_0(1)} + \frac{i_0(1,2)}{\left(1+s_0(2)\right)^2} + \cdots + \frac{i_0(n-1,n)}{\left(1+s_0(n)\right)^n}. \qquad (6.7)$$

The right side of the equation can be written as

$$\frac{1+i_0(0,1)-1}{1+s_0(1)} + \frac{1+i_0(1,2)-1}{\left(1+s_0(2)\right)^2} + \cdots + \frac{1+i_0(n-1,n)-1}{\left(1+s_0(n)\right)^n}$$

$$= 1 - \frac{1}{1+s_0(1)} + \frac{1+i_0(1,2)}{\left(1+s_0(2)\right)^2} - \frac{1}{\left(1+s_0(2)\right)^2}$$

$$+ \cdots + \frac{1+i_0(n-1,n)}{\left(1+s_0(n)\right)^n} - \frac{1}{\left(1+s_0(n)\right)^n}$$

$$= 1 - \frac{1}{1+s_0(1)} + \frac{1}{1+s_0(1)} - \frac{1}{\left(1+s_0(2)\right)^2}$$

$$+ \cdots + \frac{1}{\left(1+s_0(n-1)\right)^{n-1}} - \frac{1}{\left(1+s_0(n)\right)^n}$$

$$= 1 - \frac{1}{\left(1+s_0(n)\right)^n}$$

Then, solving for $j$, results in the at-par yield rate. The swap rate and the at-par yield rate are the same.

There is a close relationship between the yield curve of the term structure of zero coupon bond yield rates, forward rates of interest, yield to maturity of coupon bonds and at-par yield rates. The following example illustrates some of the relationships that exist under the "normal" increasing term structure.

**EXAMPLE 6.9** (*Forward rates and at-par yields*)

Suppose that the term structure of interest rates is increasing with the yield rate for a zero coupon bond maturing at time $t$-years being

$$s_0(t) = .09 - (.08)(.94)^{t-1}.$$

The spot rates are $s_0(1){=}.01, s_0(2){=}.0148, s_0(3){=}.0193,\ldots$, etc. Find the implied forward rates of interest and the at-par yield rates for the $1^{st}$ through the $60^{th}$ year and draw a graph of the three series of rates.

**SOLUTION**

To find the $n$-year forward rate $i_0(n-1,n)$ for the year starting $n$ years from now, we use the relationship $i_0(n,n+1) = \dfrac{(1+s_0(n+1))^{n+1}}{(1+s_0(n))^n} - 1$. To find the $n$-year at-par yield rate $r_n$ for an $n$-year coupon bond with annual coupons, we use the relationship $r_n = \dfrac{1-(1+s_0(n))^{-n}}{\sum_{k=1}^{n}(1+s_0(k))^{-k}}$.

The table of rates is as follows.

TABLE 6.4

| Year | Spot Rate | Forward Rate | At-Par Yield |
|------|-----------|--------------|--------------|
| 1 | 0.0100 | 0.0100 | 0.0100 |
| 2 | 0.0148 | 0.0196 | 0.0148 |
| 3 | 0.0193 | 0.0284 | 0.0192 |
| 4 | 0.0236 | 0.0364 | 0.0233 |
| 5 | 0.0275 | 0.0436 | 0.0271 |
| 6 | 0.0313 | 0.0502 | 0.0306 |
| 7 | 0.0348 | 0.0562 | 0.0338 |
| 8 | 0.0381 | 0.0616 | 0.0367 |
| 9 | 0.0412 | 0.0665 | 0.0394 |
| 10 | 0.0442 | 0.0709 | 0.0418 |
| 11 | 0.0469 | 0.0748 | 0.0440 |
| 12 | 0.0495 | 0.0784 | 0.0460 |
| 13 | 0.0519 | 0.0815 | 0.0479 |
| 14 | 0.0542 | 0.0844 | 0.0495 |
| 15 | 0.0564 | 0.0869 | 0.0510 |
| 16 | 0.0584 | 0.0891 | 0.0524 |
| 17 | 0.0603 | 0.0911 | 0.0536 |
| 18 | 0.0621 | 0.0928 | 0.0547 |
| 19 | 0.0637 | 0.0944 | 0.0557 |
| 20 | 0.0653 | 0.0957 | 0.0565 |
| 21 | 0.0668 | 0.0969 | 0.0573 |
| 22 | 0.0682 | 0.0979 | 0.0581 |
| 23 | 0.0695 | 0.0987 | 0.0587 |
| 24 | 0.0707 | 0.0994 | 0.0593 |
| 25 | 0.0719 | 0.1000 | 0.0598 |
| 26 | 0.0730 | 0.1005 | 0.0603 |
| 27 | 0.0740 | 0.1009 | 0.0607 |
| 28 | 0.0749 | 0.1012 | 0.0611 |
| 29 | 0.0759 | 0.1014 | 0.0614 |
| 30 | 0.0767 | 0.1016 | 0.0617 |
| 31 | 0.0775 | 0.1017 | 0.0620 |
| 32 | 0.0782 | 0.1018 | 0.0622 |
| 33 | 0.0790 | 0.1018 | 0.0625 |
| 34 | 0.0796 | 0.1017 | 0.0627 |
| 35 | 0.0802 | 0.1016 | 0.0628 |
| 36 | 0.0808 | 0.1015 | 0.0630 |
| 34 | 0.0796 | 0.1017 | 0.0627 |

TABLE **6.4** (Continued)

| Year | Spot Rate | Forward Rate | At-Par Yield |
|------|-----------|--------------|--------------|
| 35 | 0.0802 | 0.1016 | 0.0628 |
| 36 | 0.0808 | 0.1015 | 0.0630 |
| 37 | 0.0814 | 0.1014 | 0.0631 |
| 38 | 0.0819 | 0.1012 | 0.0633 |
| 39 | 0.0824 | 0.1010 | 0.0634 |
| 40 | 0.0828 | 0.1008 | 0.0635 |
| 41 | 0.0833 | 0.1006 | 0.0636 |
| 42 | 0.0837 | 0.1004 | 0.0636 |
| 43 | 0.0841 | 0.1001 | 0.0637 |
| 44 | 0.0844 | 0.0999 | 0.0638 |
| 45 | 0.0847 | 0.0996 | 0.0639 |
| 46 | 0.0851 | 0.0993 | 0.0639 |
| 47 | 0.0854 | 0.0991 | 0.0640 |
| 48 | 0.0856 | 0.0988 | 0.0640 |
| 49 | 0.0859 | 0.0985 | 0.0640 |
| 50 | 0.0861 | 0.0983 | 0.0641 |
| 51 | 0.0864 | 0.0980 | 0.0641 |
| 52 | 0.0866 | 0.0977 | 0.0641 |
| 53 | 0.0868 | 0.0975 | 0.0642 |
| 54 | 0.0870 | 0.0972 | 0.0642 |
| 55 | 0.0872 | 0.0970 | 0.0642 |
| 56 | 0.0873 | 0.0967 | 0.0642 |
| 57 | 0.0875 | 0.0965 | 0.0642 |
| 58 | 0.0876 | 0.0962 | 0.0643 |
| 59 | 0.0878 | 0.0960 | 0.0643 |
| 60 | 0.0879 | 0.0958 | 0.0643 |

The graph of this data is in Figure 6.6.

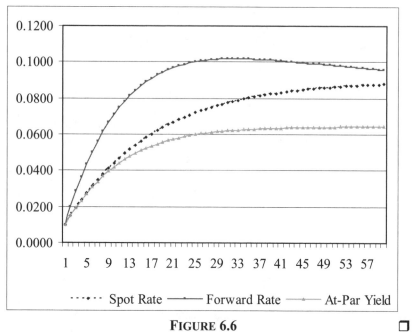

**FIGURE 6.6** ❐

There are a few features in this example that we note. The term structure of spot rates is increasing in this example. When this occurs, the forward rate for the one year period $t-1$ to $t$ is greater than the spot rate for maturity at time $t$, i.e., $i_0(t-1,t) > s_0(t)$. As can also be seen from Example 6.9, the forward rates are not necessarily increasing even though the spot rates are increasing. An increasing term structure of spot rates also results in increasing at-par yield rates as time to maturity increases. If the term structure of spot rates is decreasing, the forward rates are smaller than spot rates and the at-par yield rates are decreasing. These characteristics are considered in the exercises.

The following graph of spot rates, forward rates and at-par yield rates around early 2004 was excerpted from the website of J. Huston McCulloch, Department of Economics of Ohio State University.

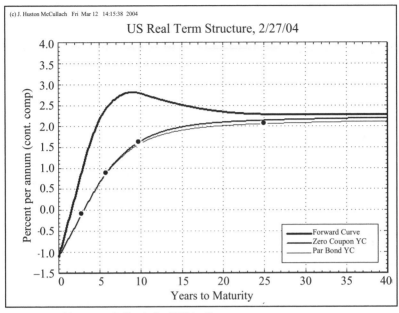

www.econ.ohio-state.edu/jhm/ts/real0204.gif

**FIGURE 6.7**

## 6.5 DEFINITIONS AND FORMULAS

### Definition 6.1 – Zero Coupon Bond

A zero coupon bond is a bond that has no coupons and has a single payment made at the time of maturity. It is also called a **discount bond**.

### Definition 6.2 – Term Structure of Interest Rates

The term structure of interest rates at the current point in time is the set of yield rates on zero coupon bonds of all maturities. This is the set $\{s_0(t)\}_{t>0}$, where $s_0(t)$ is the annual effective yield rate as of time 0 for a zero coupon bond maturing at time $t$. The term structure is also called the **zero coupon bond yield curve**. In the notation, the subscript indicates the current point in time from which interest rates are being measured.

Any set of future cashflows can be valued now using the term structure. Suppose that payments of amounts $C_1, C_2, \ldots, C_n$ are due in $t_1, t_2, \ldots, t_n$ years from now. The total present value of the series of cashflows is

$$C_1(1+s_0(t_1))^{-t_1} + C_2(1+s_0(t_2))^{-t_2} + \cdots + C_n(1+s_0(t_n))^{-t_n}. \qquad (6.1)$$

### Definition 6.3 – Spot Rate of Interest

The yield to maturity on a zero coupon bond is called the spot rate of interest for that time to maturity. $s_0(t)$ is the spot rate for a $t$-year maturity zero coupon bond. The price at time 0 of a $t$-year zero coupon bond is $\dfrac{1}{(1+s_0(t))^t}$ for a maturity value of 1.

### Definition 6.4 – Forward Rate of Interest

Given the term structure of zero coupon bond yield rates, $\{s_0(t)\}_{t>0}$, the time 0, $n$-$1$-year forward, one year interest rate for the year from time $n$-$1$ to time $n$ is denoted by the symbol $i_0(n-1,n)$, and satisfies the relationship

$$1+i_0(n-1,n) = \frac{(1+s_0(n))^n}{(1+s_0(n-1))^{n-1}}. \qquad (6.3)$$

The forward rate for the period from time 0 to time 1 is $i_0(0,1) = s_0(1)$ (not really a forward rate, since "forward rate" refers to a rate on a transaction that starts in the future, not now).

### Definition 6.5 – Arbitrage

An arbitrage is a simultaneous purchase and sale of securities in different markets in order to profit from price discrepancies.

### Definition 6.6 – Forward Rate Agreeement (FRA)

A forward rate agreement is a contract that guarantees a borrowing or lending rate for a specific amount of principal (sometimes called the **notional amount**) for a specified time period that begins at a future date.

## Definition 6.7 – Interest Rate Swaps

The practice of interest rate swapping began in the late 1970s. It has grown incredibly quickly since that time. An estimate of 1992 activity in interest rate and currency swaps is 5 trillion dollars (US), and an estimate of the same activity in 2005 is over 60 trillion dollars.

The swap rate $j$ is found from the following equation:

$$j \times \left[ \frac{1}{1+s_0(1)} + \frac{1}{\left(1+s_0(2)\right)^2} + \cdots + \frac{1}{\left(1+s_0(n)\right)^n} \right]$$
$$= \frac{i_0(0,1)}{1+s_0(1)} + \frac{i_0(1,2)}{\left(1+s_0(2)\right)^2} + \cdots + \frac{i_0(n-1,n)}{\left(1+s_0(n)\right)^n}. \tag{6.7}$$

## Definition 6.8 – At-Par Yield

Given a term structure of zero coupon yield rates, the at-par yield rate for a coupon bond maturing at time $t$ is defined to be the rate $r_t$ such that a bond with coupon rate $r_t$ that matures at time $t$ has a yield to maturity that is also $r_t$, so that the bond will be priced at par.

## 6.6 NOTES AND REFERENCES

There are a number of theories that attempt to explain the nature of the term structure and its relationship to economic conditions. A review of several of these theories can be found in *The Handbook of Fixed Income Securities* and in *Modern Portfolio Theory and Investment Analysis* by E. Elton and M. Gruber. The Elton and Gruber book also provides an extensive bibliography for stochastic models of the term structure, a topic which is beyond the scope of this book.

A good introduction to interest rate and currency swaps can be found in *Interest Rate and Currency Swaps* by R. Dattatreya, S. Venkatesh and V. Venkatesh.

## 6.7 EXERCISES

### SECTIONS 6.1 AND 6.2

6.1.1 You are given the following term structure:

$$s_0(1) = .15, \qquad s_0(2) = .10, \qquad s_0(3) = .05.$$

These are *effective annual rates of interest* for zero coupon bonds of 1, 2 and 3 years maturity, respectively. A newly issued 3-year bond with face amount 100 has annual coupon rate 10%, with coupons paid *once per year* starting one year from now.

Find the price and effective annual yield to maturity of the bond.

6.1.2 The term structure of effective annual yield rates for zero coupon bonds is given as follows: 1- and 2-year maturity, 10%; 3 and 4-year maturity, 12%. Find the price of a 4-year bond with face amount 100, and annual coupons at rate 5%. The first coupon will be paid in one year.

6.1.3 A 10% bond with face amount 100 matures in 3 years.

(a) Find the value of the bond based on each of the following term structures for zero coupon bond spot rates, where $s_0(t)$ denotes the nominal annual spot rate convertible semiannually for a $t$-year term zero coupon bond.

(i) $s_0(.5) = .075$  $s_0(1) = .0775$  $s_0(1.5) = .08$  $s_0(2) = .08$
$s_0(2.5) = .0825$  $s_0(3) = .085$

(ii) $s_0(.5) = .14$  $s_0(1) = .1375$  $s_0(1.5) = .135$  $s_0(2) = .1325$
$s_0(2.5) = .13$  $s_0(3) = .1275$

(iii) $s_0(.5) = .12$  $s_0(1) = .12$  $s_0(1.5) = .12$  $s_0(2) = .12$
$s_0(2.5) = .12$  $s_0(3) = .12$

(b) For each of the bond prices found in (a), find the corresponding yield to maturity.

(c) Repeat part (a) for an 8% bond and for a 12% bond.

6.1.4　(a) You are given the following information about two 10-year bonds. Both bonds have face amount 100 and coupons payable semi-annually, with next coupon due in $\frac{1}{2}$-year.

Bond 1:　Coupon rate 4% per year, price 85.12
Bond 2:　Coupon rate 10% per year, price 133.34.

Find the yield rate for a 10-year zero coupon bond.

(b) You are given the following term structure (effective annual interest rates) for zero coupon bond maturities up to $n$ years: $s_0(1)=s_0(2)=\cdots=s_0(n-1)<s_0(n)$ (flat term structure except for $n$-year maturity). An $n$-year bond has annual coupon rate $r > 0$ and annual coupons. Show that the yield to maturity for the bond $j$ must satisfy $s_0(n-1) < j < s_0(n)$.

6.1.5　You are given the following information for 4 bonds. All coupon and yield-to-maturity rates are nominal annual convertible twice per year.

| Bond | Time to Maturity | Coupon Rate | YTM |
|------|------------------|-------------|-----|
| 1 | $\frac{1}{2}$-year | 4% | .05 |
| 2 | 1-year | 6% | .10 |
| 3 | $1\frac{1}{2}$-year | 4% | .15 |
| 4 | 2-year | 8% | .15 |

Find the associated term structure for zero coupon bonds with maturities of $\frac{1}{2}$-year, 1 year, $1\frac{1}{2}$-year, and 2 year (quotations should be nominal annual rates convertible twice per year).

*6.1.6　Assume that the pricing of a coupon bond is consistent with its pricing based on separate coupons and redemption using the term structure of spot rates as in Exercise 6.1.1. Let $H(r,t)$ denote the current term structure for the yield to maturity of a coupon bond with coupon rate $r$ and time $t$ to maturity. Then $s_0(t) = H(0,t)$ is the current term structure for zero coupons bonds. Let $r_1 \geq r_2$.

(a) Suppose $H(0,t)$ is a decreasing function of $t$ for all $t$. Show that $H(r,t)$ is also a decreasing function of $t$, and

$$H(r_1,t) \geq H(r_2,t) \geq H(0,t)$$

for any $t$.

(b) Suppose $H(0,t)$ is an increasing function of $t$ for all $t$. Show that $H(r,t)$ is also an increasing function of $t$, and

$$H(r_1,t) \le H(r_2,t) \le H(0,t)$$

for any $t$.

(c) Suppose $H(0,t)$ is constant for all $t$. Show that $H(r,t)$ is also constant and $H(r,t) = H(0,t)$ for any $t$.

## SECTION 6.3

6.3.1 (a) Find an expression for $i_0(k-1,k)$ in terms of the $s_0(t)$'s.

(b) Show that

$$(1+i_0(0,1))(1+i_0(1,2))\cdots(1+i_0(k-1,k)) = (1+s_0(k))^k$$

for $k = 1,2,\ldots,n$.

(c) Show that $\frac{d}{ds_0(k)}i_0(k-1,k) > 0$ and $\frac{d}{ds_0(k-1)}i_0(k-1,k) < 0$.

(d) Show that if $s_0(k) > s_0(k-1)$, then $i_0(k-1,k) > s_0(k)$.

6.3.2 (a) Consider the following two yield curves (representing perhaps annual yields on two different classes of zero coupon bonds), based on the notation of Exercise 6.3.1:

(i) $s_0(k) = .09 + .001k$;
(ii) $s_0(k) = .09 + .002k - .0001k^2$, both for $k = 1,2,\ldots,10$.

For each of these yield curves, calculate the corresponding forward rates of interest for years 2 to 10, and plot the forward rates on a graph along with a plot of the yield curve.

(b) Given that both yield curves are increasing, use part (d) of Exercise 6.3.1 to create the graph of the forward rates and corresponding yield curve. Note the relationship between the curves.

6.3.3 A 6-month T-Bill of face amount 100 can be bought today for 97.800, and a 1-year T-Bill of face amount 100 can be bought today for 95.400. Find the forward rate of interest for the 6-month period beginning 6 months from today, quoted as a nominal annual rate of interest compounded semi-annually.

6.3.4   According to the current term structure of interest rates, the effective annual interest rates for 1, 2 and 3 year maturity zero coupon bonds are

1-year .08,    2-year .10,    3-year .11.

Find the one-year forward effective annual rate of interest and find the two-year forward effective annual rate of interest.

6.3.5   The following term structure is given as effective annual rates of interest on zero coupon bonds:

1-year maturity: 6%    2-year maturity: 7%    3-year maturity: 9%

(a) Find (i) the 1-year forward effective annual interest rate for a 1-year period, $i_0(1,2)$ and (ii) the 2-year forward effective annual interest rate for a 1-year period, $i_0(2,3)$.

(b) The effective annual rate of interest for a 4-year zero coupon bond is $s_4$. Find the minimum value of $s_4$ needed so that $i_0(3,4) \geq i_0(2,3)$, where $i_0(3,4)$ is the 3-year forward effective annual interest rate for a 1-year period and $i_0(2,3)$ is found in part (a).

6.3.6   The term structure of effective annual yield rates for zero coupon bonds is given as follows:

1- and 2-year maturity, 10%;<br>3- and 4-year maturity, 12%.

You are given the price of a 5-year bond with face amount 100, and annual coupons at rate 5% is 73.68. Find the 4-year forward effective annual interest rate (in effect for the $5^{th}$ year).

*6.3.7 (a) Prove each of the following relationships between $s_0(t)$ and $i_0(t-1,t)$.

(i)  If $s_0(t)$ is increasing, then $s_0(t) \leq i_0(t-1,t)$.

(ii)  If $s_0(t)$ is decreasing, then $s_0(t) \geq i_0(t-1,t)$.

(b) (i) Construct an increasing yield curve $s_0(t)$ for which $i_0(t-1,t)$. is decreasing for $t \geq 2$.

(ii) Construct a decreasing yield curve $s_0(t)$ for which $i_0(t-1,t)$. is increasing for $t \geq 2$.

*6.3.8 Suppose that $r_t$ denotes the continuously compounded yield rate on a zero coupon bond maturing at time $t$ (the term-structure). Suppose that $\delta_t$ is the continuously compounded $t$-year forward rate (force of interest at time $t$). Prove the following:

(i) If $\lim_{t \to \infty} r_t = r$ (where $0 \le r \le \infty$), then $\lim_{t \to \infty} \delta_t = r$; and

(ii) if $\lim_{t \to \infty} \delta_t = r$ (where $0 \le r < \infty$), then $\lim_{t \to \infty} r_t = r$.

## SECTION 6.4

6.4.1 Yield rates for zero coupon bonds are as follows:

> 1 year maturity, 10% (effective annual);
> 2 year maturity, 8% (effective annual).

You take the following actions:

(i) Sell a one-year zero coupon bond with maturity value 1000.

(ii) Invest the proceeds in a two-year zero coupon bond.

Which of the following represents your overall net position?

(a) One year forward investment for one year at 6%

(b) One year forward investment for one year at 12%

(c) One year forward loan for one year at 6%

(d) One year forward loan for one year at 12%

(e) Two year loan for 9%

6.4.2 Suppose that yield rates on zero coupon bonds are currently 6% for a one-year maturity and 7% for a two-year maturity (effective annual rates).

Suppose that someone is willing to lend money to you starting one year from now to be repaid two years from now at an effective annual interest rate of 7%. Construct a transaction in which an arbitrage gain can be obtained (positive net gain for net investment of 0).

6.4.3 Yield rates for zero coupon bonds are as follows:
1 year maturity, 8% (effective annual);
2 year maturity, 10% (effective annual).

You take the following actions.

(i) Sell a two-year zero coupon bond with maturity value 1000.
(ii) Invest the proceeds in a one-year zero coupon bond.

Which of the following represents your overall net position?

(a) One year forward investment for one year at 10%

(b) One year forward investment for one year at 12%

(c) One year forward loan for one year at 10%

(d) One year forward loan for one year at 12%

(e) Two year investment for 9%

6.4.4 The current term structure has the following nominal annual spot rates, $i^{(2)}$:

6-month spot rate is 8%;
1-year spot rate is 10%;
1½-year spot rate is $x\%$.

(a) Based on this term structure, a 1½-year bond with (nominal annual) coupon rate 10% has a YTM of 11%. Find $x$.

(b) Suppose that the forward rate (quoted as a nominal annual rate of interest) for the period from 1 to 1½ years is 11%. Find $x$ in that case.

(c) You predict that 6 months from now, the 6-month spot rate will be 10%. Construct a strategy to implement now, involving sale and purchase of zero coupon bonds that will make a profit for you if your prediction is correct.

6.4.5　The effective annual yield on a one-year zero coupon bond is 8% and the effective annual interest rate on a two-year zero coupon bond is 8.5%. You are able to arrange a one-year forward loan at rate $i$ for a one-year period. Suppose that under these conditions it is possible to make a riskless profit with the following strategy:

(i)　borrow amount 1 for one year at 8% effective annual,

(ii)　invest amount 1 for 2 years at 8.5% per year effective annual,

(iii)　arrange a one-year forward one-year length loan of amount 1.08 at rate $i$ (starting one year from now) and repay the loan in (i),

(iv)　use the proceeds from (ii) to repay loan (iii) at the end of the second year.

For what full range of $i$ will this strategy result in a positive amount left over after all 3 transactions are settled at the end of the second year?

6.4.6　For the term structure for Example 6.2, find the level fixed swap rate for a 4-year interest rate swap of floating rate interest for fixed rate interest.

*6.4.7　Using this book's terminology for forward rates of interest, spot rates and at-par yield rates, verify the following implications:

(a)　$s_0(t)$ is an increasing function of $t$ for all $t \Leftrightarrow i_0(t-1,t) > s_0(t)$ for all $t$.

(b)　$s_0(t)$ is a decreasing function of $t$ for all $t \Leftrightarrow i_0(t-1,t) < s_0(t)$ for all $t$.

(c)　$i_0(t-1,t)$ is an increasing function of $t$ for all $t$
$\Rightarrow s_0(t)$ is an increasing function of $t$ for all $t$
$\Rightarrow r_t$ is an increasing function of $t$ for all $t$.

(d)　$i_0(t-1,t)$ is a decreasing function of $t$ for all $t$
$\Rightarrow s_0(t)$ is a decreasing function of $t$ for all $t$
$\Rightarrow r_t$ is a decreasing function of $t$ for all $t$.

# CHAPTER 7

## CASHFLOW DURATION AND IMMUNIZATION

*"I have enough money to last me the rest of my life, unless I buy something.*
*Jackie Mason – American Comedian (1934 - )*

An investor who holds a fixed-income investment such as a bond will see the value of the bond change over time for a number of reasons. It was seen in the discussion of bond amortization in Chapter 4 that there is a natural progression of the amortized value of a bond toward the maturity value as the bond approaches its maturity date. Over the lifetime of the bond, the market value of the bond will also converge to the maturity amount as well. These longer term changes in bond values are somewhat predictable, although the market value will fluctuate to a large extent as a result of changing market conditions, such as changing interest rates and the perception of the chance of the bond defaulting on some of its scheduled payments.

The market value of a bond at a particular time is directly related to the yield to maturity that prevails in the bond market at that time. Changes in market yield rates can have a sudden and significant impact on the market value of a bond. There is no guarantee that when an investor buys a bond, the yield rate at which the bond was bought will continue to be the bond's yield rate for the entire term of the bond. In fact, the yield rate will almost surely not stay constant as time goes on. The next example illustrates one of the reasons why yield rates on a particular bond might change over time.

**EXAMPLE 7.1** (*Yield curve slide*)

Suppose that the current term structure of interest rates has the following schedule of spot rates for maturities of 1, 2, 3 and 4 years:

| Maturity | 1-year | 2-year | 3-year | 4-year |
|----------|--------|--------|--------|--------|
| Spot Rate | $s_0(1) = .05$ | $s_0(2) = .10$ | $s_0(3) = .15$ | $s_0(4) = .20$ |

Suppose a 4-year zero coupon bond with maturity amount 100 is purchased and that as time goes on, the term structure does not change, so that at any time the spot rates are the same as they are now for any time to maturity. This means that at time 1, $s_1(1) = .05$ (yield on a one year zero coupon bond issued at time 1 is 5%), $s_1(2) = .10$, etc. Find the book value and market value of the bond in one, two and three years.

| SOLUTION |

The purchase price is $100(1.2)^{-4} = 48.23$. In one year the amortized (book) value will be $100(1.2)^{-3} = 57.87$. At that time the bond will be three years from maturity, so the market yield will be 15% (we are assuming that the term structure doesn't change, so three-year zero coupon bonds will always have a yield rate of 15%). In one year the market value of the bond will be $100(1.15)^{-3} = 65.75$. Note that after one year the holder of the bond will have had a one-year *holding period return* of $\frac{65.87}{48.23} - 1 = .3657 (36.57\%)$. At the end of the second year the book value will be $100(1.2)^{-2} = 69.44$ and the market value will be $100(1.1)^{-2} = 82.64$. At the end of the third year the book value will be $100(1.2)^{-1} = 83.33$ and the market value will be $100(1.05)^{-1} = 95.24$. At the end of the fourth year the bond matures and its value (book and market) is 100. These book and market values are summarized in the following table.

| Time | Book Value | Market Value |
|------|------------|--------------|
| 0 | 48.23 | 48.23 |
| 1 | 57.87 | 65.75 |
| 2 | 69.44 | 82.64 |
| 3 | 83.33 | 95.24 |
| 4 | 100.00 | 100.00 |

The phrase "yield curve slide" in the title of this example refers to the move away from book value that the market value takes as time goes on. This occurs not because there is any change in the term structure, but because the term structure does not evolve in a way that is consistent with the original forward rate structure. For instance, at time 0, the one-year forward effective annual rate of interest is $i_0(1,2) = 15.24\%$, but when time 1 arrives, the actual one year zero coupon bond yield is 5%.

Rates of return demanded by investors may also change, which also affects the market value of the bond. If the market yield rate for the bond is higher than the bondholder's original (book) yield, then the present value of the payments represented by the bond will be less at the higher market yield rate than at the original yield rate (with the reverse occurring if the market yield is below the book yield). There is no requirement that the bondholder must sell the bond before maturity, and if the bondholder keeps the bond until maturity he will realize the original book yield-to-maturity as the internal rate of return on his investment no matter what changes in interest rates occur during the term of the bond. If the bondholder sells the bond before maturity at a price other than the book value, the bondholder's return for the period that the bond was held will most likely not be the original book yield, but will be related to the market yield at the time of sale.

Suppose that in Example 7.1 above, the investor purchases the 4-year zero coupon bond at the yield rate of 20% per year for a price of 48.23. Suppose that later that same day some significant event occurs that changes the economic and financial outlook of investors and the 4-year spot rate suddenly changes to 22%. The value of the 4-year zero coupon bond becomes $100(1.22)^{-4} = 45.14$, an almost immediate loss of 3.09. The numerical values used in this illustration are not likely to occur in the world's major financial markets, and they exaggerate the possible consequences of short term changes in interest rates. The following section presents a systematic analysis of the sensitivity of a bond's price to changes in the yield rate.

## 7.1 DURATION OF A SET OF CASHFLOWS AND BOND DURATION

The market value of any fixed series of payments is sensitive to changes in the yield rate or term structure that is used to value the payments. The conventional measure of the risk, volatility, or sensitivity of the payments to changes in the yield rate is based on the derivative (instantaneous rate of change) of the bond's present value with respect to changes in the yield rate.

## 7.1.1 DURATION OF A ZERO COUPON BOND

We will first consider the sensitivity of the value of a zero coupon bond to changes in the yield rate. Suppose that such a bond matures for amount 1 in $n$ years and is currently priced at an effective annual yield rate $i$ for $n$-year maturities. The current price of the bond is $P = (1+i)^{-n}$. If we regard the price as a function of the yield rate $i$, and we differentiate with respect to $i$, we get $\frac{d}{di} P = -n(1+i)^{-n-1}$. The derivative is negative because increasing the yield rate results in a decreasing present value ($P$ is a decreasing function of $i$).

In considering the sensitivity of the bond's price to changes in the yield rate we are mainly concerned with the magnitude of the relative rate of change in price per dollar invested. This is called the **modified duration** of the bond. The modified duration for the $n$-year zero coupon bond is

$$DM = -\frac{\frac{d}{di} P}{P} = \frac{n(1+i)^{-n-1}}{(1+i)^{-n}} = n(1+i)^{-1} = nv. \qquad (7.1)$$

We multiply $\frac{d}{di} P$ by $-1$ to clear the negative sign on the derivative, and we divide by $P$ (the amount invested) to get a quantity per dollar invested.

A related measure is $D$, the **Macaulay duration** of the bond (often just called the duration of the bond). This measure was introduced by Economics Professor Frederick R. Macaulay in 1938 in a study that he produced for the National Bureau of Economic Research.

The Macaulay duration is the modified duration multiplied by $1+i$, so that $D = DM \cdot (1+i)$. For the $n$-year zero coupon bond, the Macaulay duration is $D = DM \cdot (1+i) = nv(1+i) = n$. Duration is measured in units of years. We would say that the $n$-year zero coupon bond has a (Macaulay) duration of $n$ years. The use of the word "duration" for this measure of sensitivity is based on the fact that for a zero coupon bond, this measure of sensitivity to changes in interest rate is equal (numerically) to the "duration" until maturity.

Since it is the derivative of price per dollar invested with respect to change in yield rate, the modified duration is a more direct measure than the

Macaulay duration of the relative change in price that will occur when there is a change in the yield rate. The derivative $\frac{d}{di}P$ is the limit as $h \to 0$ of $\frac{P(i+h)-P(i)}{h}$, where $h$ represents a small yield rate change. As an approximation, for small changes in the yield rate, the change in the value of the bond is

$$P(i+h) - P(i) \doteq h \cdot \frac{d}{di}P(i) = -h \cdot P(i) \cdot DM. \qquad (7.2)$$

The differential approximation is not presented from the point of view of being an appropriate way to approximate the bond price after the change in interest rate. It is easy to calculate the exact new value of the bond at the new yield rate without relying on approximation. The main point of Example 7.2 is to illustrate numerically how the sensitivity of the bond price to changes in yield relates to the time to maturity of the bond.

**EXAMPLE 7.2** *(Duration of a zero coupon bond)*

Suppose that the effective annual yield rate is 10% for all maturities of zero coupon bonds. Find the modified duration and Macaulay duration for a 1-year, 10-year and 30-year zero coupon bond. For a bond maturity amount of 100, find the actual and the approximate change in price expected using the differential approximation for each bond when there is a 1 basis point decrease in the yield rate (a basis point is .01%).

**SOLUTION**

Using the expressions developed for modified duration and Macaulay duration, we have the following table. As a decimal, a 1 basis point increase or decrease in yield rate is a change of .0001.

| Term to Maturity | 1-Year | 10-Year | 30-Year |
|---|---|---|---|
| Bond Price $P(i)$ | 90.909091 | 38.55433 | 5.7309 |
| Modified Duration | 0.909091 | 9.090910 | 27.2727 |
| Macaulay Duration | 1.000000 | 10.000000 | 30.0000 |
| Approximate Change in Price Using $DM$ | 0.008264 | 0.035049 | 0.015630 |
| Approximate Relative Change in Price | 0.000091 | 0.000909 | 0.002727 |
| Actual Price at Yield Rate 9.99% | 90.917356 | 38.589400 | 5.746507 |
| Actual Change in Price | 0.008265 | 0.035067 | 0.015652 |
| Actual Relative Change in Price | 0.000091 | 0.000910 | 0.002731 |

□

It could have been anticipated that the $n$-year present value factor $(1+i)^{-n}$ is more sensitive to changes in $i$ when $n$ is large than when $n$ is small, although we see that the dollar change in value for the 10-year bond is greater than that for the 30-year bond. When we say that the longer term bond is more sensitive to changes in the yield rate, we mean that the relative change in value of the longer term bond is greater for the 30-year bond than for the 10-year bond. The modified duration provides a good approximation to these relative price changes. The relative change in price of the 30-year bond is about 3 times that of the 10-year bond, which, in turn, is about 10 times that of the 1-year bond.   ❏

### 7.1.2 DURATION OF A GENERAL SERIES OF CASHFLOWS

The duration measures presented above can be extended to measure the sensitivity of the present value of any series of cashflows to changes in the yield rate used to value the series. We will now suppose that a series of payments is being valued at a yield rate that is the same for each payment no matter when it occurs (a flat term structure with $s_0(t) = i$ for all $t$). This, for instance, is how a coupon bond is valued using the yield to maturity $i$.

Suppose that we consider a series of $n$ annual payments starting one year from now at an effective annual valuation rate of $i$ (the yield to maturity for valuing the series of payments). Suppose that the series of payments is $K_1, K_2, \ldots, K_n$. The present value of the series is

$$
\begin{aligned}
P &= K_1(1+i)^{-1} + K_2(1+i)^{-2} + \cdots + K_t(1+i)^{-t} + \cdots + K_n(1+i)^{-n} \\
&= \sum_{t=1}^{n} K_t(1+i)^{-t}.
\end{aligned}
$$

We can formulate a measure of the sensitivity of $P$ to changes in $i$ as the derivative of $P$ with respect to $i$. This is

$$
\begin{aligned}
\frac{d}{di}P &= -K_1(1+i)^{-2} - 2K_2(1+i)^{-3} - \cdots - tK_t(1+i)^{-t-1} - \cdots - nK_n(1+i)^{-n-1} \\
&= -\sum_{t=1}^{n} tK_t(1+i)^{-t-1}.
\end{aligned}
$$

**Definition 7.1 – Modified Duration**

The modified duration, denoted $DM$ (sometimes referred to as "volatility") of the set of cashflows $K_1, K_2, \ldots$ is

$$DM = -\frac{\frac{d}{di}P}{P} = \frac{\sum_{t=1}^{n} tK_t(1+i)^{-t-1}}{P} = \frac{\sum_{t=1}^{n} tK_t(1+i)^{-t-1}}{\sum_{t=1}^{n} K_t(1+i)^{-t}}. \qquad (7.3)$$

**Definition 7.2 – Macaulay Duration**

The Macaulay duration, denoted $D$, is usually referred to simply as "duration."

$$D = (1+i) \cdot DM = \frac{\sum_{t=1}^{n} tK_t(1+i)^{-t}}{P} = \frac{\sum_{t=1}^{n} tK_t(1+i)^{-t}}{\sum_{t=1}^{n} K_t(1+i)^{-t}}. \qquad (7.4)$$

Suppose that in Equation 7.4 we define the factor $w_t$ as $w_t = \frac{K_t(1+i)^{-t}}{P}$.

The Macaulay duration can then be written in the form $D = \sum_{t=1}^{n} w_t \cdot t$. Note

that since $P = \sum_{t=1}^{n} K_t(1+i)^{-t}$, it follows that $\sum_{t=1}^{n} w_t = 1$. The $w_t$ factors can be thought of as weights.

In this interpretation, the Macaulay duration is a weighted average of the times at which the $n$ payments are made. The weight applied to the payment at time $t$ is $w_t = \frac{K_t(1+i)^{-t}}{P}$, which is the fraction of the overall present value of the series that is represented by that particular payment at time $t$. For an $n$-year zero coupon bond, there is only one payment, and it occurs at time $n$, so the weight for that payment is 1 since it accounts for the entire present value, and hence the Macaulay duration is $1 \times n = n$. In general, duration is measured in units of years. The duration of an $n$-year zero coupon bond would be $n$ years.

### 7.1.3 Duration of a Coupon Bond

A coupon bond has relatively small coupon payments and then a large payment on the maturity date. Therefore, the weights applied to the coupons would be relatively small and the weight applied to the redemption payment would be relatively large. We would expect the Macaulay duration of a coupon bond to be close to $n$. As the coupons get larger (relative to the redemption amount) the duration should get smaller. This is illustrated in the following example.

**EXAMPLE 7.3** (*Duration of a coupon bond*)

A bond with annual coupons has face amount $F$, coupon rate $r$ per year, $n$ annual coupons until maturity, and is valued at yield rate $j$ per year. Calculate the duration of the bond for all possible combinations of parameters $r = .05, .10, .15$; $n = 2, 10, 30, 60$; and $j = .05, .10, .15$.

**SOLUTION**

The bond payments at times $1, 2, \ldots, n$ are $K_t = Fr$ for $t = 1, 2, \ldots, n-1$ and $K_n = F + Fr$. Thus, the duration is

$$D = \frac{\sum_{t=1}^{n} t \cdot Fr \cdot v_j^t + n \cdot F \cdot v_j^n}{\sum_{t=1}^{n} Fr \cdot v_j^t + F \cdot v_j^n}. \tag{7.5}$$

Note that in the numerator of $D$ in Equation 7.5, the first term is the increasing annuity-immediate $Fr(Ia)_{\overline{n}|j}$.

At a yield rate of 5% per year, the duration values are as shown in Table 7.1a.

**TABLE 7.1a**

| Coupon Rate | Coupons Until Maturity | | | |
|:---:|:---:|:---:|:---:|:---:|
| | 2 | 10 | 30 | 60 |
| .05 | 1.952 | 8.108 | 16.141 | 19.876 |
| .10 | 1.913 | 7.270 | 14.328 | 18.772 |
| .15 | 1.880 | 6.797 | 13.613 | 18.391 |

At a yield rate of 10% per year, the durations are given in Table 7.1b.

**TABLE 7.1b**

| Coupon Rate | Coupons Until Maturity | | | |
|---|---|---|---|---|
| | **2** | **10** | **30** | **60** |
| .05 | 1.950 | 7.661 | 11.434 | 11.124 |
| .10 | 1.909 | 6.759 | 10.370 | 10.964 |
| .15 | 1.875 | 6.281 | 9.987 | 10.910 |

At a yield rate of 15% per year, the durations are given in Table 7.1c.

**TABLE 7.1c**

| Coupon Rate | Coupons Until Maturity | | | |
|---|---|---|---|---|
| | **2** | **10** | **30** | **60** |
| .05 | 1.948 | 7.170 | 8.209 | 7.689 |
| .10 | 1.905 | 6.237 | 7.719 | 7.671 |
| .15 | 1.870 | 5.772 | 7.551 | 7.665 |

❏

For an $n$-year bond with annual coupons at rate $r$ per year and valued at an effective annual yield rate of $i$ per year, the Macaulay duration of the bond can be shown to be $D = \dfrac{1+i}{i} - \dfrac{1+i+n(r-i)}{r[(1+i)^n - 1] + i}$. (See Exercise 7.1.4.)

### 7.1.4 DURATION OF A PORTFOLIO OF SERIES OF CASHFLOWS

Suppose that $m$ separate series of annual cashflows are under consideration. Suppose that each set is an $n$-year series, with the payments for cashflow series $k$ denoted $c_1^{(k)}, c_2^{(k)}, \ldots, c_n^{(k)}$. At effective annual interest rate $i$ the present value of cashflow series $k$ is

$$X_k = c_1^{(k)}(1+i)^{-1} + c_2^{(k)}(1+i)^{-2} + \cdots + c_n^{(k)}(1+i)^{-n},$$

for $k = 1, 2, \ldots, m$. The Macaulay duration of the $k^{th}$ cashflow series is

$$D_k = -(1+i)\frac{\frac{d}{di}X_k}{X_k}, \text{ so that } D_k \cdot X_k = -(1+i)\frac{d}{di}X_k.$$

The aggregate present value of the collection of all series of cashflows is
$X = \sum_{k=1}^{m} X_k$, and $\frac{d}{di} X = \frac{d}{di} \sum_{k=1}^{m} X_k$. The Macaulay duration of the combination of all the series of cashflows is

$$D = -(1+i)\frac{\frac{d}{di} X}{X} = \frac{\sum_{k=1}^{m} -(1+i)\frac{d}{di} X_k}{X} = \frac{\sum_{k=1}^{m} D_k \cdot X_k}{X}. \qquad (7.6)$$

If we define the factor $v_k$ to be $v_k = \frac{X_k}{X}$, then $D = \sum_{k=1}^{m} v_k \cdot D_k$, and $\sum_{k=1}^{m} v_k = 1$. We see that the Macaulay duration of the overall portfolio of series of cashflows can be represented as a weighted average of the durations of the individual series of cashflows, where the weight applied to duration $D_k$ is $v_k = \frac{X_k}{X}$, which is the fraction of the present value of the overall portfolio represented by cashflow series $k$.

---

**EXAMPLE 7.4** (*Duration of portfolio of bonds*)

A portfolio consists of four bonds, each of which has annual coupons:

(i)   2-year bond with face amount $100,000, and 5% coupon rate,
(ii)  10-year bond with face amount $80,000, and 10% coupon rate,
(iii) 30-year bond with face amount $120,000, and 5% coupon rate, and
(iv)  60-year bond with face amount $75,000, and 15% coupon rate.

Find the Macaulay Duration of this portfolio of bonds if the term structure is flat with effective annual interest rate 10%.

**SOLUTION**

The bond prices are: (i) 91,322, (ii) 80,000, (iii) 63,439, and (iv) 112,377.

The combined price of all bonds in the portfolio is 347,138.
From Example 7.3, the Macaulay durations for the bonds are: (i) 1.950, (ii) 6.759, (iii) 11.434, and (iv) 10.91.

The Macaulay duration of the portfolio is

$$
D = \frac{\sum\limits_{k=1}^{m} D_k \cdot X_k}{X}
$$

$$
= \frac{(1.950)(91,322)+(6.759)(80,000) \\ \qquad +(11.434)(63,439)+(10.910)(112,377)}{347,138}
$$

$$
= 7.69 \qquad\qquad □
$$

## 7.1.5 PARALLEL AND NON-PARALLEL SHIFTS IN TERM STRUCTURE

Two different cashflow series that have the same present value and the same duration at a common yield rate of $i$ would have the same sensitivity to changes in the yield rate. We would describe the two series as being "matched" in the sense of present value and duration. This is a concept that will be explored further in the next section on cashflow matching and "immunization" of a series of cashflows.

Consider a bond portfolio consisting of two bonds, each of face amount 50:

(i)  a 2-coupon bond with coupon rate 5% per coupon period, and

(ii) a 60-coupon bond with coupon rate 15% per coupon period.

Suppose the yield rate for 2-coupon bonds is 5% per coupon period, and the yield on 60-coupon bonds is 15%. Since the yield rate is equal to the coupon rate for each bond, both bonds are currently valued at their par values of 50 each, so the total value of the portfolio is 100. These bonds are found in Tables 7.1a and 7.1c, with durations of 1.952 and 7.665, respectively. It follows from the comments in the previous section that the duration of the portfolio is $(.5)(1.952+7.665) = 4.81$.

Now consider a second portfolio consisting of a single bond of face amount 100, with 6 coupons and a coupon rate of 10%, valued at a yield rate of 10% per coupon period. This bond will be priced at its par value of 100. The duration of this bond is 4.79. Thus, the portfolios have the same value and almost the same duration at the current yield rates.

The yield rates can be summarized in a yield curve (Figure 7.1a). Let us consider the effect on the portfolios that result from an instantaneous change in the yield curve. Suppose that there is a +1% *parallel shift* in the yield curve (Figure 7.1b), so that the yield rates for all bond maturities increase by 1%. The value of the first portfolio becomes 95.96, and the value of the second portfolio becomes 95.77. Thus, as expected, both portfolios decrease in value by nearly the same amount as a result of the shift in the yield rate, since they have nearly the same duration. The basic notion of duration is based on parallel shifts in the term structure.

Suppose, instead, that the yield curve flattens slightly (Figure 7.1c), so that the yield on the 2-coupon bond increases to 6%, the yield on the 6-coupon bond stays at 10%, and the yield on the 60-coupon bond decreases to 14%. The value of the first portfolio becomes 102.65, but the second stays at 100. The purpose of this discussion is to point out that although two portfolios may currently have *matched* value and duration, the effects of non-parallel shifts in the yield curve may differ from one portfolio to another.

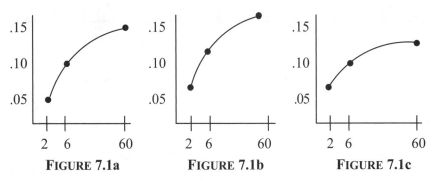

FIGURE 7.1a        FIGURE 7.1b        FIGURE 7.1c

Note that the yield curves represented here are not term structure curves but rather are graphs of yield to maturity versus time to maturity for the specific coupon bonds described above.

One of the important interpretations of duration is that two separate cashflow series that have the same duration will be affected in the same way by small changes (parallel shifts) in yield to maturity. In particular, if the Macaulay duration of a series of cashflows is $D$, then a zero coupon bond maturing in $D$ years will have the same Macaulay duration. If the zero coupon bond has the same present value as the series of cashflows, then for small changes in the yield to maturity, the change in present value of the cashflow series will be about the same as the change in value of the zero coupon bond.

It is clear that if an investor perceives that interest rates will increase, then the investor's risk of a loss in value of bond holdings is more limited with bonds of small duration, whereas if the perception is that rates will decrease, the investor's potential for gain in value of bond holdings is greater with bonds of larger duration. Duration is used to compare volatility of bond price with respect to yield rate, but would not be used in practice to actually calculate approximate changes in price as done in Example 7.2. Duration is more likely to be used to compare relative volatilities of two or more sets of cashflows.

### 7.1.6 EFFECTIVE DURATION

The definition of duration was based on a series of cashflows that wrer fixed, such as those of a non-callable bond. A series of cashflows has "embedded options". For instance, a callable bond (callable by the issuer) gives the bond issuer the option of redeeming bond at any time over a range of redemption dates. If the yield rate is above the coupon rate, the bond issuer will redeem the bond at the latest date, and if the yield rate is below the coupon rate, the bond issuer will redeem the bond at the earliest date.

Suppose we consider a callable bond and that it is past the earliest redemption date, so that the issuer can call the bond at any time. Suppose that the yield rate right now is slightly above the coupon rate. Then the bond issuer will not redeem the bond now. Suppose further that there is sudden change in yield rate and it falls below the coupon rate. Then the bond issuer will redeem the bond now. The way in which the bond price is changing is not a differentiable function of the yield rate, because the change in yield rate is not only changing present value of cashflows, it is changing the actual cashflows because the bond will be redeemed now instead of later as a result of the change in interest rates. The usual definition of duration cannot be used since it is based on the derivative of the present value of the cashflows with respect to the yield rate.

For cashflows that include embedded options which may change the actual cashflows as a result of a change in interest rate we have the notion of **effective duration**. If the current interest rate being used to value cashflows is $i_0$, then the effective duration is $\dfrac{PV_{i_0-h} - PV_{i_0+h}}{2h \cdot PV_{i_0}}$.

In this expression, $h$ represents a change in the interest rate. In practice, the value of $h$ might be from a few basis points to a full percentage point, and the effective duration will vary depending upon the value of $h$. For a series of cashflows that are fixed, the effective duration should be approximately equal to the usual modified duration, approaching modified duration as a limit as $h \to 0$.

## 7.2 Asset-Liability Matching and Immunization

In the course of conducting business, an enterprise will make commitments involving future income and outgo of capital. To maintain a viable (and profitable) position, the company will make investments so that funds will be available to provide for outgoing payments as they come due. Projected at time 0, the net outgoing payment at time $t > 0$ represents the company's *liability due* (or *outgo*) $L_t$ at time $t$. The funds available from anticipated revenue, investment income and investments maturing at time $t$ to cover that liability represent the company's *asset income* (or *proceeds*) $A_t$ at time $t$. If the company can arrange its investments so that asset income exactly covers the liability due at each point in time, so that $A_t = L_t$ for all $t$, then the projected asset income and liabilities due are said to be *exactly matched*.

Asset-liability matching is generally considered from the point of view of asset income and liability due cash flows occurring at discrete (usually equally spaced) points of time, $t = 0, 1, 2, \ldots, n$. It is also possible to consider continuous models of asset-liability matching, where $A_t$ is the *rate* of asset income and $L_t$ is the *rate* of liability due at time $t$.

**EXAMPLE 7.5** (*Exact matching of assets and liabilities*)

A small company terminating its operations has decided to provide each of its three employees with a severance package that pays 10,000 per year (at the end of each year) up to and including at age 65, plus a lump sum payment of 100,000 at age 65. In case of death of an employee before age 65, the payments continue until that employee would have been 65. The three employees are now exact ages 50, 53 and 55. The company determines that the payments due under this package can be met by the income and maturities generated by three bonds, each with a face amount of 100,000 and an annual coupon rate of 10% and with maturities of 10, 12, and 15 years. Determine the cost to the company to fund the severance package if the bonds have (effective annual) yield rates of 10% for the 10-year bond, 11% for the 12-year bond and 12% for the 15-year bond.

Applying any of the bond price formulas from Chapter 4 gives prices of 100,000 for the 10-year bond, 93,507.64 for the 12-year bond and 86,378.27 for the 15-year bond, for a total cost of 279,885.91. With the purchase of these bonds, the company's liabilities to the three employees are exactly matched.

As a variation on Example 7.5, suppose there are bonds available with a variety of coupon rates and maturity dates (including, perhaps, zero coupon bonds). The company might have several alternative combinations of investments whose asset income flows match the liabilities. Linear programming can be used to find the minimum cost combination of investments which matches asset flow to liability flow (see Exercise 7.2.1).

In Example 7.5, once the company purchases the bonds, the payments to the employees are guaranteed at the exact amounts on the exact dates needed. It may not always be possible to obtain an exact match between projected asset income and liabilities due. Example 7.6 below considers alternative ways of setting up asset cashflows in an attempt to match the liabilities that do not involve exact matching. A simpler illustration of the risk involved in asset-liability matching is presented in the following example.

| EXAMPLE 7.6 | *(Asset-Liability Matching)*

Suppose that there will be liability cashflows of amounts 1 each at times 1 and 2, so that $L_0 = 0, L_1 = L_2 = 1$. Suppose also that at time 0, the term structure is flat with yield rates of 10% for all zero coupon bond maturities. The present value at time 0 of the liabilities is

$$v_{.1} + v_{.1}^2 = 1.735537.$$

There are various ways of trying to structure asset cashflows to pay for the liabilities. Each of the following asset cashflows has the same present value at time 0 at an interest rate of 10% as the series of liability cashflows.

(i) $A_0 = 0, A_1 = A_2 = 1$. This series of asset cashflows provides exact matching with the liability cashflows.

(ii) $A_0 = 1.735537, A_1 = A_2 = 0$.   Not exact matching, but present values at 10% of assets and liabilities are matched at time 0.

(iii) $A_0 = A_1 = 0, A_2 = 2.1$. Not exact matching, but present values at 10% of assets and liabilities are matched at time 0.

---

| SOLUTION |

We can interpret each of these three cases in the following way.

(i) A one-year zero coupon bond with face amount 1 and a two-year zero coupon bond with face amount 1 are purchased to provide the asset cashflow. The cost of the two bonds is 1.735537 at time 0, and they will provide the exact asset cashflow to pay for the liabilities as they come due.

(ii) We assume that cash deposits can be made into an account earning interest at a rate of 10%. The initial asset cashflow at time 0 is a payment of 1.735537 which is deposited into the account. At time 1, the deposit account has grown to $1.735537(1.1) = 1.909091$. The liability of amount 1 due at time 1 is paid by making a withdrawal from the account, leaving a balance of .909091 in the account. At time 2 the account has grown to $.909091(1.1) = 1.000000$. The liability of amount 1 due at time 2 is paid by making a withdrawal from the account, leaving a balance of 0 in the account.

(iii) A line of credit account is set up which charges interest at a rate of 10% when money is owing to the account. The liability of amount 1 due at time 1 is paid by taking a withdrawal of amount 1 from the line of credit at that time. The amount owed to the line of credit account at time 2 is 1.1 (one year of interest is added to the balance that was owing at time 1). At time 2 when the asset cashflow of 2.1 is received, it pays for the liability of amount 1 due at time 2 and it pays off the balance owing of 1.1 in the line of credit account. This leaves a net asset-liability position of 0 at time 2.    □

The three asset cashflow series that are presented in Example 7.6 each have the same present value at 10% at time 0 of 1.735537. This matching of the present values is generally the first step in the matching of liabilities and assets. In each of these examples, we see that if the interest rate environment that was in effect at time 0 continues to be in effect during the term of the cashflows, there will be a net surplus-deficit position of 0 at the time the cashflows end. An interest rate of 10% for any zero coupon maturity was in effect at time 0, and it was assumed to continue for the two year period. We have really just restated a basic principle of compound interest that if the present values of two cashflow streams are equal at a particular point in time, then their values will be equal at any other point in time, providing the interest rate used for valuation stays constant.

### 7.2.1 REDINGTON IMMUNIZATION

In this elementary presentation of asset-liability matching concepts, we are assuming that the term structure at time 0 is flat with a yield to maturity of $i_0$ for all times to maturity. In attempting to match assets with liabilities we start out by ensuring that the present values of the two cashflow streams are equal at time 0 using $i_0$. This can be represented algebraically as follows:

$$PV_A(i_0) = \sum_0^n A_t v_{i_0}^t = \sum_0^n L_t v_{i_0}^t = PV_L(i_0). \qquad (7.7)$$

Equation (7.7) can be written in the form $\sum_0^n (A_t - L_t) v_{i_0}^t = 0$, or equivalently in the form

$$\sum_0^n (A_t - L_t)(1+i_0)^{n-t} = 0. \qquad (7.8)$$

We can interpret this last equation in the following way. At each cashflow time point $t$ there is a net cashflow received of amount $A_t - L_t$, which can be positive or negative. In Example 7.6(iii), we imagined that a line of credit account is in place in which interest is charged to the account at rate $i_0$ when the balance is negative and interest is credited to the account at the same rate $i_0$ when the balance in the account is positive. As the net cashflow amount is received at time $t$, we regard it as being deposited into or withdrawn from the line of credit account, depending upon whether $A_t - L_t > 0$ or $A_t - L_t < 0$. At each intermediate point in time there would be a net balance in the account that could be positive or negative. Equation (7.8) says that the balance in the account is 0 at the time of the final net cashflow. In other words, the net surplus-deficit position is 0 at the time the series of asset and liability cashflows ends.

The complication that arises in asset-liability matching is that although asset and liability cashflow present values may be matched at time 0 using valuation interest rate $i_0$, if there is a change in the interest rate, the present values might no longer match, and the surplus-deficit position at the time the cashflows end may no longer be 0. The imbalance that occurs depends on the relationship between asset and liability cashflow amounts.

In Example 7.6(i) it can be seen that once the 1 and 2 year zero coupon bonds are purchased to provide the asset cashflows, changes in interest rate are irrelevant in that as the bonds mature, they exactly pay the liability amounts required.

In Example 7.6(ii), the asset cashflow of amount 1.735537 was deposited into an account earning interest at rate 10%, and if the deposit account continued to earn 10% per year for the two year period, the assets would be exactly enough to pay for the liabilities. Suppose that for the first year the interest is 10% on the account, but at time 1, the interest rate on the deposit account changes to 9% for the $2^{nd}$ year. The balance in the account just after the liability payment at time 1 is still .909091, but the balance in the account at the end of the second year just before the liability payment is $(.909091)(1.09) = .990909$. After the liability payment of amount 1 at time 2, the balance in the account is $-.009091$, so there is a deficit position in the assets as compared to the liabilities.

It is impossible to know the future behavior of interest rates, so even though asset and liability cashflow present values are matched at time 0 based on the interest rate environment at time 0, future interest rate changes can put the asset and liability valuations out of balance. What we may attempt to do is structure the asset cashflows so that small changes in the interest rate do not put the asset-liability relationship into a deficit position. One way we have seen to do that is have assets exactly matched with liabilities, so that $A_t = L_t$ for all $t = 0, 1, 2, ..., n$. In that case Equation (7.7) holds for any rate $i_0$, and there will never be a surplus or deficit position in the asset-liability relationship no matter how interest rates change.

Without exact matching, there is the risk that if the valuation rate of interest deviates from its original value of $i_0$ to some other value $i$, then $PV_A(i) < PV_L(i)$ and the asset income flow will not be sufficient to balance the liabilities due.

In 1952, the actuary F.M. Redington introduced a theory of **immunization** for an asset/liability flow. According to this theory, with a careful structuring of asset income in relation to liabilities due, small deviations in the interest rate from $i_0$ to $i$ result in $PV_A(i) > PV_L(i)$, for both $i > i_0$ and $i < i_0$. Therefore, whether the interest rate increases or decreases (by a small amount), the present value of the assets at the new rate of interest will be larger than the present value of the liabilities, and the asset-liability relationship will not change from a matched to a deficit position.

The basic theory of immunization is as follows. Suppose asset income has been allocated so as to balance liabilities due at interest rate $i_0$ according to Equation (7.7). Suppose this allocation of asset income also satisfies the conditions

$$\left. \frac{d}{di} PV_A(i) \right|_{i_0} = \left. \frac{d}{di} PV_L(i) \right|_{i_0} \tag{7.9}$$

and

$$\left. \frac{d^2}{di^2} PV_A(i) \right|_{i_0} > \left. \frac{d^2}{di^2} PV_L(i) \right|_{i_0}. \tag{7.10}$$

If we define the function $h(i)$ to be

$$h(i) = PV_A(i) - PV_L(i), \tag{7.11}$$

then $h(i_0) = h'(i_0) = 0$ (from Equations (7.7) and (7.9)), and $h''(i_0) > 0$ (from Equation (7.10)). It follows that $h(i)$ has a *relative minimum* at $i_0$. In other words, for some interval around $i_0$, say $(i_L, i_U)$, if $i_L < i < i_U$ then $h(i) > h(i_0) = 0$, or, equivalently, $PV_A(i) > PV_L(i)$.

With the asset/liability flow immunized in this way, a *small change* in the interest rate from $i_0$ to $i$ where $i$ is in an appropriate interval around $i_0$ as described in the previous paragraph, results in a *surplus* position in the sense that there is an excess of the present value of asset income over liabilities due when valued at the new rate $i$. The change in the interest rate must be small enough so that $i$ stays within the interval. This immunization of the portfolio against small changes in $i$ is called **Redington immunization.**

---

**Definition 7.3 – Redingtion Immunization**

If asset cashflows are $A_t$ for $t = 0,1,...,n$ and liability cashflows are $L_t$ for $t = 0,1,...,n,$, then the liability cashflows are Redington immunized by the asset cash flows at valuation rate $i_0$ if the following conditions are met

(i)
$$PV_A(i)\big|_{i_0} \;=\; PV_L(i)\big|_{i_0}$$

(ii)
$$\frac{d}{di} PV_A(i)\bigg|_{i_0} \;=\; \frac{d}{di} PV_L(i)\bigg|_{i_0}$$

(iii)
$$\frac{d^2}{di^2} PV_A(i)\bigg|_{i_0} \;>\; \frac{d^2}{di^2} PV_L(i)\bigg|_{i_0}.$$

---

The second derivative of a function at a point is sometimes used as a measure of curvature of the function at that point. The **convexity** of a series of cashflows is related to this idea and is defined below. Equation 7.10 can be interpreted as saying that the convexity of the (present value function of the) assets as a function of the rate of interest is greater than the convexity of the (present value of the) liabilities.

---

**Definition 7.4 – Convexity**

The convexity of $s$ series of cashflows is the second derivative of the present value of the cashflows with respect to the rate of valuation divided by the present value.

$$\frac{\dfrac{d^2}{di^2} PV_A(i)\bigg|_{i_0}}{PV_A(i)\big|_{i_0}}$$

---

In Exercise 7.2.3 it is shown that Equation (7.9) is equivalent to

$$\sum t \cdot A_t \cdot v_{i_0}^t \;=\; \sum t \cdot L_t \cdot v_{i_0}^t, \tag{7.12}$$

and, if Equation (7.9) is true then Equation (7.10) is equivalent to

$$\sum t^2 \cdot A_t \cdot v_{i_0}^t > \sum t^2 \cdot L_t \cdot v_{i_0}^t. \tag{7.13}$$

It follows from Equation (7.9) that $PV_A(i)$ and $PV_L(i)$ have the same volatility (modified duration) with respect to interest rates. It is not surprising, then, that a consequence of the conditions for immunization given by Equations (7.9) and (7.10) is that at interest rate $i_0$, the assets and liabilities have the same modified duration. This says that for small changes in the interest rate away from $i_0$, the changes in the present value of the assets and the present value of the liabilities are approximately the same. Let us denote by $D(i_0)$ the common Mccaulay duration of assets and liabilities at rate $i_0$.

If the conditions in Equations (7.7) and (7.9) are satisfied, and since $D(i_0)$ is a time constant (the weighted average time to maturity or discounted mean term of the $A_t$'s or $L_t$'s), it follows that Equation (7.13) is equivalent to

$$\sum [t - D(i_0)]^2 \cdot A_t \cdot v_{i_0}^t > \sum [t - D(i_0)]^2 \cdot L_t \cdot v_{i_0}^t. \tag{7.14}$$

Therefore if Equations (7.7) and (7.9) are satisfied, the asset/liability match is immunized if the asset income flow is more "dispersed" or "widely spread" (in time) about $D(i_0)$ than the liabilities are. The liability cashflow series in Example 7.5 is used in the following example to illustrate how the conditions for immunization might be met by ensuring a greater dispersion of asset cashflows than liability cashflows.

**EXAMPLE 7.7** (*Redington immunization*)

To immunize the liabilities due in the severance package described in Example 7.5, the company purchases an investment portfolio consisting of two zero coupon bonds, due at times $t_1$ and $t_2$ (measured from the starting date of the severance package). Suppose that the term structure is flat at an effective annual rate of 10%. For each of the following pairs $t_1$ and $t_2$, determine the amounts of each zero coupon bond that must be purchased and whether or not the overall asset/liability portfolio is in an immunized position:

(a) $t_1 = 0,\ t_2 = 15$;

(b) $t_1 = 6,\ t_2 = 12$;

(c) $t_1 = 2,\ t_2 = 14$.

---

**SOLUTION**

Let $X$ be the amount of zero coupon bond purchased with maturity at $t_1$ and $Y$ the amount with maturity at $t_2$. In order to satisfy Equation (7.7) we must have $X \cdot v_{.10}^{t_1} + Y \cdot v_{.10}^{t_2} = \sum L_t \cdot v_{.10}^t = 300{,}000$ (this is the present value of the liabilities).

In order to satisfy Equation (7.9) we must have

$$
\begin{aligned}
t_1 \cdot X \cdot v_{.10}^{t_1} + t_2 \cdot Y \cdot v_{.10}^{t_2} &= \sum t \cdot L_t \cdot v_{.10}^t \\
&= 30{,}000v + 2(30{,}000)v^2 + 3(30{,}000)v^3 \\
&\quad + \cdots + 9(30{,}000)v^9 + 10(130{,}000)v^{10} \\
&\quad + 11(20{,}000)v^{11} + 12(120{,}000)v^{12} \\
&\quad + 13(10{,}000)v^{13} + 14(10{,}000)v^{14} \\
&\quad + 15(110{,}000)v^{15} \\
&= 2{,}262{,}077.228.
\end{aligned}
$$

Solving these two equations for $X$ and $Y$ in each of the three cases, we obtain the values

(a) $X = 149{,}194.85,\ Y = 629{,}950.53$;

(b) $X = 395{,}035.30,\ Y = 241{,}699.38$; and

(c) $X = 195{,}407.21,\ Y = 525{,}977.96$

The third immunization condition, Equation (7.10), requires that

$$
t_1^2 \cdot X \cdot v_{.10}^{t_1} + t_2^2 \cdot Y \cdot v_{.10}^{t_2} > \sum t^2 \cdot L_t \cdot v_{.10}^t
$$

The right-hand side of the inequality is equal to

$$30,000v + 2^2(30,000)v^2 + 3^2(30,000v^3 + \cdots$$
$$+ 9^2(30,000)v^9 + 10^2(130,000)v^{10}$$
$$+ 11^2(20,000)v^{11} + 12^2(120,000)v^{12} + 13^2(10,000)v^{13}$$
$$+ 14^2(10,000)v^{14} + 15^2(110,000)v^{15}$$
$$= 22,709,878.$$

In case (a) $t_1^2 \cdot X \cdot v_{.10}^{t_1} + t_2^2 \cdot Y \cdot v_{.10}^{t_2}$ (the left hand side of equation (7.10)) is 33,931,158, so this portfolio is immunized. In case (b) the left hand side is 19,117,390, so for small changes in the interest rate away from 10% (positive or negative), the present value of assets will be less than the present value of liabilities. In case (c) the left side is 27,793,236, so the portfolio is again immunized. ☐

In Section 7.1.6 we defined the notion of effective duration for a series of cashflows that has embedded option. We can define **effective convexity** as well. The effective convexity of a series of cash flows is defined to be $\dfrac{PV_{i_0-h} - 2PV_{i_0} + PV_{i_0+h}}{h^2 \cdot PV_{i_0}}$. As with the definition of effective duration, effective convexity depends on the value of $h$.

### 7.2.2 FULL IMMUNIZATION

In Exercise 7.2.8 you are asked to show that in case (a) of Example 7.7 the portfolio is actually *fully immunized*.

---

**Definition 7.5 – Full Immunization**

The portfolio is **fully immunized** if $\sum A_t \cdot v^t \geq \sum L_t \cdot v^t$ for *any* $i > 0$.

---

In case (c) $h(i)$ has a relative minimum at $i_0 = .10$, but $\sum A_t \cdot v^t < \sum L_t \cdot v^t$ for sufficiently large values of $i$. That is, in case (c), a deficit may occur if the change in interest is large enough so that $i$ is far enough from 10%. Thus, in case (c), the portfolio satisfies the conditions of Redington immunization at $i_0 = .10$, but the portfolio is not fully immunized. The graphs of $h(i)$ for cases (a) and (c) of Example 7.7 are shown in Figure 7.2 (not to scale).

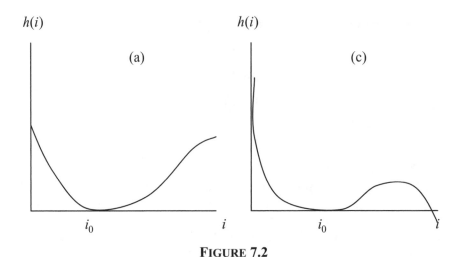

$h(i)$          (a)        $i_0$    $i$      $h(i)$        (c)     $i_0$    $i$

**FIGURE 7.2**

As time goes on, changes in interest rates may occur. This consideration, along with changing times until liabilities are due and asset income is received, may require that the asset portfolio be updated to maintain an immunized position.

We now investigate further the concept of *full immunization* defined above. Suppose liabilities due consist of a single liability of amount $L_s$ at time $s \geq 0$. Suppose also that Equations (7.7) and (7.9) are satisfied with the current values of $i_0, s, L_s, t_1, t_2, A_{t_1}$, and $A_{t_2}$, where $t_1 \leq s$ and $t_2 \geq s$ at interest rate $i_0$ per unit time. Then Equations (7.7) and (7.9) become

$$A_{t_1} \cdot v_{i_0}^{t_1} + A_{t_2} \cdot v_{i_0}^{t_2} = L_s \cdot v_{i_0}^{s} \qquad (7.15)$$

and

$$t_1 \cdot A_{t_1} \cdot v_{i_0}^{t_1} + t_2 \cdot A_{t_2} \cdot v_{i_0}^{t_2} = s \cdot L_s \cdot v_{i_0}^{s}. \qquad (7.16)$$

To simplify notation we define $a = s - t_1$ and $b = t_2 - s$. As before, the function $h(i) = PV_A(i) - PV_L(i) = A_{t_1} \cdot v_i^{t_1} + A_{t_2} \cdot v_i^{t_2} - L_s \cdot v_i^{s}$ will be the present value of asset minus liability flow, valued at interest rate $i$. With some algebraic manipulation (see Exercise 7.2.9) $h(i)$ can be formulated as

$$h(i) = v_i^s \cdot A_{t_1} (1+i_0)^a \left[ \left( \frac{1+i}{1+i_0} \right)^a + \frac{a}{b} \left( \frac{1+i}{1+i_0} \right)^{-b} - \left( 1 + \frac{a}{b} \right) \right]$$

$$= v_i^s \cdot A_{t_1} \cdot g(i) \tag{7.17}$$

We see that $h(i_0) = 0$ and $g(i_0) = 0$ and

$$g'(i) = a(1+i)^{-1} \left[ \left( \frac{1+i}{1+i_0} \right)^a - \left( \frac{1+i}{1+i_0} \right)^{-b} \right].$$

Since $a \geq 0$ and $b \geq 0$, it follows that $g'(i) \geq 0$ if $i \geq i_0$, and $g'(i) \leq 0$ if $i \leq i_0$. Therefore, $g(i)$ is increasing for $i \geq i_0$ and $g(i)$ is decreasing for $i \leq i_0$. The function $g(i)$ has an absolute minimum at $i = i_0$, and since $g(i_0) = 0$, it follows that $g(i) \geq 0$ for any interest rate $i$. Therefore $h(i) \geq 0$ for all $i$, and the asset/liability flow is fully immunized against changes in interest rates of any size.

This full immunization of a single liability due can be seen from another point of view. Earlier in this chapter we saw that the duration of a single amount payable at time $t$ in the future is simply equal to $t$. It then follows from Equation (7.14) that any allocation of asset income involving two or more non-zero $A_t$'s that satisfies Equations (7.15) and (7.16) will result in full immunization, since the right hand side of (7.14) is zero for a single liability due but the left hand side will exceed zero.

| EXAMPLE 7.8 | *(Full immunization)*

Use the method of full immunization outlined in Equations (7.15), (7.16) and (7.17) to find the values of $A_0$ and $A_{15}$ that immunize $L_{12} = 120,000$, assuming $i_0 = .10, t_1 = 0, t_2 = 15$ and $s = 12$.

| SOLUTION |

We wish to solve the two equations

$$A_0 \cdot v_{.10}^0 + A_{15} \cdot v_{.10}^{15} = 120,000 \cdot v_{.10}^{12} = 38,235.70$$

and

$$0 \cdot A_0 \cdot v_{.10}^0 + 15 \cdot A_{15} \cdot v_{.10}^{15} = 12 \left( 120,000 \cdot v_{.10}^{12} \right) = 458,828.38.$$

The solution is $A_0 = 7647.14$ and $A_{15} = 127,776.00$. Note that $h(0) = 15,423.14$, $h(.10) = 0$, $\lim_{i \to \infty} h(i) = A_0 = 7647.14$, and $h(i)$ is decreasing for $0 \le i < .10$ and increasing for $i > .10$. If the interest valuation rate were to drop to 0 from $i_0 = .10$, a profit of $15,423.14$ could be made, since some of the assets could be sold while still maintaining sufficient assets to cover liabilities at the new interest rate of 0. □

Assuming $s$, $L_s$, and $i_0$ are known, Equations (7.15) and (7.16) involve the unknown quantities $A_{t_1}$, $A_{t_2}$, $t_1$ and $t_2$. In general, given any two of these four quantities, there will be a unique solution for the other two so as to fully immunize the portfolio. (Cases may arise in which one of the $A$'s or $t$'s is negative, or there may be infinitely many or no solutions; see Exercise 7.2.11) In Exercise 7.2.4, it is shown that if each of the liabilities due in Example 7.5 is fully immunized (at $i = .10$) according to the method above, using $t_1 = 0$ and $t_2 = 15$, then the total asset income allocated for all liabilities combined is the same as in part (a) of Example 7.7.

In discussing Redington immunization and full immunization, there have been the following two implicit assumptions.

(1) The *term structure* of interest rates is constant or *flat* for all maturities.

(2) When interest rate changes occur, the change is the same throughout the term structure. In other words, there is a *parallel shift* in the term structure.

These implicit assumptions have been reflected in the examples. In practice it is not common to find a flat yield curve, and shifts in the term structure are usually not parallel, so that it may not be possible to fully immunize a portfolio. Suppose in Example 7.8 the 10% interest rate becomes 11% for the 12-year term and 11.1% for the 15 year term. Then the present value of the asset flow is

$$7647.14 + 127,776.00 \cdot v_{.111}^{15} = 33,994.58$$

while the present value of the liabilities is $120,000 \cdot v_{.11}^{12} = 34,300.90$. The portfolio is not immunized against this almost parallel shift in the yield curve. The theory of immunization can be extended to situations involving term structures that are not flat and shifts in the term structure that are not parallel, and even stochastic models of the term structure.

## 7.3 APPLICATIONS AND ILLUSTRATIONS

### 7.3.1 DURATION BASED ON CHANGES IN A NOMINAL ANNUAL YIELD RATE COMPOUNDED SEMIANNUALLY

The presentation of duration in Section 7.1 assumed that the series of cashflows had annual payments and the yield rate was an effective annual rate of interest. The presentation could have been based on any equally spaced period for the payments with a yield rate that was compounded with the same frequency as the payments are made. The units in which duration is measured would be based on the payment period, so a duration of 10 would mean 10 payment periods. In practice, the conventional units for duration are years. It is a simple matter to convert from describing duration in terms of the payment period to describing duration in terms of years.

In practice, bond coupons are paid semiannually and bond yields are quoted as nominal annual rates of interest compounded semiannually. Consider an $n$-year zero coupon bond with a yield rate $i^{(2)}$. If we define $j = \frac{i^{(2)}}{2}$ then the present value of the bond is $P = (1+j)^{-2n}$, and the Macaulay duration would be $-(1+j)\dfrac{\frac{d}{dj}(1+j)^{-2n}}{(1+j)^{-2n}} = 2n$ half-years (the interest rate $j$ is a half-year rate), which we could describe as $n$ years. If the derivative in the numerator is taken with respect to the nominal annual rate $i^{(2)}$, then the Macaulay duration becomes

$$-(1+j)\frac{\frac{d}{di^{(2)}}\left(1+\frac{i^{(2)}}{2}\right)^{-2n}}{(1+j)^{-2n}} = -(1+j)\frac{-2n\left(1+\frac{i^{(2)}}{2}\right)^{-2n-1}\cdot\frac{1}{2}}{(1+j)^{-2n}}$$

$$= -(1+j)\frac{-n(1+j)^{-2n-1}}{(1+j)^{-2n}} = n\text{-years}.$$

What has happened is that since $j = \frac{i^{(2)}}{2}$, derivatives with respect to $i^{(2)}$ are half as big as derivatives with respect to $j$.

---

| EXAMPLE 7.9 | *(Macaulay duration)*

A 10-year 5% bond has semiannual coupons and is currently valued at $i^{(2)} = 5\%$. Find the Macaulay duration of the bond (in years).

| SOLUTION |

The semiannual coupons are 2.5 each and the semiannual yield rate is 2.5%.

The Macaulay duration as measured in half-years is

$$D = \frac{\sum\limits_{t=1}^{20} 2.5t(1.025)^{-t} + 100(20)(1.025)^{-20}}{\sum\limits_{t=1}^{20} 2.5(1.025)^{-t} + 100(1.025)^{-20}} = 15.979.$$

Note that the first term in the numerator is the increasing annuity $2.5(Ia)_{\overline{20}|.025}$.

The Macaulay duration is $\frac{1}{2} \times 15.979 = 7.989$ years. ◻

---

Theoretical analysis of financial mathematics often is based on continuous compounding (force of interest) for valuations. If the yield to maturity on a cashflow series is $\delta$, then the present value is $P = \sum\limits_{t=1}^{n} K_t e^{-\delta t}$. If sensitivity is based on changes in $\delta$, then $\frac{d}{d\delta} P = -\sum\limits_{t=1}^{n} t K_t e^{-\delta t}$, and the rate of change of the present value per dollar invested is $\dfrac{\frac{d}{d\delta} P}{P} = \dfrac{-\sum\limits_{t=1}^{n} t K_t e^{-\delta t}}{\sum\limits_{t=1}^{n} K_t e^{-\delta t}}$.

Note that there is no distinction between modified and Macaulay duration when we are basing sensitivity on changes in the force of interest.

We have just described a version of duration that is based on changes in the force of interest. We can also define a version of convexity based on changes in the force of interest. The **Macaulay convexity** is defined to be $\dfrac{\frac{d^2}{d\delta^2}P}{P} = \dfrac{\sum\limits_{t=1}^{n} t^2 K_t e^{-\delta t}}{\sum\limits_{t=1}^{n} K_t e^{-\delta t}}$. The original definition of convexity given

earlier in Definition 7.4 might be described as "modified convexity."

### 7.3.2 DURATION BASED ON SHIFTS IN THE TERM STRUCTURE

The duration measure that was developed in Section 7.1 is based on the change in the yield to maturity for the cashflow series. We have seen in Chapter 6 that valuation of a cashflow series can be done using the term structure of spot rates of interest. In the duration measure considered in Section 7.1, there is an implicit assumption that the term structure is flat, with the same yield to maturity, say $s$, for payments at any time in the future. In that case, as pointed out in Section 6.1, the yield to maturity for any coupon bond will also be $s$ for any term to maturity and any coupon rate.

In practice, it is not usually the case that the term structure is flat. It is most often the case that the term structure is an increasing function of time to maturity for zero coupon bonds.

For a series of annual payments of amounts $K_1, K_2, \ldots, K_n$, the present value of the series using a yield to maturity $i$ for all payments is

$P = \sum\limits_{t=1}^{n} K_t (1+i)^{-t}$, and the modified duration is $-\dfrac{\frac{d}{di}P}{P} = \dfrac{-\frac{d}{di}\sum\limits_{t=1}^{n} K_t (1+i)^{-t}}{\sum\limits_{t=1}^{n} K_t (1+i)^{-t}}$.

The derivative in the numerator can be expressed in an alternative, but

equivalent way, $\dfrac{d}{di}\sum\limits_{t=1}^{n} K_t (1+i)^{-t} = \dfrac{d}{d\alpha}\sum\limits_{t=1}^{n} K_t (1+i+\alpha)^{-t}\Big|_{\alpha=0}$ . (evaluated at

$\alpha=0$). We are using the derivative relationship $f'(x) = \dfrac{d}{d\alpha} f(x+\alpha)\big|_{\alpha=0}$.

We will continue to use the notation introduced in Section 6.1 for the spot rates of interest, so that $s_k(t)$ denotes the yield on a zero coupon bond maturing in $t$ years from time $k$ (and $s_0(t)$ is the yield on a zero coupon bond maturing $t$ years from time 0). The present value of a series of $n$ annual payments starting one year from now with payment amounts of $K_1, K_2, \ldots, K_n$ can be expressed as $P_{TS} = \sum_{t=1}^{n} K_t (1+s_0(t))^{-t}$. Suppose that a change in the term structure occurs in which each yield in the term structure is "shifted" by amount $\alpha$, so that the yield on a $t$-year zero coupon bond becomes $s_0(t) + \alpha$. The present value of the series of payments can be formulated as a function of $\alpha$, $P_{TS}(\alpha) = \sum_{t=1}^{n} K_t (1+s_0(t)+\alpha)^{-t}$, and note that $P_{TS}(0) = P$.

The derivative of $P_{TS}(\alpha)$ with respect to $\alpha$ is

$$\frac{d}{d\alpha} P_{TS}(\alpha) = \frac{d}{d\alpha} \sum_{t=1}^{n} K_t (1+s_0(t)+\alpha)^{-t} = -\sum_{t=1}^{n} t K_t (1+s_0(t)+\alpha)^{-t-1}.$$

This derivative evaluated at $\alpha = 0$ is $P'_{TS}(0) = -\sum_{t=1}^{n} t K_t (1+s_0(t))^{-t-1}$. The modified duration of the series of payments based on the change in $\alpha$ is

$$-\frac{P'_{TS}(0)}{P_{TS}(0)} = \frac{\sum_{t=1}^{n} t K_t (1+s_0(t))^{-t-1}}{\sum_{t=1}^{n} K_t (1+s_0(t))^{-t}}.$$ Since we are assuming that the spot rates are all changing by amount $\alpha$ simultaneously, this situation is referred to as a "parallel shift in the term structure."

---

**EXAMPLE 7.10**   (*Duration based on change in term structure*)

Suppose that the current term structure of interest rates has the following schedule of spot rates for maturities of 1, 2, 3 and 4 years:

| Maturity | 1-year | 2-year | 3-year | 4-year |
|----------|--------|--------|--------|--------|
| Spot Rate | .05 | .10 | .15 | .20 |

A four year bond has annual coupons at 10%. Find the modified duration for the bond based on a parallel shift in the term structure. Find the yield to maturity for the bond. Find the modified duration for the bond based on a change in the yield to maturity.

| SOLUTION |

The bond price for a bond with face amount 100 is

$$P_{TS} = 10\left[(1.05)^{-1}+(1.10)^{-2}+(1.15)^{-3}+(1.20)^{-4}\right]+100(1.20)^{-4} = 77.41.$$

The modified duration of the bond based on a parallel shift in the term structure is

$$-\frac{P'_{TS}(0)}{P_{TS}(0)} = \frac{\sum\limits_{t=1}^{n} t K_t (1+s_0(t))^{-t-1}}{\sum\limits_{t=1}^{n} K_t (1+s_0(t))^{-t}}$$

$$= \frac{10[(1.05)^{-2}+2(1.10)^{-3}+3(1.15)^{-4}+4(1.20)^{-5}]+100(4)(1.20)^{-5}}{10[(1.05)^{-1}+(1.10)^{-2}(1.15)^{-3}(1.20)^{-4}]+100(1.20)^{-4}}$$

$$= 2.82 \text{ years.}$$

Based on the term structure, the yield to maturity for the bond is $i$, where

$$77.41 = 10\left[(1+i)^{-1} +(1+i)^{-2} +(1+i)^{-3} +(1+i)^{-4}\right]+100(1+i)^{-4}.$$

Solving for $i$ results in $i = .1847$. The modified duration of the bond based on changes in the yield to maturity is

$$\frac{\begin{array}{c}10[(1.1847)^{-2}+2(1.1847)^{-3}+3(1.1847)^{-4}\\ +4(1.1847)^{-5}]+100(4)(1.1847)^{-5}\end{array}}{\begin{array}{c}10[(1.1847)^{-1}+(1.1847)^{-2}+(1.1847)^{-3}\\ +(1.1847)^{-4}]+100(1.1847)^{-4}\end{array}} = 2.88.$$

Even with this extreme case of an increasing term structure, the difference between the modified duration based on term structure and that based on yield to maturity is not large. ❑

When changes occur in the term structure, the change is generally not a parallel shift. Short term rates tend to be more volatile than longer term rates. Suppose we consider the following model for the price of the bond based on the term structure in Example 7.10.

$$P_{TS}(\alpha) = 10\Big[(1.05{+}\alpha)^{-1}$$
$$+ (1.1{+}.75\alpha)^{-2} + (1.15{+}.5\alpha)^{-3} + (1.2{+}.25\alpha)^{-4}\Big] + 100(1.2{+}.25\alpha)^{-4}$$

Under this model, the 1-year rate is most sensitive to a change in $\alpha$, and the longer term maturities are less and less sensitive. The modified duration with respect to change in $\alpha$ is

$$-\frac{P_{TS}'(0)}{P_{TS}(0)} = \frac{\begin{aligned}&10[(1.05)^{-2} + 2(.75)(1.10)^{-3}\\ &+ 3(.5)(1.15)^{-4} + 4(.25)(1.20)^{-5}] + 100(4)(.25)(1.20)^{-5}\end{aligned}}{10[(1.05)^{-1} + (1.10)^{-2} + (1.15)^{-3} + (1.20)^{-4}] + 100(1.20)^{-4}}$$
$$= .94.$$

It is not surprising that the duration is smaller than in Example 7.10, since most of the variability is in the shortest term rates.

Although shifts in the term structure are usually not parallel, the measure of duration based on yield to maturity can be useful when comparing the interest rate risk of various bonds. If two sets of series of payments have the same duration, they have approximately the same sensitivity to a small change in yield to maturity or to a small change in the term structure.

### 7.3.3 Shortcomings of Duration as a Measure of Interest Rate Risk

As noted earlier, conventional measures of duration that we considered in Section 7.1 are based on yield to maturity and parallel shifts in the term structure. In reality, this is not the way interest rates change.

A second shortcoming is that the duration of a series of payments will change as time goes on, even if there is no change in the yield rate. For a zero coupon bond, the modified duration is the time to maturity, which decreases as time goes on since we are getting closer to the maturity date. If two series of payments valued at the same yield to maturity $i$ have the same present value and the same modified duration at time 0, then at any later time, if they continue to be valued at the same yield to maturity $i$ as they were earlier, they will continue to have matching present values and modified durations at that later time. If, however, at the later time they are valued at a yield to maturity other than $i$, their present values and durations may no longer be matched. This is illustrated in the following example.

| EXAMPLE 7.11 | *(Duration drift)*

We consider the following two portfolios of bonds

Portfolio 1:    A 10-year zero coupon bond with face amount 100.

Portfolio 2:    A 5-year zero coupon bond with face amount 41.39 combined with a 20-year zero coupon bond with face amount 86.46.

The yield to maturity for all bonds is $i = 10\%$.

Show that the present value and duration of the two portfolios are matched at any time before 5 years if the yield to maturity stays at 10%. Suppose that after one year the yield to maturity for all bonds is 11%. Find the present values and Macaulay durations of the two portfolios.

| SOLUTION |

The present values and durations at time 0 of the two portfolios are:

Portfolio 1:    $P^{(1)} = 100(1.1)^{-10} = 38.55$ and $D^{(1)} = 10$
                (for a zero coupon bond).

Portfolio 2:    $P^{(2)} = 41.39(1.1)^{-5} + 86.46(1.1)^{-20} = 38.55$ and

$$D^{(2)} = \frac{41.39(5)(1.1)^{-5} + 86.46(20)(1.1)^{-20}}{38.55} = 10.$$

At time $t$ the present value of Portfolio 1 is

$$P_t^{(1)} = 100(1.1)^{-10}(1.1)^t = 100(1.1)^{-(10-t)} = 38.55(1.1)^t,$$

and the present value of Portfolio 2 is also

$$P_t^{(2)} = \left[41.39(1.1)^{-5} + 86.46(1.1)^{-20}\right](1.1)^t$$
$$= 41.39(1.1)^{-(5-t)} + 86.46(1.1)^{-(20-t)} = 38.55(1.1)^t.$$

At time $t$ the numerator of the Macaulay duration for Portfolio 1 is

$$100(10-t)(1.1)^{-(10-t)} \;=\; 100(10)(1.1)^{-(10-t)} - 100t(1.1)^{-(10-t)}.$$

At time $t$ the numerator of the Macaulay duration for Portfolio 2 is

$$41.39(5-t)(1.1)^{-(5-t)} + 86.46(20-t)(1.1)^{-(20-t)}$$
$$= 41.39(5)(1.1)^{-(5-t)}$$
$$+ 86.46(20)(1.1)^{-(20-t)} - t\left[41.39(1.1)^{-(5-t)} + 86.46(1.1)^{-(20-t)}\right].$$

Since the durations were matched at time 0, it must be true that

$$100(10)(1.1)^{-10} \;=\; 41.39(5)(1.1)^{-5} + 86.46(20)(1.1)^{-20},$$

and therefore

$$100(10)(1.1)^{-10}(1.1)^{t} \;=\; \left[41.39(5)(1.1)^{-5} + 86.46(20)(1.1)^{-20}\right](1.1)^{t}.$$

Also, since at time 0 the present values are matched, we have

$$100(1.1)^{-10} \;=\; 41.39(1.1)^{-5} + 86.46(1.1)^{-20},$$

and therefore

$$100(1.1)^{-10}(1.1)^{t} \;=\; \left[41.39(1.1)^{-5} + 86.46(1.1)^{-20}\right](1.1)^{t}.$$

It follows that the numerators of the Macaulay durations of Portfolios 1 and 2 are equal at any time $t$ before 5 years, so that the durations are matched at any time $t$ before 5 years.

With a yield to maturity of 11% at time 1, the present values at time 1 of the two Portfolios are:

Portfolio 1: $\quad P^{(1)} = 100(1.11)^{-9} = 39.09$ and $D^{(1)} = 9$
$\qquad\qquad$ (for a 9-year zero coupon bond).

Portfolio 2:    $P^{(2)} = 41.39(1.11)^{-4} + 86.46(1.11)^{-19} = 39.17$ and

$$D^{(2)} = \frac{41.39(4)(1.11)^{-4} + 86.46(19)(1.11)^{-19}}{39.17} = 8.56. \quad \square$$

Exercise 7.1.3 shows more generally that for a series of more than one payment, as the yield to maturity increases the duration will decrease.

A third shortcoming of duration as a measure of the sensitivity of the present value of a series of payments to changes in the yield to maturity is related to the "convexity" of the graph of the present value as a function of yield to maturity. Convexity is based on the second derivative of the present value with respect to changes in the yield to maturity. A more convex present value graph results in a present value that reacts more dramatically to a change in the yield to maturity. Suppose we consider a 10-year zero coupon bond valued at an effective annual yield to maturity of 10%. The present value of the bond is $100(1.1)^{-10} = 38.5543$, and the modified duration is 9.0909. With a 1 basis point drop (.01%) in the yield to maturity, the price will be $100(1.0999)^{-10} = 38.5894$, which is a relative change in value of $\frac{.0351}{38.5543} = .000910$. Since the duration is 9.090909, we would expect a relative change of about $9.090909 \times .0001 = .000909$. Suppose instead that there is a 100 basis point drop in the yield to maturity. The price of the bond becomes $100(1.09)^{-10} = 42.2411$, which is a relative change in value of $\frac{3.6868}{38.5543} = .095626$. The actual relative change in price is further from the change suggested by the duration measure for a 100 basis point change than for the 1 basis point change because of the convexity of the present value curve. This is illustrated in the following graph. The curved line is a graph of the actual value of $(1+i)^{-10}$, and the straight line is the approximation based on the duration of the bond at $i = .10$. It can be seen from the graph that as a result of the convexity of the curve, as $i$ gets further from 10%, the actual value of the bond is further from that predicted by the linear differential approximation using the duration of the bond.

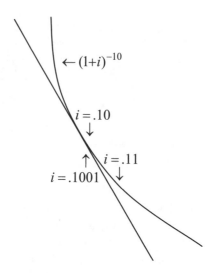

$\leftarrow (1+i)^{-10}$

$i = .10$
$\downarrow$

$\uparrow \; i = .11$
$i = .1001 \; \downarrow$

**FIGURE 7.3**

### 7.3.4  A GENERALIZATION OF REDINGTON IMMUNIZATION

Suppose that the annual asset cashflow series is $A_1, A_2, \ldots, A_n$ and the annual liability cashflow series is $L_1, L_2, \ldots, L_n$, and suppose that the current continuously compounded term structure is $\delta_{0,t}$, but after an instantaneous interest rate shock the term structure changes to $\delta_{0,t}^*$. We define the function $g(t)$ to be $g(t) = \dfrac{e^{-t\delta_{0,t}^*}}{e^{-t\delta_{0,t}}} - 1$. Then the change in the present value of the surplus (present value of asset minus liability cashflows) is

$$S^* - S = \sum_{t>0}(A_t - L_t)(e^{-t\delta_{0,t}^*} - e^{-t\delta_{0,t}}) = \sum_{t>0}(A_t - L_t)e^{-t\delta_{0,t}}\,g(t).$$

Using Taylor's expansion about 0 to the $2^{nd}$ derivative term and the weighted theorem of the mean for integrals applied to the function $g(t)$ it can be shown that

$$S^* - S = g(0)\sum_{t>0}(A_t - L_t)\,e^{-t\delta_{0,t}} + g'(0)\sum_{t>0}t(A_t - L_t)\,e^{-t\delta_{0,t}}$$

$$+ \frac{1}{2}g''(c)\sum_{t>0}t^2\,(A_t - L_t)\,e^{-t\delta_{0,t}}$$

for some value of $c$ between 0 and $n$. The value of $c$ depends on the nature of the interest rate shock. If the present value of asset and liability cashflows are matched, and the first "moment" of their present values is matched under the current term structure (before the interest rate shock), then $\sum_{t>0} (A_t - L_t) e^{-\delta_{0,t}^*} = \sum_{t>0} t(A_t - L_t) e^{-\delta_{0,t}^*} = 0$. Note that since $g(0) = 0$, the first condition is not needed, and also, in general, first moments being matched is similar to, but not exactly the same as parallel shift duration matching for effective annual interest rates. Then,

If the interest rate shock is a parallel shift in the term structure, say

$$\delta_{0,t}^* = \delta_{0,t} + \varepsilon,$$

we have

$$g(t) = \frac{e^{-t\delta_{0,t}^*}}{e^{-t\delta_{0,t}}} - 1 = e^{-t\varepsilon} - 1,$$

and

$$g''(c) = \varepsilon^2 e^{-c\varepsilon},$$

so that

$$S^* - S = \frac{1}{2}\varepsilon^2 e^{-c\varepsilon} \sum_{t>0} t^2 (A_t - L_t) e^{-t\delta_{0,t}}.$$

If the usual Redington immunization requirement for immunization is satisfied ($2^{nd}$ moment of present value of asset minus liability is positive, $\sum_{t>0} t^2 (A_t - L_t) e^{-t\delta_{0,t}} \geq 0$), then $S^* - S \geq 0$ and the assets immunize the liabilities. This analysis is valid even if the term structure is not flat.

## 7.4 DEFINITIONS AND FORMULAS

### Definition 7.1 – Modified Duration

The modified duration, denoted $DM$ (sometimes referred to as "volatility") of the set of cashflows $K_1, K_2, \ldots$ is

$$DM = -\frac{\frac{d}{di}P}{P} = \frac{\sum_{t=1}^{n} tK_t(1+i)^{-t-1}}{P} = \frac{\sum_{t=1}^{n} tK_t(1+i)^{-t-1}}{\sum_{t=1}^{n} K_t(1+i)^{-t}}. \tag{7.3}$$

**Definition 7.2 – Macaulay Duration**

The Macaulay duration, denoted $D$, is usually referred to simply as "duration."

$$D = (1+i)\cdot DM = \frac{\sum_{t=1}^{n} tK_t(1+i)^{-t}}{P} = \frac{\sum_{t=1}^{n} tK_t(1+i)^{-t}}{\sum_{t=1}^{n} K_t(1+i)^{-t}}. \tag{7.4}$$

**Modified duration and Macaulay duration of an $n$-year zero coupon bond**

$$DM = -\frac{\frac{d}{di}P}{P} = \frac{n(1+i)^{-n-1}}{(1+i)^{-n}} = n(1+i)^{-1} = nv. \tag{7.1}$$

$$D = DM \cdot (1+i) = nv(1+i) = n.$$

**Approximate change in the present value of a set of cashflows**

$$P(i+h) - P(i) \doteq h\cdot\frac{d}{di}P(i) = -h\cdot P(i)\cdot DM. \tag{7.2}$$

**Macaulay duration of an $n$-year coupon bond**

$$D = \frac{\sum_{t=1}^{n} t\cdot Fr\cdot v_j^t + n\cdot F\cdot v_j^n}{\sum_{t=1}^{n} Fr\cdot v_j^t + F\cdot v_j^n}. \tag{7.5}$$

**Macaulay duration of a portfolio**

$$D = -(1+i)\frac{\frac{d}{di}X}{X} = \frac{\sum_{k=1}^{m} -(1+i)\frac{d}{di}X_k}{X} = \frac{\sum_{k=1}^{m} D_k\cdot X_k}{X}. \tag{7.6}$$

## Definition 7.3 – Redingtion Immunization

If asset cashflows are $A_t$ for $t = 0,1,...,n$ and liability cashflows are $L_t$ for $t = 0,1,...,n$, then the liability cashflows are Redington immunized by the asset cash flows at valuation rate $i_0$ if the following conditions are met

(i)
$$PV_A(i)\big|_{i_0} = PV_L(i)\big|_{i_0}$$

(ii)
$$\frac{d}{di}PV_A(i)\bigg|_{i_0} = \frac{d}{di}PV_L(i)\bigg|_{i_0}$$

(iii)
$$\frac{d^2}{di^2}PV_A(i)\bigg|_{i_0} > \frac{d^2}{di^2}PV_L(i)\bigg|_{i_0}.$$

## Definition 7.4 – Convexity

The convexity of s series of cashflows is the second derivative of the present value of the cashflows with respect to the rate of valuation.

$$\frac{\dfrac{d^2}{di^2}PV_A(i)\bigg|_{i_0}}{PV_A(i)\big|_{i_0}}$$

## Definition 7.5 – Full Immunization

A portfolio is **fully immunized** if $\sum A_t \cdot v^t \geq \sum L_t \cdot v^t$ for *any* $i > 0$.

## 7.5 NOTES AND REFERENCES

The concept of duration was introduced by Frederick Macaulay in the book titled *Some Theoretical Problems Suggested by the Movements of Interest Rates, Bond Yields and Stock Prices in the United States since 1856*, published by the National Bureau of Economic Research in 1938. The concept of duration was not widely used in practice until the 1970s.

The early development of immunization theory can be found in the paper *Review of the Principles of Life Office Valuations*, by F.M. Redington, published in the Journal of the Institute of Actuaries in 1952. A discussion of full immunization can be found in Chapter 10 of *An Introduction to the Mathematics of Finance*, by J.J. McCutcheon and W.F. Scott, published in 1986 by Oxford: Heinemann Professional Publishing. In a presentation to the 1993 AFIR (Actuarial Approach to Financial Risks) Colloquium, S. Coutts pronounced that "Immunization is Dead." The paper outlined a number of problems with Redington immunization, including its difficulty in dealing with a stochastic interest rate environment.

## 7.6   Exercises

### Section 7.1

7.1.1   A 3-year annual coupon bond has coupons of 10 per year starting one year from now and matures in 3 years for amount 100. The YTM for the bond is 11.8% (effective annual). Find the Macaulay duration for the bond.

7.1.2   Suppose that the yield rate and coupon rate on an $n$-coupon bond are the same. Show that the duration is $\ddot{a}_{\overline{n}|}$ valued at the yield rate. Find the duration of a 6-coupon bond with coupon rate 10% per coupon period and yield rate 10% per coupon period.

7.1.3   Use a computer spreadsheet program to repeat Example 7.3 for parameter values

$$r = .04, .06, .08; \quad n = 2, \ 10, 20, 40; \quad \text{and} \quad j = .03, .05, .07.$$

Holding two of the three parameters $r$, $n$, $j$ fixed, identify the behavior of $D$ as a function of the other parameter.

7.1.4 Show that the (annualized) Macaulay duration for a coupon bond redeemable at par with annual coupon rate $r^{(2)}$ per year (payable semiannually), and yield to maturity of $i^{(2)}$ per year (payable semiannually) with $n$ full coupon periods remaining, is

$$\frac{1+j}{2j} - \frac{1+j+n(r-j)}{2r\left[(1+j)^n - 1\right] + 2j}, \text{ where } r = \frac{1}{2}r^{(2)} \text{ and } j = \frac{1}{2}i^{(2)}.$$

7.1.5 Develop an expression for the duration of a level $n$-payment annuity-immediate of 1 per period with interest rate $i$ per period, and show that it is equal to $\frac{1}{d} - \frac{n}{is_{\overline{n}|i}}$.

7.1.6 Under the current market conditions Bond 1 has a price (per 100 of face amount) of 88.35 and a Macaulay duration of 12.7, and Bond 2 has a price (per 100 of face amount) of 130.49 and a Macaulay duration of 14.6 . A portfolio is created with a combination of face amount $F_1$ of Bond 1 and face amount $F_2$ of Bond 2. The combined face amount of the portfolio is $F_1 + F_2 = 100$, and the Macaulay duration of the portfolio is 13.5. Find the portfolio value.

*7.1.7 $D(r, n, j)$ denotes the duration of a bond of face amount $F$, with $n$ coupons at rate $r$ per coupon period, and with yield rate $j$. Find

(a) $\lim_{n \to \infty} D(r, n, j)$,

(d) $\lim_{r \to 0} D(r, n, j)$,

(b) $\lim_{n \to 1} D(r, n, j)$,

(e) $\lim_{j \to \infty} D(r, n, j)$, and

(c) $\lim_{r \to \infty} D(r, n, j)$,

(f) $\lim_{j \to 0} D(r, n, j)$,

*7.1.8 For the cashflow series with payments $K_1, K_2, \ldots, K_n$, made at times $1, 2, \ldots, n$, suppose that $L = \sum_{t=1}^{n} K_t \cdot v^t$ at rate $i_0$ per payment period. Show that $\frac{d}{di}\left[L(1+i)^D\right]\Big|_{i=i_0} = 0$, where $D$ is the Macaulay duration.

*7.1.9    Consider a bond with continuous coupons at rate $r$ per period and redemption amount 1 in $n$ periods, valued at yield rate $\delta$.

(a) Express $\frac{dL}{d\delta}$ in terms of continuous annuity symbols and the factors $r$, $n$ and $\delta$. The duration is $D = -\frac{1}{L} \cdot \frac{dL}{d\delta}$.

(b) Find an expression for $\frac{dD}{dn}$. Show that it has the same sign as

$$\delta + (r-\delta)\left[r(n-\overline{a}_{\overline{n}|}) + \delta\overline{a}_{\overline{n}|}\right],$$

so that if $r \geq \delta$, then $D$ increases with $n$, but if $r < \delta$, then $D$ is increasing for $n=0$ to $n=n_0$, and then is decreasing for $n > n_0$. This accounts for the smaller durations for the 60-coupon bonds than the 30-coupon bonds in line 1 of Table 7.1b and lines 1 and 2 of Table 7.1c.

*7.1.10   Verify algebraically that the duration of a coupon bond is a decreasing function of the coupon rate.

*7.1.11   Using a 3-year 10% bond with a face amount of 100 and term structure (i) of Exercise 6.1.3, find $\frac{d}{d\alpha} \sum_{t=1}^{14} K_t \left[1 + \frac{1}{2}(i_{0,.5t} + \alpha)\right]^{-t}$ and find $\frac{d}{d\alpha} \sum_{t=1}^{14} K_t \left[1 + \frac{1}{2}(.0990 + \alpha)\right]^{-t}$ at $\alpha = 0$.

*7.1.12   It is assumed that the term structure of interest rates is flat, so that the yield on a zero coupon bond with any time to maturity is $j > 0$ per year. An investor owns a portfolio of two bonds, one of which has present value 50,000 and Macaulay duration 8 years, and the other has present value 30,000 and Macaulay duration 6 years.

The investor would like to rebalance the portfolio so that the Macaulay duration of the portfolio becomes 7 years. The rebalancing will be done by selling some of one of the bonds to decrease the holding of that bond and using the proceeds to buy more of the other bond to increase its holding. The total value of the portfolio will still be 80,000 after rebalancing. Which of the following is the correct action to rebalance the portfolio?

(a) No action is needed since the portfolio already has a duration of 7 years.

(b) Sell 20,000 of the 6-year duration bond and buy 20,000 of the 8-year duration bond.

(c) Sell 10,000 of the 6-year duration bond and buy 10,000 of the 8-year duration bond.

(d) Sell 20,000 of the 8-year duration bond and buy 20,000 of the 6-year duration bond.

(e) Sell 10,000 of the 8-year duration bond and buy 10,000 of the 6-year duration bond.

*7.1.13 It is assumed that the term structure of interest rates is flat, so that the yield on a zero coupon bond with any time to maturity is $i$ per year. Two bonds with the same face amount and the same number $(n \geq 2)$ of annual coupons to maturity are being compared. Bond 1 has coupon rate $r_1$ (per year) and Bond 2 has coupon rate $r_2$ per year. If $r_2 > r_1 \geq 0$, which of the following statements is true about the bond prices $P_1$ and $P_2$ and the bond Macaulay durations $D_1$ and $D_2$?

(a) $P_1 > P_2$ and $D_1 > D_2$

(b) $P_1 < P_2$ and $D_1 > D_2$

(c) $P_1 > P_2$ and $D_1 < D_2$

(d) $P_1 < P_2$ and $D_1 < D_2$

(e) None of A, B, C, or D is true in general.

*7.1.14 Suppose that $K_t \geq 0$ for $t = 1, \ldots, n$ and at $K_t > 0$ for at least two values of $t$. Show that $\frac{d}{dj} D < 0$.

*7.1.15 Show that for an annual cashflow series with the first payment at time 1, $\lim_{j \to \infty} D = 1$.

## SECTION 7.2

7.2.1 Liabilities of 1 each are due at the ends of periods 1 and 2. There are three securities available to produce asset income to cover these liabilities, as follows:

(i) A bond due at the end of period 1 with coupon at rate 1% per period, valued at a periodic yield of 14%;

(ii) A bond due at the end of period 2 with coupon rate 2% per period, valued at a periodic yield of 15%;

(iii) A bond due at the end of period 2 with coupon rate 20% per period, valued at a periodic yield of 14.95%.

Determine the cost of the portfolio that exactly matches asset income to liabilities due using

(a) bonds (i) and (ii) only.

(b) bonds (i) and (iii) only

(c) Show that the combination of securities in (b) minimizes the cost of all exact-matching portfolios made up of a combination of the three securities. Note that the minimum cost exact-matching portfolio does not use the highest yielding security in this case.

7.2.2 In order to match asset income to the liabilities in Example 7.5 so that $PV_A(.10) = PV_L(.10)$, a level annual payment annuity-immediate with $n$ payments is purchased to provide the asset income flow. For each of $n = 5, 15, 50, 100$, find the required annual payment and calculate both $\sum t \cdot A_t \cdot v_{.10}^t$ and $\sum t^2 \cdot A_t \cdot v_{.10}^t$. Which value of $n$ provides the nearest match to the relation $\sum t \cdot A_t \cdot v_{.10}^t = \sum t \cdot L_t \cdot v_{.10}^t$? Solve for the exact value of $n$ for which $\sum t \cdot A_t \cdot v_{.10}^t = \sum t \cdot L_t \cdot v_{.10}^t$. Determine whether this provides Redington immunization for the portfolio.

7.2.3 (a) Show that Equation (7.9) is equivalent to Equation (7.12)

(b) Show that if Equation (7.9) is true, then Equation (7.10) is equivalent to Equation (7.13).

7.2.4    For each of the liabilities due in Example 7.5 find the values of $A_0$ and $A_{15}$ at $i = .10$, according to the method of full immunization described in Section 7.2. Find the total of all $A_0$'s and the total of all $A_{15}$'s separately, and show that this gives the same asset income as that found in part (a) of Example 7.7.

7.2.5    A liability of 1 is due at time 10. An attempt is made to fully immunize this liability at $i_0 = .10$ using two zero coupon bonds of amounts $A_{t_1}$ and $A_{t_2}$ due at times $t_1$ and $t_2$, respectively. In each of the following cases, solve for the two missing quantities out of $A_{t_1}, A_{t_2}, t_1, t_2$, given the other two.

(a)  $t_1 = 5, t_2 = 15$

(b) (i)   $t_1 = 5, A_{t_1} = .40$
     (ii)  $t_1 = 5, A_{t_1} = .70$ (no solution for $t_2 \geq 10$)

(c) (i)   $t_1 = 5, A_{t_2} = .90$ (two solutions for $t_2 \geq 10$)
     (ii)  $t_1 = 5, A_{t_2} = 1.5$ (one solution for $t_2 \geq 10$)
     (iii) $t_1 = 5, A_{t_2} = .75$ (no solutions for $t_2 \geq 10$)

(d) (i)   $t_2 = 15, A_{t_1} = .80$
     (ii)  $t_2 = 15, A_{t_1} = 1.1$ (no solution for $A_{t_2} \geq 0, 0 \leq t_1 \leq 10$)
     (iii) $t_2 = 15, A_{t_1} = .01$ (no solution for $0 \leq t_1 \leq 10$)

(e)  $A_{t_1} = .40, A_{t_2} = .90$

7.2.6    A financial institution has taken over the business of another company. One of the acquired liabilities is a capital redemption policy that obligates the payment of 1,000,000 by the institution to the policyholder in exactly 12 years, and requires the policyholder to make annual premium payments (at the start of each of the remaining 12 years) of 15,000. Out of the assets of the acquired company, the financial institution wants to allocate a single asset income payment $A_{t_0}$ to be made at time $t_0$ so that, along with the asset income represented by the premiums payable by the policyholder, the capital redemption policy will be fully immunized at the current interest rate of 10%. Find $t_0$ and the asset income amount $A_{t_0}$ that must be allocated, and show that this fully immunizes the policy.

7.2.7     Liability payments of 100 each are due to be paid in 2, 4 and 6 years from now. Asset cashflow consists of $A_1$ in 1 year and $A_5$ in 5 years. The yield for all payments is 10%. An attempt is made to have the asset cash flow immunize the liability cashflow by matching present value and duration.

       (a) Find $A_1$ and $A_5$.

       (b) Determine whether or not the conditions for Redington immunization are satisfied.

*7.2.8     (a) Consider the function $h'(i)$ for the portfolio of assets and liabilities in part (a) of Example 7.7. Use one of the methods of Section 5.1 to show that $h'(i) = 0$ has only one solution for $i \geq 0$. Note that $h(0) > 0, h(.10) = 0, \quad h'(.10) = 0$ and $\lim_{i \to \infty} h(i) = 149,195$. Use these facts to conclude that $h(i)$ has its overall minimum at $i = .10$.

       (b) Show that for (very) large values of $i$, $h(i) < 0$ for the portfolio of assets and liabilities in part (c) of Example 7.7. (Try increasing values of $i$, such as 200%, 400%, and so on.)

*7.2.9     (a) Multiply Equation (7.15) by $s$ and subtract Equation (7.16) to show that $a \cdot A_{t_1} \cdot v_{i_0}^{t_1} = b \cdot A_{t_2} \cdot v_{i_0}^{t_2}$.

       (b) Use part (a) to solve for $L_s$ in terms of $A_{t_1}, a, b$ and $v_{i_0}$.

       (c) Use parts (a) and (b) to write $h(i)$ as given in Equation (7.17).

*7.2.10    For each of parts (a), (b), and (c) of Example 7.7, determine $h(i)$ for $i = .03, .08, .12$ and $.20$.

*7.2.11 Let $i_0 > 0$, $L_s > 0$ and $s$ be given. Show that in each of the following cases there is a unique solution for the unknown quantities in Equations (7.15) and (7.16), with the solution consisting of positive numbers.

(a) $t_1 \le s$ and $t_2 \ge s$, with $t_1$ and $t_2$ given

(b) $t_2 \ge s$ and $A_{t_2}$ satisfying $A_{t_2} \cdot v_{i_0}^{t_2-s} \le \frac{s}{t_2} \cdot L_s$, with $t_2$ and $A_{t_2}$ given

(c) $t_1 \le s$ and $A_{t_1}$ satisfying $A_{t_1}(1+i_0)^{t_2-s} \le L_s$, with $t_1$ and $A_{t_1}$ given

(d) $t_2 \ge s$ and $A_{t_1} \le L_s$, with $t_2$ and $A_{t_1}$ given

*7.2.12 It is assumed that the term structure of interest rates is flat at $j = .08$ per year. Suppose that a company has liabilities consisting of 10 annual payments of 1000 each starting in one year. You are given:

$$\sum_{k=1}^{10} v_{.08}^k = 6.7101, \qquad \sum_{k=1}^{10} k v_{.08}^k = 32.6869,$$

$$\sum_{k=1}^{10} k^2 v_{.08}^k = 212.9687$$

(a) The company wishes to invest in assets in order to immunize the liabilities against small changes in $j$. The assets will consist of some cash now at time 0 and a zero coupon bond maturing at time 10. The present value and duration of the assets must match the present value and duration of the liabilities. Find how much of the asset portfolio should be in cash (nearest $1).

(b) Suppose that a liability of 5000 payable in 11 years is added to the existing liability payments. An attempt to immunize is made using the same two assets as in question (a). Which of the following statements is correct regarding the additional asset amount $C$ needed at time 10?

(i) $C \leq 5000$ and the assets immunize the liabilities (for small changes in $j$)

(ii) $C \leq 5000$ and the assets do not immunize the liabilities (for small changes in $j$)

(iii) $C > 5000$ and the assets immunize the liabilities (for small changes in $j$)

(iv) $C > 5000$ and the assets do not immunize the liabilities (for small changes in $j$)

(v) $C = 0$ and the assets do not immunize the liabilities (for small changes in $j$)

*7.2.13  Cash flow 1 consists of three payments: $A$ in 5 periods, $B$ in 10 periods and $C$ in 15 periods. Cash flow 2 consists of 2 payments: $X$ in 6 periods and $Y$ in 12 periods. As of now, at yield $j$ per period for all maturities, the two sets of cashflows have the same present value and the same Macaulay duration. Suppose that one period from now the yield is still $j$ for all maturities. Show that

(a) the two sets of cash flows will have the same present value;

(b) the two sets of cash flows have the same Macaulay duration at that time; and

(c) the Macaulay duration one period from now is exactly 1 less than it is now.

# CHAPTER 8

## EQUITY AND FIXED INCOME INVESTMENTS

*"The key to making money in stocks is to not be scared out of them."*
*– Peter Lynch, Vice-Chairman of Fidelity Investments*

### 8.1 THE DIVIDEND DISCOUNT MODEL OF STOCK VALUATION

When equities are actually bought and sold on a market, the trading takes place with buyers and sellers offering "bid" and "ask" prices, respectively, with an intermediate settlement price eventually found. The amount by which the ask price exceeds the bid is the "spread." This is the difference in price between the highest price that a buyer is willing to pay for an asset and the lowest price for which a seller is willing to sell it. This terminology applies to investments of all types, bonds (Chapter 4), equities, derivative investments (Chapter 9), etc. Some assets are more liquid than others and this may affect the size of the spread.

Shares of common stock represent ownership in a corporation, entitling the stockholder to certain privileges including the right to vote on matters regarding the management of the corporation. In addition the common stock owner, from time to time, receives **dividends** that reflect a share of the profit earned by the corporation.

Among the many factors affecting the price of a stock are the nature of the company's business, the quality of the company's management, current economic conditions, and forecasts of future conditions as they relate to the company's current and prospective profitability. An investor in stock would be looking for a return on that investment in the form of future dividends and share price increases. For an investor with a long-term outlook, intending to hold the stock indefinitely, the price (or value) of the stock might be regarded as the present value of future dividends expected to be paid on the stock. If $d_t$ denotes the expected dividend payable at the end of the $t^{th}$ year (with time measured from the purchase date of the stock), and $i$ is the (long-term) annual rate of valuation for this investment, then according to the **dividend discount model for valuing stocks**, the price of the stock can be:

$$P = \sum_{t=1}^{\infty} \frac{d_t}{(1+i)^t}. \qquad (8.1a)$$

Another formulation would use separate forward rates of interest for each year for valuation, so that

$$P = \frac{d_1}{(1+i_0(0,1))} + \frac{d_2}{(1+i_0(0,1))(1+i_0(1,2))} + \cdots. \qquad (8.1b)$$

Yet another formulation is based on spot rates, $s_0(t)$, for discounting payments:

$$P = \frac{d_1}{(1+s_0(1))} + \frac{d_2}{(1+s_0(2))^2} + \cdots. \qquad (8.1c)$$

A stock is a more risky security than a government bond, so the term structure of spot rates that relate to risk-free zero-coupon bonds would not be appropriate for valuation of dividends on a stock.

**EXAMPLE 8.1** | (*Stock Valuation Using Dividend Discount Model*)

A stock is expected to pay dividends at the end of each year indefinitely. An investor wishes to receive an effective annual return of 5%. Find the stock price based on the dividend discount model in each of the following cases:

(a) dividends are level at $2 per year, and

(b) the first dividend is $2, and subsequent dividends increase by 2% every year.

**SOLUTION**

(a) The price is the present value of a perpetuity-immediate. In this case, the price is $\frac{2}{.05} = 40$.

(b)   The price is the present value of a geometrically increasing perpetuity-immediate. The price is $\frac{2}{.05-.02} = 66.67$.   □

## 8.2 SHORT SALE OF STOCK IN PRACTICE

Stocks are bought by investors who anticipate gains from dividends and increases in share prices. The typical way in which to invest in a stock is to buy the stock now, wait (and hope) for a price increase, and sell the stock later; *buy low and sell high.* IF the stock is purchased and paid fully in cash, this is referred to as an **outright purchase.** If the entire purchase price is borrowed, this is referred to as a **fully leveraged purchase.**

Owning an asset is often referred to as having a **long** position in the asset. An alternative way to buy low and sell high is to reverse the order of buying and selling. The stock investor can try to sell high (first) and buy low (later). Arranging the stock investment in this way is done by means of a **short sale** of the stock.

An investor who believes the share price of a stock will fall over a period of time can **sell short** the stock (sell something he does not own) at the current price and cover or close the short sale (buy the stock) at a later date when (he hopes) the stock can be purchased at a lower price. In theory, the short seller is "borrowing" the stock from someone who owns it then later selling it (at whatever the market price is at that time). The loan is repaid by giving the lender back the stock at the later date. This requires the short seller to buy the stock at the later date (at whatever the market price is at that time) in order to be able to repay the lender. The lender never relinquishes ownership in the stock, and is entitled to any benefits that result from stock ownership, specifically dividends. Therefore, when the loan of the stock is repaid, the borrower (short seller) must provide the lender (the actual owner of the stock) with the stock that was borrowed plus any dividends that the stock had paid during the time of the loan. If the dividends were payable before the short sale is closed, there may be interest due on the dividends from the time of dividend payment to the time of the close of the short sale, or the dividends might be paid to the actual owner of the stock as they come due.

Suppose that the value of the stock is $S_0$ at the time the short sale is opened, and the value of the stock is $S_1$ at the time the short sale is closed (the stock is bought back). When the short sale is closed, the net gain made by the short seller is $S_0 - S_1$ (the price when the stock was sold minus the price when the stock was bought). This net gain will be positive if $S_1 < S_0$, so that the stock is bought for less than the price at which it was sold. In other words, the short seller has a positive net gain if the stock price drops from the time the short sale was initiated to the time the short sale is terminated. The short seller will experience a net loss on the transaction if $S_1 > S_0$. If the stock paid a dividend of amount $D$, then the short seller must pay that amount to the original owner of the stock, and the net gain made by the short seller becomes $S_0 - S_1 - D$ (and interest will be payable on the dividend if it was payable before the short sale was terminated).

In practice, this transaction is arranged through an investment dealer. The dealer will take the position of the lender of the stock in the short sale, meaning that the investment dealer is owed the shares borrowed and sold by the short seller, with the understanding that the short seller will eventually purchase the stock and give it to the dealer. When an investor is a short seller of stock, the investment dealer who executes the transaction will usually require a certain amount of **margin** from the short seller at the time the short sale is made. This margin is "good faith" money, and may be up to 50% of the value of the stock at the time the short sale is made, and it is held in an account administered by the investment dealer (the margin account). If the stock pays a dividend before the short position is closed, the short seller must pay the dividend amount to the investment dealer, or the amount is deducted from the margin account. The money in the margin account is owned by the investor, and the dealer may pay interest on the account. A simplified view of a short sale transaction that is initiated at time 0 and completed at time 1 can be summarized as follows.

(i)   Stock price at time 0 is $S_0$.

(ii)  Margin required at time 0 is $M$.

(iii) Margin account pays interest at rate $i$ per period.

(iv)  Stock pays dividend of amount $D$ at time 1.

(v)   Stock price at time 1 is $S_1$.

| Time: | 0 | 1 |
|-------|---|---|
| | Deposit margin $M$ <br> Sell stock for $S_0$ | Margin has grown to $M(1+i)$ <br> Buy stock for $S_1$ <br> Pay dividend $D$ |

**FIGURE 8.1**

The short seller opens the margin account at time 0 with a deposit of amount $M$. The short sale is initiated at time 0. The short seller has a "short sale credit" of amount $S_0$ as a result of selling the stock for that amount. This amount $S_0$ does not appear in the margin account, since it represents money that was obtained by selling the borrowed stock, so it is not really the property of the short seller. At time 1, the original margin deposit of $M$ into the margin account will have grown with interest to $M(1+i)$. Also at time 1, when the short sale is terminated, the investor must "pay" $S_1$ to buy the stock. The net gain on the short sale transaction is $S_0 - S_1$, and this actual dollar amount is added to the margin account, increasing the balance if $S_0 - S_1 > 0$ and decreasing the balance if $S_0 - S_1 < 0$. At time 1 the dividend is payable, and that amount is deducted from the margin account. The net amount in the margin account at time 1, after interest is added to the margin account, and after the short sale is closed and the dividend is paid is $M(1+i) + S_0 - S_1 - D$. Therefore, an initial investment of amount $M$ (the original margin deposit required) has grown to $M(1+i) + S_0 - S_1 - D$ over the course of the period. The actual return or yield $j$ earned by the short sale investor over the period is found from the relationship

$$M(1+j) = M(1+i) + S_0 - S_1 - D. \qquad (8.2)$$

**EXAMPLE 8.2**   (*Short Sale of Stock*)

The margin requirement on a short sale of stock is 50% of the value of the stock, and the margin account pays 10% per year. The value of the stock being sold short is 100 at the start of the year. The stock is sold short at the start of the year, and the short sale is closed at the end of the year at the time a dividend of 5 is paid. Find the net return earned by a short seller over the one year period if the stock price at the end of the year is

(a) 90          (b) 100          (c) 110.

---

| SOLUTION |
|---|

The amount of margin required is 50 at the start of the year. The balance in the margin account at the end of the year is

$$50(1.1) + 100 - S_1 - 5 = 150 - S_1.$$

For the three cases considered, this amount will be

(a) 60                   (b) 50                (c) 40.

The net return earned by the short seller in these cases will be

(a) $\frac{60}{50} - 1 = .20$,       (b) $\frac{50}{50} - 1 = 0$,       (c) $\frac{40}{50} - 1 = -.20$.   ❏

The equity in the short seller's margin account is regularly updated when there are movements in the stock price. If the stock price increases, the short seller may be required to add to the margin account to maintain a minimum margin level (this is a *margin call*). This is illustrated in the following example.

| EXAMPLE 8.3 | *(Short sale of stock)*
|---|---|

The current price of a share of stock in Corporation XYZ is 50. Smith sells short 1000 shares of XYZ stock. Smith's investment dealer charges a commission of 2% of the value of stock purchased or sold short and also requires that Smith open a margin account for the short sale. While Smith is "short the stock," the margin account must maintain a balance of at least 40% of the value of the stock. Thus, when the short sale is initiated, Smith must deposit 20,000 into the margin account, and pay the investment dealer a commission of 1000. It is assumed that the margin account earns no interest.

(a) Suppose that the stock price drops to 40, at which time Smith "covers the short sale." If the commission on the stock purchase is deducted from the margin account, find the equity in the account after the short sale is covered.

(b) Repeat part (a) if the price rises to 60. Suppose that the price rises to 60 but Smith does not wish to cover the short sale yet. Find the amount Smith must add to the margin account to maintain the required balance of 40% of the stock value.

(c) Suppose that the stock pays a dividend of 2 per share while the short sale is in effect. Find the least amount by which the share price must drop in order that Smith not get a "margin call" to add to the margin account to maintain the 40% minimum balance.

SOLUTION

(a) When Smith sells the stock short, Smith has a credit of 70,000 (the 50,000 sale price of the stock and the 20,000 in the margin account) and owes 1000 shares of stock. At a price of 40, the cost of purchasing the stock is 40,000 plus 800 in commission. Smith's equity after the transaction is then $70,000 - 40,800 = 29,200$. Smith's overall gain is 9,200 minus the initial 1000 commission on the short sale, for a net gain, after commissions, of 8200. Smith's gain could also have been found as $1000 \times (50-40) - commission = 10,000 - 1800 = 8200$. Smith has made a gain of 8200 on an investment of 20,000, resulting in a return of 41% on the transaction.

(b) Smith must now have a margin account balance of

$$.40 \times 60,000 = 24,000,$$

and so must add 4000 to the margin account.

(c) Smith's account has 2000 deducted to pay for dividends, leaving a balance of 18,000. In order for the account to be at least 40% of the stock value, it must be the case that $18,000 \geq .40 \times 1000 \times P$. Thus, $P \leq 45$, so that the stock must drop in value by at least 5 in order to avoid a margin call. ❑

We have described how a short sale takes place in practice. In the next chapter we will look at short selling from a more theoretical financial point of view. We will refer to the method of short selling just described as the *practical method of short selling*.

It is also possible to purchase stock "on margin." This means that the stock purchaser opens a margin account with an investment dealer, but the amount required in the margin account is a fraction of the actual stock price, just as in the case of a short sale. Example 8.3 could be repeated in the case of a purchase of stock on margin.

Many types of assets other than stocks can be sold short. In theoretical models of financial markets, it is often assumed that any asset can be either purchased or sold short for the same price at any time. In practice, availability of supply will be a factor when considering a short sale. We will consider some theoretical models of financial markets in Chapter 9.

---

**Naked Short Selling**

The short sale of a stock involves borrowing the stock, selling it, and purchasing it later to repay the party from which it is was borrowed. When the short seller sells the stock, the purchaser receives the stock, or expects to receive it at some time soon after the sale. A "naked short sale" is a sale in which the short seller has not actually borrowed or arranged to borrow the stock. A risk associated with this practice is that the short seller may have difficulty actually delivering the stock to the party to whom it was sold.

On February 3, 2005 the shares of the video rental company Movie Gallery Inc, dropped 20%, the largest drop in over 10 years of trading. It was later discovered that there had been short sales of 750,000 shares that day, about 2.5% of the company's shares in the market. Daily short sales averaged 370,000 in the first week of February, 2005 and the stock price dropped 36%. It was also discovered that growing numbers of short sellers weren't delivering the shares to the buyers. There was no serious underlying financial reason for the precipitous drop in the stock price. Naked short sales accounted for much of the short selling, but the selling frenzy in Movie Gallery's shares created the impression that the company was experiencing financial difficulties and the share price was driven down.

Stock market regulations are continually reviewed and modified to try to deal with all types of improper and manipulative trading practices. For example, the SEC (Securities Exchange Commission, the main stock market regulator in the US) now has a rule that states that if a company has accumulated unsettled trades of at least 10,000 shares and 0.5% of the company's outstanding stock for five consecutive trading days, it is subject to restrictions on future short sales.

Source: www.bloomberg.com

## 8.3   ADDITIONAL EQUITY INVESTMENTS

Along with investment in (or short sale of) individual stocks, there are investment alternatives that allow the investor to own part of a group of stocks. Mutual funds and exchange traded funds are two popular investments of this type.

### 8.3.1 MUTUAL FUNDS

An investment company can pool the money of many individual investors and purchase various types of financial instruments such as stocks, and/or bonds. Each individual would own a portion of the fund determined by the amount invested as a fraction of the total value of the fund. The individual's ownership in a mutual fund is represented by a number of fund units. The price per unit would be found as the total value of the fund divided by the number of units held by individual investors. As new investors purchase units the fund managers continue to buy investments. If an investor wishes to sells units, the fund company can buy back the units and may have to sell some investments to raise money needed to pay the investor. The price per unit is usually updated at the end of each trading day. The daily updated price takes into account changes in value of the investments owned by the fund. The daily unit price would also take into account the change, if any, in the number of units of the fund being held by investors, since additional units may have been purchased or existing units may have been redeemed during the day.

The fund would be managed by investment professionals who make the decisions as to what instruments in which to invest. Some funds are designed to invest in specialized sectors of the financial markets. For instance, a fund can invest mainly in energy stocks, such as those of oil and gas exploration companies, or electrical utility companies. The investment managers would generally charge an annual fee, typically anywhere from 1% to 3% of the fund's value. There are thousands of mutual funds available, ranging in size from a few million to many billions of dollars.

An individual investing in a mutual fund has the advantage of diversifying the investment over the range of instruments owned by the fund. Another (possible) advantage is the benefit of the expertise of the investment fund manager. Mutual funds are generally quite liquid investments, with valuations updated each day.

## 8.3.2 STOCK INDEXES AND EXCHANGE TRADED FUNDS

A stock index is a portfolio of securities that represents all of, or a portion of, an overall stock market. It is generally used to track the performance of a group of stocks, which can act as valuable benchmark against which to measure the change in share price for public companies.

Indexes show trends and changes in investing patterns, and are usually expressed in terms of a change from an original or a base value. This movement of the index number up or down — or the percent change over time — gives you a good idea of the overall performance of the index.

Each index has its own calculation methodology. Most indices, however, weigh companies based on market capitalization. For example, if a company's market cap is $2,000,000 and the value of all stocks in the index is $200,000,000, then the company would be worth 1% of the index.

Popular indexes include the S&P/TSX Composite Index in Canada, the S&P 500, Dow Jones Industrial Average, and Nasdaq in the US, and FTSE in London.

One of the motivations for investing in a mutual fund is to obtain a diversified market return that has less risk than an individual stock might have. An alternative to mutual funds that has become popular in recent years is exchange traded funds. An exchange traded fund tracks a particular market index, such as the Dow Jones Industrial, or the Standard and Poor's 500 (index of 500 major stocks). The fund trades like a stock and is listed on a major market, and can be bought or sold at any time during a trading day. A mutual fund has its value updated at the end of each trading day, whereas the value of an exchange traded fund fluctuates constantly throughout the day as the price of an individual stock would. Exchange traded funds tend to have smaller management fees than mutual funds, since there is no "investment expertise" in the management of the exchange traded fund since its value always runs parallel to the index that it is tracking.

### 8.3.3 OVER-THE-COUNTER MARKET

The over-the-counter market refers to a decentralized market of securities not listed on an exchange where market participants trade over the telephone or over an electronic network instead of a physical trading floor. There is no central exchange or actual location for this market. It is also referred to as the "OTC market."

In the OTC market, trading occurs via a network of dealers, who carry inventories of securities to facilitate the buy and sell orders of investors, rather than providing the order matchmaking service seen in exchanges such as the NYSE. Although stocks that are traded over the counter are often more speculative than stocks listed on established exchanges, virtually all government and municipal bonds and most corporate bonds are traded in the OTC market. Many derivatives (see Chapter 9) are traded in the OTC market.

### 8.3.4 CAPITAL ASSET PRICING MODEL

A stock will have a certain amount of risk associated with it. The stock's price is influenced by prices in the stock market as a whole, so that part of the risk, called the *market risk* (or *systematic risk* or non-*diversifiable risk*), for an individual stock will be related to general factors that affect the overall economy. In addition, because of the specific nature of the stock's industry group and the position of the issuing corporation in that industry, there will be *non-market risk* or *diversifiable risk*. Diversifiable risk can be managed by carefully choosing the mix of stocks in the overall portfolio. If an investor's portfolio exactly matches that used to measure overall market performance, such as the portfolio used for the Dow Jones index or the Standard & Poor's index, then the risk of the portfolio will be entirely market risk as measured by the standard portfolio. The market and non-market risks are generally assumed to be independent.

The valuation rate (or sequence of rates) used in price formulas (8.1) for a specific stock, may be related to the risk classification of that stock.

The relationship between the rate of return on a stock over a period of time and the average return of a broad market portfolio such as Standard and Poor's 500 index during the same period is represented by the stock's *characteristic line*, given by

$$\underset{\sim}{R}_s = \alpha_s + \beta_s \cdot \underset{\sim}{R}_m + \underset{\sim}{e}_s, \tag{8.3}$$

where $\underset{\sim}{R}_s$ is the (random) return on the stock for the period under consideration, $\alpha_s$ is the part of the stock's return not related to the market, $\beta_s$ is the expected change in $\underset{\sim}{R}_s$, given a change of 1 unit in the market return $\underset{\sim}{R}_m$, $\underset{\sim}{R}_m$ is the (random) return on the entire market for the period, and $\underset{\sim}{e}_s$ is a random variable (with mean 0) measuring the non-market risk (usually assumed to be independent of $\underset{\sim}{R}_m$).

The factor $\beta_s$ is called the *beta* of the stock, and measures the volatility of the stock's return in relation to the return on the entire market. The larger the beta for a stock, the larger the expected return and the larger the risk (standard deviation of return). These parameters change over time; estimates of $\alpha_s$ and $\beta_s$ can be obtained using statistical regression based on historical data.

Taking the expected value of both sides of Equation (8.3) results in

$$\overline{R}_s = \alpha_s + \beta_s \cdot \overline{R}_m. \qquad (8.4)$$

Under reasonable assumptions regarding investor behavior, this relationship can be written as the **Capital Asset Pricing Model**

$$\overline{R}_s = R_f + \beta_s (\overline{R}_m - R_f). \qquad (8.5)$$

In Equation (8.5) $R_f$ denotes the risk-free rate of return available, as measured by an appropriate government security. We do not derive this model in this text.

## 8.4 FIXED INCOME INVESTMENTS

Chapter 4 considered many aspects of bond valuation. Coupon bonds and zero coupon bonds are examples of "fixed income investments." Bonds issued by the federal government provide a safe and predictable income stream. Investors who are willing to tolerate some risk of default in exchange for a (potentially) higher return can invest in bonds issued by a less secure borrower such as a municipal government or a corporation.

Some states and municipalities issue bonds that have coupons which are totally or partially tax exempt. Depending on the tax situation of an investor, this might be a desirable feature of the income received.

Bond rating agencies such as Standard and Poor's and Dominion Bond Rating Service provide credit ratings of many kinds of fixed income investments. These credit ratings are a measure of the risk that an investor faces that some of the scheduled fixed income payments might not be made due to default on the part of the bond issuer. Example 8.5 later in this chapter considers the tradeoff between higher risk and higher return on a bond. There are a number of fixed income investments besides bonds that are available to investors. In this section we will briefly describe several of these types of investments.

### 8.4.1 CERTIFICATES OF DEPOSIT

A Certificate of Deposit (CD) is a deposit that an investor makes to a bank, savings and loan, or credit union. In Canada CDs are called Guaranteed Investment Certificates (GIC). The interest rate and maturity date on a CD is usually fixed at the time the deposit is made. CDs are generally insured by the federal government through the US Federal Deposit Insurance Corporation or the Canadian Deposit Insurance Corporation for principal amounts up to $100,000. For CDs that are arranged for maturities less than a year, principal and interest are returned together at the time of maturity. For a CD that has a maturity of longer than one year, interest payments are usually arranged to be paid semi-annually or annually, with the principal amount returned at the time of maturity.

### 8.4.2 MONEY MARKET FUNDS

A money market fund is a mutual fund that invests in mostly very short term, highly secure instruments such as government treasury bills and CDs. Technically, a money market fund is a mutual fund. But practically, it is close to being a savings account without the guarantees provided with bank accounts. The fund tends to earn a higher rate of interest than is available in typical bank savings accounts, and usually pays interest every month, but it may require an initial investment that is several thousand dollars. Some money market funds allow the account holder to write checks. Money in the fund is generally available to the account holder at short notice.

### 8.4.3 MORTGAGE-BACKED SECURITIES (MBS)

When an individual takes a mortgage loan on a property, it is not unusual for the individual to have the loan insured. The Federal Housing Authority (FHA) is a US government agency that provides such insurance. This provides some security to lenders who grant mortgage loans. The Government National Mortgage Association (GNMA) provides federal government backing that guarantees the loan payments on these federally insured mortgages.

Lending institutions can pool together a number of mortgage loans and sell shares of the loans to individual investors. For mortgages that are insured by the FHA, this federal government guarantee makes Mortgage Backed Securities (MBS) very secure investments.

The investor in an MBS becomes, in a sense, the lender who then receives mortgage payments from the borrowers. An investor receives monthly payments which reflect a share of the monthly payments being made by the borrowers on the underlying mortgages.

Mortgage loans often have a provision that allows the borrower to repay principal before the scheduled end of the mortgage loan; these are called prepayments. When prepayments take place on a mortgage held in an MBS, the prepayment is spread among the various investors. There is a risk to the MBS investor that prepayments will result in the investment maturing earlier than was originally scheduled in the pool of mortgages.

MBS investments can provide a secure monthly income with annual returns that tend to be up to 2% higher than yields on medium term (5 to 10 year) treasury bonds. There is also a very liquid secondary market in MBS securities.

## The Subprime Loan Crisis

In the Fall of 2006 the housing loan market began to experience a sharp rise in mortgage foreclosures. A combination of factors led to this crisis in foreclosures.

During the early and middle part of the 2000's decade, interest rates in the US reached historical lows and mortgage loans were made at these relatively low rates. At the same time, house prices were rising rapidly and lenders were making loans to house buyers who had a small (or no) down payment on the property. In addition, many of these loans were made to high risk borrowers with no credit rating or even poor credit history. These loans tended not to be insured by a government mortgage loan insuring agency.

Interest rates began to rise in the second half of the decade, and when mortgage loan rates were reset at significantly higher levels, many borrowers were not able to carry the debt load and mortgage foreclosures resulted. It was a perfect storm of higher interest rates, slowing down (or decline) of housing prices, high debt loads, and high risk borrowers.

Lenders had packaged and resold many of these subprime loans to investors who were either not aware of the risks involved or chose to ignore them. The investments that held subprime mortgage loans were not only traditional mortgage backed securities. Subprime loans were included in many other investment packages that traditionally were considered lower risk. As these various investments began to under-perform or even collapse, a wave of fear of investing in many types of fixed income investments rippled through the financial world. This led to a liquidity crisis in which lenders who would normally be willing to finance various types of investments important for the normal operation of the economy became less willing to invest.

At the time this book is being written, the subprime crisis is not yet over, and there are efforts being made by governments and large financial institutions to restore stability to the fixed income market and, in particular, to the mortgage lending market.

## 8.4.4 Collateralized Debt Obligations (CDO)

An investment bank or other financial institution may construct a collection of assets, including mortgages, credit card debt, and other types of loans, and sell parts of that package to various investors. The investors are buying the income produced by the borrowers making debt payments.

The collateral in the loans may be real property, as in the case of mortgages, corporate bonds, and other structured debts. This collection of assets is called a collateralized debt obligation. The investment bank that packages the CDO gets income in the form of a commission for the sale of parts of the CDO. A mortgage backed security is an example of a CDO.

There can be varying degrees of risk in the assets in a CDO. The CDO might be divided into "layers" (called "tranches" in financial practice). Each tranche would have its own risk of default and its own expected return. An investor would choose which tranches in which to invest. When there is default in some of the assets in a CDO, it is the investors in the highest risk tranches that lose principal first, and losses of principal are applied in order of the risk rating of the tranches.

## 8.4.5 Treasury Inflation Protected Securities (TIPS) and Real Return Bonds

The US federal treasury and the Bank of Canada issue inflation protected bonds. The structure of a TIPS is similar to that of a standard coupon bond in that there is a coupon rate and maturity amount. The difference is that the maturity amount is regularly adjusted based on the rate of inflation that has occurred since the TIPS was issued. When it is time for a coupon payment, the coupon rate is multiplied by the inflation-adjusted maturity amount. At the time of maturity, the amount paid is the inflation-adjusted maturity amount based on the accumulated inflation rate since the TIPS was issued.

---

**EXAMPLE 8.4** (*TIPS*)

Suppose that the coupon rate on a TIPS is 5% every six months and the maturity amount of the bond is 10,000 at the time the bond is issued, with the bond to mature 2 years after it is issued. Furthermore, suppose that we set the Consumer Price Index (CPI) to 1 at the time the bond is issued. Suppose that the CPI over the next 2 years has the following values:

| Time | 6-month | 12-month | 18-month | 24-month |
|------|---------|----------|----------|----------|
| CPI  | 1.02    | 1.03     | 1.06     | 1.08     |

Determine the final maturity amount and the coupon amounts on each payment date.

| SOLUTION |

The maturity amount will be updated on each coupon payment date, and on the maturity date, and the coupon amount will be 5% of the inflation-adjusted maturity value.

| Time | 6-month | 12-month | 18-month | 24-month |
|------|---------|----------|----------|----------|
| Adj. Mat. Value | 10,200 | 10,300 | 10,600 | 10,800 |
| Coupon | 510 | 515 | 530 | 540 |

On the maturity date the maturity amount paid to the bondholder will be 10,800. ❐

## 8.4.6 BOND DEFAULT AND RISK PREMIUM

One issuer of a bond may not be as financially stable or secure as another. Based on various analyses of the bond issuer, such as historical performance as to default, the performance of the industry group with which the issuing company is associated, and so on, it may be possible to estimate probabilities of default. There are a number of bond-rating services which classify borrowers as to their creditworthiness, with ranks from AAA (highest) to C (lowest).

This concept was mentioned in Chapter 4. The risk of loss of principal or loss of a financial reward stemming from a borrower's failure to repay a loan or otherwise meet a contractual obligation is referred to as **credit risk**. Credit risk arises whenever a borrower is expecting to use future cash flows to pay a current debt, such as in the case of a bond. Investors are compensated for assuming credit risk by way of interest payments from the borrower or issuer of a debt obligation. Credit risk is closely tied to the potential return of an investment, the most notable being that the yields on bonds correlate strongly to their perceived credit risk.

---

███ **EXAMPLE 8.5** ███ (*Default risk*)

Analysis of a bond with 3 years remaining until maturity indicates an estimated probability of default of 5% in any given coupon period until maturity as long as default has not yet occurred. The bond has a nominal annual coupon rate of 14%, payable semiannually, and a face amount of 100,000. If default occurs, the bond will pay no coupon for the affected coupon period but will pay 50% of the redemption amount at the time of default and no further coupons. Using expected present value, what price should an investor pay for the bond based on an annual yield of 12%, payable semiannually?

**SOLUTION**

With a reference point of $t = 0$ (where $t = 6$ represents the maturity date), the probabilities of default each period are as follows:

| Period | Default Probability | Probability of Full Payment |
|:---:|:---:|:---:|
| 1 | .05 | .95 |
| 2 | $(.95)(.05)$ | $(.95)^2$ |
| 3 | $(.95)^2(.05)$ | $(.95)^3$ |
| 4 | $(.95)^3(.05)$ | $(.95)^4$ |
| 5 | $(.95)^4(.05)$ | $(.95)^5$ |
| 6 | $(.95)^5(.05)$ | $(.95)^6$ |

We can find the total expected present value in two ways. The first approach is to find the expected payment at each of times 1 to 6 and sum them.

The possible payments at time 1 are 7000 (the coupon if default doesn't take place during the first coupon period, with probability .95) and 50,000 (reduced redemption if default occurred, with probability .05). The expected present value is $\left[7000(.95) + 50,000(.05)\right]v$.

The possible payments at time 2 are 7000 (if default hasn't occurred during the first 2 periods, this has probability $.95^2$), 50,000 (if default occurs in the $2^{nd}$ period, this has probability $(.95)(.05)$) and 0 (if default occurred in the first period, this has probability .05), with expected present value $\left[7000(.95)^2 + 50,000(.95)(.05)\right]v^2$.

Continuing in this way to time 6, we get that the total expected present value of the coupons, default payment, and redemption amount is

$$
\begin{aligned}
&\left[7000(.95)+50,000(.05)v\right] \\
&\quad+\left[7000(.95)^2+50,000(.95)(.05)\right]v^2 \\
&\qquad+\left[7000(.95)^3+50,000(.95)^2(.05)\right]v^3 \\
&\qquad\quad+\left[7000(.95)^4+50,000(.95)^3(.05)\right]v^4 \\
&\qquad\qquad+\left[7000(.95)^5+50,000(.95)^4(.05)\right]v^5 \\
&\qquad\qquad\quad+\left[107,000(.95)^6+50,000(.95)^5(.05)\right]v^6 = 91,897.18.
\end{aligned}
$$

As an alternative approach, we can find the total present value received for each of 7 possible events:

(1) default in period 1, (2) default in period 2,..., (6) default in period 6, (7) no default. In event (1), the total present value received is $50,000v$, with probability .05. In event (2), the total present value received is $7000v+50,000v^2$, with probability $(.95)(.05)$. Continuing in this way leads to the same expected present value as the first approach.

At the price of 91,897.18, if all coupon payments are met and the redemption amount is paid, the yield on the bond would be $i^{(2)}=.1759$.

The difference between the *promised yield to maturity* of 17.59% and the *expected yield to maturity* of 12% in Example 8.5 is the *default premium* on the bond, which is 5.59%. The expected yield rate on a bond which has a risk of default will be larger than the yield on a government (risk-free) bond with the same coupon rate and time to maturity. The difference between this expected yield (12% in Example 8.5) and the yield on the corresponding risk-free bond (say 8%) is called the *risk premium*. The total of the *risk premium* and the default premium on a bond is the *yield spread* for that bond (4% + 5.59% = 9.59% in Example 8.5). ❏

## 8.4.7 CONVERTIBLE BONDS

**Convertible bond** usually refers to a bond that can be converted into a predetermined amount of the company's equity at certain times during its life, usually at the discretion of the bondholder.

Convertible bonds start out as bonds. They have a coupon payment and are legally debt securities, which rank prior to all equity securities in a default situation. Their value, like all bonds, depends on the level of prevailing interest rates and the credit quality of the issuer.

The exchange feature of a convertible bond gives the right for the holder to convert the par amount of the bond for common shares at a specified price or **conversion ratio**. For example, a conversion ratio might give the holder the right to convert $100 par amount of the convertible bonds into common shares at $25 per share. This conversion ratio would be said to be **4:1** or **four-to-one**.

The share price affects the value of a convertible bond substantially. Taking our example, if the shares were trading at $10, and the convertible was at a market price of $100, there would be no economic reason for an investor to convert the convertible bonds. For $100 par amount of the bond the investor would only get 4 shares with a market value of $40. You might ask why the convertible was trading at $100 in this case. The answer would be that the yield of the bond justified this price. If the normal bonds were trading at 10% yields and the yield of the convertible was 10%, bond investors would buy the bond and keep it at $100. A convertible bond with an **exercise price** far higher than the market price of the stock is called a **busted convertible** and generally trades at its bond value, although the yield is usually a little higher due to its lower or "subordinate" credit status.

Think of the opposite. When the share price attached to the bond is sufficiently high or **in the money**, the convertible begins to trade more like an equity. If the exercise price is much lower than the market price of the common shares, the holder of the convertible can attractively convert into the stock. If the exercise price is $25 and the stock is trading at $50, the holder can get 4 shares for $100 par amount that have a market value of $200. This would force the price of the convertible above the bond value and its market price should be above $200 since it would have a higher yield than the common shares.

Issuers sell convertible bonds to provide a higher current yield to investors and equity capital upon conversion. Investors buy convertible bonds to gain a higher current yield and less downside, since the convertible should trade to its bond value in the case of a steep drop in the common share price.

A **mandatory convertible bond** is a type of convertible bond that has a required conversion or redemption feature. Either on or before a contractual conversion date, the holder must convert the mandatory convertible into the underlying common stock. These securities provide investors with higher yields to compensate holders for the mandatory conversion structure.

## 8.5 DEFINITIONS AND FORMULAS

**Dividend Discount Model for valuing stocks**

$$P = \sum_{t=1}^{\infty} \frac{d_t}{(1+i)^t}. \qquad (8.1a)$$

**Capital Asset Pricing Model**

$$\overline{R}_s = R_f + \beta_s(\overline{R}_m - R_f). \qquad (8.5)$$

## 8.6 NOTES AND REFERENCES

A discussion of default premium and risk premium can be found in *Investments* by W. Sharpe, published by Prentice-Hall. Section 8.4.7 is based partly on a description of convertible bonds found at www.finpipe.com.

## 8.7 EXERCISES

### SECTION 8.1

8.1.1    Stock of the XYZ Corporation is expected to pay annual dividends in the years to come. The next dividend will be of amount 1.00 and is due one year from now. Dividends are expected to grow at the rate of 5% per year. A prospective purchaser plans to hold the stock for 10 years. The purchaser uses an effective annual interest rate of 15% for valuation purposes.

(a) If the purchaser anticipates a stock price of 50.00 (excluding dividend) when he sells 10 years from now, what value will he put on the stock now?

(b) Suppose the purchaser is willing to pay 20.00 now for the stock. What stock price is implied 10 years from now?

8.1.2 The stock of XYZ Corporation is currently valued at 25 per share. An annual dividend has just been paid and the next dividend is expected to be 2 with each subsequent dividend $1+r$ times the previous one. The valuation is based on an annual interest rate of 12%. What value of $r$ is implied?

Suppose the dividends are payable quarterly with the next one due in exactly one quarter. For the next four quarters the dividend will be .50 each quarter. Every year (after every 4 quarters) the dividend is increased by a factor of $1+s$. If the stock is now valued at 25 based $i^{(4)} = .12$, what value of $s$ is implied?

## SECTION 8.2

8.2.1 An investor sells short 500 shares of ABC Corporation on June 1, at a time when the price per share is $120. The position is closed out 3 months later, August 31, when the price per share is $100. A dividend of $4 per share was paid July 31, one month before the short position is closed out.

(a) Find the net gain on the transaction, ignoring any effect of interest over the 3 months.

(b) Suppose that the investor must open a margin account at the time the short position is taken. The margin required is 50% of the value of the stock sold short. The investor also earns 1% per month, compounded monthly, on the margin account. Find the investor's 3-month rate of return on the investment.

8.2.2 Today Smith sells short 1000 shares of stock in ABC Corp. Today's price per share of ABC Corp stock is 10. Smith is required to open a margin account with the investment dealer and deposit 50% of the value of the stock sold short. Smith must also pay a commission to the investment dealer, the commission being 1% of the value of the stock sold short. The margin account pays interest at effective annual rate 5%. One year after the initial short sale, Smith covers the short sale by buying 1000 shares of the stock. The stock price at the end of the year is $X$. Smith again must pay commission of 1% of the value of the stock purchased. After all transactions are complete, Smith's net gain for the year is 100. Find $X$.

8.2.3 Bill and Jane each sell a different stock short for a price of 1000. For both investors, the margin requirement is 50%, and interest on the margin is credited at an effective annual rate of 6%. Bill buys back his stock one year later at a price of $P$. At the end of the year, the stock paid a dividend of $X$. Jane also buys back her stock after one year, at a price of $(P-25)$. At the end of the year, her stock paid a dividend of $2X$. Both investors earned an effective annual yield of 21% on their short sales. Calculate $P$.

8.2.4 Jose and Chris each sell a different stock short for the same price. For each investor, the margin requirement is 50% and interest on the margin debt is paid at an effective annual rate of 6%. Each investor buys back his stock one year later at a price of 760. Jose's stock paid a dividend of 32 at the end of the year while Chris's stock paid no dividends. During the 1-year period, Chris's return on the short sale is $i$, which is twice the return earned by Jose. Calculate $i$.

## Section 8.4

8.4.1 A government is issuing a 5-year 15% bond with face amount 1,000,000,000. The perception in the investment community is that the government is somewhat unstable, and it is forecast that there is a 10% chance that the government will default on interest payments by the first or second years, a 20% chance of default by the third or fourth years, and a 25% chance of default (on interest and principal) by the fifth year. All probabilities are *unconditional* (measured from time 0, so that, for instance, the probability that the $7^{th}$ coupon will be paid is .8).

(a) Find the price to be paid for this issue for an investor to earn yield $i^{(2)} = .18$ on the expected payments.

(b) Based on the price found in part (a), find the yield to maturity if all payments are actually made.

(c) Suppose that the risk of default on the redemption amount is only 10%, but the other default risks are as stated. Repeat parts (a) and (b).

# CHAPTER 9

## FORWARDS, FUTURES, SWAPS, AND OPTIONS

*"…derivatives are financial weapons of mass destruction,
carrying dangers that, while now latent, are potentially lethal."*

> *– Warren Buffett, Chairman of Berkshire Hathaway,
> in the 2002 "Chairman's Letter" to shareholders*

A **financial derivative** is an instrument that is related to some other asset and whose value is derived from that asset. There are many types of derivatives. In this chapter we provide an introduction to forward/futures and option contracts, two of the most widely used financial derivatives. A **forward** or **futures** contract on an underlying asset is an agreement between two parties to sell and buy that asset at a specified future date for a specified price. An **option** on an asset is a contract that allows, but does not require, the holder of the option to buy the asset (call option) or sell the asset (put option) on or before a specified date at a specified price.

In Chapter 6 we introduced the concept of a forward rate of interest. We now consider the more general concept of a forward contract and the related concept of a futures contract. Some applications related to equity investments are introduced, including a simple model for pricing an option on a stock. A few of the concepts introduced in this chapter require an elementary background in probability.

It is generally assumed that there is always available a "risk-free" rate of return that can be obtained by any investor. The risk-free rate of return is often determined from government treasury bills or bonds because there is assumed to be no risk of default in treasury securities (the government can print the money needed to repay its obligations).

Another important assumption about the theoretical behavior of financial markets is that any asset can be purchased **long** or **sold short**. A long position in an asset is taken by purchasing the asset at its market value. A short position is taken by borrowing the asset and selling it with the understanding that the short seller will eventually purchase the asset and return the borrowed asset. In a short sale, the short seller must return the asset at the time the short sale is terminated. A variation on a short sale is a "naked" short sale, in which the short seller doesn't actually borrow the asset. There are regulations that limit the amount of naked short selling that can take place in an asset.

In the theoretical analysis of forward contracts and options that will be presented in this chapter, it is assumed that any amount of money can and will be invested at the risk-free rate of interest, and that loans of any amount are always available at the risk-free rate. It is also assumed that a long or short position can be taken in any asset in any fractional quantity. For instance, if a particular situation calls for a short position in one-half of a share of stock, it is assumed that such a position can be taken. If an asset is sold short, then the short seller gets the proceeds of the sale of the asset and can invest that amount at the risk-free rate, or can use the money to purchase some other asset.

A **financial position** is any combination of investments, including long and short positions in any assets, or in risk-free investing or borrowing. When describing the outcome at time $T$ of a financial position created at time 0 we make a distinction between the **payoff at time $T$** of the financial position and the **profit from time 0 to time $T$** on the financial position. The payoff at time $T$ is simply the value of the position at time $T$. The profit on the position from time 0 to time $T$ is defined as follows.

The value of the position is determined at time 0. This amount is accumulated to time $T$ using the risk-free rate of interest. The profit on the position is the difference between the payoff on the position at time $T$ and the accumulated value to time $T$ (using the risk-free rate) of the initial position value. It follows that the profit on an investment or loan at the risk-free rate is always 0. This is true because, the payoff at time $T$ of an investment at the risk-free rate is exactly the accumulated value at the risk-free rate, so when that accumulated value is subtracted, the profit is 0. This definition of profit that we will be using in this theoretical financial market context may not be the same as the definition of profit in common usage. For instance, if I invest $100 for one year and get back $110, I might regard that transaction as resulting in a profit of $10 for the year. In the version of profit that we will be using, we would subtract the risk-free part of the return from the $10; if the risk free rate of interest for the year was 6%, then profit, in our theoretical sense, would be $4.

Figure 9.1 illustrates the payoff and profit at time $T$ in a long position in an asset. The graphs are functions of the asset value at time $T$.

The payoff is simply the value of the asset at time $T$, say $S_T$. If the cost of the asset at time 0 was $S_0$, then the accumulated cost to time $T$ of creating the long position at time 0 is $S_0(1+i)^T$, where $i$, is the (annual effective) risk-free rate of interest. The profit at time $T$, is $S_T - S_0(1+i)^T$.

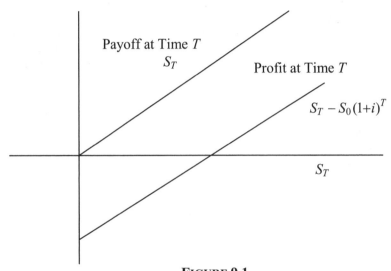

**FIGURE 9.1**

In Chapter 6, the Law of One Price was introduced. According to this rule, under the assumption that no arbitrage opportunities exist, if two financial positions have the same payoff at time $T$, then they will have the same price at time 0, and they will result in the same profit at time $T$.

In the example above the risk-free rate was used in annual effective rate form. In most financial literature, the risk-free rate is quoted as a continuously compounded rate.

## 9.1 Forward and Futures Contracts

### 9.1.1 Forward Contract Defined

---

**Definition 9.1 – Forward Contract**

A **forward contract** is an agreement to buy or sell a certain asset at a specific future date called the **delivery date**, for a specific price called the **delivery price**. Both parties of the forward contract are bound by the contract terms at the time the contract is made, with the contract being settled on the delivery date.

---

In general, the forward contract is constructed at time 0 so that no money changes hands at time 0, and the only exchange takes place at time $T$. We will see shortly how the delivery price is determined so that it is acceptable to both positions in the forward contract that no money is initially exchanged.

We will denote by $S_0$ the value of the asset at time 0, and $S_T$ will denote its value at time $T$. The value at time 0 (current price) is also referred to as the **spot price**. The spot price is the price quoted for immediate settlement, payment and delivery of a security or commodity. For a forward contract arranged at time 0 for delivery to take place at time $T$, we will denote the delivery price by $F_{0,T}$. The payoff on the long position at the time of delivery is $S_T - F_{0,T}$, and the payoff on the short position is $F_{0,T} - S_T$. It is always the case that the payoff on a short position is the negative of the payoff on a long position of the same combination of financial investments.

Since no money is initially invested for a forward contract, the profit on the delivery date is the same as the payoff on the delivery date. As with any buy/sell transaction, there are two positions that are taken on a forward contract. The party that will take delivery of the asset and pay the delivery price at time $T$ has **a long position on the forward contract**, and the party that will deliver the asset and be paid at time $T$ has **a short position on the contract**. Forward contracts are often described from the point of view of the long position. Figure 9.2 illustrates the payoff at time $T$ on long and short forward contracts. The payoff is a function of the time $T$ asset value.

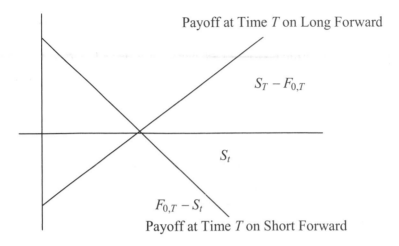

**FIGURE 9.2**

| EXAMPLE 9.1 | *(Forward contract in gold)*

At time 0, a corporation enters into a forward contract with a gold refiner to purchase 1000 ounces of gold in one year (at time $T = 1$) at the delivery price of US \$950 per ounce. Suppose that at the time of maturity the spot price of gold is US \$900. What is the payoff at time 1?

| SOLUTION |

The payoff on the long position held by the corporation is $S_1 - F_{0,1} = 1000 \times (900 - 950) = -\$50,000$. The reason for this is that the corporation is obligated by the forward contract to buy from the party that took the short position in the forward contract. The corporation must buy the gold at \$950 per ounce, even though it is available in the spot market at \$900 at time. The corporation is paying 950,000 for something that is actually worth 900,000. The payoff on the short position at time 1 would be \$50,000. ◻

### 9.1.2 PREPAID FORWARD PRICE ON AN ASSET PAYING NO INCOME

An alternative forward contract arrangement that can be made is a **prepaid forward contract**, in which the long side pays now (time 0) and the short side delivers the asset at time $T$. In this case, the amount paid now is called the **prepaid forward price**, and we will denote it $F_{0,T}^P$. For an asset which pays no income or dividends, the prepaid forward price at time 0 is equal to the spot price of the asset at time 0, $F_{0,T}^P = S_0$. The following example shows that if $F_{0,T}^P$ is not equal to $S_0$, then it is possible to create an arbitrage opportunity (as defined in Chapter 6) and obtain a positive gain for a net investment of 0.

| EXAMPLE 9.2 | *(Arbitrage on a prepaid forward contract)*

A stock has a price at time 0 of \$100. The risk-free force of interest is 10%. Suppose that an investor is willing to enter into a one year prepaid forward contract at a prepaid forward price of \$105. Show how to make an arbitrage gain under these circumstances.

| SOLUTION |

A simple, but general principle in finance is to buy low and sell high in order to make a gain. If we can "buy" for 0 and "sell" for more than 0, then we have made an arbitrage gain. Since the current price of the stock is 100, if someone is offering a prepaid forward at a price that is not 100 we can take advantage of the situation in one of two ways, depending upon what the prepaid forward price is. If the prepaid forward price being offered is more than 100, we sell the prepaid forward and buy the stock, and vice versa if the prepaid forward price that an investor is willing to accept is less than 100.

We sell to the investor the prepaid one-year forward contract on the stock (this is the "sell high" part of the arrangement). This means that the investor pays us \$105 right now (time 0), and we agree to deliver a share of stock to the investor one year from now. We use \$100 of the amount we receive to buy the stock right now (this is the "buying low" part of the arrangement), and invest the remaining \$5 at the force of interest of 10%. In one year, we have the stock to deliver to the investor to complete the forward transaction, and we have cash of $5e^1 = 5.53$. This represents positive gain obtained with a net investment of 0 at time 0. ❑

### 9.1.3 FORWARD DELIVERY PRICE
#### BASED ON AN ASSET PAYING NO INCOME

Assuming no arbitrage opportunities exist, we have seen that the prepaid forward price on an asset paying no income is the spot price of the asset. It follows that the forward delivery price for delivery at time $T$ is the value at time $T$ of the initial spot price accumulated at the risk-free rate of interest. If the continuously compounded risk-free rate is $r$ then the no-arbitrage forward price is $S_0 e^{rT}$.

That this is true can be seen in the following way. Suppose that investor A is willing to enter into a long forward contract in which he will pay a delivery price of $C > S_0 e^{rT}$. It is possible to construct the following strategy. You enter into a short position on the forward contract with investor A taking the long position in which he will pay $C$ to you at time $T$, when you will deliver the asset to him. No money changes hands now (at time 0). At the same time you enter into this contract you borrow $S_0$ at the risk-free rate and buy the asset at today's spot price of $S_0$. You hold the asset until time $T$, at which time you sell it to investor A and he pays you $C$. Since $C > S_0 e^{rT}$, you have more than enough to repay your loan at the risk-free rate. The excess is a guaranteed profit to you for a net investment of 0. The assumption that no such arbitrage opportunities exist in a market implies that such a transaction would not be possible and there would not be such an investor A. A similar argument shows that if someone was willing to sell (deliver) the asset at time $T$ at a price less than $S_0 e^{rT}$, then an arbitrage gain would be available.

It is possible to formulate the value of a forward contract (long or short position) at any point in time between the initial contract date and the delivery date.

### 9.1.4 FORWARD CONTRACT VALUE

Suppose that at time 0 a forward contract is arranged with the following characteristics: spot price at time 0 is $S_0$, delivery is at time $T$, delivery price is $F_{0,T}$, and risk-free rate (continuously compounded) is $r$. *Assuming no arbitrage opportunities exist*, it must be the case that

$$S_0 = F_{0,T}e^{-rT} \text{ or } F_{0,T} = S_0 e^{rT} \tag{9.1}$$

Suppose that at a later time, say $t < T$, the spot price is $S_t$. The value of the long position in the original forward contract at time $t$ is $S_t - S_0 e^{rt}$. The reason this is true can be seen as follows. Assuming that the risk-free rate is still $r$, a new investor at time $t$ who wants to enter into a long position forward contract that has delivery at time $T$ would agree to a delivery price of $S_t e^{r(T-t)}$ (since the time is $T-t$ until delivery, assuming the risk-free rate is still $r$). If the new investor were to take over the long forward position on the original contract, he would have to agree to a delivery price of $F_{0,T}$ at time $T$. The amount that the new investor would be willing to pay to take over the original long position in the forward contract would be the present value of the reduction in what he would have to pay at delivery; that present value is $\left[ S_t e^{r(T-t)} - F_{0,T} \right] e^{-r(T-t)} = S_t - F_{0,T}e^{-r(T-t)} = S_t - S_0 e^{rt}$. This is the present value (at time $t$) of the delivery price he would have to pay if he entered a new contract minus the delivery price he would have to pay if he took over the original contract, and it is also the current spot price (at time $t$) minus the accumulated value to time $t$ of the spot price when the original forward contract was entered at time 0.

The value of the short position of the original forward contract at time $t$ is $-(S_t - S_0 e^{rt}) = S_0 e^{rt} - S_t$ (the combined value at any time of the long and short positions is always 0).

### EXAMPLE 9.1 Continued   (*Value of a Forward Contract*)

Suppose that the spot price of gold is 975 one-quarter year after the original forward contract is made. Find the value of the long position in the forward contract at that time assuming a continuously compounded risk-free rate of interest of 5%.

### SOLUTION

When the contract was first made at time 0, the delivery price was 950. This implies that the spot price at time 0 must have been $S_0$, where $S_0 e^{.05} = 950$. Thus, $S_0 = 903.67$. Since the spot price at time $t = .25$ is $S_{.25} = 975$, it follows that the value of the long position in the forward contract is $S_{.25} - S_0 e^{(.05)(.25)} = 975 - 903.67 e^{.0125} = 59.97$. The value of the short position at that time would be $-59.97$. ☐

In the example above, gold can be replaced by any asset which does not produce any income from the time the forward contract is entered to the time the contract matures. In our simple financial market framework, we are also assuming that there would be no storage costs for holding an asset for a period of time. In practice, there would likely be some storage cost.

### 9.1.5  FORWARD CONTRACT ON AN ASSET PAYING SPECIFIC DOLLAR INCOME

We now consider a forward contract on an income producing asset such as a risk-free (government treasury) bond. The asset to be delivered on the delivery date is a bond.

Let $I_0$ be the present value at time 0, at the risk-free rate, of income to be received from time 0 until the maturity of the forward contract. With a delivery price of $F_{0,T}$, the following Portfolios A and B have the same value.

Portfolio A:  one long forward contract on the security plus cash amount equal to $F_{0,T}e^{-rT}$,

Portfolio B:  one unit of the security, combined with borrowing of amount $I_0$ at the risk-free rate.

The income from the security in portfolio B will repay the loan, and result in only the security being held at time $T$, therefore the two portfolios result in the same financial position at time $T$. Then the no-arbitrage assumption leads to

$$F_{0,T} = K = (S_0 - I_0)e^{rT}. \tag{9.2}$$

For a forward contract created at time $t < T$ with delivery at time $T$ for the security, the delivery price would be $(S_t - I_t)e^{r(T-t)}$, where $I_t$ is the present value at time $t$ of the cash income to be paid from time $t$ to $T$. The value at time $t$ of the long position on the original forward contract is $S_t - I_t - F_{0,T}e^{-r(T-t)}$. (This is the present value of the difference between what would have to be paid as delivery price on a new forward contract arranged at time $t$ and the original forward contract; we are assuming that the risk-free rate remains constant at $r$). Note that the spot price, $S_t$, includes the income to be received between now and the delivery time, but that income will not be paid to the long position holder of the forward contract, since the long position holder takes delivery after that income is paid. Thus, the delivery price should not include the income paid by the security between now and the time of delivery.

An alternative way of looking at this situation is to see that the forward price should be the amortized value of the security at time $T$. This is the initial price (spot price at time 0) accumulated to time $t$ minus the accumulated income (coupons) to time $t$. From this comment, we also see that the prepaid forward price is $F_{0,T}^P = S_0 - I_0$, which is the asset spot price minus the present value (at the risk-free rate) of all income to be paid until delivery of the asset takes place.

The following equations summarize some of the key relationships in forward contracts.

Forward delivery price at time $T$, determined at time 0 for an asset with value $S_0$ at time 0 and paying specific dollar income between time 0 and time $T$ with present value $I_0$ at time 0:

$$F_{0,T} = (S_0 - I_0)e^{rT} \qquad (9.3a)$$

Forward delivery price at time $T$, determined at time $t < T$ for an asset with value $S_0$ at time 0 and paying specific dollar income between time $t$ and time $T$ with present value $I_t$ at time $t$:

$$F_{t,T-t} = (S_t - I_t)e^{r(T-t)} \qquad (9.3b)$$

Value of long forward position at $t$ on the original forward contract initiated at time 0:

$$(S_t - I_t) - F_{0,T}e^{-r(T-t)} \qquad (9.3c)$$

**EXAMPLE 9.3** *(Forward contract on a bond)*

A coupon bond has a spot price of 860. The bond will pay coupons of 40 in 6 months and in one year.

(a) Suppose that the risk-free rate is 10% (per year continuously compounded) for both a zero coupon bond with 6 months to maturity and a zero coupon bond with one year to maturity. The delivery price for a one year forward contract on the bond, with delivery immediately after the coupon payment, is

$$F_{0,T} = \left(860 - 40e^{-.1(.5)} - 40e^{-.1(1)}\right)e^{.1(1)}$$

$$= \left[860e^{.1(.5)} - 40\right]e^{.1(.5)} - 40 = 868.40.$$

This is an illustration of Equation (9.3a).

(b) Suppose that immediately after the first coupon is paid (time .5), the continuously compounded risk-free rate of interest is still 10% for 6 month maturities. If the spot price of the bond has risen to 870, then at time .5 the delivery price for a forward contract maturing at time 1 (just after the coupon is paid) is $F_{.5,.5} = (870 - 40e^{-.1(.5)})e^{.1(.5)} = 874.61$ (Eq. 9.3b) and the value of the original forward contract entered at time 0 will be $S_{.5} - I_{.5} - F_{0,T}e^{-r(.5)} = 870 - 40e^{-.1(.5)} - 868.40e^{-.1(.5)} = 5.90$.

(c) Suppose that the risk-free rates are 8% (per year continuously compounded) for a 6-month maturity and 10% for a one year maturity. The delivery price for a one year forward contract on the bond, with delivery immediately after the coupon payment, is

$$F_{0,T} = \left(860 - 40e^{-.08(.5)} - 40e^{-.1(1)}\right)e^{.1(1)}$$

$$= \left[860e^{.08(.5)} - 40\right]e^{.12(.5)} - 40 = 867.97$$

(Eq. 9.3a) (the continuously compounded ½ year forward rate of interest at time 0 is determined by solving the equation $e^{r_0(.5,1)\times.5} = \dfrac{e^{0.10}}{e^{0.08\times.5}}$

for $r_0(.5,1)$; this results in $r_0(.5,1) = .12 = \dfrac{.1 - .08(.5)}{.5}$).

(d) Suppose that immediately after the first coupon is paid (time .5), the continuously compounded risk-free rate of interest is still 8% for 6 month maturities. If the spot price of the bond has risen to 870 at time .5, then at time .5 the delivery price for a forward contract maturing at time 1 (just after the coupon is paid) for delivery at time 1 is

$$\left(870 - 40e^{-.08(.5)}\right)e^{.08(.5)} = 865.51, \tag{9.3b}$$

and the value of the original forward contract entered at time 0 will be

$$S_{.5} - I_{.5} - F_{0,T}e^{-r(.5)} = 870 - 40e^{-.08(.5)} - 867.97e^{-.08(.5)} = -2.37. \tag{9.3c}$$

□

### 9.1.6 FORWARD CONTRACT ON AN ASSET PAYING PERCENTAGE DIVIDEND INCOME

Dividend paying stocks usually pay a dividend that is a dollar amount related to the value of the stock. If we consider a mutual fund or a stock index consisting of a mix of many different stocks, some paying dividends at different times, it may be possible to approximate the behavior of the stock index as paying dividends at a continuous percentage. It is also possible to imagine a single stock that pays periodic dividends, for which the dividend is a percentage of the value of the stock.

As an example, we could consider a stock that pays a dividend of 1% of the share price at the end of each month. The prepaid forward price for a prepaid 4-month forward contract on one share of stock would be $F^P_{0,.25} = \frac{S_0}{(1.01)^4}$. This is true because at the end of each month, the number of shares grows by a factor of 1.01, so that $\frac{1}{(1.01)^4}$ shares bought today (at a price of $\frac{S_0}{(1.01)^4}$) would grow to 1 share delivered at the end of 4 months. Note that we are assuming that the 1% dividend at the end of 4 months occurs just before delivery. Keep in mind that it is one share of stock being delivered in 4 months, and since there is the percentage dividend occurring each month, we would need less than one share ($\frac{1}{(1.01)^4}$ shares) now to grow to one share in 4 months.

Suppose that dividends are payable continuously and the continuous rate of dividend payment is $\gamma$. This is similar to a force of interest in which 1 grows to $e^{\gamma t}$ at time $t$. What is meant by a continuous rate of dividend payment is that $\gamma$ is applied instantaneously to the number of shares, so the number of shares is growing continuously at rate $\gamma$. Therefore, 1 share will grow to $e^{\gamma T}$ shares at time $T$. In order to deliver 1 share at time $T$, we need $e^{-\gamma T}$ shares at time 0, which will grow to $(e^{-\gamma T})^{\gamma T} = 1$ share at time $T$. The prepaid forward price would be the price at time 0 of $e^{-\gamma T}$ shares, which is

$$F_{0,T}^{P} = S_0 e^{-\gamma T} \tag{9.4}$$

As with the other forward contracts considered, the no-arbitrage forward price for delivery of one share at time $T$ is the prepaid forward price accumulated to time $T$ at the risk-free rate $r$,

$$F_{0,T} = F_{0,T}^{P} e^{rT} = S_0 e^{(r-\gamma)T} \tag{9.5}$$

The **forward premium** on a forward contract is defined to be $\frac{F_{0,T}}{S_0} = \frac{forward\ price}{spot\ price}$, and the annualized forward premium is $\frac{1}{T} \times \ln\left(\frac{F_{0,T}}{S_0}\right)$. If the asset pays continuous dividends at annual rate $\gamma$ then the annualized forward premium is $r - \gamma$. This annualized forward premium is also referred to as the **cost-of-carry**. It is the net rate at which cost is incurred by borrowing at the risk free rate to own the asset paying the dividend rate. If we consider a short sale of the asset, the lender would have to be paid the dividend rate $\gamma$, and this is referred to as the **lease rate**. Finance books often use $\delta$ for the lease rate, but since we have used that for other purposes in this book, we will use $\gamma$.

### 9.1.7 SYNTHETIC FORWARD CONTRACT

If two financial investments result in the same payoffs at a common time point in the future, then under the assumption of no arbitrage, they would have the same value or price today. For some types of financial contracts it is possible to replicate the payoffs by combining alternative financial instruments.

Suppose we consider a forward contract in an asset that pays dividends at continuous rate $\gamma$ (this includes the case of no dividends, $\gamma = 0$). In this case it is possible to replicate the payoffs on the forward contract expiring at time $T$ by borrowing $S_0 e^{-\gamma T}$ (the prepaid forward price) at time 0 and buying the asset. At time $T$ we own the asset which has value $S_T$, and we must pay back the loan, which has accumulated with interest to $S_0 e^{(r-\gamma)T}$. The payoff at time $T$ of this combination is $S_T - S_0 e^{(r-\gamma)T}$. The payoff at time $T$ of a forward contract is $S_T - F_{0,T}$. We have also seen that for a stock that pays dividends at rate $\gamma$, the forward price is $F_{0,T} = S_0 e^{(r-\gamma)T}$. Therefore, the loan and stock purchase combination results in the same payoff as the forward contract. We have replicated the payoff of the forward contract. The loan and stock purchase combination is a **synthetic forward contract**, which can be represented by the equation

$$\text{``forward contract} = \text{stock purchase} + \text{loan.''} \tag{9.6}$$

This can also be written as

$$\text{``forward contract} = \text{stock purchase} - \text{zero coupon bond,''} \tag{9.7}$$

since "– zero coupon bond" means shorting the bond, or equivalently, taking out a loan.

Just as the equation $A + B = C$ can be written in the equivalent form $A = C - B$, we can rewrite the "equation"

$$\text{stock purchase} - \text{zero coupon bond} = \text{forward contract}$$

in the form:

$$\text{stock purchase} - \text{forward contract} = \text{zero coupon bond.}$$

(where "$=$" means that they have the same payoff at time $T$).

We can interpret the right side of this equation as follows. At time 0 we

(i) take a long position in a forward contract (which has 0 cost at time 0) and

(ii) at the same time we invest $S_0 e^{-\gamma T}$ in a zero coupon bond maturing at time $T$.

Then at time $T$ we have

(i) a payoff from the forward contract of amount $S_T - F_{0,T}$, and

(ii) a cash amount of $F_{0,T} = S_0 e^{(r-\gamma)T}$ from the zero coupon bond.

The combined payoff on (i) and (ii) is $S_T$, the same payoff if we owned the stock at time $T$ (of course, with the forward contract, we are actually obligated to buy the stock at time $T$ at a price of $F_{0,T}$, and we have exactly the cash amount from the zero coupon bond to do that). We have used a long position in a forward contract combined with a zero coupon bond to replicate the value of the payoff of owning the stock at time $T$.

We can consider other variations on the equation $A+B = C$. For example,

$$\text{stock purchase} - \text{forward contract} = \text{zero coupon bond.}$$

"$-$" means that we are taking a short position, so the left side of this equation means that if we buy the stock and take a short position on the forward contract, we have invested $S_0 e^{-\gamma T}$ at time 0 for the stock purchase (remember that a long or short forward contract does not require any cash payment at time 0). At time $T$, our short forward contract is closed by selling the stock and receiving $S_0 e^{(r-\gamma)T}$. We have created a $T$-year investment that gives a continuously compounded return of $r$. In other words, we have replicated the payoff on a $T$-year zero coupon bond. We have created a synthetic zero coupon bond. In general, a position consisting of buying the stock and going short on the forward contract has an initial investment of $S_0 e^{-\gamma T}$, and a payoff at time $T$ of $F_{0,T} - S_T + S_T = F_{0,T}$ (sell the stock for $F_{0,T}$ at time $T$). Under the assumption of no-arbitrage, $F_{0,T} = S_0 e^{(r-\gamma)T} = S_0 e^{-\gamma T} e^{rT}$, which implies a continuous rate of return of $r$ on the overall transaction. This is the **implied repo rate** on the transaction. If $F_{0,T}$ was different from $S_0 e^{(r-\gamma)T}$, the implied repo rate would not be $r$.

We can consider any equivalent variation on the equation "$A+B=C$" and interpret "$-$" as a short position. For instance

$$-\text{zero coupon bond} - \text{forward contract} = -\text{stock purchase}$$

can be interpreted as follows. Borrowing $S_0 e^{-\gamma T}$ at time 0 at the same time as taking a short position in the forward contract has the same payoff at time $T$ as taking a short position in the stock. The payoff at time $T$ on a short position in the stock is $-S_T$ (the cost of covering the short sale). The "payoff" at time $T$ on the loan is $-S_0 e^{(r-\gamma)T}$ and the payoff on the short forward contract is $S_0 e^{(r-\gamma)T} - S_T$, for a combined payoff of $-S_T$.

### 9.1.8 STRATEGIES WITH FORWARD CONTRACTS

A long position in an investment can be hedged by taking a short position in the investment or in a related investment. An example of a hedged position is a long position on an asset and a short position on a forward contract on the same asset. This combination is referred to as a **cash-and-carry**. Suppose that the underlying asset is a stock with price $S_0$ at time 0 with continuous dividends at rate $\gamma$. The long position in stock consists of $e^{-\gamma T}$ shares at time 0, and the forward price is $F_{0,T} = S_0 e^{(r-\gamma)T}$. The payoff at time $T$ (maturity date of the forward contract) of the cash-and-carry is $S_T + F_{0,T} - S_T = F_{0,T} = S_0 e^{(r-\gamma)T}$, the sum of the payoffs on the long asset and the short forward. This corresponds to a continuously compounded return of $r$ from time 0 to time $T$ on an amount of $S_0 e^{-\gamma T}$ with no risk (risk-free return only).

A **reverse cash-and-carry** is a combination of a short position on the asset and a long forward contract on the asset. It would have the opposite payoff.

If a forward contract with a delivery price $F_{0,T}$ is available that is greater than $S_0 e^{(r-\gamma)T}$, then it possible to create a cash-and-carry arbitrage. We borrow $S_0 e^{-\gamma T}$ and "buy low," which means we buy $e^{-\gamma T}$ shares of the stock now for a price of $S_0 e^{-\gamma T}$. We "sell high," which means we short (sell) the forward contract with delivery price $F_{0,T} > S_0 e^{(r-\gamma)T}$. Then at time $T$ we deliver the stock, receive $F_{0,T}$ and repay the loan for a payoff of $F_{0,T} - S_0 e^{(r-\gamma)T}$. We have made a positive gain from an initial net investment of 0.

If a forward contract price is available with a delivery price that is less than $S_0 e^{(r-\gamma)T}$, then it possible to create a reverse cash-and-carry arbitrage by reversing the steps just described.

A variation on these situations can result in an arbitrage opportunity if the rate at which we can borrow is less than the implied repo rate. The following example illustrates this. The implied repo rate is the rate at which the initial asset value accumulated to the time of delivery is equal to the forward delivery price.

| EXAMPLE 9.4 | *(Arbitrage on the Implied Repo Rate)*

A stock which pays no dividends has a current price of $100. A one year forward contract is available with a delivery price of $110. Borrowing is available at a continuously compounded rate of 9%. Construct a cash-and-carry arbitrage.

| SOLUTION |

At time 0 borrow $100 and buy the stock, and also take a short position in a one year forward contract on the stock. At time 1, close the forward contract by selling the stock for $110, and repay the loan with a payment of $100 e^{.09} = 109.42$. A payoff of 0.58 has been made for an initial investment of 0. The implied repo rate is $r$, where $110 = 100 e^{r}$, so that $r = .0953$. Since the rate at which we can borrow is less than the implied repo rate, we know there will be an arbitrage opportunity available by borrowing at the low rate and arranging a transaction that earns the larger repo rate. We can also think of this situation as if 9% is the risk-free rate $r$, so that the no-arbitrage forward price is $S_0 e^{(r-\gamma)} = 100 e^{.09} = 109.42$, which is less than the $110 available for a forward contract. We can arrange a cash-and-carry arbitrage since $K > S_0 e^{(r-\gamma)}$. ☐

## 9.1.9 FUTURES CONTRACTS

It is usually the intention of the original parties to a forward contract to actually take part in the transaction specified for the future date, although it is possible for one of the parties to sell his side of the contract to a third party at any time before the delivery date. For both hedging and speculation on future changes in value of a particular financial instrument or commodity, futures contracts are much more widely used than forward contracts. A **futures contract** is similar in many respects to a forward contract. One of the differences is that in setting up a forward contract, there is no restriction regarding the goods to be exchanged or the future date on which the transaction will take place, whereas futures contracts are restricted to a specific group of financial instruments and commodities, and they expire on specific days (such as the second Friday of the expiry month) in various months. The existence of centralized facilities, such as the Chicago Board of Trade and International Monetary Market, for the trading and standardization of the futures contracts has led to a highly liquid and efficient market. A few examples of goods on which futures contracts are traded are the following:

(1) Japanese yen, with a standard contract size of 12.5 million yen.

(2) 8% US Treasury Bonds, maturing in 15 years, with a standard contract size of 100,000.

(3) 30-day Interest Rate Future, with a standard contract size of 5,000,000. Interest rate futures are based on an underlying government Treasury bill or corporate investment certificate with an appropriate term to maturity.

(4) Pork Bellies, with a standard contract size of 40,000 pounds.

Another distinction between a futures contract and a forward contract is that with a forward contract there is generally no exchange of goods and money until the delivery date of the forward contract, whereas with a futures contract the purchaser of long (buyer) and short (seller) position must place a fraction of the cost of the goods with an intermediary (usually a futures broker) and give assurances that the remainder of the purchase price will be paid and the item delivered when required. Usually 2-10% of the contract value (depending on the volitility of commodity) is paid to a futures broker to be held in an account, with the rest of the contract amount owed *on margin*. As will be seen shortly, futures investments tend to be highly leveraged and very risky.

Suppose a 6-month forward contract to purchase 100,000 Canadian dollars is bought on January 15 with a price of .85 US per Canadian dollar to be paid on July 15. The exchange of funds relating to this contract will not take place until July 15. On January 15, a 6-month futures contract for 100,000 Canadian dollars that expires July 15 may also have a future delivery price .85 US per Canadian dollar, but the purchaser of this futures contract will have to pay a *margin* of $1,350 US (about 1.6% of the contract value) plus a broker commission on the purchase date. If the purchaser holds the futures contract until the expiration or delivery date, then he must pay the remaining $83,650 US ($85,000 minus the original margin paid with interest). A futures contract provides considerable leverage and risk, since changes in the contract value are reflected directly in the equity that the contract holder has with the broker or investment dealer. Suppose that a short time after the contract is issued, the Canadian dollar has risen in value relative to the US dollar, and the effect on the July 15 futures price is that it has risen to .88 US. The futures contract value becomes $88,000 US and the contract holder's equity rises by the present value of 3000 due in 6 months. This is true because the holder of the long position has a contract that will allow him to buy an asset for $85,000 US that is worth $88,000 US. The long contract holder's position has more than tripled in value.

Thus a relatively small change in the value of the underlying commodity can have effects which are proportionally much larger on the equity of the contract holder. If the future price of the Canadian dollar drops any significant amount, the equity of the holder of the long position may drop enough so that the futures broker may require an additional margin payment to maintain a minimum level of equity for the futures contract holder. Suppose that a minimum 2% margin is required for the Canadian dollar futures contract just mentioned. The purchaser of a long position on a futures contract would pay $1,700 US to open the contract. If the Canadian dollar drops in value to 84 cents US, then the value of the contract has fallen by $1000 US, and the investor's equity has dropped to $700 US. When margin falls below its required level, the broker will do a **margin call**: i.e., require the futures contract holder to add an amount to the account to bring the account balance above the "maintenance margin." For Canadian dollar futures contracts the maintenance margin is $1,000 US. In the situation just described, the broker would require the contract holder to add $300 to his account.

To maintain order in the futures market, there are daily limits on the movement of future prices. At the end of each trading day, a futures account is **marked-to-market**. This essentially means that any profit or loss resulting from a change in the futures price from the previous day's close is added or deducted from the account balance. In the example cited in the previous paragraph, if the value of the Canadian dollar had dropped from 85 cents US to 84 cents in one day as of the closing of trading, then the account would be marked-to-market and the account balance would be reduced by $1,000. The investment dealer might require the investor to make an additional deposit to bring the account balance up to the maintenance margin.

Some holders of futures contracts don't intend to hold the contract until maturity, but rather hope to gain from a speculative position by selling the contract before expiration. In this case, the commodity is not received at delivery. It is settled with cash before the expiration.

The purchaser of a futures contract may be attempting to hedge a position. For example, a company may have a substantial investment in bonds or other interest-sensitive securities. The risk of adverse interest rate changes affecting the value of these securities may be reduced by the purchase (or sale) of an appropriately related futures contract. This is illustrated in the following example.

---

**EXAMPLE 9.5**   (*Futures contract*)

The holder of a 1,000,000 12% bond with a maturity of 25 years wishes to create a short-term hedge in potential changes to the bond's value by selling an appropriate number of 100,000 15-year 8% Treasury bond futures contracts which expire in a short period of time. The bondholder's objective is to neutralize the effect of a small change in interest (yield) rate on the current value of his bond. Suppose the current yield on the 25-year bond is 10% and the current yield on 15-year Treasury bonds is 9.5%, and that small changes in yield on the two bonds are numerically equal. Find the number of 100,000 T-bond futures contracts that must be sold by the bondholder to create the hedge.

---

**SOLUTION**

Let $P(i^{(2)})$ denote the price of the 25-year bond at yield rate $i^{(2)}$, and let $j = \frac{i^{(2)}}{2}$. Then

$$\frac{d}{di^{(2)}} P\left(i^{(2)}\right) = 1,000,000 \cdot \frac{1}{2} \cdot \frac{d}{dj}\left[ v_j^{50} + .06 \cdot a_{\overline{50}|j} \right]$$

$$= 500,000\left[ -50 v_j^{51} + .06(-v_j)(Ia)_{\overline{50}|j} \right].$$

With $i^{(2)} = .10$, we have $j = .05$ and $\frac{d}{di^{(2)}} P(i^{(2)}) = -10,538,299$, or an approximate decrease in value of 105,383 for an increase of 1% in $i^{(2)}$. Since the futures contract expires in a short time, we will value the 15-year bonds as of now. Let $Q(i^{(2)})$ denote the price of a 15-year 8% 100,000 Treasury bond at yield rate $i^{(2)}$, and let $j = \frac{i^{(2)}}{2}$. Then

$$\frac{d}{di^{(2)}}Q(i^{(2)}) = 100,000 \cdot \frac{1}{2} \cdot \frac{d}{dj}\left[v_j^{30} + .04 \cdot a_{\overline{30}|j}\right]$$

$$= 50,000\left[-30v_j^{31} + .04(-v_j)(Ia)_{\overline{30}|j}\right].$$

With $i^{(2)} = .095$ we have $j = .0475$ and $\frac{d}{di^{(2)}}Q(i^{(2)}) = -722,316$. In order to hedge the bond position, the required number of T-bond contracts to sell is $\frac{10,538,299}{722,316} = 14.6$.

If interest rates increase, the reduction in the value of the 25-year bond is offset by the increase in value of the futures contracts. For instance, suppose that the yield on the 25-year bond changes from 10% to 10.1% and the yield on the 15-year bonds goes to 9.6%. The price of the 25-year bond will change from 1,182,559 to 1,172,100, a drop of 10,459. The price of one 15-year bond will change from 88,135 to 87,417, a drop of 718. The drop in value of 14.6 15-year bonds is 10,483. The change in value of a short position on the futures contract in the 15-year bonds is an increase of 10,483, which approximately matches the drop in value of the 25-year bond actually being held. ❑

As another example of a hedge consider a bondholder, whose bonds will mature in six months, who plans to reinvest the proceeds in a new bond issue at that time. The price of the new purchase can be locked in now by purchasing a six-month futures contract on a bond similar to that which will be purchased. The locked-in price is the one reflected in the value of the futures contract when it is purchased. Any changes in yield over the six months will change the ultimate cost of the bonds to be purchased in six months, but if the futures contract is equivalent to the bonds to be bought, then the changes in the value of the futures contract will cancel those in the actual bond price.

Financial practice is always evolving, and new types of financial instruments appear from time to time (with some types occasionally disappearing). A futures contract is an example of a **derivative investment**.

---

**Definition 9.2 – Derivative Investment**

A derivative investment is one whose value is related to (or derived from) some underlying asset.

---

In the case of a futures contract, the value of the contract is related to the value of the underlying commodity. By the mid 1990s investment derivatives, particularly sophisticated types of options, had attained a certain glamour and notoriety.

As a result of highly risky investing in derivatives, a few companies (centuries old Baring's Investment Bank of England for example) and at least one local government (Orange County in California) have faced serious losses or even bankruptcy.

---

**Futures Trading Disaster**

The French Bank Société Générale experience a loss of about 4.9 million euros in early 2008 as a result of unauthorized trading in stock index futures by one of its employees. The trader is alleged by the bank to have fraudulently taken very large positions in European stock index futures contracts. The positions, which may have been in the tens of billions of euros in value, were discovered early in 2008 when equity markets experienced a significant drop. Closing the positions resulted in massive losses for the bank.

---

Empirically, future and forward prices tend to be very similar. Some differences can occur due to random fluctuation in the interest rate earned on a margin account. Interest rates may be correlated with futures prices, for instance for interest rate futures which are based on bond prices. A strong positive correlation between interest rates and asset price implies that futures prices are higher than forward prices and vice-versa.

There are various theories that try to explain the relationship between a forward price for an asset and what the price of the asset will be in the future. Students often ask if the forward price is the expected value of the asset at expiry. Even for a non-dividend paying stock, this would not be correct, since the no-arbitrage forward price is based on the risk-free rate of interest, whereas an investor in a stock would expect some risk premium as an expected return above the risk-free rate. Thus, on a non-dividend stock, the forward price will be less than the expected price (which goes up at the expected rate of return, which is larger than the risk-free rate).

## 9.1.10 COMMODITY SWAPS

In Chapter 6 we considered interest rate swaps. In that context, we saw how to find a level interest rate for all maturities (called the swap rate) for which the present value of a series of payments over time using the term structure is equal to the present value using the swap rate.

In general, a swap is an agreement to exchange one set of payments for another set of payments over some period of time. An underlying principle in a swap arrangement is that at the time that the swap is first arranged, the values should be the same for the two sets of payments that are being exchanged. For instance, at an annual effective interest rate of 10%, a single payment of 2 to be made at the end of one year has the same value as a payment of 1 now combined with a payment of .99 at the end of 2 years. This can be described by the equation $2v_{.1} = 1 + .99v_{.1}^2$. If the interest rate environment is defined by a term structure, the "same value" principle still applies.

---

**EXAMPLE 9.6** (Swap)

The term structure of interest rates has the following annual effective rates of interest for zero-coupon bonds.

| Maturity | Annual Effective Yield on Zero-Coupon Bond |
|:---:|:---:|
| 1 year | .0500 |
| 2 years | .0525 |
| 3 years | .0550 |

Payments of 1050.00, 1107.76 and 1174.24 are due at the end of years 1, 2 and 3. Find the level payment at the end of each year that has the same value as these payments.

---

**SOLUTION**

The present value of the payments is

$$\frac{1050.00}{1.05} + \frac{1107.76}{(1.0525)^2} + \frac{1174.24}{(1.055)^3} = 3000.00.$$

The present value of level payments of $x$ each is

$$\frac{x}{1.05} + \frac{x}{(1.0525)^2} + \frac{x}{(1.055)^3} = 2.70672x$$

Solving for $x$ results in $x = 1108.35$. ◻

In this example, we see that based on the given interest rates, we can swap the original set of payments for the set of level payments of 1108.35. We also see that a single payment of 3000 made at time 0 can be swapped for the original (or level) set of payments.

The original set of payments may represent the forward cost of some commodity or asset that will be bought at those payment times. If the commodity is paid for with a single payment at time 0, the situation is referred to as a **prepaid swap**. If the future payments are exchanged for level payments to be made over the same time frame, the amount of the level payment (1108.35) is referred to as the **swap price**. In the example above, the payments might represent forward prices at time 0 for an ounce of platinum to be delivered in 1, 2, and 3 years.

These are the no-arbitrage forward prices based on the current term structure, $F_{0,1} = 1000(1.05) = 1050$, $F_{0,2} = 1000(1.0525)^2 = 1107.76$, and $F_{0,3} = 1000(1.055)^3 = 1174.24$.

Continuing with the platinum example, the platinum buyer has a few ways of arranging to buy the platinum at the end of years 1, 2, and 3:

(i)   pay the spot price of platinum at times 1, 2 and 3;
(ii)  arrange forward contracts to pay 1050.00, 1107.76 and 1174.24 at times 1, 2 and 3;
(iii) pay 1108.35 at the end of each year for 3 years;
(iv)  make a single payment of 3000.00 at time 0.

The example above showed that (ii), (iii) and (iv) had the same present value at time 0 based on the term structure of interest rates as of time 0. They are all equivalent to paying for an ounce of platinum to be delivered at times 1, 2, and 3, so they are also equivalent to (i), even though we do not know at time 0 what the spot prices will be at times 1, 2, and 3.

A typical swap would be based on the platinum buyer wanting to lock in payment stream (iii), the level payments of 1108.35 each. Rather than an arrangement being made directly between the platinum buyer and seller, a financial intermediary, called the swap counterparty, may be willing to take a position "between" the platinum buyer and a platinum seller. The counterparty agrees to pay the platinum buyer an amount equal to that year's spot price minus 1108.35 at the end of each year. The net effect to the platinum buyer is that he was willing to pay 1108.35 at the end of each year, but under this arrangement, he receives from the counterparty an additional amount equal to the spot price minus 1108.35. With the 1108.35 he was willing to pay, this adds up to the spot price at the end of each year, and the platinum buyer can buy the platinum on the spot market. The counterparty has taken the risk of fluctuations in the price of platinum. For instance, suppose that the spot prices of platinum at times 1, 2, and 3 are 1020, 1200 and 1150. Then the counterparty pays the platinum buyer $-88.35$, 91.65, and 42.6 ($-$ means that the platinum buyer pays the counterparty) at times 1, 2, and 3. The net cost to the platinum buyer is $1020+88.35 = 1108.35$ at time 1, $1200-91.65 = 1108.35$ at time 2, and $1150-41.65-1180.35$ at time 3. The counterparty receives (from the platinum buyer) 88.35 at time 1, pays (to the platinum buyer) 91.65 at time 2, and pays 42.65 at time 3. If spot platinum prices had been higher, there would have been a greater loss to the counterparty.

We can also consider an amortization relationship associated with the platinum buyer who will pay a net amount of 1108.35 each year. There is an overpayment compared to the forward price at the end of the first and second year, but there is an underpayment at the end of the third year. These should balance out. This can be seen as follows.

The overpayment (compared to the forward price) at the end of the first year is $1108.35-1050 = 58.35$. This grows (in the amortization) from time 1 to time 2 at the forward rate of 5.25% to $58.35(1.055) = 61.56$ at time 2. Also at time 2 there is an overpayment of $1108.35-1107.76 = .59$ for an accumulated overpayment at time 2 of 62.15. This grows from time 2 to time 3 at the forward rate of 5.5% to $62.15(1.06) = 65.88$. Then at time 3 there is an underpayment of $1174.24-1108.35 = 65.59$ that cancels out the accumulated overpayment.

The counterparty can hedge his platinum price risk by making a swap arrangement with a platinum seller who wants to lock in a price of

1108.35 at the end of each year in return for selling an ounce at times 1, 2, and 3. The counterparty would agree to pay the platinum seller an amount equal to 1108.35 minus the spot price at the end of each year. If the platinum seller sells the platinum on the spot market at times 1, 2, and 3, the net amount received by the platinum seller will be

$$\text{spot price} + (1108.35 - \text{spot price}) = 1108.35$$

at each of those times. The counterparty now has a perfectly hedged position, paying $(\text{spot price} - 1108.35)$ to the platinum buyer, and paying $(1108.35 - \text{spot price})$ to the platinum seller, for a net payment of 0 at times 1, 2 and 3. Under this arrangement, the counterparty has brought the platinum buyer and seller together to create payment stream (iii) described earlier. In practice, the counterparty would charge some fee for this service.

We now consider an extension of this platinum example. No-arbitrage forward prices are set based on the current asset price and the risk free rate of interest in the current term structure. As time goes on, spot prices of an asset may change due to market fluctuations and interest rates may change as well. Suppose that at time 1, just after the first swap payment has been made, the spot price of platinum is still 1000, and the one-year zero-coupon bond yield is still 5% and the two-year zero-coupon bond yield is still 5.25%. Suppose that we now consider a platinum buyer at time 1 who would like to arrange to buy an ounce of platinum at times 2 and 3. The no-arbitrage forward prices, as of time 1, for delivery of an ounce of platinum at times 2 and 3 are 1050.00 and 1107.76. The swap price, as of time 1, for a two-year swap with swap payments at times 2 and 3, would be the level payment at times 2 and 3 that is equivalent to payments of 1050 at time 2 and 1107.76 at time 3. Using the term structure as of time 1, the swap payment is $x$, where

$$\frac{x}{1.05} + \frac{x}{(1.0525)^2} = \frac{1050}{1.05} + \frac{1107.76}{(1.0525)^2} = 2000$$

so that $x = 1078.11$.

The following time line identifies the counterparty's swap payments at times 2 and 3 under the original swap, and the swap payments under a new swap arranged at time 1.

| Time | 2 | 3 |
|---|---|---|
| Old swap payment | Spot – 1108.35 | Spot – 1108.35 |
| **New Swap arrangement** | | |
| Forward Price as of time 1 | 1050.00 | 1107.76 |
| Swap price as of time 1 | 1078.11 | 1078.11 |
| New swap payment | Spot – 1078.11 | Spot – 1078.11 |

The counterparty has different swap payments under the two arrangements. The continuation of the original swap has payments of (spot – 1108.35) at times 2 and 3, but a newly arranged swap would have payments of (spot – 1078.11). Under the assumption of no arbitrage, a newly arranged swap has value (and cost) 0 at the time it is arranged. The total value to either the platinum buyer or the counterparty at time 1 of the two new swap payments is 0. Therefore, the value to the counterparty at time 1 of the remaining original swap payments can be formulated as the present value of payments (spot – 1078.11) – (spot – 1108.35) = 30.24 at times 2 and 3. Based on the term structure as of time 1, that present value is

$$\frac{30.24}{1.05} + \frac{30.24}{(1.0525)^2} = 56.10.$$

The value to the platinum purchaser at time 1 of the remaining two original swap payments to take place at times 2 and 3 is – 56.10. This would be the market value of the swap to the platinum purchaser. We can also interpret this from the point of view of the counterparty. The original swap called for continuing payments at times 2 and 3 that are smaller than those that would be required under a new swap. The present value of the amount by which the original swap payments are below the payments required under a new swap is the value of the swap. From the point of view of the platinum buyer, under the swap, the platinum buyer receives smaller swap payments from the counterparty under the original arrangement than under a newly arranged swap. If the platinum buyer wanted to cancel the swap at time 1 after the first swap payment was made, the fair amount that the platinum buyer should pay the counterparty is 56.10. This would be the market value of the swap to the counterparty. Note that different values of the spot price and term structure at time 1 could result in a negative value for the swap at that time. Also, note that the actual amounts at risk under a swap arrangement are the swap payments, not the actual value of the underlying asset.

It is possible to arrange today for a swap to begin sometime later. This is a **deferred swap**. Using the platinum example, the platinum purchaser may wish, at time 0, to arrange to purchase platinum at the end of years 2 and 3. The purchaser can arrange a swap that begins one year from now, with swap payments occurring at times 2 and 3. The swap price $y$, would be the solution of the equation

$$\frac{y}{(1.0525)^2} + \frac{y}{(1.055)^2} = \frac{1107.76}{(1.0525)^3} + \frac{1174.24}{(1.055)^3} = 2000,$$

so $y = 1140.03$.

## 9.2 Options

An option, in the financial sense, is a contract conveying a right to buy or sell a designated security or commodity at a specified price during a stipulated period. The specified price mentioned in this definition is called the option's **strike price** or **exercise price**. A **call option** gives the holder the right to buy (or call away) a specified amount of the underlying security from the option issuer (writer), and a **put option** gives the holder the right to sell (or put) a specified amount of the underlying security to the option issuer. An **American option** allows the right to buy or sell to be exercised any time up to the **expiration date**, and a **European option** allows the option to be exercised only on the expiration date. A **Bermudan option** is an option where the buyer has the right to exercise at a set (always discretely spaced) number of times. This is intermediate between a European option – which allows exercise at a single time, namely expiry – and an American option, which allows exercise at any time (Bermuda is between America and Europe).

As time goes on, existing options contracts on a particular security expire and new option contracts are introduced. When new contracts are introduced, there are generally several contract types set up with strike prices varying from somewhat below to somewhat above the market price of the underlying security at the time the option is introduced. The contracts are set up with strike prices at increments appropriately related to the value of the underlying security. For example, if the underlying stock price is $30, options may be issued with strike prices of $25,

$27.50, $30, $32.50, etc. New options also will be introduced so that exercise dates of up to one year or more into the future are always available. When option values are quoted in a financial publication, the expiration date is given as a particular month, but it is understood that there is a specific day in that month when the option expires (usually the Saturday following the 3$^{rd}$ Friday of the expiration month).

### 9.2.1 CALL OPTIONS

There are two parties to an options contract, the purchaser of the option and the writer (or issuer or seller) of the option. For a call option, as indicated above, the purchaser has the right to buy stock at the strike price by a certain date. In exchange for receiving a payment for writing the option, the writer of the call option has the obligation to provide to the option purchaser the stock at the strike price, if the option purchaser exercises the option. The following definition describes the components of a call option.

---

**Definition 9.3 – Call Option**

The components of a call option are

(i)   the underlying security on which the option is written,

(ii)  the **strike price $K$**,

(iii) the **expiry time $T$**, **or expiration date**,

(iv)  the option type, **American** or **European** (other variations exist)

For a European call option, the purchaser (or owner) of the call option has the right (but not the obligation) to buy the security for the strike price $K$ at the time of expiry $T$. For an American call option, the purchaser has the right to buy the security for the strike price $K$ anytime up to (and including) the time of expiry $T$. The owner of the call option is said to have a **long position** on the call option. If the owner of the call option chooses to purchase the stock under the conditions of the option, the owner is said to **exercise the option**.

---

In order for a call option to exist, there must be a party willing to take a **short position** in the call option. This party is said to **write** the option and has the obligation to sell the security at the strike price $K$ to the owner of the long position if the option is exercised.

The Chicago Board Options Exchange (CBOE) is one of the main market exchanges through which options on US based securities are traded. Figure 9.3 was excerpted from the website of the CBOE after the close of trading on August 11, 2006. It shows that the AMD (Advanced Micro Devices) share price closed at $19.78. It also shows the most recent prices of several different call options on AMD stock (not all existing options are included in Figure 9.3 on the following page). The options traded on US exchanges are American options unless indicated otherwise. An option contract generally is for 100 shares of the underlying security.

The entries under the "Calls" column indicate the year and month of expiry, the strike price, and the exchange symbol for that option. The "Open Int" column indicates the open interest, which is the number of contracts currently in the market. If the owner of a long call exercises the option, the market facilitates the exercise with someone having a short position in the call option, and that contract ceases to exist, and the open interest is reduced by the number of contracts that were exercised. The exchange also facilitates the creation of new contracts by bringing together parties who wish to take long and short positions on additional call option contracts.

Using the data in Figure 9.3 for illustration purposes, suppose that on August 11, 2006 an investor purchases a long position in the "07 Jan 19.00" call option contract. The "last sale" price of $3.60 indicates the option price (also referred to as the "call premium") per share as of the last option sale. The option can be exercised on or before the expiry date in January, 2007 (close of business on January 19, 2007). Exercising the option means that the long call holder will purchase the stock for $19. An investor holding such an option would exercise it only if the share price goes above 19, since the investor could then exercise the option and buy the stock at 19 and immediately sell the stock at the higher current price. If the share price is below 19, the long call holder will not exercise.

**AMD**                                        **19.78**

| Calls | Last Sale | Net | Bid | Ask | Vol | Open Int |
|---|---|---|---|---|---|---|
| 06 Aug 15.00 (AMD HC-E) | 4.40 | pc | 0 | 0 | 0 | 681 |
| 06 Aug 16.00 (AMD HQ-E) | 4.60 | pc | 0 | 0 | 0 | 12868 |
| **06 Aug 17.50 (AMD HW-E)** | 1.95 | pc | 0 | 0 | 0 | 22951 |
| 06 Aug 19.00 (AMD HT-E) | 0.90 | pc | 0 | 0 | 0 | 7974 |
| 06 Aug 20.00 (AMD HD-E) | 0.25 | pc | 0 | 0 | 0 | 31696 |
| 06 Aug 22.50 (AMD HU-E) | 0.05 | pc | 0 | 0 | 0 | 21507 |
| 06 Aug 25.00 (AMD HE-E) | 0.05 | pc | 0 | 0 | 0 | 1437 |
| 06 Aug 27.50 (AMD HY-E) | 0.05 | pc | 0 | 0 | 0 | 4775 |
| 06 Aug 30.00 (AMD HF-E) | 0.05 | pc | 0 | 0 | 0 | 2727 |
| 06 Aug 32.50 (AKD HZ-E) | 0.05 | pc | 0 | 0 | 0 | 896 |
| 06 Sep 15.00 (AMD IC-E) | 4.60 | pc | 0 | 0 | 0 | 219 |
| 06 Sep 16.00 (AMD IQ-E) | 4.80 | pc | 0 | 0 | 0 | 98 |
| 06 Sep 17.00 (AMD IV-E) | 3.60 | pc | 0 | 0 | 0 | 303 |
| | | | | | | |
| 07 Jan 15.00 (AMD AC-E) | 6.10 | pc | 0 | 0 | 0 | 5614 |
| 07 Jan 17.50 (AMD AW-E) | 4.20 | pc | 0 | 0 | 0 | 4927 |
| 07 Jan 19.00 (AMD AT-E) | 3.60 | pc | 0 | 0 | 0 | 425 |
| 07 Jan 20.00 (AMD AD-E) | 2.55 | pc | 0 | 0 | 0 | 11304 |
| 07 Jan 22.50 (AMD AU-E) | 1.65 | pc | 0 | 0 | 0 | 26274 |
| 07 Jan 25.00 (AMD AE-E) | 1.05 | pc | 0 | 0 | 0 | 18773 |
| | | | | | | |
| 08 Jan 15.00 (WVV AC-E) | 7.50 | pc | 0 | 0 | 0 | 2602 |
| 08 Jan 17.50 (WVV AW-E) | 6.20 | pc | 0 | 0 | 0 | 2186 |
| 08 Jan 20.00 (WVV AD-E) | 4.80 | pc | 0 | 0 | 0 | 3499 |
| 08 Jan 22.50 (WVV AX-E) | 4.30 | pc | 0 | 0 | 0 | 5681 |
| 08 Jan 25.00 (WVV AE-E) | 3.00 | pc | 0 | 0 | 0 | 4852 |
| | | | | | | |
| 09 Jan 15.00 (VVV AC-E) | 9.40 | pc | 0 | 0 | 0 | 1351 |
| 09 Jan 17.50 (VVV AW-E) | 7.70 | pc | 0 | 0 | 0 | 187 |
| 09 Jan 20.00 (VVV AD-E) | 7.00 | pc | 0 | 0 | 0 | 1157 |
| 09 Jan 25.00 (VVV AE-E) | 5.30 | pc | 0 | 0 | 0 | 1454 |
| 09 Jan 30.00 (VVV AF-E) | 3.60 | pc | 0 | 0 | 0 | 748 |
| 09 Jan 35.00 (VVV AG-E) | 2.85 | pc | 0 | 0 | 0 | 2088 |
| 09 Jan 40.00 (VVV AH-E) | 2.45 | pc | 0 | 0 | 0 | 1349 |

www.cboe.com

**FIGURE 9.3**

If we consider the payoff or value of the option at the time of expiry, we see that the payoff at that time is $Max\{S_{Jan.19/07} - 19,0\}$, where $S_{Jan.19/07}$ is the stock price at expiry on Jan. 19, 2007. This is true because the option will not be exercised if the stock price is below 19, and therefore the option will have no value. If the stock price is above 19, as mentioned above, the option will be exercised and the stock bought for 19 and can then immediately be resold for $S_{Jan.19/07}$, showing that the option payoff is $S_{Jan.19/07} - 19$ in this case.

If the long call is closed out on the expiry date, the overall profit on the transaction would be the payoff minus the accumulated cost of purchasing the option. Since the option was purchased on August 11, 2006 and it is being closed out on January 19, 2007, the original $3.60 cost of purchasing the call option should be adjusted by accumulating at an appropriate rate of interest. For this period of 161 days, the continuously annual risk-free rate was about 5%, so the risk-free growth from August 11, 2006 to January 19, 2007 is about $e^{(161/365)(.05)} = 1.022$. The profit would be

$$Max\{S_{Jan.19/07} - 19,0\} - 3.60(1.022) = Max\{S_{Jan.19/07} - 19,0\} - 3.68.$$

In general, if a call option has a strike price of $K$, the payoff on the long position on the expiry date is $Max\{S_T - K,0\}$, where $S_T$ denotes the price of the underlying stock at expiry time $T$. The profit on the transaction would be the payoff minus the call premium accumulated to the time the option is exercised. If the option had an initial purchase price of $C_0$ and it is exercised at time $T$, the profit at that time is $Max\{S_T - K,0\} - C_0 e^{rT}$, where $r$ is the risk-free rate of interest from time 0 to time $T$.

Figure 9.4a illustrates the option payoff at expiry for the AMD option example as a function of $S_T$ (not counting the actual cost to purchase the option at time 0) and also illustrates the profit on the transaction. The payoff of the short position at expiry is the negative of the value of the long position and the profit is the negative of the long position profit; this graph is in Figure 9.4b. Note that the long position has an unbounded potential payoff and unbounded potential profit since there is no upper limit on the possible price of the stock. In a similar way, the short position has an unbounded potential loss and a limited potential profit. The long position will have a profit if the stock is above 22.68 on the expiry date and the short position will have a profit only if the stock is below 22.68 on the expiry date. In the graph, $S_T = S_{Jan.19/07}$ is the horizontal axis.

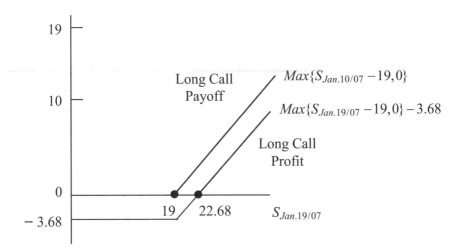

**FIGURE 9.4a**

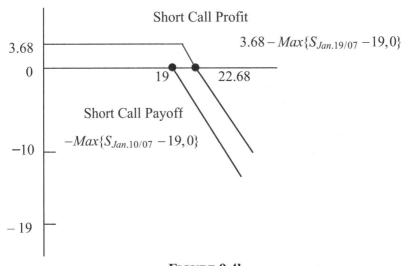

**FIGURE 9.4b**

The following equations summarize the payoff and profit at expiry of a long European call option with strike price $K$ expiring at time $T$ (initial premium is $C_0$).

$$Payoff = \begin{cases} 0 & S_T \le K \\ S_T - K & S_T > K \end{cases} \tag{9.8}$$

$$Profit = \begin{cases} -C_0 e^{rT} & S_T \le K \\ S_T - K - C_0 e^{rT} & S_T > K \end{cases} \tag{9.9}$$

Since AMD has a share price of 19.78 on August 11, 2006, the value of the January 2007 call option with a strike price of 19 is at least .78, since the option can be exercised and the stock bought for 19 and immediately sold for 19.78 for a gain of .78. .78 is the **intrinsic value** of the call option on August 11, 2006. The intrinsic value of an option is the gain that will be made if the option is exercised right now (transaction costs such as commissions are being excluded).

There is also a possibility that the stock price will increase above 20 before January 19, 2007. This suggests that the value of the option should be at least as large as the intrinsic value of .78. The value of the option above the intrinsic value is the *time value* or *time premium*, which takes into account the possible increase in the price of the underlying security before the option expiration date. There are a few examples in Figure 9.2 of in-the-money options in Figure 9.3 whose quoted prices are less than their intrinsic values. For instance, the September 2006 option with strike price 15 has an intrinsic value of 4.78 but a quoted price of 4.60. This situation may occur with an option that is "deep" in the money and is close to expiration. The transaction cost incurred if the option is exercised may cause this situation. Alternatively, the quoted price of 4.60 may have been the option price when it last traded.

A call option whose strike price is less than the current market price of the underlying security is said to be **in-the-money**. In Figure 9.3 we see that all call options with a strike price of less than 19.78 are in-the-money, and all those with strike price over 19.78 are **out-of-the-money**. An out of the money option has no intrinsic value. An option is **at-the-money** if the current stock price is the option strike price. The "09 Jan 30" option in Figure 9.3 (for example) is out-of-the-money. In spite of it having no intrinsic value, it is still priced at 3.60. The market anticipates that between August 11, 2006 and January 2009 the underlying stock price of AMD may rise above 30 (to at least 33.60 according to the option price). It is possible that the option will stay out-of-the-money until the expiration date, in which case it will expire without having been exercised.

The actual price paid for an option depends on the perceptions of investors regarding the behavior of the underlying stock's price prior to the option's expiration date. There are some fairly obvious factors that affect the value of a call option. If the stock price rises, it becomes more likely to be in the money and the value of the long call will rise. In comparing two long call options on a stock, the call with the lower strike price will have a higher value since the underlying stock can be purchased at a lower price. This is clearly illustrated in Figure 9.3. The longer the time to expiry, the more time a stock has to rise in value, and this increases the value of the call. This is also clearly illustrated in Figure 9.3. If we compare call options with a strike price of 20, we see that the January 2009 expiry has the highest price.

A call option can also be used as insurance against a short position in an asset. The following example illustrates this.

**EXAMPLE 9.7**    (*Call option as insurance for a short position*)

Suppose that a short position in 100 shares of AMD is taken just at the close of trading on August 11, 2006, when the price is 19.78. At the same time, one long call option contract (for 100 shares) is purchased with a strike price of $K$ and expiry in January, 2007. Suppose that the risk-free rate is 5% and that the option is held to the expiry date of January 19, 2007. Express the net profit on this transaction as of the expiry date as a function of the original option premium $C_0$, the expiry date stock price $S_T$ and the strike price $K$. Assume that there are no transaction costs.

**SOLUTION**

The profit on the short sale is $100[19.78(1.022) - S_T]$ and the profit on the call option is $100[Max\{S_T - K, 0\} - C_0(1.022)]$ where $1.022 = e^{(161/365)5\%}$. The overall profit on the transaction is $100[19.78(1.022) - S_T + Max\{S_T - K, 0\} - C_0(1.022)]$. If the expiry date stock price is below $K$, the overall profit is $100[19.78(1.022) - S_T - C_0(1.022)]$ and if the expiry date stock price is above $K$, the overall profit is $100[19.78(1.022) - K - C_0(1.022)]$. Without the option, the profit on the transaction would be the profit on the short sale only, which is $100[19.78(1.022) - S_T]$, which is unbounded below; and bounded above by 2021.52 (this occurs if the stock is worthless when the short position is closed). There is no limit to the possible loss. With the option, the maximum possible loss is $-100[19.78(1.022) - K - C_0(1.022)]$.    ❑

The call option in Example 9.7 "hedges" the short position in the stock. An investment is hedged by taking an offsetting position in a related investment (often an option), which reduces the risk of the original investment. Creating a hedge is one of the important uses of options.

Options are also used as speculative investments. The relatively small option price of $1.05 for the January 07 AMD call option with a strike price of $25 can result in a large percentage gain if the stock goes much above the $25 strike price. For instance, if the stock price has risen to $27 in January 2007, the profit will be close to $1 (not counting transaction costs), or about 100% return. Of course, the potential for a 100% loss may be quite large.

### 9.2.2 PUT OPTIONS

For a put option, the purchaser (long position in a put) has the right to sell stock at the strike price by a certain date. In exchange for receiving a payment for writing the option, the writer (seller or short position) of the put option has the obligation to buy the stock from the purchaser of the put option at the strike price, if the option purchaser exercises the option. The following definition describes the components of a put option.

---

**Definition 9.4 – Put Option**

The components of a put option are

(i) the underlying security on which the option is written,
(ii) the **strike price $K$**,
(iii) the **expiry time $T$**,
(iv) the option type, **American** or **European** (other variations exist)

For a European put option, the purchaser (or owner or long position) of the put option has the right (but not the obligation) to sell the security for the strike price $K$ at the time of expiry $T$. For an American put option, the purchaser has the right to sell the security for the strike price $K$ anytime up to (and including) the time of expiry $T$. The owner of the put option is said to have a **long position** on the put option. If the owner of the put option chooses to sell the stock under the conditions of the option, the owner is said to **exercise the option**.

---

As in the case of a call option, in order for a put option to exist, there must be a party willing to take a **short position** in the put option. This party is said to **write** the option and has the obligation to buy the security at the strike price $K$ from the owner of the long position if the option is exercised.

Figure 9.5 is an excerpt from the CBOE website illustrating the put option market data for AMD at the close of trading on August 11, 2006 for the same option exercise prices that are illustrated in Figure 9.3.

**AMD**          **19.78**

| Calls | Last Sale | Net | Bid | Ask | Vol | Open Int |
|---|---|---|---|---|---|---|
| 06 Aug 15.00 (AMD TC-E) | 0.05 | pc | 0 | 0 | 0 | 1115 |
| 06 Aug 16.00 (AMD TQ-E) | 0.05 | pc | 0 | 0 | 0 | 880 |
| 06 Aug 17.50 (AMD TW-E) | 0.05 | pc | 0 | 0 | 0 | 9628 |
| 06 Aug 19.00 (AMD TT-E) | 0.20 | pc | 0 | 0 | 0 | 6982 |
| 06 Aug 20.00 (AMD TD-E) | 0.65 | pc | 0 | 0 | 0 | 11105 |
| 06 Aug 22.50 (AMD TU-E) | 2.95 | pc | 0 | 0 | 0 | 8797 |
| 06 Aug 25.00 (AMD TE-E) | 5.50 | pc | 0 | 0 | 0 | 389 |
| 06 Aug 27.50 (AMD TY-E) | 8.50 | pc | 0 | 0 | 0 | 15 |
| 06 Aug 30.00 (AMD TF-E) | 10.70 | pc | 0 | 0 | 0 | 2 |
| 06 Aug 32.50 (AKD TZ-E) | 8.70 | pc | 0 | 0 | 0 | 0 |
| 06 Sep 15.00 (AMD UC-E) | 0.10 | pc | 0 | 0 | 0 | 1408 |
| 06 Sep 16.00 (AMD UQ-E) | 0.20 | pc | 0 | 0 | 0 | 1943 |
| 06 Sep 17.00 (AMD UV-E) | 0.30 | pc | 0 | 0 | 0 | 2655 |
| 07 Jan 15.00 (AMD MC-E) | 0.70 | pc | 0 | 0 | 0 | 12794 |
| 07 Jan 17.50 (AMD MW-E) | 1.50 | pc | 0 | 0 | 0 | 17064 |
| 07 Jan 19.00 (AMD MT-E) | 1.95 | pc | 0 | 0 | 0 | 130 |
| 07 Jan 20.00 (AMD MD-E) | 2.45 | pc | 0 | 0 | 0 | 18946 |
| 07 Jan 22.50 (AMD MU-E) | 4.20 | pc | 0 | 0 | 0 | 12919 |
| 07 Jan 25.00 (AMD ME-E) | 5.50 | pc | 0 | 0 | 0 | 20466 |
| 08 Jan 15.00 (WVV MC-E) | 1.70 | pc | 0 | 0 | 0 | 9330 |
| 08 Jan 17.50 (WVV MW-E) | 2.65 | pc | 0 | 0 | 0 | 6412 |
| 08 Jan 20.00 (WVV MD-E) | 3.70 | pc | 0 | 0 | 0 | 5668 |
| 08 Jan 22.50 (WVV MX-E) | 5.70 | pc | 0 | 0 | 0 | 4052 |
| 08 Jan 25.00 (WVV ME-E) | 7.70 | pc | 0 | 0 | 0 | 8690 |
| 09 Jan 15.00 (VVV MC-E) | 2.25 | pc | 0 | 0 | 0 | 572 |
| 09 Jan 17.50 (VVV MW-E) | 3.40 | pc | 0 | 0 | 0 | 524 |
| 09 Jan 20.00 (VVV MD-E) | 4.50 | pc | 0 | 0 | 0 | 701 |
| 09 Jan 25.00 (VVV ME-E) | 7.70 | pc | 0 | 0 | 0 | 1665 |
| 09 Jan 30.00 (VVV MF-E) | 10.90 | pc | 0 | 0 | 0 | 811 |
| 09 Jan 35.00 (VVV MG-E) | 15.30 | pc | 0 | 0 | 0 | 362 |
| 09 Jan 40.00 (VVV MH-E) | 19.90 | pc | 0 | 0 | 0 | 29 |

www.cboe.com

**FIGURE 9.5**

Using the data in Figure 9.5 for illustration purposes, suppose that on August 11, 2006 an investor purchases a "07 Jan 19.00" put option. The "last sale" price of $1.95 indicates the option price (also called the "put premium") per share as of the last option sale. The option can be exercised on or before the expiry date in January, 2007 (close of business on January 19, 2007). Exercising the option means that the long put holder will sell the stock for $19. An investor holding such an option would exercise it only if the share price goes below 19, since the investor could buy the stock at the lower current price and then exercise the option and sell the stock at $19. If the share price is above 19, the long put holder will not exercise.

If we consider the payoff or value of the option at the time of expiry, we see that the payoff on the option at that time is $Max\{19 - S_{Jan.19/07}, 0\}$, where $S_{Jan.19/07}$ is the stock price at expiry on Jan. 19, 2007. This is true because the option will not be exercised if the stock price is above 19, and therefore the option will have no value. If the stock price is below 19, the stock can be purchased for $S_{Jan.19/07}$ and then the option exercised and the stock sold for $19, showing that the option payoff is $19 - S_{Jan.19/07}$ in this case.

If the long put is closed out on the expiry date, the overall profit on the transaction would be the payoff minus the cost of purchasing the option. Since the option was purchased on August 11, 2006 and it is being closed out on January 19, 2007, the original $1.95 cost of purchasing the put option should be adjusted by accumulating at the risk-free rate of interest, which was about 5%. The profit would be

$$Max\{19 - S_{Jan.19/07}, 0\} - 1.95(1.022) = Max\{19 - S_{Jan.19/07}, 0\} - 1.99.$$

In general, if a put option has a strike price of $K$, the payoff on the long position on the expiry date is $Max\{K - S_T, 0\}$, where $S_T$ denotes the price of the underlying stock at expiry time $T$. The profit on the transaction would be the payoff minus the accumulated put premium to the time the option is exercised. If the option had an initial purchase price of $P_0$ and it is exercised at time $T$, the profit at that time is $Max\{K - S_T, 0\} - P_0 e^{rT}$, where $r$ is the continuously compounded risk-free rate of interest from time 0 to time $T$.

Figure 9.6a illustrates the option payoff at expiry for the AMD option example as a function of $S_T$ (not counting the actual cost to purchase the option at time 0). It also illustrates the profit on the transaction. The payoff of the short position at expiry is the negative of the value of the long position and the profit is the negative of the long position profit; this graph is in Figure 9.6b.

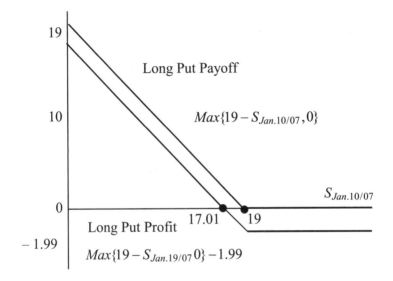

**FIGURE 9.6a**

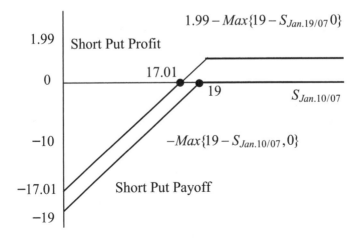

**FIGURE 9.6b**

The following equations summarize the payoff and profit at expiry of a long European put option with strike price $K$ expiring at time $T$ (initial premium is $P_0$).

$$Payoff = \begin{cases} K - S_T & S_T \leq K \\ 0 & S_T > K \end{cases} \quad (9.10a)$$

$$Profit = \begin{cases} K - S_T - P_0 e^{rT} & S_T \leq K \\ -P_0 e^{rT} & S_T > K \end{cases} \quad (9.10b)$$

Note that the long position has a bounded potential payoff and bounded potential profit as does the short position. The long position will have a profit if the stock is below 17.01 on the expiry date and the short position will have a profit only if the stock is above 17.01 on the expiry date. This put option had an intrinsic value of 0 on August 11, 2006 and was, therefore, out-of-the-money.

An example analogous to Example 9.7 would show how a put option can be used as insurance against a long position in an asset. If the asset value declines, the profit on the put option rises to compensate for the loss in asset value. If the asset value rises, the profit is reduced by the cost of the put option.

### 9.2.3 EQUITY LINKED PAYMENTS AND INSURANCE

An investment that has gained prominence in recent years is the **equity-linked CD** (certificate of deposit) also called an **equity-linked annuity**.

Certificates of deposit were briefly discussed in Chapter 8. An investor in a conventional CD is guaranteed (up to the creditworthiness of the financial institution issuing the CD) a specified interest rate for the time until maturity of the CD. An equity-linked CD has the return, or interest paid, linked to the performance of some equity (or market index). Equity-linked CDs (ECDs) can be complicated with a variety of features, but we will discuss the basic form and see how it relates to an option.

The main ingredients of an ECD are

    (i)    the equity to which the CD is linked,

    (ii)   the minimum guaranteed payment at maturity, and

    (iii)  **participation rate**.

Let us consider an ECD that is linked to the performance of the AMD stock referred to earlier in this chapter. Suppose that the ECD investor will receive a minimum of $\$P$ at maturity for each $\$1$ invested. This is the minimum guaranteed payment at maturity. The participation rate is the fraction of the growth in the equity that is paid to the ECD holder. For instance, if the participation rate is $F\%$, then the ECD holder gets a return equal to $F\%$ of the growth in the equity, but receives the minimum guarantee if this is less than $P$.

Suppose that an investor purchases an ECD on August 11, 2006 with maturity to occur on January 19, 2009. For each dollar invested, the payoff to the ECD holder will be the maximum of 1.011 (the minimum guarantee $P$) and $.5 \times \frac{S_T}{19.78}$ (participation rate 50%), where $S_T$ is the AMD share price on January 19, 2009 (2.44 years later). This can be described algebraically as $Max\left\{1.011, .5 \times \frac{S_T}{19.78}\right\}$. This can be written in the following way:

$$Max\left\{1.011, .5 \times \frac{S_T}{19.78}\right\} = 1.011 + Max\left\{0, .5 \times \frac{S_T}{19.78} - 1.011\right\}$$

$$= 1.011 + \frac{.5}{19.78} \times Max\left\{0, S_T - 1.011 \times \frac{19.78}{.5}\right\}$$

$$= 1.011 + .0253 \times Max\{0, S_T - 40\}.$$

Put into this formulation, we see that the ECD holder's payoff is equal to the minimum guarantee plus a fraction of the payoff on a call option on AMD expiring January 19, 2008 with a strike price of 40.

According to the AMD option prices in Figure 9.3, the price of this option is 2.45 on August 11, 2006. If we assume a continuously compounded risk-free interest rate of 5% until maturity, the cost on August 11, 2006 of creating the ECD payoff at maturity is

$$1.011e^{-2.44(.05)} + .0253 \times 2.45 = .957$$

When the issuer of the ECD receives $\$1$ from the investor on August 11, 2006, an investment of $1.011e^{-2.44(.05)} = .895$ can be made in a risk-free zero coupon bond maturing for 1.011 on January 19, 2009, and also purchase .0253 options on AMD with strike price 40 expiring on January 19, 2009 for a cost of $.0253 \times 2.45 = .062$. The total cost for the issuer to create this hedge on August 11, 2006 is $.895 + .062 = .957$. The remaining .043 of the $\$1$ received will be a profit to the ECD issuer.

This amount of .043 is not an arbitrage profit, because there is no guarantee that there will be a willing buyer for this ECD. An investor could get a risk-free return of $e^{2.44(.05)} = 1.130$ for the period from August 11, 2006 to January 19, 2009. An investor in the ECD would be giving up this risk-free return in exchange for the possibility that the AMD share price will rise enough to provide a greater return. In order for that to occur, the AMD share price on January 19, 2009 must satisfy the relationship $.5 \times \frac{S_T}{19.78} > 1.130$, or equivalently $S_T > 44.70$.

If the investor believes that the AMD share price will be that high on January 19, 2009, she could use the $1 to buy .41 options with strike price of 40. If the share price is 44.70 or higher at expiry, the payoff will be at least $.41 \times 4.70 = 1.93$. Of course, if the share price is below 40, the option expires worthless.

The cost of the hedge is quite sensitive to changes in either the level of the minimum guarantee and the participation rate. If the minimum guarantee is increased to 1.065 in the example above (about half of the risk-free growth for the period), the cost of the hedge is about 1.00 per $1 invested, a break even situation. If the minimum guarantee is kept at 1.011 but the participation is increased to 75%, the cost of the hedge becomes about 1.08 per $1 invested.

As seen in the previous example, an option can be used to hedge a position. It can serve as a form of insurance. It is also the case that some types of insurance behave in the same way as a put option.

Most people who own a car will purchase insurance. The insurance would likely include a component that will pay for damage to the vehicle if it is involved in an accident. There would also likely be a liability insurance component that covers the cost of damage experienced by others as a result of you being found responsible for causing damage while driving the car. We will focus on the part of insurance that covers damage to your own car.

Suppose that you purchase an automobile at a cost of $50,000. You also purchase collision insurance which will pay for the cost of repairing or replacing the car in the event it is involved in a collision. Collision insurance policies generally include a **deductible** amount. If a collision occurs and damage is below the deductible, the insurer will not pay, and if damage is above the deductible, the insurer will pay the amount by which the damage is above the deductible. Suppose that the insurance policy has a deductible of $1000 and has a one year insurance premium of $500. We will make the simple assumption that the only change in the value of the car will be due to a possible collision and will be paid at the time the collision occurs. We will also assume that there will be at most one collision in the year.

Suppose that the value of the car after a collision is $X$. The insurance will pay you the larger of $49,000 - X$ and 0. Your insurance policy is a long put option with a strike price of 49,000. It will be exercised if a collision occurs with damage of more than 1000 (bringing the value of the car below 49,000). We are assuming that this "option" can only be exercised in the event of a collision occurring.

## 9.3   OPTION STRATEGIES

There are a wide variety of combinations of long or short asset positions and long or short option positions. These varying trading strategies provide a diversity of payoff and profit outcomes. In this section we will review some of the more commonly used option strategies.

### 9.3.1  FLOORS, CAPS, AND COVERED POSITIONS

**Definition 9.5 – Protective Put or Floor**

The combination of having a long position in an asset along with a long position in a put option on the asset is a **protective put or floor** position.

An investor owning shares may have some unrealized gains from the increase in share value since they have been held. To protect against loss of the gains while still continuing to own the shares, an investor may take a protective put position by purchasing a put.

Since $\max\{S_T - K, 0\}$ is the payoff on a long call, we see that a floor has the same payoff as a long zero coupon bond maturing for amount $K$ combined with a long call, and therefore, the same profit as a long call.

$$S_T + \max\{K - S_T, 0\} = \begin{cases} K & \text{if} \quad S_T \leq K \\ S_T & \text{if} \quad S_T > K \end{cases} = \max\{K, S_T\} \quad (9.11)$$

We note that

$$\max\{K, S_T\} = K + \max\{S_T - K, 0\}. \quad (9.12)$$

Since $\max\{S_T - K, 0\}$ is the payoff on a long call, we see that a floor has the same payoff as a long zero coupon bond maturing for amount $K$ combined with a long call, and therefore, the same profit as a long call. This follows from the fact that there is no profit on zero coupon bond investments under the assumption of no-arbitrage, and therefore, if two positions have payoffs that differ by a constant at a specific point in time then those two positions must result in the same profit.

The payoff and profit graphs for the floor position are shown in Figure 9.7. Recall that $P_0$ is the put option premium. The potential loss is limited and the potential gain is unbounded with a protective put position.

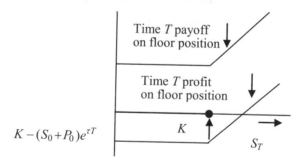

**FIGURE 9.7**

When a put is purchased at the same time as the stock, the position may be referred to as a married put position.

**Definition 9.6 – Cap Position**

The combination of having a short position in an asset along with a long position in a call option on the asset may be referred to as a **cap position**.

The payoff at time $T$ on a cap is

$$-S_T + \max\{S_T - K, 0\} = \begin{cases} -S_T & \text{if } S_T \leq K \\ -K & \text{if } S_T > K \end{cases} = \max\{-K, -S_T\}.$$

$$(9.13)$$

We note that
$$\max\{-K, -S_T\} = -K + \max\{K - S_T, 0\}. \qquad (9.14)$$

Since $\max\{K - S_T, 0\}$ is the payoff on a long put, we see that a cap has the same payoff as a short zero coupon bond maturing for amount $-K$ combined with a long put, and therefore, the same profit as a long put.

The payoff and profit graphs for the cap position are in Figure 9.8.

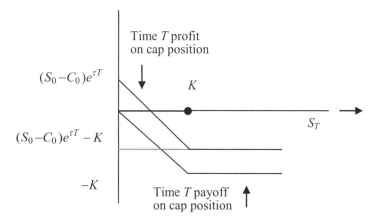

**FIGURE 9.8**

A cap position limits the potential loss that can occur with a short position in an asset.

## Covered Calls and Covered Puts

The combination of a long position in an asset with a written call option on the asset is a **covered call.** The payoff at time $T$ is

$$S_T - \max\{S_T - K, 0\} = -\max\{-K, -S_T\}. \qquad (9.15)$$

The profit at time $T$ would be the payoff minus $(S_0 - C_0)e^{rT}$. This is the same as the payoff on a short cap position.

If the call is written at the same time as the shares are purchased, the covered call might also be referred to as a "buy-write," and if the call is written after the shares have been purchased it is an "overwrite."

The covered call might be used by a bullish investor who believes the share price will experience little movement during the lifetime of the call and will gain from the income generated by writing the call.

The combination of a short position in an asset with a written put option on the asset is called a covered put. The payoff at expiry on a covered put will be

$$-S_T - \max\{K - S_T, 0\} = -\max\{K, S_T\}. \qquad (9.16)$$

This is the same payoff as a short protective put position. The profit at time $T$ would be the payoff plus $(S_0 + P_0)e^{rT}$.

Keep in mind that if two positions have the same payoff at time $T$, they have the same value at time 0 and they have the same profit at time $T$ (under the assumption that no arbitrage opportunities exist).

The payoff and profit graphs for a covered call and a covered put are shown in Figures 9.9a and 9.9b.

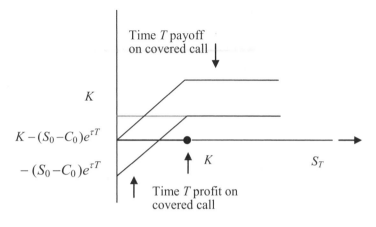

**FIGURE 9.9a**

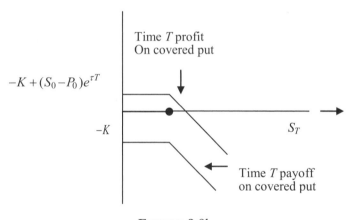

**FIGURE 9.9b**

A call option that is written by someone who does not own the asset is referred to as a **naked call**.

### 9.3.2 SYNTHETIC FORWARD CONTRACTS

We have seen that it was possible to replicate the payoff on a long forward contract on an asset by purchasing the asset and going short on a zero coupon bond (recall that "going short on a zero coupon bond" means that we are borrowing). This replicated a long position on a forward contract with the no-arbitrage forward price. We can replicate a long forward contract with any forward price by combining call and put options.

Suppose that at time 0 we combine the following positions on an asset

(i) purchased call with strike price $K$ expiring at time $T$, and
(ii) written put with strike price $K$ expiring at time $T$.
The payoff at time $T$ of this combination is

$$\text{purchased call payoff} + \text{written put payoff}$$
$$= \max\{S_T - K, 0\} - \max\{K - S_T, 0\} = S_T - K \qquad (9.17)$$

This is the same as the payoff on a long forward contract expiring at time $T$ with delivery price $K$. This combination of a purchased call and written put is a **synthetic forward**. The cost at time 0 to create this synthetic forward is $C_0(K) - P_0(K)$ (difference of call and put with strike price $K$).

A short synthetic forward contract can be created by reversing the long synthetic forward. This is done by combining a purchased put with a written call. With strike price $K$ on both the purchased put and written call, the payoff at time is

$$\max\{K - S_T, 0\} - \max\{S_T - K, 0\} = K - S_T. \qquad (9.18)$$

### 9.3.3 Put-Call Parity

The assumption that no arbitrage opportunities can exist implies that two positions with the same payoff at time $T$ must have the same cost at time 0. In fact, if the payoffs of two positions differ by a constant at time $T$, then they have the same cost at time 0 and the same profit at time $T$. We have seen that it is possible to create a synthetic forward contract with a combination of call and put options. The synthetic forward can be created with any delivery price. Earlier we saw that the no-arbitrage delivery price for a forward contract is the accumulated value of the asset at time $T$ (actually the accumulated value of the prepaid forward price). For a non-dividend paying asset with price $S_0$ at time 0, the no-arbitrage forward price for delivery at time $T$ is $F_{0,T} = S_0 e^{rT}$.

If we combine a purchased call with a written put with strike price $F_{0,T}$, we have the synthetic long forward contract with forward delivery price $F_{0,T}$. Since the cost at time 0 for the forward contract is 0, it must also be true that the cost at time 0 for the synthetic forward contract is 0.

The cost at time 0 for the synthetic forward is

$$\text{call premium} - \text{put premium} = C_0(K) - P_0(K)..$$

This should be 0 if the strike price is $K = F_{0,T}$.

Now suppose we consider a forward contract which has a delivery price of $K$ (not necessarily the no-arbitrage forward price of $F_{0,T}$). Since the price is 0 at time 0 for a forward contract with delivery price $F_{0,T}$, it follows that the value at time 0 of a forward contract with delivery price $K$ is $(F_{0,T} - K)e^{-rT}$ (this is the present value of the difference between a delivery price of $F_{0,T}$ and $K$ to be paid at time $T$). The synthetic forward made up of a purchased call and written put, but with strike price $K$, has a cost at time 0 of $C_0(K) - P_0(K)$. It follows that

$$C_0(K) - P_0(K) = (F_{0,T} - K)e^{-rT}. \tag{9.19}$$

This relationship is referred to as **put-call parity**. Note that as $K$ gets larger, the premium for a call gets smaller and the premium for a put gets larger, so the left hand side of the equation gets smaller (eventually becoming negative). It is obvious that the right hand side gets smaller as $K$ increases. An important point to note is that $F_{0,T}e^{-rT} = S_0$ under the no-arbitrage assumption (when there are no dividends).

### 9.3.4 More Option Combinations

**Bull and Bear Spreads**
A bull spread based on call options is the combination of

(i) a purchased call with strike price $K_1$ and

(ii) a written call with strike price $K_2$, where $K_1 < K_2$.

A bull spread based on put options is the combination of

(i)  a purchased put with strike price $K_1$ and

(ii) a written put with strike price $K_2$, where $K_1 < K_2$.

Suppose that we consider a bull spread made up of a call option. The payoff at time $T$ is

$$\max\{S_T - K_1, 0\} - \max\{S_T - K_2, 0\} = \begin{cases} 0 & \text{if } S_T \le K_1 \\ S_T - K_1 & \text{if } K_1 < S_T \le K_2 \\ K_2 - K_1 & \text{if } S_T > K_2 \end{cases} \qquad (9.20)$$

If we create a bull spread with put options at the same strike prices, the payoff function at time $T$ is

$$\max\{K_1 - S_T, 0\} - \max\{K_2 - S_T, 0\} = \begin{cases} -(K_2 - K_1) & \text{if } S_T \le K_1 \\ S_T - K_2 & \text{if } K_1 < S_T \le K_2 \\ 0 & \text{if } S_T > K_2 \end{cases}$$

$$(9.21)$$

The payoff and profit diagrams of a bull spread are shown in Figure 9.10.

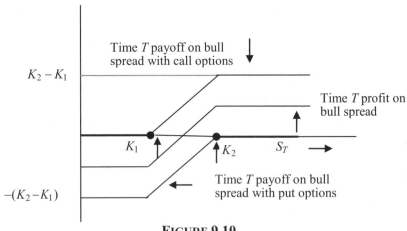

**FIGURE 9.10**

Under put-call parity, the profit at time $T$ on a bull spread made up of call options should be the same as the profit on the bull spread made up of put options because the payoffs differ by a constant.

A very bullish investor might choose to purchase the call with strike $K_1$ only to take advantage of a potential large increase in the stock price. An investor who is moderately bullish on the stock price might engage in a bull spread, earning income on selling the call at strike $K_2$.

A **bear spread** is the opposite of a bull spread. If $K_1 < K_2$, then a bear spread can be constructed by combining a written call with strike price $K_1$ and a purchased call with strike price $K_2$. The payoff would be the negative of that of a bull spread.

## Box Spreads

A box spread is a combination of

(i)  a synthetic long forward with forward price $K_1$, and
(ii) a synthetic short forward with forward price $K_2$.

The synthetic long forward with delivery price $K_1$ is constructed with a purchased call and written put, both with strike prices of $K_1$. Similarly, a written call and purchased put with strike prices of $K_2$ is a synthetic short forward with delivery price $K_2$. If $K_1 < K_2$, the payoff at time $T$ is

$$\max\{S_T - K_1, 0\} - \max\{K_1 - S_T, 0\}$$
$$- \max\{S_T - K_2, 0\} + \max\{K_2 - S_T, 0\} = K_2 - K_1 \text{ for any } S_T.$$

This box spread has the same payoff as a long zero coupon bond maturing for amount $K_2 - K_1$; there is no risk from the stock price. The cost at time 0 should be the same as the present value of this certain payoff. Reversing the position creates a short box spread that has the same payoff as a short zero.

## Collars

It was seen earlier that the combination of a purchased put and a written call, both at the same strike price $K$ and both expiring at the same time $T$ is a synthetic short forward position with delivery price $K$ at time $t$. If the written call option has a higher strike price than the purchased put option, the combination is referred to as a **collar**, and the difference between the call strike price and the put strike price is the **collar width**. If the stock is owned, the position is referred to as a **collared stock**.

For a general collar consisting of purchased put with strike $K_1$ and a written call with price $K_2$, and with $K_1 < K_2$, the payoff on the collar is

$$\begin{cases} K_1 - S_T & \text{if} \quad S_T \le K_1 \\ 0 & \text{if} \quad K_1 < S_T \le K_2, \\ K_2 - S_T & \text{if} \quad S_T > K_2 \end{cases} \qquad (9.22)$$

The profit will be the payoff minus the accumulated cost of the collar. Depending on the premiums for the two options, the accumulated cost of the collar might be positive or negative. If the stock is held along with the collar, the payoff of the collared stock will be

$$\begin{cases} K_1 & \text{if} \quad S_T \le K_1 \\ S_T & \text{if} \quad K_1 < S_T \le K_2. \\ K_2 & \text{if} \quad S_T > K_2 \end{cases} \qquad (9.23)$$

The graph of the payoff on the collar and the payoff on the collared stock are in Figure 9.11.

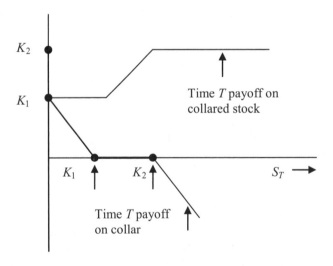

**FIGURE 9.11**

The profit diagrams would have the same shape as the payoffs, but would be shifted vertically up or down depending upon the accumulated value of the cost of establishing the collar or collared stock. It would usually be the case that when the collar is established, the put and call options chosen would be out of the money.

A collared stock is a protective put combined with a written call. An investor who has unrealized gains on a stock can protect them with the purchase of the put, and if he is only moderately bullish on the stock, he can offset the cost of the put with the out of the money written call.

A combination of a written put option with strike $K_1$ and a purchased call option with strike $K_2$ will provide a collar for a short position in the asset.

It is worth noting a more general relationship linking payoff and profit functions and diagrams. If two payoff functions differ by a constant, then this would be represented in the payoff graphs as one payoff graph being the other graph shifted either vertically up or vertically down. This corresponds to the two payoffs differing by the value of a zero coupon bond. Since a zero coupon bond always has zero profit, it follows that the profit function is the same for the two payoffs. This general relationship is true if no arbitrage opportunities exist.

**Straddle**

A straddle is a combination of a purchased call and purchased put with the same expiry and strike price. A written straddle would be the combination of a written call and a written put with the same strike price. The payoff and profit graphs are shown in Figure 9.12.

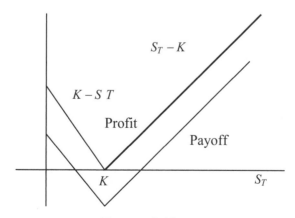

**FIGURE 9.12**

### Strangle

A purchased strangle is a combination of purchased call and purchased put options expiring at the same time but with different strike prices. The usual strangle would be a combination of out-of-the-money options, so the put strike would be less than the call strike. The payoff and profit graphs are shown in Figure 9.13 for a strangle with put strike $K_1$ and call strike $K_2$, with $K_1 < K_2$.

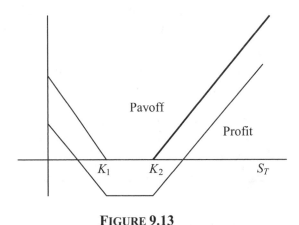

**FIGURE 9.13**

An investor believing there will be significant volatility in the stock price before the options expire will engage in a long straddle or strangle. If the stock price moves significantly higher or lower from the current position, there will be a profit in the position. Reversing the positions results in a short straddle or short strangle.

### Butterfly Spread

A butterfly spread is a combination of a written straddle with a purchased strangle. The written straddle would be at a strike price $K$ near the current stock price and the purchased strangle would have put strike $K_1$ and call strike $K_2$ with $K_1 < K < K_2$. The purchased strangle provides some insurance against the written straddle. The result is a profit if the stock price does not move far from the current level. The payoff and profit graph of a (long) butterfly spread are shown in Figure 9.14.

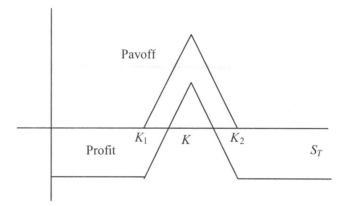

**FIGURE 9.14**

### 9.3.5 USING FORWARDS AND OPTIONS FOR HEDGING AND INSURANCE

**Hedging and Insurance for the Seller of an Asset**

Someone who holds an asset (or a producer of an asset) that will be selling the asset at a later time has various ways to limit the risk on the price to be received at the later time. Limiting the risk is referred to as hedging the risk.

A short forward contract with forward price $F_{0,T}$ locks in the amount that will be received when the asset is sold at time $T$. Assuming that the forward price is based on no-arbitrage opportunities existing, the forward contract eliminates the chance for a profit or loss. The no arbitrage forward price will be $F_{0,T} = S_0 e^{rT}$, so the "return" will be the same as the risk free rate. There is no cost for this forward contract that guarantees a price for the asset.

Buying a put option with strike price $K$ will limit, on the downside, the price that will be received when the asset is sold at time $T$. Since it is assumed that the asset is being held until time $T$, the payoff at time $T$ is $\max\{K - S_T, 0\} + S_T \geq K$. We have put in place a minimum payoff, but there is the cost of the put option needed to create this insurance hedge. The seller can trade off the potential high price for the asset by selling a call at a higher strike and creating a collared asset. The premium received from selling the call offsets the cost of the put.

Selling a call option with strike price $K$ provides income now and reduces the minimum payoff that will be received when the asset is sold at time $T$. But the payoff at time $T$ is limited to $S_T - \max\{S_T - K, 0\}$ which is $\leq K$, and which occurs if the asset value at time $T$ is $> K$ (so the call will be exercised). We are guaranteed at least the accumulated premium on the written call option, but we have an upper limit on the payoff that we will receive when the asset is sold.

A **paylater** strategy for the seller of an asset consists of buying $m$ puts at strike $K_1$ and selling $n$ puts at strike $K_2 > K_1$, so that the premium at time 0 is $mP_{0,K_1} - nP_{0,K_2} = 0$. The payoff at time $T$ is

$$m \max\{K_1 - S_T, 0\} - n \max\{K_2 - S_T, 0\}$$

$$= \begin{cases} m(K_1 - S_T) - n(K_2 - S_T) & \text{if } S_T \leq K_1 \\ -n(K_2 - S_T) & \text{if } K_1 < S_T \leq K_2. \\ 0 & \text{if } S_T > K_2 \end{cases}$$

Since $K_1 < K_2$, it follows that $P_{0,K_1} < P_{0,K_2}$, and we must have $m > n$ in order to have premium 0 at time 0. This arrangement provides no hedging for asset price above $K_2$. For asset prices between $K_1$ and $K_2$ there is a negative payoff and for asset price below $K_1$ there will be a positive payoff.

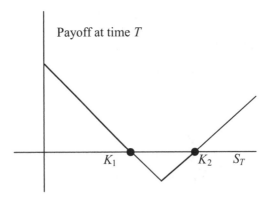

**FIGURE 9.15**

## Hedging and Insurance for the Purchaser of an Asset

The strategies that can be employed by a purchaser to hedge the price to be paid when the asset is bought are the reverse of the strategies that the seller can use. The purchaser can enter a long forward contract, guaranteeing a specific price. The purchaser can guarantee a maximum price of $K$ by buying a call option with strike price $K$.

### 9.3.6 OPTION PRICING MODELS

Since the introduction of "exchange-traded options" in 1973, a considerable amount of research has been done into the valuation of options. In order to determine the value of an option on an underlying security, a combination of selling (or buying) the option and buying (or selling) an appropriate amount of the security is made that forms a *riskless hedge* that provides the same return as would be realized over the same period when investing at the risk-free rate of return. The way in which such a riskless hedge is constructed can best be seen in an elementary illustration in which, on the expiration date, the price of the underlying security will be one of two possible values. This is called the **binomial model**.

Suppose that a stock has a current price of 100, and at the end of the current period the stock's price will be either 110 or 90. Suppose that the stock has a call option to purchase at a strike price of 105 at the end of the period. Suppose investor A writes the call option on one share and investor B purchases the call option. If the stock price is 110 at the time the option expires, the value of the option at that time will be $110 - 105 = 5$. In that case, at time 1 investor B (the holder of the option) can buy the stock from investor A for 105 when he exercises the option, and sell the stock at the market price for 110. On the other hand, investor B will allow the option to expire unexercised if the stock's price is 90, so the value of the option in this case is 0 on the expiration date.

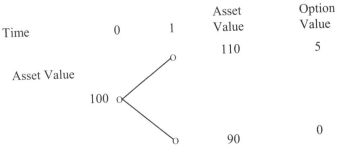

FIGURE 9.16

Suppose that at the same time investor A sells the option on one share, he also purchases ¼ share of the stock for 1/4(100) = 25. Let us denote by $C_0$ the value of the option to purchase one share at the start of the period. The net amount invested by investor A is $25 - C_0$, the amount paid for the 1/4-share of stock minus the amount received from the sale of the option. At the time of expiration, one of two events will occur; the stock price will be either 110 or 90. If the stock price is 110 at the time of expiration, then at that time the net value of investor A's combined investment is $27.50 - 5 = 22.50$ (the value of the stock investor A holds minus the cost of fulfilling the obligation to the option holder). If the stock price is 90 at the time of expiration, then the net value of investor A's combined investment is $22.50 - 0 = 22.50$. Thus, the net value of the investment at the end of the period is 22.50 no matter what the stock price is. This is a riskless hedge for investor A, in the sense that the value of the investment at the end of the period will be 22.50 with certainty.

According to the financial principle that no arbitrage opportunities exist, any riskless investment must earn the same return as the risk-free rate of interest. In order to determine the price of the option at the start of the period, investor B's riskless investment should be equivalent to a riskless investment in a government security over the same period. Suppose that the continuously compounded risk-free rate of return for the period is 1%. In order for the investment to be equivalent to a risk-free investment in the government security, we must have $(25 - C_0)e^{.01} = 22.50$, so that $C_0 = 2.72$.

In the general binomial model for stock price movement, suppose the current stock price is $S_0$, and suppose that at the end of the current period the stock price will be either $S_1^+$ or $S_1^-$, where $S_1^+ > S_1^-$. Suppose there is a call option on the stock with a strike price of $K$. The value of the option at the end of the period is either $C_1^+$ or $C_1^-$, depending on whether the stock price is $S_1^+$ or $S_1^-$. It is possible to create a riskless hedge by selling a call option on one share of stock at the same time as purchasing $h$ shares of stock, where $h = \dfrac{C_1^+ - C_1^-}{S_1^+ - S_1^-}$ is called the **hedge ratio**.

The net amount invested by the writer (seller) of the call option at the start of the period is $h \cdot S_0 - C_0$, and the value of the investment at the end of the period is $h \cdot S_1^+ - C_1^+ = h \cdot S_1^- - C_1^-$, whether the stock price goes to $S_1^+$ or $S_1^-$. If the risk-free rate of return is $r$ for the period, then

$$(h \cdot S_0 - C_0)(1+r) = h \cdot S_1^+ - C_1^+ = h \cdot S_1^- - C_1^- \qquad (9.24)$$

Since $h, S_0, S_1^+, S_1^-, C_1^+, C_1^-$ and $r$ are known, it is possible to solve for $C_0$.

This binomial model for stock prices and option valuation can be extended to a two-period scenario in which the stock price $S_0$ moves to one of two prices $S_1^+$ or $S_1^-$ at the end of the first period. For each price at the end of period 1 there are two possible prices to which the stock can move at the end of period 2, which may be different for $S_1^+$ and $S_1^-$. This generalization can be continued to more than two consecutive periods. The period can be shortened and the number of periods, $n$, can be increased, allowing a limiting case in which, as $n \to \infty$, the stock price becomes a continuous stochastic process.

The limiting case described in the previous paragraph is the **Black-Scholes option pricing formula.** The formula assumes that the stock pays no dividends prior to expiry of the option, and that $\{\ln[S_t] \,|\, 0 \leq t \leq n\}$ forms a Brownian motion stochastic process with variance $\sigma^2$ per unit time period, where $S_t$ is the stock price at time $t$. (It is possible to adjust the formulation to account for dividends). This assumption regarding the behavior of the stock's price can be more simply described by saying that the continuously compounded annual rate of return on the stock has a normal distribution with variance $\sigma^2$; in practice, $\sigma^2$ is estimated as a sample variance based on historical data for the stock. The following parameters are also required for the valuation formula:

$\delta$ - risk-free force of interest (Finance texts use $r$)

$S_0$ - current price of the stock

$K$ - exercise (strike) price of the option

$T$ - time (in years) until expiry of the option

The Black-Scholes formula gives the price of the call option at the current time as

$$C = S_0 \cdot \Phi(d_1) - K \cdot e^{-n\delta} \cdot \Phi(d_2), \qquad (9.25a)$$

where

$$d_1 = \frac{\ln\left(\frac{S_0}{K}\right) + \left(\delta + \frac{1}{2}\sigma^2\right) \cdot n}{\sigma\sqrt{n}}, \qquad (9.25b)$$

$$d_2 = \frac{\ln\left(\frac{S_0}{K}\right) + \left(\delta - \frac{1}{2}\sigma^2\right) \cdot n}{\sigma\sqrt{n}}, \qquad (9.25c)$$

and $\Phi(x)$ is the cumulative distribution function of the standard normal distribution.

---

**EXAMPLE 9.8**    (*Black-Scholes option pricing formula*)

The price on January 15 of a share of XYZ stock is 50. Use the Black-Scholes option pricing formula to find the value on January 15 of an option to buy 1 share of XYZ, with an expiration date of July 20, and with an exercise price of (a) 45, (b) 50, and (c) 55. Assume the risk-free force of interest is $r = .08$, and the continuously compounded rate of return on the stock has a standard deviation of $\sigma = .3$.

**SOLUTION**

$S_0 = 50$, $n = \frac{186}{365} = .5096$, $r = .08$, $\sigma^2 = .09$, $e^{-rT} = .9601$.

(a) $K = 45$ so $d_1 = .79$ and $d_2 = .57$ so that $\Phi(d_1) = .7852$
and $\Phi(d_2) = .7157$ implying an option price of
$50(.7852) - 45(.9601)(.7157) = 8.34$.

(b) $K = 50$ so $d_1 = 0.30$ and $d_2 = 0.08$ implying $\Phi(d_1) = .6179$ and
$\Phi(d_2) = .5319$ implying an option price of
$50(.6179) - 50(.9601)(.5319) = 5.36$.

(c) $K = 55$ so $d_1 = -0.14$ and $d_2 = -0.36$ implying
$\Phi(d_1) = .4443$ and $\Phi(d_2) = .3594$ implying an option price of
$50(.4443) - 55(.9601)(.3594) = 3.24$.    ❑

Options are available on a variety of financial instruments, including government Treasury Bonds (both long and short term) and foreign currency contracts. Options provide the investor with a certain amount of *leverage* in the investment. On a call option, the option price (or *premium*) on an in-the-money option will fluctuate in tandem, more or less, with the price of the underlying security. Thus the option investor can make a similar numerical gain as the holder of the underlying security, but the premium paid by the option investor is, typically, considerably less than the price of the underlying security. The call option buyer's potential loss is limited to the original cost of the option (but it could be a 100% loss if the option expires out of the money).

As mentioned earlier in this chapter, options are one example of the class of investments known as derivative investments or derivatives. The value of a derivative investment is derived from or tied to the value of some underlying investment; the option value is completely dependent upon the value of the underlying stock. The previous paragraph indicated that the value of an option is generally a fraction of the value of the underlying stock but may be subject to similar price changes. From Example 9.8 we see that the Black-Scholes price of the call option with strike price 50 is 2.01. If the stock price rises to 55 by the expiration date, the option value rises to 5, which is 150% increase, while the stock itself has risen from 50 to 55, which is a 10% increase. On the other hand, if the stock price drops to 45 at the expiration date, the call option has a value of 0, which is a 100% loss of the investment in the option, while the stock has had a 10% decrease in value. The call option is generally considerably more risky than the underlying stock, and this is a feature of most derivative investments. A **leveraged investment** is one for which small percentage changes in the underlying investment can result in large percentage changes in the related derivative investment. A call option is an example of a leveraged investment.

## 9.4 FOREIGN CURRENCY EXCHANGE RATES

Corporations involved in international trade that are scheduled to receive delayed payment in various foreign currencies, but whose expenditures are mainly in their own country's currency, are concerned with the fluctuation of exchange rates among the currencies. There are a number of ways to protect against adverse fluctuations in exchange rates, including the use of *foreign currency futures* and forward markets for currency exchange as discussed in Section 8.1. Forward rate contracts can be established for periods as short as one month or as long as 10 years into the future.

The economic factors that determine the relationships among foreign currencies are very complex. One important factor is the relationship between interest rates in the various countries. The following example gives a simple illustration of the effect of interest rates on the exchange rate between currencies of different countries.

| EXAMPLE 9.9 | *(Exchange and interest rates)*

Assume that today's spot exchange rate between the Canadian and US currencies, $1 CDN is equivalent to $.85 US. Suppose interest rates for the coming year are 6% in Canada and 3% in the US. Determine the one-year forward exchange rate between the values of the two currencies in order that the relationship between the currencies remains unchanged with regard to borrowing and lending for one year.

| SOLUTION |

One year from now $1.06 CDN will be required to repay a loan of $1 CDN now. Similarly, one year from now $.85 \times 1.03 = $.8755 US will be required to repay a loan of $.85 US now. In order to maintain a market balance between the currencies, one year from now $1.06 CDN should be equivalent to $.8755 US, or $1 CDN should be equivalent to $\frac{\$.8755}{1.06} = \$.8259$ US dollars. ◻

The situation in Example 9.9 can be generalized as follows. Suppose the spot exchange rate today between currencies A and B is that 1 unit of currency A is equivalent to $C_s$ units of currency B. Let the annual interest rate on currency A (in the country with that currency) be $i_A$ and the annual interest rate on currency B be $i_B$. In order to balance two one-year loans in the respective currencies, the relationship between the currencies one year from now should be $1 + i_A$ units of currency A equivalent to $C_s(1+i_B)$ units of currency B, or one unit of currency A equivalent to

$$C_f = \frac{C_s(1+i_B)}{1+i_A},\qquad(9.26)$$

where $C_f$ is the one-year forward rate of exchange.

The relationship between the spot and forward rates of exchange can also be explained in terms of the inflation rates in the respective currencies. If the real (inflation-adjusted) rates of interest over the following year are the same in the two currencies, then $i_A^{real} = \frac{i_A - r_A}{1 + r_A} = i_B^{real} = \frac{i_B - r_B}{1 + r_B}$, where $r_A$ and $r_B$ are the annual inflation rates in currencies A and B. Then

$$1 + i_A^{real} = \frac{1 + i_A}{1 + r_A} = 1 + i_B^{real} = \frac{1 + i_B}{1 + r_B},$$

so $\frac{1 + i_B}{1 + i_A} = \frac{1 + r_B}{1 + r_A}$, and therefore

$$C_f = \frac{C_s(1 + i_B)}{1 + i_A} = \frac{C_s(1 + r_B)}{1 + r_A}. \tag{9.27}$$

This relationship can be explained as follows: if one unit of currency A is now worth $C_s$ units of currency B, then to maintain the same balance of purchasing power between the currencies one year from now, $1 + r_A$ units of currency A should have the same value as $C_s(1 + r_B)$ units of currency B, which is the relationship of Equation (9.27).

Using the approximation $\frac{1 + x}{1 + y} \approx 1 + x - y$, Equation (9.26) becomes $C_s(1 + i_B - i_A) \approx C_f$, or

$$\frac{C_f - C_s}{C_s} \approx i_B - i_A. \tag{9.28}$$

The relationship in Equation (9.28) is called the **interest rate parity theorem**, which states that the percentage difference between the spot and forward exchange rates is approximately equal to the difference between the interest rates on the two currencies.

The relationships in Equations (9.26), (9.27), and (9.28) are quite simplistic, and do not account for all of the dynamics affecting exchange rates. For instance, a typical way in which a country supports its currency is by increasing the rate of interest on government securities. The reasoning behind this is that as the rate of return increases in the country's currency, there will be more foreign demand for that currency in order to invest at the higher rate, and the demand for the currency will increase its value in terms of other currencies. However if we increase $i_A$ in Equation (9.26) while keeping $i_B$ unchanged, the ratio $\dfrac{C_f}{C_s}$ must decrease. It is not clear whether this occurs because of a decrease in $C_f$ or because of an increase in $C_s$. The most likely scenario is that both $C_f$ and $C_s$ increase, but $C_s$ increases proportionally more than $C_f$ since the increased rate $i_A$ may change (decrease) before the forward exchange could take place.

## 9.5. NOTES AND REFERENCES

Practical information on the nature of forward contracts, options, and futures is available from trading exchanges such as the Chicago Board Options Exchange and the Chicago Board of Trade.

There are many good references for topics in finance and portfolio analysis. A very readable introduction to the binomial pricing model for options can be found in *Financial Calculus: An Introduction to Derivative Pricing*, by M. Baxter and A. Rennie, published by Cambridge Publishing. Discussions of the Black-Scholes option pricing model can be found in *Modern Portfolio Theory and Investment Analysis*, by E Elton and M. Gruber, published by John Wiley. The Black-Scholes formula was developed in the research paper *The Pricing of Options and Corporate Liabilities*, by F. Black and M. Scholes in the *Journal of Political Economy* in 1973. Groundwork for the Black-Scholes formula was also done by R. Merton. Merton and Scholes were awarded the 1997 Nobel Prize in economics for their work on investment derivatives (Black had died prior to the award being given). The British journal *The Telegraph* has a list of "The 20 Biggest Trading Disasters" (www.telegraph.co.uk), of which the Société Générale incident is the worst (until now).

A discussion of default premium and risk premium can be found in *Investments* by W. Sharpe, published by Prentice-Hall. There are many books on options and financial derivatives in general, but John Hull's book *Options, Futures and Other Derivatives* is an excellent reference and introductory book on mathematical finance.

## 9.6 EXERCISES

### SECTION 9.1

9.1.1   The current spot price of platinum is $2000 per ounce. The one year continuously compounded risk-free rate of interest is 5%.

(a) Find the one year forward price of platinum per ounce, assuming the price is consistent with the existence of no arbitrage opportunities.

(b) Suppose that someone is willing to enter into a long one year forward contract for platinum at $2150 per ounce. Construct a strategy from which an investor can obtain a riskless profit.

(c) Suppose that an investor takes a long one year forward position in one ounce of platinum in which the forward (delivery) price is based on no arbitrage. Six months later the price of platinum is still $2000. Find the value of the long position of the contract at that time (6 months after the contract was entered), assuming that the risk-free rate of interest is still 5% (as a continuously compounded annual rate).

9.1.2   The current spot price for one ounce of gold is 900. The continuously compounded risk-free interest rate is 8% for all maturities.

(a) Find the delivery price on a forward contract for one ounce of gold with delivery date (i) in 1 year, and (ii) in 2 years.

(b) At time $t = 0$ Smith enters a 2-year forward contract to buy an ounce of gold (long) and at the same time enters a 3-year forward contract to sell an ounce of gold (short). Find the combined value of Smith's forward contracts at time $t = 1$ as a function of $S_1$ (the spot price of an ounce of gold at time $t = 1$).

(c) Suppose that at time $t = 1$ the continuously compounded risk-free rate of interest for all maturities is 10%. Repeat part (b).

9.1.3 An investor takes a short position in a one year forward contract on a 30-year Treasury Bond. The Treasury Bond to be delivered in one year is assumed to have an 8% coupon rate (payable semiannually) and a face (and maturity) amount of 100. Assume a flat term structure, with continuously compounded annual return of 6% for all terms to maturity.

(a) Find the one year forward price, assuming no arbitrage.

(b) Suppose that the one year forward price on the bond is $125. Construct a strategy from which an investor can earn a riskless profit.

(c) Suppose that the annual yield to maturity on 31 year bonds is 6% compounded semiannually at the time the one year forward contract is entered. Suppose also that, the 6-month and 1-year risk-free rates of interest are 5% compounded continuously at the time the forward contract is entered. What one year forward yield to maturity for 30 year bonds is implied by these conditions under the assumption of no arbitrage?

9.1.4 In November 2005 an investor opens a long position on one June 2006 contract in soybeans. The contract size is for 5000 bushels of soybeans. The futures price is $4.95 per bushel on the day the contract is purchased. Initial margin required on a soybean contract is 1200, with maintenance margin of 1000. The day after opening the contract, the futures price for the June 2005 contract in soybeans has dropped to $4.90 per bushel. Find the amount that the investor must add to the margin account to keep the contract open, and find the investor's one day percentage loss.

9.1.5 A banker's acceptance is a zero coupon bond issued by a bank, with the time from issue to maturity usually being less than one year. In November 2005, a corporate treasurer expects that the company will be receiving a payment of 1,000,000 in two months (January), and plans to invest in a 3-month (¼-year) investment at that time. The treasurer wishes to hedge the investment rate that can be obtained when the investment will be made in two months, and takes a long position in one 3-month banker's acceptance futures contract (1,000,000 contract amount) with maturity in March 2006.

When the futures contract is entered today, the futures price is quoted at 94.00. In two months (January), when the 1,000,000 is received, the treasurer sells the futures contract. For each of the following scenarios, find the 3-month net return obtained for the 3 months following the receipt of the 1,000,000 that will be invested in January.

(a) 2 months from now, the 3-month investment rate is 6.5% (convertible quarterly) and the March futures contract price is 93.60.

(b) 2 months from now, the 3-month investment rate is 5.5% (convertible quarterly) and the March futures contract price is 94.40.

(c) 2 months from now, the 3-month investment rate is $i\%$ (convertible quarterly) and the March futures contract price is $100 - k$.

9.1.6    In November 2005, a corporate treasurer expects that the company will be receiving a payment of 1,000,000 in two months (January, 2006), and plans to invest in a 3-month (¼-year) investment at that time. The treasurer wishes to hedge the investment rate that can be obtained when the investment will be made in two months, and takes a long position in one 3-month banker's acceptance futures contract (1,000,000 contract amount) with maturity in March 2006. When the futures contract is entered today, the futures price is quoted at 96.00. In two months (January), when the 1,000,000 is received, the treasurer sells the futures contract, and the futures price at that time is 95.00. Find the 3-month net return obtained for the 3 month period following the receipt of the 1,000,000 that will be invested in January if the 3-month investment rate in January is 5.0% (convertible quarterly). Note that an increase of .01 in the price of a 1,000,000 3-month banker's acceptance long futures contract results in a gain of 25 in the value of the contract.

9.1.7   A speculator opens a position in a futures contract in a 3-month banker's acceptance. At the time that the position is opened, the quoted price for a contract is 98.00 (one contract is for 1,000,000 banker's acceptance). The margin required to open the account is $500. One week later the quoted price on the futures contract is 98.10. The speculator closes the account. Find the speculator's one-week rate of return on the initial investment of 500.

9.1.8   A coupon bond has a spot price of $860. The bond will pay coupons of $40 in 6 months and in one year. The risk-free rates are 8% (per year continuously compounded) for 6 month maturity and 10% for one year maturity. Find the delivery price for a one year forward contract on the bond, with delivery immediately after the coupon payment.

9.1.9   The term structure is currently flat, with zero coupon bonds having nominal annual yield rates of 10% compounded semi-annually for all maturities. A long term bond has an 8% coupon rate (payable semi-annually) with next coupon six months from now. The price of the bond today is 76.00 (per 100 face amount).

   (a) Find the no-arbitrage delivery price (per 100 face amount) for a forward contract on the bond with delivery to take place one year from today.

   (b) An individual takes a long position in a forward contract on the bond today, with delivery to take place in one year, based on the delivery price in (a). Six months from the time the forward contract in (a) was made, the term structure is still flat with zero coupon bonds having nominal annual yield rates of 10% compounded semi-annually for all maturities, and (after the first coupon has been paid) the bond price is 76.50. Find the value of the long position on the forward contract six months after the contract was made.

9.1.10 The spot price of gold today is $S_0$ per ounce and the risk-free rate of interest for a two year maturity is $r$ compounded continuously. Smith takes a long position in a 2-year forward contract to purchase gold. At the end of one year the spot price of gold is $G$ and the risk-free rate of interest for a one year maturity is $\delta$ compounded continuously. Assume that all delivery prices are determined assuming no arbitrage opportunities are available.

Find the value of Smith's contract at the end of one year.

9.1.11 The risk-free rate of interest is 8% with continuous compounding and the dividend yield on a stock index is 3% per year compounded continuously. The current value of the index is 1000. Find the 3-month futures price of the stock index.

9.1.12 At the close of trading today, the nominal annual rate of interest on a 6-month (assume ½-year) banker's acceptance is 6%, and the nominal annual rate of interest on a 3-month (assume ¼-year) banker's acceptance is 5.7%. Find the implied quoted price at the close of trading today (under the no arbitrage assumption) for a futures contract expiring in 3 months on a 3-month banker's acceptance.

9.1.13 The price today of a futures contract expiring in one year on a 10-year Government of Canada bond with 6% coupons payable semi-annually is 92.00. The price today of an 11-year Government of Canada bond with 6% coupons payable semiannually is $P$, and the risk-free rate of interest for 6-month and 1 year maturities is $r$ compounded continuously. Which of the following combinations of $P$ and $r$ result in an arbitrage opportunity?

(i) $P = 93.00, r = .06$

(ii) $P = 92.38, r = .06$

9.1.14    The continuously compounded risk-free rate of interest for the coming year is 10%. An ounce of gold can be purchased today for 900 per ounce. A one-year forward contract in gold entered into today has a delivery price of 1000 per ounce. Construct a strategy consisting of buying or selling gold in combination with going long or short on the one year forward contract, for which the strategy requires a net investment of 0 right now, but which will result in a risk-free profit one year from now. Find the amount of the risk-free profit that results from the strategy.

9.1.15    Just at the close of trading on November 16, 2005 a farmer takes a short position on a May 2006 futures contract in cotton. The contract size is 50,000 pounds. The futures price at the time the contract is opened is 0.55 per pound. The contract requires maintaining a margin account with a minimum balance of 5% of the futures price. Suppose that on Nov. 17, 2005, the closing price of May 2006 futures in cotton rises to 0.56 per pound. Find the effect on the margin account of the change in the futures price, and whether and how much the farmer must add to the account to maintain the 5% margin.

9.1.16    At time 0 the term structure of interest rates and forward prices for an ounce of platinum are as follows (yields are annual effective rates):

| Time to Maturity | 1 year | 2 year | 3 year | 4 year |
|---|---|---|---|---|
| Zero-coupon bond yield | 6.00% | 6.50% | 6.75% | 7.00% |
| Platinum forward price | 1050 | 1100 | 1150 | 1100 |

(a)  Find the swap price for platinum for 1, 2, 3, and 4 years.

(b)  A swap counterparty arranges a 4-year swap with a platinum buyer for one ounce at times 1, 2, 3 and 4. The counterparty enters into a series of long forward contracts for platinum. Show that the present value at time 0 of the net annual cash flows for the counterparty is 0.

(c)  A swap counterparty arranges a 4-year swap with a platinum buyer for one ounce at times 1, 2, 3 and 4. Find the implied loan balances at times 1, 2, 3, 4 from the point of view of the platinum purchaser.

(d) At time 0 a platinum purchaser arranges a 2-year deferred swap on platinum with swap payments at times 3 and 4. Find the swap price.

(e) A swap counterparty arranges a 4-year swap with a platinum buyer. At time 1, just after the first swap payment is made, the forward prices for platinum and zero-coupon bond yields are

| Time to Maturity (from time 1) | 1 year | 2 year | 3 year |
|---|---|---|---|
| Zero-coupon bond yield | 6.50% | 7.0% | 7.0% |
| Platinum forward price | 1150 | 1200 | 1300 |

Find the value of the swap to the counterparty at time 1 after the first swap payment is made.

9.1.17 Assume that the term structure as of time 0 is the same as in Problem 9.1.16. You are given the following swap prices for platinum for 1, 2, 3, and 4 year swaps.

| Length of swap | 1 year | 2 year | 3 year | 4 year |
|---|---|---|---|---|
| Swap price | 1100 | 1150 | 1150 | 1200 |

Find the forward prices for platinum for delivery in 1, 2, 3 and 4 years.

## SECTION 9.2 AND 9.3

9.2.1 On January 15 the share price of XYZ Corporation stock is 100, the value of a July 20 call at 110 is 1, the value of a July 20 call at 90 is 15, the value of a July 20 put at 110 is 14, and the value of a July 20 put at 90 is 1.50. For each of the following strategies, determine the profit on the transaction, after exercising the option or letting it expire on July 20, whichever is more profitable, as a function of the share price (excluding commissions and interest).

(a) On January 15 buy a call at 110.
(b) On January 15 buy the stock and sell a call at 110.
(c) On January 15 buy a call at 110 and sell a call at 90.
(d) On January 15 buy a call at 90 and sell a call at 110.
(e) On January 15 buy a put at 90 and buy a call at 110.
(f) On January 15 buy a put at 110 and buy a call at 90.
(g) On January 15 sell a put at 90 and sell a call at 90.

9.2.2    You own a house with a replacement value of $500,000. A one-year insurance policy on the house has a premium of $1500 and has a deductible of $2000. Insurance costs for damage to the house are paid, if necessary, at the end of the year. Describe the insurance policy as an option with an appropriately defined strike price and payoff and profit at the end of the year. Ignore any effect of interest and depreciation or appreciation in the value of the house over the year.

9.2.3    Smith enters into a 1 year forward contract to sell an ounce of platinum two years from now. Today's price of platinum is 2000 per ounce and the delivery price is 2100.

   (a) Find the continuously compounded annual risk-free rate of interest for a one year maturity, assuming the contract is set up with no arbitrage opportunities.

   (b) Suppose that Smith does not own an ounce of platinum right now, but plans to purchase it in one year, and then in order to complete the forward contract, Smith will immediately sell it at that time for 2100. Smith decides to buy a call option today with an expiry date of 1 year and a strike price of 2050. The price of the call option today is 80. Smith borrows 80 at the risk-free rate (found in part (a)) to buy the option. Suppose that the price of platinum at the end of the year is $P$. At the end of the year, after the forward contract and options contract expire, find Smith's gain for the year as a function of $P$.

9.2.4    A stock currently sells for $X$ per share. You *buy* one share of stock, and you *sell* a one-year European call option with strike price $X$; the call option price is $C > 0$. If the call option is not exercised at the end of the year then you will sell the stock at the end of the year. Under what circumstances will you realize a positive gain at the end of the year ($S_1$ denotes the stock price at the end of one year)? (Assume that no margin is necessary on the original short sale of stock, and no interest is earned on the proceeds of the sale of the call option).

9.2.5   A long position is taken at time 0 in a forward contract for delivery of a stock at time $T$ with delivery price $X$ (delivery price is based on the assumption of no arbitrage). Which of the following combinations of European options expiring at time $T$ has the same value $X$ as the forward contract at time $T$?

(a) Sell a put option with strike price $X$, buy a call option with strike price $X$.

(b) Buy a put option with strike price $X$, sell a call option with strike price $X$.

(c) Sell a put option with strike price $X$, sell a call option with strike price $X$.

(d) Buy a put option with strike price $X$, buy a call option with strike price $X$.

(e) None of (a), (b), (c) or (d) has the same value at time $T$ as the forward contract.

9.2.6   The price of XYZ stock at time 0 is 40. Annual effective interest is at rate 5%. Call and put option (European) values for various strike prices are:

| Strike Price | Call Price | Put Price |
|:---:|:---:|:---:|
| 30 | 12.92 | 1.50 |
| 34 | 10.32 | 2.79 |
| 38 | 8.12 | 4.32 |
| 40 | 7.18 | 5.28 |
| 43 | 6.34 | 6.34 |
| 46 | 4.90 | 8.72 |
| 50 | 3.78 | 11.40 |

It is assumed that XYZ stock pays no dividends.

(a) Formulate the payoff and profit on a protective put with a strike price of 50.

(b) Verify the put-call parity relationship for the listed option prices.

(c) Describe the payoff and profit at time 1 of a bull spread consisting of a purchased call with strike price 42 and a written call with strike price 50.

(d) Formulate the payoff and profit on a collar and a collared stock based on strike prices 40 and 50.

9.2.7    In Section 9.2.3, an example is given of an equity-linked CD with a minimum guarantee of 1.011 and a participation rate of 50%. The cost of the hedge for this ECD was shown to be .957 for each $1 invested. It is suggested after the example that if the participation rate is change to 75%, the cost of the hedge is about 1.19. Show that this is the case.

*9.2.8   The stock price at time 0 is 120. At time 1, the stock price will be either 144 or 100. The risk-free effective annual rate of interest from time 0 to time 1 is 10%.

(i)   A put option on the stock with exercise price 110 expires at time 1. Find the number of units of risk-free bond in the replicating portfolio at time 0.

(ii)  Someone is willing to sell you a call option with expiry at time 1, strike price 120. The price they will sell for is 15. Which of the following strategies at time 0 will result in risk-free arbitrage gain at time 1?

(a)  Borrow 15 at the risk-free rate and buy the call option.

(b)  Sell short .5455 shares of stock, and invest the amount at the risk-free rate.

(c)  Sell short .5455 shares of stock, buy the call for 15 and invest the remaining amount at the risk-free rate.

(d)  Borrow 80.46, buy the call and buy .5455 shares of stock.

(e)  Borrow 65.46 and buy .5455 shares of stock.

9.2.9    Repeat Example 9.8:

(a)  if the stock price on January 15 is 45, and

(b)  if the stock price on January 15 is 55.

*9.2.10  Keeping all other parameters fixed, sketch the graph of the call option price according to the Black-Scholes formula as a function of

(a) $S_0$,      (b) $K$,      (c) $n$,      (d) $\delta$, and      (e) $\sigma$.

## SECTION 9.4

9.4.1 (a) Smith has 10,000 US dollars. He can buy Canadian dollars today at the exchange rate of 1 US = 1.38 CDN., or he can sign a forward contract guaranteeing him an exchange rate of 1 US = 1.42 CDN one year from now. If he exchanges his US dollars for Canadian dollars today, he can earn interest at effective annual rate 9% on his Canadian dollars. Alternatively, he can sign the forward exchange rate contract and invest his 10,000 US at effective annual rate $i$, exchanging his US dollars for Canadian dollars next year. If he ends up with the same amount of Canadian funds in one year either way, what is $i$?

(b) Suppose Smith has just signed the forward contract. Later in the day the Canadian interest rate increases from 9% to 10%, but the US interest rate remains at $i$. What spot rate of exchange would Smith now regard as fair, assuming again that he would end up in one year with same amount of Canadian funds?

9.4.2 The Canadian dollar today is worth $.625 US. For one-year maturity, the continuously compounded risk-free rate of return in Canada is 3% and in the US it is 2%. A currency speculator believes that the Canadian dollar will increase in value to $.65 US one year from now. Formulate a strategy in which the speculator can receive a gain for a net investment of 0 if the speculator's belief turns out to be correct.

9.4.3 A recent quotation of spot and forward currency rates listed the following rates of Canadian (CDN $), United States (US $) and British (UK £) currencies.

Spot rate of exchange:
    US $1 = CDN $1.5997,       US $1 = UK £0.7090

1 year forward rate of exchange:
    US $1 = CDN $1.6100,       US $1 = UK £0.7200

The effective annual risk-free rate of interest in Canada at the time of these quotations was 2.00%. According to the no-arbitrage assumption, find the corresponding effective annual risk-free interest rate in Britain.

9.4.4 The exchange rate between the Canadian and US dollar today is US $1 = CDN $1.545. Canadian continuously compounded risk-free interest rate is 6%, 1 year maturity. As of today, the no-arbitrage one year forward contract on US dollars has a delivery price of CDN $1.540.

(a) Show that the implied continuously compounded one-year risk-free rate in the US is 6.32%.

(b) Suppose that a foreign currency dealer offers to buy or sell (long or short) a one year forward contract on US dollars with a delivery price of CDN $1.55. Construct a transaction that results in a riskless profit; you may buy or sell the forward contract, and you may borrow or invest at the risk free rates in Canadian (6% continuously compounded) and US (6% continuously compounded) dollars.

9.4.5 A recent quotation of spot and forward currency rates listed the following rates of Canadian (CDN), United States (US) and Japanese (JP) currencies.

Spot rate of exchange:
US $1 = CDN $1.5589,    JP ¥1 = CDN $0.014200

1 year forward rate of exchange:
US $1 = CDN $1.5495,    JP ¥1 = CDN $0.014997

The effective annual risk-free rate of interest in the US at the time of these quotations was 6.13%. According to the no-arbitrage assumption, find the corresponding effective annual risk-free interest rate in Japan.

# ANSWERS TO TEXT EXERCISES

## CHAPTER 1

### SECTION 1.1

1.1.1   10,400   10,816   11,248.64,   400,   416,   432.64

1.1.2   (a) 3500;   (b) 3700.61;   (c) 3714.87;   (d) 3722.16

1.1.3   11,019.70   .0081244

1.1.4   $K = 979.93$

1.1.5   (a) 10.25%;   (b)   $j = 0.091$ and $k = .084$

1.1.6   $n = 2.3$

1.1.7   (a) $i = 107.35\%$;   (b) $i = 67.59\%$;   (c) 913.32;   (d) 451 days

1.1.8   $i \leq .4069$

1.1.9   (a) 278.93

1.1.10　(a) 9.694 years;　　　(b) 9.682 years;　　　(c) 110.41 months;
　　　　(d) 11.61%;　　　　　(e) .9197%

1.1.11　(a)　$(1.0075)^{67/17} = 1.0299 < 1.03$
　　　　(b)　$(1.015)^{67/17} = 1.0604 > 1.06$

1.1.12　(a) 12.04%;　(b) −21.57%

## Section 1.2 and 1.3

1.2.1　$5000 \left[ \dfrac{1}{1.06} + \dfrac{1}{(1.06)^2} + \dfrac{1}{(1.06)^3} + \dfrac{1}{(1.06)^4} \right] = 17{,}325.53$ .

1.2.2　$25{,}000[v^{17} + v^{15} + v^{12}] + 100{,}000[v^{20} + v^{18} + v^{15}] = 75{,}686$

1.2.3　$28 = 15 + 16.50v \rightarrow v = .78779 \rightarrow i = .2692$

1.2.4　$1000 \cdot v_{.06}^3 \cdot v_{.07}^4 \cdot v_{.09}^3 = 494.62$

1.2.5　$X = 379.48$

1.2.6　1-month rate of .01, $X = 67.98$
　　　　3-month rate of .03, $X = 67.57$

1.2.7　$i = .0351$

1.2.8   (a)   $(20)(2000)[v + v^2 + v^3 + \cdots + v^{48}] = 1,607,391$ (at .75%)

        (b)   $1,607,391 + 200,000v^{48} = 1,747,114$

        (c)   $X = 1,607,391 + .15Xv^{48} \rightarrow X = 1,795,551$

1.2.9   $750 = 367.85[1 + (1+j)] \rightarrow j = .0389$ is the 2-month rate.

1.2.10   $X(1.4)^4 - 5000\left[(1.4)^{1.5} + (1.4)^{.5}\right] = X \rightarrow X = 4997.$

1.2.11   $j < k$

1.2.12   $1000(1+i)^2 + 1092 = 2000(1+i)$

        Solving the quadratic equation for $1 + i$ results in no real roots.

1.2.13   (a)   $\frac{d}{di}(1+i)^n = n(1+i)^{n-1}$        (c)   $\frac{d}{dn}(1+i)^n = (1+i)^n \ln(1+i)$

        (b)   $\frac{d}{di}v^n = -nv^{n+1}$              (d)   $\frac{d}{dn}v^n = -v^n \ln(1+i)$

1.2.14   $94.767 \leq$ Price $< 94.771.$

1.2.15   (a)   $P = \frac{1000,000}{1 + (.10)\frac{182}{365}} = 95,250.52$

        (b)   $\Delta P \doteq -45.24.$

        (c)   $-23.733.34$

1.2.17   12.68

1.2.18   (a) 13,150   (b) 13,160.27   (c) 13,150.76   (d) 13,161.12

## Section 1.4

1.4.1   $m = 2, i = .1236;$
$m = 12, i = .126825;$
$m = 365, i = .127475;$
$m = \infty, i = .127497$

1.4.2   (a) 414.64   (b) 409.30   (c) 407.94

1.4.3   $i^{(365)} \geq .144670$

1.4.4   $i = .0946$

1.4.5   $-.78\%$

1.4.6   $i^{(.5)} = .105, i^{(.25)} = .116025, i^{(.1)} = .159374, i^{(.01)} = 137.796$

1.4.7   .1365

1.4.10   $m = 4;$   nominal annual rate of 16% cannot accumulate to an effective rate of more that 17.35%

## Section 1.5

1.5.1   (a) 5187.84   (b) 5191.68   (c) 5204.52   (d) 5200

1.5.4   .1154

1.5.5    $X = 38.9$

1.5.7    $d = .0453$    (this is the nominal discount rate
compounded 4 times per year)

1.5.8    (a) $i = \dfrac{365}{n}\left[\dfrac{1}{1-d\cdot\frac{n}{365}}-1\right] = \dfrac{d}{1-d\cdot\frac{n}{365}};$ as $n$ increases, $i$ increases

(b) $t = 1, d = .099099;$   $t = .50, d = .104265;$   $t = \frac{1}{12}, d = .109001$

1.5.9    .0266

1.5.11   $i = .0909$

1.5.12   $j = .0436$

## SECTION 1.6

1.6.1    10,512.71    11,162.78

1.6.2    $i^{(4)} = .0339$

1.6.3    $k = 102$

1.6.4    $Z = 1953$

1.6.5    $X = 784.6$

1.6.6　$i - \delta = .23\%$

1.6.7　.045

1.6.8　(a) $i = .1008$

(b) $i_1 = .091629,$　　$i_2 = .099509,$

　　$i_3 = .102751,$　　$i_4 = .104532,$　　$i_5 = .105659$

(c) 821.00

1.6.9　1215

1.6.10　$i' > 2i,\ d' < 2d$

1.6.11　(a) 1044.73

(b) For $0 < t \le \frac{1}{4},\ A(t) = 1000[1 + .08t],$

for $\frac{1}{4} < t \le \frac{1}{2},\ A(t) = 1000(1.02)\left[1 + .08\left(t - \frac{1}{4}\right)\right],$

for $\frac{1}{2} < t \le \frac{3}{4},\ A(t) = 1000(1.02)^2 1\left[ + .08\left(t - \frac{1}{2}\right)\right],$

for $\frac{3}{4} < t \le 1,\ A(t) = 1000(1.02)^3\left[1 + .08\left(t - \frac{3}{4}\right)\right].$

1.6.12　(a) $\dfrac{A\left(t + \frac{1}{m}\right) - A(t)}{A\left(t + \frac{1}{m}\right)}$

(b) $d^{(m)} = m \cdot \dfrac{A(t + \frac{1}{m}) - A(t)}{A(t + \frac{1}{m})}$　　(c) $\lim_{m \to \infty} d^{(m)} = \dfrac{A'(t)}{A(t)}$

## SECTION 1.7

1.7.1    $i_{real} = -.043478$

1.7.2    $-.0309$

1.7.3    (b) The real growth in taxes paid will be 1.015873 (1.59%) and
the real growth in ATI is $.990476 = 1 - .009524$

1.7.4    Net gain is 5000 (in year-end dollars)

1.7.6    $i = 1.070175$

1.7.7    One year from now, 1000 US ≡ 1382.4306 CDN, or equivalently.
$.723364$ US ≡ 1 CDN

1.7.9    (a) Real after-tax rate of return on standard term deposit is
$\frac{i(1-t_x)-r}{1+r}$, and on inflation-adjusted term deposit is
$$\frac{r+i'(1+r)(1-t_x)-r}{1+r} = i'(1-t_x).$$

(b) If $i' = .02$ and $r = .12$, then $i$ is equal to

(i) .1424

(ii) .1824

(iii) .2224

(iv) .3224

# Chapter 2

## Section 2.1

2.1.1    $i = 6.9\%$

2.1.2    1519.42

2.1.4    19,788.47

2.1.5    (i) 715.95,    (ii) 2,033.87,    (iii) 3,665.12,    interest $= 36.65$

2.1.6    $i = .1225$

2.1.7    (a) 2328.82

2.1.8    $11S - 100$

2.1.9    $I_t = (1+i)^{t-1} - 1$

2.1.10    $n = 15,\ P = 14.53;$    $n = 20,\ P = 17.19;$    $n = 25,\ P = 20.75$

2.1.11    (a) $(1+i)^n = 2,\ i = .014286,\ s_{\overline{3n}|i} = 490$

(b) $\rightarrow\ v^n\ =\ \dfrac{2}{-1+\sqrt{1-\frac{4(Y-X)}{Y}}}$    (c) .1355

2.1.12    640.72

2.1.13   $X = 8.92$

2.1.14   An investment of amount 1 is equal to the present value of the return of principal in $n$ years plus the present value of the interest generated over the $n$ years.

2.1.15   2825.49

2.1.16   109,926

2.1.17   $X = 575$

2.1.18   $i = .0689$

2.1.19   $v^n = .858$

2.1.20   $K = 1079.68$

2.1.23   330.80

2.1.26   .6180

2.1.28   $i = .1539$

2.1.29   (a) $v_j [1+v_i] \cdot \dfrac{1}{1-v_j \cdot v_i}$          (b)  (i) $\dfrac{v+2v^2}{1-v^2}$     (ii) $\dfrac{1+2v}{1-v^2}$

2.1.31   $X = 573.76$, $Y = 449.54$

2.1.32   $17^{th}$ month

## SECTION 2.2

2.2.1   (a) $X = 447.24$    (b) December 31, 2023,  290.30

2.2.2   Derek 69,788,    Anne 65,837,    Ira  67,958

2.2.3   $Y = 9872$

2.2.4   $X = 6195$

2.2.5   $X = 3.71$

2.2.6   .088

2.2.7   1161.36

2.2.8   April 30, 2013

2.2.9   26 deposits

2.2.10  January 1, 2016

2.2.11  2.208%

2.2.12  $i = .076$

2.2.13  $i^{(12)} = .1680,\ K = 345.02$

2.2.14  $X = 39.84$

2.2.15 The 2-month effective rate is $j$

(a) $25a_{\overline{36}|j} = 150a^{(6)}_{\overline{6}|.06} = 755.83$ where $j = (1.06)^{1/6} - 1$

(b) $25v_j^4\, a_{\overline{36}|j} = 50v_{.02}^2 a^{(2)}_{\overline{18}|.02} = 724.08$ where $j = (1.02)^{1/2} - 1$

(c) $25(1+j)s_{\overline{36}|j} = 1092.02$ where $j = (.97)^{-1/3} - 1$

(d) $25(1+j)^6 s_{\overline{36}|j} = 1144.57$ where $j = e^{.01} - 1$

2.2.17 $\bar{a}_{\overline{n}|} = \dfrac{r(1-e^{-pn})}{(1+r)p} + \dfrac{(1-e^{-(p+s)n})}{(1+r)(p+s)}$

2.2.18 $K' \le 2K$

2.2.19 (a) July 1, 2006
(b) January 11, 2007

2.2.20 (a) 23  (b) 22

2.2.21 2 terms , $n = 24.8$;
3 terms, $n = 29.7$ or $300.6$ ($300.6$ is an unrealistic answer)

2.2.22 $i = \dfrac{B - A - 1}{A}$

2.2.25 $i = (1+j)^m - 1$

2.2.26 (a) $\dfrac{1}{m}\cdot s_{\overline{n\cdot m}|j} = \dfrac{1}{m}\cdot\dfrac{(1+j)^{n\cdot m}-1}{j} = \dfrac{1}{m}\cdot\dfrac{(1+i)^n-1}{(1+i)^{1/m}-1}$

2.2.27 (b) $a_{\overline{n}|i} < a^{(m)}_{\overline{n}|i} < \bar{a}_{\overline{n}|i} < \ddot{a}^{(m)}_{\overline{n}|i} < \ddot{a}_{\overline{n}|i}$

## Section 2.3

2.3.1   419,242 (419,253 based on no roundoff with calculator)

2.3.2   (i) 30,407       (ii) 59,704       (iii) 151,906

2.3.3   $k = 6\%$

2.3.4   $K = 4$

2.3.5   $R = 548$

2.3.7   $r = .0784$

2.3.8   (a) 27,823       (b) 36,766       (c) 57,639       (d) 19,974

2.3.9   $i = .0640$

2.3.10   $\frac{Y}{X} = 2.03$

2.3.11   $i = .102$

2.3.12   $X = 2729$

2.3.13   2,085

2.3.14   $n = 19$

2.3.15   $X = 44.98$

2.3.16   $25a_{\overline{25}|} + 3(Da)_{\overline{25}|}$

2.3.17   $i = .10$

2.3.19   (i)  PV before de-indexing is 168,620,
               after de-indexing it is 84,310

         (ii)  PV before de-indexing is 56,207,
               after de-indexing it is 42,155

         (iii) PV before de-indexing is 166,497,
               after de-indexing it is 83,249

         (iv)  PV before de-indexing is 164,354,
               after de-indexing it is 82,177

2.3.20   (a) $n = 505$        (b) 5,569,741

2.3.21   (a) $i = .1014$      (b) $i = .1266$

2.3.26   $i^{(2)} = .21$, $\dfrac{d}{di^{(2)}} K = 7459.13$ (or 74.59 per 1% increase in $i^{(2)}$)

         $i^{(2)} = .13$, $\dfrac{d}{di^{(2)}} K = 7101.66$ (or 71.02 per 1% increase in $i^{(2)}$)

2.3.27   $\dfrac{500,000(1+i)^t}{19}$

2.3.28   (a) $n = 185$,  $X = 532.46$
         (b) $n = 99$,  $X = 761.19$
         (c) $n = 90$,  $X = 93.85$
         (d) Total withdrawn:  (a) 185,532   (b) 148,271   (c) 144,957.

2.3.29 $i = .0820$

2.3.31 (b) $\dfrac{\ddot{a}_{\overline{k}|}}{(i \cdot a_{\overline{k}|})^2}$

2.3.40 $PV = (A-B)a_{\overline{n}|} + B(Ia)_{\overline{n}|}$ $\qquad AV = As_{\overline{n}|} + B(Is)_{\overline{n-1}|}$

## SECTION 2.4

2.4.1   (a)   (i) 7469.44     (ii) 6794.19     (iii) 3813.44

       (b)   (i) 8.30%       (ii) 13.56%      (iii) 8.81%

2.4.4   (a) 80,898     (b) 18,311

2.4.7   22,250

2.4.8   (a) 63,920     (b) 67,659     (c) $t = 8$,   $P_8 = 86,712$

2.4.9   .986

2.4.10   5000

2.4.11   36,329

2.4.12   286.3

# CHAPTER 3

## SECTION 3.1

3.1.1　(i)　4,967.68

(ii)　3,301.98

(iii)　$I_4 = 330.20,\ PR_4 = 669.80$

(iv)　867.77

3.1.2　$OB_{40} = 6889$

3.1.4　(i) Monthly payment is 445.72, $OB_{1\,yr} = 14,651$

(ii) Monthly payment is 452.61, $OB_{1\,yr} = 15,102$

3.1.5　10,857.28

3.1.8　$L = 58,490.89,\ \ PR_1 = 15.09,$

$OB_{60} = 46,424,\ I_{61} = 464.24,\ PR_{61} = 435.76$

3.1.9　97.44

3.1.11　(a) $K = 9.888857,$　　　　$OB_{1\,mo} = 1000.11,$

$OB_{2\,mo} = 1000.22,\ldots,\ OB_{12\,mo} = 1001.41$

## SECTION 3.2

3.2.2   Total interest paid is 404.15

3.2.3

| Year ($t$) | $OB_t$ | $I_t$ | $PR_t$ |
|---|---|---|---|
| 0 | 862.00 | — | — |
| 1 | 706.00 | 43.10 | 156.00 |
| 2 | 542.20 | 35.30 | 163.80 |
| 3 | 370.21 | 27.11 | 171.99 |
| 4 | 189.62 | 18.51 | 180.59 |
| 5 | 0 | 9.48 | 189.62 |

3.2.4   $t = 35$ is June 1, 2007

3.2.5   (a) $i^{(12)} = .0495$       (b) $i^{(12)} = .15$

3.2.6   (a) 67.50

   (b) Final smaller payment is on February 1, 2016 of amount 109.54

3.2.7   $X = 825$

3.2.8   $i = .09$

3.2.9   $k \le .1326$

3.2.10   (a) Example 3.1: pv of interest is 39.33, pv of principal is 960.67
   Example 3.4: pv of interest is 356.16, pv of principal is 2643.84

   (b) pv of interest is $L\left[1 - \dfrac{nv^{n+1}}{a_{\overline{n}|}}\right]$,   pv of principal is $L \cdot \dfrac{nv^{n+1}}{a_{\overline{n}|}}$

3.2.11  $K = 349.81$

3.2.12  192,858

3.2.13  (i) Total interest paid is $\frac{nL}{a_{\overline{n}|i}} - L$

(ii) Total interest paid is $Li \cdot \frac{n+1}{2}$

3.2.14  A: 541,184.58,  B: 324,710.75,  C: 134,104.67

3.2.15  $OB_{10} = 58.40$, smaller payment at time 11 is 58.98

3.2.17  $\frac{2}{3}$

3.2.18  Principal paid in the first year is 478.74

3.2.19  (i)   total interest is 161,976
(ii)   final smaller payment is 734.49 on October 1, 2019, total interest is 82,139
(iii)  112,875

3.2.20  $n = 27$

3.2.22  Difference in interest is $K\left[\dfrac{12s_{\overline{3}|}}{a_{\overline{12}|}} - 3\right]$

3.2.23  (a)  $i^{(12)} = .06$, monthly payment is 644.30, total interest is 93,290, reduced term is 1087.5 weeks, total interest is 75,170

3.2.26  479.74

3.2.28 (a) $OB_t = ta_{\overline{n-t}|} + (Ia)_{\overline{n-t}|}$, $I_t = t - 1 - nv^{n-t+1} + \ddot{a}_{\overline{n-t+1}|}$, $PR_t = t - I_t$

(b) $OB_t = (Da)_{\overline{n-t}|}$, $I_t = n - t + 1 - a_{\overline{n-t+1}|}$ $PR_t = a_{\overline{n-t+1}|}$

3.2.32 (a) 6902.98　　(b) 6699　　　(c) 6600

3.2.34

| t | OB | PR | I |
|---|---|---|---|
| 0 | 10,000.00 | — | — |
| 1 | 9400.00 | 600.00 | 900.00 |
| 2 | 8740.00 | 660.00 | 840.00 |
| 3 | 8014.00 | 726.00 | 774.00 |
| 4 | 7215.40 | 798.60 | 701.40 |
| 5 | 6336.94 | 878.46 | 621.54 |
| 6 | 5370.63 | 966.31 | 533.69 |
| 7 | 4307.69 | 1062.94 | 437.06 |
| 8 | 3152.31 | 1155.38 | 341.62 |
| 9 | 1904.49 | 1247.82 | 252.18 |
| 10 | 556.85 | 1347.64 | 152.36 |
| 11 | 0 | 556.85 | 44.55 |

## SECTION 3.3

3.3.1　$X = 13,454.36$

3.3.2　(b) $L = \dfrac{Ks_{\overline{n}|j}}{1 + i \cdot s_{\overline{n}|j}}$

3.3.3　16,856.67

3.3.4　$j = .021322$

3.3.5　(a) 100,000

3.3.6    213

3.3.7    $X = 72.00$

3.3.8    $i' = .11$

3.3.9    $L = \dfrac{\Sigma K_t v_j^t}{v_j^n + i a_{\overline{n}|j}}, \quad Y = v_j^n + i \cdot a_{\overline{n}|j}$

3.3.11   (a)  14,185.22

(b)  Amount in sinking fund at time loan is sold is 31,656.34
   (i)   87,162.04
   (ii)  75,042.37

(c)  (i)   $i_\alpha = .130206, \quad i_\beta = .135051$
   (ii)  $i_\alpha = .123749, \quad i_\beta = .128183$

## SECTION 3.4

3.4.2    (a) 17,795      (b) 16,723      (c) 16,165

3.4.4    330,117

3.4.6    (a) .1169      (b) .10      (c) .0858

3.4.8    (i)   tax rate 25%:    (a) 15,000    (b) 15,000    (c) 15,000
         (ii)  tax rate 40%:    (a) 13,323    (b) 13,967    (c) 14,301
         (iii) tax rate 60%:    (a) 11,087    (b) 12,589    (c) 13,369

3.4.9    Merchant's Rule: $X = 211.54$,    US Rule: $X = 212.16$

3.4.11   Straight-Line: 41,078.46 each year
         Actuarial: 16,058.78 in $1^{st}$ year, 82,568.81 in $20^{th}$ year

3.4.12   US Rule payment is 328,
         Merchant's Rule payment is 325

# CHAPTER 4

## SECTION 4.1

4.1.1    (a) 84.5069   (b) 84.8501    (c) 82.5199    (d) 82.9678

4.1.2    115

4.1.3    12,229

4.1.4    $21\frac{1}{2}$ years

4.1.5    .0852

4.1.6    .1264

4.1.7    109.03

4.1.9    (b) 102.79 and 102.74    (c) 3.692% and 3.690%

4.1.10  $i^{(2)} = .0525$

4.1.11  I. False      II. True      III. False

4.1.12  Coupon rates are .0225 and .045 every 6 months

4.1.13  12 years

4.1.14  908.78

4.1.15  875.38

4.1.17  97.896

4.1.19  860

4.1.20  $r = .0354$ every 6 months for 10 year issue and $r = .0417$ every 6 months for 20 year issue

4.1.21  1055

4.1.22  $i^{(2)} = \dfrac{4r_2 - 2r_1}{1 + r_1 - r_2}$

4.1.23  $H = .6446$

4.1.24  2000

4.1.25  $X = 114.28$

## SECTION 4.2

4.2.3   $n = 5$,  $j = .025$

| T | $K_t$ | $I_t$ | $PR_t$ | $OB_t$ |
|---|---|---|---|---|
| 1 | 500 | 279.04 | 220.96 | 10,940.49 |
| 2 | 500 | 273.51 | 226.49 | 10,714.01 |
| 3 | 500 | 267.85 | 232.15 | 10,481.86 |
| 4 | 500 | 262.05 | 237.95 | 10,243.90 |
| 5 | 10,500 | 256.10 | 10,243.90 | 0 |

$n = 5$,  $j = .075$

| T | $K_t$ | $I_t$ | $PR_t$ | $OB_t$ |
|---|---|---|---|---|
| 1 | 500 | 674.14 | −174.14 | 9,162.67 |
| 2 | 500 | 687.20 | −187.20 | 9,349.89 |
| 3 | 500 | 701.24 | −201.24 | 9,551.10 |
| 4 | 500 | 716.33 | −216.33 | 9,767.44 |
| 5 | 10,500 | 732.56 | 9,767.44 | 0 |

4.2.4   90.47

4.2.5   13 years or 26 coupon periods

4.2.6   (a) 8764

4.2.7   48,739

4.2.9   (a)  $P = 8117.73$,  $r = .06336$

   (b)  $P = 29,039.25$,  $r = 2483$

   (c)  $r = .60$, $P = 68,821.07$

All values of $r$ are nominal annual rates.

## SECTION 4.3

4.3.1   (a) (i) 84.95      (ii) 100.00      (iii) 117.59

       (b) (i) 12.8%      (ii) 10.0%      (iii) 7.76%

4.3.2   (a) (i) 85.93      (ii) 101.42      (iii) 120.55

       (b) (i) 12.9%      (ii) 10.16%      (iii) 8.05%

4.3.3   .0924

4.3.4   (a) (i) 859,061      (ii) 1,116,588

       (b) (i) 10.98%      (ii) 8%      (iii) 5.5%

4.3.5   1,768,084

4.3.6   92,037.62

# CHAPTER 5

## SECTION 5.1

5.1.1   (a) no real solution

       (b) $i$ is .10 or .20

5.1.3   .049301

5.1.4   $i_A = .253304, i_B = .253280$

5.1.5    (a)  .1203

(b)  .1081

(c)  1126

(d)  break even in $3^{rd}$ year

(e)  break even in $5^{th}$ year

(f)  1.0375


5.1.7    (b)  $Y \geq 938,800$


5.1.8    $i^{(12)} = .1528$


5.1.9    (b) 7.92%


5.1.10   (b) $r \geq .0388$


5.1.12   (a) .10601

(b)  .10508


## SECTION 5.2

5.2.1    .0910


5.2.2    −.25


5.2.3    .0625


5.2.4    236.25

5.2.5    time weighted rate is 0, dollar-weighted rate is .1667

5.2.6    .15

## SECTION 5.3

5.3.1    (a) .1132   (b) (i) .1034   (ii) .1081   (iii) .1132   (iv) .1188   (v) .125

5.3.3    2882

# CHAPTER 6

## SECTIONS 6.1 AND 6.2

6.1.1    .0556,   $P = 111.98$

6.1.2    78.97

6.1.3    (a)        (i)   104.05         (ii) 93.15          (iii)   95.08
         (b)        (i)   8.44%          (ii) 12.82%         (iii)   12.00%

6.1.4    (a) .0646

6.1.5    .05, .10078, .15151, .15234

## SECTION 6.3

6.3.1   (a) $i_0(k-1,k) = \dfrac{(1+s_0(k))^k}{(1+s_0(k-1))^{k-1}} - 1$

6.3.2

| $K$ | (i) | (ii) |
|-----|-------|-------|
| 1 | . 0910 | . 0919 |
| 2 | . 0930 | . 0953 |
| 3 | . 0950 | . 0981 |
| 4 | . 0970 | . 1003 |
| 5 | . 0990 | . 1019 |
| 6 | . 1010 | . 1029 |
| 7 | . 1030 | . 1033 |
| 8 | . 1050 | . 1031 |
| 9 | . 1070 | . 1023 |
| 10 | . 1090 | . 1009 |

6.3.3   .0503

6.3.4   .1204 , .1303

6.3.5   (a) (i) .0801  (ii) .1311       (b) .1001

6.3.6   .1452

6.3.7   (b) (i)   $i_0(0,1) = .2,\ i_0(1,2) = .201,\ i_0(2,3) = .2011$

(ii)   $i_0(0,1) = .2,\ i_0(1,2) = .199,\ i_0(2,3) = .1989$

Other examples can be constructed

## SECTION 6.4

6.4.1 (a)

6.4.3 (d)

6.4.4 (a) 11.09   (b) 10.33

6.4.5 $i < .09002$

6.4.6 .1774

# CHAPTER 7

## SECTION 7.1

7.1.1 2.73

7.1.2 4.79

7.1.3 $j = .03$

| $r$ | $n=2$ | $n=10$ | $n=20$ | $n=40$ |
|---|---|---|---|---|
| .04 | 1.96189 | 8.50869 | 14.5725 | 22.4642 |
| .06 | 1.94491 | 8.06690 | 13.5336 | 20.8770 |
| .08 | 1.9291 | 7.73080 | 12.8493 | 19.9706 |

7.1.6 102

7.1.7   (a)   $1 + \dfrac{1}{j}$

        (b)   1 (if $n = 1$)

        (c)   $\dfrac{(Ia)_{\overline{n}|}}{a_{\overline{n}|}}$

        (d)   $n$

        (e)   1

        (f)   $\dfrac{n \cdot \frac{(n+1)}{2} \cdot r + n}{nr + 1}$

7.1.9   (a)  $L = r\bar{a}_{\overline{n}|} + e^{-n\delta},\ \dfrac{dL}{d\delta} = -r(\overline{Ia})_{\overline{n}|} - ne^{-n\delta}$

7.1.11   $-267$ and $-247$

7.1.12   (e)

7.1.13   (b)

## SECTION 7.2

7.2.1   (a) 1.6332         (b) 1.6328

7.2.2

| $n$ | PMT | $\sum t\, A_t v^t$ | $\sum t^2\, A_t v^t$ |
|---|---|---|---|
| 5 | 79,139 | 843,038 | 2,962,020 |
| 15 | 39,442 | 1,883,680 | 16,896,161 |
| 50 | 30,257 | 3,171,124 | 60,020,920 |
| 100 | 30,002 | 3,297,823 | 69,034,390 |

Best match occurs at $n = 15$; no immunization

7.2.4   $A_0 = 25,454.55,\ A_{15} = 7,595.00$ for the liability at $t = 1$

7.2.5 (a) $A_{15} = .8053$, $A_5 = .3105$

(b) (i) $t_2 = 19.0530$, $A_{t_2} = .8432$

(ii) $A_{t_2} < 0$

(c) (i) $t_2 = 21.28$, $A_5 = .4302$ or $t_2 = 11.27$, $A_5 = .1258$

(ii) $t_2 = 31.92$, $A_5 = .5056$

(iii) no solution

(d) (i) $t_1 = 9.21$, $A_{t_2} = .2213$

(ii) no solution if $t_1 \le 10$

(iii) no solution

(e) $t_1 = 4.74$, $t_2 = 20.223$

7.2.6 $t_0 = 16.15$, $A_{t_0} = 961,145$

7.2.7 (a) $A_1 = 71.44$, $A_5 = 229.41$

(b) conditions for Redington immunization are satisfied

7.2.9 (a) $(s - t_1) A_{t_1} v_{i_0}^{t_1} = (t_2 - s) A_{t_2} v_{i_0}^{t_2}$

(b) $L_s = A_{t_1} \cdot v^{t_1 - s} \left( 1 + \dfrac{s - t_1}{t_2 - s} \right)$

7.2.10 (a) $h(.03) = 40,581$, $h(.08) = 2170$,

$h(.12) = 1595$, $h(.2) = 23,154$

(b) $h(.03) = -12,596$, $h(.08) = -690$,

$h(.12) = -514$, $h(.2) = -7524$

(c) $h(.03) = 18,968$, $h(.08) = 994$,

$h(.12) = 714$, $h(.2) = 9738$

7.2.12 (a) 3441　　(b) (iii)

# CHAPTER 8

## SECTION 8.1

8.1.1    (a)  18.33

(b)  56.74

8.1.2    $r = .04$, $s = .0418$

## SECTION 8.2

8.2.1    (a)  8000
(b)  29.63%

8.2.2    9.95

8.2.3    900

8.2.4    16%

## SECTION 8.4

8.4.1    (a) 722,854,822
(b)  25.0%
(c) 786,216,443  and  22.3%

# Chapter 9

## Section 9.1

9.1.1   (a) 2102.54
        (c) − 50.63

9.1.2   (a) (i) 974.96   (ii) 1056.16
        (b) 0
        (c) −18.92

9.1.3   (a) 126.15
        (c) .0607

9.1.4   Additional margin required is 250, one-day loss is 20.83%

9.1.5   (a) 1.523%
        (b) 1.476%

9.16    .996875%

9.1.7   −50%

9.1.8   867.97

9.1.9   (a) 75.59
        (b) .70

9.1.10  $G - Ke^{-\delta} \;=\; G - S_0 e^{2r - \delta}$

9.1.11  1012.58

9.1.12  .9388

9.1.13  (i)  arbitrage opportunity exists

  (ii) no arbitrage opportunity exists

9.1.14  5.35

9.1.15  Add 525 to margin account

9.1.16  (a)  $P_1 = 1050,\ P_2 = 1074.15,\ P_3 = 1097.71,\ P_4 = 1098.22$

  (c)  48.22 , 49.82 , 1,65 , 0

  (d)  1125.93

  (e)  $-302.20$

9.1.17  1100.00 , 1203.50 , 1150.00 , 1373.49

## SECTION 9.2 AND 9.3

9.2.1  $P$ is the stock price on July 20.

  (a) Profit is  $P - 111$  if  $P \geq 110$  (option is exercised on July 20)
   Profit is  $-1$  if  $P \leq 110$  (option is not exercised)

  (b) If  $P < 110$  Profit $= 99$
   If  $P \geq 110$  Profit $= 11$

(c) If $P < 110$  Profit $= 0$

   If $P \geq 110$  Profit $= 0$

(d) If $P < 90$        Profit $= -14$

   If $90 \leq P < 110$  Profit $= -104$

   If $P \geq 110$        Profit $= 6$

(e) If $P < 90$        Profit $= 87.5 - P$

   If $90 \leq P < 110$  Profit $= -2.5$

   If $P \geq 110$        Profit $= P - 112.5$

(f) If $P < 90$        Profit $= 81 - P$

   If $90 \leq P < 110$  Profit $= -9$

   If $P \geq 110$        Profit $= P - 119$

9.2.2   $Max\{498,000 - S_1, 0\} - 1000$  where $S_1$ is house value at the end of the year.

9.2.3 (a) .0488

   (b) $2016 - Min(2050, P)$.

9.2.4   Positive gain if $S_1 > X - C$

9.2.5   (a)

9.2.6 (a) Payoff $= Max\{50, S_1\}$

Profit is $\begin{cases} -3.98 & \text{if } S_1 \leq 50 \\ S_1 - 53.98 & \text{if } S_1 > 50 \end{cases}$

(c) Payoff is $\begin{cases} 0 & \text{if } S_1 \leq 42 \\ S_1 - 42 & \text{if } 42 < S_1 \leq 50 \\ 8 & \text{if } S_1 > 50 \end{cases}$

Profit is $\begin{cases} -2.69 & \text{if } S_1 \leq 42 \\ S_1 - 44.69 & \text{if } 42 < S_1 \leq 50 \\ 5.31 & \text{if } S_1 > 50 \end{cases}$

(d) Payoff on collar is $\begin{cases} 40 - S_1 & \text{if } S_1 \leq 40 \\ 0 & \text{if } 40 < S_1 \leq 50 \\ 50 - S_1 & \text{if } S_1 > 50 \end{cases}$

Profit on collar is $\begin{cases} 38.42 - S_1 & \text{if } S_1 \leq 40 \\ 0 & \text{if } 40 < S_1 \leq 50 \\ 48.42 - S_1 & \text{if } S_1 > 50 \end{cases}$

9.2.8 (i) Sell short .2273 shares of stock, own 29.75 units of bond

(ii) (c)

9.2.9 (a) $K = 45$, $C_0 = 4.83$; $K = 50$, $C_0 = 2.75$; $K = 55$, $C_0 = 1.45$

## SECTION 9.4

9.4.1 (a) .0593

(b) .3675

9.4.3 .0292

9.4.5 $-.0012$

# BIBLIOGRAPHY

Baxter, M. and Rennie, A., *Financial Calculus: An Introduction to Derivative Pricing.* Cambridge Publishing, 1996.

Black, F. and Scholes, M., "The Pricing of Options and Corporate Liabilities," The Journal of Political Economy, 1973.

Butcher, M.V. and C.J. Nesbitt, *Mathematics of Compound Interest.* Ann Arbor: Edwards Brothers, 1971.

"Canadian Criminal Code, Part IX, Section 347, Bill C-46," 1985, Government of Canada.

"Canada Interest Act," R.S.C. 1985, C 1-15.

"Consumer Credit Protection Act (Truth in Lending), Regulation Z," 1968, Congress of The United States of America.

Elton, E.J. and M.J. Gruber, *Modern Portfolio Theory and Investment Analysis.* New York: John Wiley and Sons, 2006.

Fabozzi, F.J., *The Handbook of Fixed Income Securities*, McGraw-Hill 2005.

Gray, *Axiomatic Characterization of the Time-weighted Rate of Return.*

Kellison, S.G., *The Theory of Interest* (Third Edition). Homewood: Richard D. Irwin, Inc., 2009.

Macaulay, F, "Some Theoretical Problems Suggested by the Movements of Interest Rates, Bond Yields and Stock Prices in the United States since 1856," The National Bureau of Economic Research, 1938.

McCutcheon, J.J. and W.F. Scott, *An Introduction to the Mathematics of Finance*. Oxford: Heinemann Professional Publishing, 1986.

Promislow, D., "A New Approach to the Theory of Interest" in *TSA*, Volume 32 (1980)

Redington, F.M., "Review of the Principles of Life Office Valuations," The Journal of the Institute of Actuaries, 1952.

Sharpe, W., *Investments*. Prentice-Hall, 1999.

"Standard Securities Calculation Methods," Securities Industry Association, 1973

Teicherow, D., A. Robichek, and M. Montalbano, "Mathematical Analysis of Rates of Return under Certainty, Management Science," Volumes 11 (1965).

Teicherow, D., A. Robichek, and M. Montalbano, "An Analysis of Criteria for Investment and Financing Decisions under Certainty," Management Science, Volumes 12 (1965).

Volume 48 (1947) of the Transactions of the Actuarial Society of America.

Venkatesh, R., Venkatesh, V., Dattatreya, R., *Interest Rate and Currency Swaps,* Chicago, IL : Probus Publishing Company, 1995.

**Websites**

Altamira Investment Services:
www.altamira.com

Bank of Canada:
www.bankofcanada.ca

Bank of Montreal:
http://www4.bmo.com

Bloomberg LP:
http://www.bloomberg.com/markets/rates/index.html

Financial Calculators from KJE Computer Solutions:
www.dinkytown.net/java/SimpleLoan.html

The Hartford Insurance Company:
http://institutional.hartfordlife.com/

J. Huston McCulloch, Department of Economics of Ohio State University:
http://economics.sbs.ohio-state.edu/jhm/ts/ts.html

US Treasury, Bureau of the Public Debt:
http://www.treasurydirect.gov/RI/OFBills

Western and Southern Financial Corp: www.westernsouthernlife.com/

Wikipedia, online encyclopedia: en.wikipedia.org/wiki/Main_Page

Yahoo: http://finance.yahoo.com/bonds

# INDEX